Defiant Prophets

Also by Hillel I. Millgram
and from McFarland

The Elijah Enigma: The Prophet, King Ahab and the Rebirth of Monotheism in the Book of Kings (2014)

The Joseph Paradox: A Radical Reading of Genesis *37–50* (2012)

Four Biblical Heroines and the Case for Female Authorship: An Analysis of the Women of Ruth, Esther *and* Genesis *38* (2008)

Defiant Prophets

Jonah, Balaam, Jeremiah and Their Rebellion Against God

HILLEL I. MILLGRAM

McFarland & Company, Inc., Publishers
Jefferson, North Carolina

LIBRARY OF CONGRESS CATALOGUING-IN-PUBLICATION DATA

Names: Millgram, Hillel I., 1931–, author.
Title: Defiant prophets : Jonah, Balaam, Jeremiah and their rebellion against God / Hillel I. Millgram.
Description: Jefferson, North Carolina : McFarland & Company, Inc., Publishers, 2022 | Includes bibliographical references and index.
Identifiers: LCCN 2021059157 | ISBN 9781476686776 (paperback : acid free paper) ∞
ISBN 9781476644721 (ebook)
Subjects: LCSH: God (Judaism) | Jeremiah (Biblical prophet) | Jonah (Biblical prophet) | Balaam (Biblical figure) | Bible. Jeremiah—Criticism, interpretation, etc. | Bible. Jonah—Criticism, interpretation, etc. | Bible. Numbers, XXII-XXIV—Criticism, interpretation, etc.
Classification: LCC BM610 .M575 2022 | DDC 296.3/11—dc23/eng/20220103
LC record available at https://lccn.loc.gov/2021059157

BRITISH LIBRARY CATALOGUING DATA ARE AVAILABLE

ISBN (print) 978-1-4766-8677-6
ISBN (ebook) 978-1-4766-4472-1

© 2022 Hillel I. Millgram. All rights reserved

No part of this book may be reproduced or transmitted in any form or by any means, electronic or mechanical, including photocopying or recording, or by any information storage and retrieval system, without permission in writing from the publisher.

Front cover image: *Jeremiah Lamenting the Destruction of Jerusalem*, Rembrandt, 1628, Dutch painting, oil on panel. Everett Collection/Shutterstock

Printed in the United States of America

*McFarland & Company, Inc., Publishers
Box 611, Jefferson, North Carolina 28640
www.mcfarlandpub.com*

For my beloved great grandchildren
DANIELLA, SHLOMIT, ITAMAR, KEDEM
EMILY and ORAN
May your numbers increase

The LORD *bless you out of Zion;*
And may you see the good of Jerusalem
all the days of your life.
And see your children's children;
Peace be upon Israel.
Psalm 128: 5–6

It is not the critic who counts, not the man who points out how the strong man stumbles, or where the doer of deeds could have done them better. The credit belongs to the man who is actually in the arena, whose face is marred by dust and sweat and blood; who strives valiantly, who errs, who comes short again and again, because there is no effort without error and shortcoming; but who does actually strive to do the deeds; who knows great enthusiasms, the great devotions; who spends himself in a worthy cause; who at the best knows in the end the triumph of high achievement; and who at the worst, if he fails, at least fails while daring greatly, so that his place shall never be with those cold and timid souls who neither know victory or defeat.

—Theodore Roosevelt, *Citizenship in a Republic,* Paris, 1910

Table of Contents

List of Maps — ix
Principal Abbreviations — x
Preface — 1
Acknowledgments — 11
Introduction — 13

Part I. The *Book of Jonah*

Introduction to the *Book of Jonah* — 25
1. The Flight of the Rebel — 35
2. In a Tight Spot — 51
3. The Great Reversal — 66
4. Endgame — 78
5. Some Second Thoughts About a Strange Book — 90

II. The Enigmatic Balaam, Son of Beor

6. Prologue: The Path to the Steppes of Moab — 103
Introduction to the *Book of Balaam* — 112
7. Come, Curse Mine Enemy — 115
8. The Mouthpiece — 132
9. The Prophet — 151
10. Retrospect — 167
11. Epilogue: The Road to Dusty Death — 184

III. A Persecuted Prophet

12. Prologue: A Tangled Three-Act Tragedy — 205
13. Problematic Beginnings — 219
Historical Interlude I. The Road to Megiddo: Playing on the Big Board — 235
14. De Profundis — 241
Historical Interlude II. Scandals in the Temple — 255
15. The Long Night — 262
Historical Interlude III. Long Day's Journey into Night — 276
16. The Anatomy of a Lifelong Agony — 284

Conclusion: A Final Accounting	299
APPENDICES	
A: When Was Jonah *Written?*	313
B: Who Was the Innovator and Who Were the Copycats?	317
C: North Moab: A Tale of Lost Lands	322
D: The Geography and Ecology of the Trans-Jordan	325
E: The Deir 'Alla Inscription(s)	327
F: The Plague at Baal-Peor	330
G: Who Was Jeremiah?	333
H: Psalm 22 and the Prayer of Jeremiah	337
Timeline I: Putting Things in Perspective	340
Timeline II: Late 7th–Early 6th Centuries BCE	343
Glossary of Terms and Place Names	345
Who's Who	358
Bibliography	363
Scriptural Index	367
General Index	371

List of Maps

The maps in this volume have been designed as aids to understanding the texts of *Jonah, Numbers* and *Jeremiah*. As such they have been simplified by excluding data unnecessary to elucidating the particular sections of the books to which they pertain. Each section has been provided with the maps necessary to its understanding, and they should be considered an integral part of that section.

MAP 1—The known world as reflected in the *Book of Jonah*, showing all the sites mentioned in the Book.

MAP 2—The route of the Children of Israel from Kadesh to the Promised Land.

MAP 3—The Trans-Jordan in the late 13th century BCE.

MAP 4—Central Israel in the second half of the 11th century to the mid–10th century BCE.

MAP 5—The Assyrian Empire at its height, c. 665 BCE.

MAP 6—The Holy Land during the reign of King Josiah, c. 610 BCE (with *The Battle of Megiddo*, 608 BCE).

MAP 7—The Division of the Spoils I: The Ancient Near East, 608–604 BCE.

MAP 8—The Division of the Spoils II: The Ancient Near East after 604 BCE.

MAP 9—Northern Judah and Benjamin, October, 586 BCE.

Principal Abbreviations

AB—The Anchor Bible
ABD—The Anchor Bible Dictionary
ANET—Ancient Near Eastern Texts Relating to the Old Testament
AV Authorized Version; the 1611 translation of the Bible into English, often called the King James Bible
BASOR—Bulletin of the American Schools of Oriental Research
BCE—Before the Common Era, equivalent to B.C.
BDB—Brown, Driver and Briggs, *A Hebrew and English Lexicon of the Old Testament*
BHS—Biblia Hebraica Stuttgartensia (ed. K. Elliger & W. Rudolph)
CBQ—Catholic Bible Quarterly
CE—The Common Era, equivalent to A.D.
HTR—Harvard Theological Review
JAOS—Journal of the American Oriental Society
JBL—Journal of Biblical Literature
JHS—Journal of Hebrew Scriptures
JPS—Jewish Publication Society Bible Translation of 1917
JPSBC—The JPS Bible Commentary
JPSTC—The JPS Torah Commentary
JQR—Jewish Quarterly Review
JTS—Journal of Theological Studies
KJB—The King James Bible, the 1611 translation of the Bible
LXX—The Septuagint, the Greek translation of the Bible
ms.—Manuscript (plural mss.)
MT—Masoretic Text
NBD—New Bible Dictionary
NEB—New English Bible
NICOT—New International Commentary on the Old Testament
NIV—New International Version
NJPS—New JPS Translation of 1985
NRSV—New Revised Standard Version Bible Translation of 1989
NT—New Testament
OL—Old Latin, the pre–Vulgate Latin translation of the Bible
OT—Old Testament
Q—Qumran, thus an abbreviation representing the Dead Sea Documents
RSV—Revised Standard Version of 1952
RV—The Revised Version of 1885, the only authorized revision of the King James Bible
Sam.—The Samaritan Pentateuch
Syr.—The Peshita; the Syriac translation of the Bible
Targ.—The Targum; the Aramaic translations of the Bible
TOTC—Tyndale Old Testament Commentaries
VT—Vitus Testamentum
Vulg.—The Vulgate; the 4th-century-CE Latin translation of the Bible by St. Jerome
ZAW—Zeitschrift für die Alttestamentliche Wissenschaft

Preface

The present work began as a project that was meant to explore the theme of rebellion as exhibited in the careers of two very atypical biblical prophets: Jonah and Balaam. However, in short order the project morphed into something else entirely: it became an in-depth study of the two Books that enshrined their tales, The *Book of Jonah* and the *Book of Balaam*.[1] These two works stand out in the Bible for their anomalous use of the Hebrew language which, at first glance, appears to be standard biblical narrative prose but on closer acquaintance proves to be something very different indeed. They also differ in content from their sister biblical works, being two blatant exceptions to the biblical rule that events be depicted in a naturalistic manner; with the result that the *Book of Jonah* has mainly become known as a fish story—"O Jonah, he lived in a whale"[2]—while Balaam has achieved fame for having been the owner of a talking donkey. When one adds to these anomalies the bizarre activities of our two anti-heroes one begins to wonder why these two tales ever found their way into the Bible.

These two strange stories—and they *are* strange—led in turn to a study of the auto-biographical disclosures of the rebellious secrets of his inner life by no less a figure than the prophet Jeremiah[3]; revelations without parallel in the Bible and, to the best of my knowledge, unique in the entire ancient world.

What emerged from this process was a focus on a trio of depictions, by different authors, of three individuals—denizens of different eras, locations and circumstances—all of them prophets in revolt; servants in rebellion against their Master. I will contend that what they hold in common is that these prophets are being presented as prototypes: that they are meant to serve as depictions of the human condition, and that the aim of these compositions is to test the limits of the humanly possible. As literary compositions they are all on a remarkably high level, extremely sophisticated and employing literary techniques that are surprisingly modern. All these compositions promote themes that were—and many still are—highly subversive of sociopolitical and religious orthodoxies. Beyond being talented writers, their authors were people who had left conventional patterns of thinking and accepted answers behind them, and were asking new questions. These were people who were thinking out of the box.

---

1. This is the name given to Chapters 22-24 of the *Book of Numbers* by the rabbis of the Talmud; see the first three paragraphs of the Introduction to the *Book of Balaam* (and especially notes 5–7) for explanation and elaboration.
2. A line from a song in Gershwin's *Porgy and Bess*.
3. Those passages in the *Book of Jeremiah* that have collectively become known as "Jeremiah's Confessions."

All of this leads us to a number of questions of our own: who were the authors of these unusual works? What were their reasons for penning them? What were they trying to say to their contemporaries? How did these problematic works come to be accepted as Scripture—that is, holy writings—and become incorporated in the Bible? And lastly: what, if anything, do they have to say to us in our day and age; questions which in turn finally morphed into a study of the problem of the role of autonomy—the concern underlying our three literary creations—its extent, and the role it plays in the life of human beings, and of how the Bible views this vexatious and contentious matter.

The issues that these works raised—all groundbreaking, or so I will contend—are as alive and pressing today as they were in their own times. They, and the issues I raised above, form the subject and the substance of this book.

We freely admit that this analysis of disparate biblical texts and the resultant preliminary exploration of some of their underlying implications cannot be fully worked out without a thorough re-examination and reappraisal of the assumptions underlying the modern Western World in which we find ourselves; the attitudes and pre-suppositions that had their birth in the "enlightenment" of the 18th century. Such an undertaking would require a widened interpretation of the past, a necessity if we wish to escape the dire insufficiencies of an increasingly ahistorical world outlook. If we don't take the trouble to review our past—which includes the wisdom of past generations—we will not have sufficient insight to understand our present condition or command our future. But such an endeavor would far exceed the scope of the present project. For the purpose of this study we will content ourselves with a preliminary survey of several issues raised in the Bible, some suggestions as to possible implications of these, and several suggestions as to their relevance for pressing issues in our current lives. For the present it will suffice us to raise the questions. The larger elaboration and clarification will have to be left to others.

As in my previous books, I find it only proper to be up front about who this book is intended for. In our day, readers of the Bible can be divided into two categories. The first group consists of academic scholars whose profession is the study of the Bible, and those in related fields such as Near East Studies. And then there is the second group, which includes everyone else. If you are an advanced-degree-bearing denizen of academia, this book is probably not for you, although you might find some of the ideas and positions of interest, and even challenging. On the other hand, if you are a member of the general public that has historically provided the overwhelming majority of the enthusiastic readership of the Bible, this book may be what you have been looking for: a work that can serve as an introduction to the world of the Bible, and one which does not require any specific background or specialized knowledge. Not being intended for a scholarly readership, it does not use language appropriate to an academic format, and as in my previous books, I will not talk down to the reader. I hold to the position that there is no idea so complex or abstruse that it cannot be explained to the average person in colloquial non-technical English. I avoid the use of academic and technical jargon, and when the use of some technical term is unavoidable, I immediately explain it. I assume no reservoir of knowledge in the fields of ancient history, Bible studies, archaeology, etc., but will provide the necessary background information on the go, telling the reader what he or she needs to know when he or she needs to know it. In a word, this book is consciously and by intention reader friendly. I recognize that, for a modern person, to enter the world of the Bible *de novo* is an experience not dissimilar to finding oneself a visitor to a foreign land lacking in modern tourist facilities. As such, I have taken upon myself the task of acting as your friendly tour guide, smoothing the way and making the unintelligible understandable.

Before we go any further, I think it is only fair that you know something about a person who is proposing to act as your guide. I personally am a religious person. This, however, does not mean that I am writing solely for a religious audience. This book is meant to be available to a secular audience as well, and my own religious beliefs are at no point introduced into the argument. My aim is to analyze a series of biblical texts that have held a place of honor in the annals of Western civilization, and through their explication to uncover both the motivations that brought them into being and their intended message. Briefly, this is not a proselytizing work.

Being a Jew, I am a descendant, both physically and spiritually, of the ancient Israelites out of whose community the authors of the Bible sprang. They being my distant ancestors, it is understandable that the text speaks to me. But two thousand years have passed since the Bible ceased to be the exclusive possession of the Jewish people. The Bible is now the common possession of all humanity, and is one of the foundations of the Western world. As such, this book is not intended for an exclusively Jewish audience, but rather for all those who see in the Bible a part of the heritage of humanity in general, and of the West in particular. It is in this light that this book has been written.

This is a book about the Bible, or to be more exact, about selected parts of the Hebrew Bible.[4] Before analyzing the biblical tales we have highlighted—those of Jonah and Balaam, and the so-called Confessions of Jeremiah—it is only proper that we be clear in our minds what exactly we mean when we speak of the Bible and precisely how we intend approaching it.

The Hebrew Bible is the creation of a people known as the Children of Israel,[5] or in shorthand, the Israelites, who were the ancestors of the present-day Jews. The thirty-nine Books[6] that became the Bible we currently possess were composed over a period of close to a thousand years. They are the end result of the sustained efforts of this unusual people to reach an understanding of itself, of its place in the world and of its tortuous, and often tortured, relationship with God. The insights reached during this millennial undertaking, known subsequently as the Biblical Age, and embedded in the Books of the Hebrew Bible, have not only shaped Judaism and its

---

4. So-called because it is mostly written in the Hebrew language (a few parts are written in Aramaic, a sister language to Hebrew). To Christians the Hebrew Bible is known as the Old Testament (OT), to differentiate it from the New Testament (NT), which is written in Greek. The Hebrew Bible is the Holy Scriptures of the Jews. It, together with the New Testament, forms the Holy Scriptures of Christianity.

5. That is, the descendants of Israel, the eponymous father of the people; i.e., the person from whom the people have taken their name. Israel was the alternate name of Jacob (see *Genesis* 32:23–33).

6. To avoid confusion, when we capitalize the word (Book) we are referring to one of the biblical Books which make up the Bible, while when we write it in lower case letters (book) we are referring to the volume you are currently holding in your hands and reading.

daughter religions, Christianity and Islam, but have determined the form and direction of civilization in the modern world.

The Bible contains literary works written in different periods and under vastly divergent conditions, and are composed in radically different literary forms. There are surges of exhortation alternating with vehement denunciation; dry legal codes side-by-side with philosophical speculation; odes of joy and sadness, comedy and tragedy, phrased either in poetry or prose, and sometimes both intermingled side-by-side with long stretches of narrative. This last includes stories, biographies and, most of all—history. Although they contain serious sections of poetry, it is within this last category—narrative prose—that we find two of the works on which we will be concentrating our attention: the *Book of Jonah* and the *Book of Balaam*, while the so-called "Confessions" of Jeremiah are mostly composed as poetry.

How did these works come into being? Obviously, someone wrote them. As we examine them we will attempt to determine when each was written and, if possible, by whom. At this stage let us simply state that our working hypothesis is that each was written in much the same way essays, stories or novels are written today: an author sitting down, organizing his or her thoughts into a composition and putting them down on paper.[7] When the subject matter was historical, as often it was, composition involved research into sources, oral and written; it was not uncommon for some of these to be incorporated in whole or part in the finished work.[8] The literary form of the final composition, the way it was structured and, of course, its moral or message were original to the author.[9]

Once written, the next concern of an author, then as now, was to get the book into circulation. Millennia before the invention of the printing press, this was a very difficult matter. All books were handwritten and were, in this aspect, identical with the original manuscript. The author would write out one or more copies (or if wealthy, could hire a scribe—a kind of professional secretary—to do it for him or her)[10] and would then circulate the copies among friends and acquaintances. These would, in turn, pass the book on to their friends. If any of these should take a special liking to the book they could have a private copy written out for personal use. No one ever thought in terms of copyright in those days; a book once circulated was the property of the public.

---

7. Jeremiah was unusual in this matter. Being sufficiently affluent, he was able to afford a private secretary to whom he dictated his works, his secretary then transcribing them into written form for him.

8. In the Biblical Era people wrote with pen and ink on sheets of papyrus or parchment (see Glossary). The sheets were then sewn together to form scrolls which were kept rolled up in cabinets or chests, and unrolled to be read. When the word "book" is used in the Bible it refers to these scrolls. (Books in the modern sense of the term, i.e., a stack of sheets bound together on one side and read by turning from one page to the next—the technical term is a codex—were only introduced into common use during Roman times.) The Torah scrolls still used in Synagogues to this day have preserved the form that biblical Books originally had. The present-day Torah being five Books (*Genesis, Exodus, Leviticus, Numbers* and *Deuteronomy*) "bound together" as one, is obviously far larger than the typical Book of biblical times.

9. The extent to which the contents of the Books of the Bible are the result of human insight and discovery, or derived from divine inspiration, has been a subject of vehement dispute within religions that look to the Bible for their authority and justification. We make no claim to resolve these questions.

10. See note 7 above.

As long as a book remained popular with the reading public it remained "in print," new copies being made as old ones wore out. If not, a book would go "out of print," no new copies replacing those lost to the natural attrition of wear and tear, accidents, wars and fires. Such was the fate of most books written during the biblical period. Of these, a number of very important books that had wide circulation in biblical times are currently known to us only by name or sometimes from quotes. While accident obviously played an important part in the survival process, the more copies in circulation, the higher the book's life expectancy. The works that are the subject of our inquiry—the Books of *Jonah* and *Balaam*, and the *Book of Jeremiah* in which his "Confessions" are embedded—seem to have been bestsellers from the start, and to have remained so as century followed century. Through the vicissitudes of the years, down to the advent of the printing press, enough people and groups cared about these books to ensure their preservation.[11]

The laborious hand-copying process ended about five hundred years ago with the invention of the printing press. In Venice, in 1524–1525, Daniel Bomberg printed what was to become the universally accepted edition of the Hebrew Bible.[12] With one exception, all Hebrew Bibles today are copies of this original edition.[13]

Endless recopying has its dangers. Being human, even the most devoted and careful scribes make mistakes. Sometimes scribes' eyes would wander, and they would skip words, or even entire sentences. Sometimes they would misread a word and replace it with something that looked superficially similar but was quite different in meaning. Despite the best of precautions and proofreading, errors would slip through. And these errors would be copied in turn. After centuries of constant recopying, a situation was created in which several versions of *Jonah*, *Jeremiah* and the *Book of Numbers* (in which the *Book of Balaam* is embedded) were in circulation simultaneously. At this time *Numbers* had already been canonized, while *Jonah* and *Jeremiah* were universally accepted as Scripture—that is, Holy Writ.[14] The circumstance of having different versions of Holy Books became intolerable to the religious authorities in Jerusalem. So, taking the best copies available in the Temple Archives, and by a process of careful comparison, they issued authorized versions of these

---

11. Or, as in the case of the *Book of Balaam*, their incorporation in later works, themselves sufficiently popular to survive the vicissitudes of the centuries.

12. Actually he published his first Hebrew Bible in the years 1516–1517, but it didn't sell. Not being a Jew (Daniel Bomberg was a devout Catholic), he hadn't realized that his main market, the Jews, wouldn't buy a Bible without the marginal Masoretic notes (see Masorite in the Glossary). Realizing his mistake, he corrected this error in the second edition (1524–1525) and had a bestseller.

13. The manuscript used by Bomberg was the text of Jacob ben Hayim, based on manuscripts from the 13th and 14th centuries CE. There is an even earlier manuscript, the ben Asher text, which is several centuries older and is preserved in the Public Library of Leningrad (now St. Petersburg) and hence sometimes known as the Leningrad Manuscript. This formed the basis of the *Biblia Hebraica* (begun under the editorship of Rudolph Kittle and completed by Paul Kahle). This text has increasingly begun to take the place of the previously used ben Hayim text as the standard version of the Masoretic Text (MT).

14. Canonization simply means the formal recognition and acceptance by an authorized body of a given Book as holy or "inspired." Works so recognized became as a consequence Sacred Scripture, writings that were authoritative and binding. *Numbers* was canonized c. 445 BCE; *Jonah* and *Jeremiah*, as parts of the biblical division named "The Latter Prophets" (see Glossary), were canonized some time after 70 CE, but had popularly been accepted as Scripture long before the formal seal of approval was given. These issues are further discussed in the introductions to the various books.

works, the most error-free editions they could achieve. These became the Masoretic Text (MT)[15] of the Bible, which has been standard to this day.

But the story does not end here. Good as these efforts were—and they were very good—problems still remain. There are phrases, and at times whole sentences, that don't seem to make sense. And there are places where quite obviously something is missing. This is where the ancient versions can help us.

More than two thousand years ago Jewish communities living in different areas of the world lost their traditional facility with the Hebrew language. No longer speaking Hebrew in their daily lives, more and more Jews lost the ability to read it. And so it became necessary to provide a translation of the Bible into the various languages these communities of Jews spoke and understood. The first such translation, into Greek, was made in Alexandria, Egypt, during the reign of Ptolemy II Philadelphus (283–245 BCE). This translation, known as the Septuagint (abbreviated as LXX),[16] is recognized today as an excellent translation, but it was often made from a different version of the various Books of the Bible than the one used by the Masorites. Comparing and editing the MT in the light of LXX can prove an enormous help in clearing up difficulties.

As the years went by, translations into other languages were made: into Aramaic, called the Targum (Targ.),[17] into Syriac (an Eastern form of Aramaic) called the Peshita (Syr.), and into Latin, called the Vulgate (Vulg.).[18] All these exhibit differences from the MT and invite comparison.

And then, in 1947, the first of the "Dead Sea Documents"[19] were unearthed in caves at Qumran on the shore of the Dead Sea. These documents and fragments—some dating back to the 3rd century BCE—contain the oldest copies of various Books of the Bible that we currently possess.[20] These also differ in many particulars from the standard Masoretic text and can be utilized in the same way as the ancient translations of the Bible to enrich our understanding of the text.[21]

While one must exercise extreme caution in the use of these alternate versions, with care they can help us to a better understanding. My translation of *Jonah*, *Jeremiah* and *Numbers* 21–25 is almost entirely based on the MT (at least ninety-eight percent). It is by far the best version we have. But in certain cases, when I feel the

---

15. See Masorite in the Glossary.

16. The Greek word means "seventy," an abbreviation of the full title, *The Translation of the Seventy Elders*. This refers to the story, related in the Talmud (see Glossary), Tractate *Megillah* 9a, that seventy-two scholars, summoned from Jerusalem, made the translation of the Torah ("The Five Books of Moses"), the first part of the Hebrew Bible. The remainder of the Hebrew Bible (The Prophets and The Writings) was translated later in stages.

17. In reality there were several different translations made into Aramaic. *Targum* is the Aramaic word for translation.

18. We are here referring to the translation made by St. Jerome from the original Hebrew, as opposed to the Old Latin (OL) version, a Latin translation of the LXX, i.e., a translation of a translation.

19. Often referred to as the "Dead Sea Scrolls," we are speaking largely of fragments; only a small number of the original scrolls have survived in relatively undamaged condition. Scholars have managed to reconstruct some 950 different documents from these fragments.

20. We possess complete or largely complete copies of a few biblical Books, such as *Isaiah*, and numerous fragments of most of the others—the Books of *Esther* and *Nehemiah* being conspicuous exceptions. Although almost all are more than 2,000 years old, they are not originals but themselves copies of copies.

21. When we rely on the Dead Sea Documents for our rendering, the citation will refer to Q (for Qumran).

ancient versions to be of help, I have not hesitated to proceed on their basis, hoping thereby to come somewhat closer to the author's original intent. In order to play fair with the reader I always indicate in a footnote when I have departed from the Masoretic Text, and on what basis; and I include the MT reading for comparison. This way it is possible for the reader to come to an independent conclusion, deciding whether to go along with my version or to prefer the MT.[22]

A Word on Translation

The portions of the Bible that will concern us—*Jonah*, *Jeremiah* and *Numbers*—were written in Hebrew; and, to make matters more daunting, in the Hebrew of 2,500 to 3,200 years ago. It is unlikely that many readers will be proficient in that tongue. This makes translation of the ancient Hebrew text into modern English a necessity, if these works are to be made accessible to most readers.

The very act of translation from one language to another is a problematic venture. Even in the case where the languages are contemporary and part of a common civilization, such as German and French, there are turns of phrase, idiomatic expressions and nuances that have no equivalents in other languages. When trying to render a literary masterwork, where these elements are often of prime importance, it is inevitable that even under the best of circumstances much will be lost; how much more so when trying to render an ancient work, written in a language whose grammar is completely different from that of modern Western languages. Still worse: we simply have no idea of what some of the words mean. These are issues with which translators of the Bible have been struggling for more than two thousand years.[23] In sum, every translation is a trade-off between comprehensibility and fidelity to the original, one which leaves no one happy; no translation is more than an approximation of the original. With these limitations in mind we return to our present case.

This volume is designed as a companion to, and a commentary on, the Books of *Jonah* and *Balaam*, and portions of *Jeremiah*. As such, it contains the full text of these works. If you are no stranger to the Bible you may be used to reading it in the Authorized Version (AV), the official title of what is known popularly as the King James Translation, first published in 1611, or in one of the more modern versions. While the AV (the King James Translation) is by far the greatest rendition of the Bible into English, the archaic language of this version no longer facilitates understanding, but

---

22. Unlike many scholars, I am extremely hesitant to second-guess the received text, substituting my own conviction for what lies before us. As a basic rule I do not approve of emending the text; that is, altering the text on one's own authority in order to make "better sense" of it. My approach is to try to make sense of what we have, and make no changes except on the authority of alternate versions. Therefore, any revisions that I have made in the MT have been on the basis of ancient versions of the text. There are several exceptions to this rule; cases were I could get no meaning from the Hebrew and no help from the ancient versions. In desperation I have been forced to offer my own understanding of the text—that is, to guess—and have indicated as much in the relevant footnote.

23. From the time of the translation of the Septuagint. See note 16 above.

instead acts as a barrier to most people.²⁴ On the other hand, I feel that many modern translations in striving to be relevant are too free in their renderings, often imposing contemporary agendas on the texts that distort the original meaning. Some modern translations I simply find wooden. And most modern versions, unfortunately, commit "the unacknowledged heresy" of using the translation "as a vehicle for *explaining* the Bible instead of representing it in another language, and in the more egregious instances this amounts to explaining away the Bible."²⁵ All this has led me to translate the text anew.

I have tried to make the translation simple and to keep it in contemporary English.²⁶ The translation is a literal one in which I have stayed as close to the Hebrew original as possible, avoiding euphemisms and paraphrases, while conforming to proper English usage. In a word, I have tried to render just what the text says while avoiding stilted and convoluted English. This not only facilitates ease of reading but also, to my way of thinking, best conveys the feel of the simple and lucid style of the original text.²⁷

---

24. Actually, the language used was already archaic in 1611 when the Authorized Version was published. "Thee"s and "thou"s had long since ceased to be used in everyday speech. The Bishops' Committee that was responsible for the translation made a conscious decision to use "old-fashioned" language in order to give its Bible a tone of solemn antiquity. The committee felt that everyday language would cheapen the text. And strangely enough, although they themselves were unaware of the phenomenon, this is exactly what the original authors of the Bible did. We are currently alert to the fact that the prose of the Bible was not in use by the people in their daily lives. Biblical prose was written in a "high literary style," employing only the most respectable and "elevated" terminology; only the best was good enough when dealing with God and His works. This explains why biblical prose vocabulary is so limited; common and every day words were excluded as a matter of principle. The solemn and stately English of the King James Translation thus accurately mirrors the kind of language employed in the Hebrew Bible.

25. R. Alter, *Genesis*, p. vii. Emphasis in the original.

26. A blatant exception to this rule is my retention of the rather archaic expression "behold!" when rendering the Hebrew term *heenai!* This demonstrative particle which expresses surprise, even shock, and signals the disclosure of a surprising and wholly unexpected development, is well rendered by the exclamation "behold," which has dropped out of current usage. But there is no adequate modern replacement. Recent translations, such as NJPS, attempt to cope with the problem with different expressions according to the context. Besides that, to my mind, the practice of rendering one and the same word in more than a dozen different ways is unacceptable (such as "just then," "they were surprised," "they found," "appeared," "and there" etc.), I find none of these replacements either felicitous or adequate. The King James Translation had no qualms about using archaic terms when they were appropriate (see note 24 above); choosing the lesser of the evils, I have decided in this, and one or two other instances, to follow suit.

27. A word about the way we refer to God in our translation of the biblical text. The Bible routinely uses two separate ways of referring to the deity: the general term *elohim* which simply means "deity" and is virtually universally rendered as "God," and what is termed "the Tetragrammaton," the four-letter personal name of God. This is often rendered by modern scholars as "Yahweh," or "Yaveh," or sometimes without vowels as "YHVH." These are current attempts to reconstruct God's personal name (a previous attempted reconstruction was "Jehovah"). But since biblical Hebrew was written with a consonantal alphabet (there were no vowels), and because we really have no idea how the consonants were pronounced in those days, all reconstructions are at best highly speculative. Jews ceased pronouncing God's name more than two thousand years ago out of a sense that it was improper to address God by name. Instead they substituted the title Lord (or *"Adonai"* in Hebrew), a convention adopted by the Bishops' Committee that issued the Authorized English Translation of the Bible (known as the King James Bible). This convention has been used in most subsequent translations down to the present day. We have continued this tradition in our translation. There is a further point to be considered, one succinctly expressed by Norman Podhoretz: "I prefer LORD because YHVH ['Yahweh'] in English willy-nilly makes God seem a tribal deity (which is in fact what some scholars—wrongly, I believe—think He was to the earliest of His Israelite devotees.)" (*The Prophets*, p. 12). Like him, I only allow this putative reconstruction into my books when I am quoting someone else.

A Word About Footnotes

I have already mentioned that this book has been designed for the general reader, and thus is not written in the format typical of academic literature. So what is all that small print doing on the bottom of the pages?

It is true that notes are a scholar's tool, the primary purpose being to facilitate peer review. Meticulous documentation of every fact and opinion with a scholarly source allows specialists to check up on each other to see how well they have done their homework, whether they are accurately reflecting the views of those upon whom they rely, and therefore how seriously one can take their conclusions. None of this is appropriate for a work that is not designed for the world of biblical scholarship, but rather for the intelligent and interested layman. In my books the notes serve different purposes entirely.

Their purposes are three. The first we have already mentioned: to play fair by letting the reader know whenever the translation departs from the Masoretic Text. As most readers will have little or no command of Hebrew, they will have no way of knowing when their guide has departed from the accepted MT. These notes are just a way of keeping the translation transparent, and of not relying on different versions without the reader's knowledge.

The second purpose is plain common courtesy. Whenever there is a direct quotation from some work it is polite to give the author credit. So whenever an author is mentioned or quoted directly that author is given his or her due.

But by far the greatest number of footnotes serves the purpose of optional enrichment. Some readers work on the principle that the shortest distance between two points is a straight line. Anything extraneous to the matter at hand is an annoyance, to be avoided at all cost. Others, myself included, far from finding digressions distracting, discover in them half the reward of reading: detours that open new vistas, expand horizons and deepen understanding. Most of the notes—those with more than one or two lines—fall into this category of short side excursions.

Assuming that at least some of my readers will have the same kind of temperament as myself, while others will prefer to get on with the task at hand, I have arranged to remove most of the side issues from the main body of the text and put them into the notes (and into a selected series of Appendices). Some of these will give a deeper understanding of the subject under discussion; sometimes they will give a view of some related field or issue. The several notes that you have encountered so far are a taste of what you can expect. Those who prefer to stay with the main text will find that it is fully self-contained. But for those inclined to explore side issues, the doors have been left open.

Acknowledgments

Being a generalist, not a specialist in any single field, this study of the sagas of Jonah, Balaam and of Jeremiah has occupied only a limited portion of my thinking life. But interest in these tales is anything but recent; my fascination with them has spanned the better part of a lifetime. As such I cannot list all my personal and intellectual debts without courting a Homeric tediousness. In the pair of decades since I took upon myself the full-time task of exploring the world of the Bible these obligations have multiplied, and I now hesitate more than ever to draw up a roster of the scholars, sages and thinkers—from the distant past to contemporaries—who have molded my thinking and guided me on the path I have pursued. Some are mentioned in the bibliography of this work, and of those of my previous books. Others remain anonymous; let them not suppose that my silence implies any failure of humility or gratitude. Nor can I overlook my debt to two magnificent institutions and their supremely helpful staffs—the National Library of Israel in Jerusalem and the superb Library of Congress in Washington, D.C.—that opened their portals and made possible much of my research into the wisdom of these past centuries of scholarship.

When I first turned to what I hoped would be serious writing for a general public I thought it would be helpful to submit early drafts to several people whose opinions I could trust. In addition to a number of colleagues, foremost among them Rabbi Yitzhak Ruben, who have read with care drafts of each chapter, corrected and commented upon them, I have turned over the years to my immediate family: my late wife Debby, and two of my sons, Elijah and Michael. Beyond the formidable editorial skills of the first two, and the expertise of the latter pair in disciplines far from my areas of competence that so usefully complement mine, their good sense and constructive criticism have proved invaluable, have encouraged me in the writing of my previous works and have emboldened me to launch into and complete this one. Rather than repeat my past enumeration of their specific contributions, I will content myself with the remark that their input has only grown with time; the present volume would not be what it is without it. Nor would it be without the graphic skills of Maya Wine who, as in my past volumes, is responsible for the maps that enhance the text and make comprehensible the topography of what to most readers are distant and unfamiliar landscapes.

My late wife, Debby, did more than give encouragement and edit the manuscript; she diligently read each draft of every chapter but the final few. Her keen eye, discerning judgment, attention to detail and challenging comments were of critical help; my heartfelt thanks to her in particular.

Lastly, I owe homage to two mentors above all others. The first, Alexander Sperber—in his day probably the outstanding scholar of the transmission of the biblical text—for introducing me to the intricacies of the process by which texts written several thousands of years ago have reached our hands. The effects of the two years spent under his supervision in an intimate seminar are evident in the following pages, and inspired the methodology of textual comparison that underlies this entire work. And as to the second, Mordecai Kaplan, my teacher—and the teacher of my father before me—I am beholden for an inestimable gift: he taught me to think "out of the box," to question unexamined premises and to approach issues from different perspectives. It was he who also encouraged me to ignore the "conventional barriers that have grown up like intellectual barbed wire,"[1] dividing the universality of human experience into so-called "disciplines," and to treat the subject of any inquiry in a holistic manner. It is because of him that I became able to profit from the wisdom of all my other guides. To all those mentioned—as well as those passed over in silence—my deepest gratitude. But for the gift of inquiring mind, I owe the deepest debt of all.

---

1. This phrase is original to Simon Schama, and is taken from the Preface to his magnificent study *Citizens*.

Introduction

By opening this book we are entering the world of the Bible; for most of us very much *terra incognita*. We will be following the adventures of three unusual individuals; prophets all. The assumptions underlying the playing field on which our protagonists—Jonah, Balaam and Jeremiah—will find themselves are very different from those with which we are familiar. Underneath the struggles and crises which we will be watching them undergo lies a monumental conflict between two worldviews, a conflict which under different names and in different guises continues to pulsate in our time. To truly understand our protagonists and their predicaments, we need some insight into the titanic struggle taking place in the background between paganism and monotheism. The tale of Jonah takes place entirely in the pagan world, with Jonah the lone and lonely monotheist. The tale of Balaam also takes place in a pagan environment, while he himself *is* a pagan. Jeremiah was a man who spent his life fighting a losing battle against paganism. The war between monotheism and paganism underlies all of our tales. Our first task will be to understand what that war was all about.

We have been very liberal in our use of the terms *pagan*[1] (and its derivative *paganism*) and *monotheism*, but usually we are less than forthright as to the exact meaning and implications of these terms. As a proper understanding of these terms is critical to follow one of the central arguments of this book, a concise examination of these subjects becomes necessary. Historically paganism preceded monotheism. Paganism appears to be the ancient—indeed primordial—spiritual-philosophical condition of human beings. Monotheism is a relatively modern phenomenon; appearing on the scene less than four thousand years ago. Hence we begin our discussion with an analysis of paganism.

Paganism 101: A Crash Course[2]

Beyond the usual derogatory connotation of the word *pagan* as "irreligious"—actually pagans often were, and are, intensely religious—in common usage *paganism*

---

1. Historically speaking, the word *pagan* comes from the Latin *paganus*, which means "rural"—someone who lives in the countryside as opposed to city dwellers. Monotheism, in the form of Christianity, made its great inroads first and foremost in the cities of the Roman Empire. It was in the rural areas that people clung to the "old time religion" and held out against Christianity. So the term *paganus*—rural dweller—came to mean someone who refused monotheism and continued to worship the old gods, with all that that implied.

2. This section is largely based on the analysis and conclusions of Yehezkel Kaufmann, as formulated in his magnum opus *Toldot Haemunah Hayisraelit* (Hebrew), Volume II, Chapter 11, "*Haellilut*" (Paganism), pp. 286–416. For the convenience of readers unfamiliar with the Hebrew language, all quotations and citations are taken from its abridged English translation by Moshe Greenberg, entitled *The Religion of Israel*.

is usually taken as a synonym for polytheism; i.e., the worship or the belief in multiple deities. This is an error: while it is true that all forms of paganism are polytheistic, polytheism is but one facet of paganism, and far from its most significant feature. Rather, the central insight common to all paganism, and to be found in all its religions in all their varying forms, is that the gods—whoever they may be and whatever forms they may take—are neither autonomous nor supreme. The foundational belief of paganism is that behind the reality that we perceive lies a pre-existent primordial realm which gave birth to the world we know. This primordial realm also gave birth to the gods, and as such they—no less than we—are subservient to it. Or as Yehezkel Kaufmann puts it, "there exists a realm of being prior to the gods and above them, upon which the gods depend, and whose decrees they must obey. Deity belongs to, and is derived from, a primordial realm."[3]

This concept is to be found in all the varying forms taken by paganism—from the most primitive, such as the religions of the Australian aborigines, to the most elevated and sophisticated, such as philosophical Hinduism—and is its distinguishing characteristic. The gods emerged from this pre-existing realm; the gods are thus the personal embodiments of those various seminal forces inherent in the primordial realm. The natures and destinies of the various gods are therefore determined by the nature of these various forces. The multiplicity of deities that is so typical of paganism in all its forms is a direct consequence of the multiple forces belonging to the primordial realm. It is these that set the eternal limits to the domains and powers of each and every pagan deity. "It is not the plurality of the gods per se ... that expresses the essence of paganism, but rather the notion of many independent power-entities, all on a par with one another, and all rooted in the primordial realm."[4]

To recapitulate: as paganism sees it, "the gods are not the source of all that is, nor do they transcend the universe. They are part of a realm precedent to and independent of them. They are rooted in this realm, are bound by its nature, and are subservient to its laws.... Transcending them is the primordial realm, with its pre-existent autonomous forces."[5] It is this fundamental dichotomy between the inherent autonomous forces of this preexistent primordial realm and the powers of the gods which are subservient to them that give birth to the two main manifestations of paganism: myth and magic.

Myth

Myth is the story of the pagan gods: their biographies. In it the gods appear not only as actors but also as subjects acted upon. It tells of their births, their relationships with each other and with human beings, their characters, their destinies and their fates. They are subject to the conditions of gender—they are male and female—and by their nature they are subject to sexual needs, copulating with each other and with human beings.

---

3. Kaufmann, *Religion of Israel*, p. 21.
4. *Ibid.*, p. 23. Kaufmann goes on, page after page, in wearisome detail, documenting these fundamental concepts in different pagan religions from every corner of the earth.
5. *Ibid.*, p. 22.

They procreate, giving birth to multiple generations of deities, and are often surpassed and deposed by their progeny. They are subject to the limitations of their physical conditions—they eat and drink—and are involved in the process of time. Above all, they are subject to abstract necessity; their destinies are pre-determined and unalterable.

Their characters and their natures are also predetermined. Throughout paganism we find good gods and evil gods, equal in their divine rank and power, because both are derived independently from the primordial realm. Their unending struggles form one of the staples of the tales of the gods.

Myth, even more than the artistic depiction of the gods, is the unique form taken by paganism to express the face it presents to its devotees. It opens the doors to paganism's inner essence and it is its primary literary expression. At the heart of myth is the tension between the gods and other forces that shape their destinies. In myth, we find Fate apportioning lots to the gods, even as they do to men. "This is a great symbol of paganism's fundamental idea: the existence of a realm of power to which the gods themselves are subject."[6]

Magic

The fundamental idea of paganism not only finds poetic expression in *myth*, it also finds practical expression in *magic*. Since there are two realms—that of divine powers and another of what Kaufmann calls the realm of the meta-divine—pagan man finds himself subject to, and in need of, both. He prays to the gods, but is conscious that they are specific embodiments of a more generalized power. For this reason paganism could never content itself with being merely religious; that is, satisfied with service only to the will of the gods. This realm of the gods (the religious sphere) was always, of necessity, qualified by the sphere of powers beyond the gods.[7] Thus paganism was necessarily and essentially magical as well.

When we speak of the role of magic in the ancient—hence pagan—world, we must put aside any notion of stage magicians pulling rabbits out of hats. Magic was the "science" of the pagan world: first and foremost, a sophisticated methodology for manipulating the forces of the natural world for the benefit of humankind (or of specific groups and persons thereof) by accessing and drawing upon the powers of the more basic primordial world that underlies it. And as the gods are part of the natural world—both gods and world are equally derivative from the meta-divine, primordial realm—the gods also can be manipulated. In the understanding of pagan man, through the practice of religion—prayer and ritual—humans can serve and attempt to influence the gods to benefit them. By the practice of magic—by accessing and drawing upon the meta-divine powers of the primordial realm which gave birth to the gods—pagans could pressure the gods, and force them to do their will.[8] The class of professional magicians held a position of public esteem in the ancient world not

---

6. *Ibid.*
7. *Ibid.*, p. 24.
8. The operational aspects of magic are elaborated on in Chapter 10, the section entitled An Enlightening Ordeal.

dissimilar to that held by scientists in our world today. Priest and magician form the two dominant elites of paganism.

The Monotheist Revolution as an Alternative to Paganism[9]

Even as the use of the term *paganism* to connote an entire worldview is the product of historical accident,[10] so the choice of the term "monotheism" to signify the underlying basis of Judaism, Christianity and Islam is based on a profound misconception: that the number of deities worshiped is the key to these religions and the factor that sets them apart from paganism.[11] Just as the fact that all paganism is polytheistic does not begin to capture its distinguishing characteristics, the fact that Judaism and its daughter religions, Christianity and Islam, recognize but one deity distracts us from what distinguishes them.

There is a second misconception—an outgrowth of the first—that needs to be put to rest before we can proceed: that "monotheism" is a developmental outgrowth of "polytheism"; the product of a process of refinement that progressively cut down the number of deities recognized and worshiped until but one remained. But just as the invention of the alphabet was a radically new and different way of rendering language into written symbols—a unique and revolutionary event in the history of human writing—and not the result of a developmental outgrowth of previous complicated and inefficient systems,[12] so the appearance of "monotheism" was a revolutionary conceptual break from all past religious beliefs and understandings: a new way of looking at God and His relationship with the world, and of the role of human beings within it. While many rites and practices of paganism lived on in monotheism, out of cultural habit and momentum,[13] and give a superficial impression of continuity, the monotheistic revolution entirely rejected the core beliefs of paganism—first and foremost, in the existence of a primordial realm with meta-divine forces prior to, and underlying, our world. In monotheism what you see is what there is.[14] Secondly, in place of a primordial realm which gave birth to the world we know—and to a plethora of gods dependent on and subject to it—monotheism holds there to be an eternal God Who created the world and all that there is: a world which depends on Him and not He on it. From this core insight, summed up in the seminal statement with which the Bible opens,

---

9. Portions of this section previously appeared in slightly different form in my previous works *The Invention of Monotheist Ethics*, *The Elijah Enigma* and *Judges and Saviors*.

10. See note 1 above.

11. Along with this focus on the number of deities one finds the unspoken assumption of "the fewer the better." According to this view Zoroastrianism, which recognizes but two deities, is infinitely more "advanced" than Hinduism, with its several million gods.

12. The invention of the alphabet somewhere in southern Canaan some 3,500 to 4,000 years ago was a one-time event, never duplicated so far as we know in the entire course of human history. All alphabets to the present day stem from that one original prototype.

13. For example, animal sacrifice. In paganism sacrifice played a central role: pagan gods had physical needs—they needed to eat—and animal sacrifice was their food. In the monotheistic view, the Creator of the universe has no need for food; He is incorporeal and doesn't eat. In the Israelite religion sacrifice served no central function; it was simply the way things were done, a holdover from time immemorial.

14. God, of course, being incorporeal, cannot be seen but only experienced second hand through what He created. Outside of His creation there is nothing: so what you see is what there is.

In the beginning, God created the heavens and the earth (Genesis 1:1)[15] everything follows. New and very different horizons open up to those able to accept this fundamental postulate.

> The basic idea of Israelite religion is that God is supreme over all. There is no realm above or beside him to limit his absolute sovereignty. He is utterly distinct from, and other than, the world; he is subject to no laws, no compulsions or powers that transcend him. He is, in short, non-mythological. This is the essence of Israelite religion, and that which sets it apart from all forms of paganism. This idea was not a product of intellectual speculation, or of mystical meditation, in the Greek or Indian manner. It first appeared as an insight, an original intuition.[16]

Or, if one wishes, one can substitute "original revelation" for "original intuition" at the close of the quotation.

In a very real sense, all the Hebrew Bible is an exposition of the logical implications of this axiomatic concept.

> The dominant tenet of Hebrew thought is the absolute transcendence of God. Yahweh[17] is not in nature. Neither earth nor sun nor heaven is divine; even the most potent natural phenomena are but reflections of God's greatness.... The God of the Hebrews is pure being, unqualified, ineffable. He is *holy*. That means that he is *sui generis*[18].... It means that all values are ultimately attributes of God alone.... It has been rightly pointed out that the monotheism of the Hebrews is a correlate of their insistence on the unconditional nature of God. Only a God who transcends every phenomenon, who is not conditioned by any mode of manifestation—only an unqualified God can be the one and only ground of all existence.[19]

The chasm between the pagan Ancient Near East and the Israelite belief in the one transcendent God Who created the universe and sustains it became evident almost at once. Unlike the pagan world in which the religious impulse supremely manifested itself in the portrayal of the gods, the Israelite society rejected images. Any physical representation of a God Who is pure being cannot but be seen as belittling; a transcendent deity could not but be offended, no matter what the good intentions. Unlike the pagan world which saw nature as divine and worshipped its manifestations, the Israelites, believing that both they and nature were alike the creations of an Omnipotent Deity, related to their natural environment much the way we do—as raw material for human use (and hopefully not for abuse).[20] And especially,

---

15. There are some who prefer to render *Genesis* 1:1 into English as follows: *When God began to create heaven and earth...* (cf. NJPS, etc.), but the central point remains the same: it is God who created heaven and earth, not some primordial realm that created God.
16. Kaufmann, *Religion of Israel*, p. 60.
17. On the name "Yahweh," see Preface, note 27 above.
18. I.e. unique.
19. Henri Frankfort et al., *The Intellectual Adventure of Ancient Man*, p. 367–369.
20. There is one basic difference between the ecological attitudes of biblical and modern men. Those living within the biblical world took as given the position expressed in Psalm 24: *The earth is the LORD's and the fullness thereof; the world, and they that dwell therein.* Mankind is no more than God's steward. Man is given the use of this world but will be called to account if he abuses it. The clear understanding that mankind does not own the world and is held accountable by the Owner placed severe limitations upon biblical man. James Bar puts this into the context of our modern ecological crisis: "I would say that the great modern exploitation of nature has taken place under the reign of a liberal humanitarianism in which man no longer conceives of himself as living under a Creator, and in which therefore his place of dominance in the universe and his right to dispose of nature for his own ends is, unlike the situation in the Bible, unlimited." (Bar, "Man and Nature: The Ecological Controversy and the Old Testament," p. 73)

monotheism broke down the coercive and stifling power of the collective, and cleared space for the individual to emerge into the world and stand alone—a phenomenon previously unknown.

> All this may help to explain the strange poignancy of single individuals in the Old Testament. Nowhere in the literature of Egypt or Babylonia do we meet with the loneliness of the biblical figures, astonishingly real in their mixture of ugliness and beauty, pride and contrition, achievement and failure. There is the tragic figure of Saul, the problematical David; there are countless others. We find single men in terrible isolation facing a transcendent God: Abraham trudging to the place of sacrifice with his son, Jacob in his struggle, and Moses and the prophets. In Egypt and Mesopotamia man was dominated, but also supported, by the great rhythm of nature. If in his dark moments he felt himself caught and held in the net of unfathomable decisions, his involvement in nature had, on the whole, a soothing character. He was gently carried along on the perennial cosmic tides of the seasons. The depth and intimacy of man's relationship with nature found expression in the ancient symbol of the mother-goddess. But Hebrew thought ignored this image entirely. It only recognized the stern Father....[21]

In freeing the individual from the bonds of nature and granting men and women autonomy, monotheism imposed upon liberated humanity a terrifying burden of moral responsibility. One would be free to choose, but one would have to bear the consequences of one's choice.

Needless to say, all the foregoing is a radical oversimplification of an extremely complex issue. However, its purpose is not to exhaust the subject but to give the reader a framework, rough-hewn though it be, that can make some of the matters dealt with in the larger work a bit more intelligible.

Prophets and Prophecy

Leaving for a moment the organizing principles that underlie the two worldviews which we call paganism and monotheism, and the struggle between them that forms the grand theme of the Bible, we turn to those individuals whom its pages highlight as monotheism's primary exponents: the prophets. As the central protagonists of all three of the tales that are the subjects of our proposed inquiry fall into this category, it becomes necessary at the start to clear the ground by banishing certain misconceptions. Just as, in our discussion of the pagan world's magicians, we had to rid our minds of pictures of rabbits being pulled out of hats, so in the case of biblical prophets must we dispel any ideas we may have of persons—with or without crystal balls—with the power to predict future events. While it is true that the English word "prophet" has, as one of its primary meanings, *one who prophesies future events, a predictor,*[22] the use of this term to translate the Hebrew *nabi*, the term used in the Bible, is misleading. The term *nabi* comes from the West Semitic root whose basic meaning is "to call." There is no hint of prediction inherent in this root. The *nabi* is thus one who has been especially called by God for a purpose, one who has a call or vocation from God.[23]

---

21. Henri Frankfort et al., p. 371.
22. The word *prophet* is derived from the Greek *prophetes*, which comes from *pro* = forth and *phanai* = to speak; hence one who speaks forth, a predictor.
23. J. Huehnergard, "On the Etymology and Meaning of the Hebrew *Nabi*," *Eretz-Israel* 26, p. 88–93. See also W. F. Albright, *From the Stone Age to Christianity*, p. 303.

Introduction

We can best understand the role of the biblical *nabi* through an examination of how the Bible treats him. After his call at the burning bush Moses—the prototypical "prophet"[24]—attempts to beg off from his calling by claiming unfitness: he is not a persuasive speaker.[25] God does not dispute Moses' claim but rather proposes a solution:

Is there not Aaron, your brother Levite?[26] I know that he can speak well.... And you shall speak to him and put the words in his mouth.... And he shall speak for you to the people; and it shall come to pass that he shall be to you a mouth, and you shall be to him like God [Exodus 4:14-16].

And later God amplifies his instructions thus:

And the LORD *said to Moses: "See, I have set you in God's stead to Pharaoh, and Aaron your brother shall be your prophet.[27] You shall speak to him* [i.e., Aaron] *all that I command you, and Aaron your brother shall speak to Pharaoh"* [Exodus 7:1-2].

The analogy is plain: just as God speaks to a prophet, puts His words into the prophet's mouth, with the prophet then delivering His message, so will Moses tell Aaron what to say. Moses will play God's role to Aaron, and Aaron, acting as Moses' prophet, will speak the words to Pharaoh. Thus the prophet or *nabi*, when he speaks, is first, last and always a messenger of God, delivering His Word.[28]

This does not preclude outlining the future consequences of current behavior, but only to the extent that we do the same. The prophets believed implicitly, no less than we, in cause and effect. Current behavior has inevitable, and often predictable, consequences. But over and beyond this, they believed totally in a just God and in a moral order as absolutely as we believe in natural law. Cause and effect to them were as binding and irrevocable in the moral realm as in the physical. So their worldview enabled them to project the future outcomes of moral and immoral behavior with the same confidence as the worldview of today's scientist enables him to predict the outcomes of chemical reactions or the movement of stellar bodies.

This is the human side of the equation. But to the extent that we are willing

---

24. Despite its inadequacy and unfortunate connotations, we will continue to use the term *prophet* to translate the Hebrew term *nabi* since, due to the constraints of the English language, there is no better substitute.

25. The Hebrew is *k'vad peh uk'vad lashon anochi* (*Exodus* 4:10); literally, *heavy of mouth and heavy of tongue*. This can refer to anything from a speech impediment to a simple lack of natural eloquence; in colloquial terms, he lacked "the gift of gab."

26. Hebrew, *ahicha halevi*. This rendition follows Y. Kaufmann, *Toldot Haemunah Hayisraelit, Vol. I*, p.175, note 15 (Hebrew).

27. Hebrew, *nebiecha*.

28. In the last years of the First Commonwealth (see Glossary), some 650 years after the call of Moses, when his distant spiritual descendant, Jeremiah, was rededicated to his calling as a prophet, God employs the same metaphor:

"If you return [to duty], *and I* [agree] *to restore you,*
  [Then] *you shall stand before Me.*
And if you bring forth the priceless from the worthless,
  As My mouth you **[again]** *shall be."* (*Jeremiah* 15:19)

For the context see below, Chapter 15, the final section entitled Reinstatement.

to entertain the notion that the prophets were actual messengers of God, then we must be willing to accept that woven within their words were elements that cannot be explained in purely human terms. This was their claim; that through their words God made His will known to humanity. The consensus of the Jewish people, based on the thousand-year experience with prophecy and almost 2,500 years of subsequent reflection on this experience, is that they were indeed the spokesman of the Almighty. The prophets believed, as did most of their contemporaries, that through them God actually spoke.

And here we have to take a step backward in order to take account of some of the basic underlying assumptions of the Bible if we wish to proceed. Just as the Bible begins by postulating the existence of God:

In the beginning God created the heavens and the earth [*Genesis* 1:1]

as a corollary, Scripture holds as axiomatic that there exist channels of communication between God and His creatures Whom He created in His image.[29] The channels by which God makes His will known to humans are three in number:

1. Signs imprinted in the natural world that can be read and interpreted by humans.[30]
2. Through dreams.[31]
3. By means of prophets.

But communication is not understood to be a one-way street. There are understood to be channels that allow humans to access the realm of the divine:

1. Prayer: this means is open to all.[32]
2. In the pagan world, by means of magic.[33]
3. By means of prophets: prophets, through serving as God's spokesman delivering His messages to humans, are, by virtue of their calling, in close contact with the Almighty, and hence uniquely placed to intercede with Him for sinful humanity; both for individuals and especially for groups, nations and all humankind.

For these reasons the prophet is seen in the Bible as holding a key role: he is the prime interface between God and humanity. Through the prophet God makes known to humans His will. The prophets are God's messengers, and because they are the bearers of His word, they are never left in the dark by God as to His intentions. God makes a point of keeping His agents in the loop.

---

29. *Genesis* 1:26–27; 5:1–2.

30. This is the primary means used by pagans to ascertain the will of the gods, either through the mediation of their clairvoyants or by the casting of lots. (For examples, see Chapter 1, note 35 and relevant text). For Israelites this channel is restricted solely to the use of *Urim* and *Thumim* (see Glossary), a mechanical device manipulated by priests capable of giving answers to simple questions. Among Israelites, use of these means to pose questions to God fell out of use during the course of the 10th century BCE.

31. In the ancient world everyone—pagans and Israelites alike—believed that dreams could contain divine messages, usually coded and hence obscure. This did *not* mean that all dreams were divine messages; it was understood that most dreams were simply dreams. See below Chapter 7, the section entitled The Veto.

32. During the biblical age there were no fixed and regular liturgical services. People prayed spontaneously—"whenever the spirit moved them"—and frequently, on a daily basis.

33. See the subsection above entitled Magic.

Certainly the Lord GOD *does nothing,*
without revealing His intention
to His servants, the prophets [*Amos* 3:7].

The prophet, privy to God's purpose before He acts on it, is thus uniquely in a position to intercede should he be convinced that intervention is necessary. Thus along with his (or her[34]) role as a messenger or spokesperson of God, the prophet also serves as a sort of defense counsel for sinful humanity—in whole or in part—before the bar of divine justice.[35] And just as the first appearance in the Bible of a prophet (Moses) serving as an evangelist—proclaiming God's word to humankind—is accompanied by a descriptive vignette clarifying this new role and defining its function,[36] so does the Bible introduce the prophet's mission as intercessor for sinners by an illustrative incident taken from the life of Abraham.[37]

While the office of the *Nabi* or prophet is clearly defined in the Bible, the prophets themselves appear and act very differently from one another. The role is uniform but the persons who fill it over the centuries of the biblical age cover the entire spectrum of human types and personalities. As such, the way the office is filled at any given time is obviously colored by the unique personality of the individual who occupies it. Inevitably there were some who were enthusiastic about the role they had been called upon to perform, and some who were less so. And among the latter, it is hardly surprising that there were those who found the demands of the calling sufficiently intolerable as to drive them beyond the limits of their endurance. It is three such—each very different from his fellow rebels—that form the subject of this book.

A Final Word

This book, of necessity, will be dealing with subjects that are overtly religious: primarily God, His word, and His ways with the human denizens of the world which He created and governs. This, after all, is what the Bible as a whole is all about. The religious reader takes this for granted as a matter of faith (which does not mean, of course, that he may not have serious problems with the various aspects of God's ways with His creatures as set forth in the Bible; indeed the biblical works we have selected for this study focus on this very issue). But what of those who are not believers, or are

---

34. There were female prophets as well as male.

35. A prime example of this function is displayed by Moses concerning the incident of the Golden Calf. While on Mount Sinai, Moses is informed by God of what the children of Israel have done in his absence—relapsed into idolatry—and therefore He intends to wipe them out and designate Moses as the father of a new people to be in their place. Moses will have none of this; he mounts a strong plea for the sinful people, and convinces God to renounce His intention to destroy them. (*Exodus* 32:7–14) This does not imply that prophets were always successful. Even the best of lawyers can at times fail to convince the court that their client deserves the benefit of the doubt or, failing that, another chance.

36. That is, as God's "mouth," cf. *Exodus* 4:4–16; 7:1–2. See above.

37. *Genesis* 20:1–7. The King of Gerar has taken Sarah into his harem, thinking that she is an unmarried woman. In a dream, God informs him of his mistake. He then orders the king: *"Now restore the man's wife, for he is a prophet (nabi), and he will pray for you, and you will live."* (*Genesis* 20:7) That is, as a prophet Abraham has both the ability and the duty to intervene and gain forgiveness for even a sin as great as wife stealing, resting his case on the fact that it is forgivable because done in ignorance.

skeptical or unsure of where they stand with regard to the belief system that underlies the Bible and is proclaimed by it? Are such persons—usually thought of, and often self-defined as secular—by definition excluded from the prospective readership of this book?

In the Preface the statement was made that this book was "meant to be available to a secular audience." This pledge was meant seriously. The Bible is now the heritage of all humanity, as are, say, Dante's *Divine Comedy* or the *Confessions of Saint Augustine*, not to mention the *Iliad* of Homer or the poetry of Pindar. One does not have to belong to the faith communities of those who produced these masterpieces of the human spirit to be able to appreciate and learn from them.

But to do so there is one urgent requirement. We must renounce our natural tendency towards condescension. It is almost second nature in our culture to see the past as simply a process leading up to us, and hence as somehow simpler, less developed and even childish or naïve in comparison with ourselves. This attitude tends to blind us to the worth of past ages, and to the fact that true sophistication lies in appreciating the truth embodied in the statement of Leopold von Ranke, dean of 19th-century German historians, that every period in history stands justified in the sight of God. In other words, every era has its own worth, and its creations have their own unique and imperishable value. They also have something to teach us. And to be able to appropriate their singular virtues and what they have to offer us we must learn to put aside our current ideas and prejudices for the time we contemplate these works of the past, and look with sympathy on the values and ideas of that age which inform their creations.

William Butler Yeats, contemplating the tendency of human beings to become set in their ways, stultified and petrified of soul, counseled as the only remedy that

> *Soul clap its hands and sing, and louder sing*
> *For every rent in its mortal dress,*
> *Nor is there singing school but studying*
> *Monuments of its own magnificence.*[38]

Looking upon the Books of the Bible as monuments to some of the greatest outpourings of the human soul—even if we may find the idiom of these outpourings strange to our modern sensibilities—can expose their richness even to those who do not share their religious premises. And more, it can open our eyes to the universal human issues with which they wrestle, issues that are as alive today as they were millennia ago when their authors walked the earth.

---

38. W. B. Yeats, "Sailing to Byzantium."

Part I

The *Book of Jonah*

A wise man should so write … that wise men only should be able to commend him.—Thomas Hobbes, Works

Introduction to the *Book of Jonah*

Jonah is one of the shortest books in the Bible, and of biblical books written in narrative prose it is the shortest.[1] At forty-eight verses comprising a mere six hundred and eighty-nine words, the Book is a marvel of compactness, containing enough content to fill to overflowing a work at least five times its length. At first glance *Jonah* seems simple and disarmingly straightforward, but on closer examination it proves to be an extraordinarily complex and difficult book. It contains multiple layers, and it works on several different levels simultaneously. Its plot is replete with surprises; time and again, just when we think we finally have a handle on what is going on, the plot takes an unexpected twist and dashes all our expectations. There are multiple allusions to different parts of the Bible, including quotes from different biblical works, which only seem to confuse the issue. And central to the book is a complex and sophisticated theological argument that weaves through the narrative and is, we will argue, one of the most radical theses to be found in the entire Bible. These are merely some of the factors that make this little book both so intriguing and so difficult to understand. Unless we want to start with some a priori assumption and try to force the tale into that theory's procrustean mold—a not uncommon procedure—we will have to study in some depth this seemingly simple tale before we will be in a position to arrive at any conclusions as to what it is all about, what it means and what are its implications. It is this in-depth analysis that therefore will be our first task. Only when we have a firm grasp as to what the *Book of Jonah* actually says that we can begin to consider what it means. But before we can begin, we need to be clear as to what problems we will face.

Jonah is a book that is glaringly out of place in the Bible. We find it among The Latter Prophets—to be exact, it is one of the twelve so-called Minor Prophets[2]—sandwiched in between the *Books of Obadiah* and *Micah*. It is the only work of narrative prose among all the Books of The Minor Prophets,[3] where it sticks out like a

---

1. Counting by number of sentences (verses) only *Obadiah* at 21, *Haggai* at 38 and *Nahum* at 47 are shorter. These works are all exhortatory orations, two of them written in poetry. Of biblical works composed in narrative prose the closest competitor in conciseness is *Ruth* at 85, almost twice as long.

2. The section of the Hebrew Bible entitled "The Latter Prophets" comprises those works allegedly authored by the prophets themselves; the collections of their sermons, exhortations and denunciations. The so-called "Minor Prophets" is a subcategory, not minor in importance but rather minor in the sense that the sum of their surviving writings and sermons are shorter in length than those of the so-called "Major Prophets": *Isaiah*, *Jeremiah* and *Ezekiel*.

3. It should be mentioned that while both the *Book of Isaiah* (for example *Isaiah* 36–39) and the *Book of Jeremiah* (for example *Jeremiah* 26:1–30:3; 36 etc.) contain sections of third-person narrative prose of a biographical and/or historical nature—added to the words of the prophets to provide context and background—they are very different in style and content from the prose of *Jonah*.

sore thumb. Its placement seems to testify to the assumption of the Canonizers of the Bible that the Book had been written by the 8th-century-BCE prophet Jonah ben Amittai,[4] a belief that is almost certainly mistaken.[5]

Not belonging with the Latter Prophets, and seeing that its own protagonist seems to be a prophet, the Book might perhaps be better placed among those historical works that have prophets as part of their subject matter—*Joshua, Judges, Samuel* and *Kings*[6]—or conversely, as the central subject of *Jonah* is philosophical and theological, its place might seem more properly to be with works such as *Job* and *Ecclesiastes*, or perhaps with narrative works such as *Ruth* and *Esther*. The unhappy fact is that *Jonah* does not find a good fit anywhere. The book is *sui generis*, odd man out, unique. There is nothing quite like it in all Scripture.

Then What Kind of Book Is Jonah?

If we raise the question, to what literary category does *Jonah* belong, we can say with certainty that it is not a typical prophetic work. Aside from the fact that, with practically no exceptions,[7] the classical prophets wrote poetry and *Jonah* is written as narrative prose, the clincher is that the prophets preach, and sermonic exhortation is the common denominator of all their books. But the *Book of Jonah* doesn't preach. Its message is delivered by indirection. Moreover, despite the central protagonist of *Jonah* bearing the name of a well-known 8th-century-BCE prophet,[8] and despite the fact that in the *Book of Jonah* our protagonist performs many of the functions of a prophet, the author is careful never to name him as such. The word *nabi*, prophet, never appears in the Book. The most that one can say on this issue is that *Jonah* seems to use a format similar to that used in the historical sections of the Pentateuch and the Former Prophets[9] which contain tales *about* the prophets and their deeds, but almost never quote much more than snippets of their sermons and sayings.

So if *Jonah*, despite its place in the Canon among the Books of the Prophets, is not itself a prophetic book, then what is it? There have been two main answers given to this question. The first and by far the dominant definition is that *Jonah* is a work of history. Like the tales concerning the doings of Moses, of Samuel, of Elijah, etc., embedded in the various works of historiography that comprise so large a part of the Bible, *Jonah* is intended to be a factual account of several incidents in the life of "Jonah ben Amittai, the prophet, who was of Gath-hepher."[10] As such, the book was meant to be read literally, and so it mostly has been for more than two millennia. It is this literalist reading that has led to the various controversies—especially those

---

4. The order of the Books of The Minor Prophets is intended to be chronological.

5. The truth is that we do not know who wrote the Book; neither is there any consensus as to when it was written. More on this matter later.

6. These Books of the Hebrew Bible are termed "The Former Prophets."

7. Haggai, along with Ezekiel, are two prophets whose books are largely in prose. Other prophetic books do have prose additions, but these are by third parties and not by the prophet himself. See note 3 above.

8. He figures prominently in the account of the reign of King Jeroboam II of Israel (*2 Kings* 14:25).

9. *Joshua, Judges, Samuel* and *Kings*. See note 6 above.

10. A town in the Lower Galilee, about 2 miles from modern Nazareth (*2 Kings* 14:25).

concerning the real-world possibility of a human being surviving for three days in the bowels of a giant fish—that have swirled around the Book, as well as scholarly concerns with regard to perceived contradictions within the text itself. Despite these problems, to this day a literalist reading of the Book is the way it is approached by a majority of its readers.

But while *Jonah* shares many of the traits typical of the tales of the prophets, such as the stories of Elijah and Elisha that are to be found embedded in the pages of the *Book of Kings*, it lacks the specifically historical elements that frame and run through them, and which may justify a literal reading. To my mind at least, *Jonah* lacks the least vestige of the historical concreteness that would warrant categorizing it as historiography.[11] It is this absence of chronological and even geographic specifics that would argue against reading the book literally. The avowedly fabulous nature of the narrative—the very fact that *Jonah* is best known as a "fish story" speaks for itself—only strengthens the case against a literalist reading. All of which argues for finding some other way of understanding *Jonah*.

There have always been those who have rejected a literalist approach to *Jonah* in favor of the alternative of reading it as a fable; a common genre in the literature of the ancient world. A fable may be defined as a fictitious narrative—usually of supernatural or highly marvelous happenings—which under the guise of the events related conveys a moral or spiritual truth. As this is the interpretive approach I will be following in my exposition, it seems appropriate to digress for a few moments to discuss some aspects of this literary category.

Probably the most famous of all known composers in this international style of literature was the early 6th-century Greek fabulist Aesop.[12] The fables attributed to him pretty much define the genre. One example will suffice:

> A crow has found a piece of cheese and has retired to a tree branch to eat it. A fox, seeing the crow with a piece of cheese in its beak and wanting it for himself, stations himself under the branch. Calling to the crow he butters her up, praising the gloss of her feathers, calling her the most beautiful of birds and wondering out loud if it is true what he has heard that the beauty of her voice exceeds that of her appearance. The crow, immensely flattered, condescends to give the fox a demonstration of her singing voice. As she opens her beak to give a harsh caw the cheese falls down, whereupon the Fox snaps it up, and, chuckling, ambles off.

Fables were part of the literary repertoire of ancient Israel and a number are to be found in the Hebrew Bible. One of the most famous of these is known as Jotham's Fable[13]:

> The trees of a forest decide to elect one of their number to be king and to rule over them, but

---

11. Normal biblical historical narrative routinely states where and when the events occurred, names the principal "actors" and defines their roles. *Jonah* does none of these. There are no chronological markers in the text, while the vagueness of its geographic references borders on the mythological. God's call to the story's main protagonist, Jonah son of Amittai—the event which drives the entire tale—is neither dated nor located; it, as all the events depicted in the little book, occurs in a sort of timeless void. If we wish to identify the hero with the historic Jonah ben Amittai, then we are free to assume that the tale takes place in the eighth century BCE. But nowhere in the story is this assumption confirmed or, for that matter, denied.

12. Beyond the approximate dates of his life (620–560 BCE), and that he was a slave, little is known of him. The collections of the fables attributed to him are legion.

13. Jotham lived in the eleventh century BCE, almost 500 years before Aesop. But the tale told in his oration at Shechem was not even original to Jotham; it was simply a reworked version of a more than 1,000 year-old fable that scholars have traced back to third millennium Mesopotamia. See my *Judges and Saviors*, pp. 214–216.

candidate after candidate—the olive tree, the fig tree, even the grapevine which is properly not even a tree—decline the offer. They are all productive and have better things to do than devote time and effort to the thankless task of ruling their compatriots. Finally, for want of any other option, the trees turn to the worthless bramble-bush whose only use is to serve as kindling to start fires. Not being productive, it has time on its hands and consents to be king on condition that it will rule with an iron hand, and it warns that if any of the trees should dare disobey, it will start a fire and burn the entire forest down! [*Judges* 9:8–15]

Sometimes fables spell out the moral at their end and sometimes they don't, leaving the reader to figure it out for himself or herself. But always the story has a moral: that is the entire point of its being a fable. And always, the precise details of the tale matter far less than the moral. The crow could just as well have been a raven or a buzzard, and the fox some other animal; the whole point is that it is the height of foolishness to allow empty words to flatter one into relinquishing real benefits. Or again, it didn't have to be an olive or a fig tree; oak trees and cedars could just as easily be substituted for the proud and smug masters of the forest community. The danger of abandoning civic leadership to worthless and nonproductive riffraff is what Jotham's Fable is about.

What we will contend is that *Jonah* falls into this category of literature and should be read as such; the fabulous elements of the tale should be seen as window dressing and the lesson or moral being conveyed as the essence of the matter. Whether this method of reading the Book will justify itself is a question that will only be answerable after we have tried it. Our analysis of *Jonah* will be the test of this thesis.

The Assumptions Underlying This Study

In the interest of transparency we have stated up front our considered assumption that *Jonah* is neither a work of prophecy nor of history, but a fable meant to convey some moral or spiritual thesis. This is one of our starting points, and as such one of our two main working hypotheses. The second, which is more than a bit controversial, is that the *Book of Jonah* that we hold in our hands today is a unified composition. It is this work as we now possess it that is our sole interest. We will not be concerned with the prehistory of the Book, the stages of its composition, if any, and the sources upon which it may have drawn (all literary works have at least some prehistory and all serious authors have sources upon which they draw). These have been the subjects of innumerable studies and we have no interest in going over well plowed ground. Our interest resides solely in the finished product: to try to understand and appreciate the *Book of Jonah* as it is now. We furthermore will treat *Jonah* not as a compilation of patched-together sources or as a core overlaid with editorial additions—both not uncommon scholarly assumptions—but as a unitary work, composed by a single author, which has come down to us in virtually pristine and unaltered form, pretty much as its author originally wrote it.[14] This assumption implies a comprehensive plan to the book that informs its construction and its literary style, and a unified purpose

---

14. MT (The Masoretic Text; see Glossary) in its Leningrad Codex version, dating from 1009 CE, is singularly well preserved and is the one that we follow. With one exception (*Jonah* 1:8) it is virtually identical with the LXX version (see Glossary).

that works its way through to a resolution of the issues that lie on the surface—the plot—and those that lie beneath—what the book is about; its moral or meaning. This will be our second working hypothesis, and again only time will tell if it is justified.

The Author

If we begin with the working assumption that *Jonah* is a unified composition and not a hodgepodge patched together by editors, then it must have had an author. What can we postulate about this author? To begin with we know neither the name nor even the gender of our author.[15] All that we can say with relative certainty is that whoever he or she was, the intricate and sophisticated plotting and composition of the work testify to a writer of genius. Moreover, unlike Shakespeare, who had probably the largest active vocabulary of any author in the history of world literature, we can state that the author of *Jonah* has one of the tiniest. Even in comparison with the other authors of Books of the Bible, the vocabulary of our author is remarkably small. This paucity is unlikely to be the product of social deprivation; the author is intimately acquainted with biblical books with much more extensive vocabularies.[16] It would seem rather that the author—for ideological or stylistic reasons—has purposely restricted the Book's vocabulary, even as he or she has curtailed to a minimum the number of words contained within the confines of the work. On the other hand, the author seems under no compunction to select those words he or she chooses to use from the standard biblical vocabulary, but feels free, as did Shakespeare, to coin words and phrases not found elsewhere in Scripture.[17] One can only marvel at what the author manages to achieve with this restricted vocabulary. In *Jonah* we are beholding one of the most remarkable literary gems in world literature, and its author proves to be one of the greatest literary stylists of all time.

One further fact about our author becomes apparent upon probing deeply into the contents of our little book: he or she is far from being a conventional thinker. The *Book of Jonah* reveals its author to be a radical, one not afraid to challenge and overturn one of the central pillars of the faith of Israel. It must have taken great courage to propose, even in the guise of a fabulous tale, so fundamental a departure from conventional orthodoxy as *Jonah* affirms. What this revolutionary doctrine is will have to wait on the author's sense of timing—in matters of both plot and meaning the author keeps us dangling until almost the very last words—but suffice it to say at this point that the repercussions of this revisionist interpretation have not only deeply influenced the Israelite understanding of morality, but also have deeply impacted Israel's daughter religions, Christianity and Islam.

---

15. This assumption rejects the possibility that the *Book of Jonah* is a somewhat fictionalized autobiographical work, authored by the historical eighth century BCE prophet Jonah ben Amittai.

16. This is not speculation. As we shall see, the author quotes and alludes to a surprising number of these works.

17. Just two examples of such, taken from the final two verses of the Book: *bin-laila* (4:10), literally *son of a night* which we rendered as *in a night*, and *asher lo yada bain yemeeno lesmolo* (4:11), which we render as *who do not know their right hand from their left*. They are unique to *Jonah*.

The Problem of the Date of *Jonah's* Composition

Like speculation regarding the authorship and prehistory of *Jonah*, the question of the date of the Book's composition has exercised the minds of countless commentators. The reason for this focus is the conviction that if we could but know when the Book was composed, the knowledge of the historical context—the political and social situation, the issues that dominated the period, the ideas floating around at that time—would be decisive in clarifying many of the ambiguities in the text and would provide the necessary context into which to fit the book and thus understand its purpose. Unfortunately, despite centuries of speculation and of effort, no consensus has emerged. Magonet sums up our current situation: "critical opinion gives such a wide range of dates … from the 9th to the 2nd century for 'Jonah' … that no clear-cut historical relationship can be evoked."[18] I do not find this diversity of opinion especially disturbing, because my contention is that the entire issue is irrelevant to our concerns and of academic interest only. If we accept the position detailed above, that Jonah is not a historical narrative but a fable, then we are in a timeless realm where dating has no place. A fox, a crow and a piece of cheese are not restricted to any specific period of time, and the moral regarding the danger of succumbing to flattery is not specific to any given century. And as we have seen, Jotham, living in 11th-century-BCE Israel, could appropriate and adapt to his own uses and needs a local fable which the Canaanites had themselves appropriated from its original birthplace in Mesopotamia more than 1,000 years before. Its moral remains as valid today as it was over 4,000 years ago when it was first coined.[19] By their very nature those fables that survived the centuries are both timeless and universal in use and application.[20]

Jonah as a Work of Art

Last on our agenda, but far from least in order of importance, is the issue of the artistic nature of this little work. Before we can begin to appreciate *Jonah* as a great religious work which, as we will contend, advocates what amounts to a complete revision of our understanding of humanity's relationship with the divine, we must first recognize the Book as a literary masterpiece; a work of art of the highest caliber. The *Book of Jonah* is universally considered to be a literary gem, one of the finest examples of narrative prose in the Bible. To a reader not steeped in the discipline of literary criticism this evaluation might seem unusual, seeing that at a mere 689 words the entire Book barely passes the halfway mark of the first chapter of *Oliver Twist*, a point where the novel has not even gotten underway.[21] To pack as much content as the book contains into so little without making the resulting narrative seem heavy

---

18. Jonathan Magonet, *Form and Meaning*, p. 78.
19. See note 13 above.
20. For those who are nevertheless interested in the matter, I survey in Appendix A some of the arguments involved and, for what it is worth, come to an answer that, although irrelevant to our present study, I find more compelling than some of the others that have been proposed.
21. The first chapter of Charles Dickens' novel, *Oliver Twist*, is comprised of a little less than 1,100 words, a quite short chapter as things go. Chapter 2 is more than three times as long.

and overloaded, is an extraordinary tour de force, only made possible by meticulous literary construction. One cannot even begin to achieve an adequate appreciation of the Book without taking this factor into consideration.

But if the purpose of the work is—as we shall maintain—to present its readers with a radical revision of what is expected of them as they try to better their lives, then why not simply come out and say it, rather than invest what must have amounted to enormous effort and painstaking labor in encasing the message in so concise a work of art? This question is relevant not only in the case of *Jonah*; narrative prose throughout the Bible is unfailingly characterized by a surprisingly high level of literary quality and a well developed sense of style. Large or small, all these Biblical works see themselves as works of art, and strive mightily for excellence.[22]

Beyond an obvious attempt to woo an audience habituated to a sophisticated literary style,[23] we must never lose sight of the fact that the authors of the Books that eventually made it into the Bible were consciously writing works of *religious* import. These were compositions whose subject was God and His ways with humankind, intended, if not necessarily, as Milton put it, to "justify the ways of God to Men,"[24] then at the least to illuminate them. To these biblical authors, works dealing with God deserved only the best, the most artistic and exalted efforts of which one was capable. Even as the sculptors who ornamented medieval cathedrals would never have dreamt of leaving roughhewn and unfinished those parts of their works that would have been invisible to future viewers[25]—these works were meant for the glory of God, and God sees all—so to authors of the biblical age penning *religious* works it was a matter of the utmost urgency to present these topics clothed in the noblest literary style of which they were capable. Thus biblical narrative prose is, with only rare exceptions, sculpted into works of high art.

When meaning is artistically presented, the artistic medium becomes an integral part of the message; the message can only be fully understood when taking the medium into consideration. Therefore it becomes worthwhile to invest a number of pages in acquainting readers, most of whom are non-specialists, with some of the elements that make *Jonah* one of the outstanding gems of the literature of the ancient world. So as to keep our discussion within reasonable bounds we will choose all of our examples from the first chapter of *Jonah*.

We begin by returning to the minuscule size of the Book: 48 verses or sentences.

---

22. This is true as well of those works written in poetry—Books such as *Amos*, *Isaiah* and *Jeremiah*—are consciously composed as works of art.

23. We must never forget that the 36 Books that eventually were chosen for inclusion in the Canon—becoming part of what we now know as the Hebrew Bible—were originally but a miniscule portion of an extensive literature created by the Israelites over a period of 1,000 years, the best of it—judging from the biblical Books that have survived—achieving a remarkably high artistic level. Those Books that were canonized were preserved for us. Some that were not are preserved for us in collections known as the Apocrypha and the Pseudepigrapha, but the vast bulk of ancient Israelite literature is irretrievably lost.

24. John Milton, *Paradise Lost*, I, l. 22.

25. We, who can now view the gargoyles that embellish the roofs of the great Gothic cathedrals of Europe from hovering helicopters—a possibility never conceived of by the medieval sculptors—can now see that the tops of these fantastic figures, which were then invisible to human eyes, are as finely carved and finished as the lower parts which were the object of the fascinated gaze of the throngs of worshipers going in and out of these houses of worship.

When we narrow our focus to the first chapter, we find ourselves with a total of only 16 verses or—in the original Hebrew—only 253 words; barely enough to make a decent paragraph. Yet how much has been packed into these few phrases! The conciseness is remarkable. There is not a single superfluous syllable; each word is made to count. Indeed, words are often made to serve several purposes at the same time. We will need to pay attention to each word and how it is used, each turn of phrase.

Yet despite its compact form, this first chapter is itself divided into three distinct units: an Introduction (1:1–3) which also serves double duty as the Introduction to the entire Book, the Main Body (1:4–15) and an Epilogue (1:16). As such, the chapter forms a complete mini-composition that can stand by itself. Further, the Main Body exhibits an inner structure: should one count ninety-four words in the Hebrew beginning with verse 4, and ninety-four words backwards from the end of verse 15, we arrive at the exact center of the Main Body where we find Jonah's self-identification and his confession of faith, both being the focus of this section and its turning point:

> "A Hebrew am I, and the Lord, the God of the heavens do I revere,
> Who made the sea and the dry land." [1:9][26]

Not only does the artistic form taken by the architecture of the chapter and its parts serve to direct our attention to the meaning the author intends to convey, but another literary technique—that of keywords—serves much the same purpose. Martin Buber's description of this biblical artistic technique remains definitive[27]:

> A *leitwort* [keyword][28] is a word or a word-root that recurs significantly in a text, in a continuum of texts, or in a configuration of texts: by following these repetitions, one is able to decipher or grasp a meaning of the text, or at any rate, the meaning will be revealed more strikingly. The repetition, as we have said, need not to be merely of the word itself but also of the word-root; in fact, the very difference of words can often intensify the dynamic action of the repetition. I call it "dynamic" because between the combinations of sounds related to one another in this manner a kind of movement takes place: if one imagines the entire text deployed before him, one can sense waves moving back and forth between the words. The measured repetition that matches the inner rhythm of the text, or rather, that wells up from it, is one of the most powerful means for conveying meaning without expressing it.

These keywords, blatantly obvious in the original Hebrew, are often obscured in modern translation by the use of synonyms and by paraphrase, due to an often slavish adherence to Western literary style.[29] In my translation I have made every effort to preserve the keywords wherever the dictates of the English language permit.

---

26. This artistic conceit of reserving the exact center by word count of a composition for a statement, either of what the literary unit is all about or of stressing its main point, is not unique to *Jonah*. For example, *Psalm* 23 employs the same artistic construct. Leaving out the superscription and beginning with the words (in the Hebrew of course) *The Lord is my shepherd*, and then counting 26 words, and from the end of the Psalm backwards 26 words, one finds at this numerical center point the words *ki atah eemadee*; *For You* (God) *are with me*; the entire point of the Psalm.

27. Almost a century ago, Martin Buber and Franz Rosenzweig were the first to analyze this technique of purposeful repetition of words, recognizing it as a distinctive convention of biblical prose.

28. Literally, "leading-word." The quotation is from Buber's book *Darka shel Miqra* (Hebrew). Jerusalem, 1964, p. 284. The translation is by Robert Alter in *The Art of Biblical Narrative*. New York: Basic Books, 1981, p. 93.

29. On the other hand, due to its close adherence to the original biblical text, the King James Bible often preserves the keyword phenomenon quite well.

Two examples of keywords in chapter 1 of *Jonah* are the word *yare* (to *fear*, to *revere*, to *stand in awe of*—the precise meaning in each case dependent on the context), repeated six times, and the word *yarod* (to *go down*) repeated three times.[30]

The first, *yare*, appears as follows:

vs. 5—The storm breaks out and the sailors are *afraid* (*vayeeru*)
vs. 9—Jonah declares that he *reveres, he stands in awe* (*yare*) of the LORD
vs. 10—Now the men [the sailors] *feared with a great fear* (*vayeeru ... yeerah gedolah*)
vs. 16—Now the men felt *measureless awe* (*vayeeru ... yeerah*)[31]

The storm breaks out and the sailors are *afraid*, but Jonah is not; he knows what is happening and why, and he informs the sailors that he *stands in awe* of the LORD, that he *reveres* Him Who is the cause of the storm. The storm gets worse and the sailors' terror increases: they now *fear* with a very great *fear*. Jonah now offers himself as a sacrifice to save the ship and the lives of the sailors; they throw him overboard and the storm abruptly ceases. Now the phrase from verse 10, *vayeeru haanashim yeerah gedolah* is repeated (verse 16) but with a completely different meaning: they are no longer afraid but are experiencing *immeasurable awe* of the LORD; Jonah's *reverence* and *awe* of the LORD (verse 9) has been transferred to the pagan sailors. (When we analyze the chapter in detail we will discuss the significance of these shifts of meaning and of the locus of these emotions.)

The second example of a keyword is the root *yarod* (to *go down*). In this case we have a progression: Jonah is running away from the LORD.

vs. 3—he *went down* [from the highlands] to Jaffa
vs. 3—he *went down* into her [the ship]
vs. 5—now Jonah *had gone down* into the lowest recesses of the ship (i.e., the hold of the vessel) and was fast asleep (*vayeradem*).

Although a completely different word, this term for being in a deep slumber contains the same three consonant letters as *yarod*, and would have been recognized by the original audience of the Book as a further stage in the progression: from the highlands to the seashore, from the dock downwards into the ship, from the deck down into the hold, and now from consciousness to the oblivion of sleep—always downward. In the next chapter we will find Jonah *gone down* (*yaradetee*) to the bottom of the sea.

The emphasis on Jonah's descent, spiritual as well as physical, is relentless.

There are several other keywords in chapter 1—*arise* (*kum*), *evil* (*raah*), *to cast* (*haytayl*) etc.—which will be dealt with ad. loc.

The purpose of the foregoing analysis has been to sensitize the reader to some of the artistic dimensions of the narrative we are about to pursue, and to the literary artifacts employed by the author of our chapter to give to a limited number of words, arranged in a mere sixteen sentences, a weight and complexity of implication that would be hard to match with a straightforward exposition of five times the length.

---

30. The appearance of this keyword a fourth time in chapter 2, continuing the sequence, is one of several connecting links that linguistically bind together the Book.

31. See Chapter 1, note 54 on the grammatical construction of this phrase which prevents a literal translation into English.

Where Do We Go from Here?

Søren Kierkegaard once remarked that if one wishes to sew, one must first tie a knot in the thread. One has to make a beginning, and to have a beginning one must have a starting point. The two working hypotheses I have detailed above are positions I took before beginning the course of study and research that led to this book. They are my two knots in the thread, my twin starting points.

Having completed the process of getting to know and at least partially understand the *Book of Jonah*—a lengthier process as it turned out than I had anticipated—I have been rewarded by the discovery that my twin knots did not lead me astray. They provided me with a suitable starting point. All the rest of the various conclusions and insights that I have outlined above or hinted at are the results of my journey of discovery. How I arrived at them will become apparent in the pages to come.

The path I took followed the course of the Book. At times my research led me into cul-de-sacs and blind alleys, and I was forced to retrace my steps. The author of *Jonah* had a macabre sense of humor, and must have been chuckling while writing the Book as, time and again, he (or perhaps it was she) set the reader up and then pulled the rug out from under him or her. But ultimately, I discovered, if one perseveres, one is rewarded; the author comes clean at the end, or so it seems. But then again, does he?

I have elected to take you, my readers, down the path of discovery that I followed, including one or two of the blind alleys I stumbled into and some of the false turns that I took. In this way, as I retrace my steps we will become partners in unraveling the carefully plotted puzzle designed by a remarkable writer in the distant past.

Chapter 1

The Flight of the Rebel

I fled Him down the nights and down the days;
I fled Him, down the arches of the years,
I fled Him down the labyrinthine ways
Of my own mind....
From those strong Feet that followed, followed after.
—Francis Thompson, *The Hound of Heaven*

Now it came to pass,[1] *that the word of the* LORD *came to Jonah, son of Amittai, saying, "Arise, go to Nineveh, the Great City,*[2] *and cry out against her; for their evil has risen up before Me." And Jonah arose to flee from before the* LORD *to Tarshish. Now he went down to Jaffa and found a ship bound for Tarshish; so he paid the fare* [for the passage],[3] *went down into her*[4] [in order] *to go with them*[5] *to Tarshish from before the* LORD [1:1–3].

These three verses, which serve as both Introduction to this chapter and Introduction to the Book as a whole, begin, without preamble, by introducing the two main protagonists of our tale: the LORD and Jonah, son of Amittai. The introduction takes place with neither setting nor context; as it were in a vacuum. We are told neither where the confrontation takes place nor when.[6] Out of space and time, the LORD is shown as confronting a human being with an unequivocal command: Arise—that is, get up—go to Nineveh (defined as a "Great City") and because their behavior has become intolerable to Me make proclamation against them (that is, against the inhabitants of Nineveh).

---

1. Hebrew *vayehee*, a term used in the Bible to signal the opening of a work (cf. *Joshua* 1:1, *Ezekiel* 1:1, *Ruth* 1:1, *Esther* 1:1 etc.), the opening of a new section within a given Book (cf. *Jonah* 3:1), or even at times to mark a sudden turn of events that introduces a completely new situation or theme (cf. *Jonah* 1:4, i.e., the storm). For my decision to, at times, revert in my translation of the biblical text to phraseology that is archaic and has dropped out of current usage, see my treatment of the problems of translation in the Preface, especially note 26.

2. That is, "Greater Nineveh," an urban complex which included Rehaboth-ir, Caleh and Resen which served as satellite cities, and together with Nineveh formed a large urban sprawl. In *Genesis* 10:11–12 these three together with Nineveh are referred to as *"the Great City."*

3. Literally, *her fare.*

4. I.e., from the dock down into the ship.

5. Oddly we hear of no other passengers. The only alternative would then seem to be that this is a reference to the crew.

6. While we will be able to make some educated guesses from what we are told, the customary temporal anchorage routinely given at the opening of biblical Books and the geographic setting are conspicuous by their absence. For comparison, see the opening verses of the Books referred to in note 1 above.

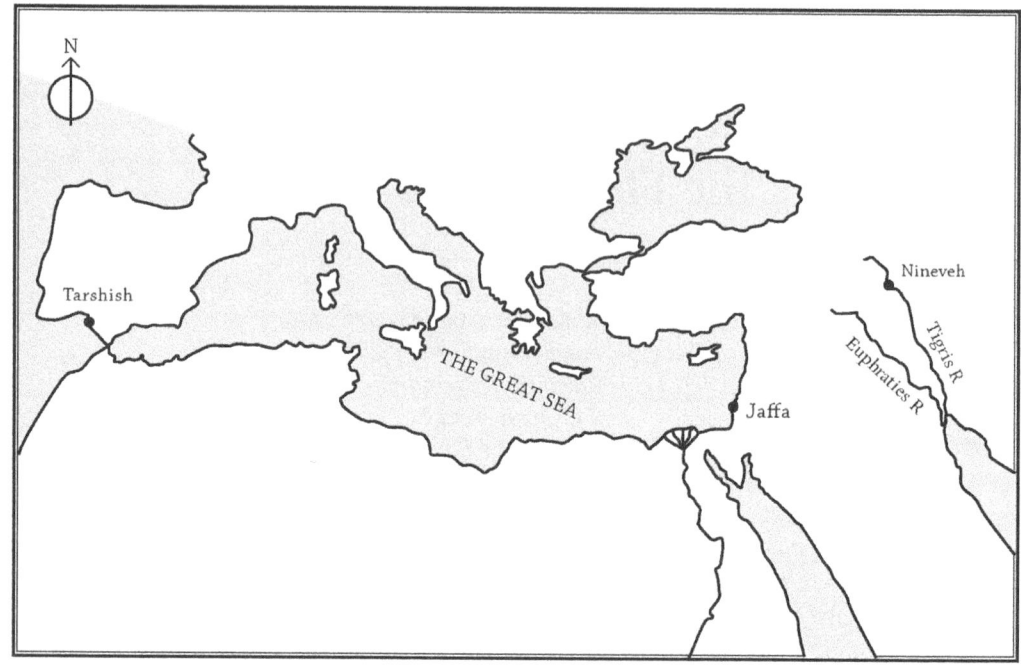

Map 1

The known world as reflected in the *Book of Jonah* showing all sites mentioned in the book.

Who the Lord is the author most probably expects his readers to know, although to make assurance doubly sure he will in short order arrange for his use of this proper noun, the Lord, to be explicitly defined.[7] But our second protagonist, the hero—or possibly the anti-hero—of our tale, is not accorded such complete disclosure; he is left in a curiously ambivalent status throughout the narrative. True, the author has our protagonist unmask his ethnic identity as a Hebrew (but note, not an Israelite), and proclaim himself to be a worshiper of the Lord (although never does he state, or even imply, that he is a monotheist).[8] True, by giving us his name, complete with patronymic, he has allowed us to identify him with a historic personality—the famous 8th-century-BCE prophet Jonah, the son of Amittai—but never does he refer to him as a prophet. We are left free to make the identification and draw all sorts of inferences therefrom, but nowhere does he *explicitly* confirm either his protagonist's identity, or any of our resultant assumptions. About the only thing that we can say with complete certainty about Jonah as he is presented to us in this tale is that he is a human being with all the strengths and weaknesses to which humanity is prone; in other words, *everyman*.

At any rate, sticking to the bare bones of our narrative, while Jonah is never

---

7. See 1:9 (from this point onward until the end of this section, all verse references without citation of a specific Book, are to the *Book of Jonah*).

8. We, from our perspective, tend to equate the belief in the Lord with monotheism, but to the pagans whom Jonah is addressing the Lord is simply one god among many. Jonah never denies the existence of any gods but the Lord (monotheism), nor even claims that among the plethora of choices he worships the Lord exclusively (monolatry).

explicitly defined as a prophet we are shown him being called upon to perform one of the tasks of a prophet. God speaks to him and commands him to proclaim His word to humankind. We are not told at this point what he is to proclaim; presumably the doom of the Ninevites. Getting a bit ahead of ourselves, when later Jonah is quoted as proclaiming:

"*Yet forty days and Nineveh shall be overthrown!*" [3:4]

it is likely that this is what he had originally been commanded to say.

However, even though one of the Children of Israel,[9] Jonah is not being sent to preach the word of the Lord to his own people,[10] but to a city of pagans. This is hardly unprecedented: Moses was sent by God to proclaim His word to Pharaoh, King of Egypt.[11] Elijah was commissioned by God to go to Damascus and anoint Hazael to be king over Aram.[12] The Lord is God over all the earth and, from time to time He will send Israelite prophets to pagan peoples to proclaim His word; Israelite prophets routinely directed prophecies to the nations.[13] The mission of Jonah, while unusual, would be nothing out of the norm.

What is extraordinary is Jonah's reaction. He begins by complying: he has been called upon to arise, so he rises. But as to the command to go to Nineveh, instead of obeying, without a word he turns and sets off in the opposite direction! This is no error on his part; he knows perfectly well in which direction Nineveh lies. His purpose, we are told, is to "flee from before the Lord to Tarshish."[14] His move is an act of open rebellion. He does not waste his breath on explanation or argument. He at once takes steps to implement his decision. He goes down to Jaffa,[15] a major Mediterranean port, locates a ship due shortly to depart for his chosen destination, books passage, goes down from the dock and boards the boat. So that there should be no mistake, the author repeats his destination three times: Jonah is setting out for the very end of the known world, as far as he could possibly get from the place where he was commanded to go. And with his act of boarding the boat the conditions that will determine all that will take place in the Book are fixed.

Two critical questions are raised by Jonah's actions and what we have been told of his intentions in "fleeing from before the Lord." Does Jonah really think that he

---

9. Even if we refrain from identifying our Jonah with the historic Jonah, son of Amittai, the name itself is an almost certain indication of his being an Israelite.

10. As was the historic Jonah, son of Amittai. See *2 Kings* 14:25.

11. *Exodus* 3:10; 4:21–23; 5:1–5 etc.

12. *1 Kings* 19:15. Elijah never lived to fulfill this mandate. After his death it was his disciple and successor, the prophet Elisha, who fulfilled it for him.

13. For example see *Amos* 1:3–2:3 and *Jeremiah* 46:1–51:64.

14. Probably the Phoenician colony of Tartessus, beyond the Mediterranean on the Atlantic coast of Spain is meant. This was the last port of call to the far West which any shipping line reached. *Isaiah* 66:19 groups the inhabitants of Tarshish with nations so far distant from the center of things (i.e., the land of Israel) that they have never heard of the name of the Lord.

15. With the mention of Jaffa we complete the sparse list of geographic markers given by our author: *Nineveh*, on the Eastern bank of the Tigris River in Iraq, opposite present-day Mosul, a bit more than 550 miles as the crow flies northeast of the Land of Israel, *Tarshish* (see previous note), and now *Jaffa*, a major port on the Eastern Mediterranean shore (see MAP 1). From the fact that Jonah *descends* to Jaffa (presumably the closest point where he could expect to find a ship sailing to Tarshish), we might infer that Jonah received his commission to go to Nineveh somewhere in the Highlands of Israel.

can get away with it? Does he believe that by changing his geographic location—even to the ends of the earth—he can escape from God? And secondly, what is it that is driving Jonah to rebel against the Lord?

As to the first, considering the pagan world of the 8th century BCE in which ostensibly Jonah finds himself embedded—a world which believes that specific gods have jurisdiction over particular territories—it might seem reasonable to conclude that Jonah thought that if he could only "get out of town," i.e., out of God's area of authority, he could put himself out of His reach. But Jonah is no pagan; he is a committed monotheist. He doesn't believe in multiple gods, each with his own limited jurisdiction, but in the Lord, Creator and Ruler of the entire universe. As he will proclaim in his forthcoming declaration of faith:

> "*The* Lord, *the God of the heavens, do I revere,*[16] *Who made the sea and the dry land*"[17] [1:9].

And as we shall learn, he really believes this. He may harbor a hidden hope that if he shifts his location, out in the boondocks he may have a stroke of luck and escape notice—people do buy lottery tickets in the rather forlorn hope that lightning might strike, despite knowing the odds to be a million to one against—but rationally Jonah knows perfectly well that God's reach extends beyond the three-mile limit. There is no escaping His dominion in Tarshish. Then what can be the purpose of his flight?

Jonah, unlike his great predecessor Moses,[18] refuses to argue or remonstrate with God. He is beyond words. His flight is, in itself, his answer to God's command; his running away is probably no more and no less than a dramatic expression of outrage over his mission and his rejection of it. He knows that ultimately he cannot escape, and he knows full well the punishment for rebellion against God. But what he is being called upon to do so violates his most deeply held convictions that he is willing to give up his life rather than betray his principles. I believe that in embarking for Tarshish it is likely that Jonah is consciously setting out on the path of martyrdom.[19]

In taking this interpretive approach I am rejecting the line of argument that what is driving Jonah is the fear that the mission will fatally tarnish his reputation. This line of reasoning goes somewhat as follows: God has pronounced doom upon Nineveh and has commissioned Jonah as a prophet to proclaim their coming destruction. But Jonah knows God's nature[20] and understands that if God is sending

---

16. Or *do I stand in awe of*.

17. *The sea and the dry land* is a *merism*, a figure of speech in which a totality is expressed by two contrasting extremes, such as *near and far, thick and thin, old and young* etc. Thus the phrase *the sea and the dry land* simply stands for *everything, the entire Earth*. The use of merisms as a rhetorical device is typical of our author's style: beyond this instance we have *days/nights* (2:1), *greatest/least* (3:5), *man/beast* (3:7, 8), and *human beings/cattle* (4:11).

18. Upon being commissioned by God to go down to Egypt, confront Pharaoh and liberate the Children of Israel, Moses makes a sustained effort to argue himself out of the job, until God, having had enough, tells Moses to just get going. Moses then capitulates, stops arguing and starts on his mission. (*Exodus* 3:11–4:17)

19. By martyrdom we mean the willingness to give up one's life in the service of one's ideals, be they what they may. The term itself is neutral and has no necessary connection with religion in general, or any given religion in particular. One can opt to sacrifice one's life—i.e., become a martyr—for one's nation, for political ideals, etc.

20. See 4:2.

him to warn them, then the Ninevites are being given the option of repenting. And should they do so, God will spare them. Should this occur Jonah will appear to the world as a false prophet, a charlatan; he proclaimed the destruction of Nineveh and it didn't happen. This loss of face is something he will be unable to endure. He would rather die than suffer such humiliation.[21] I find attributing such motives to Jonah as demeaning. It turns him into a petty individual; the plot of the Book becomes a squalid struggle over reputation. If this is all there is to the Book I cannot see what it is doing in the Bible.

As I see the Book, it involves a struggle—to the death from Jonah's point of view—over principle. Ibn Ezra, the medieval biblical commentator (see Glossary), in his comment on 1:1, makes a crucial distinction between a common biblical expression *levroaḥ mipnai* (*to flee from the face of*) and the almost identical *levroaḥ milifnai* (*to flee from before*): they are *not* synonymous. The former connotes flight induced by fear, while the second (which is the expression used regarding Jonah's flight to Tarshish) refers to turning one's back on someone, breaking contact and distancing oneself for reason. The repetition of this latter expression as the closing statement of this Introductory section to the Book would seem to indicate the author's wish to emphasize his view that Jonah's flight is one based on principle.

But what principle? What is driving Jonah? In this question, we will discover, lies the crux of the Book, and on this issue opinions are deeply divided. In over two thousand years of heated argument not even the beginning of a consensus has developed. We have briefly outlined above one of the opinions which, perhaps too hastily, we have summarily rejected. There are a number of others which we might consider far more serious, all with impressive lineages. Allow me to present one of them which, at this early stage of our investigation, seems to me highly compelling.[22]

This approach to the *Book of Jonah* and to the character of its central human protagonist was first proposed about five hundred years ago by the statesman, financier and biblical commentator, Don Isaac Abravanel.[23] He begins by accepting the identification of the hero of the Book with the historic figure of the prophet Jonah, son of Amittai. This allows him to anchor our hero in the history of the world of the 8th-century-BCE Ancient Near East. We know from *2 Kings* 14:25 that Jonah was a contemporary of King Jeroboam II (793–753 BCE), who presided over the last great age of the Kingdom of Israel. It was the rise and westward expansion of the Assyrian Empire that brought this golden age to a close, eventually destroying the Kingdom in

---

21. This thesis has been advanced by as varied proponents as J. G. Herder and Thomas Paine (*The Age of Reason*).

22. The other main contenders will not be overlooked. In due course they too will be presented for consideration.

23. Abravanel, *Commentary on the Latter Prophets* (Pisaro, 1520). No cloistered, ivory-towered scholar, Abravanel was very much a man of the world. Three times over a self-made millionaire, court financier and trusted counselor to kings—and more to the point, respected by the oligarchs who ruled the Venetian Empire (of all the tough-minded rulers of that turbulent age, the Venetian oligarchs were among the toughest)—Abravanel was a deeply religious person, a great biblical scholar and a man of inflexible principle. I believe that it is possible to read elements of his own character into the way he sees Jonah. Certainly it took a statesman with a wide experience in the ruthless world of international power politics to arrive at the conclusions Abravanel reached.

722 BCE, and permanently exiling the survivors of the devastation.[24] Nineveh was the capital of the Assyrian Empire when it was at its height.

Abravanel sees Jonah as a fervent patriot and a devoted lover of his people. Foreseeing the forthcoming devastation of his land and the annihilation of his people, Jonah wishes nothing more fervently than the destruction of this "Evil Empire," this ravisher of the nations and exterminator of entire peoples. The news that the crimes and atrocities of Assyria have finally moved God to decree doom upon the empire's capital is music to Jonah's ears, but his announced role in the coming divine drama fills him with dread. His being sent to proclaim their doom implies a second chance for these monsters. Should they heed his warning and change their ways God may yet spare them; and Jonah does not want them spared. Let them off the hook and the chances are that they will resume their westward drive and destroy Israel. Jonah, with all his heart, wants Nineveh destroyed, wants Assyria to implode, wants his land and his people spared destruction. Rather than become the instrument of Assyria's possible salvation and Israel's subsequent annihilation, Jonah would rather die. In fleeing from before the LORD Jonah is rejecting any possibility of playing a part in such an abhorrent scenario. In his rebellion against his Master Jonah is fully cognizant that he is committing suicide. So be it; in choosing martyrdom he will be saving his people.

There are several incipient problems with this reading, but at the present stage of our investigation of the *Book of Jonah* this seems the most viable of the available solutions to the mystery of Jonah's motives, and as such we will provisionally adopt it as our working hypothesis. As we progress we will see how well it holds up in the face of the many surprising twists and turns that will be taken by our marvelous tale.

The Storm

At this point in our analysis we need to pause for a moment and take stock. In our treatment of the plot we may seem to be relating to the tale as though it is an account of events that actually took place, and that Jonah was a real person whose personal motives we are trying to unravel; in other words, we are taking a literalist approach to the Book. But recall, one of our main assumptions is that *Jonah* is a fable, not an account of actual events. That means that the central protagonist of our story, Jonah, is not a real person but a fictional character created by the author of the Book—a character possibly based on a real person but a fictional creation nonetheless—and that the events to be related are no more than a gripping tale designed by the author as a vehicle to transmit some moral thesis. How then can we treat Jonah as though he were a real person?

And here we confront the mystery of fiction penned by great authors: their ability to create characters that appear three-dimensional, that so possess the patina of reality that they compel us to empathize with them and to relate to them as though they were real. This is the mark of great art: that on reading a tale created by such an author we are drawn into it to the degree that its protagonists seem more real than people that we know, that in their lives and struggles we see our own, and in so doing

---

24. The so-called "Ten Lost Tribes."

Chapter 1. The Flight of the Rebel

come to better understand ourselves and the world in which we find ourselves. In other words, great fiction can dissolve the barrier between fact and fantasy, and draw us into a world peopled with characters and events that we relate to as though they were actual people. And through this "suspension of disbelief"[25] we become aware of truths about ourselves and, in the case of fables and other similarly purposed fiction, truths about the world and how it works.

So while never losing sight of the fabulous nature of our tale, nor for a moment abandoning our ultimate objective, which is to discover what is the moral lesson or thesis that *Jonah* is trying to convey, we will suspend our disbelief and, for the length of time it takes us to read the tale and follow its involved plot, relate to Jonah as though he were real and that the tribulations he undergoes might be happening to us as well as to him. Behind our often dry analysis of this chapter, and the three following ones, is a living and pulsating tale. To the extent that we allow ourselves to be carried along by its stream, to that degree will we be enriched.

We return to Jonah as his getaway ship clears Jaffa harbor and heads out to sea.

Although Jonah is well aware that God will not pass lightly over his audacious dereliction of duty, it is likely that he doesn't expect an immediate reaction. After all, everything has gone smoothly on his descent to Jaffa and getting aboard his getaway vessel. Maybe God has not yet noticed his absence. He will be quickly disabused. The boat has put out to sea and may yet be in sight of land when a sudden squall lashes the waters. Instead of abating, the cloudburst intensifies into a full-fledged storm. The heavily laden vessel begins to founder in the troughs between the ever-growing waves. Panic takes hold of the sailors—a motley pagan crew of diverse origin—and they begin crying out for help, each to his own national and ancestral gods. Desperate to avoid being swamped, they undo the lashings and begin dumping the cargo overboard to lighten the craft. The relief is only temporary. As the waves, rising ever higher, batter the boat, the timbers begin to give way under the strain; the ship is in imminent danger of breaking up.

One person alone refuses to succumb to panic. Jonah has gone below to the boat's hold and there has composed himself; he seems to have come to the recognition that what is happening is God's doing. The LORD has caught up with his fugitive agent. Jonah has resigned himself to his fate. It is there that the master of the vessel finds him, fast asleep.

Now the LORD *hurled a great wind at the sea*,[26] *and there came to pass* [such] *a*

---

25. This phrase was created by William Wordsworth and Samuel Taylor Coleridge, at the launching of what became the Romantic Movement in English literature, to describe the necessary attitude to be able to read and appreciate the "new literature" to which they were giving birth.

26. That there be no doubt in any of our minds as to what is the nature of the sudden storm that is engulfing the ship, both the word order and the vocabulary employed by the narrator explicitly charges God with the responsibility. Normal Hebrew sentence structure places the verb at the head of the statement, before the subject. Here the author reverses the order, putting the subject—the LORD—first; it is *He* Who is behind the Tempest, *He* Who has caused the storm by *hurling* a great wind at the sea. To *hurl a wind* is not an idiomatic Hebrew expression. The phrase is an invention of the author. The word *hayteel* is normally used of hurling an offensive weapon, such as a javelin, at some inoffensive object; it calls starkly to mind the incident where Saul, in a paroxysm of fury, hurls his javelin at David as he is playing his lyre, with the intention of pinning him to the wall (*1 Samuel* 18:11). The impression is given that the LORD is furious at Jonah for not only refusing to obey orders but also for having the audacity to turn his back on his Master and try to run away.

great storm on the sea that the ship threatened[27] *to break up. And the sailors were afraid, and they cried every man to his god; and they hurled*[28] *into the sea the cargo*[29] *that was in the ship in order to lighten it. Now Jonah had gone down to the lowest recesses of the vessel; he lay down and was fast asleep*[30] [1:4–5].

And now the verbal progression of descent we have previously noted rises to a crescendo. Jonah has gone down to Jaffa; he has gone down from dry land into his getaway ship. Now we learn that he has gone down within the ship to its deepest recesses and he has fallen (or gone down) into the oblivion of a deep slumber.[31] Jonah's flight from God is not only taking place horizontally on the face of the earth—he has set out from the land of Israel to what he deems to be the furthest reaches of the world—but it is vertical as well. Turning his back on God involves a remorseless descent. Of the physical aspect of this descent he is undoubtedly cognizant; it has been part and parcel of his horizontal getaway. But that his physical descent is concurrently the mirror of a parallel spiritual decline is a fact of which he has yet to be made aware.

There is a delicious irony in the position in which the shipmaster finds him. In his attempt, now aborted, to flee his mission and his God horizontally to the ends of the earth, he has managed to descend to "the lowest reaches of the vessel,"[32] the very bottom of the boat which is actually below the waterline. He has reached the end of his rope; he has gone as deep as he can go—or so he thinks. Only death can now release him from his predicament and as we shall learn, for this he is prepared.

The master of the vessel sees things very differently. There is no indication that he was specifically looking for Jonah. The ship is on the verge of breaking apart and in this crisis the whereabouts of his passenger is the least of his concerns. It is likely that he went down to the hold merely to check whether the ship had sprung any leaks. Coming upon his peacefully slumbering passenger he is scandalized. "What are you doing sleeping at a time like this!,"[33] he cries as he shakes him awake. "If you can't help the men with lightening the load, the least you can do is to pray! Get up and call on your god. We need all the prayers that we can get."

---

27. Literally, *she* [*the ship*] *thought that she would be broken up*, metaphorically attributing consciousness to the ship: she is as terrified as the sailors! The word *ship* in Hebrew is feminine, hence *she*. Once again in Hebrew the word order is reversed, putting the emphasis on the ship.

28. The same word used for God's action: He *hurls* a great wind at the sea, while the sailors *hurl* their cargo at the sea in response.

29. Possibly bronze vessels, if we accept the description in *Ezekiel* 27:13 of the essence of the Levant-Tarshish trade as relevant to our tale.

30. This phrase recalls Job's description of the finality of death:

So man lies down and never arises,
Till the heavens are no more he will not awake,
Nor will he be roused from his sleep. (Job 14:12)

Uriel Simon is of the opinion that the word order indicates simultaneous action, i.e., at the same time that the sailors are imploring their gods and throwing the cargo overboard, Jonah, in stoic disregard of the crisis, goes below deck, lies down and goes to sleep.

31. For the significance of the Hebrew term *vayeradem*, see the discussion of *keywords* in the Introduction to the *Book of Jonah*.

32. The Hebrew term *s'finah*, here rendered as *vessel* (this is the only use of this term in the Bible), designates a boat designed for long distance voyages that is fully decked over, hence a boat with an enclosed hold.

33. Though phrased as a rhetorical question, this figure of speech, *mah lecha!* (literally, "What's with you?!"), is really an explosive rebuke, virtually an expletive, used by a person in authority when dressing down an inferior.

Chapter 1. The Flight of the Rebel

Now the shipmaster came up to him and said to him, "What are you doing sleeping! Arise, cry out to your god; perhaps the god will take thought of us and we not perish." And they said, every man to his fellow, "Come and let us cast lots, that we may know on whose account this evil has [befallen] us." So they cast lots, and the lot fell upon Jonah. Now they said to him, "Tell us, please, [you] on whose account this evil has [befallen] us,³⁴ what is your business and from where do you come? What is your country and of what people are you?" [1:6-8]

The irony persists: in his wake-up call to Jonah the shipmaster is unknowingly echoing God's original commanded to Jonah: *kum k'rah*, Arise, cry out... (1:1). The difference between them only surfaces in their following words: God's command is to cry out *against* Nineveh; the shipmaster demands that Jonah cry out *to* God. As before Jonah complies with the first part of the demand: he gets up (we will shortly find him back on deck). But we are never told that he accedes to the primary demand: that he pray to his God for His intervention. How can he? He is a fugitive from the very God to Whom he is being asked to turn. God does not need to be entreated to intervene; He already has. By now Jonah knows full well that the storm is a targeted strike directed against him. Under these circumstances the only prayer that would have any chance of being efficacious would be one of submission: "Okay, LORD, you've got me. You win; I'll do what you want." But this Jonah is not willing to do. Anything but that! Death is preferable to surrender. Tightlipped, Jonah allows himself to be herded back up onto the deck where he joins the cowering crew.

Jonah is not the only one who is beginning to grasp the true nature of the predicament that they are in. The crew's suspicions—that this tempest is no natural phenomenon—have now hardened into a certainty. This is a manifestation of divine wrath. The ship must be harboring an enemy of the gods. If so, there is something that the sailors can do. By means of divination³⁵ they can discover the cause of the disaster in which they have been swept up. No sooner said than done, and it is Jonah who, metaphorically speaking, draws the short straw. But this does not close the matter. To rely on divination alone can be dangerous; the results may be misinterpreted and mistakes can be made. The next step is to interrogate the suspect: who is he, where is he from, how and why did he anger the gods?

Having been outed, Jonah speaks freely. Although he must have spoken in order to book passage—and indeed we are specifically told that he has explained to at least some of the crew his reasons for wishing to travel as far as Tarshish³⁶—as far as the Book is concerned, up to this point everyone but Jonah has been portrayed as speaking. God has spoken, the shipmaster has spoken and the speech of the crew has been

---

34. This rendering follows Arnold Ehrlich, who takes the Hebrew *le-mi* as equivalent to a possessive (see also David Kimchi ad loc. [see Glossary]). On the other hand these words—which are a repeat of the phrase found in the previous verse, and are missing in some versions of LXX and some Hebrew codicils—are considered by many scholars to be a dittography and are excised. In either case, the overall meaning of the verse is not changed.

35. Divination was a practice universal in the ancient world. "Divination is ... predicated on the assumption that the course of events is predictable: its advanced notices are imprinted in natural phenomena or discernible in man-made devices" (Jacob Milgrom, *JPSTC Numbers*, p. 472, henceforth *Milgrom*). One common form the practice took was the casting of lots, which often worked by a process of elimination. (See *Joshua* 7:14-23 and *1 Samuel* 14:38-43 for examples of the procedure as practiced in Israel.)

36. 1:10.

quoted. It is only Jonah who has been conspicuous for keeping his mouth shut. But now when finally forced to speak, what he has to say proves of pivotal significance. Not only has his silence up to this moment enhanced the shock value of his little speech, but its importance is highlighted by the author having situated it precisely at the center of the Main Body of the chapter.[37] Not only is Jonah disclosing who and what he is—a Hebrew and a worshiper of the LORD—but this confession of faith lays the foundation for our ultimate understanding of what the Book is all about.

> *And he said to them: "A Hebrew am I, and the* LORD, *the God of the heavens, do I revere,*[38] *Who made the sea and the dry land"*[39] [1:9].

When summoned to give testimony under oath a witness is called upon to swear "to tell the truth, the whole truth and nothing but the truth." By these strict standards this declaration of Jonah reveals itself as considerably less than candid. It is not that Jonah does not tell the truth; he emphatically does. It is just that he does not tell the whole truth. It is in his omissions that the trouble lies. His statement conceals more than it reveals.

The first of these evasions has been widely noted, and substantial efforts have been made to excuse Jonah's dodging. When asked "from where do you come? What is your country and of what people are you?," he does not forthrightly reply, " I come from the Kingdom of Israel and I belong to the people who call themselves 'The Children of Israel.'"[40] He answers, "A Hebrew am I," that is, I am a member of that well-known ethnic group, the Hebrews,[41] but by so doing he is concealing the fact that he is one of that unique subset, the Children of Israel; i.e., a Jew.[42]

---

37. See Introduction to the *Book of Jonah*, note 26 and related text. The phrase "the God of the heavens," as an appellation of the Lord, is first found in the mouth of Abraham (*Genesis* 24:3, 7) and makes its appearance in the climactic verse of the great liturgical Psalm 136. Its use will become common in the post-exilic period (in the books of *Ezra*, *Nehemiah*, *Daniel* and *Chronicles*).

38. Or *do I fear*. For reasons that will become evident, our translation preserves the word order of the original Hebrew.

39. This apposition of these two opposites, *sea* (*yam*) and *dry land* (*yabashah*), is a merism (see note 17 above) and means simply "everything." But more of interest, these two words appear together in this order in only two other contexts in the entire Bible: Creation (Psalm 95:5) and the crossing of the Red (or reed) Sea (*Exodus* 14:16, 22, 29). This last becomes significant when (a) this reference is repeated a few verses further on (1:16), and (b) when we realize that *Exodus* 14 is referred to three more times in the course of the *Book of Jonah*. For the present we will defer all discussion of the author's purpose in his repeated references back to this formative moment in the early history of the Children of Israel. We will return to this question at a later point when we analyze the repeated use of quotations and echoes from other parts of the Bible that appear in *Jonah*.

40. Or in modern parlance, the equivalent of, "I come from Israel and I am a Jew."

41. *Hebrew* (or its plural, *Hebrews*) is a term that appears some thirty times in the Bible. In our present state of knowledge the word appears to be the designation of an ethnic grouping that was widely dispersed throughout the Ancient Near East; the Israelites belonged to this larger entity. Abraham, for instance, is defined as a Hebrew, differentiating him from his military ally, Mamre, who is described as an Amorite, a member of a different ethnic group (*Genesis* 14:13). The term *Hebrew* in narrative texts is restricted to the earliest stages of Israelite history. By the time of David's consolidation of Israel's tribes into the United Monarchy the word *Hebrew* had vanished from the lexicon. Its use in *Jonah* 1:9 is thus doubly unique: not only is it the only use of the term in a post-Davidic context, it is also the only use of the term by an Israelite as a means of self identification. (The use of the word *Hebrew* to designate the language spoken and written by the Israelites is a post-biblical development. In the Bible, this language is called *yehudit*, "Jewish" or "Judean" (*2 Kings* 18:26, 28) or *s'fat c'naan*, "the language of Canaan" (*Isaiah* 19:18)).

42. It should be recognized that the use of the term *Jew* in the present context is anachronistic. The word *Jew* (in its current meaning) first appears as a term of self-identification in post-exilic Books such as *Esther* and *Daniel*. See my *Four Biblical Heroines* for an extended discussion of the historical and sociological context that led to the emergence of this term.

Chapter 1. The Flight of the Rebel

For well over a century this equivocal reply has been excused on the grounds that the sailors—heathens all—could not have been expected to have heard of the Children of Israel—a small minority in the Ancient Near East—or to have had any idea of who they were. Jonah, therefore, identified himself by referring to the larger ethnic group of which the Israelites were a subset, certain that at least they would know who the Hebrews were.[43] But when we analyze the situation in which Jonah finds himself in our tale, this explanation does not really hold water. Jonah found the boat—a long-distance commercial vessel bound for the other side of the Mediterranean—docked in Jaffa port. Indeed, he expected to find a "Tarshish-ship"[44] either docked or expected there; that is why he went down to Jaffa in the first place. Jaffa was one of the two main seaports handling the maritime trade of the Kingdom of Israel. In these circumstances it is hard to imagine that the very sailors who handled her trade had never heard of the Kingdom. Furthermore, the Israelites were not some obscure family or tribe. David created an empire that had stretched to the Euphrates. Even after the collapse of the Empire the Kingdom of Israel had remained a significant factor, and at times a major player, on the international scene in the Ancient Near East. The idea that the statement "I come from the Kingdom of Israel and I am an Israelite" would have been met with blank incomprehension is really not a very credible proposition.[45] We will have to look elsewhere for explanations of Jonah's evasiveness.

Not only in matters of who he is does Jonah exhibit a lack of forthrightness. His reply concerning his beliefs is equally problematic. He identifies by name his God—the LORD—and delineates the realms of His jurisdiction—the Heavens and the Sea (and hence it is He Who is the putative cause of the storm), and the Dry Land (without regard for national boundaries)[46]—but stops short of either asserting that He is the one and only God, or of denying the existence of the gods of the sailors.[47] Thus his statement is, by implication, little more than an admission that his God, THE LORD, is responsible for the mess they are in; what it most decisively is *not* is a proclamation of monotheism. For one who was designated by the LORD to proclaim His word to the Gentiles, even though not defined by the author as a prophet, Jonah's "confession of faith" displays a disturbing lack of candor.

As to the query, "What is your business?"—that is, what is your profession?—this seems to be an issue that he prefers to ignore.

The question of exactly what Jonah is hiding, and why, will have to be left open for the present.

---

43. This explanation rests on the fact that almost all the uses of the term "Hebrew" in the Bible are in cases where Gentiles are referring to Israelites, or in a context of Gentile-Israelite relations.

44. A "Tarshish-ship" was a technical term for a long-distance cargo vessel designed for the trans-Mediterranean trade (and, by extension, any long-distance trade route such as the Red Sea-India Ocean trade). See *1 Kings* 10:22; *Isaiah* 2:16; 23:1; 60:9; *Ezekiel* 27:25; *2 Chronicles* 20:36f, etc.

45. All references to Hebrews in the Bible by Gentiles, or references to them by the narrator as Hebrews to differentiate them from non–Israelites, take place *before* the rise of David, when the Israelites were no more than a family or a number of obscure tribes. Once David put Israel on the map references to Hebrews vanish. *Jonah* 1:9 is the sole exception.

46. That is, *everything!* See note 17 above.

47. See note 8 above.

Martyrdom

The focus of our tale now shifts from Jonah—and from any suspicions his problematic declaration may have raised in our minds—to the members of the crew. Considering their diverse ethnic and national backgrounds, and the well-known nature of the polyglot crews of cargo vessels, many of us probably have very low expectations as to the character of these pagan sailors. We have a surprise awaiting us. Instead of the assemblage of roughnecks and cutthroats Jonah may have been expecting, he finds himself dealing with a group of very decent individuals. Having discovered who the proximate cause of their misery is, they turn to question him with neither violence nor fury, but with a politeness that is astounding considering the circumstances. They even prefix their demand that he answer their questions with a "please"! Upon hearing that the god he is fleeing—the Lord—is the Master of the heavens above and the sea and dry land beneath, a deep dread falls upon them. The exclamation of shock called forth by his confirmation of their suspicions is not a remonstrance over his having brought disaster upon them. They don't blame him. They are horrified that he has been as foolhardy as to have infuriated such a powerful deity. "What is this that you have done!?," they cry rhetorically.[48] Further, in place of turning on him they consult with him: "You know your god and what he wants. Tell us what to do that we may escape his wrath."

> Now the men feared greatly[49] and said to him, "What is this that you have done!" (for the men knew that he was fleeing from before the Lord, because he had told them). Now they said to him, "What shall we do to you that the sea quiet down for us?," for the sea grew more and more tempestuous. And he said to them, "Take me up and hurl me to the sea and the sea will quiet down for you, for I know it is because of me that this great storm is upon you" [1:10–12].

Jonah is now forced to face the wider consequences of his behavior. Up to now he has been focused solely on himself, and has resigned himself to his fate. If he has given any thought to the sailors and what is about to happen to them he has probably written them off; considering the scum they undoubtedly are they will only be getting what is coming to them. But now, his eyes opened by their unexpected decency to him, he for the first time sees them as fellow human beings. For all his pig-headed adherence to principle, Jonah is at core a profoundly moral person. That he is willing to die for his beliefs is one thing, but to drag uninvolved and innocent people down with him is another matter entirely. His priority now becomes to avoid turning the sailors into "collateral damage." So his response to the crewmen is, "You are right, I am the cause of this crisis. I have been running away from the Lord; His anger is directed at me alone. Get rid of me and you will be out of the line of fire. Treat me just

---

48. This is not a request for information but an exclamation of shock that will recall to sensitive readers God's appalled cry of remonstrance to Eve when He learns that it was she who gave the forbidden fruit to Adam and induced him to eat of it: "*What is this that you have done!*" (*Genesis* 3:13). The sense of the utterance is, *How could you?!*

49. Literally, *feared a great fear*. For an explanation of this grammatical construction, technically known as the *infinitive absolute*, a way of strongly emphasizing the issue at hand, see note 54 below. Other examples can be found in 1:16 and 3:2.

as you treated the cargo. Take me up and throw me into the sea and the storm will stop. I am lost; save yourselves."

The sailors have their out; Jonah has given them carte blanche to do what needs to be done. But they don't take him up on the offer. The idea of throwing one of them—his offer of self-sacrifice has made him one of their company in their eyes—to the wolves to save the rest revolts them. They are all in this together. Rather than treat him as a piece of disposable merchandise they will risk the boat breaking up and make one supreme effort to reach land. The fury of the storm ever rising and their sail, if it still exists, useless, they take to the oars—in vain. Exhausted they admit to failure. They now have no choice but to take up Jonah's offer or to die with him.

Their dilemma is severe. They only have Jonah's word that by throwing him overboard they can save themselves. They have no guarantee. And whatever the outcome, to dump him is nothing less than murder. Even if they succeed in emerging unscathed from this traumatic moment, the stain of blood guilt will cling to them ever after. The gods do not look kindly on men with innocent blood on their hands, and nemesis ever dodges the footsteps of such miscreants. Before acting they must make peace with the gods, and especially with this unknown LORD Who has so remorselessly pursued their luckless shipmate. So the crewmen turn to prayer.

Now the men strained at the oars[50] *to bring* [the ship] *back to dry land but they couldn't, because the sea*[51] *was growing more and more stormy upon them.*[52] *So they cried out to the* LORD *and said, "Please, O* LORD*, we beg You,*[53] *let us not perish for the life of this man, and lay not upon us innocent blood, for it is You, O* LORD*, Who are doing as You wish." And they picked up Jonah and hurled him* [in] *to the sea; and the sea ceased its raging!* (1:13–15)

"Please, LORD, we are not doing this of our own free will. It is You Who have forced our hand. So let Thy will be done; we can neither stop You nor resist You. But please don't hold us guilty." What Jonah has adamantly refused to do—*cry out*—first against Nineveh (1:2), and then to the LORD (1:6), the sailors, taking matters into their own hands, have now done. They have *cried out to the* LORD. They are now, willy-nilly, conscious instruments of the LORD. Then, just as the LORD *hurled* a great wind on the sea the sailors, in response and in imitation, pick up the unresisting Jonah and *hurl* him to the sea.

And wonder of wonders, the clouds disperse, the wind stops, the waves die down and the sea becomes as calm as a mill pond.

---

50. Literally, *dug* [with their oars into the water].

51. *Dry land, sea*: Once again these two terms appear in close proximity. See note 39 above.

52. Throughout the Main Body of the chapter, the ferocity of the storm has been increasing. It begins in 1:4 as a "great storm." By 1:11 it becomes "the sea grew more and more tempestuous." Finally, at the climax (1:13), it has escalated to "the sea was growing more and more stormy upon them." Then suddenly, in 1:15, everything stops: the Main Body concludes with the words "the sea ceased its raging." The Main Body begins with the opening of the storm, and ends with its cessation.

53. "The prayer of the sailors is phrased in the most urgent language of entreaty, using the particles *'annah* and *na*'" (Limburg, *Jonah*, p. 56): thus, "*please, O Lord, we beg You.*"

Epilogue

The sudden cessation of the storm leaves the sailors in a state of shocked relief. On the one hand there is a profound sense of gratitude for the fact that they are still among the living. On the other hand, they are experiencing a sense of immeasurable awe at the power of this previously unknown-to-them deity, the Lord, and the boundless extent of His sway. They select one of the animals that have been taken aboard to serve as a source of fresh food during the next leg of the journey (hopefully the best among them). And there, on the deck of the ship, they offer it as an impromptu sacrifice of thanksgiving to the Lord—this God introduced to them by their late passenger, Jonah—in gratitude for His sparing their lives.

> *Now the men felt measureless awe*[54] *for the* Lord[55]*; so they offered a sacrifice* [of thanksgiving][56] *to the* Lord*, and vowed vows* [1:16].

Six times this multifaceted word, *yeerah*, has appeared in this chapter, and it would be well at this point to examine its uses. It first makes its appearance in describing the condition of the sailors when they are introduced in our mini-drama: they are in a state of *fear* bordering on stark terror, crying out to their gods to save them from the storm (1:5). The term then reappears in a radically heightened form close to the midpoint between the first appearance of the sailors and their final bow (1:16): *now the men feared greatly* (1:10),[57] their terror of the storm now coupled with a new cosmic fear of having learned that they have been appealing to the wrong gods.[58] The curtain descends on the scene with a repetition of the phrase used in 1:10. The sailors, having called upon the Lord and having been answered, are experiencing a radically heightened sense of *yeerah*, but the word has transmuted in meaning; it now connotes *awe* and *reverence*. The sailors—pointedly referred to as *the men*[59]—have undergone an epiphany; their physical terror has been transformed into a revelatory experience.

---

54. Literally, *they awed a great awe* (or *feared a great fear*). The Hebrew verb *yeerah* (awe/fear) is in the *infinitive absolute* construction (see Glossary) which is almost impossible to render adequately in English except for those rare instances where the construction appears in the English language itself (an example paradoxically appearing at the very end of this verse: *they vowed vows*). In biblical Hebrew the effect of the use of the infinitive absolute construction is to immeasurably strengthen the action delineated by the repeated verb; in this case that the awe felt by the men was absolutely overpowering. The accepted way of dealing with this problem of translation is to replace one of the verbs with an adjective; thus in place of "they awed a great awe" (an impossible construction in English) to render it as "they felt an immeasurable awe."

55. *Vayeeru haanashim…et Adonai* (*Now the men…stood in awe of the lord*) (1:16). This phrase is the second of a series of quotes and echoes that refer back to *Exodus* 14 (the dramatic episode of the crossing of the Red (reed) Sea), this to *Exodus* 14:31b; *Exodus* 14:31c will be echoed in *Jonah* 3:5. We are being invited to compare and contrast our situation with that depicted in *Exodus* 14. See note 39 above.

56. Hebrew *zebaḥ*: the most common type of individual and/or group offering in the ancient world, Gentile and Israelite alike. For more detail see Glossary. Note the singular (*a* sacrifice); the entire crew participates in making an offering on behalf of them all.

57. *Vayeeru haanshim yeerah gedolah* (literally, *now the men feared with a great fear*); the term *yeerah* twice repeated for emphasis. See note 54 above.

58. The men have just learned from Jonah that it is the Lord Who has caused the storm, and thus it is only He, and not their gods, Who can save them.

59. This is hardly the first time. After their first mention, and concurrent with manifestations of their behavior as decent human beings, they have consistently been referred to as simply "men" and not "sailors" (verses 7, 10, 13 and now 16).

The one remaining use of the term *yeerah* appears in the mouth of our anti-hero, Jonah. In his centrally positioned "declaration of faith" (1:9) he proclaims that *the* LORD, *the God of the heavens, do I revere.*[60] There is no reason to doubt his sincerity. Jonah knows perfectly well with Whom he is dealing: the Lord of all creation. He may disagree with Him, rebel against Him, turn his back on Him and try to flee from before Him; and he realizes that he can never escape Him. His boundless *awe* and *reverence* for his God is the true measure of his audacity in taking a stand against Him. The contrast between Jonah and the heathen sailors who have just come to a very partial and imperfect knowledge of the LORD couldn't be starker. In matters of simple human decency it is the sailors who show themselves in the best light; while it is Jonah who introduces them to a knowledge of the LORD, it is they who, by their behavior, have prompted Jonah to his first reported acts of humanity and compassion.

The sailors, having given expression to their overpowering emotions by their spontaneous on-the-spot sacrifice, do not leave matters there. They vow vows (note the plural), each sailor individually; most probably that when they reach land each of them will worship the LORD by offering a formal sacrifice in a proper sanctuary. There is a widespread belief that this implies their rejection of their gods and their conversion to monotheism. I agree with Kaufmann who holds that there is no hint of this in the text.[61] The sailors do not abandon their ancestral and national gods; they remain pagans. What they have done is to add the LORD to the pantheons of the gods that they worship. Perhaps they even accord the LORD the status of *primus inter pares*, first among his peers. They have come to partial knowledge of the LORD and their respect and reverence for Him is immense, but this is as far as it goes.

And in all this there is a great irony. Jonah was called by the LORD to go to a pagan city, Nineveh, to make the LORD known to them—and he refused. Now, inadvertently, as a side effect of his rebellion against the LORD, he has made Him known to the pagan sailors of his escape ship. Despite himself he has performed the function of a prophet: he has brought the knowledge of the LORD to the heathens; he has magnified the name of the LORD among the nations.[62] Not only can he personally not escape his God, he cannot escape his vocation as His servant.

Summation

With Jonah cast to the waves, and the sailors offering sacrifice to the LORD and making their vows to Him, the curtain falls on our dramatic tale. As we contemplate it we realize that what has been presented to us in miniature—a mere sixteen verses—is a Samson story.[63] Like Samson, Jonah has been entrusted with an exalted mission: Samson, even before his birth, has been charged with initiating the deliverance of

---

60. *Anee yarai: I revere, I stand in awe.*
61. Y. Kaufmann, *Toldot Haemunah Hayisraelit*, volume 2, p. 281–282 (Hebrew).
62. Both Elijah and Elisha are recorded as having excelled in this mission, the former in Zarepath (*1 Kings* 17:8–12) and the latter among the Aramaeans (*2 Kings* 6:8–23; 8:7–13, etc.). In post-exilic times the achievement of magnifying the name of the Lord among the nations had become a prophetic ideal: *For from the rising of the sun to its setting My name is great among the nations.* (*Malachi* 1:11)
63. *Judges* 13–16. For an exhaustive analysis of the Samson story see my *Judges and Saviors*, pp. 283–358.

Israel from Philistine hands, while Jonah has been commanded to bring God's word to that great but evil city, Nineveh. Both, for personal reasons, have rejected their missions: Samson passively, preferring to fraternize with the Philistines rather than fight them; Jonah actively, by turning his back on God and heading off in the other direction. But neither finds themselves able to evade their destiny, not by passively ignoring it nor by actively running away from it. The responsibilities they tried to avoid pursue them, enmesh them and ultimately destroy them both. Samson ends his short and misspent life a suicide, pulling down a pagan temple over his head and on the heads of the Philistines he so yearned to befriend. Jonah ends his abortive flight to Tarshish also a suicide, cast into the sea at his own behest. In both cases the moral is the same: there is no escaping the tasks delegated to us by God. Or to put it in non-theological terms: any attempt to evade the responsibilities that life lays upon us is doomed to failure; one way or another the responsibilities we refuse to face will resist our attempts at avoiding them, relentlessly pursue us and, if we persist in turning our backs on them, will destroy us.

And worse, one finds oneself forced to fulfill one's destiny, at least partially, despite oneself. The more one tries to evade one's responsibilities the more they entangle one. The more Samson tries to fraternize with the Philistines the more he finds himself enmeshed in conflict with them, becoming their number one nemesis, and they his. On the other hand Jonah, fleeing his task of bringing the knowledge of the LORD to pagan Nineveh, by his flight and suicide only succeeds in fulfilling his mandated destiny with the pagan ship's crew. There is no escaping God and the tasks He assigns us.

We rise from our seats and prepare to leave the theater, marveling at what is basically the same tale that was told of Samson—essentially the same plot, the same conclusion, the same moral—but, in the case of Jonah, compressed into less than one sixth the length of Samson's saga, yet complete with Introduction, Main Body and Epilogue.

And then we stop; the curtain is rising once more. We were wrong. It now appears that what we mistakenly took for the complete work was actually only the first act. But the play should be over. What is there left to be said? Baffled, we settle back into our seats as the drama of Jonah resumes.

Chapter 2

In a Tight Spot

*Now of that long pursuit
Comes on at hand the bruit;
That Voice is round me like a bursting sea:
"And is thy earth so marred
Shattered in shard on shard?
Lo, all things fly thee, for thou fliest Me!"*
—Francis Thompson, *The Hound of Heaven*

We were wrong because we made the same mistake that Jonah made. We thought that Jonah's death concluded the drama, even as Jonah was certain that being hurled into the sea would end his life. His game with God was over: he had cast the dice, lost, and was resigned to paying the forfeit; he even asked the sailors to throw him in. But he had it all wrong. He tried to flee from before God to the ends of the earth in order to escape performing the mission he had been assigned. But suicide is merely another form of escape, and God refuses to let Jonah off the hook. Like it or not, God will not let Jonah sidestep his designated task.

Now the LORD *had prepared a great fish[1] to swallow Jonah; and Jonah was in the bowels of the fish three days and three nights* [2:1].

Instead of agonizing death by drowning, expected and even welcomed, Jonah finds a giant maw gaping wide to receive him. And even as the earth was reported to have *opened its mouth* in the wilderness and have *swallowed* Korah, Dathan and Abiram, so that they and all that was theirs *went down alive into Sheol*,[2] so does Jonah find himself swallowed,[3] and as the huge fish dives he finds himself carried down, alive, not to Sheol but to the very bottom of the sea. And there, encased in a pitch black-dungeon of living flesh, Jonah is left to come to terms with his situation and

---

1. The currently accepted version of the story is that Jonah was swallowed by a whale. But the author, who in all probability knew of whales (see for example *Psalm* 104:26) said *fish*, not whale. To us this could be significant. Anatomically these are two completely different orders of marine life. A whale is a mammal, and thus closely related biologically to humans. A fish, no matter the size, is a cold-blooded non-air breathing creature, a far more alien form of life, with which humans have little if any sense of fellow-feeling.

2. *Now the earth opened its mouth and swallowed them and their households... so that they and all that belonged to them went down alive into Sheol; and the earth closed over them and they vanished from the midst of the congregation.* (Numbers 16:32–33) For Sheol—the Netherworld, the realm of the dead—see *Glossary*.

3. "The verb 'to swallow up' never has a positive connotation in the Hebrew Bible. Korah and his followers were swallowed up by the earth/Sheol, as were Pharaoh and his chariots. (*Num.* 16:28–34. *Exod.* 15:12)." (J. Ackerman, "Jonah," pp. 236–237)

with himself. In the hold of the boat he thought he could go no deeper. He now realizes how wrong he was. There will be no escape.

Three days he endures this horrid incarceration; then finally Jonah breaks.

Roadmap

Once again we must remind the reader not to be put off by the fabulous elements of our tale. If we can accept with equanimity talking foxes and crows—and more marvelous still, foxes and crows that, despite being different species, speak the same language and so can hold discourse with one another—then we should equally take in our stride giant fish that can engorge human beings without digesting them, and then vomit them up alive and unharmed. We accept these elements of our tale as the conventions of the type of literature we have determined that we are reading—parable or fable—and press on to see where our tale will lead us.

Just as the first chapter formed a self-contained unit complete in itself, so does its sequel: an Introduction (2:1), a Main Body (2:2–10) and an Epilogue (2:11). We have just concluded the Introduction.

The Main Body of the chapter opens with the words:

> *Now Jonah prayed to the* LORD *his God from the bowels of the fish, and he said...* [2:2–3a]

The remainder of the Main Body, and hence almost the entire chapter, consists of Jonah's prayer which takes the form of a psalm. And here we must digress to briefly discuss the forms taken by prayer in ancient Israel.

In the first place we must keep in mind that, with virtually no exception, everyone prayed on a regular basis in those days; but not in the formats with which we are mostly familiar. There were no formal prayer services, nor was prayer restricted to specific days or times of the day. Prayer was almost completely individual and spontaneous: people prayed when the spirit moved them.[4] It was the meaningful moments in one's life that would move one to prayer, and it was at these moments, or immediately thereafter, that one would pray. The wording of the prayer would be made up on the spot[5]—short and concise or long and rambling as the case might be—and would be specific to the moment or event that prompted its composition.

But there would be times when such a spur-of-the-moment composition would

---

4. The one apparent exception to this rule was the formal ceremonies on set occasions in shrines, such as the Temple in Jerusalem, where Levitical choirs (usually with orchestral accompaniment) would chant certain psalms; sometimes the congregation would join in with set responses. For the average person, participation in these events was a rare occurrence, and was not perceived as part of his or her ongoing spiritual rhythm of life.

5. We have many examples of such prayers scattered through the pages of the Bible. The best analysis of private prayer in biblical times, as well as a full catalog of the examples of this type of prayer in the Bible, can be found in Moshe Greenberg, *Biblical Prose Prayer as a Window to the Popular Religion of Ancient Israel* (University of California Press, 1983). Two examples of such prayers, one concise almost to the point of brusqueness and the other verbose and rambling—both by David—can be found respectively in *2 Samuel* 15:3 and *2 Samuel* 7:18–29. And in our own *Book of Jonah* we have seen one such, the prayer of the sailors before hurling Jonah into the sea (1:14).

not be considered sufficient; only a more lofty and literary format would be deemed appropriate. A thanksgiving prayer to accompany an offering made in a sanctuary, commemorating some momentous turning point in one's life, say; the recovery from a desperate illness or perhaps a petition for the safety of a loved one leaving for war. On such occasions one would want the resonance of poetry and would turn to the format of the psalm.[6] If one had poetic ability—David is an outstanding example—one would sit down and compose a psalm appropriate to the occasion. But of course most people lacked this talent. For these, the custodians of shrines—the spots where most people felt the need for such inspiring compositions—had anthologies of psalms available to meet the needs of tongue-tied worshipers. Unlike spontaneous prayers, which were in prose and were always specific to the person and to the events that prompted it, psalms—composed in poetry—were framed vaguely, in metaphoric language which allowed the user to read his own specific needs into the inexplicit and ambiguous phraseology.[7] Even when one composed a psalm for one's own needs—and indeed most psalms had their origin in an upsurge of a poet's religious emotions at a specific moment of his or her life—these were invariably composed in this unspecific format; such was the convention of the psalm form. No matter the specifics of the inception, from the start a psalm was meant for reuse, to meet the needs of others. Many of these compositions are to be found scattered throughout the Bible. Chapter 2 of *Jonah* contains one of these.

Enormous quantities of ink have been spilled arguing over whether it was the historical Jonah who composed the psalm or the author of the Book, whether the author chose an existent Psalm for insertion at this point because he thought it was appropriate, or whether it was not part of the original *Book of Jonah* but the addition of some later editor; all to no universally accepted conclusion.[8] However, for our purposes debate can be put aside. Our interest is in the *Book of Jonah* as we have it today—a finished creation—and not in the putative stages of its composition. For us, the psalm is an integral component of the Book, and so we will treat it.[9]

---

6. The psalm was simply a type of poem that was common in those days, just as the sonnet is a type of poem that is part of the poetic repertoire of modern European languages. Like the sonnet, the psalm was an international poetic format and its earliest forms predated the emergence of the Israelites as a people. Adopted by Israelite poets, it became one of the prime vehicles for the expression of deep religious passion in the Biblical Age.

7. Some of the best of these psalms were collected and are now known as the Psalter or *Book of Psalms*.

8. J. Magonet summarizes and evaluates the various arguments, pro and con, for all these positions in "Jonah, Book of," *ABD III*, p. 939–940. As to his own position, he tends to view the psalm as an integral part of the Book, based in part on the analysis of J. Ackerman. See note 9 below.

9. James Ackerman shows quite convincingly that the narrative part of the Book seems to be dependent on the actual content of the psalm itself ("Satire and Symbolism in the Song of Jonah"). Additionally, it is important to realize that most of the "contradictions" between the narrative portions of the *Book of Jonah* and the psalm of Chapter 2 that have so troubled readers and critics over the centuries have their origin in a literalist reading of the text. If one reads *Jonah* as a work of historiography then there *are* contradictions, just as if one reads the Book as a naturalistic or scientific description of events one encounters absurdities. But if one reads the work, as we do, as a parable or fable, the stumbling blocks evaporate and cease to bother us. Seen in this light, the psalm, regardless of its origin, will be shown to be extremely appropriate to its setting, its "inconsistencies" serving the purpose of raising serious questions with regard to the larger issues of Jonah's character and motivations, which in turn impinge on the overall meaning of the Book.

The Anatomy of a Psalm

The "Psalm of Jonah" is preceded by a formal introduction or superscription:

Now Jonah prayed to the L<small>ORD</small> *his God from the bowels of the fish* [2:2].

Many psalms are preceded by such a notice, either delineating the authorship of the composition or the conditions which prompted its writing. When both are present it is usually a signal that, while the prayer is available for reuse by anyone who finds it can express his or her needs, *we as readers* should keep constantly in mind the context in which it is set.[10]

Up to now prayer (in the sense of petitioning God for aid or forgiveness due to deep distress) has been expressed by the euphemism "to cry out to God" (1:5, 6, 14). That this is the first time the actual word for prayer is being used should alert us that something different than what we have become accustomed to will now be taking place.

To prefix a psalm by calling it a prayer (*t'philah*) or to say someone prayed it (*hitpalel*, the verbal form of the same root) is unusual but hardly unknown.[11] In our case, the use of the word *pray* highlights its difference from previous instances of prayer in Chapter 1. These were described by the euphemism: "crying out." The difference resides not so much in the formal poetic construction of the composition, as opposed to the spontaneous prose informality of the prayers of the sailors, but more importantly, in the *nature* of the prayer. All the previous prayers offered (and in Jonah's case, the prayer that was demanded of him which he refused to articulate) were petitions, asking for help.[12]

But the present psalm, although composed and delivered—so we are told—by a renegade entombed in the bowels of a giant fish at the bottom of the sea, is not a cry for help but a paean of thanksgiving. We are being forced to confront the stark contrast between the *context* of the psalm's genesis, insisted upon by the superscription, and the *contents* of the psalm. Having called attention to this glaring incongruity, we will defer attempting to understand it until after we have examined the psalm itself.

The construction of the psalm proves to be relatively straightforward:

2:3 A short statement of the theme of the psalm
2:4–8 The personal testimony of the writer of the psalm
2:9–10 The conclusions drawn from his experience

These conclusions can be broken down as follows:

What he has learned [2:9]
What he will therefore do [2:10]

---

10. As examples, see *Isaiah* 38:9, *Psalm* 34 and *Psalm* 51. In our case, of course, we are expected to take the entire background of *Jonah* 1:1–2:1 into account when reading Chapter 2.

11. *Psalm* 90 commences with the superscription: *A Prayer of Moses, the man of God*, while the psalm attributed to Hannah opens: *Now Hannah prayed and said* (1 *Samuel* 2:1).

12. Or, in the case of the sailors' prayer, prior absolution for the crime of murder which they were about to commit.

The Prayer of Jonah

We begin with the statement of the psalm's theme.

And he said:
"I cried out to the LORD *from out of my straits,*
And He answered me;
From the belly of Sheol[13] *I called for help;*
You heard my voice" [2:3].

This verse amounts to a brief summary of the writer's personal testimony. Yet it would be unwise to simply leave it at that and move on. There are at least three aspects of this short couplet that deserve our attention. The first is the word order of the Hebrew.[14] The stanza opens with the word *karati* (*I cried out*). This placement emphasizes the action of *crying out* which defines everything that follows. This is a phrase—in the Hebrew one word: *karati*—with which we have become familiar: the entire first Chapter has been dominated by this term. God has commanded Jonah to go to Nineveh and *cry out* against her (1:1), the shipmaster has ordered him to *cry out* to his god (1:6) and in both cases he has adamantly refused. The sailors, on the other hand, have no qualms about *crying out* to the LORD, a deity of whom previously they had never even heard (1:14). And now, finding himself at the bottom of the sea—so the narrator informs us—his dire situation has moved him finally to pray. And in the first word that he is quoted as uttering to the LORD *his God*, he defines his action as *crying out*; that which he had previously refused to do. Jonah has not merely broken; he has turned around 180 degrees.

We have said that when a psalm is prefixed by a superscription detailing the context which gave birth to its composition, this amounts to a set of instructions directing us to read it in light of this context. In identifying the opening phrase of Jonah's prayer—*I cried out*—as one of the keywords of Chapter 1 we are, in effect, reading the psalm as a continuation of the preceding narrative.

This keyword will prove to be but one of several links between the psalm and the narrative that frames it. And so, while never losing sight of the generalized and non-specific manner in which the psalm is formulated—designed as a vehicle for public use—in our exposition we will continually draw attention to those elements that fit the psalm into Jonah's story.

Yet another aspect of the opening words of this stanza is the double entendre contained in the words *out of my straits*. The word which we have translated as "straits" means something like "trouble," or "affliction" or "distress," and so it is generally rendered.[15] But its basic root meaning is "a narrow space," i.e., "a tight spot,"

---

13. I.e., from the depths of the Netherworld, conceived of as being deep under the sea bottom. The use of this strange expression, *the belly of Sheol*, is obliquely reminding us of Jonah's current condition. This particular expression appears nowhere else in the Bible.

14. Following the Hebrew word order, as our translation does, creates an awkward sentence in English, but prioritizing English style, as most translations do, puts the emphasis in the wrong place: on the psalmist's troubles.

15. As in *Psalm* 118:5; *Lamentations* 1:3; *Jeremiah* 19:9; *2 Samuel* 24:14 etc.

and all the other meanings are derivatives of this central meaning. So the phrase can mean—as it is usually taken—"out of my trouble" or "out of my affliction" I cried out to the Lord. But in the context of *Jonah* it can also be understood in its literal sense: "Out of the 'tight spot' in which I find myself"—inside of a fish—"I cried out to the Lord."

The third aspect of this superscription worth noting is the strange shift in person: of who it is that is being addressed. The writer, speaking in the first person, begins by describing how he called upon the Lord and the Lord answered him. Then, in a very next line, we find him talking *to* the Lord. To address the Lord is appropriate for one who is writing what is described as a prayer, but who is he speaking to in the first line when he is telling *about* his relationship with the Lord? This opening couplet sets the pattern for a disquieting series of shifts in the person addressed that runs through the psalm: sometimes the writer is talking *to* God, and at other times he is talking *about* God and His deeds. When talking *about* God,[16] who is he telling it to?

James Limburg makes a telling observation at this juncture: "The statements assume the presence of a listening congregation and thus point to the use of the psalm and of the entire book of *Jonah* in the context of a gathered community."[17] In other words, we have to remember that our psalm was designed to serve three separate functions: it was included in our book in a way so as to be an integral part of the Jonah story, it was written so as to enable inarticulate individuals to find the words with which to open their lips to God in prayer, and it was also composed with the aim of filling a liturgical role within the community of the faithful.[18]

To design a Psalm for three separate and not necessarily compatible purposes requires the skill of a juggler keeping several balls in the air simultaneously. The result is a complex reality hiding behind an apparently simple surface, capable of several very different, yet authentic, readings. Our reading, as we have intimated, will follow the first alternative: our aim, after all, being the explication of the *Book of Jonah*.

The main body of the psalm consists of the personal testimony of the psalmist. Having introduced his psalm by a brief summary of its theme, the writer now proceeds to elaborate on what he went through:

You have cast me into the deep,
Into the heart of the sea;
And the flood was all around me,
All Your breakers and billows
Passed over me.[19]

---

16. 2:3a; 2:8a; 2:9; 2:10b.

17. Limburg, *Jonah, A Commentary*, p. 66.

18. This latter role the psalm has served, along with the entire *Book of Jonah*, by having been designated as one of the two Prophetic Readings in the liturgy for Yom Kippur, the holiest day in the Jewish calendar.

19. The final line of this verse, from *All Your breakers...* is duplicated in *Psalm* 42:8b. Its appearance in the context of this Psalm is suggestive. "In this Psalm we have a pathetic lament by one whose delight had been to participate in the Temple Service but was now prevented from doing so." (A. Cohen, *The Psalms*, p. 130.)

"As for me," I said, "I am driven out[20]
From before Your eyes,
Nevertheless I will continue to look
Toward Your Holy Temple.[21]
The waters closed over me,[22]
That deep was all around me;
Weeds wound round my head."

I went down to the roots[23] *of the mountains,*
The bars of the earth closed to me forever.
Yet You brought my life up from the Pit,
O Lord my God!

When my soul was fainting within me,[24]
I called the Lord to mind;
And my prayer came to You,
To Your Holy Temple [2:4–8].

While at first glance this all may appear rambling, this personal testimony is logically constructed. The writer opens by hurling an accusation at God: it was not the sailors; it was *You* who are responsible for my distress!

<u>You</u> *have cast me into the deep,*
Into the heart of the sea;
And the flood was all around me,[25]
All <u>Your</u> breakers and billows
Passed over me.

He continues, still addressing God:

"As for me," I said, "I am driven out
From before Your eyes,
Nevertheless I will continue to look
Toward Your Holy Temple" [2:4–5].

In other words, despite what You are doing to me—turning Your back on me, driving me away from You—my faith in You remains unaltered; looking toward God's Holy Temple being used as a metaphor for faith in God.

Following his accusation and his defiant declaration to God of his unwavering

---

20. This term also carries the connotation of divorce.

21. The 2nd century Greek translation of Theodotion, reading *aich* (how) in place of MT *ach* (nevertheless), takes the second line of this stanza as a question: "How ever again shall I gaze upon Your Holy Temple?" Many moderns follow his lead. We prefer to remain with MT.

22. The text reads literally, *Waters encompassed me to my very soul*, an idiom which means that "I was within an inch of losing my life."

23. Literally, *the extreme bottom*.

24. Literally, *on me*.

25. Hebrew, *yisov'vainee*; surrounded me, engulfed me. The word is repeated in 2:6, where the writer fleshes out his depiction of drowning.

faith, the psalmist ceases speaking to God and turns to a harrowing description of the agonies of drowning.[26]

> *"The waters closed over me,*
> *The deep was all around me,*[27]
> *Weeds*[28] *wound round my head.*
>
> *I went down*[29] *to the roots of the mountains,*
> *The bars*[30] *of the earth closed over me forever"* [2:6–7a]

His drowning body now at the very bottom of the sea, and nowhere left to descend but to Sheol, the realm of the dead, he feels death closing him off forever from the land of the living.

> *Yet You brought my life up from the Pit,*[31]
> *O* LORD *my God!*
>
> *When my soul was fainting within me,*
> *I called the* LORD *to mind;*
> *And my prayer came to You,*
> *To Your Holy Temple* [2:7b–8].

At this moment of despair, when he had given up all hope, suddenly the God Who had *cast me into the deep* now unexpectedly, miraculously, *brings his life up* from death. As he describes it, as he was dying—*my soul was fainting within me*[32]—his last thought was of God and, miracle of miracles, his despairing cry for help gets through![33] He has lived to recount his experience.

This final section of the writer's personal testimony—a virtual explosion of pent-up emotion—veers wildly between fervent exclamations directed to God and an explanatory exposition addressed to his listeners before whom he is bearing witness; and ultimately to us, the readers of his words. He concludes his soul-wrenching account with the word picture of something very concrete, the Holy Temple; probably the Temple built by Solomon in Jerusalem is meant. But the writer is perfectly clear: the Holy Temple is no more than a symbol representing the invisible LORD, Creator and Ruler of the universe and Director of the destiny of all flesh. If we read

---

26. Although the language can be read as metaphoric—and indeed it was meant to be read as such by those who would reuse the psalm for their own needs—these passages are only exceeded in vividness by Clarence's account of his dream of drowning in Shakespeare's *Richard III*, I: 4.

27. See note 25 above.

28. I.e., seaweed. Another possibility would be "rushes" or "reeds," c.f. *Exodus* 2:3, 5 and *Isaiah* 19:6, the basic idea being that he has been entangled and trapped in marine vegetation that prevents him from swimming to the surface.

29. We remember this word, *yarad* (went down), one of our keywords, from Chapter 1. Jonah is now acknowledging the remorselessness of the descent he initiated when he *went down to Jaffa* in order *to flee from before the Lord.*

30. The gates of ancient cities were locked by the use of iron bars. Once the gate was locked (or "barred"), you were walled in; there was no escape, hence the graphic metaphor for death.

31. The Pit is a synonym for Sheol.

32. An expression for when one is on the point of death, one's life ebbing away. See *Psalm* 107:5 for another use of this expression, in that case of people dying of thirst in the desert.

33. Once again, the Temple serves as a symbol for God. See note 21 above.

the psalm as the prayer of Jonah, then we can infer that Jonah has made his peace with his situation. The rebellion is over.

So what has he learned from his experience? He tells us.

They who cling to worthless vanities[34]
Abandon their [hope of] *grace.*[35]

This statement, couched in the form of an aphorism or epigram, is so elliptical and obscure as to be almost totally enigmatic. In the first place, the word here rendered as "they who cling," *m'shamrim*, comes from the root *shamor*, which has the meaning of "to keep," "to watch," "to preserve." Thus *m'shamrim* would mean something like "those who keep" or "those who pay regard to" (a usual rendition in the current context). But what are the "worthless vanities" that are being "paid regard to" or "clung to"? The phrase "worthless vanities" is often taken as a euphemism for idols. While this usage is well attested,[36] to take "idols" as the exclusive meaning of this phrase would seem to be overly restrictive. Within the context of a monotheistic worldview idols are certainly "worthless vanities," but they are not the only ones; physical idols are merely a subset of a much vaster category.

We may get a better idea of what is being talked about when we examine the only other use of this phrase, "worthless vanities," in the Bible, in Psalm 31:7.

I hate those who cling[37] *to worthless vanities;*
But I trust in the LORD.

Here "clinging to worthless vanities" is clearly the opposite of "trusting in the LORD." This certainly includes trusting in idols, but can encompass far more. It is here that I find the insight of Calvin most helpful: he defines *worthless vanities* as "all inventions with which men deceive themselves";[38] in other words, not so much "idols" as idolatries.

Through the ages humans seem to have a propensity for finding alternatives to God in which to repose their trust—be they power, technology,[39] charismatic leaders or pernicious philosophical doctrines, of either a religious or a secular nature. To these they cling, often with a single-minded devotion that should be reserved only for God. Today we call them substitute religions, false doctrines or simply idolatries. The writer of our psalm and the author of Psalm 31 preferred to term them *worthless vanities*, focusing on their ephemeral nature and lack of value; just when you need them most is when they let you down. Putting one's trust in one of these in place of

---

34. Hebrew *hebel*; literally, "a breath"; hence something insubstantial and intrinsically valueless, here today and gone tomorrow. The term serves *Koheleth* (Ecclesiastes) as an antonym for something of value; thus, *Vanity of vanities, says Koheleth, all is vanity* (*Ecclesiastes* 1:2), where *hebel* is rendered as "vanity."

35. Hebrew, *ḥasdam*, i.e., their *ḥesed*. *Hesed* is a basic attribute of God, often rendered as "grace," i.e., granting human beings benefits above and beyond what they deserve on the basis of their behavior or achievements. See *Glossary*.

36. This reading is based on *Jeremiah* 8:19 and *Deuteronomy* 32:21, where *vanities* is used as a synonym for "idols" in the first case, and for "no-gods" (also a euphemism for "idols") in the second.

37. Or "I hate those who pay regard to worthless vanities."

38. John Calvin, *Commentaries on the Minor Prophets*, quoted by S. Goldman in "Jonah," *The Twelve Prophets*, p. 144.

39. See L. Kass on the Egyptian trust in their technological expertise and the biblical argument against basing a society on such foundations. (Kass, *The Beginning of Wisdom*, p. 626)

trust in God, Jonah is saying, is not only to turn one's back on God, but also means abandoning any expectation of receiving God's grace. The essence of *hesed* (grace) is that it is undeserved.[40] Jonah, who has just experienced God's grace in his own person and in a most extreme and unexpected form, is painfully aware of how little his behavior merited his astounding deliverance from death. Yet here he is, returned to the land of the living.

Beyond expressing his gratitude in a psalm of thanksgiving, like the sailors before him he vows a vow:

But as for me,[41] *with voice of thanksgiving*
I will make offerings[42] *to You;*
That to which I have vowed I will perform.
Salvation belongs to the Lord. (2:10)

Not being in a position to make immediate sacrifice as did the sailors, Jonah has to content himself with a vow that on the first suitable occasion, should one be afforded, he will make the appropriate offering. At the same time he insists that he is not one who makes promises, and then under altered circumstances conveniently forgets to keep them. What he has vowed, that will he fulfill.

The final affirmation with which the psalm concludes, *Salvation belongs to the* Lord—a two-word declarative pronouncement in the Hebrew—is not simply the polar opposite of what Jonah so decisively rejected in his epigraphic pronouncement in the previous verse. He will cling to the Lord, not to "worthless vanities." But more, he is also proclaiming a complete revolution in his understanding of God. In his declaration of faith to the sailors he avowed:

The God of the heavens do I revere,
Who made the sea and the dry land.[43] (1:9)

This statement of belief in God the Creator—or to put it in more philosophical language, in God as the First Cause—would seem to be a sincere confession of where he was at the time. Three days later, after what he has undergone, Jonah apparently has radically revised his understanding of God. From an essentially cerebral reverence for the Majestic Creator of heaven and earth he has come to an *experiential knowledge* of the Lord as *his* Savior. God has become transformed in his eyes.

This revolution finds its first voice just past the midpoint of the psalm, when he experiences the Lord's salvation:

You brought my life up from the Pit
O Lord *my God!*

This addition, *my God*, has never before been recorded as issuing from the mouth

---

40. See *Hesed* in *Glossary*.

41. In contrast to his prior use of this phrase—our rendering of the emphatic first-person singular *vaanee*—in (2:5), which was an admission of total despair, it now precedes an exclamation of joyous affirmation and commitment.

42. Hebrew *zebah*, the same term used for the sacrifice of the sailors but in its verbal form. See Chapter 1, note 56.

43. In our comments, we expressed serious reservations about this avowal of faith, but only about what was *not* said. What Jonah *did* say about his belief in God was the unvarnished truth.

Chapter 2. In a Tight Spot

of Jonah. From a distant transcendental deity God has become close and intimate; a very present help in time of trouble. But it is not God Who has been transformed, it is Jonah. It is the shattering experience of almost drowning and then being restored miraculously to life that has completely altered Jonah's understanding of and relationship to God. And note: it is only after this internal revolution that Jonah has spontaneously turned to God in prayer. It is only now, as we recognize what happened to him, that the full significance of the narrator's superscription to the psalm can be appreciated.

Now Jonah prayed to the LORD *his God from the bowels of the fish.* (2:2)

With this change we find ourselves in a new ball game.

We have alluded in passing to various alleged "contradictions" between the contents of the psalm and the narrative parts of *Jonah* (i.e., Chapters 1, 3 and 4), "contradictions" endlessly pointed to by critics, ancient and modern alike. Most of these prove to be artifacts of the way these commentators choose to read the text.[44] But there is a glaring incongruity embedded in the structure of the text itself that cannot be made to disappear by reading the tale of Jonah as a parable. The preamble or superscription to the psalm (which is part of the narrative text) tells us that Jonah prayed while inside the great fish. This establishes the context of the prayer, and the subsequent words "and he said": establishes the psalm as Jonah's prayer. As we have pointed out, the reading instructions attendant on the psalm insist that we read the psalm in the light of this context. In that case, we are being told to read the psalm as uttered by Jonah while at the bottom of the sea, and while imprisoned within the living flesh of a giant fish. This would seem to call for a cry for help; an appeal for deliverance. Yet what we find is a psalm of thanksgiving, couched in the perfect tense[45]; an account of some crisis in the past from which the LORD has delivered Jonah.

We have taken note of this inherent contradiction—which we've referred to as a "glaring incongruity"—but deferred confronting it until we had completed our analysis of the psalm itself. Having completed this task, and having come to some understanding of the structure and dynamics of the psalm, the time has come to confront this discrepancy.

The answer to this problem that is advanced by many modern scholars[46] is that the psalm doesn't belong in the *Book of Jonah* at all; it is a foreign element shoehorned in by a later editor after the Book had been completed. As Uriel Simon puts it, "The tension between the psalm and the circumstances in which it is uttered is largely dissipated if we assume that there is no literary reason for ascribing its composition

---

44. See note 9 above.

45. The perfect tense in biblical Hebrew denotes an action that has been completed. It is usually rendered in English as a past tense (see Glossary).

46. The medieval commentators were also aware of this problem and grappled with it. We are limiting our discussion to the scholars of the modern era because the solutions of the medieval writers appear unconvincing to modern sensibilities. For example, I. Abravanel, to whom we have previously referred, found his solution to the problem that the psalm is in the perfect tense (see previous note) by relying on a Midrashic identification by the rabbis of the Talmudic Period of Jonah with the son of the widow of Zarepath, who died and was brought back to life by the prophet Elijah (*1 Kings* 17:17–24). So according to Abravanel, when Jonah is praying, he is giving thanks for the miracle wrought by Elijah that brought him back to life. Conclusions such as these, which were deemed perfectly acceptable to medieval thought, seem fanciful to us.

to Jonah or even to the author of the book."[47] The basic problem with this thesis is that it assumes that the editor and his contemporaries were not alert enough to realize how inappropriate his choice of a psalm was—an issue that has been perfectly obvious to subsequent generations down to modern times. Simon is aware of this discrepancy and alludes to it in passing, referring to the postulated editor as "someone who was less sensitive than the author to the character of the prophet."[48] But this dismissive comment really doesn't address the issue: if one is choosing a psalm to insert so as to "enrich" the existent text, why not choose a psalm that is an appeal for help while in deep trouble? There was no shortage of such psalms.

We contend that this theory, that a foreign psalm has been intruded into the Book by some later editor, simply won't work.[49] In the first place, there are too many linguistic and literary connections between the psalm and the prose narrative. We have called attention to several keyword sequences that find their continuation in the psalm.[50] These are simply two or three instances of many.[51] The second reason, which we have already raised, is that this solution is too simplistic. What is obvious to us would have been obvious to the original audience of the Book as well. This response is less an answer than an evasion.

What we need, therefore, is a line of reasoning that would have made sense to the original audience of the Book. Indeed, once we accept the unity of *Jonah*, the divergence of the content of the psalm from what the context leads us to expect is so blatant as to suggest that it is intentional.[52] Taking this as our new starting point, let us see where this leads us.

What I would suggest is as follows: taking the text we currently possess as a given—that is, the psalm as the original continuation of the narrative of 1:1–2:2—we turn our attention to two surprising anomalies which are integral to it. The first is Jonah's act of turning to God in prayer. The man who received God's command to go to Nineveh with not a word of protest or even a comment and who then fled in stubborn silence, and even in the crisis of the storm adamantly refused to address God and ask for His help, now suddenly breaks his silence and turns to Him—so the narrator informs us—in prayer! And in the very first word of his prayer, *karati* (I cried out), he does what for the entire first Chapter he has adamantly refused to do. The second is the turnabout embodied in his acceptance of the LORD as *his* God and Savior, a revolution not only proclaimed in the psalm (2:7) but also explicitly confirmed by the narrator (2:2). In my view, these two surprising developments are actually two

---

47. Simon, *Jonah*, p. 16. Simon is hardly alone in the assumption that some editor picked an existent psalm off-the-shelf, as it were, and simply intruded it into the text in order to "improve it." During the last fifty years or so, among those that have propounded this view, besides Simon, are W. Rudolph, G. Vanoni and H. W. Wolff.

48. *Ibid.*

49. I say "we" because I am not alone in holding to the belief that the psalm was an integral part of the *Book of Jonah* from the beginning. In addition to J. M. Sasson and J. Magonet whom we have cited above, we can name K. Craig, H. Gese and J. Limburg, who also adhere to this position.

50. See notes 29 and 44 above. Also the first paragraph of the section entitled "The Prayer of Jonah."

51. J. M. Sasson presents an entire list of unifying features. (AB *Jonah*, p. 19–20).

52. Incidentally, this argument applies equally to a postulated later editor as well. Assumptions of mental laxness on the part of hypothetical ancient "editors" are more often than not signs of mental laziness on the part of the critics who so postulate.

sides of the same coin. This transformation of Jonah's attitude to God, which defies all our expectations, is what leads him to attempt to reopen communication with his God.

We must not be dismayed by the sudden switch being pulled on us. We cannot allow ourselves to forget that our author began Chapter 2 by pulling the rug out from under our feet. Chapter 1 ended with Jonah committing suicide: he asked the sailors to throw him overboard and they complied. At the time, we stressed how this neatly wrapped up the crime and punishment theme of the Chapter—the punishment for treason to God being death—rounding out the moral that there is no escape from God and His demands. Then, with the opening of Chapter 2, everything is turned upside down. Instead of dying, Jonah is swallowed by the fish. As God uses the storm to block Jonah's flight to Tarshish, God uses the fish to thwart his attempt at suicide. And now added to this we are treated to a second surprise: he who turned his back on God and fled from before Him now has turned around and embraced Him as his Savior. This, as we shall discover, is our author's style: to build up our expectations, only to dash them with a sudden change of direction. As our tale has been written, nothing will turn out as we will think we have every reason to expect; it is the unexpected that will prove to be the norm.

So if we abandon what we thought was obvious about Jonah and his character, and accept the astounding picture of our ex-rebel praying in the bowels of a huge fish to the God Whom he fled, and amazingly uttering a psalm of *thanksgiving* for God's salvation (in the past tense[53] no less), we will be beginning, in a sense, a new chapter in the life of Jonah.

So taking Jonah's present position in the fish as a given, and keeping in mind what got him there, let us start all over and try to reimagine the frame of mind that would lead him to give thanksgiving to God for his current situation. The fact is that Jonah gives us our answer. All we have to do is to abandon our previous assumptions and to take seriously what he tells us in his psalm.

Jonah rebelled against the Lord and God punished him by *casting him into the deep*. Jonah accepts his punishment as just, and resigns himself to death by drowning. But it is one thing to resign oneself to die for one's principles, even to court death, and quite another matter indeed—as Jonah now horrifyingly discovers—to experience the fate of drowning. The agony, the terror and despair so movingly depicted in his psalm exceeds all his expectations. The fish swallowing him and ending his agony is experienced by Jonah as revelatory.

> *You brought my life up from the Pit,*
> *O* Lord *my God!*
> *When my soul was fainting within me....*
> *Salvation belongs to the* Lord.

Now we can understand the perfect tense.[54] The thanksgiving psalm refers to his near-death experience and his being saved from drowning. Finding himself alive

---

53. Actually, the perfect tense. See note 45.
54. See again note 45.

after that terrifying ordeal is what has led to a new understanding of God—not as a remote transcendental divinity but as close and immediate—as his Savior. He is his God. Whatever God will do to him now, or demand of him now, he will perform as God's faithful servant. It is the difference between the worship of a distant and impersonal God and the experience of God's salvation as an act of *hesed*[55] that has revolutionized Jonah. It is the new-forged relationship that makes sense of and rectifies the "contradiction" between our expectations and a psalm of thanksgiving. Jonah does not call for help because he has already been helped; he is overwhelmed and gives thanks for the experience of his salvation. What God does with him now is immaterial. If he returns to the land of the living he will offer sacrifice—the conventional act of giving thanks for God's grace—and if not, also fine. In the splendor of his dazzling new intimate relationship with *his* God—this epiphany—all that he can think about is his salvation; his newly discovered and conclusive truth: *Salvation belongs to the* LORD. It is only when Jonah finds himself at the end of his tether and cut off from the consolations of all that seemed so solid and earthy in the daily round of his life—that seemed so reliable and satisfying as long as this routine was accepted without question—that he could open himself to God's grace and be transformed. Jonah has made the leap from the realm of the political to the soul's search for salvation. With this declaration Jonah rests his case.

Epilogue: Back to Square One

And God responds. With the formal recognition of the LORD as *his God* and Savior, Jonah's rebellion has become a thing of the past. God responds accordingly:

And the LORD *commanded*[56] *the fish, and it vomited Jonah out onto dry land.* (2:11)

The term *vomit* conveys a sense of rejection and disgust.[57] The fish did not swallow Jonah by chance, or even of its own free will; God had assigned it the task. For three days and three nights it had been compelled to harbor this noxious indigestible creature, and now at long last, free from the compulsion, it can rid itself of this foreign body. So it vomits it out—but not anywhere in the sea; the compulsion to fulfill God's will still holds the fish in its grip—but onto the shore that the sailors, by their desperate unaided efforts, had failed to attain.

Having reached this point let us recap. But inasmuch as most of us have never had the experience of drowning and being resuscitated, perhaps we can better understand Jonah's testimony in his psalm if we translate it into a 21st-century context, that of an employee in a large corporation who has messed up on the job and been fired by the CEO.

---

55. Grace; see note 35 above.
56. Literally, *said to*.
57. *Proverbs* 23:8 and 25:16 (the only other uses of the verb in the Bible), speak of nausea induced by hypocrisy and by gluttony, making one sick to one's stomach, while the noun *vomit* in *Proverbs* 26:11 speaks for itself:
   As a dog returns to his vomit,
   So does the fool repeat his folly.

"You are the one who fired me. You are the one who ruined my reputation and broke my spirit. I have never been able to hold a job since you threw me out. I've become unemployable, unable to pay rent and hence homeless. I have been reduced to scavenging in garbage cans for food. In my wretchedness I took to drink, then drugs and have become a hopeless addict. I was at my wit's end.

"Then, in my despair, I remembered your reputation for decency and fairness. I wrote to you and you took notice of me. You read my letter. You took the time to hunt me down. You lifted me out of the gutter and, at your own expense, committed me to a rehab program in a closed mental hospital. The rehab has been hell, but infinitely better than where I was before because there I had no hope. I was finished.

"You saved my life. You promised me a job. You gave me a future. You are my savior. You have won my eternal gratitude and loyalty. Whatever you ask of me I will do. Wherever you send me I will go. You are my Boss forever."

These testimonies—by our hypothetical employee and by Jonah—are descriptions of epiphanies, experiences that totally transform the personalities of the persons who undergo them; that revolutionize the way they see themselves in relation to the world and in relation to their own lives.

To return to our tale, the only question that remains for Jonah, as he wades through the surf and climbs onto the shore, is how long this glorious sense of gratitude and loyalty will last. Is the transformation permanent, or will it fade with time and the older Jonah—the rebel—reassert himself?

As the curtain falls on Jonah, full of resolve, starting on his journey to God's Temple to make good his vow, we do not stir from our seats. Having learned our lesson at the end of the first act, we have looked at our programs. There are still two acts left to our drama. Jonah may think that his main duty now is to bring closure to this dramatic turning point in his life by making a formal offering of Thanksgiving to his Savior in His Holy Temple. The act of grace bestowed upon him deserves no less. But perhaps God has other plans for His now willing servant.

Chapter 3

The Great Reversal

> *The Eternal of Israel neither lies nor changes His mind[1];*
> *He is not a man that He should change His mind.*
> —*1 Samuel 15:29*

> *Then the word of the* Lord *came to me and said: "…At one instant I may speak concerning a nation and concerning a kingdom, to pluck up, to break down and to destroy it; but if that nation turn from their evil, because of which I have spoken against it, I change My mind about the evil I thought to do to it."*—*Jeremiah 18:5-8*

Introduction: The Message Delivered

Jonah has hardly begun his journey from the seashore back to the highlands to fulfill his vow when his plans are suddenly changed for him.

> *Now it came to pass, that the word of the* Lord *came to Jonah a second time, saying: "Arise, go to Nineveh, the Great City, and cry out against her the proclamation[2] that I tell you." So Jonah arose and went to Nineveh in accordance with the word of the* Lord [3:1-3a].

We seem to have come full circle and have returned to our starting point, but have we? As in the case of our two previous chapters, we again find ourselves confronted with a complete and carefully structured compositional unit, comprising an Introduction (3:1-3a), a Main Body (3:3b-9) and an Epilogue (3:10). We have just read the Introduction, set apart from the rest of the chapter by opening and closing with the same phrase, *"the word of the* Lord."[3]

This would seem to be a repeat of the Introduction to Chapter 1 (1:1-3), but although the similarity is striking it is in the differences—small though they seem—that the interest lies. In the first place, our hero is referred to as simply Jonah; he is missing his patronymic.[4] This is no oversight. Simon reminds us that this is standard

---

1. Hebrew *yenahem*, to repent of a decision one has made; to change one's mind.
2. Literally, *the cry.*
3. The bracketing of a section of text by either a given word or phrase, or two versions thereof, is a common way biblical authors signaled that we should read the text between the "brackets" as a self-contained unit.
4. In Chapter 1 he is referred to by his full name: Jonah, son of Amittai.

biblical procedure: when first mentioning a protagonist the full name is given. For subsequent references his given name is deemed sufficient.[5] In this way the author is subtly reminding us that this is not a new beginning but a continuation of what went on before; we are being expected to know who our protagonist is, and what has happened to him up to now. However, if the reader is expected to remember Jonah's patronymic from Chapter 1, then he can equally remember what God said. What need is there for God to repeat what He already said to Jonah? But the point here is that God is not repeating himself; the seemingly insignificant differences throw God's current commission to Jonah into an entirely different light. It is in effect a new mission.

As we shall learn, the reason for the assignment remains the same,[6] and therefore merits no repetition. What is new is that God substitutes for the reason he gave previously a command to declare *the proclamation that I tell you*, that is, the exact words you are to speak.[7] Moreover, it is the wording of this mandate that is especially significant: it is phrased in such a manner as to remind us of the commissioning of Moses to go down to Egypt and confront Pharaoh.

And the LORD *said to Moses, "I am the* LORD; *speak to Pharaoh, King of Egypt,* all that I tell you"[8] [*Exodus* 6:29].

The point of the comparison lies in the following verses. Moses, having been told what to do and what he is to say, wants no part of the assignment and tries to talk his way out of it, claiming to be unqualified to deliver the message.[9] However, Moses is given no option. Where God wants him to go there he will go, and what God wants him to say that he will say. Jonah, we are being reminded, is following in the footsteps of his great predecessor.

The difference being highlighted between Moses and Jonah lies in their responses. Moses is open and aboveboard as to his feelings and his objections for taking on the assignment while Jonah remains characteristically tightlipped; his silence leaving us—but not God—in the dark as to the causes of his original refusal to accept his mission, the degree to which his recent experiences have altered his former resolve and what he currently feels about the assignment for which, not so long ago, he had been ready to offer up his life rather than perform.

But even under the worst of interpretations, Jonah has learned his lesson: there is no use trying to run away. He will now do what he is told. But in what spirit, and with what mental reservations the narrator will not tell us, nor will Jonah himself see fit to enlighten us. He will remain as tightlipped and enigmatic as ever, and we will continue to be in the dark.

---

5. Simon, *Jonah,* p. 4, and again 26.

6. *For their evil has risen up before Me.* (1:2)

7. The original assignment given to Jonah was of a more general nature; the subject given, Jonah apparently would be free as to how to word the message. Now this putative freedom is being taken from him.

8. *Asher anochi dover ailecha*; the same four words in the Hebrew. The mandate to both Moses and Jonah end in exactly the same manner.

9. The text is unclear as to whether Moses is asking to be disqualified for having a speech impediment, or whether he is claiming a lack of rhetorical skill to deliver the message in a sufficiently forceful and convincing manner.

The Doomed City

At this point in our tale we take leave of our hero (or anti-hero). He has no role in the rest of the chapter except for a cameo appearance at the very beginning. The Main Body of our installment is about Nineveh, its population and its ruler. And as the tale unfolds we perhaps will begin to grasp in however imperfect a manner why God was so determined to send his messenger to "The Great City."

But before beginning we must disabuse ourselves of any inclination to identify the Nineveh of the *Book of Jonah* with the Nineveh of history: the great metropolis on the Tigris, the city of the warlords Sennacherib and Assurbanipal, capital of the Assyrian Empire whose ruins so amazed Xenophon and whose shards and remnants clutter some of our best museums. Our Nineveh is a dream city, a fantasy: a mythical City-State in a far-off never-never land, a resplendent "Emerald City" in an imaginary Land of Oz, or for those too young to remember *The Wizard of Oz*, the "Gotham City" of *Batman*. The two cities have nothing in common except their respective names, and to seek Jonah's Nineveh in the bloody annals of the history of the Ancient Near East or in the partially excavated ruins opposite Mosul in Iraq would be an exercise in futility. Once divorced from history and geography our Nineveh takes on a life of its own in the realm of our imaginations, for its role is not of brick and stone but that of symbol. This said, we return to our tale.

Now as for Nineveh, it was[10] a great city in God's eyes,[11] a walk of three days![12] So Jonah began to enter into the city [a distance of] *one day's walk, and he cried out, saying, "In forty days and Nineveh shall be overturned!"[13]* [3:3b–4]

Our narrator begins by stressing the monstrous size of this fabulous city. If we calculate that the distance an average man could walk in a day as about 15 miles,[14] this would make Jonah's Nineveh almost 50 miles across. But as Wolff correctly comments: "The reader is not supposed to do the arithmetic. He is supposed to be lost in astonishment."[15] So Jonah proceeding one day into the megalopolis will have been

---

10. Hebrew *haytah*. Many scholars make much of the fact that this word is in the perfect tense, a grammatical construction that is usually rendered in Western languages as a past tense, i.e., "was." Starting from this point they contend that the implication of the text is that Nineveh at one time *was* a great city but *now* it no longer is. From this they deduce that *Jonah* was composed long after Nineveh was destroyed by the Medes and the Babylonians in 612 BCE. Thus, in penning this opening statement of the Main Body of the chapter, "He [the author] takes him [the reader] back to 'time immemorial.'" (Wolff, *Obadiah and Jonah*, p. 147) But the perfect tense in ancient Hebrew is *not* a past tense: it signifies an action or process that has come to its conclusion as opposed to one that is still ongoing (which is signaled by use of the imperfect tense). Thus the use of the perfect tense in our verse simply means that Nineveh has grown from a town into a huge urban sprawl, and at the time the tale is taking place the process of absorbing the satellite cities (see Chapter 1, note 2) has been completed, turning the city into a megalopolis. Therefore I do not believe that from this verse any inference as to the time of composition of the *Book of Jonah* can reliably be made.

11. Literally, *a city great to God*, i.e., a huge city, even from God's point of view. For the real Nineveh which gave birth to its legendary namesake, see Chapter 1, note 2.

12. The reference is clearly to diameter, not circumference. That is, walking in a straight line from one side of the urban megalopolis to the other would take a minimum of three whole days.

13. Literally, *is overturned*, in the present tense singular, giving the warning "greater certainty and immediacy" (Simon, p. 29) than a prediction phrased in the future tense, and hence not immediate.

14. The Rabbis of old had a more optimistic view of adult capability, increasing our estimate to about 20 miles. (*Talmud Pesahim* 94b)

15. Wolff, p. 148.

conceived by the narrator to have traversed the suburbs and have reached the center—the core city proper—before beginning to deliver his message. Then having made his pronouncement, Jonah disappears from the narrative for the remainder of the chapter. The focus is now solely on Nineveh.

Be that as it may, while Jonah himself vanishes, the proclamation he has made lives on and only gathers strength with the passage of the days. Before we can turn to how the Ninevites react to this bolt from the blue—and as we shall see, this is exactly how they take it—we must examine the message itself and its implications:

"In forty days and Nineveh shall be overturned!"

The first thing that strikes us is the shocking brevity of the pronouncement, a mere five words in the Hebrew. Is this all Jonah has to say? There are two ways that this short statement can be taken. A prophetic pronouncement of doom usually includes three elements: an indictment listing the crimes allegedly committed, the verdict convicting the accused of the crimes, and the sentence.[16]

Jonah's oracle consists solely of the sentence, both indictment and verdict are missing; it lacks even the name of the Judge who pronounced the sentence! There are those who hold that the oracle pronounced by Jonah in the squares of Nineveh was a full-fledged prophetic proclamation containing both indictment and verdict. In order to keep the narrative concise and to enhance the shock effect, these have been omitted in our narrative and only the sentence has been stated; the bottom line as it were. On the other hand there are those who take these five words as the complete oracle that Jonah proclaims. Simon (p. 28f), for example, explains that the brevity "reflects the fact that he is not sent to reprove Nineveh for its sins, but only to inform it of the sentence passed upon it."[17]

Turning to the contents of the oracle itself,[18] two aspects of this brief sentence stand out as having far-reaching implications. The first is the crux of the decree: that Nineveh is doomed to be not merely destroyed but "overturned."[19] The Hebrew term *nehepachet* denotes a total and terminal destruction; an annihilation so absolute and final that the city will never be rebuilt, but will remain an everlasting desolation. It is the term used to describe the blotting out of Sodom and Gomorrah, the archetypes of urban evil and annihilatory punishment in the Bible[20]—an event so horrific that it haunted the memory of the Israelites throughout the Age of the Bible—and the use

---

16. See *Amos* 1:3–2:16 for a series of examples.

17. A second issue that troubles many Bible commentators is in what language did Jonah proclaim his oracle to the Ninevites, Aramaic or Akkadian? Was he even conversant with these languages? Hebrew, of course, would be unintelligible to the inhabitants of Nineveh. But this question, like so many of the "problems" and "inconsistencies" that plague these scholars rests on cleaving to a literalist reading of the text: seeing *Jonah* as an account of a historical event. Once one reads the Book as a fable, the issue vanishes. If, when reading fables, we are not troubled by animals or even trees speaking, then the ability of the Ninevites to understand spoken Hebrew should hardly trouble us.

18. We use the term *oracle* because, although not proclaimed in the name of any deity, it was clearly taken by the Ninevites as a revelation of the will of the gods.

19. *Overturned*: like a bowl turned upside down with all its contents spilled out into the dirt.

20. *Genesis* 19:21, 25, 29; *Deuteronomy* 29:22; *Isaiah* 13:19; *Jeremiah* 20:16; 49:18; 50:40; *Amos* 4:11; *Lamentations* 4:6.

of this term would invariably recall that event to mind. This, Jonah proclaims, is the destiny decreed for Nineveh.[21]

But not immediately; the decree includes a stay of execution. Only after an indeterminable but finite period will the doom descend upon the "Great City."[22] This divinely mandated postponement of the execution of sentence amounts to a grace period that will give the Ninevites an opportunity to save themselves, either by fleeing the doomed city or by seeking a pardon. The first option has a precedent (known to every Israelite): having been warned, Lot and his daughters flee Sodom and so escape the doom of the city (*Genesis* 19:12–26). To seek a pardon from impending punishment is also not unprecedented: David seeks pardon for the doom he brought down on his infant son by his sin with Bathsheba—but in vain (*2 Samuel* 12:13–23).[23] After the 8th century many readers of *Jonah* would also have known the story of the mortal illness of King Hezekiah (715–686 BCE) and his success in gaining, if not a pardon, then a fifteen-year reprieve (*2 Kings* 20:1–11). And within the confines of our tale we can assume that our hero is well aware of at least the first two of the above-mentioned precedents.

Under these circumstances we could assume that Jonah would immediately grasp the implications of the stay of sentence included in his mandated pronouncement: that the Ninevites are being offered an opportunity—if they believe the warning—of escaping the impending doom. But, as we have learned, this is the last thing that Jonah wants. It is this offer of a second chance, we have surmised, that originally led Jonah to refuse any part in God's mission. This time around Jonah knows that he has no choice. Due to either his new born trust in "his God," or to *force majeure*, Jonah complies and delivers the message.

At the Book's beginning this was the hypothesis that we tentatively adopted, and at that time we may have found this reasoning compelling. But this reading only applies to the real world. Having come to the conclusion that *Jonah* is fable and not history, and taking into consideration all that Jonah has undergone in the last two chapters since we considered Abravanel's reading, it becomes necessary to reconsider. In Chapter 1 we commented that Jonah was aware that refusing to obey orders was tantamount to rebellion against God, and that the penalty for such defiance was death. By running away Jonah was courting martyrdom, and by telling the sailors to throw him into the sea he was accepting this fate. This time around Jonah has learned

---

21. Limburg (p. 80) points out that, metrically, the oracle is cast in the *kinah* rhythm, the poetic format used for laments and dirges in biblical Hebrew—a fact that would have been instantly evident to the original audience of *Jonah*.

22. "Forty is frequently used [in the Bible] as a symbolic number, and forty days represents a significant period of time" (Sarna, *Exodus*, p. 155), i.e., a fairly long time but with a definite terminus point. Examples are: "*I will make it rain upon the earth forty days and forty nights.*" (*Genesis* 7:4), *Now it came to pass that Moses was on the mountain* [Mount Sinai] *forty days and forty nights.* (*Exodus* 24:18; also with variations 34:28; *Deuteronomy* 9:9, 11, etc.), and [Elijah] *went on the strength of that meal forty days and forty nights as far as Horeb, the Mountain of God* (*1 Kings* 19:18), etc. Leon Kass, quoting Robert Sacks, notes that 40 weeks is the average length of a human pregnancy. Thus the number 40 also symbolizes a period of time during which nothing happens, yet without which nothing can ever happen. (*Beginning of Wisdom*, p. 164, n. 17)

23. Interestingly from the perspective of our tale, David adopts the same measures in seeking a pardon as the Ninevites will implement: lying on the ground, fasting, self-mortification and prayer. These two precedents would have been known to most eighth century Israelites (the putative time the story is taking place).

his lesson; he obeys his orders to the letter. Moreover, I would contend that it is even likely that he does so willingly; after his revelatory experience in the bowels of the fish he now sees God as his Savior. But has he abandoned his former reservations as to God's purposes?

Let us try to look at his mission and its probable outcome through Jonah's eyes, not for Nineveh but for himself. Whether in terms of the real world or within the confines of a story, Jonah could hardly expect his mandated message of doom to be popular with the Ninevites. Those of the population who hear him would be likely to react with fury; the authorities would be likely to see him as preaching sedition. If they should fail to arrest him on the spot—and he knows from grim report that he could expect little mercy if he is seized—then there would be every likelihood that his listeners, turned into an infuriated mob by his words, would lynch him. By accepting his mission has Jonah once again resigned himself to martyrdom?

Let us now take this line of speculation a step further. Could we entertain the suspicion that Jonah may not have abandoned his reservations about God's intentions; that as the days have passed on his journey to Nineveh Jonah has at least partially reverted to the Jonah of old? If so, then is it further possible to postulate that he now holds to the hope that should he be martyred—it matters not whether by the authorities or by the public—this murder of a prophet of the Lord in the act of proclaiming His word would so infuriate God as to tip the balance and insure Nineveh's destruction? In other words, is Jonah's compliance with his orders a wholehearted obedience to God's will, or is his outward acquiescence merely a cover for an inner determination to force God's hand and assure the doom of Nineveh? We currently have no way of knowing with any certainty. Jonah has yet to show his hand.

With these uncertainties as to the motives of our protagonist, we take our leave of Jonah and turn now to Nineveh, an abstraction that is as yet for us little more than a name.

Turnabout

Up to this point in our tale all that we have been told about Nineveh and its inhabitants is the city's size—it is huge—and that its inhabitants are evil, in fact so evil that the situation has become intolerable in God's eyes. Of what this evil consists we have not been told, although the language employed has hinted that we would do well to look to the case of Sodom and Gomorrah for guidance in this matter. We have also speculated on how a population so steeped in evil as to merit divinely ordained annihilation is likely to react to the public announcement of its impending doom. We might anticipate disbelief, rejection and even fury at such a pronouncement. And inasmuch as the divine source of the proclamation is beyond its reach, we could reasonably look forward to the population turning its rage upon the messenger proclaiming that which they so do not want to hear, and rending him limb from limb.

Our author, however, as is his wont, never ceases to surprise us. Against all expectation, and indeed against all logic, he informs us that the inhabitants of Nineveh actually believe the unpalatable message. More: In their panic over their impending doom they do not abandon their homes and flee the doomed city, leaving it to its fate while running for their lives. Instead they opt to abase themselves before the gods and petition for a stay of sentence.

> *Now the men of Nineveh believed in the gods*[24]; *and they called*[25] *a fast and put on sackcloth, from the greatest of them even to the least of them. And the matter*[26] *reached the King of Nineveh, and he rose off his throne, and cast his* [royal] *robe from off him and put on sackcloth and sat in ashes*[27] [3:5–6].

Fasting and donning sackcloth[28] in place of one's usual garments were traditional ritual expressions of self abasement, contrition and grief throughout the Ancient Near East. By these signs the general population of the city begins to express regret for whatever wrong they had done, and thus to petition the gods for a stay of sentence. Word of these goings-on reaches the palace, the report including the contents of Jonah's declaration. Even though not explicitly proclaimed as a divine oracle,[29] it is universally accepted by the Ninevites as such. We can assume that reports of the growing popular hysteria are also passed on to the king.[30] And wonder upon wonders, despite not having heard the oracle from the prophet's mouth but only second or third hand, he also believes it. He goes even further than those whom he rules: he divests himself of the paraphernalia of his royal office—his throne and his royal robes—and to further abase himself, in place of these he puts on sackcloth and seats himself on a heap of ashes.[31]

But the king is more than a private person. The responsibility for the welfare of the city and all its inhabitants rests upon his shoulders. This is a state emergency and the king takes matters in hand.

---

24. That is, they believed that the proclamation was a divine oracle revealing the true intention of the gods. The term *elohim*, is grammatically in the plural. When the term is used by or about a monotheist it is rendered as "God," the plural being understood as the "plural of Majesty." When used by or about pagans—who are polytheists—it is rendered as "gods." As the inhabitants of Nineveh are all pagans, we render it here and in all future uses regarding them as "gods" or as "the gods," the meaning being that the Ninevites stood in awe of the realm of the divine, as manifested by their various deities. But see note 34 below.

25. Literally, *"cried out"* (*karah*) *a fast*, echoing the word used by God in His command to Jonah to cry out against Nineveh (1:2, 3:2).

26. Hebrew *hadavar*: "the word" or "the thing," i.e., word of Jonah's proclamation, and possibly also the public reaction to it.

27. Literally, *on the ashes*, i.e., on an ash heap.

28. Sackcloth was a coarse material used for baling agricultural produce. Worn against the skin for any length of time it would become intolerably uncomfortable.

29. Note that the Lord is never mentioned by Jonah as the source of the oracle.

30. This office is entirely fictional, the invention of the author. There never was a "King of Nineveh" in the first millennium before the Common Era, if indeed ever, any more than there was ever a "President of New York City." The real Nineveh was a very ancient, large and important city in Mesopotamia. At a late stage of the Assyrian Empire, in 705 BCE, the great warlord Sennacherib moved the capital of the Empire to Nineveh. From then until the fall of the Empire and the destruction of Nineveh in 612 BCE it served as the administrative center of the Empire and the residence of its kings. The author does not seem to know anything about Nineveh as an Imperial Capital. He portrays Nineveh as an independent city-state with its own king. It cannot be overly stressed that we are not in the real world of the Ancient Near East; we are in the Land of Oz or the world of Batman.

31. There is no need for the author to state that he fasted; it can be taken for granted. What the common folk have taken upon themselves amounts to the minimum of personal abasement which the king, in order to maintain his moral authority, must also adopt and then surpass.

And he had it proclaimed throughout Nineveh: "By the authority[32] of the king and his nobles, let neither man nor beast, neither cattle nor sheep, taste of anything; they shall neither graze nor drink any water. Let both man and beast be covered with sackcloth, and let them cry with all [their] might upon [the] gods; let every man turn from his evil way, and from the violence which is in his hands.[33] Who knows but the gods may turn and relent and turn from His fierce anger[34] that we not perish" [3:7–9].

The Intolerable Evil

This royal proclamation, to which the king's nobles[35] add their imprimatur, explains the remarkable uniformity of the popular response to Jonah's declaration: everyone, without exception, donning sackcloth and fasting.[36] As a consequence of this edict royal troops can now be counted upon to ensure that any individuals who initially had abstained from voluntarily joining in the general frenzy of self abasement and contrition would now be compelled to do so. But more importantly, in his decree the king has clarified for us an issue that has been nagging at us from the opening verses of *Jonah*: what exactly is the evil that is so intolerable to God as to lead to His decision to wipe Nineveh off the map? The king does not have to appoint a commission of inquiry to figure out why the gods have passed a sentence of doom upon his city; he knows. And so do his nobles. For years the level of h̲amas—ferocious violence—has been inexorably rising in our mythical city of Nineveh; it has now reached intolerable and uncontrollable levels. The sentence comes as no surprise.

---

32. This rendition of the term *mitaam* follows Sasson, pp. 253–254.

33. In contradistinction to the ancient rabbis, and to some modern scholars as well, who understand the phrase *"turn from... the violence which is in his hands"* to refer to the proceeds of violence, i.e., loot, and thus a demand to return any stolen property that may be in one's hands to its rightful owners, Simon (p. 33) points out that this would require the word *turn* to be a transitive verb. But as in this verse the verb is intransitive, followed by the preposition *from*, the meaning can only be a demand for fundamental behavioral change: to stop the violence and bloodletting. What is in their hands is not loot but blood, c.f. Isaiah's rebuke to the Jerusalemites:
And when you spread forth your hands,
  I will hide My eyes from you;
Even when you make many prayers
  I will not hear;
Your hands are full of blood! (Isaiah 1:15)

34. This is a literal translation of MT. Since it is a pagan king speaking who knows nothing of monotheism, we render the term *haelohim* in this context as "the gods" despite the fact that strangely the verbs modifying *haelohim* are all in the singular. This dissonance is forced upon the author—who is quite conscious of the incongruity—by the fact that the following words are a quotation from *Exodus* 32:12 (see below) which is in the singular. He has already been forced to mangle his source by inverting the position of the two phrases from their original order so as to fit them into the context of Chapter 3. Perhaps our author felt that also changing the tense of the phrases would exceed acceptable limits of quotation and render the original unrecognizable. The author is, of course, a monotheist, and to him *haelohim* means simply the one and only God. Although he determinedly refuses to refer to the lord, and is playing with the ambiguity inherent in the term *haelohim*, there are theological limits beyond which he cannot allow himself to go, even for the sake of grammatical consistency.

35. "The Assyrians were already familiar with 'the great men' (*rabutu/rabani*) who were at the king's side; the phrase is used for the princes, the civil servants who were in charge of administrative affairs, and the king's advisers." (Wolff, p. 152)

36. The phrase *from the greatest of them even to the least of them* (3:5) is a merism (see *Glossary*), it means simply "everyone without exception."

The term *ḥamas* needs some elucidation. It refers to bloody acts of an extreme nature perpetrated in civilian context, both by individuals and by groups of men.[37] Abimelech's barbarous massacre of his family—seventy screaming relatives slaughtered systematically at one spot, like a contingent of cattle at an abattoir[38]—is referred to as *ḥamas*; ferocious, vicious violence.[39] In the account of the great flood, the evil which brought down judgment upon mankind is described as *ḥamas* (*Genesis* 6:11, 13). Indeed, *ḥamas* can be taken as an "equivalent of 'shedding blood.'"[40]

A second point needs to be made: the term seems to be reserved for cases of bloodshed that take place in an urban setting.[41] This fact is important. Fixated as we tend to be on the historic Nineveh, the capital of the Assyrian Empire in the 7th century BCE, we imagine her crimes to be those of the blood-drenched world conqueror so painstakingly recorded in her annals and so vividly depicted in her art: the destruction of nations and the annihilation of whole peoples; genocide, mass torture of prisoners, rapine and gratuitous slaughter of helpless civilians. But neither the Assyrian Empire nor Assyrians find even a passing mention in the *Book of Jonah*, nor do any of the atrocities committed by the Empire.[42] As we must keep reminding ourselves, we are being treated to the picture of a fantasy "Great City" situated in a Never-Never Land, an imaginary city-state, beset with crime, whose social fabric is rapidly unraveling to the horror of its rulers and its minuscule remnant of law-abiding citizens. Our Nineveh is not a capital set on imperial conquest but "Gotham City," beset by civic violence, urban crime, bloodshed and—if we can draw on an example from Sodom—perversion, without Batman to save it from itself. This picture of Nineveh as an urban jungle has this much basis in reality: the prophet Nahum, who was a contemporary of Nineveh's fall near the close of the 7th century, describes the city as *a city of crime* [*or blood*], *utterly treacherous, full of violence, where killing never stops.* (*Nahum* 3:1)[43] We now realize that it is not the Evil Empire we are being shown, but the Evil City; or to put it in language closer to our own experience, the "Great City" has become "The Asphalt Jungle."

Now that we have begun to realize what Jonah's mission is all about in our tale, and why God has determined to terminate the existence of the Great City, it would be well to summarize our new understanding and some of its implications. In the first place, the great evil that has doomed the city is rampant urban bloodshed that has reached intolerable levels. Secondly, this situation seems to be known

---

37. The term does not seem to apply to the bloody violence of warfare.
38. See the account in *Judges* 9:5.
39. *Judges* 9:24.
40. Wolff, p. 153.
41. Limburg (p. 83) refers to *Psalm* 55:10; *Jeremiah* 6:6–7; *Ezekiel* 7:23 and *Micah* 6:9–12 as examples of the term *ḥamas* being used in explicit urban contexts. There seem to be no examples of the use of this term in explicitly non-urban settings.
42. The contrast between *Jonah* and the *Book of Nahum* in their treatment of Nineveh is illuminating. *Nahum's* listing of her crimes is exclusively of atrocities committed against others in the course of Empire; *ḥamas* finds no mention. Unlike Jonah, Nahum was celebrating the destruction of the *real* Nineveh, and giving voice to the outrage of the entire Ancient Near East at the crimes against humanity perpetrated by the Assyrian Empire.
43. Translation by U. Simon, p. 33.

to everyone, and further is understood by all concerned to be insufferably evil. Thus no one is really surprised by the announcement that the gods have had enough and have decided to close down the Evil City and its inhabitants. May we further speculate that many Ninevites may have been half-expecting such an outcome? So in our tale Jonah's pronouncement would be falling upon the ears of a population prepared to hear such words as his; which could account for their ready acceptance. Further, they neither rebel against the punishment nor even protest it because, having admitted this evil, they believe they deserve it. The remorse triggered by Jonah's proclamation is not simply a show; it is genuine.

To these understandings three further points need to be made about the king's remarkable decree. The first concerns the bizarre insistence on including domesticated animals (cattle and herds)[44] on an equal footing with human beings in the edict to perform the traditional rituals of self-abasement and contrition, as well as the command to *cry with all* [their] *might upon* [the] *gods*.[45] This seems to stem from a realization that these sentient partners of humans that dwell in such close proximity one with the other share a common fate should Nineveh be destroyed.[46] This sense of a common shared destiny for God's creatures—humans and animals alike—is an understanding that is to be confirmed by God in His final remarks (4:11).

A second point is that the edict exhibits the realization that ritual expressions of remorse—no matter how sincere the feelings underlying them—are insufficient to move the gods to reconsider their stand. Only repentance might induce them to reverse themselves, and repentance requires not only remorse over past behavior but also behavioral change. The violence—the bloodshed, the daily killings—must cease forthwith, conflict must give way to cooperation. An entire philosophy of human relations lies embedded in these few words.

That this is hardly a pagan point of view is beside the point. Indeed the author subtly underlines the fact that this is a central Israelite doctrine that he is projecting onto a pagan king by having the king quote in his decree from Moses' plea to God, that He forgive Israel for the sin of worshiping the Golden Calf (*Exodus* 32:12).[47] By reversing the two phrases and adding the words *who knows*, he has the king turn the plea into a pious hope that the gods will (perhaps) respond to him the way God responded to Moses (*Exodus* 32:14).

Moreover, in this final clause of the king's declaration:

---

44. Cattle consist of bovines (bulls, oxen, cows, etc.), herds in those days consisted of sheep and goats.

45. The ancient rabbis took literally this command to ensure that the beasts would also cry out to the divine source of the impending doom, and speculated as to how this goal was to be accomplished. One method proposed the removal of the nursing calves from their mothers. This would result in the cows bellowing in anxiety for their young while the hungry calves would be bleating to be fed, thus resulting in a cacophony of "crying out." The rabbis obviously had no high opinion of the Ninevites' concern for the welfare of their creatures.

46. In Israel and Judah, living conditions were such that these domestic creatures shared living arrangements with their human masters: the ground floor of the typical family structure served as a barn for stabling domestic animals while the second floor provided the living quarters for the human family. (See my *Invention of Monotheist Ethics*, Excursus iv, p. 115–117, for a detailed description of living conditions in ancient Israel). Was our author unrealistically projecting Israelite living arrangements on the Ninevites, or was the assumption of a close human-animal relationship based on intimate knowledge of the Ninevite reality?

47. *Turn from Your fierce anger, and relent from the evil* [You intend] *for Your people.* (*Exodus* 32:12) Note that in *Jonah* 3:9 the phrases have been reversed to fit better into the context,

> "Who knows[48] but the gods may turn and relent and turn from His fierce anger that we not perish" [1:9].

By the addition to the quote from *Exodus* of the words "*who knows*," the author is indicating a very real sense on the king's part of the highly uncertain nature of the entire process being undertaken. The gods have a will of their own. There is no way to force their hand. Neither ritual properly performed, nor remorse, nor even the complete behavioral change of true repentance can guarantee averting the looming disaster. What is being undertaken is an extremely uncertain path with very limited probability of success, but the king is willing to take the chance. The odds are against us, but *who knows?*

And with these words we conclude the Main Body of this chapter. But before we get to the Epilogue which contains the dénouement, we must pause and evaluate the larger significance of where our analysis of the king's decree has led us. If it is true that the Nineveh of our tale is not the historic capital of the predatory Assyrian Empire but a mythical city-state situated in some fairy-tale land—in other words, that our tale is not history but parable—and that the evil of which our Nineveh is accused is an orgy of urban violence and not the march of a nation-destroying military machine, then we will have no choice but to once and for all abandon any lingering nostalgia for Abravanel's reading of the *Book of Jonah*,[49] which is based on the premise that the Nineveh of our tale is the historic capital of the Assyrian Empire in the 7th century BCE, well advanced on its bloody path to world conquest. We will have to cast about for some other explanation for Jonah's original refusal to carry out God's orders and deliver His proclamation of doom to Nineveh.

Epilogue: God Changes His Mind

As we have pointed out, the climax to the king's edict, in which he voices the reason for the extraordinary regimen of contrition and repentance he has imposed upon his people—that who knows, maybe repentance may induce the gods to change their minds and cancel the decree of doom that hangs over them—is actually a quotation from the 32nd Chapter of *Exodus* (slightly rearranged to better fit into the context of the king's decree).[50] Those of us who have grasped this fact and are acquainted with the story related in *Exodus* 32, should not be surprised by the startling culmination of our own chapter. The Epilogue to our chapter states:

> *And God[51] saw their deeds—for they had turned from their evil ways—and God*

---

48. An expression parallel to that made by the Shipmaster in Chapter 1, "*perhaps the god will take thought of us and we will not perish* (1:6b) and carrying much the same burden of meaning.

49. The premise that Jonah is an Israelite patriot who sees the relentless approach of the Assyrian war machine that threatens to annihilate his beloved country, who wants God to destroy Nineveh before it can destroy Israel, and who therefore is ready even to sacrifice his life to ensure that Nineveh will not escape the fate it deserves. See Chapter 1.

50. *Exodus* 32:12.

51. Literally, *the God*, i.e., the one and only God. The narrator is now speaking, not the king, and the biblical narrator is of course the spokesman of monotheism, so we here render *elohim* as God. See note 24 above.

relented from the evil that He said that He would do to them[52]; *and He did it not* [3:10].

This statement itself embodies another quote from *Exodus*, indeed the decisive turning point of that tale: God changes His mind and rescinds the judgment on Israel that He had decreed.[53]

We must keep in mind that the author of *Jonah* is an Israelite, and that the audience for whom he is writing his Book is composed of Israelites. By twice quoting from *Exodus* 32, he is calling to mind the story of the Golden Calf and is thus suggesting to his readers that this episode and the tale of Jonah in Nineveh are parallel narratives. Don't be so startled by the thought of God changing His mind and canceling the well-deserved death sentence that He has decreed, the author is implying to his readers. God does change His mind. Remember your own history: how He decreed a sentence of annihilation upon your ancestors in the wilderness and then canceled His decree. Then it was the intercession of the great prophet Moses that effected the change of heart, now in the case of Nineveh it is the repentance of the people. Pay heed, the author may also be implying: what worked for them in their hour of need may also work for you in yours.

But what worked for the Ninevites in the story were not their prayers but *their deeds—for they had turned from their evil ways*. Words are cheap and intentions insubstantial; it is behavior that is decisive in the eyes of God. Indeed, the author drives home this point by embedding no less than three derivatives of the verb *asah*—to do—in this single verse.[54] This is no accident, Sasson insists. "This dense repetition anchors an important reflection: deeds—and not just good intentions—are necessary for forgiveness."[55]

Even more; if we remove the concluding subordinate clause, *and He did it not* (two words in the Hebrew) from the concluding verse of the Epilogue (3:10), we find in the exact center of the main body of the verse two terms—*raah* (evil) and *nahem* (repentance, change of mind)—that will highlight the central themes of the next chapter. The author is preparing us for the climactic conclusion of the Book. It is amazing how much he is able to pack into the mere eighteen words of verse 10.

As the Main Body of the chapter concludes with the curt statement (two words in the Hebrew) in which the king sums up his entire purpose—literally, *"that we perish not"* (3:9), so does the Epilogue end with an equally brief yet definitive statement of God's decision (also two words in the Hebrew, with the same construction): *and He did it not*. On this notice of convergence between the purposes of God and king the curtain drops on Chapter 3 of the *Book of Jonah*.

---

52. An almost exact quote of *Exodus* 32:14, the only significant difference being that in line with his policy of not mentioning the Lord in the Main Body and in the Epilogue of Chapter 3 (the Ninevites and their king being pagans, they never have heard of the Lord) the author has substituted the generic *haelohim*.

53. *Exodus* 32 tells the tale of Israel's great lapse into idolatry. Moses has ascended Mount Sinai to receive the Ten Commandments. In his absence the Israelites construct a golden calf and commence worshiping it. God is furious at this betrayal and proclaims to Moses that He will destroy this "stiffnecked people," but Moses intercedes for the Israelites—successfully as it turns out—and God changes His mind: *And the Lord relented from the evil which He said He would do to His people*. (*Exodus* 32:14) This, the author is suggesting, is a precedent that can be relied on.

54. *And God saw their deeds (maasayhem) ... and God relented from the evil that He said He would do (laasot) to them; and He did (asah) it not*.

55. Sasson, p. 264.

Chapter 4

Endgame

But He, being compassionate,
Forgives iniquity and does not destroy;
He often restrains His anger,
And does not stir up all His wrath.
He remembers that they [humans] *are but flesh,*
A breath of wind that passes away and does not return.
—Psalm 78:38–39

Is my gloom, after all,
Shade of His hand, outstretched caressingly?
—Francis Thompson, *The Hound of Heaven*

Fury Unbounded

We now take leave of the repentant "Great City" of our tale and return to our hero; or more properly, our anti-hero. We left him in one of the many public squares of Nineveh, having just concluded his proclamation and, considering his likely frame of mind, bracing himself to meet the violent reaction of his audience.[1] All that followed—his audience's acceptance of his message, the panic and hysteria, the wave of contrition, the king's decree and its implementation, and finally God's change of mind—can hardly have consumed much less than a week; likely a fair bit more. What has Jonah been doing all this time? How does our story picture the way Jonah takes the amazing series of events that he has triggered by his proclamation? Our author now turns back the clock to pick up where he left off, with the crowd of Ninevites listening in shock to Jonah's words—"In forty days and Nineveh shall be overturned"—and, amazingly, believing what they hear.

Now [this][2] *incensed Jonah enormously,*[3] *and he became furious. And he prayed to*

---

1. Was this all Jonah does? In real life it would be more reasonable to believe that Jonah repeats his proclamation several times in different parts of the city over the next two or three days, bringing his message to as many of the city's vast number of inhabitants as he can and fanning the flames of the growing hysteria. But this is a fable, and in a fabulous setting once is more than enough.

2. I.e., that the Ninevites *had turned from their evil ways—and God relented from the evil that He said that He would do to them, and He did it not.* (3:10)

3. Once again the infinitive absolute construction (see Chapter 1, note 54); literally, *It was evil to Jonah with a great evil*, i.e., it angered him tremendously. The contrast between Jonah's reaction to the salvation of Nineveh and the response of the sailors to the salvation of their ship—*Now the men felt a measureless awe for the lord* (1:16, also tellingly in the infinitive absolute construction)—hardly redounds to Jonah's credit. (Simon, p. 36)

Chapter 4. Endgame

the LORD, *saying, "Please,* LORD*! Isn't this just what I said while I was still on my own soil?*[4] *That is why I arose to flee to Tarshish, for I knew that You are a compassionate and merciful God, slow to anger*[5] *and abounding in loving-kindness,*[6] *and ready to change Your mind about punishing.*[7] *And now,*[8] *O* LORD, *please take my life from me, for it is better for me to die than to live!"* [4:1–3]

Considering our analysis and speculation up to this point, our hero's disappointment at the repentance of the Ninevites and God's subsequent change of mind, reversing Himself, may not be completely unexpected, but Jonah's outburst is shocking. He has completely lost his cool. In his fury he has let slip the tightlipped stoic front that he has been maintaining and at long last bares his soul. "I knew it! I knew it! I knew it from the moment we started on this charade, back in the land of Israel! I knew You would never stick to Your word. I know Your nature: You are a compassionate and merciful God, slow to anger and abounding in *ḥesed*, and ever ready to change Your mind about doing what needs to be done.[9] That is why I tried to run away to Tarshish.[10] I wanted nothing to do with Your games. But You forced me. And now look at what You have made me complicit! It is just what I feared from the start: You have let them off the hook. This is too much! Take away my life, O LORD; life is no longer worth living."

Jonah is absolutely beside himself. And he is not exaggerating; for him, this is truly a matter of life and death. It is not simply that God has spared Nineveh—for Jonah, we shall discover, this is a matter of principle—but there is also a deep personal aspect to the issue at hand. In his rant, in the course of two verses (4:2–3) the first person singular—I, me, mine—appears in the Hebrew no less than nine times.[11] For Jonah his involvement is total: this is where I take my stand!

To have this tirade defined as a prayer[12] seems more than a little bizarre until we notice that, tacked on at the very end is a petition asking God to take back the life that He originally gave to Jonah. The rant is no more, in a formal sense, than an

---

4. I.e., in the land of Israel. Note how Jonah consistently refuses to verbally acknowledge his status as an Israelite. See Chapter 1, note 40, and related text.

5. I.e., long-suffering.

6. Literally, abundant in *ḥesed*; see Glossary. These words are a direct quote from God's revelation of His Attributes in *Exodus* 34:6, but note the omission of the concluding word of that verse, *veemet (and truth)*!

7. This is Lindbergh's (*Jonah*, p. 89) rendition. A literal translation of the Hebrew would read *and relenting from doing evil*, but Lindberg's paraphrase better captures the thrust and intent of this crucial phrase.

8. Hebrew, *v'atah*, And now, "when succeeded with an imperative (*take my life*), implies that the time to discuss a matter is over and there is not much to do now but to fulfill what is being asked." (Sasson, p. 283)

9. We are now at the theological heart of the Book: the author has put into Jonah's mouth the central confession of faith of biblical Israel, but a confession altered, both by omission and by commission, so as to affect a radical transformation of the faith of Israel. Not to unduly interrupt the flow of the tale we will defer our consideration of this theological shift until the author brings his tale to its moving conclusion. And only then will we be in a position to address the question of the roots of Jonah's revolt against his God and Savior.

10. Three times in Chapter 1 the narrator stressed that Jonah fled *from before the lord* (twice in 1:3 and again in 1:10) which, as we then pointed out, amounts to a charge of rebellion against God. Magonet (*Form and Meaning*, p. 93) calls attention to the striking omission of the words "from before the lord" in Jonah's explanation of why he ran away. Even at this late date Jonah is holding back, refusing to admit to his rebellion against God.

11. Wolff, p. 168.

12. *And he prayed to the lord, saying...* (4:2a)

introduction to his request and an attempt to justify it. When we compare this "prayer" to the other prayer attributed to Jonah—the beautifully structured and poetic Psalm composed and delivered in the bowels of the fish—we can begin to gauge to what extent the recent turn of events has unsettled him.[13]

But what has triggered this outburst? That Nineveh is caught up in a paroxysm of contrition and self-abasement Jonah could see. But how does he know that this has induced God to change His mind and rescind His decree of doom? Our author does not tell us; as in so many other instances he is leaving us to puzzle it out for ourselves. And the question is not necessarily a trivial one, for the way we answer it will determine our understanding of the Main Body of the chapter.

There seem to be only two alternatives within the parameters of our tale: either God so informed Jonah, or he discovered the truth for himself empirically. If the former is the case, then we can postulate that after the initial wave of panic in Nineveh has settled down into widespread contrition and repentance, formalized by the king's decree, and God sees that they really mean it—the crime wave having halted in its tracks and the bloodshed ceased—God changes His mind about Nineveh and decides to grant Nineveh a stay of sentence. So in line with standing policy to keep His agents, the prophets, updated as to His intentions,[14] He informs Jonah of His change of plan. In this case, probably only a week or a bit more has elapsed between Jonah's proclamation and his "enlightenment."

We now turn to the Main Body of our chapter to follow up this option in detail.

The Set Up

As was the case in the three previous chapters, Chapter 4 is also structured as a self-contained unit with its own Introduction (4:1-3), Main Body (4:4-8) and Epilogue (4:9-11). With Jonah's histrionic declaration that *"It is better for me to die than to live"* we have concluded the Introduction. And with God's sardonic dismissal of Jonah's temper tantrum

Now the Lord *said, "Is it good that you are so furious?"* [4:4]

we begin the Main Body of our chapter.[15]

---

13. Note how his death wish (4:3) is the polar opposite of his thanksgiving for God saving his life in his previous prayer (2:7-8).

14. The prophet Amos, whose prophetic career took place toward the end of the reign of Jeroboam II (793-753 BCE), states as an axiomatic truth that:
 Indeed, the Lord God will do nothing
   without revealing His secret
   to His servants the prophets. (*Amos* 3:7)
That God has informed Jonah of His intention to spare Nineveh is the position taken by David Kimchi and Isaac Abravanel. See Glossary.

15. This verse is usually taken to be God's response to Jonah's eruption of pent-up anger, but this is not the way the *Book of Jonah* that has come down to us is structured. Both the Masoretic Text (the normative Hebrew text—MT) and the Dead Sea Scrolls (the oldest extant Hebrew Versions—Q) break the narrative at the end of Jonah's tirade and begin a new section with God's remark (4:4). Our understanding of *Jonah* follows this classic arrangement, treating 4:3 as the conclusion of the Introduction to the chapter, and 4:4 the opening verse of the Main Body. This pair of phrases—Jonah's request to die and God's sardonic dismissal—will also mark the conclusion of the Main Body and the start of the Epilogue.

Chapter 4. Endgame

What this way of dividing the chapter means in practice is that Jonah gets no response whatsoever to the charges that he has laid at the feet of God and, as we shall see, Jonah is laying some very serious charges against God's management of His cosmos. What is more, it means that God's remark about Jonah's distraught emotional state is actually the starting point of the climax of the Book, which is the role of the Main Body of Chapter 4. When looked at in this manner—as a very provocative opening—this verse is pouring salt on an open wound. For Jonah, this is adding insult to injury. This dismissive attitude—which Jonah can only understand as God not taking him seriously—merely infuriates him further. Jonah's response to this put down is to cut off communication with God. As far as he is concerned, they are no longer on speaking terms. It causes him to turn his back on his God and to storm out of the city in a blind fury, thus initiating the train of events that will bring the Book to a head. Thus our tale has it that it is really God Who initiates the train of events that comprise the Main Body of the chapter, prodding Jonah to react, and Jonah responds to the divine provocation.[16]

So Jonah departed from the city, and sat [himself] down to the east of the city. Now he made himself there a sukkah[17] and sat under it in the shade; [there he waited] until he would see what would happen in the city[18] [4:5].

Jonah seems to feel that the remorse and repentance of the Ninevites is not real; it is all an act. And even if it is genuine it can't last; give it a couple of weeks and those monsters of iniquity will relapse into their old ways. Jonah simply cannot believe that even the best of intentions can prevail against the ingrained habits of a lifetime. He is betting on a relapse, leading to God having no choice but to reverse Himself once again, and therefore give the Ninevites what they deserve.[19] So Jonah heads east[20] and

---

16. James Limberg (p. 91), in his analysis of Chapter 4, points out that up to now the action in all the episodes has also been initiated by God; Jonah simply reacts. God speaks to Jonah and commands him to go to Nineveh, and Jonah responds by running away (1:1–3). God sends a storm to intercept the boat and Jonah reacts by offering himself as a sacrifice to save the ship (1:4–16). God sends a fish to swallow Jonah, and he responds by praying to God (2:1–11). God commands Jonah a second time to go to Nineveh, and this time Jonah obeys (3:1–10).

17. *Sukkah*: a booth; a "rude or temporary structure…made of boughs, in which people lived at harvest time." *BDB*, p. 697.

18. Three times in this one verse the word *city* is repeated. The alert reader should remember that this is not the first appearance of this phenomenon: in 1:3, when Jonah first turned his back on the lord and fled to Tarshish, the name of that city was also repeated three times in the one verse. Then Jonah turned west, now he turns east. By this means of reminding us of Jonah's previous act the author may also be suggesting that Jonah has so far learned nothing and that he has not changed; he still is in rebellion against God. He may also be hinting that, as his earlier act of rebellion was checkmated, so will Jonah's current move be stymied.

19. This reading is what lies behind the Targum's (Targ.) expansion of the text, adding the word *besof* (in the end) so as to read: *until he would see what in the end would happen in the city*. It is also that of David Kimchi who sums up Jonah's motive: "Perhaps they will not persevere in their repentance."

20. Why eastward? We have already suggested a literary-symbolic reason (see note 18 above), but perhaps the reason for the directions taken by Jonah were simply dictated by geography, and the author is only locating his fable in a well known topographical setting. When Jonah's original rebellion occurred he was, as he puts it, *on my own soil* (4:2)—in the land of Israel—and he had been commanded to go to Nineveh which lay to his East, so instead he headed in the opposite direction: West. Now he finds himself in Nineveh and wants to put enough distance between himself and the city so as to be safe, yet also wishes to be in a position to be able to have a front-row seat to its annihilation. Geographically his choices are limited: to the West the Tigris River blocks his path, as does the Kosen River to the North (Nineveh lies in the angle between these two major bodies of water). To the south of the city, hugging the bank of the Tigris, stretches a vast urban sprawl. To the east, however, sufficiently distant, lie several low hills which should offer an unobstructed view of the walls and towers of Nineveh proper over the roofs of the surrounding suburbs.

picks a good vantage spot where the sun will be at his back on the dawn of the day after the conclusion of the grace period, while brilliantly illuminating the doomed city. There he builds himself a *sukkah*—a simple temporary structure to give him some protection from the blazing Near Eastern sun—and settles down[21] to await "the day," never for a moment suspecting that he has been set up.

> *Now the* LORD *God had prepared a kikayon*[22] *which grew up over Jonah, providing shade for his head and delivering him from his evil*[23]; *and Jonah was overjoyed at* [the presence of] *the kikayon.* [But] *as the dawn came up next day God had prepared a worm which smote*[24] *the kikayon, and it withered. Now it came to pass that as the sun rose, God had prepared a scorching*[25] *east wind* [to blow], *and the sun beat*[26] *on Jonah's head and he collapsed*[27] *and begged for death,*[28] *saying, "It is better for me to die than to live!"* [4:6–8]

A *sukkah* was a crude structure made of interwoven boughs,[29] its roof consisting of a few leafy branches. As the leaves would rapidly wither and dry up, the "roof" would progressively provide less and less protection from the sun. But God has provided for this contingency by speeding up the growth of an adjacent *kikayon*, so that even as the roof-branches wither away the plant's broad leaves spread over the *sukkah*, and indeed intensify the shade in which Jonah reposes.[30] He is overjoyed by this "stroke of luck" and properly grateful to the *kikayon* for the comfort it provides. But a bit more than this is implied by the remark:

Jonah was overjoyed at the [presence] *of the kikayon* (4:6)—literally, *Jonah was happy with a great happiness*—once again the infinitive absolute construction. This reminds us of Jonah's emotional state only five verses ago: *Now this incensed Jonah enormously* (4:1)—literally, *It was evil to Jonah with a great evil*—also in the infinitive absolute construction.

The author seems to be using the grammatical construction of the infinitive absolute to make several points, one of them being that he is calling attention to

---

21. Sasson (p. 289) points to the sardonic contrast between the king who seats himself on an ash heap in contrition and repentance (3:6), and Jonah who sits himself down to watch (and undoubtedly rejoice at) the annihilation of an entire city (4:5).

22. *Kikayon*: this term is a *hapex* (see Glossary); probably *ricinus communisor* (the castor-bean plant) is meant; a fast-growing broad-leafed plant that grows from 3 to 12 feet or more in height and provides a deep shade. (Moldenke & Moldenke, pp. 203–204)

23. Or *misery*; i.e., the effects of direct exposure to the Near Eastern sun, and/or the deep state of anger and depression he has been in (literally, *now it was evil to Jonah with a great evil* [4:1]) since God informed him of His change of plan. See note 31 below.

24. I.e., attacked it, gnawed through its root.

25. While the Hebrew adjective *horeesheet* is of uncertain meaning, the substance of the entire phrase is clear: a blistering desert wind (Arabic *Hamsin*, the North-African *Siroco*; in California it is called a *Santa Anna*), stifling and debilitating, springs up.

26. Literally, *smote*, the same word as used for the activities of the worm in verse 7. At God's direction all elements conspire to destroy Jonah's comfort and joy created by the shade of the God-given plant.

27. Literally, *fainted*. Wolff, citing *Psalm* 121:6 and *Isaiah* 49:10, defines the cause as sunstroke. (p. 172)

28. Literally, *begged his soul that he might die*.

29. *Nehemiah* 8:15.

30. A *kikayon* is a fast-growing plant, but not *that* fast. Leafy branches wither quickly in arid zone conditions. It would need a divine boost to keep pace with the shriveling of the leaves.

a number of disparate situations: the contrast between Jonah and the pagan sailors to deliverance—in his case an entire city, and in their case their ship (see note 3 above)—and our current contrast between his furious reaction to the news that Nineveh won't be obliterated and his joy over his personal comfort. The contrast between the deep depression[31] and anger in which we found Jonah at the start of the chapter—caused by his discovery that God had changed His mind and would not obliterate an entire city—and his "high" over the comfort of a patch of shade on a hot day, casts a very dubious light on his scale of values. It also highlights the violent mood swings to which Jonah is pictured as being subject.

However, Jonah is not slated to remain long in his euphoric state. God has a nasty surprise in store for him. Although he is unaware of the fact, Jonah has been shown to be the subject of divine manipulation from the very start of the story. We began our tale by watching him rebel against God and trying to run away to Tarshish but God, we discovered, *had prepared a great fish to swallow Jonah* (2:1). That time Jonah learned that you cannot run away from your responsibilities, and came to recognize and accept God as his Savior. But it seems that in God's eyes this is far from sufficient. This time around Jonah does not rebel externally; he does exactly what he is told. But at heart it would seem that Jonah has not changed. Inside he is still seething with rebellion. He thinks that God is making a catastrophic mistake in sparing Nineveh. In effect, he is convinced that he knows better than God how to run the world.

God doesn't argue with Jonah. He refuses to answer Jonah's accusations (and as we have suggested, Jonah has a serious position on which to take his stand); and besides, as we may remember, God and Jonah are no longer on speaking terms. So God will have to manipulate Jonah into a condition where he is willing to resume conversation. And in the process God will be teaching Jonah a lesson using nonverbal means. God *had prepared a kikayon*; now we are informed that He also *had prepared a worm* to destroy His *kikayon*, and additionally He *had prepared a scorching east wind* to make life utterly intolerable for Jonah.

Four times, like a drumbeat, the word *vayeman* (*now He prepared*) is repeated, driving home the point that Jonah has been set up, that the critical events happening to him are neither accident nor coincidence; there is a Purpose that is driving him toward a predetermined end, as yet unforeseen by him.

As our tale has been progressing, the pace of events has been speeding up. From the moment the Ninevites first hear what is in store for them and hysterically try to avert their fate by contrition and repentance, until the moment that God comes to the conclusion that they are sincere and aborts His rain of fire and brimstone, we estimated a lapse of a week or perhaps ten days. Adding a couple of days for Jonah's tantrum, his starting out of the city proper, traversing the suburbs and his arriving at the location of a significantly distant spot to be safe from the effects of the cataclysm, but yet with a good line of vision to be able to observe the anticipated overthrow of the

---

31. "*His evil*" can mean not only the misery of direct exposure to the Near Eastern sun from which the shade cast by the *kikayon* had *delivered him* (4:6), but probably also alludes to the emotional turmoil induced by the knowledge that the hated Nineveh will be spared, which is there referred to as *a great evil* (4:1). See also note 3 above.

hated city, and possibly adding one more day for him to gather the necessary materials, build his *sukkah* and settle in, we still probably haven't completed much more than two weeks from the day he first entered Nineveh. Now matters speed up even more.

In one day, perhaps two at the most, the roof of his *sukkah* begins to wither and the *kikayon* grows up to supply the deficiency in shade. Then we are informed that in the hour or so between first light and sunrise of the next day God *had prepared* a worm which attacks the plant and kills it, causing its leaves wither. Then, with the rising of the sun, the Sirocco that God *had prepared*—the blistering dry desert wind—begins to blow while the sun beats down with ever-increasing strength on Jonah's unprotected head. Before the day is out, dehydration and direct exposure to the sun have accomplished their purpose: he collapses from sunstroke.

His collapse is more than merely physical; it involves spiritual dimensions as well: Jonah has broken. He is no longer capable of maintaining his sulking attitude. He cannot bring himself to initiate a resumption of his conversation with God, but he will no longer refuse to respond should God take the initiative. More, he even tentatively hints his willingness to backtrack and pick up the dialogue where he broke it off. Taking care not to phrase his probe as a prayer but simply as a world-weary lament—in the words of that old play, "Stop the world, I want to get off"—and carefully omitting all reference to his tempestuous challenge to his Savior's good sense (4:2), he repeats, word for word, his previous death wish, "*It is better for me to die than to live*" (4:3, 4:8c).[32]

Of course, while attempting to save face, he is fooling no one. The narrator caustically comments on Jonah's remark, in words identical to those that describe Elijah's death-wish in the desert (*1 Kings* 19:4), "*and he begged for death.*"[33] God has been waiting for this moment. And on this note of a resumption of communication between the rebellious prophet and his God the Main Body of our chapter concludes.

An Alternative Reading

If we think that God did not inform Jonah of His decision, and left it for Jonah to work it out on his own, then we must assume that after having delivered his warning Jonah abandoned the doomed city, removed himself to some vantage point a safe distance away, and settled down to wait out the grace period[34] that he had proclaimed and then enjoy his front-row seat to the ensuing fireworks.

---

32. Suicide is not an option for Jonah; the words Shakespeare put into the mouth of Hamlet could apply equally to Jonah in his present wretched mood:
 O that this too too solid flesh would melt,
 Thaw, and resolve itself into a dew,
 Or that the Everlasting had not fixed
 His canon 'gainst self-slaughter. O God, God,
 How weary, stale, flat and unprofitable
 Seem to me all the uses of this world! (*Hamlet* I, 2)
One's God-given life is not one's own, and the religious prohibition against self-murder is a line that neither Hamlet nor Jonah would cross.

33. Literally, *he begged his soul that he might die*. But just as Elijah doesn't get his wish, neither will Jonah.

34. This assumes that Jonah takes the forty days of his proclamation to be literally 40 days.

Chapter 4. Endgame

At long last the forty-day grace period draws to its close and—nothing happens! Maybe it takes several days until the awful truth sinks in: nothing will happen. God is not going through with it. Jonah explodes in fury. This is too much; he can't take it and asks for death.

O Lord, *please take my life from me, for it is better for me to die than to live!* [4:3]

What this reading means is that Jonah's explosion takes place only following his discovery that God has changed His mind about destroying Nineveh, and that this discovery only takes place, not in Nineveh, but on a lonely hilltop some forty days after he had begun his proclamations in the city. If this is the case, then what follows the outburst in the text (4:5–6) is a flashback, explaining how Jonah got to the hilltop, and what he has been doing with himself during the previous month.[35]

In either case the end is the same: Jonah has been put through a harrowing experience which seems to him to be pointless. Not only has he learned nothing, but he is emotionally back where he started. The Main Body of Chapter 4 began with Jonah wishing to die, and it ends with him repeating his wish in identical words. The only difference appears to be the reason: then it was hurt over violation of deeply held principle, and now it is over spiritual exhaustion brought about by physical collapse. Once again Jonah doesn't get the point. It will have to be spelled out for him in a simplistic analogy. For this we will have to turn to the Epilogue.

But to properly understand the Epilogue we need to go back once more over the narrative we have been analyzing. As Phyllis Trible has perceptively pointed out, there is a critical piece of information that is missing.[36] God has been putting Jonah "through the hoops": first He *prepares* a *kikayon* to provide shade for Jonah, then the He *prepares* a worm to destroy the *kikayon*, and lastly He *prepares* an east wind to dehydrate Jonah and set him up for sunstroke.[37] In the first incident we are told how Jonah reacts to the unexpected appearance of the *kikayon*:

Jonah was overjoyed at [the presence of] *the kikayon* [4:6].

And in the final incident we are informed of Jonah's reaction to the effects of the east wind and the sun:

He collapsed and begged for death, saying, "It is better for me to die than to live!" [4:8]

Conspicuous by its absence is any mention of a response on Jonah's part to the withering of the *kikayon*. Does this silence imply that Jonah was indifferent to the death of the plant? This is hardly credible considering the joyous reaction on the previous day produced by its shade. We read, literally:

Jonah was happy with a great happiness at the [presence] *of the kikayon* [4:6].

---

35. This reading was pioneered by Abraham Ibn Ezra (see Glossary) in the twelfth century CE, and is quite popular with many modern scholars. It understands the verbal forms in 4:5 to be in the pluperfect tense. Therefore we would render the text as follows: *Now Jonah had departed from the city, and he had seated* [himself] *to the east of the city. Now he had made himself there a sukkah and sat there in the shade;* [there he waited] *until he would see what would happen in the city.* (4:5)

36. Trible, *Rhetorical Criticism*, p. 195–226.

37. There is no need for God to do anything about the sun; in the normal course of events it will be there.

We have the right to expect some sort of reaction, and therefore we could suspect that the lacuna might be the result of a decision on the part of the author to withhold the information from us.[38] And we would be right. Only in the next to the last sentence of the Epilogue will the missing information be sprung on us, causing a complete revision of our evaluation of Jonah's character.

Having further whetted our appetites for the grand resolution of all (or almost all) of the issues raised in the *Book of Jonah*, we now at last pass on to the Epilogue.[39]

Epilogue: The Concluding Argument

Both with regard to structure and content, the Epilogue flows directly from the earlier portions of the chapter. Jack Sasson has demonstrated the meticulous construction of the dialogue between God and Jonah,[40] and the subject matter of the Epilogue is an unbroken continuation of, and conclusion to, the tug-of-war between Jonah and his God. The Main Body concluded with Jonah expressing his wish for death.

The sun beat on Jonah's head and he collapsed and begged for death, saying, "It is better for me to die than to live!" [4:8].

As we have noted, this remark is not directed to God.[41] Jonah has previously prayed for death and God has refused his petition; he has no hope for succor from that quarter. He is simply a man at the end of his tether giving voice to his exhaustion and despair. But he is also a man who, at last, is in a more receptive mood; Jonah is finally prepared—emotionally as well as intellectually—to converse and, what is more important, to listen. God resumes the dialogue where Jonah broke it off, repeating the question that prompted His reluctant emissary to refuse to answer and to march off in a huff.

---

38. This would not be the first time the author has played this game with us. From the opening lines of the Book we have been bothered by not having been told Jonah's motive for refusing to obey the Lord and attempting to flee to Tarshish. Only in the final chapter of the Book has the missing information at long last been given us (4:2). Nor will this be the last time we are being played with.

39. Just as the opening lines of the Book (1:1–3) did double duty as both Introduction to the Book and also to Chapter 1, so the closing lines (4:9–11) serve as both Epilogue to Chapter 4 and Grand Epilogue, wrapping up the Book as a whole.

40. Pp. 317-18. We begin with Jonah's tantrum, a thirty-nine word rant (4:2-3), followed by God's three word comment (4:4), Jonah's follow-up remark also consisting of only three words (4:8). God next queries Jonah (five words) and Jonah responds also with a five word reply (4:9). Then God sums up, stating His position in a thirty-nine word declamatory inquiry (4:10–11). The pattern thus, by word count, is:

Jonah	God
39 words	------
3 words	3 words
5 words	5 words
------	39 words

a balance that gives equal opportunity to both sides of the dialogue for expression of their positions, with Jonah opening the conversation and God having the last word.

41. Simon notes that the opening words of the Epilogue—*And God said to Jonah*—are highly unusual. In biblical dialogue, "there is no need to specify that the response is addressed to the previous speaker. Here, however, the narrator emphasizes that God is responding to a speech that was not addressed to him." (p. 44)

And God said to Jonah, "Is it good that you are so furious about the kikayon?" [4:9a]

But this is not quite the same question as before. All that has passed since Jonah's explosive rant and God's resultant query have dictated the need for modification. Originally, in the aftermath of Jonah's frenzied eruption, God saw no need to specify the target of his rage when He formulated his follow-up question. He simply asked, *"Is it good that you are so furious?"* It could be taken as a given that it was God Who was the object of Jonah's vehemence. But the second time around God directs attention away from Himself and focuses on Jonah's feelings concerning the plant and what happened to it. And now we begin to learn something that we had no suspicion of before: Jonah claims that he cares deeply about the *kikayon* and is absolutely furious over what became of it.

And he said, "I am indeed furious, even unto death!"[42] [4:9b]

This is the datum missing from 4:7, whose absence we suspected was due to its having been suppressed: Jonah's reaction to the death of the *kikayon*. Due to its absence we have been forming a skewed picture of Jonah's personality, seeing him as a cold and self-centered individual who is concerned first and foremost with himself and his creature comforts; a person who is passionately concerned with abstract principles and cares little for his fellow creatures, seeing them simply as statistical ciphers. And now this man who keeps himself and his emotions under such strict control, who has presented to us such an impenetrable front, has for the second time in our tale let slip his stoic façade. The first time was due to the shock of learning that God had aborted His promised strike against Nineveh—a matter of principle yet to be explored—and he reacted with fury. Now, once again, the façade slips and once more we are given a glimpse of Jonah's naked soul. Once again the reaction is fury, this time over the death of a living thing: a bush! We begin to suspect that Jonah has been conceived as a person who cares and cares deeply, not just about principles but about his fellow creatures. We may also sustain the surmise which we have tentatively entertained: that this passionate concern is an emotion that Jonah struggles to keep under tight control lest it run away with him. It is this that may be the reason for the impenetrable façade he attempts to maintain.

We return to Jonah's response:

And he said, "I am indeed furious, even unto death!" [4:9b]

God accepts Jonah's claim, and by accepting it He confirms it.[43] He then contrasts the level of Jonah's emotional involvement with the *kikayon* with the extent of his

---

42. Sasson cites Winton Thomas' proposal that the phrase *ad mavet* (*even unto death*) is a colloquial expression meaning "very much," or some such superlative (p. 307).

43. By biblical narrative convention, statements made by human beings—the "players" in the narrative plot—are unreliable. The person may be speaking the truth, he may be speaking what he *believes* to be the truth (but isn't), or he may be lying. Unless we can verify his statement from some other source it remains suspect. On the other hand, God (and the narrator) always speak the truth. In our present case, by accepting Jonah's statement and then building His argument upon it, God has validated Jonah's assertion that he cares deeply about the plant and was infuriated by its wanton destruction; any suspicions we might harbor that Jonah cared only for the shade that the plant provided and not for the plant itself are unwarranted and must be dismissed.

physical connection to it: Did you plant it? Did you water it? Did you nurture it? These are all rhetorical questions; Jonah would have no choice but to admit that he had had nothing to do with the plant. As far as he was concerned, it appeared yesterday and died today. Yet in that short space of time the author has had him develop a deep emotional relationship with it.

> *And the* Lord *said, "You cared*[44] *about the kikayon* [over which] *you did not labor, nor nurture its growth; it came up in a night and perished*[45] *in a night"* [4:10].

And in this simple factual statement God establishes what will be the foundational premise of His attempt to bring Jonah into line; this will be the fulcrum which will provide Him the leverage with which He hopes to move Jonah. The argument will run as follows: "If you can become so attached to an insignificant insentient bush—a mere plant—with which you were never actively involved, and after an acquaintance of less than twenty-four hours, should not I, God, care for a Great City full of myriads of sentient creatures, humans and animals alike, with whom I have been actively involved for millennia? You would have prevented the plant from perishing if it had been in your power to do so. Then should not I, Who do have the power, spare the city from annihilation?"[46]

> *And as for Me, should not I care for Nineveh, the Great City, that contains more than twelve times ten thousand*[47] *human beings who do not know their right hand from their left,*[48] *and also much cattle?* [4:11]

The argument now proceeds to a more rarefied plane: "You care deeply for a lowly, immobile plant with which you share no common traits except life itself. Then shouldn't I, all the more so, care about the masses of bumbling humanity who inhabit

---

44. Hebrew, *Hus*, a word meaning to care for, to be concerned about, to pity and to spare; often used in tandem with its close synonym *hamal* "to express a compassionate decision not to harm or punish" (Simon, p. 44). Cf. *Deuteronomy* 13:9; *Ezekiel* 7:4, 9; *1 Samuel* 15:15, etc.

45. Hebrew, *abad*, the same word used by the shipmaster (*"perhaps the god will take thought of us and we will not perish"*—1:6) and the king (*"who knows but the gods may turn and relent and turn from His fierce anger that we do not perish"*—3.9), expressing their deepest fears.

46. This type of argument is known in Hebrew as *kal vehomer* (in Latin *a fortiori*, or sometimes *a minori ad maius*), an argument of proceeding from minor premise to major conclusion: i.e., if you accept the correctness of the minor premise, how can you reasonably reject the major conclusion which is merely the minor premise writ large? Examples of this kind of argument can be found in *Genesis* 44:8; *Deuteronomy* 31:27; *2 Kings* 5:13.

47. This number, 120,000, is not given as the population of Nineveh but as that portion of the population that God feels should not be held responsible for their actions, i.e., "Forgive them, Father, for they know not what they do" (*Luke* 23:34). At its height in the days of Sennacherib, the population of Nineveh proper is estimated as at least 300,000, not counting the suburbs (Sasson, pp. 311–312). For the eighth century BCE, the period in which our story is set and when Nineveh was not yet the capital of the Assyrian Empire, the population would have been considerably less. In these circumstances the figure of 120,000 souls might be considered to have been intended to encompass at least half of the population, perhaps more.

48. There are commentators who think that the phrase "who do not know their right hand from their left" (an idiom unique to *Jonah*, and which seems to mean an inability to distinguish right from wrong) refers to very young children, and therefore conclude that Nineveh was spared "for the sake of the children." This interpretation, while emotionally appealing, is almost certainly wrong. As Wolff points out (p. 175), the phrase in question is a relative clause that is modifying the term *adam*, a collective noun which means human beings in general, including women and children; it cannot refer just to children (see also Sasson, p. 314). The expression would thus seem to refer to the greater part of the population (see previous note) whom God deems to be lacking in clear moral sense, who are morally deficient.

this earth, many, if not most of them, morally obtuse? And what about all those cattle—also my creatures, but who have no moral sense whatsoever—that, if I were to vent My anger on the human beings of Nineveh, would be dragged to their doom through no fault of their own?" This level of argument glances obliquely at one of the roots of Jonah's moral outrage, although it fails to meet it head on.[49]

When one comes right down to it, Jonah is being confronted with an emotional appeal to which he has no ready answer. To continue to maintain his rebellious stance in the face of this assertion would appear churlish, to say the least. It would seem that God feels that only on an emotional level has He a chance of breaking through Jonah's defenses. But while we now realize that Jonah is a person who cares deeply, we have learned from the start that he is also a person who takes principles with extreme seriousness. Will this argument appeal to his head as well as his heart? To this question we at this point have no answer.

In the Book it is God Who has the last word, but that last word is framed not as a declarative statement but as a question; a question to which there is no record of a reply. Has Jonah been convinced, and his silence taken as an assent?[50] Or does Jonah understand God's question to be rhetorical, in which case his silence could be taken as a refusal to be maneuvered into a coerced acceptance? In either case, Jonah's lack of reply leaves the question open, and in effect drops the question into the reader's lap.

The *Book of Jonah* ends as it begins: with the word of the LORD. It opens with God's command to Jonah, the act which triggers the plot of the Book. It concludes with God's explanation of His original command and why things turned out as they did. But the Book is not merely about events that once happened. It is about events that always happen, and why they happen; it is about how the world works and why it works as it does, what our responsibilities are and how we should fulfill them. It is about principles that should govern our lives and how we should prioritize among them when they conflict.

We are given no final answers; the author does not preach. The book concludes without closure. The ball is being passed to us, and it is we who are left to ponder and reach our own verdicts.

---

49. This question of principle will be dealt with in the next chapter.

50. The contrast with the *Book of Job* is illuminating. There, following God's extended presentation of His position (the Voice from the whirlwind, *Job* 38:1–41:26), Job responds, capitulates and admits that he was wrong:
    And therefore have I uttered that which I understood not,
      Things too wonderful for me which I knew not....
    Wherefore I despise my words and I repent,
      Seeing that I am [but] *dust and ashes.* (*Job* 42:1–6)
In contrast, Jonah, after his one outburst, reverts to the tightlipped posture he has exhibited from the beginning; he admits to nothing.

CHAPTER 5

Some Second Thoughts About a Strange Book

Let us learn by the example of Jonah not to measure God's judgment by our own wisdom.
—John Calvin, *Commentaries on the Minor Prophets*

Over the years it would seem that most readers of the *Book of Jonah* have found God's concluding argument convincing; they have accepted it and assumed that Jonah did likewise. This assumption grants closure to the Book and has spawned the two dominant theories of what *Jonah* is all about. One of these holds that the central issue of the Book is the conflict between the principles of Justice and Mercy, with Jonah—the champion of Justice—having to be taught by God that Mercy trumps Justice. Or as a contemporary philosopher, citing an English fourteenth-century poet puts it: "Jonah is at first distressed by God's putting off the destruction of Nineveh ... but has to learn that it is only because God is patient and slow to anger that this wicked world is allowed to survive at all."[1] The other theory claims that the question around which the Book revolves is the struggle between provincialism and universalism, with Jonah—the proponent of the primacy of the in-group—having to learn that he and his "in-group"—his people—have no monopoly on God; that the LORD is not only his God but the God of all humanity and all creation, and that he has to widen his horizons accordingly.[2] Both of these theories see the *Book of Jonah* as a sort of instructional primer, a tale of the education of a prophet by God, whose purpose is to school the reader by the example of Jonah's enlightenment.

But there have always been those who have found these theories unconvincing, largely because they failed to find God's argument persuasive; the problem being that God's answer doesn't address Jonah's central challenge. And being myself among those unsatisfied by God's side-stepping of Jonah's objections, as well as by the absence of a definitive resolution to the Book like that of the *Book of Job*,[3] I have

---

1. Alasdair MacIntyre, *After Virtue*, p. 177–178. A current forceful proponent of this thesis is Uriel Simon.

2. This theory has a long history, counting among its proponents Augustine and Luther, and among Jewish medieval exegetes Rashi and Ibn Ezra. Among more recent scholars who champion this popular thesis can be cited G. A. Smith at the start of the twentieth century and J. Magonet and H. W. Wolff toward its end.

3. See Chapter 4, note 50. It seems that the ancient rabbis of the Talmud were equally troubled by the lack of closure to *Jonah*. They resolved this problem by decreeing that when the *Book of Jonah* was read as part of the Yom Kippur liturgy, the last three verses of the *Book of Micah* (*Micah* 7:18–20) be added, serving as the "missing answer" of Jonah in which he, as it were, recants his rebellion.

a powerful suspicion that we may be missing something. And that something might even be the key to the Book. So having done our homework and having completed our analysis of the *Book of Jonah*—its structure, its plot, some of its literary allusions as well as a few of its linguistic subtleties[4]—we are now in a better position to try at last to get to the bottom of a problem that has been bothering us from the very start of the Book: what was it that prompted Jonah's rebellion against God? I believe that the results of this investigation may lead us to what the *Book of Jonah* is really all about.

To begin our inquiry we return to the pair of pivotal statements made by Jonah which we have identified as being the central axes on which the Book turns: his two "declarations of faith."

"*A Hebrew am I, and the* Lord, *the God of the heavens, do I revere, Who made the sea and the dry land*" [1:9].

and

"*...for I know that You are a compassionate and merciful God, slow to anger and abounding in loving-kindness, and ready to change Your mind about punishing*" [4:2b].

The first we have already discussed at some length, stressing both its importance—its insistence on the universalism of God's domain, that the Lord is the God of all creation and all mankind—as well as its problematic nature; the second will prove critical as well as equally troubling.

We have already demonstrated how the importance of the first declaration has been structurally highlighted by having been situated at the exact center of the Main Body of Chapter 1.[5] The vital nature of the second is likewise underscored by having Jonah's explosive rant which contains it similarly centered.[6] It is this second, his assertion of what is the true nature of the Lord his God, which will be our present focus.

Jonah begins by quoting God's revelation of His Attributes as He is recorded to have disclosed them to Moses. It would be well to review the dramatic account. Moses has ascended Mount Sinai to receive the Ten Commandments. In his absence the Children of Israel relapse into idolatry, construct a golden calf, and proclaiming it the god[7] who had delivered them from Egypt commence worshiping it. God

---

4. We have on the whole avoided commenting on the elaborate wordplay and paronomasia that pervades the Book; a fascinating subject in itself. But as these aspects of our little Book are largely opaque even to many modern native Hebrew speakers (the language of the Book is the Hebrew of close to 3,000 years ago), much less to those to whom Hebrew is a foreign language (wordplay is, by its very nature, virtually untranslatable), we have regretfully left the subject to the various studies that have devoted themselves to it. For those interested, one can make a start with Ackerman, Sasson and Trible, who devote considerable space to the subject (see Bibliography).

5. See introduction to the *Book of Jonah*, note 26 and related text.

6. Jonah's outburst occurs in the Introduction to Chapter 4. It is framed by an eleven word mini-prologue which introduces it, and Jonah's eleven word prayer asking for death which follows it.

7. Or more properly "gods;" (*elohim*) is in the plural form and the demonstrative pronoun (*eleh* = these) and the verb (*he'elucha* = brought you up) are also in the plural, thus: "*These are your gods, O Israel, who brought you up out of the land of Egypt.*" (Exodus 32:4)

announces that in punishment for this apostasy He will destroy them, but Moses intercedes for the Israelites and God relents.[8] Emboldened by his success, Moses makes an outrageous request:

> "And now, please, if I have [indeed] *found favor in Your eyes, please let me know Your ways, that I may know You, that I may* [continue] *to find favor in Your eyes"…. And the* LORD *said to Moses, "I will also do this thing that you have asked, for you have* [indeed] *found favor in My eyes"* [*Exodus* 33:13, 17].

Nahum Sarna describes Moses' request as follows:

> From God's response to this request, as given in [*Exodus*] 34:6–7, it is clear that Moses here asks to comprehend God's essential personality, the attributes that guide His actions in His dealings with humankind, the norms by which He operates in His governance of the world.[9]

God then makes good His promise in a revelatory declaration:

> *"The* LORD, *the* LORD, *a merciful and compassionate God, slow to anger and abounding in loving-kindness*[10] *and truth"* [*Exodus* 34:6].

We pause here to note that in quoting from what, in biblical times, served alongside the Ten Commandments as the central affirmation of faith,[11] Jonah is straying from the original in two matters. He has inverted the order of the terms "*merciful*" and "*compassionate*"—an error that may be no more than a slip of the tongue—and, far more serious, he has omitted the phrase "*and truth.*"[12] This last, as we shall see, is hardly inadvertent. But God's self-revelation does not end here. It continues:

> *Extending loving-kindness to the thousandth generation,*[13] *forgiving iniquity, transgression and sin*[14] [*Exodus* 34:7a].

---

8. *Exodus* 20:18; 31:18–32:14.

9. Sarna, *Exodus*, p. 213. For this understanding, Sarna relies on *Psalm* 103:7–8, which he defines as the earliest commentary on this text. Furthermore, "Moses' request… rests on the postulate that God is not capricious but acts according to norms that human beings can try to understand." (*Ibid.*)

10. Literally, abundant in *hesed*, i.e., treating people far better than they deserve. See Glossary.

11. The central confession of faith, *Hear, O Israel, the lord our God, the lord is one*, etc. (*Deuteronomy* 6:5–9)—popularly known as the *"Shema"* from its first word—seems to have only achieved its current status during the periods of the Babylonian Exile and the Second Commonwealth (see Glossary). Before the 6th century BCE these verses were accorded no especial significance above and beyond that accorded to the other verses in *Deuteronomy*, and certainly were completely overshadowed by *Deuteronomy* 5:6–28 (The Ten Commandments) which preceded them and to which *Deuteronomy* 6:6 refers.

12. In Hebrew one word: *ve'emet*: while the primary meaning of *emet* is *truth*, it also has the meaning of *reliability* and *faithfulness*. In this context the sense is that humans can rely on God to keep His word; that He is absolutely reliable, eternally dependable.

13. Hebrew *la'alaphim*, literally *thousands*. The parallel text in *Deuteronomy* 7:9 which reads *le'eleph dor* (*to the thousandth generation*), indicates that our expression *la'alaphim* is being used synonymously as a one-word abbreviation of *eleph dor*.

14. These three terms are not synonyms being used for literary effect or for stylistic variation. They denote three separate and distinct modes of human wrongdoing:
(a) *Sin* (in Hebrew *het*) literally means "missing the mark" (as in shooting at a target with a bow and arrow). It refers to wrongdoing due to error, ignorance or carelessness.
(b) *Iniquity* (in Hebrew *avon*) literally means "crookedness." It refers to committing a conscious act "with malice aforethought": doing something one knows from the start to be wrong.
(c) *Transgression* (in Hebrew *pesha*) literally means "rebellion." It refers to persisting in an extended conscious course of wrongdoing.
It is significant that what became in Israel a doxology focuses on deliberate and conscious evil, moving from sporadic deliberate acts to wrongdoing as a way of life, with sin (*het*) only tacked on, as it were, as an afterthought.

Chapter 5. Some Second Thoughts About a Strange Book

This optimistic assurance that there is no manner of wrongdoing, however egregious, that God will not forgive,[15] and that God's *hesed* is, for all practical purposes, everlasting (i.e., a thousand generations)[16] is not, however, the final word. The catalog of God's Attributes continues:

> *But He will by no means clear* [the guilty],[17] *visiting the iniquity of fathers upon children, and on children's children unto the third and fourth generation [Exodus 34:7b].*

God may be willing to forgive the wrongdoer for doing his deeds, but the evil actions he has done cannot be undone. Actions have consequences, and the wrongdoer remains responsible for these consequences. These consequences live on, as does the responsibility, spanning the generations and ensnaring his descendants. And because this is so, every generation inherits a heavy burden, for good and for ill, from its forbearers.

All this is hardly news; the simple fact that every generation willy-nilly receives as its inheritance both the fruits and the debts of its predecessors was a truth long known and appreciated by the ancients. What *is* new, and what Moses and the Children of Israel will struggle to absorb, is that contrary to the accepted wisdom of the pagan world, so well expressed by the words Shakespeare put into the mouth of Mark Antony—

> *The evil that men do lives after them,*
> *The good is oft interred with their bones*[18]

—the revelation received on Mount Sinai proclaims the opposite: that it is the *hesed*, the good that we perform, that lives on long after us, its effects gaining momentum as it courses down the generations, while it is the evil we do and its consequences that burn themselves out in a matter of three or four generations. The bottom line of what is to become a central declaration of the faith of Israel, and is to become embedded in its liturgy,[19] is that *hesed* (acts of loving-kindness) trumps *avon* (iniquity), *pesha* (transgression) and *het* (sin).

> *It is the good that men do that lives after them,*
> *The evil is interred with their bones, and the bones of their children.*

Now we are in a better position to understand Jonah when he proclaims:

> *"I know that You are a compassionate and merciful God, slow to anger and abounding in loving-kindness"* [4:2].

How does he know? His source is God's revelation to Moses, the wellspring of Israelite understanding of the nature of the God they worship; what they can expect of

---

15. The underlying assumption being that forgiveness is conditional on repentance.

16. Or alternatively, this expresses the idea that *human* acts of *hesed* have long-range effects: a sort of domino effect for good that is self-reinforcing and cumulative, and whose influence reaches far into the future.

17. Hebrew *v'nakeh lo yenakeh*; once again in the infinitive absolute construction; literally, *acquitting He will not acquit* or *cleaning He will not clean*, i.e., God most certainly will not wipe the wrongdoer's slate clean.

18. William Shakespeare, *Julius Caesar*, III.

19. Called "The Thirteen Attributes of God" (*shelosh esrai middot*), it is recited in the Synagogue on Festivals, and especially in the penitential prayers recited during the High Holy Days.

Him and what He expects of them. Moses sought to know God's ways in order that he might adjust his behavior so as to conform to them.

"Please let me know Your ways, that I may know You, that I may [continue] *to find favor in Your eyes." [Exodus 33:13].*

It is because of God's response to Moses' request that Jonah possesses his certainty; that he can say, *"I know...."*

But now Jonah does a shocking thing: he cherry-picks God's revelation. He quotes the first part of God's declaration but deletes the second. By this deletion Jonah has, in effect, created a radical new theology, and he nails down this transformation by replacing the concluding word of *Exodus* 34:6, *"and truth"*[20] with the phrase *"and ready to change Your mind about punishing."*[21] With this phrase Jonah summarizes what he thinks being *a compassionate and merciful God, slow to anger and abounding in loving-kindness* (*hesed*) means to God: that punishment is essentially repugnant to Him, a measure to be resorted to only as a last resort.

This has nothing to do with mercy or with God's forgiveness of sin. Jonah has no argument with either. His bone of contention lies in the area of accountability. As far as Jonah is concerned, it is right for God to be merciful; if a sinner repents it is only proper that God should forgive him his evil acts. But what about the damage he has done, the *consequences* of his evil acts? What sticks in Jonah's craw is that he believes that God is not only forgiving the sinner, but that forgiveness includes not holding the sinner to account for the damage that he has done.

All this, of course, is predicated on the assumption that the wrongdoer has sincerely repented. But repentance cannot cancel the blood spilt, the children orphaned and the wives widowed, the lives permanently ruined. Is no one to be held to account for these? Is there to be no punishment for the *consequences* caused by the evil? Specifically, in the case of Nineveh—the Great City steeped in bloodshed (*hamas*)[22]—will repentance wipe the slate clean? The voice of the blood of the murdered cry to God from the ground[23]; the cries of the widows and the orphans rise to heaven and there is to be no answer? Is this to mean that simply saying one is sorry earns one a "Get-Out-of-Jail-Free" card? This, as a matter of principle, Jonah cannot accept. Forgive the sincerely repentant sinner, yes; but he must be called to account for the *consequences* of his sin; and to be held responsible means punishment.

This is the classic position of Israelite faith: that actions have consequences and that the one who was the cause of these consequences is to be held accountable for them. In this context we once again turn to Shakespeare:

Use every man after his desert, and who should 'scape a whipping?[24]

---

20. This is the axiomatic statement that God is absolutely dependable, that His Word is rock solid and can be relied upon. See note 12 above.

21. Hebrew *ve'neeham al haraah*, a phrase extremely difficult to render into English literally and still adequately convey its meaning; hence our adoption of Lindbergh's paraphrase. See Chapter 4, note 7.

22. See Chapter 3, the first three pages of the sub-section entitled The Intolerable Evil, where the true nature of Nineveh's *evil* is clarified.

23. See *Genesis* 4:10–12.

24. William Shakespeare, *Hamlet*, II.

Chapter 5. Some Second Thoughts About a Strange Book

This is a proposition that finds God and Jonah in total agreement. So how is one to deal with erring humanity? In Jonah's opinion they should get the whipping they deserve. He thinks God is being too easy on them; He is giving them a free pass. From this it emerges that Jonah is really an archconservative; he is taking his stand on the classic position revealed by God to Moses:

He will by no means clear [the guilty] ... [*Exodus* 34:7]

But if this is God's revealed position, and if this is where Jonah takes his stand—that is, that Jonah is willing to defend this position, even to the death—then in heaven's name who is Jonah fighting against and what is he combating with such vigor?

In posing a question such as this we need to step back and remember that the *Book of Jonah* is *not* a historical account but a fable, and that our Jonah is not a real person but a character in a story. The radical revision of classic Israelite theology that we have been discussing is not the creation of any of the characters in the Book; it is the brainchild of its writer. Jonah is no more than a literary creation, a character in a fable, speaking the words put in his mouth by the author of the Book. It is the author who is the revolutionary, using the Book he has written as a launching pad for a new conception of how God should treat erring and sinful humanity, and even, in the author's opinion, how He *does* treat us. To present his idea of how the faith of Israel should be understood, and what he thinks Israel's religion is all about, he has created the character he calls Jonah—an arch conservative—as a Don Quixote to tilt with windmills, whose fruitless struggles serve to highlight and throw into high relief the author's radical new theology. Let us now examine this new doctrine and see of what it consists.

At bottom it amounts to answering with a "yes" our previous question; Saying "I'm sorry" *is* all it takes to get one a "Get-Out-of-Jail-Free" card. If our aim is to make better people, then if a person of his own free will sincerely repents—and we must remember that true repentance involves a complete behavioral makeover—then we have already achieved optimal results. What need is there for punishment beyond satisfying our own atavistic desires for revenge? There is no need for punishment; under the new dispensation repentance alone satisfies all requirements for divine forgiveness. The doctrine is succinctly summed up by Jonah as the true nature of God:

"I know that You are a compassionate and merciful God, slow to anger and abounding in loving-kindness, and ready to change Your mind about punishing" [4:2b]

This, with its new summary phrase, says it all. And now we can understand why the word *ve'emet* (see notes 12 and 20 above) has been replaced. If God is ever-ready to change His mind one cannot rely on His Word. What this means is that not only are God's judgments conditional but His promises are as well. What this amounts to is that from a Deity Who can be relied on absolutely, in this revisionist theology God is seen as essentially capricious.[25]

---

25. I am far from certain that our author was aware of these implications, but to later generations they were to become abundantly evident. On this point see Appendix B.

The blatant utopianism of this doctrine fuels its most basic critique. As an ideal it is wonderful, but experience teaches that most people, mired deep in their habitual ways of life, are quite incapable of reinventing themselves in so radical a fashion, and then going the distance without relapsing. This is a doctrine for a spiritual elite. The experience of the Children of Israel argues against it. Exposed to the dazzling vision of monotheism at Sinai, when Moses temporarily absents himself they almost immediately relapse into idolatry. And for the next seven hundred years, the tale of the First Commonwealth is one long chronicle of such relapses. Martin Luther, who read *Jonah* literally and took it to be a historical account, commenting on the mass repentance of the entire population of Nineveh, voiced, in all seriousness, the opinion that "none but saints inhabited the city."[26] That is, average people would be incapable of so suddenly reinventing themselves. The deletion of the word "truth" in the revised doctrine may also be, among other things, symptomatic of a disinclination to grapple with certain hard facts of human nature. This, or something not too dissimilar, would be a capsule presentation of the possible reasons for Jonah's rejection of the revised doctrine.

But we will never hear words to this effect proceeding from Jonah's lips. The author of the Book has no interest in having Jonah explain himself. As the whole purpose of the Book, we contend, is to launch a radical revisionist theology; the last thing the author needs is that, in the interests of "fair play," he undermine his revised doctrine at its inception with a cogent counter-argument.[27] Jonah will only be allowed, in the course of proclaiming the new doctrine, to indicate his violent objection to it, but never to voice his reasons for his opposition. Nor will God be permitted by the author to address Jonah's concerns. Any counterargument to the new doctrine has to be suppressed. The new doctrine must stand unopposed at the Book's end. This, of course, allows for Jonah's silence at the Book's end to signify not agreement but continued opposition. Jonah is unconvinced by God's appeal to his emotions and refuses to buckle under.

And now we can begin to understand the reasons for a second problem that has been bothering us throughout our reading and analysis of *Jonah*: the puzzling and at times incomprehensible way in which the Book is written. As we have noted, time and again the author builds up our expectations only to dash them. Repeatedly, just as we think we have grasped what the story is about and where it is going, the tale takes a sudden turn and once again we find ourselves at sea, the one constant of the story being our confusion while reading it. Worse, the author doesn't play fair, concealing from us vital information that we need in order to make sense of what we're reading. Why should the author write his book in this manner? This is a problem with which we have been struggling from the very start. Now that we have completed the Book we are in a position to address this issue.

We have been concentrating on the problems that we have faced in reading the Book, but perhaps we need to shift our focus to the issues which the author faced in

---

26. *Luther's Works: American edition*, volume 19, p. 85.

27. For the reasons for my contention that this new doctrine is original to the author of *Jonah*, see Appendix B: Who Was the Innovator and Who Were the Copycats?

writing his Book. If we are correct in our assumption that he was trying to launch and achieve maximum acceptance for a radical new theology, he faced two major obstacles. The first was interest; the simple fact that, then as now, most people are not all that captivated by theological issues. If he wanted to get his message out to as wide an audience as possible, he would have to package the message in an attractive wrapping, one that would appeal to a general public.

But this approach would hold its own dangers. We must remember that the author was attempting to promote a revolutionary change in the accepted religious understanding of his time, an about-face that would shock much of the public and be seen by many as subversive of morality and revealed religion; by some even as heresy. And the more widely his ideas spread the more intense and even violent the reaction was likely to be. Only if the proposed doctrine could be confined to an elite few, who were sufficiently intelligent and mature to be able to coolly consider it on its own merits, was the author likely to be able to hope for a fair hearing, without provoking a violent reaction. These two requirements would seem to be mutually contradictory.

The author's solution to this dilemma would seem to have been to write a story that would captivate and intrigue a general audience, but to so encode the underlying message (while beclouding and misleading the reader) that only the most intelligent, sophisticated and persevering members of the audience would ever catch on to what the author was really driving at. If so, our author would hardly be unique. Since antiquity some of the greatest writers have resorted to this technique. The 17th-century philosopher, Thomas Hobbes, commenting on criticisms of the writing of the great Greek historian Thucydides, observes, "Marcellinus sayeth, he was obscure on purpose; that the common people might not understand him. And not unlikely: *for a wise man should so write, (though in words understood by all men), that wise men only should be able to commend him.*"[28]

If this indeed was his intention the author of *Jonah* succeeded brilliantly. Without promoting excessive controversy or violent opposition, his little Book became a "bestseller" in his own time, and has remained enormously popular ever since. The story of Jonah is one of the best-known tales in the Bible. And at the same time enough of HAZAL[29] (the rabbis of old) grasped the Book's meaning to ensure it being designated as Scripture and finding its place in the Bible.

Returning to the doctrine itself: despite the literary brilliance of the little Book that served as its launching platform—no small matter in promoting the acceptance of the new doctrine—and the inherent attractiveness of the idea that sincere repentance can expunge one's past and cancel all responsibility for past acts—not to mention the notion that punitive measures are primitive and are to be outgrown—this doctrine never really caught on among the Children of Israel. In the final reckoning, Israel in the biblical age chose to reluctantly pass on the option of attempting to navigate a world of conditional promises and judgments, and stick with a God on Whose Word it could unconditionally rely. In due time, with the shift of formal worship

---

28. Thomas Hobbes, *Works* xxix.

29. An acronym used to designate the Ancient Rabbis. The term literally means, "Our wise men, may their memory be a blessing."

away from sacrifice to prayer, the emergent liturgy will be based on *Exodus* 34 and not on *Jonah* 4:2.[30] In the Bible itself, besides *Jonah*, only the *Book of Joel* pays serious attention to the doctrine of the superfluity of punishment and the sufficiency of repentance.[31] As far as the Canonizers of the Bible were concerned, this concept was very much a minority point of view. Considering that it concerned theological issues of so sensitive a nature, the fact that they allowed it to have a voice within the parameters of Scripture, even as a sort of minority report, has broad implications.

The *Book of Jonah* can be seen as part of a tradition of tolerating, and indeed at times looking with favor on principled dissent, even to the extent of challenging God Himself. This attitude can be found embedded in the earliest annals of the faith of Israel. The tale of Abraham confronting God over His intention to destroy Sodom entered the lore of Israel as a model to be emulated. The audacity of daring to challenge the wisdom and the morals of the Deity is astounding. But the point of the tale is that Abraham was standing up to God not out of caprice or ego, but as a matter of conscience.

> *"Will You indeed sweep away the righteous with the wicked? Perhaps there are fifty righteous [persons] within the city; will You indeed sweep [them] away and not forgive the place for the sake of the fifty righteous [persons] that are within it? Far be it from You to do such a thing, to bring death upon the righteous along with the wicked, so righteous and wicked fare alike! Far be it from You! Shall not the Judge of all the earth do justly?"* [*Genesis* 18:23–25]

God not only tolerates the challenge but accepts its premises, debates the issue with Abraham, and even though Abraham loses the argument God approves of his having had the courage to take a principled stand.

As the faith of Israel would seem to have it, human beings are free agents, not puppets. And while behavior is rigorously circumscribed—for example murder, adultery, robbery and perjury (bearing false witness) are expressly forbidden and harshly to be punished—thought and belief are not. Extremely heterodox ideas could be tolerated by the mainstream so long as they did not eventuate in forbidden acts. More: Scripture seems to indicate that stands taken against universally accepted doctrines or beliefs, when founded on principles basic to the faith, could even generate a modicum of grudging approval within certain circles, and even inclusion as

---

30. The liturgical proclamation (see note 19 above), while based on *Exodus* 34:6–7 is a censored version thereof, the second half of verse 7 being omitted. Furthermore, not only is the statement *visiting the iniquity of fathers upon children and on children's children, unto the third and fourth generation* omitted, but the preceding phrase (which we have rendered idiomatically as *But He will by no means clear* [the guilty] (the Hebrew is *v'nakeh lo yenakeh*, literally, *acquitting He will not acquit*), by chopping the grammatical phrase in half the rabbis completely reversed its meaning. The liturgical version of *Exodus* 34 thus reads:

The Lord, the Lord, a merciful and compassionate God, slow to anger and abounding in loving-kindness and truth; extending loving-kindness to the thousandth generation, forgiving iniquity, transgression and sin, and acquitting.

This edited version suggests that the ancient rabbis, although tempted by the vision of total absolution through repentance, but troubled by some of the same reservations that prompted its rejection in the radical form proposed by the author of *Jonah*, decided to attempt to split the difference.

31. To Joel we might also want to add Jeremiah and Ezekiel (see note 27 above) and also possibly the author of *Psalm* 103 who, in verse 8, in quoting *Exodus* 34 omits the word *emet* (truth), and in the following verses extols God's limitless mercy and compassion.

Minority Reports within Scripture itself. It is within these norms that the author of *Jonah* wrote his Book and launched it; it was these norms that allowed this heterodox little Book to enter the corpus of Scripture and become part of the Bible, and indeed it was because of these parameters that the author could picture his anti-hero standing up and defying God Himself. Both the author of the *Book of Jonah* and the character he created to be the central protagonist of his Book rely on the apparent practice that so long as one has the courage of one's convictions, and these convictions, no matter how seemingly heretical, are rooted in principles central to the faith of Israel, quite literally the sky is the limit. The boundaries of the free market of ideas were enormously elastic in Ancient Israel.

And as the author has God tolerating Jonah's rebellion in his Book, so he hoped that God—not to mention his fellow Israelites—would show forbearance to his audacity in challenging God's attitude to those who perform iniquity, transgression and sin as He revealed it to Moses. And it would seem that they did. It is a fact that his little Book was admitted into Scripture and has remained enormously popular to this day. And while it has not displaced the normative doctrine, its "Minority Report" has remained an intriguing alternative constantly before the readers of the Bible.

But *Jonah* is hardly the only challenge to God and orthodoxy in the Bible. We now turn to another of God's refractory agents, who for different reasons and in different ways challenges his God.

Part II

The Enigmatic Balaam, Son of Beor

"*There has not arisen in Israel a prophet like unto Moses*"
—*Deuteronomy* 34:10,

but among the Gentiles there has, i.e., Balaam.
—*Sifre* on *Deuteronomy* 34:10

Chapter 6

Prologue: The Path to the Steppes of Moab

To take a long circuitous route, after enticing the enemy out of the way, and though starting after him, to contrive to reach the goal before him, shows knowledge of the artifice of deviation. He will conquer who has learned the artifice of deviation. Such is the art of maneuvering.
—Sun Tzu, The Art of War—500 BCE

In turning to our new protagonist—or shall we say our new antihero—Balaam, son of Beor, we have in effect entered a time machine, and emerging find that we have turned back the clock some 500 years. We discover ourselves displaced in space as well as in time: Nineveh has vanished and we learn that we are in the Trans-Jordan, in the Kingdom of Moab, east of the Dead Sea.[1] What are we doing here? We will have to pause for a few moments, catch our breath and reorient ourselves. This is the purpose of the current chapter, the Prologue to the tale of Balaam: to put us into the picture and prepare us for the new circumstances in which we find ourselves. Without what amounts to a background briefing it is doubtful that we will be able to make head or tail of the drama we are about to encounter. Even with preparation it promises to be a wild ride. So as we catch our breath let us brace ourselves to adapt to the world we now inhabit, and to conditions radically different from those we have just recently learned to live with.

I

Almost forty years have passed since that decisive moment when the Children of Israel[2] had been liberated from the slavery of Egypt. During the succeeding harsh and precarious wilderness years an entire generation has passed from the world; with only a handful of exceptions, there soon will remain no one who can recall experiencing as an adult the degrading experience of slavery. By the simple fact of natural attrition a people has been transformed. A new nation, conceived in liberty, hardened by

---

1. See MAP 2.
2. We prefer to use when possible the biblical phrase "Children of Israel," rather than the more current "Israelites;" this was the name by which the tribes collectively knew themselves, and by which they were known by their neighbors, friends and enemies alike. In our use the two terms are synonymous.

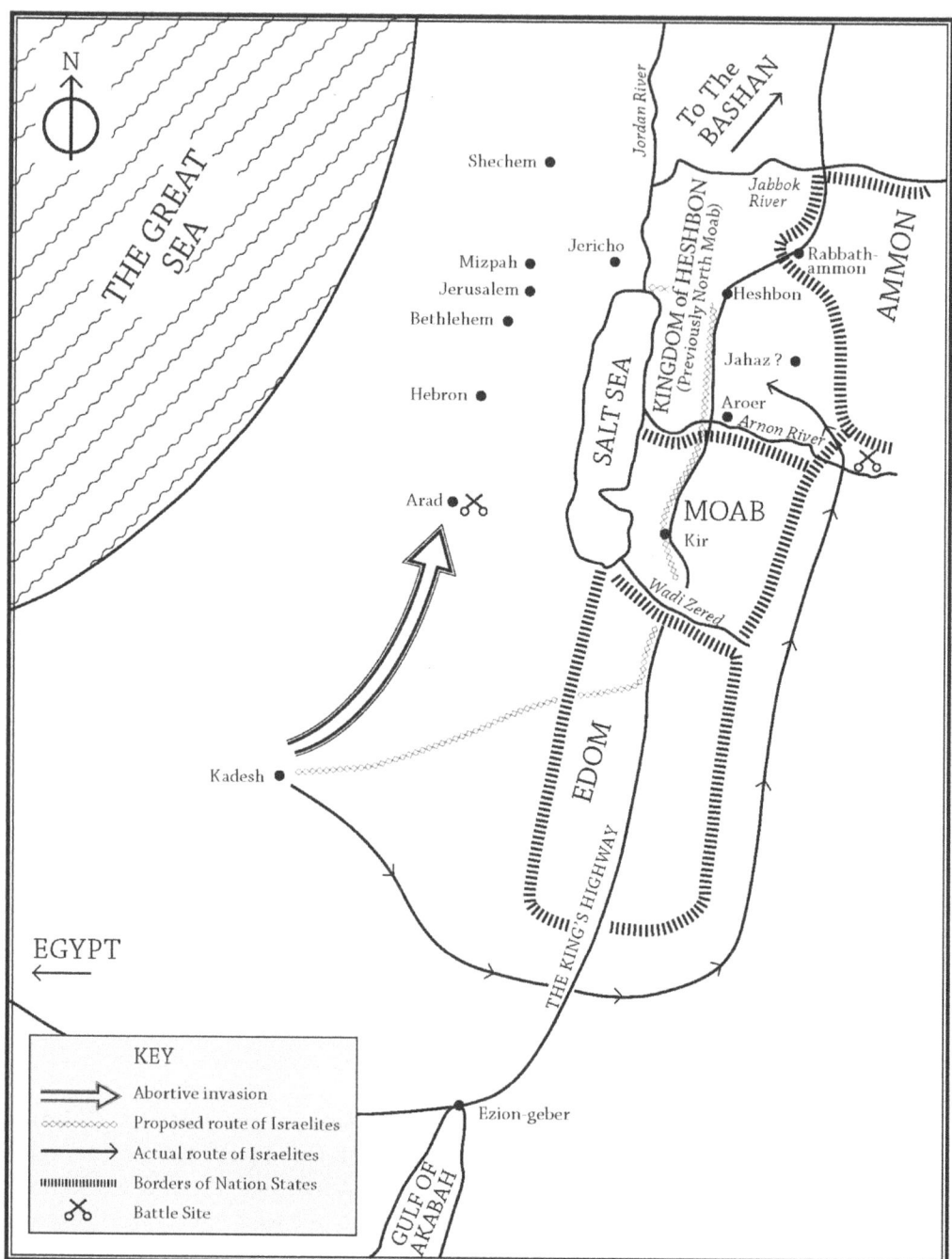

Map 2

The route of the Children of Israel from Kadesh to the Promised Land.

adversity and hungry to take possession of the land promised to its forefathers is now ready to enter into its destiny. The time has arrived to get moving.

The Children of Israel have made Kadesh[3] their base "for many days."[4] The question they now face is how are they to proceed to their goal, the Promised Land? The obvious path is the direct approach: to advance north across the Negeb wasteland and penetrate the heartland of Canaan from its south. The problem with this choice is twofold: the part of Canaan to their north consists of a relatively narrow land corridor surrounded on both sides by water; on the west the Great Sea—the Mediterranean—and on the east a chain of bodies of water—the Sea of Galilee, the Dead Sea to its south, and the Jordan River which connects them.[5] To attack from the South means fighting one's way up that corridor against a stack of enemies, one kingdom after another, one city-state after another, while undergoing remorseless attrition in the process. Sooner or later one is almost certain to run out of momentum. The second problem with the direct approach is that this is a traditional invasion route into Canaan, both by nomadic barbarian hordes and by professional Egyptian armies. The Canaanites have been there before—more times than they care to remember—and they are well prepared for such an eventuality. Israel[6] tried this route many years ago, not long after the Exodus from Egypt, and suffered a bloody repulse; a shock they have never forgotten.[7]

But there is another possibility, an indirect approach: to drive into the Canaanite heartland from the east, cut Canaan in two and deal with each half separately. This approach would entail turning east, not north, detour around the southern end of the Dead Sea, swinging around its eastern shore and penetrating into Canaan by crossing the Jordan River to the Sea's north. It is this more sophisticated strategy—the strategy of the indirect approach—that Moses decides to explore. The major obstacle to its implementation is that the Eastern side of the water-barrier of the Sea of Galilee, the Jordan River and the Dead Sea—the Trans-Jordan—is occupied by a number of kingdoms; to get to the Jordan in order to cross it would require traversing several of them. Now Israel has no intention of battling her way through these kingdoms—at a very minimum the Kingdoms of Edom, Moab, Heshbon, and possibly Ammon as well—nor has she any quarrel with them. She will need their permission to peaceably transit their territories. This may prove expensive to obtain but it would be worth the price.

Moses opens diplomatic consultations with the first of these kingdoms, Edom, pledging to stay on the highway[8] and offering to purchase for cash all supplies that

---

3. The location of Kadesh is well established: the current Ain el-Qudeirat (see MAP 2), an oasis in the wilderness where the Sinai merges into the Negeb. The question raised by some scholars as to whether the launching point of our tale is the main oasis—Kadesh-barnea—or the less lush adjacent Ein Kadesh is, as far as we are concerned, geographically irrelevant.

4. *Deuteronomy* 1:46.

5. See MAP 2.

6. A collective term that serves as an abbreviation for "the Children of Israel."

7. *Numbers* 14:39–45.

8. One of the main highways connecting Egypt with Mesopotamia—known as the "King's Highway"—ran through the Trans-Jordan, traversing Edom, Moab and Ammon. It is this route that Moses wishes to use. In all these matters refer to MAP 2.

might be required, even including well water. Despite the kinship ties between the two peoples,[9] the King of Edom refuses point-blank to allow the Children of Israel to even enter his kingdom, much less transit it. Any attempt to cross the border will be considered an act of war. A second attempt at negotiation by Moses only prompts an Edomite mobilization, and the movement of an Edomite army to the border. In the face of this display of force Moses backs off.[10]

It would appear that this rebuff leads Israel to once again attempt the direct northern approach. Our account is far from clear, but it seems that a probe northward into territory controlled by the Kingdom of Arad results in serious losses, which include some Israelites taken captive.[11] This defeat prompts a furious reaction on the part of the Children of Israel. Vowing a war of annihilation, they launch an all out assault on the kingdom, defeat it, and raze Arad and its dependent towns to the ground.[12]

This encounter, despite its victorious conclusion, must have proven costly because Israel does not follow it up. They have not even gotten to Canaan proper and already they have incurred serious losses. Several more such Pyrrhic victories will bleed them to death. The northern approach is abandoned once and for all.[13] It testifies to how far the confrontation with Arad had disillusioned the Israelites with the direct approach that they prove willing to endure prolonged and arduous hardships rather than repeat their mistake: at any cost they will assault Canaan from the east, from the Trans-Jordan. Since the direct and easy route here—the King's Highway through Edom and Moab—is barred to them, they will have no choice but to circumvent these kingdoms as well. This will involve a grueling and extended trek through a harsh wilderness terrain.[14] But if this be the price of final possession of the Promised Land, so be it. The children of Israel break camp and turn southeast to skirt the bottom of the Kingdom of Edom, then north, well beyond its Eastern border. They reach the Wadi Zered.[15] Crossing it they are now advancing in the arid wilderness to the east of the Kingdom of Moab. Finally, crossing the Arnon River they are now at the border of the Amorite Kingdom of Heshbon; the last obstacle between them and the River Jordan.

---

9. Both Edom and Israel acknowledge a common ancestry. Father Isaac's two sons, Esau and Jacob, are the progenitors of Edom and Israel respectively. For Esau see *Genesis* 36; for Israel as the alternative name of Jacob see *Genesis* 35:9–15.

10. *Numbers* 20:14–21.

11. This was considered by Israel as far more serious than men being slain. Prisoners in those days were routinely sold as slaves, an idea understandably anathema to the Israelites.

12. *Numbers* 21:1–3.

13. On the other hand, instead of assuming that Moses was wavering between these two approaches, it is equally possible that Moses had already made up his mind to use the indirect approach through the Trans-Jordan. In this scenario the probe northward into the Kingdom of Arad would have been meant simply as a distraction; a show of force to cover his real intention to move eastward. If so, this was a diversion that got out of hand—as military maneuvers have a way of doing—embroiling Israel in a series of unforeseen and unwelcome consequences. However, whatever the origins of the campaign, the annihilation of the Kingdom of Arad must have had the effect of focusing the attention of the entire South of Canaan on the Negeb, fostering the certainty that a new invasion of Canaan from the South was looming, and diverting their attention from their eastern flank.

14. Not only will the conditions be brutal, but the distance to be traveled will be more than twice as long as the route through the kingdoms by the King's Highway.

15. A *wadi* is a seasonal river (see Glossary) but though called a *nahal* (wadi) the Zered boasts a perennial stream. The Zered delineates the border between the Kingdoms of Edom and Moab.

II

The previous section summarizes the itinerary of the Children of Israel contained in *Numbers* 20:1–21:20, along with a minimalistic analysis of the significance of the various moves, and omitting the numerous incidents embedded in the narrative—the death of Miriam, the death of Aaron, the investiture of Aaron's son, Eleazar, as High Priest, the plague of poisonous snakes etc.—as irrelevant to our purpose.[16] But from this point onward, as the focus of the biblical narrative and our focus converge, we will stop synopsizing and henceforth stay very close to the text.

The goal of the Children of Israel is to reach and cross the Jordan, but between them and the River lies the Amorite[17] Kingdom of Heshbon. Once again Moses attempts to negotiate passage.

> *Now Israel sent messengers to Sihon, King of the Amorites,[18] saying: "Let me pass through your land; we will not turn aside into field or vineyard; we will not drink well water; we will go by the King's Way[19] until we have crossed your border."*
> [21:21–22][20]

All settled lands with their backs to the wilderness are the natural targets of the nomadic peoples who sparsely inhabit it. In times of drought and privation necessity drives them to raid the rich farmlands; in times of plenty the prospect of loot acts as a magnet. The struggle between farmland and the barrens, between settled societies and nomads, has been a constant of the history of human civilization, since its beginning. The states bordering on the Dead Sea and the Jordan are no exceptions to this rule. The struggle to maintain themselves against nomadic incursion was an unending fact of life. We must understand the currently unfolding events in the light of this reality.

The sudden appearance of a nomadic people on his wilderness frontier is to Sihon an immediate cause for alarm. That they claim peaceful intent—that they mean no harm and merely want to pass through—is simply not credible to the King of Heshbon and his government; in the light of their experience with nomads this is hardly surprising. Even if they now mean what they say, once this beggarly horde—these so-called Children of Israel—enters the Kingdom and sees with its own eyes the, to them, undreamed of wealth of a prosperous agricultural society, what is to prevent them from changing their minds and deciding not to move on but to stay?

---

16. It is important to realize that these "incidents" are the real focus of the biblical narrative, while the movement of the tribes of Israel from their wilderness base in Kadesh to their present position north of the Arnon River is being used by the text merely as a chronological framing device. But as our purpose lies in ascertaining how the Children of Israel found themselves on the Steppes of Moab we have focused our attention on the framework: the account of the historical movement of the tribes into the Trans-Jordan north of the Dead Sea, and what it was that brought them there.

17. See Glossary.

18. LXX and Sam. add *with an offer of peace*, as in *Deuteronomy* 2:26.

19. Not the main Egypt-Mesopotamia international highway of note 8 above, but an east-west route branching off from the main highway at Heshbon, and connecting the capital of the Kingdom with Jericho across the Jordan.

20. From this point onward, all verse citations are to the *Book of Numbers* unless otherwise noted.

Once let them in, and they will be a hundred times more difficult to deal with than when they are outside. The response of King Sihon is almost a given:

However Sihon did not permit Israel to cross his border; and Sihon gathered all his people and went forth against Israel to the wilderness. He came to Jahaz[21] and fought against Israel [21:23].

Probably having a poor opinion of the fighting ability of the scraggly-looking semi-nomadic Children of Israel, when contrasted with his battle hardened militia spearheaded by his professional troops, Sihon, wedded to the idea that attack is the best defense, decides to take the offensive. He mobilizes his people (the militia) and along with his professional army moves to the border, basing himself on Jahaz. From there he launches an attack on the Israelites, aiming to shatter them and drive the remnants back into the wilderness. He has a surprise awaiting him.

And Israel smote him with the sword[22] and took possession of his land, from the Arnon to the Jabbok [Rivers], even to the Children of Ammon[23]; for the border of the Children of Ammon was strong[24] [21:24].

The outcome of the battle is a startling upset. It is Sihon's army that is shattered, and instead of being driven back into the wilderness, it is the Israelites who occupy the now defenseless kingdom, right up to the Jordan on the west and the border of the kingdom of the Children of Ammon[25] on the east; from the Arnon in the south to the Jabbok in the north. They seize all its towns as well as the capital, Heshbon, and make themselves at home. By the time Israel is ready to cross the Jordan and enter into the Promised Land proper, two of the tribes, Reuben and Gad, will feel so much at home that they will decide to forgo their allotted portions of the Promised Land and opt to stay in the Trans-Jordan.[26] The concluding verse of this section looks forward to this outcome.

So Israel took all the cities, and Israel dwelt in all the cities of the Amorites; in Heshbon and all her dependent villages,[27] for Heshbon was the city of Sihon, King of the Amorites [21:25–26a].

---

21. A city on the eastern border of the Kingdom whose exact location is currently unknown. See Glossary and MAP 3.

22. I.e., crushed him and his army.

23. The Ammonite border; see Glossary. Also see Appendix D: The Geography and Ecology of the Trans-Jordan.

24. *Az*, not a place name but the adjective "strong," i.e., well fortified. This may also be a reference to the precipitous Jabbok Canyon which formed Ammon's western border. The text seems to be implying that the reason Israel at this time didn't make a clean sweep of the kingdoms north of the Arnon is that Ammon was in too strong a position, i.e., it would have been too tough a nut to crack. *Deuteronomy* gives a different reason: that the Ammonites were distant kin to the Israelites, being descendant from Lot, Abraham's nephew (*Genesis* 19:36–38). See *Deuteronomy* 2:9, 16–19.

25. The name by which the Ammonites knew themselves, and by which their neighbors knew them. In the Bible, with only two exceptions, they are always referred to as "the Children of Ammon." At this period they had formed a strong and well established state. See Glossary.

26. The final accommodation that will be reached is that the fighting forces of these two tribes will cross the Jordan with the other tribes and participate in the conquest of Canaan and then, at the conclusion of the campaign, will return to the Trans-Jordan and settle there permanently.

27. Literally, *her daughters*. See Cities and Daughters entry in the Glossary.

III

At this point the account of the conquest of the Trans-Jordan breaks off, and the narrative digresses into the history of the territory Israel has just entered, serving as necessary background for the geopolitical realities of the region. The explanation is highlighted by a powerful piece of Amorite poetry, a triumphal paean which ironically celebrates the conquest from its previous possessors of what they in turn have just lost to the Israelites. To maintain the continuity of our tale we will skip over this digression and continue our description of the course of the escalating momentum of the Transjordanian campaign. In Appendix C will be found a full account of the verses we have deleted, i.e., 21:26b–31, and an analysis of what they imply.[28] We return to our tale.

The battle that broke the Amorite army took place in the wilderness, well beyond the borders of the Kingdom, somewhere to the southeast of the capital of Heshbon.[29] This had been a preemptive strike against a perceived enemy that had gone disastrously wrong. With the destruction of the Amorite army and the death of its king,[30] the Israelites follow up their victory by crossing the frontier and investing Heshbon, the Kingdom's capital.

After mopping up the administrative core of the Kingdom, Moses turns his eyes northward, first of all to the Kingdom's northern half. He begins with Jazer, the main city of a discrete region bordering the neighboring Kingdom of Ammon. This was probably the most dangerous potential center of resistance, and therefore the first to be dealt with.[31]

> *Now Moses sent to spy out Jazer, and they took her and her villages*[32]*; and they drove out the Amorites who were there* [21:32].

This is the paradigm of all that will follow: an intelligence mission to gather tactical and topographic information, immediately followed by a lightning campaign of conquest and the eviction of the local populace. With this example, there is no need to enumerate location after location so treated; the narrative passes in silence over the Israelite sweep northward to the Jabbok River and moves on to the next big thing.

> [Then] *they turned and went up the road to the Bashan,*[33] *and Og, King of the Bashan, went out to meet him in battle, he and all his people, at Edrei*[34] [21:33].

The campaign that is now opening will be radically different from that which

---

28. Appendix C: North Moab: A Tale of Lost Lands.
29. The Kingdom took its name from the capital city.
30. *Deuteronomy* 2:33 adds that Sihon's sons also shared his fate.
31. Jazer was almost directly north of Heshbon, on the western side of the Jabbok, about 10 miles southwest of Rabbath-ammon (the site of the present day Amman). See MAP 3.
32. Reading with LXX.
33. Both the name of a district—bounded by Mount Hermon on the North, Jebel Druze on the East, the hills east of the Sea of Galilee on the West, and a line about 6 miles south of the Yarmuk River to the South (see Appendix D: The Geography and Ecology of the Trans-Jordan)—and the name of the Kingdom that ruled the region.
34. The modern Der'a, on the Yarmuk River near the southern border of the Bashan.

conquered Heshbon. That conflict opened with an Amorite attack on the Israelites, at a time when they were encamped outside the borders of the Kingdom and were attempting to negotiate passage. From the perspective of the Children of Israel, it was for them a defensive war in which they emerged victorious; and to the victors belong the spoils. It was not they who initiated the hostilities. But once Israel crossed the Jabbok it was she who was the aggressor. What is more, the text clearly differentiates between the two conflicts ideologically. God is never so much as mentioned with regard to the war and subsequent conquest of Heshbon. In the Bashan campaign God is depicted as initiating the conflict, promising Israel victory and awarding her the possession of the Bashan.

> *And the* Lord *said to Moses, "Do not fear him, for I have given into your hand him, and all his people and his land; you shall do to him what you did to Sihon, King of the Amorites, who dwelt in Heshbon"* [21:34].

How can we explain this difference between these two campaigns that seem so similar, indeed, simply two phases of one war? To answer this question requires us to turn back the clock to the last third of the 16th century BCE, the beginning of the period in Egyptian history known as "The New Kingdom" or alternatively "The New Empire."[35] Under a string of energetic and imperialistic Pharaohs—notably Tuthmosis III and Amenophis II—Egypt carved out an empire in Asia that for a time stretched well into northern Syria.[36] The Egyptians gave their Asiatic conquests the name of "Canaan." As a result of the civilizational collapse that brought the Bronze Age to a close at the end of the 13th century BCE, the Egyptian army was forced to evacuate their Province of Canaan.[37] The relevance of this snippet of ancient history to our tale only became evident in the middle of the last century.

About seventy years ago the distinguished historian and "dean" of biblical archaeologists, Benjamin Mazar, conclusively demonstrated that the borders of the Promised Land as set forth in the continuation of our narrative (*Numbers* 34:1–15) correspond exactly with those of the Egyptian Province of Canaan during the Age of the New Empire.[38] In other words, the land promised by God to the Children of Israel was none other than the territory of what had not so long before been the Egyptian Province of Canaan.

What this means to the unfolding of our tale is that everything north of the Yarmuk River is part and parcel of the Promised Land. While Israel had no mandate to possess, nor any interest in, the Kingdom of Heshbon, and its conquest was purely

---

35. This period, which covers the reigns of the Eighteenth and Nineteenth Dynasties (circa 1567–1200 BCE), began with the expulsion of the Asiatic Hyksos who had traumatized Egypt by their conquest and foreign rule. In reaction Egypt became an imperialist power, expanding into Asia under the slogan "No security except on the Euphrates."

36. The northern border of the Egyptian New Empire only stabilized c. 1270 BCE with the signing of a peace treaty with the rival Hittite Empire, delineating their border as a roughly east-west line a bit north of the city of Biblos in central Syria.

37. However, the name the Egyptians gave to the region stuck, as did the term *Canaanites* as a catchall designation for the polyglot inhabitants of what had been the Egyptian province.

38. B. Mazar, "Canaan on the Threshold of the Age of the Patriarchs" (Hebrew). *Eretz Israel 3* (1954). These findings were independently confirmed by R. de Vaux, "Le pays de Canaan." *JAOS 88* (1962).

due to historical coincidence and secular contingencies, the Bashan, as a part of the Promised Land, was a different matter entirely. Israel very much had a divine mandate to take possession of the Bashan, and when what amounted to almost half of the tribe of Manasseh eventually settled there, they were entering into their designated inheritance. Unlike the tribes of Reuben and Gad, whose decision to remain in the Gilead[39] was from the first problematic and was never considered completely legitimate, the right of the tribe of Manasseh to straddle the East-West divide, part in the Cis-Jordan south of the Jezreel Valley and part in the Trans-Jordan, in the Bashan, was never questioned.

With the Gilead (Heshbon that was) and the Bashan in his pocket, Moses now turns his eyes westward toward the Cis-Jordan, the heartland of Canaan. The Children of Israel terminate their northern drive,[40] turn on their heels and retrace their steps southward. Their destination is their original target, the fords of the Jordan opposite Jericho, which are the entry portal to central Canaan. This had been their goal when they were attempting to negotiate passage through the Kingdom of Heshbon, the denial of which had led to their long and ultimately costly diversion in the Trans-Jordan.[41]

[Then] *the Children of Israel set out* [from there] *and pitched camp in the Steppes*[42] *of Moab, across the Jordan from Jericho* [22:1].

With these words the epic saga of Israel's progress from Egypt to the Promised Land breaks off; it will only resume in *Numbers 25*. For the present we leave the Children of Israel encamped on the Steppes of Moab, opposite Jericho, and shift our attention southward, across the Arnon River, to the Kingdom of Moab. There, completely unbeknown to the Children of Israel, will play out a drama that will concern, at the deepest level, her very existence and destiny. And at the center of this drama we will become acquainted with our second central protagonist, Balaam, the son of Beor.

---

39. The Gilead is the name given to the region between the Arnon and the Yarmuk Rivers. See MAP 3.

40. The Aramaean Kingdoms of Geshur (on the eastern bank of the Sea of Galilee) and Maaca (to its north), though also part of the Promised Land, were never touched.

41. Israel was never to take complete possession of the Cis-Jordan. Kaufmann (*Conquest of Canaan*, p. 53) is of the opinion that the primary reason was that they didn't need all the territory. The decision of two tribes—Reuben and Gad—to settle in the Trans-Jordan meant that at least 15 percent of the Children of Israel never entered into the Promised Land, and room for them was no longer necessary. The pockets of non–Israelites that therefore remained were to prove serious problems for centuries.

42. Hebrew *Arbot Moab*, the eastern portion of the lower Jordan plain before it empties into the Dead Sea, as distinct from *Sedai Moab*, "the plains of Moab" which refers to the larger Moabite plateau (cf. *Genesis 36:35, Ruth 1:1–2* etc.). The name of this semi-arid area opposite Jericho is a holdover from the days the region was part of Moab. See Appendix C.

Introduction to the *Book of Balaam*

O My people, remember now what Balak, king of Moab, plotted,
And what Balaam, son of Beor answered him;
From Shittim even to Gilgal,
That you might know the righteous acts of the LORD.
—Micah 6:5

What I tell you three times is true.
—Lewis Carroll, *The Hunting of the Snark*

Our new protagonist, Balaam, son of Beor, is a very different proposition than was Jonah, son of Amittai. For one thing, although both Jonah and Balaam were historic personages,[1] their tales have been preserved for us in two very different literary genres. While our contention is that the story of Jonah is presented as a fable, that of Balaam takes the form of historical narrative, and is to be found embedded in the record we have just been reading of Israel's epic journey from Sinai to the Promised Land. Thus, while the Tale of Jonah is situated in a world of archetypes—out of time and space—and therefore necessitated our treating it solely in terms of itself, the drama of Balaam, set in the real world, compels us to take its context into serious account. For this reason, our treatment of the Tale of Balaam has been preceded by a Prologue and will be succeeded by an Epilogue, both of them framing the drama, and anchoring it in the wider historical process.

The Tale of Balaam is to be found in the *Book of Numbers*, Chapters twenty two–twenty four.[2] These chapters form a discrete literary unit, highly structured in form and very sophisticated in style and content. In this sense we will find ourselves dealing with a self-contained composition quite similar in many respects to the *Book of Jonah*. It is important to note that both in style and vocabulary the chapters encompassing our drama bear no similarity to the chapters that precede and follow them; i.e., the Prologue and the Epilogue.[3] Nor do the contents of this unit have any connection with

---

1. Jonah, as we have seen, was an older contemporary of the eighth century BCE prophet Amos (see introduction to *Book of Jonah*, note 8), while Balaam was a figure of note on the international world stage some 500 years previously, in the thirteenth century; a younger contemporary of Moses. For extra-biblical evidence for Balaam see Appendix E: The Deir 'Alla Inscription(s).

2. There are several references to Balaam in various Books of the Bible which both continue the tale and comment on it. These will be dealt with in due course.

3. Nor, for that matter, to any other part of the Bible. We find terminology in this unit that is unique to it. For an example see Chapter 9, note 14.

the preceding and following chapters.[4] None of the protagonists featured in the preceding and following chapters appear in *Numbers* 22–24, nor do the actors who star in this periscope make an appearance in the framing chapters. We repeat, the narrative of Israel's journey during the Wilderness Years (which includes the conquest of the Trans-Jordan) has broken off abruptly at the end of Chapter 21, and will only resume in Chapter 25. Chapters 22–24 can thus be defined as an intrusion; an autonomous composition that has arbitrarily been shoehorned into the text of *Numbers*.

This realization is hardly new. Already in late antiquity, the sages of the Talmud[5] recognized these chapters as an autonomous unit, and named it "The Book of Balaam."[6] "Clearly the rabbis believed that the Balaam story was composed independently and only later inserted into the Pentateuchal corpus."[7] Accepting this understanding of the *Book of Balaam* (as we shall hereafter refer to *Numbers* 22–24), our first task will become to appreciate it in its own terms, and only afterwards to investigate its place within the larger context of the *Book of Numbers*.

Beginning with the *Book of Balaam* as we now have it, our first question must be the nature of the composition: is it a unitary work composed by a single creative mind—i.e., can we speak of an author?—or is it an editorial compilation, patched together from several disparate sources? Its literary form is that of narrative prose, interspersed with a number of oracular utterances written in archaic poetry.[8] Is the combination seamlessly organic, the connection between the poetry and the prose a natural outgrowth of their intrinsic unity, or is their juxtaposition (as many scholars believe) artificial and arbitrary? Further, within the narrative prose there seem to be serious internal contradictions that have led many commentators to conclude that the prose itself is a patchwork of different accounts that don't always agree with one another. We will state our initial premise upfront: that the *Book of Balaam*, as we now have it in *Numbers* 22–24, is a coherent and self-consistent work composed by a highly talented author, built around a series of poetic oracles dating from an earlier age. Our contention is that the tale surrounding the oracular poems—the description of the conditions under which the oracles were uttered—dates from the time of the composition of these self-same oracles (see below). At a significantly later date, the person whom we have termed "the author" reworked the story into the sophisticated narrative we have today, while retaining the oracles—i.e., the "Words of God," and hence holy—un-altered, as he had inherited them.

This point requires some clarification. As could be expected, the oracles embedded in the *Book of Balaam* were originally uttered within a historical context. In the ancient world oracles were never uttered ex cathedra; in a vacuum, as it were. Either they were delivered upon the request of some interested party[9]—usually for pay—or

---

4. The only connection is spatial and temporal: the events related in *Numbers* 22–24 take place at the time when the Children of Israel have arrived on the Steppes of Moab, their last stopping place before entering the Promised Land, and are encamped there. See MAP 3.

5. For Talmud and related terms see Glossary.

6. Tractate *Baba Batra* 14b, Munich MS.

7. Milgrom, *Numbers* (hereafter simply Milgrom), p. 185. Rabbi Johanan held that the Torah was put together from different scrolls, the *Book of Balaam* being one of them. (Tractate *Gittin* 60a.)

8. These poetic passages are four in number, the last being itself composed of four separate oracles.

9. Or were on occasion provoked, as was oracle number four in our case (*Numbers* 24:15–19).

they were uttered at the command of a deity. Always oracles addressed some set of social, political or historical circumstances. When oracles were deemed worthy of being preserved for posterity, it was natural to append some record of the circumstances that had called them forth; oracle and circumstantial account thus becoming an integral package.[10] In our case, the language in which "Balaam's oracles" are couched—both vocabulary and grammar—are archaic. On the other hand, the language of the narrative in the *Book of Balaam* is more recent; more modern by at least a century or two, possibly more. This leads us to account for the linguistic discrepancy by postulating a writer (our postulated "author") inheriting from "olden times"—either in oral or written form—the "Balaam oracles," packaged together with some explanation of the accompanying circumstances of their nativity. This description he then transformed into the complex and subtle account we currently possess.

A further point needs to be made. We maintain that the so-called self-contradictions in the narrative pointed to by numerous scholars are the results of a profound misunderstanding of the text on the part of these commentators. Their error is primarily due to an overly narrow reading of the text; a misreading caused by a lack of appreciation of the high level of the author's literary sophistication.

These will be our working hypotheses, and our analysis of the text will either vindicate or refute them. We will revisit these issues in the summary chapter to the *Book of Balaam* and reevaluate our conclusions in the light of the textual evidence.

We have alluded to a disparity between the time when the poetic oracles scattered within the *Book of Balaam* were composed and the era in which the prose account that frames them was put into its present form, using phrases such as "date from an earlier age" and "a significantly later date." It is time to become more specific. Our dating of the composition of the poetry and that of the prose (which means the *Book of Balaam* as we have it today) will be based on the conclusions of W.F. Albright.[11] Relying primarily on philological and especially orthographical analysis, he sums up his findings as follows: the poems were most probably *composed* in the latter half of the 13th century BCE and certainly no later than the 12th,[12] while the prose and the first *written* versions of the oracles date in or about the 10th century BCE.[13] Placing the composition of the oracles in the latter part of the 13th century to the early 12th century BCE would make them contemporaneous with the lifetime of Balaam, strengthening the case for taking the narrative description of their genesis as being based on a substratum of hard fact.

With this brief introduction to the account of our second protagonist, Balaam, son of Beor, and to some of the assumptions that underlie how we will treat his tale, we begin the remarkable drama that the rabbis of old named the *Book of Balaam*.

---

10. Without this account, within a decade or two the oracles themselves would become unintelligible. As Jacob Milgrom puts it with regard to the *Book of Balaam*: "Without the narrative, the poetic oracles would make no sense, and all their allusions to personalities, nations and events would be incomprehensible.... the many interlocking details and the parallel development of identical themes in the prose and poetry demonstrate that chapters 22–24... form an organic unity." (*Milgrom*, pp. 467–468)

11. Although his magisterial article, "The Oracles of Balaam," was written a good three quarters of a century ago, first seeing the light in 1944, I know of no subsequent study that either seriously challenges or modifies the conclusions that he reached with regard to the dating of the oracles and the surrounding prose.

12. "Oracles," p. 226.

13. *Ibid.*, p. 210.

Chapter 7

Come, Curse Mine Enemy

*The will
And high permission of all-ruling Heaven
Left him at large to his own dark designs,
That with reiterated crimes he might
Heap on himself damnation.*
—John Milton, *Paradise Lost*, I

Seeking a Savior

The sudden eruption of the Children of Israel from the eastern wastelands, the shattering of the Amorite armies of Sihon and Og, and the seizure and occupation of their kingdoms have sent shockwaves through the entire region both east and west of the Jordan.[1] The move of the Israelites from their conquest of the Bashan southward to the Steppes of Moab sends the clear signal that the Kingdom of Moab itself is likely to be Israel's next target. Balak, King of Moab, panics. It is too late now to regret his denial of transit rights to this horde which calls itself the Children of Israel, and his unnecessary open display of hostility to them.[2] He has incurred their wrath, and after their fearsome display of military prowess he accepts as a given that, should they turn their attention to him and his kingdom, he will be powerless to stop them.[3] Balak, seeing disaster staring him in the face, initiates what defensive measures he can muster.

> *Now Balak, son of Zippor, saw everything Israel had done to the Amorites. And Moab was in great dread of the people, because it was so numerous; Moab was*

---

1. In *Joshua* 2:9–14 we learn from the mouth of a resident of Jericho how not merely the governments but also the general populations of the city-states west of the Jordan have been hanging on the reports cascading in of the annihilation of the kingdoms of Heshbon and Bashan, of the identity and background of their conquerors and of the resultant wave of terror sweeping the region.

2. In *Deuteronomy* we learn of the lasting animosity this hostile behavior left in the collective memory of Israel: *No... Moabite shall ever be admitted into the congregation of the Lord... because they did not meet you with bread and water on your way when you left Egypt* (*Deuteronomy* 23:4–5).

3. In Appendix C: North Moab: A Tale of Lost Lands, we discuss the Amorite invasion of the Gilead south of the Jabbok River, then part of the Moabite Kingdom. Balak (or possibly his immediate predecessor) had proved to be no match for the Amorites. Sihon had defeated him and had shorn him of half his kingdom: everything north of the Arnon River. But now Israel had crushed the formidable Amorite war machine with an ease that was frightening. No wonder Balak was terrified.

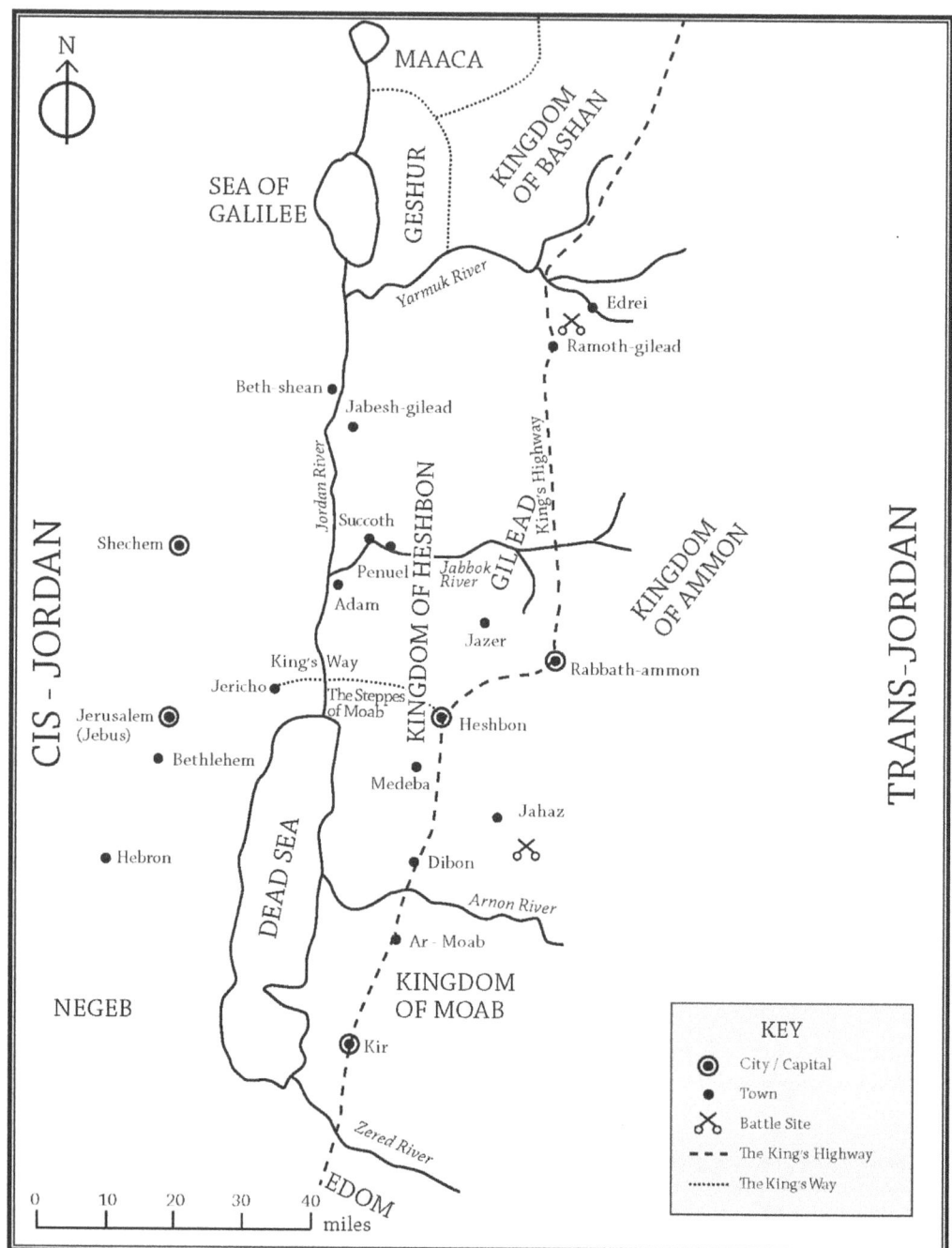

MAP 3

The Trans-Jordan in the late 13th century BCE.

terrified of the Children of Israel. So Moab said to the elders of Midian, "Now this[4] horde will lick up all that is about us as the ox licks up the grass of the field" [22:2–4a].

Balak's first move is to try to recruit allies. He turns to the Midianites,[5] stressing the danger that this people which had come out of Egypt, now on a rampage, poses to both of them. He seems to have been successful in convincing at least some of the Midianite tribes to enter into a mutual defense alliance with him directed against Israel. But, as both Balak and the Midianites suspect, even together they will not be able to prevail against an Israelite assault. Something more will be necessary.

Now Balak, son of Zippor, who was King of Moab at that time, sent messengers to Balaam, son of Beor, at Pethor, which is by the Euphrates[6]—the land of his kin— to summon him, saying, "Behold, a people has come out of Egypt, and behold, they cover the face of the earth[7]; and it has settled [down] next to me. And now,[8] please come and put a curse upon this people for me, for it is too multitudinous for me; perhaps [then] I will be able to smite it and drive them from the land, for I know that whom you bless is blessed, and whom you curse is cursed" [22:4b–6].

Who is this Balaam, son of Beor, to whom the King of Moab appeals, and what exactly does he expect from him? Now beyond what we know of him from the Book that goes by his name, and a scattering of references in various parts of the Bible— which we shall in due course draw upon—Balaam holds the distinction of being one of that small handful of biblical personalities of whom we know from extra-biblical sources.[9] Balaam was a *kosem*, a diviner[10]; an expert with an international reputation in the "science" of forecasting future events.[11] But Balak is not looking for a prediction of things to come; he sees Balaam as a person who can determine outcomes, who, through blessings and curses, has the power to influence how things turn out. In a word, he confuses a diviner with a sorcerer. He wants to engage the services of one who can put a hex on Israel, a curse that will destroy their morale, weaken their resolve and dissolve their cohesion. He wants someone who can "set the Israelites up"

---

4. Reading with LXX, Vulg. and Syr. MT omits the word *this*.

5. *Midianites* is an ethnic term used to describe a loose and constantly shifting coalition of nomadic tribes roaming the wastelands of the Sinai, the Negeb and the regions east of the fertile belt of settled land of the Trans-Jordan in which kingdoms had coalesced. But why turn just to the Midianites? Why not to the Kingdom of the Bnai-ammon, the strongest remaining non-Israelite state in the region? Probably Balak did turn to them as well, but without success. For whatever reasons, Ammon preferred not to get involved and sat it out. As a result, they emerged from this turbulent period as an unscathed neutral.

6. Probably Pitru, about 12 miles south of Carchemish. See MAP 5.

7. Literally, *they cover the eye of the earth*, i.e., they hide the earth from view; an idiom usually used of a plague of locusts and sometimes, by extension, of an invading army.

8. See Chapter 4, note 8 for the implications of this expression.

9. See Appendix E: The Deir 'Alla Inscriptions.

10. *Joshua* 13:22. In the Deir 'Alla inscriptions he is called a *hozeh*, a clairvoyant, a specific branch of divination: foreseeing.

11. Divination was considered a science in the Ancient Near East, and its practice was deemed effective. The Bible concurs with this estimate, but prohibits its use by Israelites (*Deuteronomy* 18:10), possibly due to the connection of its practitioners with pagan rites. In their place the Children of Israel are directed to its prophets (*Deuteronomy* 18:15). For Balaam, a non-Israelite, the practice of divination was perfectly legitimate with no stigma attached.

so that he and his allies can defeat them in battle and drive them from the land. For he knows:

that whom you bless is blessed, and whom you curse is cursed [22:6].

And it is on this basis that he will dispatch a delegation to Mesopotamia to secure his services. And for these services Balak is willing to pay, and pay extravagantly.[12]

Where does Balak get the idea that Balaam is a sorcerer who not just predicts outcomes but also determines them? In our sources Balaam never makes this claim. Indeed, in the *Book of Balaam* (22:3–24:25) he insists time and again that while he can ascertain the will of God (or the gods, as the case may be) and thus what the future holds in store, he has no power to alter it; he can only do what God (or the gods) want him to do and say what He (or they) want him to say. But obviously the image of Balaam as a man whose word can determine the future—that those he blesses *are* blessed while those he curses *are* cursed—is not the invention of King Balak. He is simply reflecting general opinion. Balaam may deny it—perhaps not too strongly—but, as we shall see, his protestations are not taken very seriously. The image of the all-powerful sorcerer who can bend the future to the benefit of him who can afford to pay his fee sets Balaam apart from his competitor diviners and puts him into a league of his own.

With this image of Balaam firmly fixed in his mind, and having convinced the Midianites to go along with this plan, a joint delegation is dispatched by Balak to Pethor on the River Euphrates bearing his message.

So the elders of Moab and the elders of Midian set out with divination in their hands,[13] and they came to Balaam and spoke to him the words of Balak. And he said to them, "Lodge here tonight and I will bring back word to you as the LORD *may speak to me." So the Moabite officials stayed with Balaam* [22:7–8].

The Veto

Up to this point in the narrative we know Balaam only by reputation. Now, as we are being introduced to him in person, as it were, it will be worth our while to pay close attention to what he does and says, and to how the author of his tale treats him. Balaam, we shall begin to discover, is far from a transparent personality. In fact, at first acquaintance, his character begins to exhibit clear signs of ambiguity. His opening remark, straightforward though it may seem, is both revealing and at the same time enigmatic.

---

12. If Balaam ensures that Balak can "drive the Children of Israel from the land," that could mean that Moab might regain its northern territories lost to Sihon. Is this possibility part of King Balak's calculations?

13. This is a literal rendition of the Hebrew *ukesamim beyadam*. Most commentators take this to mean the fee (or "honorarium") paid to a "seer" or "diviner" for his services. On the other hand Milgrom (p. 187), pointing out that Balaam was to be paid *only after* he had successfully accomplished his projected mission (24:10–11), renders the Hebrew phrase as "versed in divination," i.e., that the emissaries sent by Balak were themselves diviners, "colleagues ... present for the purpose of honoring him." As the Hebrew term *to honor* can also have the connotation, as we shall see, of "to present with 'sweeteners,'" or of "to grease his palm," I feel it better to stick with our author's refusal to spell his meaning out, and to leave the ambiguous phrase stand as is.

"Lodge here tonight and I will bring back word to you as the LORD *may speak to me."*

Balaam is here claiming that he, a denizen of this world, is in communication with the realm of the divine. More, that he has a direct pipeline to the LORD, the God of Israel, the very people—although Balak was careful not to name them[14]—that are the subject of the king's proposed commission. Further, he is implying that he doesn't have to wait for the LORD to initiate conversation, but that he has the ability to make contact when and where he pleases. Balaam is guaranteeing Balak's emissaries an answer by tomorrow morning. Secondly, Balaam is averring that he is not a free agent. Whether or not he accepts Balak's commission depends upon the LORD's prior approval. As to the factors that may determine the LORD's attitude, Balaam preserves a studied silence.

Unmentioned, but undoubtedly understood by all, is that the consultation with the LORD will take place in the dead of night through the medium of a dream. In Israel, as in the entire Ancient Near East, divine visitations by means of dreams were an accepted way of the gods making their wills known to select human beings. That Balaam claims the ability not simply to receive but also to initiate such contact from the human side—to actively transmit as well as simply to passively receive—emphasizes the loftiness of the status he claims, and perhaps partially explains his inflated popular reputation.

And it turns out that Balaam is not bluffing. That night, in a dream, Balaam holds a conversation with God.

Now God came to Balaam[15] *and said, "Who are these men with you?" And Balaam said to God, "Balak, King of Moab, sent for me* [saying], *'Behold, a people*[16] *that has come out of Egypt covers the face of the earth,*[17] *and now come and put a curse on it for me, perhaps* [then] *I will be able to fight against them and drive them off.'" And God said to Balaam, "Do not go with them; you shall not curse the people for it is blessed"* [22:9–12].

The query with which God opens the conversation is not concerned with the identity of Balaam's visitors but with their business. It amounts to the question: "What do these men want with you?" This is more than just a request for a dry informational report. It is really a leading question, aiming to probe Balaam's attitude to the proposition being made to him. Balaam refuses to rise to the bait. Playing his cards very close to the chest he simply responds with a slightly abbreviated version

---

14. In his appeal to Balaam, Balak, although fully aware of the name by which the conquerors of Heshbon and Bashan knew themselves, and by which they were known, refers to them only as "a people has come out of Egypt."

15. This is the standard language used in the Bible for a divine visitation in a dream to a Gentile; cf. *Genesis* 20:3 (with Abimelech) and *Genesis* 31:24 (with Laban). In 22:20 the full formula will be used: *And God came to Balaam by night and said....* As we have already been told that Balaam would be speaking to God that night, the final word of the formula, *by night* (one word in the Hebrew) can be omitted from our present statement for the sake of brevity. It is well to note that this formula is never used in the case of a divine visitation with an Israelite.

16. Reading with LXX, Targ. and Sam. MT reads *the people*.

17. See note 7 above.

of Balak's summons, without any overt indication as to how he feels about it. The implied question being posed in turn by Balaam is: "Am I free to accept this commission or not?" God's response is an immediate and unequivocal no! You may *not* go with these emissaries of Balak. You may *not* curse this as yet unnamed people. And then God unbends and supplies the reason for this unilateral prohibition: this is a people whose status has already been determined; they may not be cursed because they are already blessed.[18]

Comes the dawn and Balaam gives the emissaries his answer to Balak's proposition:

Now Balaam rose in the morning[19] *and said to the officials*[20] *of Balak, "Go [back alone] to your land, for the* LORD *refuses to give me leave to go with you"* [22:13]

We are beginning to learn something about Balaam. His response to the king's emissaries is two-faced: it is true and at the same time it is misleading. It is true in that God did forbid Balaam to accept Balak's commission and to return with them to Moab. But the reason for the prohibition—that an attempt to fulfill the king's proposition would be an exercise in futility: this people cannot be cursed, for it already is blessed—has been omitted. This studied omission has the effect of making the divine refusal seem irrational and capricious, and invites doubt as to its authenticity. Why should the great seer and diviner—an intimate of the gods[21]—be denied by them the opportunity to practice his trade and to pocket a nice fat fee? Perhaps the gods really have nothing to do with the matter; perhaps Balaam is simply playing hard to get and using the alleged prohibition of this God, the LORD, as a convenient excuse, the real issue being the size of his "honorarium." This line of reasoning is more than uncertain speculation. Arguing in its favor is the fact that in their report to the King of Moab the envoys omit all mention of Balaam's claim that the LORD refused to give him permission to accept their offer. As they report it, Balaam's rejection of Balak's proposal is solely of his doing.

So the Moabite officials rose up and came to Balak, and they said, "Balaam refused to come with us" [22:14].

---

18. God is not here revealing something new, but simply informing Balaam of a long-standing fact, that this is a people created for a special destiny and blessed by God at the moment of its formation, which was the call of Abraham: *And the Lord said to Abram, "Get you forth out of your country, and from your native land and from your father's house, unto the land that I will show you. And I will make of you a great nation, and I will bless you, and I will make your name great; and [therefore] be a blessing. And I will bless those who bless you, and he who curses you will I curse; and in you shall all the families of the earth be blessed."* (Genesis 12:1–3)

19. This phrase introduces a report of a nighttime divine visitation. The same phrase is used of Balaam in the Deir 'Alla inscription. See Appendix E.

20. Up to now they have been called "elders," dignitaries of high respectability and prestige, whose presence in the delegation is meant to be a flattering tribute to Balaam's sense of worth. But now, when they have failed to charm him into accepting the commission, their true identity stands revealed: they are nothing more than *sarim*, government officials, high-level bureaucrats in the service of the king. From this point onward all talk of "elders" ceases and we will hear only of *sarim*, officials and government functionaries.

21. Like the *Book of Job*, the cast of characters in the *Book of Balaam* is composed exclusively of Gentiles, i.e., pagans. To them the term *elohim* (grammatically a plural) means "gods." And when the narrator speaks about them this is the term he uses. (See also Chapter 3, note 24 for the way a different author deals with this issue.) Balaam is the sole exception to this rule. Despite being a pagan he alone speaks of the LORD and to the LORD. Is he a Gentile monotheist (there is such a thing) or is he a polytheist who sees the LORD as one among many deities—perhaps even the most powerful among them—with Whom he has a special relationship? For the present we leave the question open.

Under the circumstances we can hardly blame Balak for concluding that either the delegation was insufficiently flattering and persuasive, or that the fee proposed was not sufficiently opulent to sway him; or perhaps both. He will have to try again.

One thing seems certain: when Balaam declined the offer he failed to persuade the emissaries that when he said no he really meant no. And in this less-than-convincing refusal lies the nub of our tale.

If at First You Don't Succeed...

Not daunted by the rebuff, and more than half convinced that Balaam's refusal was nothing more than a standard Near Eastern bargaining ploy, Balak determines to meet Balaam on his own ground; he will up the ante. Considering the crisis he thinks he is facing he really has little choice. As he sees things, Balaam offers his only chance to avoid the fate that overtook Sihon and Og. He must have the services of the world famous Balaam at any price.

So once again Balak sent officials, more in number and more honorable than they. And they came to Balaam and said to him, "Thus says Balak, son of Zippor[22]*: 'Please do not refuse to come to me. For I will most certainly honor you greatly,*[23] *and everything you tell me to do I will do; so please go and curse this people for me'"* [22:15–17].

By sending a delegation composed of some of the kingdom's highest ranking officials with an offer that amounts to a blank check—you can name your own reward, just curse this people for me, *please*—Balak has cut through the haggling process with what he considers an irresistible offer. Bearing in mind the oblique, subtle and torturous stages of the normal negotiating process in the Ancient Near East,[24] Balak's having come so quickly and openly to so magnanimous an offer is a true measure of his desperation. He is in the incipient stages of panic. Balaam's reply is revealing.

And Balaam replied and said to the servants of Balak, "[Even] if Balak were to give me his palace[25] *filled with silver and gold I could not do anything, great or small,*[26] *to violate the word of the* LORD *my God"* [22:18].

If Balaam were to conclude matters with this ringing declaration of principle—I said no and I meant no—that would be that. But he doesn't.

"And now,[27] *you also please stay here overnight and I will see what more the* LORD *will say to me"* [22:19].

---

22. In the diplomatic parlance of the Ancient Near East, this is the language a king uses to address an equal. Not only has the status of the delegation been raised but so has the level of discourse.

23. A polite euphemism for "I will richly reward you," a promise immeasurably strengthened by the use of the infinitive absolute grammatical construction. See Chapter 1, note 54.

24. For an example, see my *Judges and Saviors*, p. 255–266, an in-depth analysis of negotiations between the Israelite Judge Jephthah and the King of Ammon which, incidentally, casts a retrospective light on the background of our tale.

25. Literally, *his house*.

26. A merism (see Glossary), i.e., anything at all.

27. Once again this expression "And now," followed by an imperative; meaning that the time for talk is over and the time for getting down to the nitty-gritty has arrived (see Chapter 4, note 8). The last time it was Balak who used it (see note 9 above), now it is Balaam.

What Balaam is saying here, translated into plain and blunt English, is: "Now that I have put on record my noble principles, stay overnight while I see what I can do about your revised proposal." As time passes, the two sides of Balaam are becoming more and more evident.

What is Balaam thinking? He knows that the LORD his God (his own words) has forbidden him to accept Balak's commission. He knows that he cannot curse the people Balak wants him to curse because they are already blessed—presumably by the LORD Himself—and therefore are "immunized" against any curses. Yet it seems that the lure of that blank check he has been offered is overwhelming. Does Balaam entertain the hope that, somehow, he can get the LORD to change His mind? Is he perhaps toying with the idea of getting God to go along with a little hanky-panky, possibly with a counterfeit cursing ceremony that would fool Balak into paying his fee while leaving this as yet unnamed people in their state of blessedness? After all, he has always been a faithful servant of the LORD. Doesn't the LORD's loyal servant deserve a little slack? Perhaps Balaam himself doesn't quite know exactly what he wants, except that he wants to eat his cake and somehow have it. And amazingly he seems to get the slack that he has been dreaming of.

And God came to Balaam by night and said to him, "If the men came to call you, arise and go with them. However, the thing[28] that I speak to you, only that shall you do" [22:20].

How did Balaam manage to get God to change an absolute prohibition into a partial and conditional permission? That, we suggest, is what we are about to learn.

Travels with a Donkey and Other Absurdities

Up to now we have been perusing what purports to be a historical drama, a straightforward tale that proceeds along perfectly comprehensible and naturalistic lines. Now suddenly the plot takes an unexpected turn, and before our astonished eyes the play transmogrifies into the theater of the absurd: the world has turned surreal, Balaam's donkey suddenly takes center stage and steals the limelight from her master, nothing makes sense and everything has been turned upside down.

It is not only that the donkey breaks into speech. She—yes, the donkey turns out to be a jenny, a member of the female sex—she also emerges as the most perceptive and levelheaded member of the cast, while her master proves himself the true ass. We might label this episode "The Saga of the Talking Donkey"—the name under which the story of Balaam has become world-famous—were it not for other anomalies. For example, we might title it "The Mystery of the Missing Ambassadors"; Balaam begins his journey in the company of the delegation which had been sent to fetch him, only to have them mysteriously vanish, leaving Balaam with only two servants as companions. Then they disappear, leaving poor Balaam all alone with only his donkey

---

28. Hebrew *hadabar*, a term with two distinct meanings: *thing* and *word*. So with equal accuracy we could render this phrase as *the word that I say to you*... Native Hebrew speakers (the ancient Israelites, the original audience of this tale) would hear both the meanings simultaneously and understand what follows accordingly.

for company. And if this is not enough, Balaam is on the wrong road. He set out for Moab to meet with King Balak, a route that traverses the desert, but the road on which he finds himself is passing through rich farmland and grape-laden vineyards. Where is he? And now things go from bad to worse: a new character enters the plot, a killer Angel flourishing a sword, and his target is none other than poor Balaam! We have fallen into a nightmare.

For several thousand years people have been struggling with little success to make sense of this weird saga of Balaam as he tries to wend his way to Moab.[29] In my estimation, so much effort with so little to show for it indicates that some of our basic assumptions may be wrong: we have been asking the wrong questions. The general lines of approach have been theological, source-critical or folkloristic. None having resulted in what I would consider acceptable results, I propose that we abandon them. For myself, I intend to approach this section as a purely literary problem.

What we should find most disturbing about this section of our tale is that it violates one of the cardinal rules of biblical narrative prose: we might term this the rule of naturalistic presentation.[30] This is the norm, but Balaam's journey to Moab is not the only exception to this rule; there are close to a dozen other surrealist episodes in the Bible. For instance, there is this account, as related by Pharaoh, King of Egypt:

"And behold, I was standing on the banks of the Nile. And behold, up out of the Nile came seven cows, fat-fleshed and with beautiful bodies, and they grazed upon the reed beds. And behold, seven other cows came up after them, scrawny, extremely ill-favored and emaciated, such as I have never seen so bad in all Egypt. And the emaciated and ill-favored cows ate up the first seven cows! And when they had been taken into their stomachs,[31] you could not tell [from their appearance] that they had been taken into their stomachs; their appearance was just as bad as at the start" [Genesis 41:17–21].

Or these accounts related to his family by the young Joseph:

"Behold, we were binding sheaves in the field, and behold, my sheaf arose and stood upright, and behold, your sheaves gathered round and bowed low to my sheaf.... And behold, the sun and the moon and eleven stars were bowing low to me!" [Genesis 37:7, 9]

Or again, in this account related by a Midianite warrior to one of his comrades:

---

29. We will make no attempt to catalog the various "solutions" and "explanations" that have been proposed, none of which have gained much of a following. In modern times, beyond a general consensus that the tale of the donkey is probably a foreign element artificially intruded into the Balaam narrative (and that if removed its loss is hardly felt), it appears that no one can convincingly explain what it is doing in our narrative or why it should have been "intruded" in the first place. The reasons proposed—to liven up the tale, to mock Balaam (David Marcus claims that "this story constitutes the first example of anti-prophetic satire in the Hebrew Bible" whose purpose is "to belittle Balaam and expose him to ridicule" (*Balaam to Jonah*, pp. 31, 41), while Meir Sternberg terms this episode a "hatchet-job" (*Poetics*, p. 94)), or simply because the "folk tale" existed and an editor felt that it shouldn't be left out—are surprisingly weak. None of these suggestions really explains very much.

30. Unlike fabulous literature, such as that of Aesop, the Bible does not abound in talking animals; Balaam's donkey is unique. Sternberg points out that this section's "very incongruous effect derives from a violation of the Bible's rule of naturalism." (*Ibid.*, p.174)

31. Literally, *into their midst*.

> "*Behold ... a [giant] round of barley bread*[32] *tumbled into the camp of Midian; it reached the [Headquarters] Tent and struck it, and it fell and turned upside down, [while] the [Headquarters] Tent collapsed!*" [*Judges* 7:13].

All these episodes, as well as others of their ilk, are presented as accounts of dreams. In this context, as a dream sequence, our doings would seem far more in place than as a description of a waking episode. We have spoken metaphorically of Balaam's journey as a scene out of a nightmare. Perhaps instead of a metaphor that is exactly what we are dealing with: the description of a nightmare and not a portrayal of actual events.[33]

Understanding *Numbers* 22:21–35 as the report of a dream makes sense within the context of the narrative. We have just been informed that on the night of the arrival of the Moabite delegation, in a dream, God gave Balaam conditional permission to accompany the emissaries to Moab (22:20). This permission is the operative essence—the bottom line as it were—of the dream. Now, I would contend, the narrator backtracks and gives us a detailed description of the dream as a whole, and what led up to God's shocking reversal of his previous prohibition.[34]

In support of this suggestion that the coming account of Balaam's journey with his donkey is not a chronological continuation of the account that we have been following but rather a flashback—giving a detailed description of Balaam's dream following the arrival of the new delegation from Moab—is the fact that our author saw fit to enclose this chronicle of bizarre happenings in brackets. The account opens with the phrase:

> *So Balaam rose in the morning and saddled his donkey, and went with the Moabite officials* [22:21]

and closes with an abbreviated repetition of this key phrase

> *So Balaam went with the officials of Balak* [22:35b]

the two phrases acting as brackets and serving to signal the reader to remove the bracketed account from the natural sequence of events; i.e., not to read it historically but to understand it as an account of a dream.[35]

---

32. Bread made from barley was poor farmer's food, coarse-ground and unrefined. It was baked in thick round loaves. The warrior is recounting the paralyzing sight of a giant round of barley bread, rolling on its side down the mountain, smashing into the Midianite camp and crushing the Headquarters of the Midianite army.

33. I am not the first by any means to have come to this conclusion. Moses Maimonides proposed this understanding over 800 years ago; for that matter so, more recently, did Isaac Abravanel. (See Glossary)

34. This procedure of giving a brief synopsis highlighting the main point or the moral of an episode—especially a dream—and then turning back and going over the episode in detail is hardly an unknown phenomenon in the Bible. Abram's mystic dream, "the covenant between the pieces," begins with a statement of the entire point of the vision: "*I am the Lord Who brought you out from Ur of the Chaldees to give you this land as a possession.*" (*Genesis* 15:7) Then the text goes into detail: the preparation for the vision, Abram falling into a trance, the full contents of the dream and, at its conclusion, the full promise which *Genesis* 15:7 briefly summarized (*Genesis* 15:8–21). Another example is the episode of Jacob, after twenty years in Paddan-aram, where we are given the basic message (*Genesis* 31:3) "*Return to the land of your fathers, the land of your birth, and I will be with you.*" Then the text backtracks and details the dream of which this was the bottom line (*Genesis* 31:10–13).

35. We have previously encountered this biblical literary device of the use of brackets to set off a segment of narrative from the surrounding text, so as to delineate it as a discrete unit to be understood in its own terms, most recently in *Jonah*, Chapter 4. The Main Body of the chapter (4:4–8) is set apart from the Introduction and the Epilogue by being bracketed by God's rhetorical question, "*Is it good that you are so furious?*" (4:4) and its repetition (4:9a). See Chapter 4, note 15.

But if the coming section is a description of the dream that Balaam dreamt the night after receiving Balak's revised proposal, then we must read it as dreams have to be read, i.e., symbolically. Of course we will have to interpret the dream using the interpretive tools of the Ancient Near East, the way dream symbolism was understood by the author and by his original audience.[36] Taking this approach, let us see what sense we can make of the outré happenings in what is to come.

The Dream of Balaam

So Balaam rose in the morning and saddled his donkey, and went with the Moabite officials. Now God[37] *was furious that he was going with them, and a messenger*[38] *of the* LORD *stationed himself in the road to oppose him.*[39] *He was riding on his donkey and his two servants were with him* [22:21–22].

In these two verses lies the crux of a problem that has perplexed commentators for centuries: If God just gave permission for Balaam to go with the delegation, then why is He furious when Balaam avails himself of this permission? But the readers baffled by this section, laymen and scholars alike, have been taking these lines as a depiction of actual events. If we read them as a description of a dream the question vanishes. We have been informed that God, in a dream, gave Balaam permission to go (22:20). We are now in the dream itself, but no permission has as yet been given (it will only come at the very end of the dream). In the dream's opening, Balaam, although he knows perfectly well that God has forbidden him to go, gets up, saddles his donkey, and leaves for Moab with the delegation. Is it any wonder that God is furious with him?

Let us get the timing of the events clearly in mind. The delegation arrives in Pethor and presents Balaam with Balak's new and radically revised proposal. Balaam makes his ringing declaration of principle, tells the emissaries that he once again will take up the matter with God that very night, and promises them his answer on the morrow. He then goes to bed, and in the night a dream does come. In the dream it is morning; he is saddling his donkey and departing with the delegation, all this despite God having forbidden him to do so. Despite his declaration that he always obeys God's commands, in his dream he is openly flouting His orders. Naturally God is infuriated by this insolent disobedience. So He sends a messenger, an angel with a sword, to confront His rebellious servant who is accompanying the large caravan of mounted Moabite high officials on the way back to Moab.[40] And unexpectedly

---

36. Dream interpretation was a highly skilled profession in the Ancient Near East, one in much demand. Joseph's remarkable proficiency in unlocking the symbolism of dreams was the key to his spectacular rise from foreign slave to the position of Viceroy of Egypt.

37. Sam. reads Lord in place of God, as do some mss. of MT and LXX.

38. Hebrew *malach*; often rendered in English as "angel." The word "angel" is the English form of "angelos"—the Greek word meaning "messenger"—the term the Greek translators of the Septuagint (LXX) used to translate the Hebrew *malach*. A "messenger" (angel) can be human (a prophet, a "man of God", as in *Judges* 2:1), a supernatural being (cf. *Judges* 6:21–23) or, as probably in our case, a manifestation of God Himself.

39. Or, *as an adversary to him*, i.e., with hostile intent.

40. In those days horses were not used for riding, only for pulling chariots. Kings and princes ("royals" in modern parlance) rode in chariots. Important personages, and people sufficiently well-off to be able to afford them, rode donkeys. Everyone else walked. Balaam, as a very important person and sufficiently well-heeled to be able to afford a donkey and its upkeep, was among the riders in the procession, and not among the riffraff who walked in their dust.

the dream, as dreams sometimes do, begins to turn nightmarish. The procession—the high officials in their splendidly embroidered robes, their colorfully caparisoned mounts, their swarms of servants trailing along in their wake—all of a sudden vanishes. Balaam finds himself alone on an empty road with two servants straggling along on foot after him. Then, as we noted, the servants likewise vanish leaving Balaam alone with only his donkey for company. And awaiting him just down the road, although he cannot see him, awaits the LORD's messenger full of menace. But remarkably, the donkey has no difficulty perceiving what stands in their way.

> *Now the donkey saw the messenger of the* LORD *stationed in the road, and his naked sword*[41] *in his hand, and the donkey swerved from the road and went into the field. And Balaam beat the donkey to turn her back to the road* [22:23].

The donkey—seeing things as they are, and sensible creature that she is—in order to avoid that menacing figure blocking the road turns off into the neighboring field. And this is very strange, for they are supposed to be on the road to Moab, and there should be desert on either side of them and not cultivated fields. Balaam, seeing only empty road before him, can't understand why his donkey has strayed off the road. Commands and pulling on the reins having no effect, he begins to beat his mount (probably with his rider's crop) to try to get her back on the road. The donkey, having by this time made a wide detour around that fearsome figure, allows herself to be directed back to the road by her angry master. But they are not yet through with the angel.[42] Not committed to one spot, he simply repositions himself down the road at a place where walled-in vineyards will prevent the donkey from repeating its maneuver.

> *So the messenger of the* LORD *stood in a sunken lane*[43] *between the vineyards, with a stone wall on either side.*[44] *Now the donkey saw the messenger of the* LORD, *and she pressed herself against the wall and crushed Balaam's foot against the wall, so he beat her again* [22:24–25].

To Balaam the road remains open and unobstructed, but the donkey is fully aware of what lies in wait for them. So veering onto the shoulder and pressing herself against the wall, she manages to get around the ominous figure at the price of crushing and scraping Balaam's foot against a stone wall. Balaam reacts with rage, beating her vehemently.

Balaam is being beset by a rising crescendo of events designed to frustrate his aims: three times his donkey will refuse to go the way he wishes, each subsequent time in a more annoying manner; she wanders off the road, she crushes his leg against the rough stone wall, she will lie down and refuse to move. This is caused by the angel three times blocking the road, each time in a more inaccessible spot. Even the text

---

41. Literally, *his drawn sword*.

42. For "angel" see note 38 above.

43. A *hapex* (see Glossary). The term seems to be derived from the word for the hollow of the hand, hence a hollowed or sunken lane.

44. "Curiouser and curiouser"; instead of desert on either side of him, the cultivated fields give way to walled vineyards. Balaam, however, seems oblivious to the fact that he must be on the wrong road.

reflects this rising crescendo: each time the angel sets up a roadblock the incident is related in the Hebrew in a greater number of words: the first time in 6 words, the second in 9 and the third time in 13 words. The cool and self-possessed Balaam is being driven into a frenzy, and finally loses all control over himself.

> *And the messenger of the* LORD *went ahead and stood in a narrow place where there was no room to swerve either to the right or to the left. Now the donkey saw the messenger of the* LORD, *and she lay down under Balaam; so Balaam was furious*[45] *and he beat the donkey with* [his] *staff* [22:26–27].

Having been left no options, the donkey simply lies down in the road and refuses to advance. Seeing nothing, understanding nothing, for the third time thwarted by the outrageous behavior of his mount, Balaam is driven into a fury. Abandoning his riding crop he seizes his staff and begins to belabor the donkey like a madman. And then, suddenly, everything shifts. Like a kaleidoscope that has been turned, the pieces that make up our drama abruptly assume a new configuration: the donkey suddenly breaks into speech and rebukes Balaam for his beastly behavior.

> *Now the* LORD *opened the mouth of the donkey,*[46] *and she said to Balaam, "What have I done to you that you have beaten me these three times?" And Balaam said to the donkey, "Because you have been playing with me*[47]; *would that I had a sword in my hand for then I would kill you"* [22:28–29].

While we tend to focus on the talking donkey, what is truly revealing about this episode is the reaction of our protagonist. An animal opening its mouth and speaking would have been greeted with as much shock three thousand years ago as it would be today, and that the incident is related in the Bible in no way mitigates this fact. As we have mentioned, the Bible has no convention of talking animals; Balaam's donkey is unique in Scripture.[48] Nor is it a violation of the Bible's rule of naturalistic narrative, being—as I contend—not a report of an actual occurrence but of an episode in a dream. As is normal in dreams, the unusual and bizarre creates neither shock nor alarm. Far from exhibiting surprise, without hesitation Balaam enters into a conversation with his donkey "as though he was accustomed to having daily domestic wrangles with his asses."[49] The donkey reasonably asks her tormentor what she has done to deserve three beatings.[50] Balaam replies that she has been playing with him, and

---

45. Literally, *his anger was kindled*, the same idiom used of God in 22:22 above (also there rendered as "furious"). First Balaam rouses God's anger by his actions, now the donkey in turn rouses Balaam's anger by her actions.

46. This is a phrase used in the Bible to describe the inspiration of a prophet (cf. *Ezekiel* 3:27, 33:22); the implication is that of the two, it is the donkey that is the prophet, having vision of spiritual things (i.e., the presence of the angel) to which Balaam is blind.

47. In the sense of capriciously making fun of me.

48. The only other case of a "speaking animal" in the Bible is the serpent in the Garden of Eden (*Genesis* 3). But I believe that Leon Kass is correct when he proposes "an allegorical reading of the serpent: an embodiment of the separated and beguiling voice of autonomous human reason speaking up against innocence and obedience, coming to us as from some attractive source outside us that whispers doubt into our ear." (*The Beginning of Wisdom*, p. 82)

49. R. Alter, *Art of Biblical Narrative*, p. 106.

50. Note the emphasis on the number three; more on this in Chapter 8.

in the process making a fool of him. It is this humiliation that so infuriates him. "You complain about getting beaten? Be thankful I only have this staff in my hand. Had I a sword, in place of beating you I would have killed you!" Instead of being angered by this display of rage the donkey, the very voice of calm reason, replies, "You have been riding on me for years. Have I ever acted this way before?" This question pulls Balaam up short. He has no choice but to admit that her behavior is unprecedented.

Suddenly, once again the kaleidoscope turns and the pieces of our dream-drama fall into a new pattern. As the donkey was granted power of speech in the last iteration, so now Balaam's eyes are empowered, and with vision unimpaired he now can see what has been standing in what to him had seemed an open road. He now grasps what has been the cause of the outlandish behavior of his donkey.

> *And the donkey said to Balaam, "Am I not your donkey upon whom you have been riding all your lifelong to this day? Have I been in the habit of doing this to you?" And he said, "No." Now the* LORD *unveiled the eyes of Balaam and he saw the messenger of the* LORD *stationed in the road with his naked sword in his hand*[51]*; and he bowed and fell on his face. And the messenger of the* LORD *said to him, "Why have you beaten your donkey these three times? Behold, I went forth to oppose you,*[52] *for your road*[53] *is twisted*[54] *before me. The donkey saw me and swerved away from me these three times. Had she not swerved away from me, surely now it is you I would have killed while her I would have let live"* [22:30–33]

At this sudden appearance, realizing on the instant what it is that is confronting him, Balaam throws himself facedown on the ground in deep obeisance. One thing that can be said for Balaam: he knows a manifestation of God when he sees it. The messenger now takes over the conversation from the donkey. Rebuking Balaam for his threefold unwarranted abuse of his inoffensive creature—three times her prompt action has saved Balaam's life while she herself was never at any risk of harm—the angel now makes clear exactly what his attitude to Balaam is, and why. His stance is hostile, and the reason is that the road that Balaam has chosen to take is unacceptable: he is going the wrong way. But far more is being implied than that God doesn't want Balaam to go to Moab. This we already know. It is Balaam's motives in choosing to take this road that are being called into question. The life-path that Balaam has chosen is twisted and devious in the eyes of God.[55] The unsheathed sword in the hand of the messenger is a warning to Balaam to straighten himself out or else. Balaam is being put on notice.

At this point we begin to get to the heart of our drama: the question of what is driving Balaam to act as he does. The world did not have to wait for Sigmund Freud to

---

51. See note 41 above.

52. See note 39 above.

53. Reading *darkecha, your road* with LXX, Vulg. and Sam., i.e., your purpose, your destination. MT reads *the road*.

54. I.e., devious, aberrant. The Hebrew *yarat* is again a *hapex* (see Glossary). We have rendered the word in accord with the suggestion of Ibn Ezra, Ramban and Abravanel.

55. Either the angel is speaking in the name of God or—in my opinion more likely—the dream-apparition in the road is a manifestation of God Himself. If so, then the word *me* should be capitalized, thus: *for your road is twisted before Me.*

realize that what ever else may be signified by dreams,[56] they also often reveal something about the inner life of the dreamer; his hopes, his fears, his deep-set desires. The ancients were perfectly aware of this fact and so, if this sequence is indeed Balaam's dream, we can reasonably expect to get some insight from it as to what lies behind his behavior. Let us begin to briefly explore this avenue.

We have already noticed signs of dissonance between Balaam's pronouncements on the one hand and his behavior on the other. He insists, and will continue to insist with ever-increasing vigor, that he can only do or say what the LORD his God will allow him to do or say. He will not and cannot violate the command of his God. Yet there seem to be signs that he doesn't necessarily always mean what he seems to be saying. His contemporaries don't seem to take his "no" seriously, and we ourselves have noted indications that he appears at times to be waffling. And here in this dream—if it is a dream—we get our first clear instance of a blatant contradiction between Balaam's public stance and his acts.

We have been told on unimpeachable authority[57] that God expressly forbade Balaam to go with the Moabite emissaries, and this is what Balaam reported to them. But despite God's prohibition, and despite the Balaam's public declaration that he cannot in any way violate the word of the LORD his God (22:18), here we find him dreaming of doing just that: getting up in the morning, saddling his donkey and setting out for Moab in their company while knowing that what he is doing is forbidden. What the dream seems to be revealing is that there is a fundamental conflict between Balaam's principles (public and probably private as well) and his innermost desires.

But why? Can the answer be greed? Can the lure of that blank check be overpowering Balaam's scruples as well as his fear of divine retribution should he flaunt God's command? Up to this point this looks like the most probable cause, and if so then our drama will revolve about the inner struggle in Balaam's soul between his higher calling as a seer or prophet,[58] and crass materialism; his irrepressible longing for undreamed of wealth. But perhaps this facile interpretation is too simplistic, underestimating the complexity of Balaam's character. We are still too early in our account to be able to draw definitive conclusions. The question will have to remain open until we have more information to work with. We return to our tale.

We remember that Balaam, upon becoming aware of the messenger of the LORD confronting him, had thrown himself down on the ground in an attitude of worship.

---

56. The ancients believed that in addition to being conduits for messages from the realm of the divine (i.e., the gods), dreams often contain, in an encoded form, predictions of future events. This is true in our case as well: the recurring reiteration of triads—groups of 3 events, such as the angel setting up 3 roadblocks, Balaam administering 3 beatings to his donkey, etc.—foreshadows what awaits Balaam in Moab, which will also occur in groups of 3. This point will be elaborated in the next chapter.

57. We are told this by the narrator (22:12), and by biblical narrative convention the narrator is absolutely trustworthy.

58. On a superficial level these two terms are synonyms, the former term (seer) in the process of being replaced in common usage by the latter (prophet): *Formerly in Israel, when a man went to inquire of God he would say, "Let us go to the seer (haroeh)," for he that is now called a prophet (nabi) was formally called a seer.* (1 Samuel 9:9) But actually, as we shall become aware, this shift in terminology marks a profound shift in meaning. Suffice it to say that for the present the term "seer" is Balaam's proper title, and it is with this term that the text is and will continue to be playing.

While being addressed by the angel he has been lying, facedown in the dust of the road beside his donkey. Now, while still prone, he raises his head to reply.

> *And Balaam said to the messenger of the* LORD, *"I have sinned,*[59] *for I did not know that you were stationed in the road to oppose me. And now, if it is evil in your eyes, I will go back"* [22:34].

This is disingenuous. To begin with, Balaam is trying to make light of his actions, claiming that his error lay in the fact that he couldn't see the angel and therefore didn't know that he was there. This would be analogous to an employee, caught on camera helping himself from the cash drawer, trying to excuse himself by saying that he didn't know that the security system was on. Balaam's act was not *het* (sin) but *avon* (iniquity): consciously committing an act which he knew from the start to be wrong.[60] Who does he think he is kidding? Then he tops this "confession" with the offer that *if* God doesn't like what he is doing he is willing to turn back. What does he mean by *"if"*? He knows perfectly well that there is no "if." God commanded him not to go and he went. This is nothing other than an attempted plea bargain: confessing to a lesser crime and then agreeing to give back what he had been caught taking. And this is a trusted servant of the LORD! What is God to do with such as he?

God doesn't react to his attempted evasions, or reprove him for flouting His command. There is a sense of weary resignation in His response to his "faithful servant."

> *And the messenger of the* LORD *said to Balaam, "Go with the men. However, only the word that I shall speak to you, that shall you speak"* [22:35a].

God has countermanded his prohibition. Why? In those cases where we are not specifically told, it is at best a risky proposition to try to pin down the reasons for God's actions. What it comes down to is that our only option is to try to put ourselves into God's shoes and, knowing what we do, try to assess how we would act. But we are a poor fit to take God's place—our feet are too small and our knowledge far too paltry—and as such our estimates are bound to be badly off. But as the text at this point virtually begs us to make a guess as to God's motive in reversing himself, while keeping our caveat in mind, we will make a stab at guessing the reasons for God's perplexing action.

We begin by noting that of the two prohibitions that God laid upon Balaam, the second and by far the more serious—that Balaam is forbidden to curse this people that has come out of Egypt—remains uncompromised. Indeed, it is this that the whole issue is all about; it is this that Balak wants Balaam to do for him, and the matter of going with the delegation to Moab is strictly secondary. The only reason that I can see for God's prohibiting Balaam from going with the emissaries might possibly be God's wish to shield His servant from getting involved with Balak in the first place. But Balaam proves to be incorrigible; he longs to get involved. Moab will prove to be

---

59. Hebrew *ḥatati*, that is, I committed a *ḥet*, an infraction committed by mistake, or an act not known to be wrong.

60. See Chapter 5, note 14 for a listing of the various terms used for wrongdoing in the Hebrew Bible, along with their specific meanings.

a quagmire, and in his heart of hearts Balaam knows this. He is enmeshing himself in a mission impossible: he is accepting a contract to curse a people who are uncurseable because they are already blessed, and he knows this. By nevertheless going, Balaam will be setting himself up for failure and a nasty debacle. As I see it, this is something that God would wish to spare his servant, but Balaam simply cannot see it. So God gives in: "All right, if that is what you have set your heart on, go ahead and learn the hard way." God is simply giving Balaam a large length of rope.

The permission that Balaam has wrung from God is limited and conditional. He can go to Moab, but he pays for this concession with his liberty. He will be kept on a tight leash. He will lose the freedom to say what he deems appropriate; he will be able to utter only those words that God will put in his mouth. In a word, Balaam will be reduced to acting in the role of a ventriloquist's dummy; it is God, the Ventriloquist, Who will be speaking through his mouth.

And with this pronouncement the dream ends, Balaam awakes and finds himself still in Pethor.

If this conditional permission is the best Balaam can manage to promote, does he still want to go to Moab, for it is under this mandate he will henceforth have to function? Balaam, undoubtedly elated at having gotten the absolute prohibition canceled, and perhaps speculating that if he was able to get the LORD to go along with him thus far he may possibly be able to wrangle a bit more, decides to take advantage of what he sees as his new freedom of action. He will go to Moab and reap the benefit of whatever opportunities lie open there for his exploitation.

So Balaam went with the officials of Balak. (22:35b)[61]

---

61. This is the closing bracket that terminates the dream flashback. With Chapter 8 the chronological narrative resumes.

Chapter 8

The Mouthpiece

God is not a man that He should be capricious,
Nor mortal, that He should change His mind....
Now let it be said of Jacob,
And of Israel: "What hath God wrought!"
—Numbers 23:19, 23

An Acrimonious Arrival

Up to this point, both in narrative report of Balaam's words and actions, as well as in the account of his dream, we have been seeing matters from Balaam's point of view. Now, for the first time, we are to be treated to a change of perspective: we will be given a glimpse of how things look through King Balak's eyes.[1]

Now Balak heard that Balaam was coming, and he went out to meet him at Ir-moab, which is on the Arnon border,[2] at the furthest point of the border.[3] And Balak said to Balaam, "Did I not send for you honorably[4] to summon you [the first time]? Am I not able to honor[5] you?" [22:36–37]

After going all the way to the border to be the first to welcome him to the kingdom, Balak then spoils the effect of his gesture by his surly opening remarks, chiding Balaam for not coming at once when summoned. "What's the matter? Weren't the emissaries sufficiently high up on the pecking order for you? Did you think that I couldn't (or wouldn't) meet your high expectations for remuneration? Why didn't you come immediately?" It seems that the time factor has been pressing on Balak; the fear that with all this back and forth Israel might make its move before Balaam would arrive to stop it. Balak's actions and his speech are in blatant contrast with each other. They seem to mirror a fundamental ambivalence in his attitude. On the one hand he is enormously exhilarated, not to mention relieved, that Balaam has consented to come and curse Israel for him. On the other hand, now that Balaam's arrival has

---

1. It is true that in 22:1–6 we are introduced to the panic that leads to the decision to summon Balaam, but beyond the office that he holds and the terror that grips him, Balak remains largely an enigma. It is only at this point that we will begin to get to know the third central protagonist of our tale.
2. See Appendix C, note 2.
3. I.e., at its northernmost point where Balak would first cross into Moabite territory; a singular honor to be greeted at this point by the king in person.
4. Balak uses the infinitive absolute construction to signify the high level of the first delegation. I.e., were they not good enough for you?
5. See Chapter 7, note 23; "honor" in this context having the meaning of "adequately compensate."

put to rest the fear that he might refuse or come too late, perhaps the thought of that blank check he offered, and what it will cost him to honor it when it becomes due, is beginning to temper his euphoria. Can the kingdom really afford such extravagance? Is this Balaam using the present crisis to extort obscenely exorbitant sums, more than his services are reasonably worth? Or, if it is not the anticipated damage to his pocketbook, then it may be that Balak takes Balaam's refusal to jump when summoned as a personal insult. Something has soured Balak's mood and turned his words of greeting into a rebuke. Or is he simply trying to intimidate Balaam, and thus assert his dominance over their relationship?

Balaam's reply is instructive. He rebuffs Balak's rebuke with a curt "I am here now," in effect refusing to give any consideration to his remarks. Then, with equal bluntness, he lays down the law with regard to the terms of his employment: phrased as a rhetorical question, he makes it clear that his allegiance is owed solely to God,[6] and that it is He, and not Balak, Who dictates what Balaam can and will say. It is to God's summons that he jumps; the king, he implies, should be grateful that he, Balaam, has consented to grace Moab with his presence. If Balak has any response to this put down, he keeps it to himself. His attempt, if it was one, to assert an ascendancy over Balaam has fallen flat.

And Balaam said to Balak, "Behold, I have come to you now. Can I speak a single thing [of my own free will]? The word that God will put in my mouth, that will I speak" [22:38].

This statement of commitment to his God is powerful, but uncalled for in the present circumstances. What has prompted Balaam to lay down the law in this definitive manner? Is it simply that Balak's reproach has gotten his back up, and he feels that he needs to put the king in his place? But then again it may not be a question of momentary pique but deeper reasons; it could be that on the journey from his home to Moab he has had the time to reassess his situation. Let us diverge of bit from our direct story line to explore this alternative.

As we have noted, considered objectively, Balaam's decision to accept Balak's summons to come to Moab has placed him in an impossible position. He has accepted a commission to curse a given people, but is forbidden by God to do so. His revelatory dream has sharpened matters even beyond this: not only is he forbidden to curse, under the conditions of his permission to go to Moab—a sort of parole— he now *cannot*. He will now be able to speak only the words scripted for him by God. Worse: Balaam has understood the full significance of the sword in the hand of the messenger of the LORD in his dream; the penalty of cursing is death!

We repeat, in the Ancient World dreams were conceived as revelatory, but their meaning was cloaked in symbolism.[7] Balaam was, first and foremost, a *roeh*, a seer—

---

6. This is strange. Balaam, when speaking, has exclusively referred to God by His proper name, the Lord (22:8, 13, 18 and 19); see Chapter 7, note 22. This is the first time he has referred to Him using the generic term *elohim*, God. Perhaps because *elohim* is grammatically in the plural, and thus can be understood as "the gods," Balaam uses this term, rather than the name of a deity of Whom Balak has probably never heard, to make certain that his point gets across: he owes his allegiance to no man but exclusively to the realm of the divine.

7. See Chapter 7, note 56.

one who possesses the ability to see through appearances into the realms of reality and spirituality—one who sees into the true nature of things past, present and future.[8] He was also by reputation a *kosem* and a *hoze*, a diviner and a clairvoyant[9]— an expert in interpreting signs and unraveling the symbolism of dreams—having gained international renown for his successes in these arcane arts. He has understood the significance of the sword, and now knows better than to even think of cursing if he values his skin. But what has he made of the rest of his dream?

Given the time at his disposal while on the way to Moab to ponder deeply this seminal experience, I think we can be confident that he grasped what scores of later biblical commentators have been able to gather; first and foremost, that in the dream Balaam and his donkey have exchanged roles. In the dream he, the seer, is blind while it is the dumb donkey that sees the messenger of the LORD. It is the donkey who is intelligent while it is he who is stupid. It is the donkey who acts sensibly, avoiding danger while it is he who acts irrationally, wanting to head into peril, flying off the handle, beating the beast that is saving him and generally acting in an asinine manner. In sum, it is the donkey that fills the role of seer, while it is he who is the ass. By the time Balaam arrives in Moab I believe he has grasped the personal significance of the dream: in going to Moab he will be assuming the role of the donkey. Just as in the dream the donkey was caught in an impossible situation, trapped between the naked sword in the hand of the Apparition in the road and the stick in the hand of Balaam beating her mercilessly, so now will he be trapped in Moab between the demands of Balak to curse and the inability to do so imposed by God.

I do not think that Balaam was aware of any of this when he first awoke from his dream. At that point in time all he gathered from the dream was its bottom line: that he was free (subject to some minor conditions) to go to Moab. And on this understanding he agreed to accept the commission. But now, having had time to consider, he realizes that he has maneuvered himself into a no-win situation. However, by this time things have gone too far; he no longer has any way of backing out. So beyond establishing the ground rules for what is to come, is Balaam in his opening declaration to Balak also laying the foundations of his excuse for what he now realizes will be inevitable failure: I warned you that I could only speak the words that God (or the gods as the case may be) will put in my mouth; I have had no choice in this matter?

Since we have begun to examine the dream of Balaam, let us take the analysis a step further. We have said that in those days people believed that dreams contained encoded forecasts of future events.[10] The very literary format of the dream, as it was related in the previous chapter, is constructed in such a way as to reflect this contention. The dream is organized in a triadic structure, that is, in groups of three: three confrontations with an angel, three attempts at evasion by the donkey, three

---

8. See Chapter 7, note 58.
9. See Chapter 7, notes 10 and 11.
10. For example, Pharaoh's dreams of seven scrawny cannibal cows devouring seven fat and sleek cows, and seven wind-blasted ears of grain swallowing up seven solid and full ears of grain—as decoded by Joseph—contain an agricultural forecast: seven years of bumper crops to be followed by seven years of crop failure (*Genesis* 41:1–4, 25–32). Or again, the dream of the Midianite warrior of a giant round of barley bread rolling down Mount Gilboa, smashing into their camp and flattening the Midianite headquarters—as deciphered by his companion—being a forecast of Gideon's impending victory over the Midianite horde. (*Judges* 7:13–14)

beatings administered by Balaam, etc. All these prefigure what will happen to Balaam in Moab.[11] Getting a bit ahead of ourselves, we will see Balaam maneuvered into three confrontations with Israel which will result in three oracles. Three times Balaam will fail to deliver the curses demanded of him and will get a verbal beating from Balak, and so on. It is extremely doubtful that Balaam grasped to what degree his dream was foreshadowing what would happen to him should he decide to implement the opportunity offered and go to Moab.

This symmetry between the events in the dream sequence and those that subsequently take place in Moab argues against the general opinion that the donkey tale was not part of the original Balaam narrative, but rather a foreign element intruded into it. It argues rather that a single author wrote both the dream sequence with the donkey and the account of Balaam in Moab, specifically crafting the events in the dream to foreshadow what will happen to Balaam in Moab. This symmetry is too specific to be the product of coincidence.

The degree of symmetry—the literary construct of the author of our tale—can only be understood in retrospect; its value for us lies in its embodiment of the beliefs of that age. These details are simply refinements of the central meaning of the dream—that God didn't want Balaam to go to Moab, that his wanting to go was rebellion against God, that his motivations were under deep scrutiny, and that not only was cursing the people in question forbidden but would indeed be impossible—and the overall import of the dream was fully appreciated by Balaam. The point is that, nevertheless, he made the decision to go. From that decision all that was to come followed.

The Fiasco

The initial meeting between Balaam and Balak has descended into an animosity-filled confrontation, barely kept within the bonds of civility. Having reached a standoff, Balak decides not to prolong a meaningless argument, but rather to get on with the business at hand. He escorts Balaam from the border to a town abutting the proposed theater of operations. It is from nearby that Balak proposes to launch his first strike against Israel, and it is here that he has prepared a lavish welcoming banquet in honor of Balaam, a grand gesture perhaps intended to smooth ruffled feathers. Balak may be having second thoughts about the effects of his acrimonious greeting of his honored guest; he wants him in a positive mood for what is to come. But at one and the same time the feast is also a religious ceremony to propitiate the gods, and so intended to prepare the ground for Balaam's impending action against Israel.[12] So here, along with the high Moabite officials that accompanied him from Pethor joined with Balak's retinue, Balaam wines, dines and gorges himself with no thought for the morrow.

---

11. In 22:28, in the donkey's remonstrance with Balaam, the author made a point of calling our attention to these three times, for the number will be important in the second half of the story. (Alter, p. 106)

12. In the Ancient Near East most instances of meat consumption took place in the context of a *zebah* offering (see note 14 below); thus lavish feasting and religious ritual were almost indissolubly associated.

So Balaam went with Balak, and they came to Kiriath-ḥuzoth.[13] *And Balak sacrificed*[14] *cattle and sheep, and had them served to Balaam and to his officials that were with him* [22:39–40].

Balaam undoubtedly expects some time after his exhausting journey—several days at the very least—to pull himself together, come up to speed and make his esoteric preparations for the ceremony that is expected of him. But Balak has other ideas. Too much time has already been lost. Who knows what the Israelites are planning? Any further delay in cursing them may prove fatal. So the incipient panic that has been driving Balak leads to a surprise for his guest. Comes the dawn and Balaam finds himself shaken awake and hurried out to get on with the business for which he was summoned. No further delay will be allowed.

And behold,[15] *in the morning Balak took Balaam and brought him up to Bamoth-baal,*[16] *and from there he could see the tail end*[17] *of the people* [22:41].

The term *Bamah* is often rendered in English as "High Place" because *bamot* (the plural of *bamah*) were universally located on high points—hilltops, mountain ridges, promontories—where one was more likely to make contact with the gods. This was a sacred precinct, in modern terms a source of power that Balaam could draw upon to energize his curse. Equally relevant, it was ideal as an observation point where Balaam could establish visual contact with the object that was to be cursed: a prerequisite deemed essential for a curse to be effective.[18] Balak has done what he can; he has positioned Balaam in an ideal spot to launch a curse. Now it is up to him.

Balaam, suffering from travel fatigue, over-eating and probably a hangover, rises to the occasion and takes charge. He issues terse instructions: build seven altars and prepare seven bulls and seven rams for sacrifice.[19] Balak gives orders to his entourage; the altars soon rise, wood is piled upon them, the animals are slaughtered and a bull and a ram are placed on each altar for incineration. None of this is surprising; Balak

---

13. Literally, "town of streets," or "town of markets," possibly the reference is to Kiriathaim, a town northwest of Dibon.

14. The word rendered as "sacrificed" is not *vayakrib*, the term conveying the entire range of sacrifices, but *vayizbaḥ*, a word derived from the name of a specific type of sacrifice, the *zebaḥ*, in which the meat of the slaughtered animals is consumed by the celebrants in a communion meal along with their gods. See Glossary for *Zebaḥ*.

15. The Hebrew *vayehee* is, among other things, an expression of surprise, seemingly uncalled for unless it is intended to indicate that Balaam was not expecting to be rushed into action.

16. Literally, *the High Places of Baal*, apparently the site of a cluster of shrines dedicated to the service of Baal, one of the chief deities of Canaan. (LXX reads in the singular, *the High Place of Baal*). It possibly is the same location as the *Bamoth* of 21:19.

17. Literally, *the end*. "Hebrew qaseh [*ketzai*] in geographical descriptions, seems to refer to the nearest contact point, as seen by the eye of the beholder" (Levine, *Numbers 21–36*—hereafter simply Levine—p. 160); thus, the nearest part of the people but not the whole people.

18. Cursing was universally regarded in the Ancient Near East as part and parcel of the practice of magic, and thus was highly ritualized. "The practitioner of magic is regarded as controlling a ritual key to a super-human power source…. This magical ritual activity could not affect distant human enemies through natural cause-and-effect, but it was viewed as producing results through some kind of supernatural energy guided to its target" (R. Gane, *Leviticus-Numbers*, pp. 703–704); thus the need for eye contact with the object of the curse.

19. The altars are simple platforms built of stones gathered at the site. Upon being hurried out in the morning, Balaam undoubtedly instructed Balak as to what animals would be required and the number to bring.

and his staff were all expecting something of this sort. The first stage of any magical ceremony always involved summoning the gods by sacrifice.[20]

And Balaam said to Balak, "Build for me here seven altars, and prepare[21] for me here seven bulls and seven rams." So Balak did as Balaam had spoken, and Balak and Balaam offered up a bull and a ram on each altar.[22] And Balaam said to Balak, "Station yourself by your offering[23] [while] I go off. Perhaps the LORD *may chance to appear to me and speak; what ever He reveals to me[24] I will tell you." And he walked off to the bare height[25]* [23:1–3].

This entire procedure may seem to us exotic, but it was fairly standard practice in the pagan world of the Ancient Near East: parallel sacrifices on multiple altars[26] to summon the god or gods, and then the *kosem* removing himself to some solitary place in order to enable contact with the realm of the divine so as to be able to draw upon the power to perform that which was in his heart to do. Here the sacrifices are offered jointly by the king (the main sponsor)[27] and Balaam, his agent who is to transact his business with the gods. Balaam, who is orchestrating the proceedings, instructs Balak and company to remain positioned besides the blazing altars as the carcasses are being reduced to ashes,[28] while he seeks the solitude of the bare height where he hopes to make contact with the deity. It is important to keep in mind the inner contradiction inherent in this narrative, a contradiction that was shockingly evident to its audience of First Commonwealth Israelites, although less blatant to readers today: the contradiction between ends and means. Balaam wants to establish contact and receive revelation from the LORD, the God of Israel, yet the means that he is employing are exclusive to the pagan world. Roy Gain makes this point clearly: "Israelite prophets were never required to offer sacrifices before they receive divine messages. It appears that God meets with Balaam *in spite* of the sacrifice."[29]

But this contradiction is a product of the human perspective. As Balaam and

---

20. See Introduction, the section entitled Paganism and Monotheism.

21. Hebrew, *vehachen*, i.e., prepare for sacrifice; cf. *Zephaniah* 1:7.

22. "The use of multiple altars for a single ritual is unattested anywhere else in Scripture. Hence it must derive from a pagan practice." (Milgrom, p. 194) We have numerous examples of such in the pagan Ancient Near East.

23. Hebrew *olatecha*, literally, *"your whole burnt offering,"* a type of offering which, unlike the *zebah*, was not shared with the worshipers but was entirely consumed by fire on the altar; i.e., devoted whole to the deity. The *olah*, or "whole burnt offering," was considered the sacrifice most pleasing to the gods because it was not shared. Using bulls and rams—the most expensive sacrificial animals—and multiplying the offering times seven, would, in the opinion of Balak and Balaam, make the offering absolutely irresistible to any deity.

24. Literally, *shows me*.

25. Hebrew, *shefi*, a *hapex* (unless we accept the *ketib* of *Job* 33:21; see Glossary for *hapex* and *ketib*). This word has been variously rendered as "alone" (NJPS), "silently" (Levine, AB), "forthwith (NEB) etc. In the plural, *shefayim* does appear eight or nine times in the Hebrew Bible in the meaning of "bare heights." But rendering *shefi* as the singular of *shefayim* is no better than a guess.

26. See note 22 above.

27. The reason for the ceremony is Balak's—to bring a curse upon this people, the Children of Israel—and it is he who is providing the animals for the sacrifice.

28. This also was standard: at all sacrifices the offerer (or his proxy) had to be physically present. The term *hityatzev, station yourself*, is "used to characterize the stance of those in attendance upon deities." (Levine, p. 166)

29. Gain, p. 700. Emphasis is in the original.

Balak see things, Balaam needs to confer with a specific deity—the Lord[30]—and the sacrifices are the means to summon the Lord to conference. But God cannot be summoned at will like a servant. God manifests Himself to humans when and where it pleases Him. Balaam is unique in being highly attuned to God, and thus often able to anticipate when his God will wish to manifest Himself to him, but he knows that he is not always right. There are times when he is out of sync with his Creator and gets it wrong. This is what lies behind his "*Perhaps the* Lord *may chance to appear to me and speak*" (23:3). Balaam understands perfectly well that he may go through the standard pagan motions of summoning the Lord, but whether He will manifest Himself or not is up to Him. Balaam may need to speak to God, but does the Lord want just now to interact with him? Dealing with God involves a large measure of uncertainty.[31] So with a final promise that should God appear to him he will let Balak know exactly what He said, Balaam turns his back on king, entourage and alters and wends his way up to the bare height.

> *Now God appeared*[32] *to Balaam, and he* [Balaam] *said to Him, "I have set up seven altars and have offered up a bull and a ram on each altar." And the* Lord *put a word in Balaam's mouth, and He said, "Return to Balak, and thus you shall speak"* [23:4–5].

This time Balaam gets it right; not only does he need to consult with God but God needs to tell him what to say. Upon God manifesting Himself, Balaam opens the conversation in the standard pagan manner on such occasions: he calls God's attention to his proper concern with ritual detail in issuing his opulent summons to conference; seven (count them, seven!) altars, with no less than an entire bull and an entire ram on each! The Lord does not deign to comment on this prodigal display, but simply implants in Balaam's mouth—like a cassette or a MP3 file—a *dabar* (*a word, a thing*)[33]: the oracle he is to recite. And with a curt "Go back to Balak and play back to him the oracle that I have implanted in you," Balaam is dismissed.

Balaam had been warned: this was the condition upon which he had been allowed to proceed to Moab. Indeed, this is exactly what Balaam proclaimed to Balak when first they met: "*The word that God will put in my mouth, that will I speak.*" (22:38) Balaam undoubtedly meant the phrase to be metaphoric; a dramatic way of saying that God would tell him what to say, and that then he would proclaim it in his

---

30. To Whom Balaam refers to as "my God." (22:18)

31. And with this (Hebrew) word *ulai*, "perhaps" (23:3), we are back with the pagan shipmaster in *Jonah* 1:6 and the *mi yodayah*, "who knows," of the King of Nineveh in *Jonah* 4:9. In the eyes of both of our authors, pagans are more than aware of the lack of certainty in predicting how deity will react to human initiatives. Nor is this realization restricted to the *Books of Jonah* and *Balaam*; see *1 Samuel* 6:5 for the same expression of uncertainty in the mouths of the pagan priests and diviners of the Philistines. Lastly, this understanding is hardly unique to pagans; Moses himself expresses uncertainty as to how God will receive his attempted intercession on behalf of the Children of Israel (*Exodus* 32:30). In the Bible, among sensitive pagans and monotheistic Israelites alike, it is understood that in dealings with the Divine uncertainty is a prime factor in the equation.

32. Hebrew, *vayikar*, *appeared*, *manifested Himself*, a term used exclusively for divine manifestations to pagans (*Numbers* 23:3, 15, 16) or in talking *to* pagans *about* divine manifestations (*Exodus* 3:18; 5:3); for the appearance of God to Israelites the term used is *vayera* (cf. *Genesis* 18:1).

33. See Chapter 7, note 28.

own words. It may come as a shock to Balaam to realize that the phrase is no metaphor but the literal truth: he has been reduced to a mere mouthpiece of God, a kind of mechanical device to transmit God's words into the human realm, and nothing more.

> *So he returned to him* [i.e., Balak], *and behold, he was* [still] *stationed beside his offering, he and all the officials of Moab. Now he* [Balaam] *uttered his oracle,*[34] *saying:* [23:6–7a]

Following instructions, Balaam returns to the king. He finds him and his entire staff of officials where he left them: standing in attendance by the still smoking altars. Balaam positions himself; he, as it were, clicks the switch, and at full volume out pours his oracle.

But wait a moment: we have been told that God put a word—His word—into Balaam's mouth, which Balaam would have to spew out verbatim, and now we are speaking of Balaam's oracle? So which is it, God's oracle or Balaam's oracle? My contention will be that it is both. And to understand this point we will have to digress into the question of how oracles were framed and delivered in the Ancient Near East.[35]

Oracles were nothing new in the thirteenth and twelfth centuries BCE, the era in which our tale is set.[36] Balaam was practicing his trade of *roeh* or seer within the confines of a very ancient tradition that, while leaving the contents of the oracle to the particular divine inspiration, rigidly prescribed the format in which it was to be delivered. The two traditional specifications relevant to our case are, first, that oracles were to be proclaimed in a high literary style, which meant never in street language—in prose—but always in verse; poetry was the universal format of oracular pronouncements. This meant that seers were expected to be poets,[37] and as we shall learn, Balaam happens to be a very good one. And secondly, an oracle was expected to have an introduction which would provide information about the circumstances that have led to its proclamation, or to the identity of the seer delivering it; ideally both. What this meant was that an oracle always contained two components: the core content believed to be of divine origin, and the elaboration (introduction, biographical material, context etc.) whose source lay in the talent and the psyche of the seer.

Let us return to the poetic format. In the "Prayer of Jonah" (Chapter 2 above), we were introduced to the Hebrew verse of the classical Biblical Age, the poetry typical of the last centuries of the First Commonwealth. The language and the poetic forms of Balaam's oracles are archaic by comparison with those of Jonah, dating from at

---

34. Hebrew, *vayisa m'shalo*. This phrase appears seven times in the *Book of Balaam*. In its nominal form (*massa*), the word means an oracle. Thus *vayisa*, the verbal form, means to utter an oracle. *M'shalo*, his *mashal*, refers to the literary form the oracle takes: a poetic utterance of the "wisdom" variety.

35. As opposed to how oracles were proclaimed in cultures outside the Ancient Near East, for example those in Greece, where tradition prescribed very different formats and means of delivery.

36. W. F. Albright strongly argues that this was also the period in which the oracles embedded in *Numbers* 23–24 were composed. See above, Introduction to the *Book of Balaam*.

37. It was the seer who was responsible for formatting, often spontaneously but not necessarily so, the contents into the form demanded by tradition.

least five hundred years earlier; they are among the oldest to be found in the Bible.[38] When we ask what it was that distinguished ancient Hebrew poetry from prose, the answer is *not* rhyme—rhyming played no part in the versification of the Bible—but rather the meter, or rhythmic beat, and what is termed "parallelism." This is a phenomenon that is best explained through illustration.

Let us take the opening lines of Balaam's first oracle as our example. The oracle consists of fourteen lines, divided into seven couplets of two lines each.[39] It opens thus:

From Aram has Balak brought me,
The king of Moab from the Mountains of the East:

The first line makes a statement; the second line echoes it, restating it in different words. The title, *king of Moab,* is substituted for the name *Balak*; while *Aram*, a region comprising northern Syria and Upper Mesopotamia, is replaced by *the Mountains of the East*, a traditional metaphoric description of a portion of that region. This pattern of statement and echo is what we mean when we speak of "parallelism." Note that monotony has been avoided by reversing the order of place and person. If we label the place *Aram* as A and the person *Balak* as B, while we label the parallel terms *king of Moab* as B' and *Mountains of the East* as A,' then the structure of the first couplet is:

A—B
B'—A'

This is not always the rule. Often the structure is a simple

A—B
A'—B'

but the order will be switched from time to time to prevent the composition from falling into a boring repetitive pattern.

One further variation on simple parallelism needs to be pointed out: there are times—often at a critical moment or a turning point in the poem—that instead of merely restating the first line in different words, the second line states the corollary or implication of the first, thus advancing the argument; moving the theme a step or two forward. This is a way archaic Hebrew poetry has of highlighting the main point of the poetic composition. With these few remarks we should find that we have at least a minimum of the tools needed to help us make sense of the form Balaam's oracles will take.[40] With these under our belts, we now turn to what will prove to be the first of a series of utterances.

The First Oracle

"From Aram has Balak brought me,   A
The king of Moab from the Mountains of the East[41]

---

38. The closest comparable poetry in the Bible would be the "Song of the Sea" (*Exodus* 15:2–18) and the so-called "Song of Heshbon," *Numbers* 21:27–30 (see Appendix C).

39. We will try to keep the explanation simple and in everyday English, avoiding technical terminology such as cola, bicola etc.

40. A slightly more extensive exposition of the issues involved in the reading of biblical poetry can be found in my *Judges and Saviors*, p. 115–119. For those interested in a fuller and more sophisticated analysis of biblical parallelism, it is recommended that the reader turn to Robert Alter's *The Art of Biblical Poetry*, p. 3–26.

41. Or *the Mountains of Kedem*, if we take Kedem to be a place name.

Chapter 8. The Mouthpiece

'Come, curse me Jacob,	B
Come, pronounce Israel's doom.'	
How can I damn whom God[42] has not damned?	C
How can I doom whom the LORD has not doomed?	
For from the mountain peaks I see him,	D
From the high hills I behold him.[43]	
This is a people that shall dwell alone,	E
Not reckoned among the nations.	
Who can count the dust of Jacob?	F
Who can number[44] the dust-clouds[45] of Israel?	
May I die the death of the upright,	G
May my end be like his!"[46] (23:7b–10)	

In launching our attempt to understand this remarkable utterance we begin by returning to the question which led to the digression which preceded this oracle: who is the author of the oracle under question, God or Balaam? We then suggested that the answer is both. The time has come to elucidate this rather cryptic statement. We have said that in the Ancient Near East an oracle was made up of at least two parts: the core which contained the central message, believed to be of divine origin, and the elaborate framework provided by the seer who proclaimed it. The former, which I will contend is the "word" or "thing" that God implanted in Balaam, is presented by him embedded in a flowery framework of traditional poetic exposition. It will be our task to differentiate and untangle one from the other. While our theological interests will center on God's "word," we will give extended attention to Balaam's contribution as well, for it is this that is most relevant to his unfolding tale.

My contention is that couplets E and F constitute the "word" that God "placed in Balaam's mouth"; the remainder, couplets A–D and G are Balaam's elaboration. What this division means is that most of the oracle is Balaam's. What is remarkable about Balaam's contribution to what God is forcing him to proclaim is that it has next to nothing to say about the subject of the oracle, Israel. It is God Who talks about Israel; Balaam talks about himself.

The contents of the oracle can be briefly described as follows:

1. A long Introduction by Balaam:
   a. How *he* got where *he* is and why   A & B

---

42. Hebrew *el*; in Canaanite mythology *el* was the chief God, the head of the Pantheon. By using *el* as parallel to the Lord, Balaam is using the two terms as synonyms and thus identifying them one with the other. As such, it is reasonable to treat *el* as a variant or singular form of *elohim*, and thus render it as God. This is the way *Genesis* treats it: as one of the names by which Abraham, Isaac and Jacob knew their God: c.f. *Genesis* 14:18–20; 46:1–3, etc.

43. The object of the verbs *see* and *behold*, i.e., *him*, is *a people* in the next couplet, i.e., *Israel*.

44. Reading with LXX and Sam. MT runs the two words *mi saphar* (who can number—the verb) together to form the single word *mispar* (number—the noun).

45. Since *et* does not appear in ancient Hebrew poetry, we read with Albright, "Oracles," p.213, note 28, *tarbaat* (dust-clouds) for MT *et ruba* (a quarter); adopted by NJPS and NICOT among others.

46. For ease of reference we have labeled each couplet with a letter of the alphabet.

b. *His* excuse why *he* can't perform what has been asked of *him*   C
   c. How from *his* vantage point *he* can see *his* target   D
2. THE WORD OF GOD about Israel   E & F
3. A conclusion by Balaam, the result of growing enlightenment: G
   the realization that *he* is on a slippery slope, which generates a prayer for *himself*.

The various interpretations of these oracles that have been offered over the years differ amazingly; they range from the pedantic to bizarre flights of the imagination. Especially in the case of the first oracle, but indeed with regard to all, they seem to act as Rorschach blots, stimulating the imagination and leading many of the interpreters to read their theologies, biases and fantasies into the utterances. We will make no attempt to catalog the numerous different interpretations of these oracles, but at this stage of the analysis simply to try to expound the surface meeting of the words themselves: to clearly explain what the text says, what it meant in the context of the language and the cultural setting of the 13th century BCE, and hopefully to get some grasp of how late-13th-century–early-12th-century-BCE Israelites would have understood it. We will also be interested in how Balaam—a sophisticated and highly intelligent pagan—understood what he himself was uttering. But we will we will leave the larger questions of theology and meaning in a twenty-first-century humanistic setting to the Summary Chapter.

What I will be contending in the coming pages is that, to me at least, the first two oracles (or at least those parts that are clearly of Balaam's authorship), taken in conjunction with the prose narrative in which they are embedded, reveal a soul in violent conflict with an irresistible compulsion to proclaim a thesis that sticks in his craw, a message that he does not want to deliver. He appears to be desperately trying to assert his own personality in a situation where he feels overpowered by the presence of God, and he seems to be trying to contain a growing sense of resentment at the way God is imposing on him and using him. Along with this we see a growing sense of enlightenment. Balaam's eyes are being opened to things about Israel—this people that has come out of Egypt—that he never dreamed: he is intelligent enough to sense that its emergence on the stage of history will prove to be a game changer. At the same time, he is becoming aware of things about himself to which he has previously been oblivious: of the "crooked road" upon which he has so recklessly embarked, and a growing suspicion of what its end is likely to be. With this as a preamble, let us now plunge into the first oracle.

In the first three couplets of his Introduction to the "word" that he must deliver, Balaam concisely summarizes what has led up to this moment, a tale that has already taken up more than a chapter of prose: that Balak has brought him from afar, that the reason that he has been fetched is to curse Israel, and that it cannot be done for God will not have it.[47] This brings him to the present moment, encapsulated in the fourth and final couplet of his lead-up, where he finds himself standing on a high point overlooking the distant encampment of the people he has been brought to curse, and where now he must utter the "word" which God has implanted within him:

---

47. Once again, as in his initial response to Balak's summons, Balaam suppresses the fact that Israel is in fact blessed.

> *This is a people that shall dwell alone,*
> >   *Not reckoned among the nations.*
> *Who can count the dust of Jacob?*
> >   *Who can number the dust-clouds of Israel?*   E & F

    Each of these couplets makes a critical point. The first is that this people is like no other on the face of the earth. It is unique, but in what way is not stated. The second point relates to the numerical size of this people. It is enormous. This would seem to relate to more than the numbers that had originally panicked Balak. It would appear to be predictive, hinting at a future exponential expansion that, like the dust motes in a desert storm, are spread to the four corners of the earth. Together these two couplets form a classic oracle: powerful, cryptic, ambiguous in meaning, yet pregnant with obscure implications.[48]

    Important as this divine pronouncement is, our attention is drawn to the concluding couplet, Balaam's coda to the "word" he has been compelled to utter. His focus lies neither in the oracle he has just uttered nor in its subject, but in himself. It is simultaneously a cry of terror and despair, and a prayer. It would seem to have been engendered by the very act of uttering God's "word" and the feelings that it has aroused within him, a sudden upsurge of antipathy—toward God? toward Israel?— that he never knew that he harbored within him. Perhaps we are getting a bit ahead of ourselves, but maybe we should consider the possibility that the words of the Apparition on the road in Balaam's dream has suddenly come home to him:

> *"Behold, I went forth to oppose you, for your road is twisted before me"* [22:32].

Balaam, in his dream, had set out for Moab in defiance of God's prohibition. He has been told that the road that he has embarked on is twisted, crooked, displeasing to God. He is still on that road, playing a game with God: outwardly complying with God's orders—not willingly but due to force majeure—and covertly trying to maneuver God into letting him have things his own way. I think it's more than merely possible that what brought the cry of terror and despair to Balaam's lips was a sudden vision of the abyss opening at his feet, the realization of where the road he was on might lead. Playing games with God could be a thousand times more dangerous than playing with fire. Balaam has just proclaimed the unique status of Israel and gathered a glimpse of its blessedness. The contrast between that positive future and his sudden insight as to what he was in the process of becoming, and where he was heading, might have been what brought the cry to birth; a cry that morphs into a prayer:

---

48. To us, who have read *Genesis*, there is nothing here that is really new. All that Balaam proclaims has been prefigured in God's promise to Abraham, the father of this unique people that is to come into being, in his Call (*Genesis* 12:3, see Chapter 7, note 19) and the confirmation of the Promise: *"I will absolutely bless you, and I will certainly make your descendants as numerous as the stars in the heavens and the sand on the seashore; and your descendants shall inherit the gates of their enemies. All the nations of the earth shall be blessed by your descendants, because you have hearkened to My voice"* (*Genesis* 22:17–18). To this add God's promise to Jacob in his dream of the ladder to heaven: *"And it shall come to pass, that your descendants shall be* [as numerous] *as the dust of the earth... and all the families of the earth shall be blessed in you and your descendants"* (*Genesis* 28:14). Of course neither Balaam nor Balak had ever heard of these divine proclamations, so that to them Balaam's oracle is revolutionary.

> *May I die the death of the upright,*
> *May my end be like his!* (23:10)   G

The Second Opinion

To say that this was hardly what Balak was expecting is a prize understatement; anticipating a hideous curse Balaam's utterance completely throws him.

> *And Balak said to Balaam, "What have you done to me? I've brought you to damn my enemies, and behold, you have explicitly blessed them!"*[49] *And he answered and said, "Should I not be careful to speak* [only] *that which the* LORD *places in my mouth?"* [23:11–12].

Balaam has his excuse ready: I warned you that I am the LORD's agent. And then, rhetorically, he throws the question into Balak's face: "As the LORD's agent, don't you think that I should proclaim exactly what the LORD orders me to say?" To this question Balak has no answer. His response takes the form of a new initiative.

One thing we have learned about Balak is that he is persistent; he refuses to take "no" for an answer. When Balaam refused to accept his first summons he simply redoubled his efforts. Here too he will not admit defeat. If he can't get a favorable oracle one way he will simply have to try another approach. Maybe this particular site is not propitious; perhaps another place will prove better for launching a curse.[50]

> *So Balak said to him, "Come with me, please, to another place from where you will see him*[51]*—however only his extreme tail end will you see,*[52] *but his whole you will not see—and damn me him from there." And he took him to S'dai-zophim,*[53] *to the very summit of The Pisgah.*[54] *So he built seven altars and offered up a bull and a ram on each altar. And* [Balaam] *said to Balak, "Station yourself here by your offering. As for me, I will go and seek an encounter here* [with God]*"* [23:13–15].

The point of the shift of locale seems to be that from the new lookout site an even smaller proportion of the Israelite camp will be visible than from the previous location; perhaps Balak is reacting to the stress on the numbers of the Children of Israel in Balaam's oracle, and thinks that if Balaam can't see as many Israelites he will be able more easily to curse them. We are not directly told how Balaam is taking this search for a second opinion, but we will be able to infer his contempt from the words that he will soon utter. It would seem that throughout the entire shift of venue and the ritual that follows he holds his tongue, breaking his silence only to repeat his instructions to the king and his retinue to remain in attendance at the altars while he goes to seek a solitary encounter with his God.

---

49. More literally, *blessing have you blessed them*, the infinitive absolute.
50. Why this should be so remains obscure. Milgrom (p. 198) suggests a superstitious belief that changing one's place can lead to changing one's luck.
51. That is, Israel. The pronouns referring to Israel are in the masculine singular; "Israel" in the singular is here being used as a collective noun that encompasses the entirety of the Children of Israel.
52. I.e., only a small portion of him will you see. See note 17 above.
53. Literally, *The Fields of the Watchers*, apparently a prominent location for lookouts.
54. "*The Pisgah* is a collective term for the headlands of the Moab plateau, which falls off quite sharply to the Dead Sea. This term may also refer to the north end of the Arabim range of mountains." (Ashley, p. 415)

And the LORD *appeared to Balaam and put a word into his mouth, and He said, "Return to Balak and thus shall you speak." So he came to him* [i.e., Balak] *and behold, he was still stationed beside his offering, and the officials of Moab with him. And Balak said to him, "What did the* LORD *say?" Now he* [Balaam] *uttered his oracle,*[55] *saying:*[23:16–18a].

Once again the LORD manifests Himself, once again He puts His word in Balaam's mouth and once again He sends him back to Balak. But this time, instead of waiting in silent expectation for the word from on high, the tension under which Balak is laboring breaks down all restraint; he bursts forth with a "So, what did God say?" As it will turn out, this proves to be the wrong question, a reflection of his mistaken understanding of the situation in which he finds himself. Balaam's subsequent proclamation is not a response to the king's impulsive query, but rather addresses the larger issue that faces them both.

The Second Oracle

"Arise, O Balak, and hear!	
Give ear to me, O son of Zippor!	
God is not a man that He should be capricious,	
Nor mortal,[56] *that He should change His mind.*	B
Will He declare[57] *and He will not do it?*	
Speak and not bring it to pass?	C
Behold, I was summoned[58] *to bless,*	
He has blessed and I cannot reverse it.	D
No iniquity can be perceived in Jacob;	
No wrong can be seen in Israel.[59]	E
The LORD *his God is with him,*[60]	
And a King's proclamation[61] *is in his midst.*	F
God Who brings them out of Egypt	
Is for him like the towering horns of the wild ox.[62]	G

---

55. See note 34 above.
56. Literally *son of man*; a common synonym for "man."
57. Literally, *said*.
58. Reading with Albright, *lukahti* ("Oracles," p. 214, note 35); also LXX and Syr. MT reads *lakahti, I took*.
59. Taking the terms *aven* and *amal* in their moral meanings, as in *Habakkuk* 1:3
Why do You show me iniquity? (*aven*)
Perceive wrong? (*amal*)
where the prophet uses the identical terms—the identical verbs and the same parallelism—and the context is unambiguously moral. See also *Habakkuk* 1:13.
60. His... him... his: all these third person singular pronouns refer, of course, to "Israel," i.e., the people of Israel. See note 51 above.
61. Hebrew *teruah*: a long series of short blasts on a shofar (see Glossary) or trumpet; also a euphemism for a human shout of joy. The shofar was sounded to proclaim the crowning of a king, in this case the lord, cf. *Psalms* 47 and 98:6.
62. The wild ox was a traditional Ancient Near Eastern symbol of unrestrained and irresistible power; his horns are perceived as the focus of this power.

> *For no enchantment can be effective against Jacob,*
> *No magic*[63] *against Israel.*[64]   H
>
> *Now let it be said of Jacob,*
> *And of Israel: 'What hath God wrought!'*[65]   I
>
> *This is a people that will rise up like a lion,*
> *Like the king of beasts*[66] *will leap up.*   J
>
> *He will not lie down until he eats prey,*
> *And drinks the blood of the slain."*[67] (23:18b–24)   K

This second soaring oracle that Balak's persistence has called forth is lengthier than the first (eleven couplets in place of seven) and far more explicit than its predecessor. It also consists of two parts: the "word" God implanted in Balaam's mouth and Balaam's embellishment of that core. Let us begin our analysis by outlining the logical structure of the pronouncement.

It begins with Balaam calling to Balak to pay close attention to what he will be told (A).[68] The next two couplets inform Balak in no uncertain terms that his basic premise in seeking a "second opinion" is mistaken: God is not a human being.[69] Humans are capricious, they change their minds, they waffle. God, on the other hand, is reliable: when He makes up His mind He sticks to it, when He promises He follows through (B & C). Balak may have brought Balaam to curse Israel, but God has summoned him to bless. Why? Because God Himself has blessed Israel and Balaam is powerless to reverse God's blessing (D).

So far Balaam has been correcting Balak's misapprehensions. Now we come to the core of the oracle: the "word" God has placed in Balaam's mouth. Why has God blessed Israel? Because He can find nothing wrong with this people: they are inherently blameless and thus deserving of blessing (E). For this reason God is present in the midst of this people Israel, and they have proclaimed Him their king (F). It is God Who empowers Israel; it is He Who brought Israel out of Egypt; He is all-powerful and unstoppable[70]

---

63. Literally, *divination* (*kesem*). Both *enchantment* (*naḥash*) and *divination* are being used as euphemisms for "magic," a practice ubiquitous to the pagan world which involves the manipulation of nature and the gods (who themselves are part of nature) through power drawn from the primordial meta-divine realm which was perceived as underlying and sustaining nature. (See the General introduction, the section entitled Paganism and Monotheism, and especially the sub-section entitled "Magic" for an elaboration of this fundamental idea of pagan religion.)

64. Taking with Albright the prepositional *bet* before *Jacob* and *Israel* to connote opposition (p. 215, note 49), i.e., no magic employed against *Jacob/Israel* can be effective.

65. We return to the King James translation of the Hebrew exclamation *ma paal el*, as the phrase has become famous because with these words Samuel Morse opened the Age of Telecommunications on May 24, 1844, by transmitting them from Washington, DC to Baltimore as the world's first telegraph message.

66. Hebrew *labi, ari*: two words both connoting "a lion." There are seven different words for lion in Hebrew—designating among other aspects various stages of biological development—but only one word for the animal in the English language. This plethora of near synonyms makes poetic parallelism easy in Hebrew, but almost impossible to render in English without the use of euphemisms, as here.

67. Ashley points out that "*dam*," 'blood,' in the singular (as here) refers to the organic material found in the body. In the plural (*damim*) it refers to 'bloodshed,'" i.e., the liquid flowing in the veins. (p. 475, note 22)

68. The letters in parentheses identify the relevant couplets.

69. Or, for that matter, neither is He like one of the pagan deities which, in these matters, are just like the human beings on whom they are patterned.

70. This is the meaning of the symbol of the horns of the wild ox.

(G). And don't think that you can destroy Israel by magic, or use enchantment to deter Israel from its destiny. Because God has blessed it and is in its midst, no magic directed against Israel will work (H). This is something unheard of; something completely new.[71] One can only respond to this unique phenomenon with an exclamation of wonder: "What a wondrous thing God has created!" (I) And what is it that God has wrought? A people as fierce as a lion and completely unstoppable. (J and K)

With this outline as a guide let us discuss some implications of selected issues raised in this oracle, the first being Balaam's startling shift from an obsessive preoccupation with himself in the first oracle to a focus on the issue at hand, and the second: Balak's compulsive desire to reverse, or at the very least to cancel, God's previous pronouncement. The content of the "words" God implanted in Balaam exhibit a basic consistency of theme, the second "word" being in effect a partial clarification of the first. It is in Balaam's additions to God's "words" that we mark a real development bespeaking a growing enlightenment.

We have noted the indications that, despite the seer's incessant pro forma declarations that he can only do or say what the LORD will tell him to do or say, Balaam has a will of his own that often seems to run counter to the will of God. In his dream he saddles his donkey and departs for Moab in open defiance of God's specific prohibition, revealing more than a little of where his heart really lies. We have watched him, while awake, trying to game God, and actually succeeding in wringing a conditional permission to fulfill his heart's desire, but at the price of losing his freedom of action. We have seen him accept a commission that in the normal course of events he knows he can never fulfill, and laying the groundwork for his future exoneration in the event of his inevitable failure. When we add to all this his obsessive focus on himself in the first oracle, we must admit that all the signs point to a heart that is not at one with his God. It is this spiritual state that makes Balaam's dressing down of Balak so startling: is he really speaking only to Balak or is he, in truth, also preaching to himself?

There is a new candor in the words Balaam addresses to Balak in his second oracle. For the first time he reveals what he has known from the first but never publicly admitted: the reason why he cannot curse this people is because Israel is already blessed by God.

He has blessed and I cannot reverse it. D

It is becoming clear to Balaam that this state of blessedness is neither new nor provisional. It is a hard fact: set in stone and eternal. There is a clear sense from his words that Balaam, for the first time, has begun to accept this fact and make peace with it. In effect, we seem to be seeing the signs of a man whose horizons are beginning to widen beyond his immediate self and take in a vision of at least some of God's purposes for the world.

Balaam's contribution to the second oracle, his harangue addressed to Balak, is much more than a public dressing down of the king for his presumption in demanding "a second opinion." It is above all a mini-lecture in theology by this pagan seer that, given its polytheistic context, is revelatory and expressive of a growing

---

71. This couplet is a corollary of the fifth couplet of the first oracle: *This is a people that shall dwell alone, Not reckoned among the nations.* (23:9b)

understanding of the LORD Whom he serves. Unlike the gods known to the nations of the world, the LORD is *not* capricious; once He makes up His mind, you know He won't backtrack. He is absolutely reliable; this is one of His main attributes. Which brings us back to Jonah and his refusal to accept the revision of Israel's faith in a God Who is completely trustworthy.[72] And because the Creator is reliable, His creation is a universe of natural law and a place of order. The ramifications of this simple postulate are central to the worldview of the nascent monotheistic faith of Israel.

What follows in the oracle—that is, the "word" implanted by God in Balaam for his delivery—opens with the premise that Israel is in a state of blessedness.[73] As has been pointed out, we, who have read *Genesis*, know that this blessed state is due to God's fulfillment of His promises to the progenitors of this people: Abraham, Isaac and Jacob (otherwise known as Israel). This is a people especially created by God to bring blessing to all humanity.[74] But this is not the reason given in the oracle. Balaam knows nothing of the prehistory of this people Israel, nor does he know of God's relationship with its forefathers. Neither does Balak. Nor would telling them do much to enlighten them, lacking as they do the monotheistic frame of reference which gives overriding force and meaning to a divine promise.[75] Rather a completely different reason is given:

No iniquity can be perceived in Jacob;
No wrong can be seen in Israel.[76]   E

This people Israel is blessed because it is blameless. Or to put it another way, it is not deserving of being cursed because it has done nothing wrong. Now to Balaam and Balak, who know little about this people beyond that they have come out of Egypt and have recently been on a roll, riding roughshod over the Amorite kingdoms of Heshbon and Bashan, this oracular statement undoubtedly carries weight.[77] But to us it sounds weird. Remember that we, who have read the *Book of Genesis* and so have learned of God's promises to Abraham and Jacob, have also opened the *Book of Exodus* and even glanced, however fleetingly, at the earlier chapters of the *Book of*

---

72. Israel's prototypical confession of faith, later to be termed the *shelosh esreh middot* (the Thirteen Attributes of God), is stated to have been revealed to Moses on Mount Sinai only a generation prior to the time in which our tale is set; Moses is still alive. Its opening utterance is *"The Lord, the Lord, a merciful and compassionate God, slow to anger and abounding in loving-kindness and truth."* (Exodus 34:6). The final word (*emet*), which we have rendered as "truth," also has the meanings of *reliability* and *faithfulness*, and in this context the sense is that humans can rely on God to keep His word; that He is eternally dependable. As we have seen, the replacement of this word *emet* by the phrase, *and ready to change Your mind about punishing* (Jonah 4:2), is the crux upon which the entire *Book of Jonah* turns. See Chapter 5 above.

73. Since Balaam was obviously aware of the contents of the "word," it is reasonable to assume that he tailored his introductory remarks specifically so that they would lead up to this point.

74. For God's promise to Abraham see Chapter 7, note 18. For further expansions on this promise, see note 48 above.

75. From a pagan point of view, in a world with multiple deities, all in conflict with each other, a divine promise by one deity, which can always be countermanded by another, holds little weight in comparison with such a promise within a world view in which there is only one God Who gives His word.

76. In the oracles, the terms "Jacob" and "Israel" are routinely treated as synonyms, which indeed they are, being two alternative names for the same person. See *Genesis* 32:23–30 for the incident where father Jacob receives his alternative name of Israel; hence his descendants becoming known as the Children of Israel.

77. This is not Balaam speaking; this is the opening couplet of God's "word" which He implanted in the seer.

Numbers. Thus we cannot avoid being aware that ever since it has come out of Egypt this people Israel has been engaged in one unending cascade of transgressions and rebellions against their Savior and Redeemer.[78] Far from being blameless, this is a people charged with being stubborn, stiff-necked and rebellious, and which has been sentenced to death.

But this is precisely the point: the rebellious generation that left Egypt is gone. Thirty-nine years have passed since the Exodus. In the months to come, of all those who were adults at the time of the Exodus only Moses, Joshua and Caleb will remain alive; that entire generation will have died off, and of those who remain Moses also will be dead before the year is out. A new generation has replaced them, comprised of those who were children when they accompanied their parents out of Egypt, and those born during the years of the wilderness. It is of this new generation that never experienced slavery as adults, that grew up in the wilderness facing the harsh realities of freedom that the oracle speaks; a generation that, until and unless it sins, possesses a presumption of innocence. This new generation does not the bear the onus of its parent's sins. It is about them that the oracle declares:

> *The* LORD *his God is with him,*
> *And a king's proclamation is in his midst.*   F

It is God Himself Who empowers them. As long as they remain loyal to their God they are insulated from any magical incantations. They are something new to a pagan world, whose only reaction can be uncomprehending wonder. This is a phenomenon that can only be understood as having its origin in the will of God.

The phrase *"What hath God wrought!"* is multifaceted: it can be taken as an exclamation, as we have been reading it, but it can also be understood as a rhetorical question. And in this reading, the final two couplets of the oracle would then fill the role of answer to the query: God has created a fierce and powerful people—compared to a ravaging lion tearing nations to pieces and gorging itself on its prey—that is terrifying in its invincibility.

> *This is a people that will rise up like a lion,*
> *Like the king of beasts will leap up.*   J
>
> *He will not lie down until he eats prey,*
> *And drinks the blood of the slain.* [23:23–24]   K

And it is on this note of "look what you are up against" that Balaam's second oracle concludes.[79]

---

78. Beginning immediately upon their liberation from slavery Israel exhibits gross ingratitude at every difficulty (*Exodus* 16:1–3; 17:1–7 etc.), while at Sinai they fashion a golden calf and worship it (*Exodus* 32:1–6). Their rebelliousness reaches a climax when, at the report of the spies sent to reconnoiter the Land of Canaan, the Children of Israel lose their faith in God and panic; and He condemns them all to die in the wilderness and never see the Promised Land (*Numbers* 11–14).

79. It is an open question as to whether these last two couplets are part and parcel of God's "word," and thus is as revelatory to Balaam as they are to Balak, or if, as in the first oracle, Balaam has added these couplets as his own peroration. In that case God's "word" would close with the phrase *"What hath God wrought."* If these final lines are Balaam's, then the seer is demonstrating that he is on a steep learning curve; he at least has gotten the message. Balak will be correct in taking these words to be a blessing.

Aftermath

And Balak said to Balaam, "Neither damn them nor bless them!" And Balaam answered and said to Balak, "Did I not speak to you saying, 'Whatever the Lord *speaks, that I must do'?"* [23:25–26]

Balak's reaction to this pronouncement is an explosion of baffled fury. Both the phrases we have rendered as *damn*[80] and *bless*[81] are in the infinitive absolute construction; in other words this is as strong a statement as Balak can make. The force of it would be something like, "For God's sake, if you can't curse them at least don't bless them! It would be better if you said nothing! Shut up!" Balak is absolutely beside himself. Balaam, for his part, resorts to his mantra in reply, reminding Balak of the terms he lay down for accepting employment. The two of them, king and seer, are at complete loggerheads.

What the king has understood from Balaam's recitation is clear; what Balaam has learned is less so. Apart from the overall logic of God's word which we have discussed, I would like to draw attention to one couplet which, while at first utterance probably had no special significance to Balaam, but with the passage of days will begin to loom large in his eyes:

No iniquity can be perceived in Jacob;
No wrong can be seen in Israel. (23:21a)　　　　　　　　　　　　E

A seed has been planted in what will prove to be fertile soil: the fruit it will bear will prove bitter to all concerned.

---

80. *kob...tikabenu.*
81. *baraich... tibarchenu.*

Chapter 9

The Prophet

set upon a golden bough to sing
To lords and ladies of Byzantium
Of what is past, or passing, or to come.

—W. B. Yeats, *Sailing to Byzantium*

The Mind Cage

Now Balak said to Balaam, "Come now, please, I will take you to another place. Perhaps it will be acceptable[1] in the eyes of the gods[2] that you damn them for me from there." So Balak took Balaam to the top of the Peor,[3] which overlooks the Wasteland.[4] And Balaam said to Balak, "Build for me here seven altars and prepare[5] seven bulls and seven rams for me here. So Balak did as Balaam said, and offered a bull and a ram on each altar" [23:27–30].

Balak and Balaam—the employer and, as he sees it, his hired help—make an unlikely pair. From the start they have never been on the same page. While Balaam is a self-proclaimed seer with highly developed professional skills as a diviner,[6] Balak insists on regarding him as a sorcerer, the possessor of occult powers that enable him not simply to foresee the future but also to shape it: the ability to influence the gods to bend future events so as to determine their outcomes. It was on the basis of this belief that Balak was willing to go to extraordinary lengths to acquire Balaam's services. Despite numerous attempts by Balaam to correct the king's misapprehensions, and undeterred by two stinging failures to achieve his ends, Balak remains firm in his belief in Balaam's powers.

For his part, Balaam's behavior has proved problematic and his motives murky. He has gone to Moab in defiance of God's explicit directives and has accepted a

---

1. Literally, *be straight, be upright in the eyes of...*
2. The literal translation of the Hebrew *ha-elohim*. See Chapter 7, note 21. We must never forget that both Balak and Balaam are pagans.
3. "Probably the name of one of the peaks of the Arabim range that overlooks Israel's encampment." (Milgrom, p. 201) For *Arabim* see Glossary.
4. Hebrew, *ha-yeshimon*. This term, "with the definite article, as here, indicate[s] the wasteland of Judah north of the Dead Sea, both on the eastern and western shores." (Ashley, p. 415)
5. I. e., prepare for sacrifice. See Chapter 8, note 21.
6. One alert to omens—signs with the design of coming events imprinted upon them—and skilled in interpreting them.

commission he knows he cannot fulfill. We have not been told what it was that induced him to embark on the road that has led to the cul-de-sac in which he now finds himself, nor will we be told. This will remain one of our central puzzles. What is clear to us, and is becoming increasingly evident to Balaam, is that this is a partnership based on falsehood and is irredeemably dysfunctional, kept alive only by the compulsiveness of a king driven by panic and clinging to the hope of a magical happy ending.

We said that Balak asked the wrong question when he burst forth with the words "So what did God say?"[7] It is time that we clarify this remark. Balak's question was based on the assumption that the problem created by Israel's sudden appearance on the scene was susceptible to correction: Israel could somehow be made to implode or vanish. Balak's question was really: so did God tell you how to make Israel go away? And ironically, whether the king realized it or not, the oracle that Balaam immediately proclaimed does contain an answer to his question. Taken on a literal and simplistic level, it corrects Balak: the question is not "what did God *say*?" but rather "*What hath God wrought?*" i.e., what has God *done*? The entire oracle is an answer to this rhetorical question. God has created a unique people—Israel—that is an established fact which won't go away. This is the new reality, and the nations of the world, beginning with Moab, will have to learn to live with this new "lion" in their midst.

This is not an answer the king is capable of hearing, much less accepting. Instead of taking it to heart and cutting his losses, he brushes it aside, doubles down and forces a third round. Balak simply can't let go. A remark, attributed to Albert Einstein, is pertinent to our situation: "The definition of insanity is doing the same thing over and over again, but expecting different results." Balak's behavior has lost all contact with reality; it has become compulsive and irrational. Once again he forces a change of location; once again he erects seven altars; once again he offers a bull and a ram on each altar. Like a creature self-locked into a squirrel cage, he doubles down and runs with an increasingly fanatical determination. Faster and faster spins the cage, but no matter how hard he runs he remains in exactly the same place. A different result eludes him.

The cage in which Balak finds himself trapped is not a physical cage—a squirrel cage—but a state of mind: a mind cage. Balak is a pagan, and it is the pagan worldview that is driving him into compulsive and irrational behavior.

> Paganism, with its notion that divine powers can be manipulated by a cast of professionals through a set of carefully prescribed procedures, is trapped in the reflexes of a mechanistic worldview while from the biblical perspective reality is controlled by the will of an omnipotent God beyond all manipulation.[8]

It is this mechanistic worldview that is preventing Balak from breaking out of the increasingly maddening situation into which he finds he has locked himself, while at the same time it is Balaam's dawning realization of the true meaning of God's immunity to human manipulation and the immutability of His freewill that

---

7. 23:17.
8. Robert Alter, *Art of Biblical Narrative*, p. 106–107.

is beginning to transform him from a pagan seer into something radically different. What we are reading can be seen as a tale of the enlightenment of Balaam.

Metamorphosis

The *Book of Balaam* opened with the verb *vayar (now he saw)*[9]:

Now Balak, son of Zippor, <u>saw</u> everything Israel had done to the Amorites [22:2].

The King of Moab may be awake to what is going on about him; however, what he is alert to are the political realities of his surroundings, the changes in the balance of power in the region. But although he opens the *Book of Balaam*, Balak is not its central protagonist. The central figure of the *Book* is Balaam, son of Beor, a "seer," a *roeh*.[10] Now, at this late stage of our tale, we are told that for the first time he too has begun to see. But unlike Balak, this seer (*roeh*) does not focus on the ephemeral world of politics and power but rather he now sees (that is, comprehends) God's purpose, and therefore begins to understand how he should reorient himself.

Now Balaam <u>saw</u> (vayar) that it was good in the eyes of the LORD *to bless Israel* [24:1a].

And what leads Balaam to this understanding? It would seem that at least one person has taken seriously the words of the second oracle, and that person is Balaam himself:

Behold, I was summoned to bless,[11]
He has blessed and I cannot reverse it. (23:20)   D

There is a second couplet that apparently Balaam has taken to heart:

For no enchantment can be effective against Jacob,
No magic against Israel. (23:21)   H

The acceptance of the reality of these passages is leading to a complete behavioral change on the part of Balaam. Balak may not be getting the message, but Balaam is.

Now let us see this passage in its entirety:

Now Balaam <u>saw</u> that it was good in the eyes of the LORD *to bless Israel, so he dispensed with his previous enchantments,*[12] *but turned his face to the wilderness. And Balaam raised his eyes and he <u>saw</u> Israel encamped in tribal array,*[13] *and the spirit of God came upon him* [24:1–2].

---

9. Unlike the English translation, the original Hebrew word order, in opening with the verb, puts the emphasis *not* on the subject—Balak—but on his *act of seeing*. We are being put on notice: this is a tale about "seeing": both in the meaning of visual perception and especially that of mental comprehension.

10. *Roeh*—the nominal form of the verb *vayar*—is here being used as the descriptive title of one who, due to his relationship with God, can *see* beneath surface appearances into the true nature of reality. This term is often used as a synonym for "a man of God." See Chapter 7, note 58.

11. I.e., by God. Balak summoned him to curse but God summoned him to bless Israel, so he has no choice but to do God's will.

12. Literally, *he did not, as in previous occasions, go to encounter enchantments.*

13. That is, in military formation, organized in accordance with its tribal subunits and arranged in a square around the Tabernacle housing the Ark of the Covenant (*Numbers* 2), i.e., a people whose encampment mirrors their inner reality: a people centered on God.

These verses are revelatory. In the first place we are explicitly informed why Balaam has, on two previous occasions, left Balak and his retinue standing by their altars and wandered off alone. We surmised that it was to commune with God, but now we discover that despite his constant claims that he could only say and do what God (or the gods) told him to say or do, in reality Balaam has, after all, been attempting to fulfill his commission. He needed the solitude in order to be able to perform enchantments.[14] It would appear that Balak was right after all: that while Balaam had gained international renown as a diviner—a predictor of the future—he also could and did dabble in sorcery.[15]

But the enchantments haven't been working. Two times running the bucket has come up dry from the well. Instead, God has put "words" in Balaam's mouth; not curses but blessings. Balaam is not stupid. His two-time failure, confirmed by God's pronouncement in the second oracle that Israel is blessed, and furthermore that no magic will be effective against Israel, has been taken to heart. So Balaam abandons his attempts to hex Israel. Having given up on enchantments he no longer needs the secrecy in which to practice his magic, so this time he does not wander off. Instead he turns his back on king and altars to face the wilderness where Israel is encamped.

And Balaam raised his eyes and he <u>saw</u> *Israel encamped in tribal array* [24:2a].

On previous occasions he had had no opportunity to get a panoramic overview of what was to have been the intended recipient of his curse. As part of the targeting operation, he had been positioned by the king at places where he could only glimpse the outlying fringe of the Israelite encampment. Nor was more required: a line-of-sight view of any portion of the people would be sufficient to allow him to guide the curse to its destination.[16]

Once the curse would impact any portion of the Israelite encampment it would immediately spread and infect them all. But this time Balaam is not trying to take aim at an enemy; he has accepted that Israel is blessed and that his "guided missiles" won't work. For the first time Balaam lifts up his eyes and looks at what lies before him; for the first time he actually *sees* the people whom the LORD has brought out of Egypt and has blessed. The result is electric; and amazingly he finds himself free to react. Having abandoned his "enchantments"—*his attempts to coerce his God*—Balaam finds God's restraints upon him lifted. God will no longer put "words" in Balaam's mouth, but instead He rests His spirit upon him, heightening his perception and inspiring him.

And the spirit of God came upon him [24:2b].

Balaam has ceased being a seer; his eyes have been opened and he has metamorphosed into a prophet.

---

14. Hebrew *nehashim*, the plural of *nahash* (23:23). As a noun these are the only two appearances of this term in the Bible; both in the context of the *Book of Balaam*. The reference may be to the recitation of magical incantations or some other magical practices.

15. See Chapter 8, note 63.

16. "It is implicit that having the target of the curse in sight is requisite to the efficacy of the pronouncement." (Levine, p. 215) See also Chapter 8, note 17.

The oracle that will now issue from his lips bespeaks a sea change. The prologue which introduces it is something radically new, as is the oracle's source. Up to now it was God Who dictated the content—placed the "word" in Balaam's mouth; Balaam the seer would be free to tack on some elaborative material—mainly biographical or contextual—at the beginning and at the end of the "word." But from here on in we will no longer be dealing with a seer but with a prophet, and his oracles become something different, not only in degree but in kind. Inspired by God's spirit, his inner eye immeasurably energized, it is Balaam who now is the author of his oracles. From a mouthpiece of God, a sort of mechanical transmitter of God's word, we now find ourselves confronted with a human being infused with God's spirit and inspired to reveal God's truth as he now is capable of perceiving it. From God's puppet he has graduated to being God's partner. All this he attempts to put into words in his prologue, beginning with the threefold repetition of the word *neum* (*utterance*), one of the two explicit signatures of prophecy.[17]

His prologue, beyond introducing his proclamation of an enlightened vision concerning Israel, is simultaneously a confession. Balaam not only has learned something about this new people Israel and of God's intentions for it, but also something about himself: what he has been, what he now is and what he might become. One who once thought he could see into the heart of things, now knows that he has been blind; one who had an overweening conception of himself, who saw himself as a towering figure, now knows that he is next to nothing; one who once relied on his vast fund of knowledge and esoteric expertise, now knows that all wisdom comes from God. In his prologue, he decries his past blindness, extols his privilege of being privy to God's word and vision, admits his fallen state and celebrates the fact that finally his eyes have been unveiled and he can at last truly see.

The Third Oracle

Now he uttered his oracle, saying:

"The utterance of Balaam, the son of[18] *Beor,*
And the utterance of the man whose eye [has been] *sealed shut,*[19]

The utterance of him who knows the words of God,
[*And who knows the thoughts*[20] *of the Most High*][21]

---

17. Hebrew *neum*: this word indicates a divine utterance and is a synonym for "oracle." Its parallel indicator is the phrase *Thus says the* Lord.

18. Hebrew *beno*; the suffix "o," the remnant of the archaic nominative case ending, is vivid testimony to the early date of this poem. (Albright, "Oracles," p. 216, note 54.)

19. Reading *satum* with Vulg. This is a variant spelling of the common Hebrew word meaning "closed," "stopped up," as in *Lamentations* 3:8. MT vocalizes the consonantal text as *shatum*: a rare term found only in Aramaic and late (Rabbinic) Hebrew with the specific meaning of boring a small hole in a wine cask or an amphora to draw a sample for tasting. As *shatum*, the word occurs only here in the Hebrew Bible. It seems to me more than a stretch to interpret this rare word as "open" in general, to apply it to eyes in particular, and then to project its use back more than a thousand years, all without any attestation. In another though hardly superior option, Albright, following Wellhausen and citing a Phoenician incantation for support, renders the phrase as "whose eye is perfect." ("Oracles," p. 216, notes 56 & 57.)

20. Literally, *knowledge*. MT vocalizes in the singular, but most likely it should be in the plural (*dayot*) as in 1 Samuel 2:3.

21. Metrically a line is missing after *the words of God*. This prologue to the oracle is repeated below in 24:16, where it contains the missing line. Along with almost all recent commentators we propose restoring it to the present verse.

Who views visions from The Almighty,[22]
Fallen down, yet with eyes unveiled."[23] (24:3–4)

The main body of the oracle which immediately follows is an unrestrained eulogistic outpouring, a poetic flood praising Israel. Beginning in the present with the overwhelming impression Israel-the-lovely has made upon him, Balaam, through a cascade of similes and metaphors, pictures the future prosperity of a God-empowered Israel; her political ascendancy and, under divine guardianship, her triumphs over her enemies.

Returning to the metaphor of a lion, he pictures Israel's place among the nations as something irresistibly wonderful. The panegyric comes to its climax in the concluding couplet, which is a repetition of God's pledge to Abraham,[24] restating the promise as an accomplished fact.

How fair[25] *are your tents, O Jacob,*
Your dwelling places, O Israel!   A

As wadis [that the Lord*] has stretched out,*[26]
As gardens beside a river,   B

As aloes planted by the Lord,
As cedars beside [many] waters.[27]   C

Water flows from his buckets,[28]
And their roots have abundant water.   D

His king[29] *shall be raised up higher than Agag,*[30]
And his kingdom shall be exalted.   E

---

22. Hebrew *Shaddai* (possibly originally meaning "The One of the Mountain"), was a common designation of the Lord in the Age of Abraham. In the Deir 'Alla inscriptions, *Shaddai* in the plural (*shaddaiim*) is used as a synonym for *elohim*, and clearly means "gods." The term is archaic, and in Israel it became simply an alternate designation for the Lord. The common English translation, which we use, "The Almighty," comes from LXX (*ho pantokrator*) and Vulg. (*omnipotens*). (Ashley, p. 488)

23. Note: In his dream, God unveils Balaam's eyes in his third encounter with the angel, and when he sees the angel he falls down (prostrates himself). Here, in his third oracle, he confesses himself as fallen yet with eyes unveiled (same word as in 22:31).

24. *Genesis* 12:3. See Chapter 8, note 48. It is almost an exact quote of Isaac's blessing of Jacob, only the order of the clauses is reversed (*Genesis* 27:29).

25. Hebrew *tobu* (the plural of *tob*, "good"); in the sense of "pleasing," as in *Canticles* 4:10.

26. A wadi is a wilderness riverbed that only flows with water during the rainy season. As a result of the water then absorbed, it presents a verdant, even lush, contrast to the surrounding parched environment.

27. Albright suggests adding the word *rabim* (many) from verse 7, both because of the meter and because *mayim rabim* "is a standard Hebrew topographic expression, used for a place with pools." ("Oracles," p. 217, note 67) To nomads in a desert surrounding, an abundance of water is a paradise only to be dreamed of.

28. Reading with Rashi. The picture is that of a person striding from a well bearing two buckets filled to the brim, with water slopping over the sides.

29. This bestowal of a future king upon Israel is again a reflection of God's pledges to Abraham (*Genesis* 19:6, 16) and Jacob (*Genesis* 38:11), that they would be progenitors of kings.

30. A king of the Amalekites (see Glossary). Some commentators deny that "Agag" is a personal name and see it as an Amalekite dynastic name, or as a title like "Pharaoh" in Egypt. In the thirteenth century bce the Amalekite horde was a power to be reckoned with. The entire oracle—its imagery and its political context—bears witness to its nomadic and wilderness setting.

God brought him[31] *out of Egypt,*
He [God] is for him like the horns of a wild ox.[32]   F

He shall devour the nations, his enemies,
He shall crush their bones
And with his arrows he wounds them.[33]   G

He crouches; he lies down like a lion;
Like the king of beasts,[34] *who [dare] rouse him?*   H

Blessed are they that bless you,
And they that curse you are accursed. (24:5–9)   I

In the first two oracles, the ones which the LORD "put in Balaam's mouth," the subject was the LORD's past election of Israel. Now, inspired by God's spirit, Balaam shifts the focus to Israel's future as it is nourished, sustained and ultimately empowered by God.[35] The final couplet of the oracle, making explicit what has been becoming increasingly evident as it progressed, not only confirms Israel's state of blessedness but damns all who would curse it.

Sacked

This, for Balak, is the last straw. Confronted with this unequivocal pean of praise[36] in place of the curses he was anticipating, he explodes in fury.

Now Balak was furious with Balaam,[37] *and he struck his hands together [in anger]. And Balak said to Balaam, "I summoned you to damn my enemies, and behold, all that you have done is to bless them*[38] *these three times! And now, get out! Back to where you came from!*[39] *I said that I would assuredly honor you,*[40] *but behold the* LORD *has denied you the honor"* [24:10–11].

Balak's patience is at an end. Not only has Balaam not fulfilled his contract

---

31. *Him*: the third person singular pronouns in this verse and the next refer to Israel except where otherwise indicated. See Chapter 8, note 51 and 60.

32. See Chapter 8, note 62 for this imagery.

33. Both metrically and in content this line is extremely problematic. This rendition can be no more than a guess.

34. See Chapter 8, note 66, for this euphemism.

35. The poetic picture of Israel's future prosperity harps on the theme of water. Five times in the course of two verses (24:6–7) water in the various forms it takes (wadis, river, water) recurs like a drum beat. Beyond water being a source of life, it also serves as a symbol of God; cf., God comparing Himself to *a fountain of living waters* (Jeremiah 2:13). Only in couplets F–H we return to the theme of the God Who brought Israel out of Egypt, and will empower it to triumph over all its enemies.

36. There are commentators who take some of the allusions in the oracle to be messianic.

37. Literally, *Now Balak's anger was kindled against Balaam*. This is the third use of this idiom. First it was used to describe God's fury with Balaam (22:22), and then to depict Balaam's fury with his donkey (22:27). Now it is Balaam who is the victim of Balak's fury.

38. Literally, *blessing have you blessed*, the infinitive absolute.

39. Literally, *And now, flee away, you; back to your place!*

40. I.e., richly reward you. See Chapter 7, note 23.

and cursed Israel, but he has done the opposite: he has explicitly blessed them. The king summarily fires Balaam, withholding all pay. And anticipating another repeat of Balaam's excuse—that he only says what God tells him to say—as a parting shot he tells Balaam that if he has any complaint about being sent home with empty pockets, he should take it up with the Lord his god. It is He Who is responsible for making you break your contract; an accusation that holds more truth than Balak realizes as he holds Balaam responsible for the fiasco, and his remark is meant sarcastically.

Balak is not the only one who is furious. Balaam, frustrated by his multiple failures and publicly humiliated by being fired in the presence of the king's entire retinue—his nobles, his high officials and the entire train of attendants he brought along on this expedition—has himself been driven to the boiling point. This is no way to treat an internationally renowned seer! In a rage he opens his retort with his now mantra-like excuse, backdating it to the early stages of their negotiations:

> *And Balaam said to Balak, "Did I not speak to the messengers that you sent to me, saying, '[Even]* if *Balak were to give me his palace filled with silver and gold I could not do anything, good or evil, contrary to the command of the* Lord. *What the* Lord *says, that must I say'?"*[41] [24:12–13]

In other words, by agreeing to engage me under these conditions it is you who are breaking contract.

Of course, there is no court where Balaam can sue for breach of contract, and no way he can force Balak to pay what he owes; it is the king who possesses the soldiers. There is only one avenue open to Balaam before he must make his shamefaced exit. It is in the realm of the spirit—the one arena in which he reigns supreme—in which he possesses the tools to get his own back. And even in his rage Balaam reacts with moderation; he makes no attempt to lay Balak or Moab under a curse. He responds neither as a seer nor as a sorcerer, but as the prophet that he has become. As Balak publicly humiliated him so will he retaliate: humiliating the king by publicly revealing to one and all what lies in store for them. So Balaam raises his voice and proclaims:

> *"And now, behold, I go back to my people."*

That is, you have the power to withhold my honorarium and to throw me out of your kingdom. But before I go,

> *"Come, I will advise you*[42] *as to what this people* [Israel] *will do to your people in the days to come"* [24:14].

---

41. That the messengers apparently never delivered that message is irrelevant to Balaam's current complaint. Balaam certainly did put himself on official record with regard to his non-negotiable conditions for entering Balak's employ, and under those conditions Balak hired him.

42. Hebrew, *iyatscha* (from the root *yiuts*). On the basis of the Proto-Semitic Inscriptions, Albright contends that the basic meaning of *yiuts* originally was "to utter an oracle," with especial reference to a prediction of the future. (*The Proto-Semitic Inscriptions and Their Decipherment*, pp. 21 and 43) "Since people who sought an oracle could use it as a guide, the meaning 'to advise' developed." (Ashley, p. 499)

Chapter 9. The Prophet

The Fourth Oracle[43]

Now he uttered his oracle, saying:	
"The utterance of Balaam, the son of Beor,	
And the utterance of the man whose eye [has been] *sealed shut,*	A
The utterance of him who knows the words of God,	
And who knows the thoughts of the Most High	B
Who views visions from The Almighty,	
Fallen down, yet with eyes unveiled.[44]	C
I see him, but not in the present,[45]	
I behold him, but not soon"[46]:	D
A star[47] *strides forth from Jacob,*	
A scepter[48] *arises*[49] *from Israel.*	E
He smashes the borders[50] *of Moab,*	
The territory[51] *of the Children of Seth.*[52]	F
And Edom shall be dispossessed,[53]	
Yea, dispossessed shall be Seir[54];	G

---

43. The text of this oracle is difficult, as evidenced by the many notes, but verses 24:18–19 (couplets g and h) are exceptionally problematic, both textually and structurally. This has led us to depart from our normal procedure of translating the received text (MT) as is, and then dealing with its problems. In the case of these two verses, we have tampered with MT (in what for modern biblical commentators would be considered a minimal fashion)—moving one word, transposing (that is switching the order) of two lines, and re-dividing two words—in order to improve both the meter and the clarity of the poetry. By so doing, while preserving the overall meaning of the text (as well as we can currently understand it), we also think that we have significantly improved, as a piece of poetry, the seemingly muddled text we currently possess. Whether we have achieved our purpose of restoring the received text to something closer to its original is, however, an open question. For purposes of comparison, we append a rather literal version of these verses:

Moab will become a possession,
   And Seir, his enemies, will be a possession;
And Israel is triumphant.
A victor emerges from Jacob,
   He will destroy the remnant from the city.

From this, in our translation in the main body we have
1. moved the last words (in Hebrew one word) from the end of line 2 to the end of line 4.
2. switched the order of lines 3 and 4.
3. repointed the last word of line 3 from *ir* (city) to *ar* (the name of the former capital of Greater Moab, cf. 22:36 and 21:28).

44. For textual comments see notes 18–23 above.
45. Hebrew *lo attah*; literally *not now*. The word *attah* is a consistently temporal term.
46. Hebrew *lo karob*; literally *not near* in a temporal rather than a spatial sense; *karob* has both meanings.
47. I.e., a king; as in *Isaiah* 14:12 where the king of Babylon is poetically depicted as the morning star.
48. *Scepter*; again a euphemism for a king, he who holds the scepter, cf. *Genesis* 49:10.
49. *Arises*: with a hostile intent, as in *Numbers* 10:35. (Milgrom, p. 208)
50. Albright suggests the meaning of "borders," "frontiers" for *paatai*, based on its meaning in Ugaritic. ("Oracles," p. 220, note 80)
51. From Akkadian, where *qaqqaru* means "ground," "territory." (Milgrom, p. 323, note 66)
52. *Children of Seth*: "A general designation for all the nomadic groups descended from Abraham (see *Gen.* 25) … over whom Israel was promised dominance in the patriarchal blessings, as in *Genesis* 27:29." (Milgrom, p. 208)
53. Hebrew *yerushah* from the verb *yrash*. Reading it as a passive participle we get the meaning *to be dispossessed*. (Albright, "Oracles," p. 221, note 92) The translation follows the Hebrew word order: abba.
54. Edom is the name of the nation (i.e., the people) situated just south of Moab. Seir is the name of the territory and of the mountain range that forms its backbone. The two names are often used as synonyms in the Bible.

> *Jacob shall rule over his enemies,*
> *And Israel shall do mightily,*
> *Destroying the remnant of Ar.*[55] (24:15–19)   H

This oracle, and the three immediately following, differ from Balaam's first three not merely in degree but in kind. The first three were descriptive and interpretive, singling out specific aspects of the past and immediate present and identifying their significance. The present oracle and its successors shift their perspective exclusively to the future, focusing solely on distant outcomes. As a result, beyond the uncertainties of textual integrity and archaic terminology which plagued our efforts of interpretation of Balaam's first oracles, we now also have to contend with a number of problems that bedevil our understanding of all biblical visions of things to come. In our case, these can be summed up as follows. First, there is the use of ambiguous terms, which the text does not bother to explain; the context itself is ambiguous and the ancient versions give little help, either using equally unclear terminology or simply translating the text that we find in MT with all its difficulties. And secondly, we are burdened with what later interpreters, both in the Bible and in the post-biblical period have understood these oracles to mean. These traditions of interpretation cannot help but influence our perceptions.

Beyond a heightened awareness of the pitfalls confronting us, we embrace Timothy Ashley's advice: the "lack of certainty over the author's exact meaning ought to keep the interpreter from making definitive pronouncements on the specific referent in the text.... One must first suggest what the MT, as far as it is intelligible, meant [to its original audience], then recognize that these oracles will have a fuller meaning as they are placed in their wider biblical context."[56] All that we will attempt at this juncture, therefore, will be to get some insight into how Balaam and his thirteenth-century-BCE audience—pagans all—might have understood his words.

The immediate context of our oracle is Balaam's furious reply to the king's public termination of his services and his being kicked out of the country:

> *"And now, behold, I go back to my people. Come, I will advise you as to what this people* [Israel] *will do to your people in the days to come"* [24:14].

The key word in this verse is "people," repeated three times: *my people, this people* [Israel] and *your people.* Balaam begins by disassociating himself and his people from the arena of conflict between the Israelite people and the Moabite people; he has no part in their future and is purely an impartial outside observer reporting what objectively he sees. The burden of the oracle is clear[57]: *this people,* i.e., Israel, is going to pulverize *your people,* i.e., Moab. Sometime in the future, *not soon,* a ruler will arise in Israel, decisively defeat and rule over Moab (and incidentally, also over Edom, Moab's southern

---

55. Or more properly, *Ar-moab,* the former capital of "Greater Moab" before its northern territories between the Arnon and Jabbok Rivers were sliced off and incorporated into the Amorite Kingdom of Heshbon. (See Appendix C: North Moab.) In the late thirteenth century BCE *Ar* was still one of the most important population centers in Moab.

56. Ashley, p. 498.

57. While many of the details in the oracle are obscure, and all renditions are debatable, the overall thrust is beyond doubt.

neighbor).⁵⁸ This is my legacy that I leave to you, Balak: your worst fears will ultimately be realized. The people you wanted me to destroy for you will eventually destroy your people. This is guaranteed. Your only comfort is that it will not be in your time.

In the heady days of the Davidic Empire some three hundred years later, there were those who saw David's conquest of Moab (and incidentally Edom) around 990 BCE as the fulfillment of Balaam's prediction. But David's empire, as empires do, came to an end, and Moab (and Edom) regained their independence. In the post-biblical era the interpretative emphasis of the *star* and the *scepter* shifted from an earthly ruler to a messianic figure. Beyond this there is not much that can be said that is not mainly conjecture.

The Final Words

The relationship between Balaam and Balak had been an uneasy one from the start, full of tension and beset by cross purposes. Balaam had been summoned from afar, hired to curse Israel but instead blessed them, and was consequently fired and sent back where he came from. But it is Balaam who has had the last word—a devastating rebuff—and considering the circumstances he has delivered a magnificent exit line. Anything further would be an anticlimax; at this point he should just leave, but he doesn't. He pushes on, another three oracles' worth. Perhaps, having entered into some sort of prophetic trance, the momentum of prophesying simply swept him on. In other words, the matter was not fully under his control.⁵⁹

*Now he saw Amalek,*⁶⁰ *and he uttered his oracle, saying:*

"First of the nations is Amalek,
*Yet his end is to perish for ever!"*⁶¹

And he saw the Kenite, and he uttered his oracle, saying:

"Everlasting is your dwelling place,
Your nest set among cliffs;
*None the less Kain*⁶² *shall be consumed,*⁶³
Your dwelling place a heap [of ruins] *and a garbage dump."*⁶⁴

---

58. Does this imply some future alliance between these two peoples directed against Israel?

59. Another possibility is that he did leave, and the following three short oracles, also by Balaam but delivered in some other context, were tacked on by an editor. Why they would have been appended we cannot say with any certainty, but perhaps to bring the total number of oracles up to the mystic number seven. Levine, on the other hand, thinks the purpose to be "so as to give Balaam a reputation as a prophet to the nations." (p. 237)

60. As opposed to 24:2, when *Balaam raised his eyes and he saw Israel encamped in tribal array*. Unlike the process of putting a hex on a subject, which necessitated the target being in direct line of sight, a prophetic vision had no such requirements. In this triad all references to seeing are with the inner eye.

61. Reading with Sam. MT reads *his end will be destruction*.

62. Taking the singular, *Kain* (smith), as a collective noun for the Kenites (who were a nomadic tribe of metalworkers), even as *Amalek* in 24:20 serves for the Amalekites. On the other hand, the original audience would have been aware that there is a word play taking place here. The Hebrew word for *nest* in the previous line is *kain* (with an identical spelling as our proper noun), so this line could also be read: *None the less the nest shall be consumed*.

63. Literally, *burnt up*.

64. Taking the *daled* (D) of *ad* in MT as a misread *resh* (R), then reading *ad-ma* as *aremah, a heap* [of ruins], c.f. *Nehemiah* 3:34. Thus the *Biblia Hebraica* proposes reading the line as *arema weashpot moshabecha*, which rendition we adopt for want of a better.

And he uttered his oracle, saying:

"The isles shall be gathered from the north,
And ships from the furthest reaches of the sea,[65]
They shall afflict Ashur and they shall afflict Eber,[66]
So he also shall perish for ever!" (24:20–24)

Outside of their common introductory phrase—*he uttered his oracle, saying*—these three oracles seem to have nothing in common with the four major compositions that preceded them. In comparison with the sometimes difficult but relatively comprehensible language of their predecessors, the wording of these three is so uncertain, obscure and ambiguous as to produce radically disparate and conflicting renditions by different translators. In fact, all English versions of the original Hebrew are little more than scholarly guesswork. This makes any attempt at interpretation problematic in the extreme. The most that one can say with any certainty is that, in contradistinction to the first four oracles which are, in sum, blessings; in this triad of mini-oracles what unites them is their negativity. They all predict calamity and doom.[67]

Amalek

Now he saw Amalek and he uttered his oracle, saying:

"First of the nations is Amalek,
Yet his end is to perish forever!"

The heading of the first of our triad identifies its subject as Amalek, a nomadic conglomerate horde made up of a sizable number of tribes and clans, all related in some fashion by common descent or ties of marriage. Its range of movement and domination was the Sinai, the Negeb and possibly a segment of northern Arabia. They were the first "nation" or "people" encountered by the Israelites shortly after the Exodus from Egypt, when the Amalekites attacked their column.[68] This confrontation proved traumatic for Israel. It was deemed a miracle that the Amalekites failed to exterminate the Israelites and were driven off.[69] The event seared itself into the national consciousness. We are informed that, immediately after the encounter, God instructed Moses:

"Write this for a memorial in a scroll, and read it aloud to Joshua, for I will utterly blot out the memory of Amalek from under the heavens." So Moses built an altar,

---

65. Following Albright, "Oracles," notes 107–111. With the exception of again reading a *daled* (D) as a misread *resh* (R), i.e., *miyarketai yam* in place of *miyad kitim*, Albright does not depart from the consonantal text of MT.

66. Reading with Sam., *veyaanu*, in the imperfect plural, i.e., "they shall afflict."

67. This statement requires qualification: even in this point there is no unanimity: both C. F. Keil (*The Book of Numbers*, Edinburgh, T. & T. Clark, 1869, p. 196–197) and F. C. Coole (*The Fourth Book of Moses Called Numbers*, London, Murray, 1871, p. 747–748) read into 24:22 a positive meaning.

68. Probably merely a segment of Amalek, no more than a tribe or two; Israel at that point could hardly have survived an assault by the entire horde.

69. According to *Exodus* 17:8–13, only the act of Moses, managing to hold aloft his staff, "the rod of God," for the entire day insured the divine aid that allowed the Israelites to barely beat off the assault.

and named it Adonai-nisi.[70] *And he said:* "[The name means] *'Hand upon the throne of the Lord: The Lord will wage war with Amalek from generation to generation'"*[71] [*Exodus* 17:14–16].

The passing of that generation did nothing to dim the memory of the trauma. In *Deuteronomy* this intention and oath will be codified as an injunction:

Remember what Amalek did to you on the way as you came out of Egypt. How he fell on you on the road, when you were faint and weary, cutting down all the stragglers in your rear; he had no fear of God! Therefore, when the Lord your God has given you rest from all your enemies around you, in the land that the Lord your God is giving you as an inheritance, to possess it, you shall blot out the memory of Amalek from under the heavens. You shall not forget! [*Deuteronomy* 25:17–19]

The ritualized enmity was destined to persist, Amalek becoming the paradigmatic enemy of Israel—and ultimately of all decent humanity—a symbol of endemic evil to be extirpated. And it is in the light of this background that the Israelites, when they became aware of the existence of this oracle, undoubtedly understood it: although mighty and threatening now, Amalek is destined to vanish from the earth. And so it did.[72] The evil that Amalek represented is another matter entirely. It lives on in the hearts of men, taking new forms in each generation.

The Kenites

And he saw the Kenite, and he uttered his oracle, saying:

"Everlasting is your dwelling place,
Your nest set among cliffs;

None the less Kain shall be consumed,
Your dwelling place a heap [of ruins] *and a garbage dump."*

The heading of the second mini-oracle of our triad declares its subject to be "The Kenite," a people positioned at the opposite end of the spectrum from the Amalekites. While the Amalekites were the hostile horde whose very name became the symbol of evil and unending hostility toward Israel, the relations between the Kenites—a clan of nomadic metalworkers (*Kain* means "smith")—and the Israelites were uniformly positive. Connected by marriage—Moses married into the clan (*Exodus* 2:16–22)[73]—the Kenites acted as guides for the Children of Israel during their years of wandering in the Wilderness[74] and are destined to act as military allies, actively participating in the

---

70. I.e. *"The Lord is my banner."*
71. I.e. eternally.
72. Circa 1020 BCE, in a major campaign in the northern Negeb, King Saul delivered a massive body blow to Amalek, throwing the horde onto the defensive. His successor, David, decisively defeated the Amalekite horde, reducing its remnants to subservience. The last recorded mention of Amalek occurs during the reign of King Hezekiah (716–687 BCE) when the destruction of the last remnants of the Amalekites, who had fled to Edomite territory, is recorded (*1 Chronicles* 4:43).
73. In those days the Kenites had been part of the Midianite Confederation. At a later date the clan, or at least a portion of it, detached itself from the Midianite conglomerate and settled in the Negeb south of the tribe of Judah (*Judges* 1:16).
74. *Numbers* 10:29–32.

campaigns to conquer Canaan.⁷⁵ We know that relations continued to be good through the days of Saul and David, some 250 years after the times of Balaam.⁷⁶

With regard to their relationship with Israel, the Kenites are the very antithesis of the Amalekites. And just as the evil done by the Amalekites was not forgotten in Israel—*you shall not forget* (Deuteronomy 25:19)—so was the good received from the hands of the Kenites not consigned to oblivion.

In this regard it would be well to recall a dramatic episode from King Saul's campaign against the Amalekites. Upon preparing to attack, Saul discovers a Kenite encampment in the vicinity.⁷⁷ Saul thus faces a dilemma. If he launches his attack, the Kenites will inevitably be caught between the opposing forces and decimated. Instead of taking the position that these are the fortunes of war—or as Napoleon is reputed to have said, "If you want to make an omelet, you have to break eggs"—Saul decides to warn the Kenites and give them a chance to escape. By doing this he knowingly gives up his trump card, the element of surprise. But he cannot see his way clear to countenancing the sacrifice of the friendly Kenites on the altar of expediency.

> *Saul said to the Kenites, "Go, depart, get you down from among the Amalekites, lest I destroy you with them; for you showed kindness to all of the Children of Israel when they came up out of Egypt." So the Kenites departed from among the Amalekites* [1 Samuel 15:6].

The price paid in Israelite blood for this act of magnanimity must have been high, but there seems no reason to doubt that Saul was authentically representing the feelings of the Israelites in this matter. All of which leads us to some very puzzling conclusions, for despite the relationships between Israel and these two peoples being polar opposites, Balaam's oracles consign both to an equivalent doom. But in his first four oracles Balaam clearly and decisively identified his position with that of Israel. This leads one to suspect that these two oracles—against Amalek and against the Kenite—despite their proximity to the first four have nothing to do with them⁷⁸ and do not belong here at all, or conversely, that while belonging where they are, there is something very wrong with the Kenite oracle.

The suspicion that the latter may be the case is strengthened by the fact that outside of the heading—*And he saw the Kenite, and he uttered his oracle and said:*—the body of the oracle does not, on the face of it, seem to have anything to do with Kenites. The Kenites were nomads, breeders and raisers of livestock, with additional skills as metalworkers. As such, they were tent dwellers of no fixed abode,⁷⁹ constantly migrating—

---

75. Several generations later, Jael, "the wife of Heber the Kenite," a contemporary of Deborah, became a national hero to the Israelites, due to her spectacular assassination of the Canaanite general Sisera during Israel's Third War of National Liberation (Judges 4:17–22). For a detailed account of this war and the part played by Jael, see my *Judges and Saviors*, pp. 95–113, 132–133.

76. 1 Samuel 15:6; 30:29.

77. After the conquest of Canaan, the Kenites chose to locate themselves in Amalekite territory; Judges 1:16 (LXX reading *and they went and settled among the Amalekites*).

78. As postulated by some scholars; see note 59 above.

79. In her victory pean, Deborah describes Jael the Kenite as:
Most blessed of women be Jael –
  The wife of Heber the Kenite –
Of tent-dwelling women most blessed. (Judges 5:24)

seeking grazing for their flocks, and customers in need of their skills—their habitat the wilderness, the semi-arid lands that separate desert from the cultivated fields of the Fertile Crescent. But this is not the description of the people being consigned to oblivion:

Everlasting[80] is your dwelling place,
Your nest set among cliffs.

This is the image of a sedentary people that has embedded itself in mountain strongholds, the very antithesis of nomads. Indeed the description sounds remarkably similar to the prophet Obadiah's denunciation of the Edomites.[81]

The hubris of your heart has deceived you,
O dweller in the clefts of the cliffs,

Who sets his habitation in the Heights;
Who says in his heart:
"Who can bring me down to the ground?"

Though you make your nest as high as the Eagle,
Yea, even if you set it among the stars,
From there I will bring you down:
an oracle of the LORD. (*Obadiah* 1:3–4)

This leads to the suspicion that Balaam's sixth oracle may be addressed not to the Kenites but to the Edomites. If so, then it logically becomes an extension or annex to couplet G of the Fourth Oracle, that puzzling digression in an oracle primarily directed against Moab. It also resolves the problem of Balaam impartially dispensing predictions of doom upon Israel's foes and friends alike. Edom became an inveterate enemy of Israel, destined to disappear from the political map[82] and then to live on as a symbol: the name applied to Rome, and then to successor states that persecuted the Jews. In this regard Amalek and Edom form a pair, and should we accept the possibility of the sixth oracle being intended for Edom, then it is possible to see symmetry in these two oracles and a connection with the first four.

The final oracle is unique in that it has neither a national nor an ethnic subject; it is addressed to everyone in general and to no one in particular. It is also the most obscure of all Balaam's utterances, and thus its rendition into English the most problematic. The only interpretive rule I can suggest is: the more that the words group together into phrases that seem to make sense, the more guesswork has been employed.[83] In our rendition it reads:

---

80. Hebrew *aitan*; with the connotation of "permanent," "secure."

81. In his "Oracles to the Nations," Jeremiah uses virtually identical language in his denunciation of Edom (*Jeremiah* 49:16).

82. The Edomites were eventually dispossessed from their homeland by the Nabataeans, pushed westward into the Negeb, and eventually converted to Judaism by the Hasmonaean King John Hyrcanus (135–106 BCE).

83. Just on the simplest level, it must be remembered that in biblical times the alphabet contained no symbols to represent vowels, but only letters that represented consonants; there were also no spaces between words. The reader was presented with an unbroken string of consonants and it was up to him to break this string into words and supply the appropriate vowels to make sense of these resultant groups of letters. It therefore has not been uncommon for there to be serious disagreement between different readers as to not only what the biblical text means but even as to what exactly the text *is*. It is here that the practice of educated (hopefully) guesswork begins.

And he uttered his oracle, saying:

"The isles shall be gathered from the north,
And ships from the furthest reaches of the sea,[84]
They shall afflict Ashur and they shall afflict Eber,
So he also shall perish for ever!" (24:23–24)

Balaam has outdone himself in obscurantism. What seems possible is that he might be envisioning an age of chaos let loose upon the world, such as occurred in the general collapse of civilization that brought the Bronze Age to its disastrous conclusion.[85] There are those who have seen in these two verses (24:23–24) allusions to the so-called "Peoples of the Sea" who spread slaughter, fire and destruction along the shores of the Mediterranean and far inland. There is no real idea, much less a consensus, as to who or what Ashur or Eber refer to, and as to the identity of the "he" who will "perish forever," no one seems to have the least idea; perhaps Balaam is referring to a world that has vanished with the storm never to return. And with these mysterious words, Balaam emerges from his possibly trance-like state to confront once again a king and his court reeling with shock, and his new status of *persona non grata* in the land of Moab.

So Balaam arose and left, and returned to his place; and Balak also went his way [24: 25].

With these words, depicting our two protagonists—angry, embittered, each profoundly dissatisfied by the outcomes of their expectations—turning their backs on each other and stalking off to their respective homes, the *Book of Balaam* concludes. Of Balaam at least we could hope that:

> *He went like one that had been stunned,*
> *And is of sense forlorn:*
> *A sadder and a wiser man,*
> *He rose the morrow morn.*
> —Samuel Taylor Coleridge, *The Rime of the Ancient Mariner*

---

84. Following Albright; see note 65 above.

85. For a brief overview of this devastating civilizational debacle which commenced in the 13th century BCE and stretched into the 12th, see my *Judges and Saviors*, pp. xxx–xxxii.

CHAPTER 10

Retrospect

He who is now called a prophet was formerly called a seer.
—1 Samuel 9:9

Having concluded our close reading and analysis of Chapters 22–24 of the *Book of Numbers*, let us draw together the various insights we have reached. We have been treating these chapters as an autonomous literary composition: the *"Book of Balaam"* as the rabbis of the Talmud named it. If it indeed is such, then the time has come to try to reach some conclusions as to its nature and meaning. It would seem that the proper place to begin is by passing in review our original hypotheses and evaluating their validity in the light of our analysis of the text. How well have they stood up to the test?

Beginning with the oracles themselves, we would contend that we have found nothing in their contents, vocabulary or grammar that is incompatible with the late-13th–early-12th-century date for their composition that we postulated.[1] This would mean that the oracles are contemporaneous with the lifetime of Balaam as depicted in the narrative, and this buttresses the credibility of its claim that they were indeed originally proclaimed by him.

That the *Book of Balaam* is a unitary work, composed by a highly talented and refined author, and not an editorial composite, has been borne out by our close reading and analysis of the text. Virtually all of the so-called "contradictions" that have been taken by various biblical scholars as "proof" of multiple sources, editorially patched together, we have found to be the products of an overly literalistic (and simplistic) underreading of the text. With a proper appreciation of the author's cultivated and subtle literary technique, most of the "internal contradictions" have vanished into thin air, while those remaining have been adequately explained. We are left with a remarkable work of literary art built around seven oracles—archaic pagan poems, the products of an alien world and dating from days of old—possessing a new life and a meaning all of its own.

And finally, our close reading of the text of the *Book of Balaam* has also confirmed our initial impression of the disconnect between the factual account of the events related in the tale and the tone and thrust displayed by the narrative which relates them. The characters in the story are all pagan, as is the environment—mental

---

1. This estimation was based on the philological and orthographical analysis of W. F. Albright. See introduction to the *Book of Balaam* above.

as well as physical—in which the tale plays itself out. Yet the entire tone of the narrative,[2] and the ideological assumptions underlying it, are robustly monotheistic. Much like the *Book of Job*, it would seem to be a tale set in the pagan world that is being told by a monotheist, i.e., an Israelite. This also fits in with our original hypothesis that eventually the oracles, along with the accompanying tale of the events that led to their proclamation, found their way from the pagan world which spawned them into Israelite circles. In the course of time, a talented Israelite author was inspired by them to compose the *Book of Balaam* that we now possess,[3] building his work around the original oracles—retained as he had inherited them—and using the accompanying tale as the primary source for his account of their genesis. Starting with the main facts to which he fell heir, he built upon them the sophisticated and enigmatic narrative masterpiece we now possess.

If this be accepted, then we must confront the question: what was the purpose of the author in composing his work? What was his agenda—all authors have agendas—and what was he driving at? Our suggestion will be that, first and foremost, the *Book of Balaam* was written to be a tale of enlightenment; primarily it is a tale of perception, of growth and of transformation.

The Seer

What steers us toward this assertion is the prominence of the root *raah*, which in its various verbal forms has the meanings of *to see, to perceive, to understand* (that is, to mentally grasp), *to consider* and so on, while as a noun it denotes the designation *"seer,"* the calling of the hero of our tale, Balaam. This term serves as a keyword that accents the central theme of the *Book of Balaam* as the author plays on its various meanings.[4] The *Book* opens with this word:

Now Balak, son of Zippor, <u>saw</u> *everything Israel had done to the Amorites*[5] [22:2].

Further, the critical turning point of the narrative is signaled by a strikingly similar phrase:

Now Balaam <u>saw</u> *that it was good in the eyes of the* LORD *to bless Israel....*[6] [24:1]

The most intensive use of the term occurs in the prophetic dream sequence, where Balaam and his donkey exchange roles: four times the donkey proves herself to be the true *"seer"* when she is able to *see* (i.e., perceive) the presence of the angel while Balaam demonstrates that he is the ass by his inability to do so.[7] Only when the LORD

---

2. As distinct from the oracles themselves.
3. Probably in the tenth century BCE. See note 1 above.
4. The root *raah* appears eighteen times in the *Book of Balaam*, three times in the oracles themselves (more on this later) and fifteen times strategically distributed by the author in the surrounding narrative.
5. Because of the constraints of English grammar, it is impossible to retain the Hebrew word order when translating this phrase. The original Hebrew verse begins with the word *vayaar* (*now he saw*), placing the opening emphasis on the *act of seeing* (and not on the subject of the sentence who was doing the seeing), and thus sounding the opening note of what will be the central theme of the work. See Chapter 9, note 9.
6. Once again the word *vayaar* (*now he saw*) heads the sentence (see previous note).
7. 22:23, 25, 27, 33.

Chapter 10. Retrospect

intervenes and unveils Balaam's eyes can he *see* what his donkey has *seen* all along[8]; the point being that vision (including understanding) is a God-given gift. Without His help even the most gifted of humans is a blind ass.

The author repeatedly plays with the term. The tale opens with the King of Moab *seeing* what is taking place around him, but due to his pagan frame of reference he doesn't *perceive* the significance of what he *sees*. Locked in by his pagan mindset, he remains frozen in place and never progresses. While three times he instructs Balaam as to what he should *see*,[9] fixated on a superficial operational level he lacks any *insight* into the significance of the drama that is taking place before his eyes.

It is Balaam, the hero of the tale, who exhibits growth and development. From one who could only *see* Israel partially,[10] he progresses to a *vision* of Israel in its entirety.[11] From one blind to the presence of an angel, he advances to a point where he can *see* the future of entire peoples.[12]

This transformation is both appreciated and acknowledged by Balaam in the preamble he composes to open both his third and fourth oracles:

The utterance of Balaam, the son of Beor,
And the utterance of the man whose eye [has been] *sealed shut,*

The utterance of him who knows the words of God,
And who knows the thoughts of the Most High

Who views visions from The Almighty,
Fallen down, yet with eyes unveiled.[13] (24:3–4, 15–16)

In this startling confession he now recognizes the justness of his relegation to the role of the ass in his prophetic dream: his blindness at a time when he believed himself to be the all-knowing and all-seeing *"seer."* Now that his eyes have been unveiled, his drastic drop in his own estimate as a result of the puncturing of his overinflated ego has brought on a new humility, a more realistic self-appraisal that has opened his eyes to visions beyond the wildest expectations of his former self. This new understanding of himself is part and parcel of his revised grasp of God's purpose and of his proper place in the scheme of things. We can term it Balaam's enlightenment, as announced by the critical comment:

Now Balaam saw *that it was good in the eyes of the* Lord *to bless Israel….*

that is, he now grasped God's will and accepted it.

And the spirit of God came upon him [24:1–2].

It is at this point in the *Book of Balaam* that our central protagonist abandons his attempts to assert himself in opposition to his God, and accepts his role as God's servant; metamorphosing in the process from a seer into a prophet.

---

8. 22:31.
9. 23:13.
10. 22:41.
11. 24:2.
12. 24:20, 21.
13. 24:3–4, 15–16. For textual notes see Chapter 9, notes 17–23.

An Enlightening Ordeal

The *Book of Balaam* opens with Balaam ensconced in the role of an illustrious pagan seer, one who has earned an international reputation as a clairvoyant—a foreteller of the future who has proven extraordinarily accurate in his predictions—and who also is not above dabbling in sorcery.[14] All indications are that he is a polytheist, yet he has a special—indeed, a privileged—relationship with the LORD. For a pagan this poses no problems; the LORD to Balaam would be one deity among many, possibly even the most powerful in his estimate. Not being an Israelite, he is not a partner to the Sinai Covenant which demands loyalty to the LORD to the exclusion of any other deities.[15] How this special relationship was born we have no way of knowing; all we know is that according to Balaam the LORD is his God,[16] and to Him he turns. We never hear of him speaking of or to any other deity. And to him the LORD speaks on a regular basis. From both sides the relationship is deep and intimate. Yet, strangely, although in our tale the ostensible subject of the give and take between Balaam and the LORD is the Children of Israel, until the receipt of God's "word" that he will deliver in his second oracle, there is no hint that Balaam is aware that "his God" is also the God of Israel. Nor, as a pagan, is there any reason that he should have known this. Unless God had seen fit to so inform him, there was no reason in the normal course of events that Balaam was likely to be otherwise informed of this special relationship. In the aftermath of the first oracle it is possible that Balaam might have guessed it to be the case. The "word" received for delivery in the second oracle would then have definitively confirmed any guesses he might have made. From this point he knew.

But before we can proceed we need to step back and go a bit more deeply into our initial statement that, first and foremost, Balaam is a pagan. Being a pagan means more than being a polytheist. Paganism involves a complex worldview, an understanding of reality that is radically different from our modern views, which have been decisively shaped by several thousand years of monotheism. The ancients believed that, hidden from our senses by the realm of nature in which we are embedded, lies another realm, that of the primordial transcendent forces which underlie and sustain nature and the natural world. As the gods were perceived as part of nature, they too are subject to the forces of this meta divine dimension. The ancients believed that through the use of magic humans could access this realm of the meta divine, siphon off some portion of its transcendent forces and through them manipulate and control nature. As the gods were part of nature, they too were controllable and subject

---

14. That is, through the practice of magic attempting to determine the shape of the future. Although throughout the *Book* Balaam denies being a sorcerer and insists that he is merely a clairvoyant—one who foresees the future—in 24:1 we are informed that behind the cover of his denials, in an attempt to fulfill his contract with Balak, Balaam has preceded the pronouncement of his first two oracles with magical enchantments in an attempt to force God to change His blessing of Israel into a curse, only to discover that his magic will neither work on God nor against Israel. Not only can God not be coerced (23:20), but He has blessed Israel, and thus immunized her against Balaam's magic (cf. 23:23).

15. The Ten Commandments begins: *I am the Lord your God Who brought you out of the land of Egypt, from the house of bondage. You shall have no other gods besides Me.* (Exodus 20:2–3; Deuteronomy 5:6–7)

16. "The Lord my God," Balaam's own words in his declaration to Balak's emissaries (22:18).

to manipulation.[17] So when we are told that after going through an elaborate ritual to summon the LORD to conference,[18] Balaam removed himself to a state of solitude and performed magical incantations,[19] we can understand from this that he was simply trying to do what all pagan sorcerers did: he was attempting to bring the power of the meta divine realm to bear on his God, and to force Him to change His mind about cursing Israel. He had been forbidden to curse Israel. More, he had been told that indeed this people was blessed.[20] Balaam wants to get his God to reverse His former decision; not only to allow him to fulfill his mandate but, if possible, to get God to be the very source of the curse. And if, as he has begun to suspect, that it was the LORD Himself Who was the One Who had originally bestowed a blessing upon this people that had come out of Egypt, then he wishes to use the leverage of the meta divine forces to get the LORD to rescind His blessing; in effect to change His blessing into a curse.

In all this Balaam is not acting weirdly or abnormally. He is indeed rebelling against his God, but he is acting rationally within the "scientific" worldview of his era. Through his magic he will bend God to his will, and the same magic will protect him from any divine retribution. But to his surprise, the magic doesn't work. Instead of God acceding to his desires, the LORD roughly implants two "words" (*debarim*) in Balaam's mouth. Balaam finds himself forced by an irresistible compulsion to embellish these with preludes and conclusions in the traditional manner, and to proclaim these as oracles. In the light of this analysis let us reexamine these first two oracles.

In the first case, God appears to Balaam when summoned. Balaam apprises his God (as though He didn't know) of the massive magical apparatus that he has assembled to enforce his demands:

Now God appeared to Balaam, and he [Balaam] *said to Him, "I have set up seven altars and have offered up a bull and a ram on each altar"* [23:4].

But instead of the LORD responding with some conciliatory statement such as

"What is it that you desire, my son?"

He brusquely puts His "word" into Balaam's mouth and orders him to deliver it—suitably embellished—and proclaim it to the king whose hireling he is:

And the LORD *put a word in Balaam's mouth, and He said, "Return to Balak, and thus you shall speak"* [23:5].

Beyond the shock and dismay at the failure of his magic to succeed in bending the LORD to his will, what did Balaam learn from this incident? On his way back to the waiting king from the lonely spot he had chosen for his confrontation with his God, what thoughts and emotions must have been swirling within him? Besides having to compose extempore the rhetorical frame for the "word" he was being forced to

---

17. See the section entitled Paganism and Monotheism in the General Introduction for a more detailed exposition of the subject and of the role magic played in pagan thinking.
18. 23:1–3, 14–15; we must remember that cursing was an integral part of magic.
19. 24:1. See also Chapter 9, note 12, and related text.
20. 22:12.

utter—with the exception of his excuse for not delivering what was expected of him,[21] all the rest of the introduction was pro forma and routine, a task an accomplished and experienced poet and seer could compose mentally in a minute or two. He must have been struggling with the task of coming to terms with both the failure of his magic and the blowback he could expect when instead of a curse he would deliver what would be perceived as a blessing.

I would suggest that foremost in his mind was the cul-de-sac in which he found himself. By having the temerity to resort to magic against his God he had crossed a line: this was an open act of rebellion against the LORD, and I feel it more than likely that on his way down from the mountain peak the memory of the angel with the naked sword in his prophetic dream had returned to haunt and terrify him. He had well understood the warning in that sword, yet in his blind confidence in the efficacy of his magic—pure hubris—he has dared to rebel against the direct command of the LORD and worse, to attempt to coerce His agreement. Why didn't the LORD strike him down on the spot? Probably, he reasons, because God still had a use for him: to proclaim the "word" placed within him, declaring the uniqueness and blessedness of this people Israel.[22] But what awaits him once he has declaimed God's "word"? As I see it, he is consumed with terror at the thought of the abyss on whose edge he finds himself standing. It could well be the panic induced by the thought of what he can look forward to from an angry God that brings to his lips the desperate prayer with which his oracle closes:

"May I die the death of the upright,
May my end be as his!" [23:10b]

Having declaimed the oracle he has been forced to proclaim, having endured Balak's infuriated subsequent tongue lashing and having reiterated what will become his stock excuse—that he can only say what God demands that he say—Balaam finds himself still alive. Surprisingly, now that he has completed his divinely mandated task of proclaiming God's word, the LORD has not struck him down for his audacity and rebelliousness. But he is far from being home free. Dragooned into a repeat performance by the compulsiveness of the king, Balaam finds himself being trundled to a new launching site for the curse that Balak persists in believing will solve all his problems. And on the lengthy trek to the summit of the Pisgah,[23] the terror of imminent annihilation temporarily stilled,[24] for the first time since his disastrous confrontation with his God Balaam has a chance to consider his situation.

Two matters, we can assume, must have dominated his thoughts at this time, the first being the question of how he can best handle the impossible situation in which he finds himself. Here he is caught between an angry king determined to get from Balaam, one way or another, what he had contracted to deliver, and on the other

---

21. *"How can I damn whom God has not damned?*
    How can I doom whom the Lord has not doomed?" (23:8)
22. He now at last knows the name of this people that had come out of Egypt.
23. See Chapter 8, note 54.
24. Both rebellion against his God and an unsuccessful attempt to coerce Him by means of magic were both understood to be unforgivable offenses punishable by death.

Chapter 10. Retrospect

hand the image of that wrathful angel, with a sword poised to extract vengeance in the name of a God furious at Balaam for his presumptuousness and defiance. He now finds himself fulfilling the role of the donkey in his dream: trapped between the threat of the sword in the hand of the angel and the stick beating her in the hand of her master. (Does Balaam realize at this moment how prophetic the dream was?) What will the king do to him if, for a second time, he fails to come across? What went wrong with the magic? Did he do something wrong, make a mistake in procedure? Dare he make a second attempt to force the Lord's hand? His current status is no better than that of a stay of execution. A second failure would guarantee immediate death. He is trapped. To which party should he yield? Decision is imperative because act he must.

The second matter roiling Balaam's mind is the divine "word" that he has just proclaimed. What meaning is being hinted at by those two enigmatic couplets? And more important, what significance lies in them for him? Could he but decode them, their implications might provide the key directing him how to act in his current situation. As our conflicted and increasingly desperate hero might well have thought in this manner, let us turn our attention first to the oracle.

As we have previously determined, the "word" itself consisted of the two following couplets:

This is a people that shall dwell alone,
Not reckoned among the nations.

Who can count the dust of Jacob?
Who can number the dust-clouds of Israel?[25] (23:9b–10a)

In our preliminary analysis of these two couplets we noted that each makes a central point: the first, that this people Israel is unique among the nations of the earth. From this one might deduce that the principles that apply to the functioning of the various nations, and hence what could be expected of them—the "Realpolitik" or "ways of the world" with which experienced and sophisticated pagans such as Balaam and Balak were well acquainted and routinely practiced—did not necessarily apply to this new entity. The existence and destiny of Israel are likely to be governed by different rules, and the old tried and tested ways of dealing with nations would not necessarily work with her. Of this point, Balaam would seem to have a certain amount of empirical confirmation: Israel did not seem to be subject to magical manipulation. Uniquely, Israel was not curseable.

The second part of God's word, employing the metaphor, *the dust of Jacob*,[26] would seem to imply the large and ever-increasing numbers of the Children of Israel, while the metaphoric use of the phrase *the dust-clouds of Israel*[27] in the following line

---

25. For textual notes, see Chapter 8, note 45.

26. *Jacob* can be taken as used simply as a synonym parallel to *Israel* in the next line, with which it is paired. In this case the metaphor would be implying the huge size of the current Israelite population. Or, and more probably, *Jacob* is being used primarily as a reference to the progenitor of this people (as in *Genesis* 28:14; see Chapter 8, note 48), and hence as a metaphor for the promised geometric multiplication of his descendants until they are as countless *as the dust of the earth* (ibid.).

27. "Jacob" and "Israel" are not only two alternative names for a given people or nation, but primarily the alternate names of one given person who was the progenitor of this people (*Genesis* 32:23–31).

would suggest the spreading of this people worldwide, even as dust motes in a desert storm are blown to the furthest reaches of the earth. Thus much Balaam might milk from the enigmatic "word" that God had implanted within him, but what direction this could give him as to how to conduct himself in the trial he was now facing is far from clear. Ultimately, it would seem that, for want of any better idea, Balaam appears to have decided to stick with his previous modus operandi. He would go along with the king's demand for a repeat performance; expecting a better result from a change in locale did not seem likely, but on the other hand the king didn't seem to be in any mood to listen to reason. A repeat performance the king demanded, so a repeat he would get.

So once again Balaam orders up seven altars, seven bulls and seven rams. Once again he absents himself from human company, and in seclusion performs the proper incantations prescribed by occult tradition—probably taking extra care this time to get every word, act and gesture of the arcane ritual exactly right—and once more his God appears in answer to his summons. To Balaam's deep dismay this confrontation turns out to be an exact replica of the first; nothing has changed. Again the LORD has nothing to say, neither acknowledgment nor rebuke; as before He implants a "word" in Balaam and curtly orders him to disgorge it before his employer. Having learned nothing from his previous experience, it would appear that the second round is being used by Balaam's God—at least in part—to bring home to Balaam certain fundamentals that the LORD had hoped he would have already grasped. In other words, not only is King Balak designated as recipient of the "word," but at least in part Balaam himself is being instructed. It is almost as though Balaam is being treated as a slow student.

And this time Balaam finally gets the message. Two successive failures to get his way, added to the contents of God's "word," finally penetrate. As in his dream, the kaleidoscope turns and everything changes. The convictions of a lifetime disintegrate and the pieces reform into a new pattern. Let us take this transformative experience as Balaam perceived it happening to him. And with our change of perspective we can expect some changes from our former analysis.

Balaam already knew that this people that had come out of Egypt—his designated target—was blessed; God had so informed him.[28] That was why his God had forbidden him to curse it. But he knew that, should he be driven to this extremity, he always had a fallback remedy to this prohibition in magic; through sorcery he could force God to rescind His ban, and nullify any blessing, no matter what the source. This is not a course that he would willingly take, for it would be certain to infuriate his God and possibly fatally damage his relationship with Him. But he had maneuvered himself into an impossible situation, one from which he had no way of backing out. Not only was the exorbitant honorarium—a blank check no less—at stake, but his reputation as well. Failure to deliver would be fatal to his prospects of future

---

28. 22:12. Being a polytheist and believing in the existence of many gods, Balaam had no way of knowing the source of the blessing. Note that God did not say to Balaam, as He could have, that it was He Who blessed them. Nor did God inform Balaam on that occasion why this people was blessed. Our knowledge of God's promises to the progenitors of this people (see Chapter 7, note 19, and Chapter 8, note 48 above)—promises that a reliable deity would inevitably honor—were a closed book to Balaam.

commissions, as well as to his future influence. As he must have seen it, to protect his interests he had had no choice but to resort to magic to force the issue with God, and it had failed him; not once but twice. Why? This was as unthinkable as the sun failing to rise in the east. How could this be? And in the "word" that God had implanted within him he receives his answer.

As Balaam slowly retraces his steps down the mountain—he was in no rush to face the increasingly irascible king—let us review with him the contents of God's "word" and its implications. In the first place he has learned the identity of this people that had come out of Egypt. It is named "Jacob," or alternatively "Israel." Secondly, he now understands why it is blessed: it is a people in which neither wrong nor iniquity (not necessarily the same things) exist.

No iniquity can be perceived in Jacob;
No wrong can be seen in Israel [23:21].

Further, Israel did not simply come out of Egypt; it was *brought out*, and by none other than God Himself:

God Who brings them out of Egypt... [23:22]

That vague and enigmatic statement in God's first "word,"

This is a people that shall dwell alone,
Not reckoned among the nations [23:9].

is beginning to assume an unexpected meaning and a frightening significance. Not only is this people, known as "Jacob" or alternately "Israel," blameless, but it stands in a special relationship with the Lord. He has brought them out of Egypt and they have proclaimed Him as their King. It is God Who empowers them and is behind the amazing *Blitzkrieg* that, in a matter of weeks, has swept the Kingdoms of Heshbon and Bashan from the map. Worse, this is a people against whom magic will be ineffective.

For no enchantment can be effective against Jacob,
No magic against Israel [23:23a].

No wonder his enchantments didn't work. With a people like this loosed on the world, things will never be the same. What has God done to us?

Now let it be said of Jacob,
And of Israel: "What hath God wrought!" (23:23b)

In the time it takes Balaam to reach the site of the altars where the king awaits him—perhaps half an hour at most—his entire world has fallen apart and he has begun to come to terms with a new perspective on life.

This new understanding becomes immediately evident in his attitude to the king. Their relationship has from the start contained an underlying stratum of mutual hostility, increasingly manifest as their conflicting expectations, driven by the pressures to which they are subject, intensify. Both parties are experiencing progressively greater difficulty in maintaining a façade of politeness. Upon Balaam's reappearance the king, unable to contain himself, bursts out with an impatient demand, "What did the Lord say?" For his part Balaam, abandoning his previous apologetic surliness, disdains to even acknowledge the king's question. On the way down from the Heights he has been mentally composing his contribution to the oracle: the prelude to God's "word" which he must deliver. This will consist of two elements: a theological lecture consisting of the revolutionary conclusions that Balaam has just reached, framed as a dressing down to be administered to Balak, and a confession of failure on his own part. In the first section of his prelude the king will receive answer enough to his compulsive outburst.

Balaam opens by demanding the king's full attention; these words are meant especially for you. Addressed directly by name, Balak is scathingly rebuked for demanding a "second opinion." God doesn't waffle or change His mind; once He comes to a decision you can rely on Him to not only stick to it but also to follow it up.

Arise, O Balak, and hear!
Give ear to me, O son of Zippor!

God is not a man that He should be capricious,
Nor mortal, that He should change His mind.

Will He declare and He will not do it?
Speak and not bring it to pass? [23:19]

This from Balaam is revolutionary. He is beginning to get his first glimpse into the inner meaning of monotheism. Not only is there no multiplicity of deities that can, at least theoretically, be played off against each other by a wise and competent sorcerer, but the very basis of the pagan worldview—Balaam's worldview—is being challenged; the existence of a meta divine dimension that sustains nature is being called into question. Moreover, if the Lord is not capricious and cannot be made to change His mind, then He must not be subject to the natural order. That means that He must exist *outside of the realm of nature*. In other words, in place of a meta divine realm of primeval forces sustaining nature, it must be the Lord Who exists outside of nature and sustains it. I very much doubt that Balaam could have put this flash of insight into words as we have, but his glimpse of the foundations of monotheism did lead to the revelation of the absolute freedom and sovereignty of the Lord his God, a deity unhampered by external restraints; incoercible and absolutely reliable. His word is final, so don't expect Him to change it. This is followed by an admission:

Behold, I was summoned to bless,
He has blessed and I cannot reverse it. (23:20)

I.e., I've tried, and found that even I could not do it. Forget it.

[Then there follows God's "word," which we have already discussed.]

The final two couplets, as we have previously mentioned,[29] could be either part of God's "word," or they could be a coda, added by Balaam, as in the first Oracle. If the former, then the phrase, *What hath God wrought!* is meant as a semi-rhetorical question to which these final lines are the answer: a new and unique people which is

---

29. Chapter 8, note 79.

as strong as a lion has been loosed to ravage the nations. If the latter, then the same phrase should be taken as an exclamation of shock which ends God's "word." In that case, the final lines are Balaam's. If so, then the seer can be seen to be getting his own back. In his prelude he stuck his knife into Balak, publicly rebuking him for having dared to try to get God to change His mind. In that case, in the coda, he is turning the knife in the wound by confirming the king's worst fears: yes, Israel *is* unstoppable, strong as a lion, and three guesses what that lion will first maul and then devour?

Transformation

We have now reached the turning point of our tale. Something has been happening to Balaam, a progressive widening of his horizons. This change has been implicit in the two oracles he has delivered. We have already taken note of the self-preoccupation displayed in the material he composed to frame the "word" he was compelled to utter in the first oracle. By the second oracle, his attention has shifted from himself to God (and if the last two couplets of the oracle are also his, then Israel shares with God the focus of his concerns). Now the narrator makes explicit Balaam's growing understanding of God and his appreciation for His concerns, with the remark,

Now Balaam saw[30] that it was good in the eyes of the LORD *to bless Israel...* [24:1a]

It is not simply that it is the LORD's will that Israel be blessed; Balaam has been pretty well convinced of this all along. The point of the remark is that Balaam at long last accepts the full implication of God's decision, and appropriates it as his own. The self-centered rebel, chaffing at God's restrictions, is dissolving away, and a new person is in the process of emerging: Balaam is now the faithful servant of the LORD, one who knows his place in the scheme of things. Objectively nothing has changed; it is just that Balaam sees things in a new light. Or to put it another way, he is finally willing to see things through God's eyes rather than through his own.

This change manifests itself on two fronts. When the compulsive king forces yet another round—perhaps on the principle of "third time lucky"—Balaam abandons all attempts to get his way by means of magic.

... So he dispensed with his previous enchantments, but turned his eyes to the wilderness [24:1b].

This is doubly surprising. Balaam has once more gone through the preliminary routine—seven altars, seven bulls and seven rams—preparatory to the incantations that are supposed to force the deity to do his will. But then, instead of departing to some "island of solitude" to perform his sorcery, he remains beside the altars, turns his back on king and entourage, and gazes toward what had been his designated target. And for the first time he *sees* Israel, not through the eyes of self-interest—the eyes of

---

30. As in the opening line of the *Book of Balaam* (22:2), the first word of the pivotal verse of the *Book* (*vayaar—Now he saw*—24:1) places the emphasis on *seeing*, in this case in the meaning of finally understanding. See above, the section entitled "The Seer," and especially notes 5 and 6, and Chapter 9, note 9.

a hired assassin—but through God's eyes. And seeing Israel as God sees it, the LORD no longer needs to use Balaam as a ventriloquist's dummy, but can let him speak for himself. So He rests His spirit upon Balaam, heightening his vision, and Balaam gives birth, in the words of James Ackerman, "to the most far-reaching and positive visions of Israel's future found in the entire Pentateuch."[31] Balaam is no longer the Balaam of old, a pagan clairvoyant; his enlightenment has transformed him into a prophet of the LORD.

Prognosis

In the last century a sardonic slogan achieved a wide currency: "My mind is made up; don't confuse me with the facts." This pithy expression not only addresses the widespread unwillingness of people to abandon their pet prejudices in the face of empirical evidence, but also reflects a deeper truth: that every era exhibits its own unique way of thinking that very few can find the courage to challenge. We have spoken of the pagan worldview, which has been driving Balak's increasingly compulsive and irrational behavior, as a mind cage. Trapped by the preconceptions of his time, the king is incapable of coping with the realities of the situation in which he finds himself. He is locked into a compulsive repetition of failure. Balak is far from unique; he is a typical denizen of his age.

It is Balaam who is unique. Under God's tutelage and prodding, he has broken out of the cage. He has begun to question the pagan mindset on which his profession—and indeed his entire life—has hitherto rested. It is this breakthrough that the author of our tale highlights by his repeated use of the word *vayaar* (*and he saw*)—as well as other variations of the same root, in all its multiple meanings—and which he now brings to a head in the sentence:

Now Balaam <u>saw</u> *that it was good in the eyes of the* LORD *to bless Israel* [24:1a].

And it is to this breakthrough that we refer when we speak of Balaam's "enlightenment." Having been brought, and having brought himself, to question some of his most basic presuppositions, Balaam is now becoming able to see the facts that lie before him, accept them as such and draw the appropriate conclusions; he can adopt a new perspective—and he does. The results of his liberation from what we have called the pagan mind cage, his dawning new perspective and his new understanding of himself—all this he encapsulates in the preamble he composes for his third and penultimate oracle:

The utterance of Balaam, the son of Beor,
And the utterance of the man whose eye [has been] *sealed shut,*
The utterance of him who knows the words of God,
And who knows the thoughts of the Most High
Who views visions from The Almighty,
Fallen down, yet with eyes unveiled.[32] (24:3–4; 15–16)

---

31. Ackerman, "Numbers," *Literary Guide*, p. 87.
32. For textual comments see Chapter 9, notes 17–23.

Chapter 10. Retrospect

And with enlightenment comes a new way of seeing and a new freedom. Balaam can now see Israel as it really is and finds himself liberated from his old mental shackles, as well as from the restraints God had placed on him. He no longer is a sort of mechanical device to spew forth the "word" implanted in him by God. The spirit of God now rests upon him and he finds himself free to express himself as he will.

And Balaam raised his eyes and he <u>saw</u> Israel encamped in tribal array, and the spirit of God came upon him [24:2].

With his preamble, the third oracle pours out; a prophetic lyrical panegyric culminating in a reaffirmation of God's pledge to Abraham's seed:

*Blessed are they that bless you,
And they that curse you are accursed*[33] [24:9].

The new vision has found its expression in prophecy.

Now, in retrospect, we are in a position to realize that Balaam's first two views of Israel preceding his first two oracles—partial views of the fringes of the camp—can be seen as being used by the author as a metaphor for partial blindness, the inability to see the whole picture. Or in terms of our tale, what is being implied is that unless God unveils our eyes—that is, removes the preconceptions that have locked our minds—the fragmentary views of our surroundings that we perceive give us a false picture of our world. A partial or disjointed picture amounts to a lie. Only when Balaam can see the whole of Israel, our tale suggests, can he, with the help of the spirit of prophecy, grasp what lies before him.

But beyond the widened vision and deeper understanding that Balaam's enlightenment has afforded him, another radical change has occurred. A shift in the focus of his vision has taken place. As a *roeh* or seer—a time when he *thought* that he was seeing—at the most he was only able to grasp past and current reality. Even the "words" implanted by God within him encompassed only these. But with the spirit of God coming upon him—that is, with his transformation from a seer into a prophet—the focus of Balaam's oracles shifts to the future. In the first and second oracles, God's "word" was limited to the explication of the *past* and the *present*; seeing the world as it really was and is. But in the third and subsequent oracles the horizon expands to take in the *future*—the *outcomes* of the past and the present. The bottom lines of these oracles lie not in their details but in their essences: Israel has a future; Moab, Amalek and Edom have none. This shift from a perception of current reality to the ability to

*look into the seeds of time,
and say which grain will grow and which will not,*[34]

amounts to a sea change, a difference not in degree but in kind. The gap between pagan seer and prophet of the LORD is so profound as to be revolutionary. Balaam is no longer the same man.

---

33. *Genesis* 12:3. See Chapter 8, note 48.
34. William Shakespeare, *Macbeth* I.

And Now a Word About Our Author

The picture we have been drawing of Balaam's enlightenment and of his transformation from pagan seer to some sort of proto-monotheistic prophet is based on the narrative portion of the *Book of Balaam*, and is, of course, the literary construct of the author of the work. We have postulated that along with a handful of late-thirteenth-century-BCE oracles,[35] our author inherited—either in oral or in written form—a story telling about the origin of these selfsame oracles and their proclamation. This tale forms the basis of the narrative we now possess. But while a legendary tale might very well contain the outline of what was to become the main plot line of our *Book*, such traditions rarely contain the wealth of detail or the subtlety of interplay and allusion of the type our work exhibits. These we have to attribute to the creative genius of our author. But it is on these—the keywords, the subtle allusions and the interplay of the subplots—that the deeper meanings rest; and from them most of our analysis is drawn. The question therefore arises: to what extent do the conclusions we have tentatively been reaching have a basis in the life of the historic Balaam and the oracles he uttered? Could they simply be the products of our author's overactive imagination? Or to put the matter more concretely: where did our author ever get the idea that the saga of Balaam was a tale of enlightenment?

My contention will be that the author got both the idea and the keyword he uses to convey the concept from the oracles themselves.[36] We have mentioned that the root *raah* (to *see*, to *perceive*) appears no less than eighteen times in the *Book*,[37] and serves the function of a keyword for the entire work. We have discussed at some length the fifteen times it occurs in the narrative, and the role it plays in some of these various contexts, but until now we have passed over in silence its presence in the oracles. The time has come to remedy this omission.

We begin with the circumstance that the threefold appearance of the root *raah* in the oracles is not random. Its occurrence exhibits a discernible pattern, being distributed in the first, second and fourth oracles, one occurrence in each. It first turns up in Balaam's preamble to his premier oracle, where he announces the physical fact of his catching sight of his target:

For from the mountain peaks I <u>see</u> him,
From the high hills I behold him [23:9].

The subject of this verse is Balaam; the object is this anonymous "people" he has been summoned to curse.

The placement of the second occurrence of the root *raah* is in the following oracle. It appears not in Balaam's preamble but in God's "word," with the object of the "seeing" no longer an anonymous people but Israel (or alternatively named "Jacob"):

---

35. To be exact, seven in number: four major oracles and three oracular mini-pronouncements. If Albright's analysis is even remotely accurate (see Introduction to the *Book of Balaam*) then between 250 to 300 years separate the composition of the oracles from the writing of the narrative we have been discussing.
36. It is always possible that this theme was embedded in the legend that accompanied the ancient oracles, but not possessing the original tale to which the author was privy we have no way of knowing this. We are therefore left only with the oracles as his primary sources.
37. See note 4 above.

No iniquity can be perceived in Jacob,
No wrong can be <u>seen</u> in Israel[38] [23:21a].

Here as well a progression has taken place in the person of the subject; from a human viewer (Balaam) to God Himself (*the* LORD *his God*).

The third time the verb *raah* occurs is in Balaam's fourth oracle, his prophetic outpouring revealing the future destinies of the two subjects of the looming showdown between Israel and Moab.[39] Following his preface in which he, as it were, affixes his signature to the oracle (24:15–16), Balaam begins his prophetic vision with the word *erenu* (*I see* him):

<u>I see him</u>, *but not in the present,*
I behold him, but not soon:

A star strides forth from Jacob,
A scepter arises from Israel[40] [24:17].

The entire pattern (in tabular form) now stands revealed as:

Oracle number	Source of statement in which the root *raah* appears	Temporal focus of vision	Sense in which root *raah* is being used
1	Balaam's PREFACE to the oracle	Present	Catching sight of the physical location of the object of the oracle
2	God's "WORD" mechanically implanted in Balaam	Present	Perception of spiritual state of the object of the oracle
4	WORD OF GOD (*neum*) conveyed via a prophetic vision/trance	Future	Vision of the future of the object(s) of the oracle

The use of the root *raah* in the oracles can be seen to be neither static nor random. There appears to be a clear pattern of progression: in source, from human composition to divine implantation to prophetic vision; in temporal focus, from present to future; from use of the term, in the sense of location of an object in space, to its use in the sense of understanding the spiritual state of the object in question, to envisioning future developments. A careful reading of the oracles would seem to indicate that the root *raah* was deployed carefully and intentionally in the oracles for the purpose of indicating some sense of movement and development. What we wish to suggest by all this analysis is that the author of what was to become the *Book of Balaam*, in studying the 13th-century oracles, became aware of the patterned use of the various forms of the root, and it was this that suggested to him the theme of Balaam's enlightenment, and also the use of the root *raah* as a keyword with which to convey this theme. In other words, what is being suggested is that the author's construction of the *Book of Balaam*, and of the themes and meanings that he has built into it, if not original to the tale he inherited was at the very least implicit in, and was developed from, the oracles

---

38. Our translation, for reasons of English grammar, is in the passive tense (*can be seen*), but in the original Hebrew the verse is grammatically active (*He has not perceived… He has not seen*), the subject being *the Lord his God* in the second half of the verse (23:21b).

39. That is, the perceived imminent Israelite invasion with which the *Book* opened, and the fear of which has driven the entire narrative.

40. For textual comments see Chapter 9, notes 45–49.

themselves. Thus the roots of the unity of the 13th-century oracles and 10th-century narrative in the text of the *Book of Balaam* that we possess today go back to the 13th century BCE, the deeper meanings of the *Book* being an organic outgrowth nurtured by our author.

But this does not address what should be to us a more basic question. Granted that the *Book of Balaam* is a tale of enlightenment, and granted that this theme is not something superimposed by our author upon an ancient tale accompanying a handful of antique oracles, but an organic outgrowth from its ancient roots, the real issue is what drew our author to Balaam in the first place? If his concern was to pen a tale of enlightenment and spiritual growth, why turn to pagan sources? By the 10th century BCE, could not our author, himself obviously an Israelite, find candidates aplenty among his own people to choose from to serve as the protagonist for a tale of enlightenment and transformation? Why go outside of Israel to recruit a pagan clairvoyant as his hero?

And here, perhaps, we can permit ourselves to speculate on what the author's original motivation for writing his little book was. It would seem that he intended far more than penning an interesting tale about the struggles and adventures of an ancient individual, even about the enlightenment of some seer of days gone by. We might entertain the possibility that the story is meant to be representative; its protagonist intended as a prototype for mankind in general, and the path traveled is being treated as a metaphor for humanity's projected journey—prodded on and mentored by God—from darkness to light.

If his aim was to convey such a message, to choose an Israelite—Moses, say—would obviously not do; it would willy-nilly restrict the stage in the eyes of the reader to Israel alone. If we accept the hypothesis that the author's vision encompassed all God's children, then to give point to the universalism of his dream, a well-known historic figure like Balaam—a prominent pagan abhorred by many Israelites for his reputed animosity to their people[41]—would make an excellent fit as a prototypical pagan, a stand-in for the superior type of non–Israelite. It is my suggestion that this agenda, as much as the contents of the oracles themselves, explains the surprisingly positive spin given to Balaam in our author's presentation.

To sum up this thesis, let us suggest that the author of the *Book of Balaam* wished to write a work promoting the ideal of universal human enlightenment. In his time only the people whom the LORD had brought out of Egypt—Israel—recognized Him as their Sovereign. And for most Israelites this was quite sufficient; He was their God, and all others could continue to dwell in darkness as pagans, worshiping gods of wood and stone. But there were those—the author of the *Book of Jonah* for one—who could see beyond the narrow horizons of clannish provincialism to the inherent logic of monotheism, *as could our author*. If there is but one God, Creator of everything that is, then all human beings are His children, and in the fullness of time all humanity will come to know this and will acknowledge Him as their Father and King, even as Israel does at present. It is this universalistic vision, I believe, that

---

41. As we shall see below, the historic Balaam was destined to become well-known to the Children of Israel as a particularly dangerous enemy, whose memory was accordingly abhorred.

animates the work that he wrote, a dream that would be definitively put into words by the 6th-century prophet Zechariah[42]:

And it shall come to pass, that the LORD *shall be King over all the earth;*
In that day shall the LORD *be One, and His name one* [*Zechariah* 14:9].

It is my suggestion that it was this larger meaning that led, by a circumlocutory route, to this little book finding its way into the Bible.

---

42. Zechariah was one of the last of the Hebrew prophets. He was born during the Babylonian Exile, and following the Edict of Cyrus that freed the Jews, he returned from exile to Jerusalem in 536 BCE. His call to prophecy came sixteen years later, in 320 BCE.

Chapter 11

Epilogue: The Road to Dusty Death

Such subtle covenants shall be made,
That peace itself is war in masquerade.

—John Dryden, *Absalom and Achitophel*

For extreme illnesses extreme remedies are most fitting.

—Hippocrates, *Aphorisms*

Collapse![1]

Having completed the *Book of Balaam*, the *Book of Numbers* returns to the tale of Israel's adventures in the Trans-Jordan from where it was broken off.[2] For the Israelites, the military campaigns they have so successfully undertaken against the kingdoms of Heshbon and Bashan have been little more than an unwelcome but necessary diversion. Their primary goal was, and remains, the territories west of the Jordan River: the Promised Land. Now at last they are in a position to cross the Jordan and commence the task for which they have been waiting ever since they left Egypt. But first they will need some time to reorganize, apply the lessons learned in the course of the Trans-Jordanian campaigns, and prepare for what is to come.[3] There is a further reason for this pause: Moses is visibly aging. There will have to be a transfer of power and authority to a new leadership before Israel can commit itself to the vast undertaking of entering and taking possession of the Cis-Jordan. The crossing of the Jordan will have to be put off for a while. And then, as one thing leads to another, the months stretch out. During this hiatus Israel will find itself unexpectedly confronted by a new diversion.

Now Israel settled down in Shittim,[4] *and the people profaned themselves*[5] *by*

---

1. Early versions of the first part of this chapter, under the title "A Zealous Exemplar," appeared as Appendix 6 in my book *The Elijah Enigma*, and as Appendix 11 in *Judges and Saviors*.
2. In *Numbers* 22:1, we were informed that following their conquest of the Bashan, the Children of Israel turned southward, finally pitching camp in the Steppes of Moab at a location not far from the River Jordan, to the east of the city of Jericho which lies on its far side.
3. This will include the updating of their mobilization lists. Since the last census almost four decades have elapsed; a new census is imperative on which to base new mobilization tables.
4. Literally, "in the acacias." The full name of the site was Abel-shittim (Abel of the acacias), located according to Josephus approximately seven miles from the Jordan River. It was the final camping spot of the Israelites before crossing the Jordan. See *Numbers* 33:49.
5. Reading with LXX (as in *Leviticus* 19:29 and 21:9). MT reads *they began to whore with*.

whoring with the daughters of Moab.[6] *They* [the daughters of Moab] *invited*[7] *the people* [of Israel] *to the sacrifices*[8] *of their gods, and the people ate, and worshiped*[9] *their gods. So Israel joined itself to Baal-peor,*[10] *and the anger of the Lord was kindled against Israel* [Numbers 25:1–3].

The wilderness generation, inured to the rigors of a nomadic existence, arrives in a settled agricultural area and for the first time is thrown into contact with a breed of woman infinitely more worldly and accomplished than any they have previously encountered. Fraternization with these wildly enticing women leads directly to the delights of a new religious experience—the worship of Baal, whose fertility rites involve ritual coupling. It is thought that the worshipers believed that through their sexual union they could induce Baal to send his rain and so insure the fertility of the fields for the coming year.[11] A breakdown in sexual restraints leads directly to an attachment to the worship of the god who sanctions, and indeed promotes, unrestrained sexual license. This development, needless to say, is hardly pleasing to the Lord, the God of Israel.[12]

Amazingly, Moses seems at first to be oblivious to the seriousness of the developing crisis, or at a loss as to how to deal with it. It takes a direct order from God to prod Moses into some sort of action.

And the Lord said to Moses, "Take all the officers[13] *and have* [their bodies] *publicly impaled before the Lord,*[14] *so that the Lord's wrath may turn away from Israel." So*

---

6. Were these Moabite women remnants of the original North Moabite population that had remained subsequent to the Amorite conquest of the region (see Appendix C: North Moab: A Tale of Lost Lands), or did the establishment of the Israelite encampment act as a magnet attracting "ladies of loose virtue" from Moab proper south of the Arnon River?

7. Literally, *they called.*

8. The Hebrew word used here, that we have translated by the generic term "sacrifices," is *zevah*. This is the term used for an animal sacrifice whose meat is eaten by the offerer. These were freewill offerings that were brought to a sanctuary and presented to the priests for consecration as a sacrifice. After slaughter small segments of the animal (among Israelites it was fat, kidneys and a lobe of the liver) were burned on the altar. A part of the animal was reserved for the priest's personal use. The offerer, his family and invited guests consumed most of the animal as a communion meal with their deity. The *zevah* was the most common form sacrifice took among Israelites and pagans alike.

9. Literally, *bowed down, prostrated themselves before.*

10. The Baal whose place of worship was Mount Peor. Able-shittim was sited at the foot of Mount Peor.

11. These seductive rituals, once learned, were hard to unlearn. Despite the best efforts of the prophets and several reforming kings, the practices refused to disappear. Some six hundred years later these fertility rites were still being practiced, prompting the prophet Jeremiah to exclaim:

Upon every high hill
And under every leafy tree
There you sprawled a-whoring! (Jeremiah 2:20),

a charge both symbolic and descriptive of actual practice.

12. The phrase "the anger of the lord was kindled against Israel," beyond its obvious surface meaning can also be a euphemism for the outbreak of an epidemic. See *Numbers* 17:11; 31:16; *Psalm* 106: 29 etc. There are some who postulate that the epidemic might have been of venereal origin.

13. Literally, "the heads of the people"; i.e., those officers in command of the levies provided by the various clans. We are speaking of a war camp, with the Israelites currently organized as an army in military formation.

14. Literally, *impaled before the sun*, i.e., where everyone can see them. See *2 Samuel* 12:12 for the euphemism.

> *Moses said to the commanders*[15] *of Israel "Every one of you slay those of his men who have joined themselves to Baal-peor"* [*Numbers* 25:4–5].

We are not told whether Moses turned to God for instruction as to how to deal with this completely unforeseen breakdown of moral and religious discipline, or whether it is God Who takes the initiative to spur Moses out of his lassitude. God orders Moses to execute the entire lower leadership echelon—note the *entire*—and to have their bodies impaled on stakes in the midst of the camp as a public example to the entire people! The Israelites are currently organized on a military basis as an invasion army. It would seem that God holds the officers in direct command of the various units personally responsible for allowing things to have gotten out of hand, and orders Moses to make an example of their failure of leadership. This is drastic medicine, and an implied stinging rebuke to Moses for his failure to take preventive measures and avert the outbreak of defection to Baal.

Shockingly, Moses fails to comply. Instead of implementing the instructions he has received, he disregards them. Mustering the commanders of the very leaders he has been ordered to execute, he orders them to identify those men who, along with their female partners, had involved themselves in the worship of Baal and to execute them. In other words, only acts of commission—that is, active participation in the worship of Baal—will be punished, but acts of omission will be condoned. This absolves the various levels of leadership from responsibility for the debacle, and throws the onus on the lower ranks. This is passing the buck on a grand scale.[16]

We are left to speculate why Moses disobeyed the orders he received.[17] Is it simply a failure of nerve, or is it the inability to face executing subordinates that he has worked with for years? Moses, we must remember, is in the last year of his long life. It may simply be that he is no longer constitutionally capable of taking hard and decisive action.

In the event, neither order is carried out. The breakdown of religious fidelity brought about by the collapse of sexual discipline in the ranks is paralleled by a total failure of resolve on the part of the highest echelon of the leadership. Instead of acting, the next scene finds the leaders of Israel simply sitting at the entrance to the Tent of Meeting in solemn assembly, fruitlessly debating, weeping and bewailing the appalling situation! This abdication of leadership brings matters to a head.

> *Now behold, a man—one of the Children of Israel—came and brought a Midianite woman*[18] *to his kinsmen*[19] *in the sight of Moses, and in the sight of the entire*

---

15. Hebrew *shoftim*. "The Hebrew root SHPT has no judicial meaning as its primary connotation, but rather it is to be translated as 'to issue orders, to exercise authority, to rule, to govern, to administer' and the like." (Ishida, p. 41) Thus the *shoftim* here refer to officers of staff rank, probably those commanding the levies of entire tribes, while the "heads of the people" in verse 4 is referring to the lower echelon officers of the smaller units that made up the tribal levies. See *Exodus* 18:21.

16. The underlying assumption, that the breakdown is confined to the lower ranks, while the upper ranks of the leadership were free from contagion, will shortly be disproved. The rot has reached the highest levels.

17. It has been suggested that Moses is here trying to intervene with God on behalf of the sinning officers (as he has on occasion pleaded the case for Israel as a whole), but this explanation avoids the fact that Moses is not arguing with God; he is simply refusing to implement a direct order.

18. Literally, *the Midianite woman*; i.e., a very specific woman. Every mention of this woman is preceded by the prefix denoting the direct object: cf. 25:14 and 15. She was not just any woman; she was a princess, and perhaps something more (see on below).

19. I.e., his family.

assembly of the Children of Israel; who were weeping at the entrance to the Tent of Meeting.[20] *Now Phinehas, son of Eleazar,*[21] *son of Aaron the priest saw it, and he rose up from the midst of the assembly; he took a javelin*[22] *in his hand and followed the Israelite man into the pavilion*[23] *and thrust both of them, the Israelite man and the woman, through her belly!* [Numbers 25:6–8]

In the vacuum created by the complete breakdown of discipline and the abdication of leadership, anything goes. Flaunting his brazen behavior in front of the entire assembly, an Israelite introduces the Midianite woman that he has picked up to his family, and then takes her into a small pavilion to fornicate with her in what amounts to an act of public defiance.[24] The entire assembly, comprising the highest leadership echelon and including Moses, is dumbstruck and sits in impotent dismay.

This is more than Moses' grandnephew, Phinehas, can take. Laying hold of his javelin, he follows them into the pavilion and with one powerful thrust skewers the copulating couple through their abdomens, pinning them to the ground.

Thus the plague was stayed from the people of Israel. Now those that died in the plague were twenty-four thousand.[25] *And the Lord spoke to Moses, saying, "Phinehas, son of Eleazar, son of Aaron the priest has turned back My wrath from the Children of Israel by his extreme zealousness for Me in their midst,*[26] *so that I did not wipe out the Children of Israel in My zeal. Therefore say, 'Behold, I grant him My covenant of peace; and it shall be to him, and to his seed after him, an eternal*

---

20. The premises where Moses would go to receive his instructions from God; a part of the sacred compound.

21. Aaron, the High Priest, has already died; his son, Eleazar, is now High Priest while Phinehas, his son, in turn has succeeded to what was his father's former position (*Numbers* 3:32); he now heads an elite armed Levitical unit—the sanctuary guard—tasked with preventing encroachment on the sacred precinct, and especially the Tabernacle, by unauthorized individuals. (See *1 Chronicles* 9:20) He is currently on duty, which explains both his presence at the entrance to the Tent of Meeting and his having a weapon ready to hand.

22. Not a long-shafted spear "but a short-shafted pike, which could be held in both hands, and, like a modern bayonet, thrust downward upon a recumbent body." (Milgrom, p. 215)

23. Hebrew *kuba*, possibly a small red leather tent with a domed top. It may have been pitched in sacred precincts which would have added sacrilege to blatant immorality. The term is often rendered as "chamber," but this gives the impression of a fixed structure, which it almost certainly was not. The use of this very rare term (S. C. Reif renders it as "tent-shrine," a term he claims specifies a portable pagan shrine used for their cultic practices; "What Enraged Phinehas?" p. 204–206) can be explained by its apposition to the similar-sounding word *kubatah* (*her belly*, the spot where the woman is pierced by Phinehas' javelin), itself a euphemism for her womb. What we seem to be encountering here is an intentional wordplay by the author implying that the woman, due to her licentious act on behalf of her god, is getting what she deserved: i.e., the punishment fitted the crime.

24. A strong case can be made that the sexual act was not merely for pleasure but was an integral part of the worship of Baal-peor. Thus we are speaking of an act of ritual intercourse taking place right in front of God's sanctuary, and in the presence of the assembly of the religious and secular leadership of Israel—an intentional and maximal provocation.

25. "Later tradition, interpreting 'plague' as slaughter, claims Phinehas's example was followed by his loyal supporters [in the sanctuary guard], and it was they who slew the twenty-four thousand Israelites" (Milgrom, p. 217), taking as their precedent the purge carried out by Moses following the worship of the Golden Calf (*Exodus* 32:25–28). For a further exploration of the question of the "plague" see Appendix F: The Plague at Baal-Peor.

26. Literally, "in his becoming zealous with My zealousness." The verb *kana* "in Arabic and Syriac means 'became intensely red' and refers here to the visible effects of anger on the face. God becomes 'impassioned,' that is aroused when Israel flirts with other gods… [thus] this phrase most likely means Phinehas's passion matched that of God's." (*Ibid.*, p. 216)

covenant of priesthood, because he was zealous for his God, and made atonement for the Children of Israel'" [Numbers 25:8b–13].

One decisive action and the rot is halted. Authority has been reasserted and order is restored.

It should never have come to this; the entire shameful episode is a devastating comment on the collapse of Moses as a leader. Age has taken its toll. Moses is no longer able to provide the kind of leadership required. It was he who allowed things to get out of hand in the first place; when they had, he abdicated his responsibility to deal with the emergency. Even when matters had reached crisis proportions, with his authority being publicly flouted and harsh measures unavoidable, the offenders should have been dealt with through established judicial procedures. Moses' breakdown was directly responsible for a collapse of due process and the vacuum, where only vigilante action could save the day. All parties seem to realize this. In the near future we will find Moses turning over the reins of leadership to his disciple, Joshua, reserving only his authority as a religious teacher, which he exercises to the end.

The text, in its summary, endorses these conclusions. The situation had reached a point where the very future of Israel was at stake. Unless someone acted, all would be lost. Phinehas acted in the most drastic way possible so as to make a statement, and we are informed that God approved his intervention. The moral collapse, had it continued unabated, would have led to God writing off the Children of Israel. By his zealous act, which is specifically defined as zealousness for the Lord God of Israel, disaster has been averted. And as a reward for stepping into the breach and saving the situation, Phinehas is granted two rewards: God's "covenant of peace" and a permanent privilege—both he and his progeny (seed)—of being the only ones to serve God in His sanctuary.

But this accolade does not end our tale. The couple, who were caught *in flagrante* and killed by Phinehas, are not a couple of nobodies, mere riffraff. They were part of the elite, the setters of style and standards of their time. In a postscript we are apprised of their identities.

> *Now the name of the man of Israel who was slain—the one who was slain with the Midianite woman—was Zimri, son of Salu, Prince of a Simeonite Beth-av.*[27] *And the name of the Midianite woman who was slain was Cozbi, daughter of Zur; he was the Chieftain*[28] *of a Beth-av in Midian* [Numbers 25:14–15].

It took exceptional courage to dare to act against both a prince of his own people and a foreign princess: personages of note from noble families with motive and the means to avenge their deaths. Phinehas richly merited his commendation and reward.

The Source of the Rot

Up to this point, the focus of our narrative has been on Phinehas and his solitary intervention; his taking matters in hand and turning around a crisis situation.

---

27. Literally, "a Father's House," i.e., one of the basic hereditary Houses that composed the clan in ancient Israel. There were five clans to the tribe of Simeon; there had been six but one apparently died out during the Wilderness Period; the tribe of Simeon seems to have suffered a loss of almost two thirds of its members.

28. He is termed a king in *Numbers* 31:8. The Midianite Chieftain (Hebrew *Rosh Umah*) is clearly the leader of a much larger body than that headed by Zimri.

But now the camera, so to speak, zooms out and our attention is directed to the larger national ramifications of what has been going on. Phinehas' act, while saving the day, has been a mere stopgap measure which did not address the source of the rot. It is Cozbi, Princess of Midian, who points us to the true cause of the infection that has taken hold in Israel.

In the aftermath of Phinehas' action, God prods Moses to come out of his torpid lapse of leadership and once again take charge by dealing with the root of the crisis. God informs Moses that the cascade of events which led to the debacle was not fortuitous; Israel had been set up, and the ones who had orchestrated the emergency were none other than the Midianites. It is they who must be dealt with.

> *And the* LORD *spoke to Moses, saying: "Assail the Midianites and smite them. For they have assailed[29] you by their wiles[30] by which they beguiled you in the matter of Peor and the matter of their kinswoman, Cozbi, daughter of a prince of Midian,[31] who was struck down at the time of[32] the plague, on account of Peor"[33]* [25:16–18].

In other words, fraternization was not initiated by the Israelites but was instigated by the Midianites—largely using Moabite women[34] to front for them and to obscure the role that the Midianites were playing—with the purpose of seducing susceptible Israelite men to transfer their allegiance from the LORD to Baal. In sum, God considers that the Midianite actions at Peor were a premeditated attack on Israel, and should be responded to as such.

But where do the Midianites come into the picture? After all, we have been informed that it was Balak, King of Moab, who was the one who panicked and who was in the forefront of the efforts to undermine Israel. True, as his first step he recruited at least some of the Midianite tribes as allies (see *Numbers* 22:4, 7), but the *Book of Balaam* portrays the Midianites as largely silent partners, content to remain in the background and allow King Balak and the Moabites to lead. But now we are being informed that—perhaps due to the failure of Balak's plan to employ Balaam to curse Israel—it is the Moabite leadership that seems to be taking a rear seat, while it is the Midianites who appear to have taken over the direction of the anti–Israelite campaign.

---

29. "The Hebrew verb ṣ-r-r [assail, attack] bears the sense of military aggression (*Exod.* 23:22, *Num.* 10:9, 33:55).... What the Midianites have perpetrated by these deceptions was tantamount to war, and warrants referring to them as *ṣorerim* 'aggressors.'" (Levine, p. 291). With regard to the first use of the term, we read in the imperative—*assail*—with the Samaritan Pentateuch (Sam).

30. "The Hebrew *niklehem*, from the root n-k-l, connotes deception" (ibid..), hence *wiles*.

31. In 25:15 she is cited as being the daughter of a Chieftain (Hebrew *Rosh Umah*; see note 28 above), while in 31:8 he is referred to as one of the five Kings of Midian; it would seem that he held several offices in the loose tribal confederation of that nomadic horde. In any event, regardless of which hat he was wearing at any given time, her father is cited as a person of high rank, and not to be taken lightly.

32. Literally, *in the day of*.

33. The expression *al davar* is repeated no less than three times in this single verse. The first two times we have translated it as *in the matter of*, the third time we render it as *on account of* because it is giving the reason why Cozbi was killed: she being a key figure in the seduction of Israel to the worship of Baal-peor. Thus the three-fold repetition of the phrase serves to emphasize the three aspects of the affair: the moral and religious collapse, the killing of princess Cozbi and what flows from it, and assigning to Cozbi the responsibility for what led to her demise.

34. See note 6 above.

God's directive consists of four parts: first, directing attention to the Midianites as the true enemies of Israel, and branding them as the ones responsible for the debacle at Peor. Secondly, it then defines their actions at Peor as unprovoked aggression: the launching of an undeclared war; it mandates Israel to consider itself as being at war with Midian. Thirdly, it then orders Israel to retaliate with an armed counter-strike. In effect, the Midianites have launched a clandestine campaign against the Children of Israel. Israel, in reply, must therefore enter into an open armed conflict with them. So far so good; but then the last part of God's directive to Moses—almost half of it by word count—is devoted to Cozbi, who had originally been presented to us as nothing more than a promiscuous young lady of good family who was unlucky enough to have been caught "carrying on" at the wrong time and in the wrong place. Why does God keep harping on her?

Let us begin our speculation by asking a question: what was Cozbi doing in the area of the Israelite encampment in the first place? We accounted for the Moabite women by postulating that they were locals (the area in which the Israelites are encamped had been, until fairly recently, Moabite territory), or that they were Moabite prostitutes in search of new customers (Moab's current border was not that far away), or possibly both. Either way, there must have been more than a few to have produced the impact that they did. Are all these promiscuous women fired with missionary zeal?

They [the daughters of Moab] *invited the people* [of Israel] *to the sacrifices of their gods, and the people ate, and worshiped their gods* [25:2].

Where did the animals for the sacrifices come from? Who supplied them? Sheep, oxen, etc., are not inexpensive. This entire affair begins to smell of a choreographed production, well organized and well financed. God's accusation merely confirms these suspicions. But organization implies organizers, and finance implies paymasters. And then suddenly we encounter a Midianite woman, originating from the highest circles of the Midianite power elite, enjoying the intimate companionship of one of the Israelite ruling establishment. How did they meet? The Plains of Moab are at the western edge of the Trans-Jordan, at a considerable distance from the wilderness abode of the Midianites. Need we assume that their meeting was fortuitous; the relationship based solely on mutual attraction, with the Israelite as the leading partner? Or, on the other hand, dare we harbor a suspicion that Cozbi's presence is not unpremeditated and her activities neither casual nor undirected? Certain it is that her demise appears to have brought matters to a standstill. Is this only because her dramatic termination, and that of her paramour, Zimri, presented a warning to all and sundry; a warning that could not be ignored? Or could we entertain the further supposition: that a key figure in the operation has been removed from the playing field?

Whatever conclusions we reach in our speculations, certain it is that Cozbi's horrific skewering—while ostensibly in the performance of an act of religious worship—has created a situation that no one can ignore. The bloody dispatch of a Princess of Midian cannot but provoke a violent reaction from, at the very least, her father's entire tribe, and probably from other tribes as well who are bound by ties of

Chapter 11. Epilogue: The Road to Dusty Death

blood, marriage and treaty to her father's family. This is a *casus belli*. Given the conventions of those days, open warfare must commence. This throws a special light on God's instructions to Moses. God is commanding Israel to act before Midian does; to launch a preemptive strike. And Moses, having gotten his act together, emerges from his lassitude and comes to life.

But suddenly, once again the narrative screeches to a halt. We read:

Now it came to pass after the plague... [25:19a]

To this fragment the Masorites[35] add the following note: "A break [here] in the middle of the verse,"[36] which not only indicates a break in the narrative, but implies that, even as the *Book of Balaam* (*Numbers* 22–24) has been editorially introduced into the text, so has the block of material that follows (*Numbers* 26–30).[37] The narrative will continue from the place where it broke off in *Numbers* 31:1 with the account of the Midianite war.[38] So let us back up a step or two, repeat the lead-up to the truncated verse (25:16–18), put the two pieces of the verse together and continue as though the editorial intrusion had never occurred.

> *And the* LORD *spoke to Moses, saying: "Assail the Midianites and smite them. For they have assailed you by their wiles by which they beguiled you in the matter of Peor and the matter of their kinswoman, Cozbi, daughter of a prince of Midian, who was struck down at the time of the plague, on account of Peor." Now it came to pass after the plague that the* LORD *spoke to Moses saying: "Vindicate*[39] *the Children of Israel*[40] *with regard to the Midianites*[41]*; afterward you shall be gathered to your people"*[42] [25:16–19a, 31:1–2].

---

35. See Glossary.
36. Hebrew, *piskah be'emtza pasuk*.
37. Philo preserves the original order of the text, *Numbers* 31 following immediately after *Numbers* 25.
38. The block of material intruded into the narrative (*Numbers* 26 through 30) is comprised of:
    1. The account of the second census (*Numbers* 26), which concludes with a note that the census showed that of the entire generation, age 20 and over, that exited Egypt only Joshua and Caleb remain alive (26:63–65).
    2. Along with the military purpose of the census, its secondary purpose is for use in the future apportionment of the Promised Land, once seized, among the tribes and clans of Israel (26:52–56).
    3. This leads to the case of the appeal of the five daughters of Zelophehad (27:1–7), which in turn leads to a revision of the laws of inheritance (27:8–11).
    4. There follows the expected appointment of Joshua to succeed Moses as leader of the Children of Israel, and the formal transfer of authority (27:12–23).
    5. As opposed to his civil responsibilities, Moses retains his religious authority (both in regard to his role as teacher and as religious legislator) until his death (*Numbers* 28–30).
        a. Moses inaugurates the Religious Calendar of Holy Days, and their ritual ceremonies as they are to be observed in the Promised Land; i.e., the public sacrifices (28:1–30:1).
        b. Moses initiates rules of vows and their annulment (30:2–17).

    We skip over this intrusion and continue with the narrative.
39. Hebrew, *nekom*, often translated as "revenge." But Mendenhall has demonstrated, to my mind convincingly, that positive vindication is a more appropriate translation. (G. Mendenhall, "The Vengeance of Yaweh," p. 99)
40. Hebrew, *nekom nikmat benai yisrael*; literally, "vindicate the vindication of the Children of Israel"; i.e., redress the wrongs done to the Children of Israel by the Midianites; exact retribution from them.
41. Literally, *from the Midianites*.
42. I.e., your kin. This is an idiom used only of Israel's forefathers, and of Moses and Aaron. "It is an act that takes place *after dying but before burial*.... It means 'be reunited with one's ancestors' and refers to the afterlife." (Milgrom, p. 170)

The skein has run out: Moses' drastic mishandling of the Baal-Peor disaster—a crisis that should never have been allowed to develop in the first place—has brought the curtain down on his leadership role. God informs him that he is through, and in the most drastic manner possible: *you shall be gathered to your people*, i.e., in short order you will die. But before you will be removed from the scene, you will have one last task to perform, that of providing a decisive response to the covert campaign the Midianites have launched against the Children of Israel.

Moses rouses himself to meet this last challenge. Rather than declare war and mobilize for a major campaign against an amorphous nomadic horde, a course that at best can only prove drawn out and costly, Moses opts for a quick surgical strike against that Midianite tribal grouping he has reason to believe has been directly responsible for the Baal-peor operation. In place of mass he will pin his hopes on surprise. As a general mobilization cannot but signal his intentions, he will use the troops that each tribe currently has under arms and rely on stealth, suddenness and shock to carry the day.[43]

For a brief moment Moses seems almost his old self. In short order he convinces the tribal leaders that the supposedly friendly Midianites are really their enemies, of the soundness of his strategy of a surprise attack, and he gets them to donate a regiment each for the campaign. Moses' plan works; the Midianites suspect nothing. Caught completely unprepared and from the first thrown completely off-balance, the result is a slaughter. Our author doesn't bother with details. He merely informs us that once resistance collapses the Israelites make a thorough job of it. They systematically kill every male, young and old alike, making of their victims an example to the remaining tribes of the far-flung horde as to what happens to those who have the effrontery to involve themselves in the internal affairs of the Children of Israel, and simultaneously guaranteeing that those tribes guilty of such "involvement" will not be able any time soon to regroup and exact revenge. And last, but hardly least, the Israelites make a special point of executing the leadership echelon that was responsible for launching "Operation Baal-peor."

So Moses spoke to the people, saying, "Detach[44] from your midst men for the campaign,[45] and let them fall upon[46] Midian in order to exact the LORD's *vindication upon Midian. A regiment[47] from each tribe, a regiment from each tribe, from all the*

---

43. We must never forget that the Israelites have been living for an entire generation in a semi-nomadic state; their economy is based not on agriculture but on animal husbandry. They are burdened with large flocks and herds which require constant and intensive care. A full mobilization of military manpower removes most of those responsible for the care of the animals and can therefore be tolerated only for relatively short periods. We can thus take as a given that the conclusion of the campaigns against the kingdoms of Heshbon and Bashan was followed by a general demobilization. Needless to say, each tribe would keep a certain proportion of its manpower under arms as a necessary and elementary security precaution. It is these battle ready units—relatively few in number but immediately available—that Moses proposes to use for his strike against the Midianites.

44. Hebrew, *hayhaltzu*. The root *h-l-tz* has two basic meanings: 1. *To remove, to extract* and 2. *To gird* (for battle), *to arm*. With Levine (p. 450–451) I prefer the first as more suited to the context.

45. Hebrew, *tzava*. "Campaign [is] the sole meaning of the word in this chapter. It connotes more than a battle. It embraces the total operation of a military campaign or any other group service." (Milgrom, p. 256)

46. Hebrew, *veyeheyu al*. As in *2 Samuel* 11:23 the idiom means to attack, to fall upon. (*Ibid*.)

47. Hebrew *eleph*. This Israelite term for their basic military unit, which we have rendered by its rough modern equivalent of "regiment," also has the meaning of "a thousand," which was its ideal or "book" enrollment. In real life the *eleph* rarely if ever came up to its full manpower complement.

tribes of Israel shall you dispatch for the campaign." So from the regiments of Israel there were provided[48] *a regiment per tribe; [a total of] twelve regiments*[49] *equipped for the campaign. And Moses sent them, a regiment per tribe, to the campaign; them and Phinehas, son of Eleazar [to serve as] chaplain*[50] *in the campaign, [who was] bearing with him*[51] *the sacred implements*[52] *and the trumpets for blowing. And they campaigned against*[53] *Midian as the* LORD *had commanded Moses, and they killed every male. And in addition to the others whom they slew, they killed the kings of Midian: Evi, Rekem, Tzur, Hur and Reba, the five kings of Midian. And Balaam, son of Beor, they put to the sword*[54] [31:3–8].

The Return of Balaam

Wait a minute, what's this about Balaam? What is he doing here? When we last heard of Balaam he had just been declared *persona non grata* and had been expelled from Moab. We were then informed that he *returned to his place* (24:25), i.e., to Pethor in Mesopotamia.[55] What is he now doing among the Midianites? For that matter, why have the Israelites killed him, and why does our author bring his account of the operational phase of the Midianite war to its climax with the report of Balaam's death? Only in the wake of the war will we gain the insight necessary to find answers to these questions.

Rather than follow our normal procedure of quoting the subsequent text and analyzing it carefully—it deals with issues remote from our present concerns—we will content ourselves with simply summarizing it in order to arrive at the parenthetical comment that will prove to be the key to our problem. We are informed that, following the battle and the ensuing slaughter, in line with universal custom of those days the Israelite troops fall to looting the Midianite encampments.[56] And again in accordance with international practice of that period, the women of the vanquished pass into the hands of the victors. So the triumphant Israelites, after setting the Midianite encampments and semi-permanent structures ablaze, return to their camp at Shittim burdened with the possessions of the Midianites: their movable goods, their cattle and sheep, and of course their women.

Accompanied by Eleazar the High Priest and all the leaders of the community, Moses goes out to greet the victors. When he sees what they have brought with them

---

48. Reading with LXX, Syr. and Targ. MT reads "they committed" as in "to commit a trespass."
49. Thus excluding the priestly tribe of Levi, which never participated in military matters due to its calling.
50. Literally, *priest*.
51. Literally, *in his hand*, i.e., in his possession.
52. Probably this refers to the Breastplate of the High Priest which contained the *Urim and Thumim* (see Glossary); we know that these were often present in battles, in the possession of the priest serving the army, to enable him to ascertain, in real time, God's will as the battle progressed. (See for example *1 Samuel* 14:36–45)
53. In the sense of "waged war"; "took the field against" (see *Isaiah* 29:7–18; 31:4 for this usage).
54. Literally, *killed with the sword*.
55. See Chapter 7, note 6.
56. We must remember that nonprofessional soldiers—i.e., militia—were not paid for their services. Their only compensation for risking their lives and spilling their blood was, if victorious, what loot they could amass from the enemy.

he explodes. Focusing his anger on the military commanders he cries, "What have you done? These are the very women with whom you fornicated and who seduced Israel into idolatry: the worship of Baal-peor! And you are now reintroducing them into the camp of Israel as your slaves and concubines!" And here we find the remark that acts as our key, opening the door to a completely new understanding of everything that has gone on up to this moment.

> *These [women] are the very ones who, at the instigation[57] of Balaam, caused the Children of Israel to commit sacrilege[58] against the* LORD *in the matter of Peor...* [31:16]

Moses is here publicly charging Balaam with being the Machiavellian conniver who was behind the covert operation at Baal-peor. This revelation throws the entire complex of events which have been preoccupying us into a completely different light. It confirms our suspicions that the fraternization of the Israelites with the pagan women—first described as Moabite but now revealed to be largely Midianite—was anything but fortuitous boy meets girl occurrences, but rather a planned program of seduction. The women did not just happen to be on the way to a religious festival, and happen to spontaneously invite their new acquaintances along to join in the fun; rather, the participation of thousands of Israelites[59] in the worship of Baal—an act that amounted to high treason against the LORD, the God of Israel—was actually the purpose of what is now being revealed to be a cleverly orchestrated plot. And it reveals the initiator and orchestrator of the operation to be none other then Balaam, son of Beor.[60]

Now we can understand the act of the triumphant Children of Israel in killing Balaam along with the five Kings of Midian; we are once again confronted with a lethal combination of a head of state—this time a collective of five confederate "kings"[61]—joined by an outside "expert."[62] And while at this point in time the Israelites may not yet be aware of Balaam's role in Balak's attempt to neuter Israel,[63] they were most certainly and painfully aware of the trauma that they had undergone at Peor and, we are now being told, who was responsible for it.

By this time the perceptive among us will have become more than aware of the yawning gap that has opened between the author of the *Book of Balaam* on the one hand, and the author of the narrative account in the *Book of Numbers*, of the vicissitudes of the Children of Israel in their progress to the Promised Land,[64] on the other.

---

57. Literally, *word*.

58. Reading with LXX and Targ. *limol maal*, "to trespass," "to commit sacrilege." MT reads *limsor* ("to count" or possibly "to provide" as in 31:5), meanings which make little sense here.

59. If we accept the figure of those who died in the "plague"—24,000—as the number of those who were inducted into the worship of Baal (see note 25 above), we are speaking of an enormously successful plot that came close to undermining the morale and cohesion, indeed the very existence of the Children of Israel.

60. The role of Balaam as the Machiavellian instigator of "Operation Baal-peor" was recognized by the rabbis of the Talmud (see Tractate *Sanhedrin* 106b). This led to the majority opinion of Balaam as a virtually Satanic figure. But see note 66 below.

61. Or perhaps more properly, in our parlance—tribal heads or overlords of tribal groupings.

62. In the first instance Balak, King of Moab, with Balaam in the role of clairvoyant and sorcerer for hire, in our present case the five Kings of Midian with Balaam, here in the role of advisor and implementer.

63. Due to God's intervention Balaam never managed to put a hex upon Israel.

64. I.e., the author of the account contained in *Numbers* 21, 25 and 31.

Chapter 11. Epilogue: The Road to Dusty Death

They hold strikingly different estimates of Balaam's character. The author of the *Book of Balaam* (*Numbers* 22-24) pictures him in a very positive light, as a person who has long served the LORD "his God" as His seer, and after a bout of rebelliousness has learned his lesson, accepted his proper role as a trusted servant of the LORD, and as a result been raised to the status of a prophet. The author of the *Numbers* narrative contained in Chapter 21, 25 and 31 sees Balaam in a very different light: a Machiavellian plotter lurking in the shadows, the malevolent enemy of Israel, designer of the nefarious plot to seduce Israel into the betrayal of its God at Baal-peor and thus to self-destruction. How can we account for this radical divergence?

If we accept the analysis of Albright[65] that the *Book of Balaam* was composed in the 10th century BCE, then it is reasonable to assume that its author was fully aware of the 13th-century Baal-peor affair, and that Balaam was to be blamed for having been behind it. Yet this in no way seems to dampen his enthusiasm for his "hero." He simply closes his "Book" before the incident and doesn't take it into account. Similarly, the editors who shoehorned the *Book of Balaam* into the *Numbers* account seem to have had no qualms about placing the positive portrayal of Balaam cheek and jowl with the picture of a foul villain.[66] It is hard to believe that they were unaware of the conflict. As opposed to many modern scholars, I do not believe that biblical editors were obtuse. What is obvious to us must have been evident to them as well. Which means that they did not see the conflict between the two ways of understanding Balaam as irresolvable; they had a way of subsuming the two into one comprehensive view. The rest of this chapter will therefore be an attempt to reconstruct something approaching their viewpoint, harmonizing these two perspectives into one vision of this complex and ultimately tragic figure.

In the first place we must ask ourselves: what could have been Balaam's purpose in devising the scheme of seducing large numbers of Israelite men to partake in the worship of Baal-peor? If we postulate that his aim was malignant—and I think that we have every reason to assume this—then we have only to go back to God's revelation to discover the genesis of Balaam's scheme. For his second oracle God put the following words into Balaam's mouth:

> *No iniquity can be perceived in Jacob;*
> *No wrong can be seen in Israel.*
>
> *The* LORD *his God is with him,*[67]
> *And a King's proclamation is in his midst....*

---

65. See the concluding paragraphs of the introduction to the *Book of Balaam*.

66. These two points of view—saint or villain—continued to reverberate down the centuries. From earliest times, many saw Balaam's protestations that he could only say and do what God commanded as a statement of the literal truth. In the 8th century the prophet Micah (6:5) clears Balaam of all blame, laying the onus for desiring to curse Israel solely on Balak. In the post-biblical period some of the rabbis even saw Balaam as the equal of Moses (*Sifre* on *Deuteronomy* 34:10), while there were those who considered him in some respects as even greater (*Numbers Rabba* 14:20). But the preponderant view was distinctly negative. From *Deuteronomy* 27:4-7 to *Nehemiah* 13:2 (which quotes *Deuteronomy*)—both basing legislation on their negative interpretation of the Balaam episode—to the New Testament (*2 Pet.* 2:15-16, *Jude* 11, *Rev.* 2:14) to the age of the rabbis, the stereotype of "Balaam the Wicked" grew into the mainstream view. To this day most people reflexively continue to see Balaam as the paradigm of wickedness.

67. *His...him...his*: these third person singular pronouns refer, of course, to "Israel," i.e., the people of Israel.

> *For no enchantment can be effective against Jacob,*
> *No magic against Israel.* (23:21, 23)

Seen from Balaam's point of view, these words were revelatory. He already knew—God had so informed him while he was still at home in Pethor—that this people was blessed and therefore uncurseable.[68] Now God informs Balaam of the reason for Israel's state of blessedness: it is blessed because it is blameless; having done nothing wrong, it is immune to any and all curses and magical incantations. Now while Balaam may have accepted this statement at face value we, who have access to the record (*Exodus, Leviticus* and the first twenty chapters of *Numbers*), would find this statement so blatantly far from the truth as to be absurd. In our discussion of these verses,[69] we pointed out that the only way this pronouncement could make sense would be for it not apply to the generation of ex-slaves that came out of Egypt; after all, for their multitudinous sins they had been condemned to die in the wilderness. Rather, it describes their children who, not being held responsible for the sins of their parents, currently rest under a presumption of innocence. The parents' generation is in the last stages of dying off,[70] and it is their children who now hold center stage. Of them no serious sin has as yet been recorded. For this reason God's presence dwells in their midst and empowers them to the ferocity and invincibility of lions. And it is precisely in this soaring panegyric that the shrewd and penetrating mind of Balaam perceives opportunity. As he sees it, in revealing His reason for blessing the children of Israel, God has inadvertently exposed their fatal vulnerability, their Achilles heel. Should the current generation be induced to sin—to betray the Lord their God—their advantage will be gone; they will be irretrievably weakened.

What we are therefore proposing is, that it is this vulnerability that Balaam elects to exploit. Where he failed in the supernatural realm—his efforts to curse Israel embarrassingly frustrated—he will succeed using mundane means. Instead of fatally weakening Israel by occult devices, he will achieve the same end through the application of his worldly wisdom. Balaam is revealing himself to be a dedicated man; come what may, he will fulfill the contract he entered into with Balak. The author of the *Book of Balaam* was right about Balaam's enlightenment. But enlightenment does not cause him to abandon his mission; rather it shows him an open path to achieving it. Balaam will remain steadfast to the end.

In my opinion, it would be wrong to disregard the personal element behind this development. Balak began with an exalted opinion of Balaam and had become bitterly disillusioned by Balaam's failure to deliver the expected outcomes. He had severed their relationship by publicly humiliating Balaam, withholding payment and expelling him from the land. Balaam's retaliatory oracle, predicting Moab's future defeat and subjugation at the hands of this despised people, was far from sufficient to salve the mortification and shame to which this proud man had been subjected. Only the eventuality of being able to confront Balak and throw his success in the king's face could hold the promise of assuaging the hurt to his pride. While this is hardly

---

68. *"You shall not curse the people for it is blessed."* (22:12)
69. See above, Chapter 8, the section entitled The Second Oracle.
70. By the year's end, of this entire generation only Joshua and Caleb will remain among the living.

the whole story of what leads to Balaam's attempt at a comeback, it is almost certainly a major piece of the complex of motives that led to Balaam's organizing and launching his clandestine assault—one that but for Phinehas' intervention, might very well have succeeded.

But for a man like Balaam, injured pride alone could hardly provide the sole reason for launching an assault on a people under the Lord's protection, and for deciding to disregard the sword in the angel's hand. Balaam was a brilliant and experienced clairvoyant: he had taken note of and understood the significance of that element of his dream: that the naked sword represented a warning as to what awaited him should he persist on the "twisted road"[71] on which he was embarked. Yet persist he does. And so the deeper question remains: what is it that is driving Balaam's self-defeating and ultimately self-destructive behavior? And to address this question we have to leave the conclusion of our tale and return to its beginning.

At the start of our account we remember being pulled up short by a basic inconsistency in Balaam's behavior: the contradiction between his pronouncements and his actions. In speech he is a saint. In pronouncement after pronouncement he avers that he is merely a servant of his God, that he can only say and do what the Lord tells him to say or do. But again and again his actions belie his avowals. He issues ringing declarations of principle such as:

"*[Even] if Balak were to give me his palace filled with silver and gold I could not do anything, great or small to violate the word of the* Lord *my God*" [22:18].

And,

"*Can I speak a single thing* [of my own free will]? *The word that God will put in my mouth, that will I speak*" [22:38].

And again,

"*Should I not be careful to speak* [only] *that which the* Lord *places in my mouth?*" [23:12]

And yet again,

"*Did I not speak to you saying, 'Whatever the* Lord *speaks, that I must do'?*" [23:26]

Yet again and again we have seen Balaam attempting to defy his God. He starts by attempting to get around a direct prohibition forbidding him to go to Moab,[72] and finally succeeds in wringing a conditional concession from God.[73] He accepts a commission to curse the Children of Israel, a commission that God has told him is impossible to fulfill.[74] He moves on from attempting to game God to attempts to coerce Him through the use of magic, and only desists after his attempts fail to bend God to

---

71. 23:32.
72. *And God said to Balaam, "Do not go with them* [Balak's emissaries]." (22:12)
73. *And God came to Balaam by night and said to him, "If the men came to call you, arise and go with them. However, the thing that I speak to you, only that shall you do."* (22:20)
74. *"You shall not curse the people for it is blessed."* (22:12)

his will.⁷⁵ His dream reveals him openly defying God. Not only do his actions betray a will retrograde to the will of God, but even more to the point, none of his contemporaries seem to take his pronouncements seriously. They appear to understand what he says as either statements for the record or excuses, and take it as a given that his heart lies elsewhere. It is to this conclusion that we too have belatedly come.

So why did Balaam want so badly to go to Moab? What led him to accept a commission that he knew he could not fulfill? Why, despite this knowledge, did he make every effort to achieve the aims he had contracted to achieve? We tentatively postulated an overpowering greed—that blank check that he had been offered that would enable him to satisfy his every worldly desire—and left it at that. But the solution does not really fit the bill. Balaam has been increasingly revealed to us as far more than a crass money-grubber. Money alone could never explain his adopting an adversarial role to his God. Nor can it explain his return from Pethor and his role as an advisor to the Midianites or his crafting of "Operation Baal-peor," that brilliant and incisive identification of Israel's greatest vulnerability and the means by which to exploit it. Money in this context is never mentioned; it seems to be off the table. So what is there in all this for Balaam? What has been driving him all through this complex and ultimately sordid saga?

The Rude Eye of Rebellion

From the start Balaam has been proclaiming himself to be no more than a humble servant of the Lord. Again and again he repeats this claim. These repeated disclaimers sound hollow; one is reminded of the remark of Gertrude in Hamlet:

*The lady doth protest too much, methinks.*⁷⁶

It almost seems as if Balaam is trying to convince the world—and possibly himself as well—that he is content to remain in his condition of mere servant to the Lord. One suspects that for some time the status of servant—of messenger boy—to the Almighty has become increasingly irksome to him. No one likes to be continually told what to say or do. One begins to surmise, therefore, that increasingly he has yearned to shake off the restraint under which he has been laboring and carve out a role of his own. In a word, the wish to be free of God's direction—the wish to be autonomous and not simply a servant—has become an overpowering urge. With the arrival of the first of the Moabite and Midianite deputations bearing Balak's proposals, matters come to a head.

The issue is not so much the tempting offer, one speculates, as the fact that Balaam has been told "no" by God once too often. Balaam has reached the point where he finds it impossible to keep on simply taking orders; he wants to make some decisions on his own. He simply can't continue to hold his peace and take orders anymore. The issue is not this "people who have come out of Egypt." By all indications, at this point Balaam knows next to nothing about the Children of Israel, and could

---

75. *He dispensed with his previous enchantments.* (24:1)
76. William Shakespeare, *Hamlet*, III, ii.

care less one way or the other. To Balaam, Israel is simply a test case: does he always have to do as he is told, or can he, at least from time to time, get his own way and do what he sees fit, rather than what God wants? May we conclude, therefore, that what we are seeing is nothing less than Balaam's attempt to break free and assert his freedom of action?

God must have seen this coming. We already have pointed out that the prohibition to go to Moab was superfluous. The basic issue was the matter of cursing this people. The concession that Balaam wrests from his God—that if his heart is so set on going, permission granted, but with these conditions—is meaningless. What is the use of going if, once you are there, you will be unable to fulfill the terms of your contract and put a hex on Israel? But Balaam does not see things this way. He sees breaking free of God as a drawn-out process. He has taken the first step, and won the first round. God has issued a decree and he has gotten God to back off. And the concession that he has had to make—that he could only say what God will tell him to say—is nothing new; it is simply a reaffirmation of the rules under which he has always been operating. But as he has finessed God into backing down on the first restriction, so does Balaam see himself succeeding with the second, and so on, until all restrictions on his actions are lifted. Maurice Samuel, who has reached similar conclusions by a different route, puts it this way:

> To Balaam it is unacceptable that he is doomed forever to be God's public crier, without a role of his own in the ordering of world affairs.[77]

And so, from Balaam's point of view, Israel is irrelevant. In this struggle between himself and God the question is whether or not Balaam can break free from God. What happens to Israel in the process is simply collateral damage.

If Balaam's motives are dark and convoluted, God's are almost totally opaque. It would seem that God is fully aware of what is going on with Balaam. He appears to see in Balaam a highly talented servant in danger of going off the rails. As we previously speculated,[78] God's original intention was to keep Balaam out of temptation's way by keeping him away from Moab. This ploy failed. But God does not need automatons for servants. Balaam has freedom of choice and he insists on pushing the envelope. God then warns him in a dream where the road on which he is embarked will end.[79] Balaam understands the warning, but ultimately disregards it. In Moab he tries, twice, to influence God through magic to turn His blessing into a curse, and twice he fails. And then comes a critical turning point: it is Balaam who backs off. He accepts that he cannot succeed in his attempts to game God, and resigns himself to his role as a servant of the Lord.

> *Now Balaam saw that it was good in the eyes of the* Lord *to bless Israel, so he dispensed with his previous enchantments,*[80] *but turned his face to the wilderness* [24:1].

---

77. M. Samuel, "Perverted Genius," p. 52.
78. In the last paragraphs of Chapter 7, the wrap-up of the analysis of Balaam's dream.
79. The naked sword (22:23, 31), repeated twice for emphasis.
80. Literally, *he did not, as in previous occasions, go to encounter enchantments.*

God responds to Balaam's abandonment of his struggle, and his acceptance of his role as God's mouthpiece, by rewarding him:

...and the spirit of God came upon him [24:2].

Instead of simply putting His words into Balaam's mouth for him to spew out verbatim, God rests His spirit upon him. Balaam has been promoted; from a *seer* or clairvoyant he has been raised to the rank of *prophet*, the highest status a human can attain. He now is not only privy to the will of God but has the privilege of conveying it as he understands it, and in his own words. And this he does, proclaiming his transformation with the three couplets he prefaces to both his third and fourth oracles.

The utterance of Balaam, the son of Beor,
    And the utterance of the man whose eye [has been] *sealed shut,*
The utterance of him who knows the words of God,
    And who knows the thoughts of the Most High
Who views visions from The Almighty,
    Fallen down, yet with eyes unveiled [24:3–4, 15–16].

It is at this point that the rabbis of old considered Balaam to have become the equal of his contemporary Moses, the greatest of the prophets.

There never arose in Israel another prophet like Moses' (Deuteronomy 34:10)—*in Israel* there never arose another, but among the nations of the world there did arise another [namely Balaam].[81]

After his promotion, had he been content to remain in the service of the Lord as prophet and devoted servant, our tale would have had a different ending and the world might have benefited from another spiritual titan. But it was not to be. Perhaps the humiliation he was forced to endure at the hands of Balak irretrievably embittered his spirit and clouded his vision. Maybe the urge for autonomy had grown too overwhelming to be appeased by God's resting His spirit upon him. Probably there were other elements involved of which we know nothing. But either on the long road home or back in Pethor itself, the decision crystallized in Balaam's mind not to close the book on the Moab venture but rather to open a new chapter. Which means in effect that he would not rest content to remain a mere servant of the Lord; the struggle for his autonomy would continue; the battle for a space in God's world that he could call his own, where he could be "master of his fate and captain of his soul." And since it had so fallen out that the first round turned on a struggle over the fate of this people called the Children of Israel, the second round—perforce its sequel—would also have to turn on Israel's fate. If he could manage to bring low this people whom God had blessed, and of whom He expected great things, this would signal Balaam's success in wresting his autonomy from God's grasp.

The strategy decided, there remained but the determination of what tactics to use. In the first round the field of battle had been determined by Balak:

---

81. Sifre Habrekhah 357, cited and translated from the Hebrew, A. J. Heschel, *Heavenly Torah*, p. 526. Heschel also cites rabbinic opinions that in certain aspects Balaam was even greater than Moses.

Chapter 11. Epilogue: The Road to Dusty Death

"Please come and put a curse upon this people for me ... for I know that whom you bless is blessed, and whom you curse is cursed" [22:6].

This had looked like favorable ground on which to fight; was not the realm of the spirit his forte? But in retrospect Balaam realizes that he had made a serious mistake. His opponent was not a man but a god. And for a god—especially a god such as the LORD—the spirit is home ground. No wonder he had been bested. This time he will know better. He will avoid challenging the LORD on his home ground; rather, he will pick the field of battle—human ground—and triumph by way of a flank attack on human weakness. He will use sexual attraction and male lust to lead Israel to betray its God. Once Israel proves unfaithful to its God, He will have no option but to abandon them, and Balaam will have won: indisputably forcing God's hand and countering God's plans. This is a well-thought-out plan of action, and Balaam is masterful in its implementation and orchestration, bringing it to the very cusp of success. In the zealousness of Phinehas Balaam meets his match, and in the Israelite reaction provoked by his tactic Balaam will meet his doom.

But Balaam had been doomed long ago, at the very start of the tale. Two roads had lain before him: the road to prophecy and the road to Moab. One road was open, the other "twisted" and forbidden. But from the first moment his preference was for the second, which was in essence the path of self-aggrandizement. I see God looking with despair on what is taking place with His talented servant. He tries to head him off by forbidding the "twisted road," but Balaam will not take no for an answer. God does not want coerced service; Balaam will remain free and the choice will be his. God warns him what the consequences of the choice of the road to Moab will be—Balaam grasps the meaning of the naked sword in the angel's hand in his dream—but persists nonetheless. Rather than close Balaam down, God patiently gives him more rope, gives him time to discover for himself that he is on a fool's journey, clearly intimating to Balaam in the dream that he is being an ass—a nuance that Balaam also grasps (he is not stupid)—but to no avail. Balaam's heart is set and nothing can dissuade him in his pursuit of personal autonomy.

What divine prohibition and warning could not achieve, the bitter experience of public failure seems to accomplish. Twice, drawing on the accumulated wisdom and experience of a lifetime, this world-famous seer attempts to curse Israel, to force his God to cancel His blessings, and to permit His people to stand cursed—and fails miserably, finding himself blessing instead of cursing. And finally Balaam breaks. He recognizes the blunt fact that he cannot game God. God is immutable and immovable, and Balaam gives up his fool's quest. And God recognizes Balaam's surrender by laying His spirit upon him. God's faith in His servant and His patience with him has seemingly paid off.

Balaam's resultant elevation from seer to prophet has raised the stakes considerably. God is investing a great deal of hope in Balaam's resolution, while Balaam now has so much more to lose should he waver and relapse into rebellion. God is giving Balaam every incentive to remain on the high road. But it seems that Balaam's pride—we would call it ego nowadays—and his overpowering ambition to be free, to be his own man, will prove irresistible. As far as Balaam is concerned, no matter how high the promotion, God will just have to learn that Balaam cannot be bribed into submission. So with grim resolution, and a new strategy firmly in mind, Balaam retraces his steps, but this time his destination is Midean.

While his overall aim is the same, the means Balaam intends now to employ have altered drastically. The first time he was open and forthright: the internationally renowned seer openly practicing his profession by cursing a people unknown to him for a high fee. This time around we find Balaam in a new role: as a Machiavellian plotter skulking in the shadows and orchestrating a devious plot against the people that he now knows to be both blameless and blessed. He himself, as a prophet of God, had eulogized this people Israel in terms of soaring beauty and grandeur. He himself had proclaimed this people's uniqueness, a very creation of God destined to fulfill His purposes. And now Balaam proposes to drive a wedge between this people and its God. As he has betrayed his God, so will he seduce them to betray Him. As he has rebelled against the Lord, so will he draw them into his path of rebellion and so destroy them. Again it is crucial to remember that Balaam has nothing against this people Israel. To him they are simply the tool he will use for his own aggrandizement. Their destruction will, so he seems to think, purchase for him his autonomy from God.

And this is why I cannot feel sorry for Balaam as, now clear in his mind as to exactly what he will be doing, he once again sets out from Pethor, on the road to Midean, and thus to his own doom. He is knowingly setting out to destroy the good and the beautiful in order to advance his own sense of worth. From the heights of prophecy Balaam has lowered himself to the point where he has become an active force for evil in the world. He had been warned where all this would lead should he persist in following this "crooked road." Nevertheless, the man who would not be the servant of God, the man who wanted to be free like God to do as he wished, chose the road to Midean—the road of rebellion—so: *and as for Balaam, son of Beor, the diviner, the Children of Israel slew with the sword, along with the rest of those they slew* [in Midean] (*Joshua* 13:22).

Two roads diverged in a yellow wood,
And sorry I could not travel both
And be one traveler, long I stood
And looked down one as far as I could
To where it bent in the undergrowth;
Then took the other....

I shall be telling this with a sigh
Somewhere ages and ages hence:
Two roads diverged in a wood, and I—
I took the one less traveled by,
And that has made all the difference.

—Robert Frost, *The Road Not Taken*

Part III

A Persecuted Prophet

The strongest man in the world is the man who stands alone.
—Henrik Ibsen, *An Enemy of the People*

Chapter 12

Prologue: A Tangled Three-Act Tragedy

And moreover I saw under the sun,
In the place of justice there was wickedness,
Yea, in the place of righteousness, wickedness was there!
—*Ecclesiastes 3:16*

In the autumn of 1934 Winston Spencer Churchill had a dream.

He dreamt he was standing on the brow of a hill overlooking a wide plane. Clad in bright uniforms two armies—pitifully small by modern standards—were commencing battle. Commanding the army clothed in red was an inspiring figure on horseback, whom Churchill instantly recognized as his illustrious ancestor, General John Churchill, to be known to history as the first Duke of Marlborough. In his dream Winston saw the Duke turn his head and for a long moment look his distant descendant in the eye. In his later accounting of his dream he never could be certain whether or not the Duke had smiled at him. But of one thing he was confident: he had been present in spirit with his glorious ancestor, somehow sharing with him his moment of triumph at the resounding victory of the Battle of Blenheim.

Himself born in one of the many bedrooms of Blenheim Palace,[1] Winston Churchill's life was indelibly colored by his consciousness of his ancestry and origins. For his entire life he felt the eye of the First Duke upon him, urging him on to dare greatly. For Winston Churchill, his ancestry determined his destiny.

The case of Winston Churchill is not unique. There have been many others who have been deeply conscious of the heavy hand of past generations—of illustrious ancestors and of deeds, both glorious and infamous—which weighed heavily upon their shoulders. One such is the subject of our present section: the prophet Jeremiah. Just as one cannot understand the character and resolve of the Winston Churchill who rallied an England on the brink of defeat and led her to victory in World War II without knowing of John Churchill, first Duke of Marlborough, who had lived with Winston in his consciousness as his mentor and model since childhood, so we lack the key that will enable us to grasp the character—his fortitude, his courage and his weaknesses—that made Jeremiah what he was if we do not know something of his

---

1. Blenheim Palace—named after Marlborough's stunning victory—was a grateful nation's gift to their brilliant soldier and statesman. It was Queen Anne who provided the land and Parliament that voted the funds for its construction. From 1733, the date of its completion, Blenheim Palace has remained the ancestral home of the Churchills.

past. Thus we begin our tale not with the birth of our protagonist near the middle of the 7th century BCE, but almost five hundred years earlier.

Act I

The Curse

We find ourselves in the first half of the 11th century BCE in Shiloh[2]; not the little town itself, but the sanctuary against which it nestles. In these days the Shrine of Shiloh is the holiest site in all the land of Israel, for it is here that Moses' successor, Joshua, back in the days following the conquest of Western Canaan, deposited the Ark of the Covenant[3] containing the original Ten Commandments. This now is the religious center of all the tribes of Israel. It is here that the High Priest Eli officiates, as well as his sons who serve under his direction.[4]

> *Now the two sons of Eli, Hophni and Phinehas, were priests unto the* LORD *[in Shiloh].... However the sons of Eli were base men,[5] they knew not the* LORD. *And the custom of the priests with the people was, that when any man offered sacrifice, while the flesh was cooking in the pots a servant* [of one of the priests] *would come with a three-pronged fork in his hand, and he would strike it into the pan, or the kettle, or cauldron or pot[6]; whatever the fork brought up the priest took. So they did to all Israel that came there to Shiloh. Even before the fat was made to smoke* [on the Altar][7] *the priest's servant would come and say to the man who sacrificed, "Give meat to grill for the priest; he won't take stewed meat from you but* [only] *rare!" And the man would say to him,[8] "First let the fat smoke upon the Altar, then take as much as your soul desires." Then the servant would say, "No![9] You give it to me now. If not I will take it by force!" And the sin of the young men was very great before the*

---

2. A town located approximately 21 miles north of Jerusalem.

3. This is an abbreviation of the full title: *The Ark of the Covenant of the Lord of Hosts Enthroned upon the Cherubim*. It was an oblong box, made of wood overlaid with gold, the repository of the Ten Commandments; the original stone tablets that Moses had brought down from Mount Sinai. It was designed for carrying. Its cover, made of solid gold, was surmounted by gold figures of winged cherubim; representations of two mythological creatures with the bodies of lions and human faces, whose outstretched wings covered the Ark from above. In popular imagination these wings formed the support upon which the invisible God sat enthroned.

4. The role of High Priest is hereditary, inherited from Aaron, the first High Priest, who was the brother of Moses.

5. Literally, *"sons of Belial."* Belial is the Netherworld, the Realm of the Dead. Cross and Freedman (*Studies in Yahwistic Poetry*, p. 22, n.6) find the root meaning of the term is "the place from which none arise," i.e., a euphemism for the underworld, the pit, hell. When used in conjunction with *man, men, son/daughter* (as in our case "sons of Belial") it means something like "one destined for hell," a worthless, vile person, a base person with no good in him.

6. The "pan" (Hebrew *kiyor*) was a shallow, wide-mouthed vessel; the "kettle" (*dud*) was a deep, round-bottomed, two-handled cooking pot; the "cauldron" (*kalahat*) was a one-handled cooking jug, while the "pot" (*parur*) seems to have been similar to the *kalahat*. As this was a shrine the vessels were probably made of metal. (King and Stager, *Life in Biblical Israel*, p. 65)

7. I.e., before the part of the sacrifice dedicated to God was even offered

8. Reading with LXX; MT reads *And the man said to him...*

9. Reading with *Qeri*, LXX and Q. The *Ketib* (see Glossary) of MT reads *then he would say to him: "You give..."*

LORD *for the men dealt contemptuously with the offering of the* LORD [*1 Samuel* 1:3; 2:13–17].[10]

As the curtain rises we are being treated to a view of multiple abuse on the part of officiating priests. Of every sacrifice brought to the sanctuary by a layman, a given portion of the animal was reserved for the priests as a fee for officiating at the ceremony.[11] But Eli's sons are breaking all the rules. They refuse to limit themselves to their prescribed shares and, adding insult to injury, they insist on serving themselves before God. This indeed is the crux of the matter: they are men dedicated to the service of God who are using their office to serve themselves.

Things do not stop here; they rarely do. We are further told that the sons of Eli use the authority of their office to

lay the women who served at the door of the Tent of Meeting [2:22].

In blunt terms we are being told that they are sexually abusing the female employees of the shrine who are under their supervision.[12]

What does their father have to say about the actions of his sons? He is old and retired from active priestly duties—he has left those to his sons—and may be initially unaware of what is taking place, but if so it is a situation that cannot last. As scandal grows, it is merely a matter of time before it will be brought forcibly to his attention.

Now Eli was very old, and he heard all that his sons did unto all Israel, and that they did lay the women who served at the door of the Tent of Meeting. And he said to them, "Why are you doing things like these—evil things—of which I hear from all the people? Don't [do them], *my sons, for this report*[13] *which I hear the* LORD's *people spreading about is not good. If one man sin against another, God may intervene for him. But if a man sin against the* LORD, *who is there to intervene for him?"* [2:22–25a]

Eli's reaction is surprisingly weak, lacking in moral urgency. Indeed, from his remonstrance it is hard to tell what is really bothering Eli: the *actions* of his sons or the *rumors* that are circulating? And if it is the deeds of his sons, then it is enlightening that his theological mini-lecture focuses on his sons' ritual malfeasance and not

---

10. Throughout this prologue, unless otherwise stated, all verse references are to the *First Book of Samuel*.

11. Priests in those days were not supported by the state—there was no state—nor did most have any private income. They lived on free-will donations of laymen and the fees they received for officiating: a "cut" of each offering. This cut was limited to the breast and right thigh of the animal; the breast to be divided among all those priests serving in the sanctuary, while the thigh was the personal fee of the priest who did the actual work of officiating. The prescribed procedure was as follows: an animal was brought as a *zebah*, presented to the priest and slaughtered. Only a small symbolic portion was designated for the Altar (part of the fat, kidneys and a lobe of the liver) and these would be "made to smoke," i.e., burnt. Only then the priest's fee would be detached and removed from the carcass. Finally the rest of the animal would be consumed by the offerer and family, on the sanctuary premises, as a Communion Meal "before the Lord." In other words, first God is served, and only then the priest and the layman. See *zebah* in Glossary.

12. Besides clergy, all shrines, then as now, employ lay staff—female as well as male—to perform the routine clerical, administrative and maintenance work that every shrine requires in order to keep functioning. For every priest there were probably anywhere from three to half a dozen male and female employees attached to the shrine. (On seeing these women as shrine employees rather than as worshipers, see Carol Myers, "Women at the Entrance to the Tent of Meeting.")

13. *Report*; in the sense of gossip, a circulating rumor.

on their predatory behavior with their female employees. It is hardly surprising that his sons pay little attention to their old man's tut-tutting.

> *But they did not listen to the voice of their father, because the* LORD *would slay them* [2:25b].

They are young and very full of themselves; and no parental lecturing would cause them to turn back from their self-destructive course.

The text lays heavy blame upon Eli for his son's behavior. But what could he have done? Here we need to remember that Eli is not only their father but, as High Priest, also their boss. He bears the responsibility, both as father and as supervisor, to take action to rectify the situation. Instead of enforcing behavioral norms, he has taken the easy path: first, avoidance of an unpleasant situation, and then indulgence. Unable to summon either the strength or the conviction to discipline his children, God holds him responsible for their clearly criminal behavior. The charge that he honors his sons above God will be a just verdict upon his behavior, as he himself will ultimately acknowledge.

Retribution is not long in coming.

> *Now there came a man of God[14] to Eli, and he said to him, "Thus says the* LORD: *'Did I not reveal Myself[15] to the House of your father, when they were in Egypt, slaves to the House of Pharaoh?[16] And did I not choose him out of all the tribes of Israel to be My priest, to go up to My Altar, to burn incense* [to Me and] *to wear an ephod[17] before Me? And did I not give to the House of your father all the offerings made by fire of the Children of Israel? Why then do you look with a greedy eye[18] at My sacrifice and at My offering which I have commanded in My habitation, and honor your sons above Me, to make yourselves fat with the choicest of all the offerings of Israel My people? Therefore'*—[this is] *an oracle of the* LORD, *the God of Israel*—*'I said indeed[19] that your House and the House of your father should walk before Me for ever; but now'*—[this is] *an oracle of the* LORD—*'be it far from me![20] For they that honor Me will I honor, and they that despise Me shall be lightly esteemed'"* [2:27–30].

Speaking in the name of God, the prophet begins by reminding Eli of how God chose his ancestor Aaron, while he was still in Egypt, to be His first priest, and granted the Office of Priesthood—with its exclusive rights and privileges—to him and to his direct male descendants in perpetuity. Then follows the accusation: the charge of malfeasance in office, of rank ingratitude, and of their underlying cause: *"You honor your sons above Me!"* By his actions, Eli has made clear where his priorities lie. What

---

14. A euphemism for *a prophet*, i.e., a spokesman of God speaking in His name.
15. A pronouncement framed as a rhetorical question, in the infinitive absolute construction for emphasis.
16. Reading with LXX and Q. MT lacks *slaves*.
17. An ephod was a distinctive white linen garment worn by priests and, at times, by laymen when performing sacred duties.
18. Reading with LXX. MT reads *kick at*.
19. Once again the infinitive absolute construction for emphasis.
20. I.e., I revoke My promise.

is more, not only is Eli, in effect, showing contempt for God by his preference for his sons, but he is also personally profiting from it. And here the man of God becomes bitingly personal. Eli, as we shall learn, is a very fat man.[21] Being old, Eli no longer officiates on a daily basis at the Altar; the operative side of the Priesthood having been turned over to his sons. So the food that he is eating, by which he is making himself *"fat with the choicest of all the offerings of Israel"*—to quote the man of God—is made up of those very choice cuts his sons are arrogantly extorting from the people. By his indulgence of the behavior of his sons, Eli has made himself an accomplice to his son's crimes; an accomplice both before and after the fact. Eli may think that because the High Priesthood is hereditary, an integral component of the Sinai Covenant, he and his House (that is, his children) will hold the office in perpetuity.[22] He is now informed that this is far from the case. The position is conditioned upon proper behavior while in office.[23]

The charge has been laid; now the punishment:

Behold, the days are coming that I will cut off your strength,[24] and the strength of your father's House, that there shall not ever be an old man in your House. Then in distress you shall behold with envious eye[25] all the good which shall be done to Israel; and there shall not be an old man in your House for ever. And the man of you that I shall not cut off from My Altar, shall weep out his eyes and grieve his heart; and all the increase of your House shall die by the sword[26] [2:31–33].

The curse that is being pronounced upon Eli will rest not only on him but also upon his descendants to all time: his descendants will all die young—*there shall not be an old man in your House forever*. Status and respect were linked to age in the Ancient Near East. The term for community leader, a person usually possessing judicial authority, was *Zaken*, usually rendered as "elder." Early death would prevent one from ascending the ladder of leadership. In effect, the curse laid upon the House of Eli amounts to a permanent decree that the family would not only lose the office of High Priesthood, but also would never again have any status or influence in Israel. The House of Eli will be deposed from office, and the High Priesthood will be bestowed on another branch of the family.

But the man of God has not finished:

And this shall be the sign to you,[27] that which shall come upon your two sons, on Hophni and Phinehas: in one day both of them shall die. And I will raise Me up a faithful priest that shall act according to that which is in My heart and My mind;

---

21. See 4: 18.
22. *Exodus* 29:9 and 40:15. At the foot of Mount Sinai Aaron and his sons were promised the priesthood in perpetuity.
23. *They that honor Me will I honor, and they that despise Me shall be lightly esteemed.* (2:30)
24. Literally, *your arm, and the arm of your father's House,* seeing *arm* as a metaphor for *strength.* LXX reads here *descendants.*
25. Reading with LXX; the meaning of MT is uncertain.
26. Reading with LXX; MT reads *shall die men.*
27. This will be the event that will authenticate to you that these words I have spoken are true, and that the judgment that you now hear will indeed come to pass.

and I will build him a faithful²⁸ House; and he shall walk before My anointed forever. And it shall come to pass, that everyone that is left of your House shall come and bow low to him for a piece of silver and a loaf of bread, and shall say: "Please put me into one of the priest's offices so that I may eat a bit of bread" [2:34-36].

We are not informed of Eli's response to this terrible judgment. Perhaps he makes no reply but merely sits there stunned. Some years later the curse is confirmed in Samuel's call to prophecy.²⁹ By now Eli has had time to brood over his sons' behavior and his indulgence of them. He has become resigned.

*He said: "It is the L*ORD*. He will do what is right in His eyes"* [3:18]

Confirmation: The Ax Falls

*Now it came to pass in those days that the Philistines mobilized for war against Israel,³⁰ and Israel went out to battle against the Philistines, and encamped besides Eben-ezer³¹.... And the people sent to Shiloh, and they carried from there the Ark of the Covenant of the L*ORD *of Hosts Enthroned upon the Cherubim³²; and the two sons of Eli, Hophni and Phinehas, were there with the Ark of the Covenant of God.... And the Philistines fought [with Israel] and Israel was routed, and they fled, every man to his tent; and there was a very great slaughter for there fell of Israel thirty thousand foot soldiers. And the Ark of God was captured, and the two sons of Eli, Hophni and Phinehas, were slain!*

Now a man of the [tribe of] Benjamin ran from the battle and arrived that same day in Shiloh, his clothing torn and earth upon his head. And when he arrived, there was Eli sitting on the seat on the arm [of the gate] overlooking the road,³³ for his heart trembled for the Ark of God.... And the man said to Eli: "I have come from the battle, and I fled today out of the battle." And he said: "How went the matter, my son?" And he who brought the news answered and said: "Israel has fled from before the Philistines, and also there has been a great slaughter among the people, and also your two sons, Hophni and Phinehas, are dead and the Ark of God has been captured!" And when he mentioned the Ark of God, he [Eli] fell backwards off his seat, down from the arm of the gate, his neck broke and he died; for he was an old man and heavy; and he had judged Israel for forty years [4:1, 4, 10-14, 16-18].

Eli's seat is perched on the low wall connecting the two gates to the city. The man doesn't pull his punches. Directly, almost brutally, he delivers his report: defeat; massive slaughter; your two sons dead; the Ark captured by the Philistines! Eli reels under the hammer blows. Even the death of his two sons on the same day—validating the curse on his House—he can take with resignation (he had written them off

---

28. I.e., a sure House, one that will last and not collapse; a *faithful* House for a *faithful* priest.
29. 3:12-14.
30. Reading with LXX. This entire phrase is missing from MT.
31. A site near the source of the Yarkon River, about 20 miles west of Shiloh; see MAP 4.
32. See note 3 above. In the popular imagination, bringing the Ark to the battlefield was equivalent to bringing God to be with the army.
33. A two-meter high outer wall enclosing the entryway to the town.

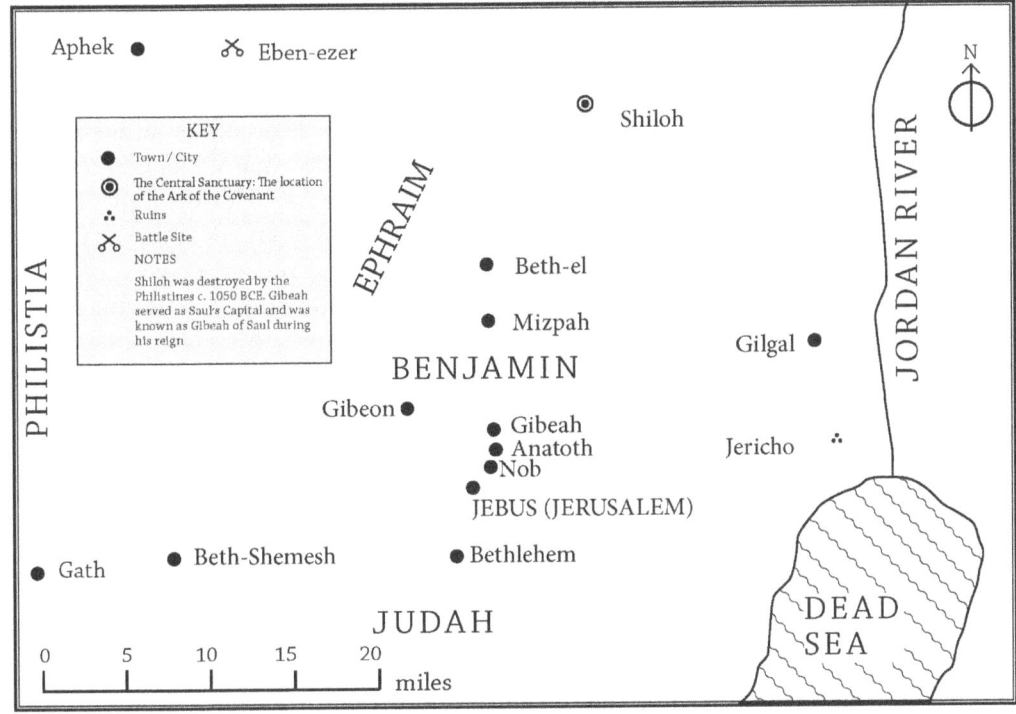

MAP 4

Central Israel in the second half of the 11th century to the mid–10th century BCE.

long ago). It is the loss of the Holy Ark, of which he was the guardian, that finishes the old priest.[34] He faints at the news, falling off the wall and dying of a broken neck. For forty years the High Priest had been the dominating figure of his age. His death marks the end of an era.

The calamity is national and the results appalling. Yet the real disaster in the eyes of the Israelites is not their military defeat and the resultant subjugation to the Philistines, but rather the loss of the Sacred Ark of the LORD. For if, in the popular mind, God is enthroned upon the Cherubim over the Ark, then with the Philistines carrying off the Ark captive, God Himself has also been carried off into captivity and exile! It is the horror of this thought that prostrates old Eli and kills him. Now this same horror will finish off his daughter-in-law.

> *Now his daughter-in-law, the wife of Phinehas, was with child, close to being delivered. And when she heard the news of the capture of the Ark of God, and that her father-in-law and her husband were dead, she bowed herself and gave birth, for her labor pangs came suddenly upon her. And at the time of her death the women attending her said: "Do not fear, for you have given birth to a son." But she did not answer nor give any heed. And she named the child Ichabod, saying: "Glory is exiled from Israel," because of the capture of the Ark of God, and because of her*

---

34. He was 98 years old (4:15).

father-in-law and her husband. She said: "Glory is exiled from Israel for the Ark of God is captured!" [4:19–22]

The shock of the news sends her into premature labor. She begins to hemorrhage uncontrollably. The narrator insists that it is the news of the death of her father-in-law and of her husband, as well as that of the capture of the Ark, that kills her. Her own statements belie this. She mentions neither Eli nor Phinehas. Her thoughts center exclusively on the loss of the Ark. As life drains out of her she refuses to be comforted by the tidings that she has borne a healthy son. Her mind is fixed exclusively upon the spiritual catastrophe that has befallen Israel. She names her son—it was customary for the mother to name her child—*Ichabod*, which means something like *No-Glory* or *Dishonor*. Her dying words are: "Glory (or Honor) is exiled from Israel because the Ark of the LORD is captured."

With this scene, approximating in pathos and horror a scene from a Greek tragedy, is born the first of a long line destined to live under the cloud of the cursed House of Eli, a line that will eventually culminate with the prophet Jeremiah.

Act II

The Massacre at Nob

We fast forward more than half a century. Israel has become a monarchy and Saul sits on the throne. He has undone the disastrous consequences of the Battle of Eben-ezer,[35] and managed to extricate Israel from the grasp of Philistine occupation, but the war with Philistia continues. Israel may have regained her independence, but her very existence is precarious, to say the least. Beset with enemies on all sides, war never ceases, if not on one front, then on another. Thus a military career is not only patriotic but also the Golden Path to rise from obscurity.

One of Saul's most outstanding regimental commanders is young David. Just entering his twenties, he has shown himself to be courageous, charismatic and a born leader of men. Brilliantly successful and wildly popular with the public, he has won the hand of his king's younger daughter, Michal. But his very success has planted the seeds of his downfall. Saul—never the most stable of personalities, and increasingly paranoiac under the pressure of recurrent crises—has come to see David as a threat to his hold on the crown. As Saul sees it, David has become too popular with the public to be tolerated. Saul decides that David must go.

Now that very night, Saul sent agents to watch David's house, so as to kill him in the morning. But Michal, David's wife, told him: "If you do not flee for your life tonight, tomorrow you will be killed."[36] So Michal let David down from a window, and he fled away and escaped [19:11–12].

The path of David's flight takes him to Nob, a town containing a shrine and a large population of priests to serve it.[37] It would seem that this was the refuge found

---

35. The great victory of the Philistines over Israel. See previous section.
36. It seems that, as Saul's daughter, she was keeping au courant of her father's moods.
37. Nob was located not far from Saul's capital at Gibeah, and within sight of Jerusalem to its south.

by the survivors of Eli's family after the destruction of Shiloh by the Philistines in the wake of their victory at Eben-ezer. Here we find Ahimelech, great-great grandson of Eli, serving as Chief-Priest of the shrine.

David is hungry and weaponless—his arms are in the state armory; had they been at home he would have taken them with him when he fled by the back window. His first need is to arm and provision himself. As he enters Nob he is gambling that he has outpaced the news of his falling out with the king; that they do not know that now he is a hunted fugitive. His proverbial luck holds, but his bedraggled appearance and the fact that he lacks his usual escort, armor and arms raises questions, and forces him to brazen it out.

> *So David went to Nob, to Ahimelech the priest, and Ahimelech was very nervous as he came out to meet David: "Why are you alone, and no man with you?"*[38] *And David said to Ahimelech the priest: "The king has commanded me [to go on] a mission; he said to me: 'Let no one know anything about the matter on which I have ordered you.' And as to the soldiers, I have arranged to meet them at such and such a place"* [21:2–3].

The sight of David appearing unsummoned and alone, unarmed and disheveled is unsettling. Ever glib, David quiets Ahimelech's uncertainties by inventing a plausible story to explain his appearance: he is on "His Majesty's Secret Service." Ahimelech calmed, David gets down to business.

> *Now one of Saul's officials was there that day, detained before the* LORD, *and his name was Doeg the Edomite, the chief of Saul's herdsman.*[39] *And David said to Ahimelech: "You don't happen to have in your possession a spear or a sword? For I have taken neither sword nor weapons with me, for the king's business was urgent." The priest said: "The sword of Goliath the Philistine, whom you killed in the Vale of Elah, is here, wrapped in a cloth behind the Ephod.*[40] *If you wish to take that, take it; for there is none but that one here." And David said: "There is none like it. Give it to me"* [21:8–10].

Ahimelech may be a bit gullible, but then David is very persuasive. So without giving thought to the possible consequences of his actions, David takes the sword along with several loaves of bread which the priest gives him,[41] and departs. His needs have been met.

> *So David departed from there, and escaped to the cave of Adulam. And when his brothers, and all his father's House heard, they went down there to him. and everyone who was in distress, and everyone who was in debt and everyone who was embittered gathered to him, and he became their leader. There were about 400 men under him* [22:1–2].

The city of Adulam, about 10 miles southeast of Gath, had been destroyed about two centuries before David's days by Joshua. Once a rich and densely populated area,

---

38. I. e., Where are your troops?

39. His presence in the sanctuary of Nob is explained by the fact that he is undergoing ritual purification for some defilement. Being present, he is witness to David's dealings with Ahimelech.

40. Actually the sword belonged to David, the spoils of his victory over Goliath. He had originally deposited it in the sanctuary for safekeeping and as a memorial. For *Ephod* see note 17 above.

41. 21:4–5.

it now lay desolate, a no man's land between Philistia and Judah; it was a good place of refuge. As the word gets around that the great war hero has assumed the role of outlaw in the wilderness, David finds himself a magnet for all the malcontents of the kingdom. Eventually David finds himself the commander of a band of approximately four hundred desperados; men with nothing left to lose.

But inevitably, word of David's whereabouts reaches the ears of the king.

> *Now Saul heard that David had been located, and the men who were with him. Saul was sitting at Gibeah on the height, under the tamarisk tree, with his spear in his hand,*[42] *and all his retainers were standing about him. And Saul said to his retainers standing around him: "Hear now, men of Benjamin, will the son of Jesse*[43] *give to every one of you fields and vineyards? Will he give to every one of you command of regiments and companies? For you have, all of you, conspired against me, in that no one informed me when my son made a pact with the son of Jesse, not one of you cared to reveal to me that my son has stirred up my servant against me as an enemy,*[44] *as at this day!"* [22:6–8]

When paranoia gives birth to crass demagoguery it distills a potent brew. Following up on the theme that his son Jonathan has joined David in a conspiracy against him, Saul now is accusing all his key officials of a conspiracy of silence. No one tells him anything! In effect, Saul is challenging his staff to prove its loyalty.

> *Then up spoke Doeg the Edomite, who was standing among Saul's retainers, saying: "I saw the son of Jesse coming to Nob, to Ahimelech the son of Ahitub. He inquired of the* LORD *for him*[45] *and gave him provisions, and gave him the sword of Goliath the Philistine"* [22:9–10].

Delivering a report like this one when Saul is in one of his paranoiac tempers is nothing less than criminal provocation. Saul reacts instantly.

> *Then Saul sent, summoning Ahimelech the son of Ahitub the priest, and his entire father's House, the priests that were in Nob. And all of them came to the king. And the king said: "Hear now, son of Ahitub." And he said: "Here I am, my lord." And Saul said to him: "Why have you conspired against me, you and the son of Jesse, in that you have given him bread, and a sword, and have inquired of God for him that he should rise as an enemy*[46] *against me, as at this day?" Then Ahimelech answered the king, saying: "Who among all your servants is as trusted as David, the king's son-in-law and captain over your bodyguard*[47] *and honored in your House? Is today the first time I have inquired of God for him? Far be it from me! Let not the king impute anything to his servant nor to all my father's House, for your servant knows nothing of this matter, neither little nor much"* [22:11–15].

---

42. This spear serving as his scepter, his symbol of power.
43. I.e., David. To refer to someone not by his proper name but by his patronymic is belittling and insulting.
44. Reading with LXX. MT reads *to lie in ambush*.
45. That is, produced an oracle for him.
46. Reading with LXX. MT reads *to lie in ambush*.
47. Reading with LXX and Targ. MT reads *giving heed to your bidding*.

Ahimelech is not lacking in courage. He stands his ground before the King, admitting all the facts but insisting that he acted in all ignorance, being totally unaware of David's status. The argument is, however, deeply flawed. Ahimelech may have been ignorant then (he was, it will be remembered, suspicious) but much time has passed since then. David's defection is now common knowledge. So why didn't the priest come forward and report when he learned the true state of affairs? Out of loyalty to David? Out of fear for his own skin? Either way, the priest will now pay the penalty for his silence. What punishment did he fear would be visited upon him? Removal from office perhaps; at the worst banishment. No more than that; after all he is a priest of God. But Saul is in no mood for half measures. He is seeing red, and the red he sees is blood.

The king said: "You shall surely die, Ahimelech, you and all your father's House!" And the king said to the guard that was standing in attendance: "Turn and kill the priests of the LORD, *for their hand is also with David, for they knew that he fled and did not inform me." But the king's servants would not raise a hand to injure the priests of the* LORD [22:16–17].

The king is demanding of his servants not only murder but also sacrilege. No one moves. They will not strike down their priests. In this impasse Saul turns to the Edomite foreigner among them, the unscrupulous informer. You started this business, now you finish it.

So the king said to Doeg: "You turn, and strike down the priests." And Doeg the Edomite turned, and struck down the priests. And he killed on that day eighty-five men, wearers of the linen ephod! And Nob, city of the priests, he put to the sword, men, women, and children alike, even infants; oxen, asses, and sheep, [all] to the sword! Now one of the sons of Ahimelech, the son of Ahitub—Abiathar by name— escaped. He fled to David. And Abiathar told David that Saul had killed the priests of the LORD. *Then David said to Abiathar: "I knew that day that Doeg the Edomite was there, and that he would surely tell Saul. I have caused the death of all the members of your father's House. Stay with me. Do not fear, for he who seeks my life seeks your life; you will be safe with me"* [22:18–23].

So who was guilty for the massacre at Nob? Was it the paranoid King Saul, or was it David whose thoughtless actions set up the priests of Nob? In the verdict of the court of public opinion of that day it was neither. People in those days, learning of the massacre, would have remembered with a feeling of horror the words of the man of God more than half a century before: "All the increase of your House shall die by the sword." The curse on the House of Eli was doing its dread work.

Of all the descendants of Eli, now only Abiathar remains.

Act III

Deposition

Having little choice, Abiathar stays with David. And as the years pass the bond, born of common necessity, becomes one of deep loyalty. During David's outlaw years,

Abiathar assumes the role of chaplain to the band, and the prime source of spiritual guidance to its leader. With David's election to the throne of the Kingdom of Judah,[48] he brings Abiathar with him, installing him in the office of Chief Priest of his capital of Hebron. When he conquers Jerusalem and makes it the capital of the United Kingdoms,[49] there is Abiathar by his side. And when he brings the Ark of the Covenant to Jerusalem,[50] he appoints Abiathar as its custodian, and as High Priest. And so the situation remains for almost thirty years. The fortunes of the House of Eli have been restored; the curse seems to have worn thin with time and has become little more than a fading memory.

But as is the way of this world, men grow old. David, now in his sixties, is showing his age. He is clearly losing his grip. He continues to reign, but the rule—the day to day running of things and the ongoing decision-making—is increasingly slipping out of his hands and into the hands of his Cabinet, chaired by his nephew Joab, Commander in Chief of the Army. The major issue on the agenda is the question of the succession: when David dies, which among his many sons will be the one to inherit the throne? The various contenders have their backers and the Cabinet is split.[51]

The matter finally boils down to two sons: David's oldest surviving son, Adonijah, a man now in his mid- to late thirties, and Solomon, son of David's favorite wife, Bathsheba.[52] And it is at this point that Abiathar[53] makes a bad mistake: he backs the wrong candidate for the crown. When Bathsheba forces the issue and persuades David to name her son Solomon as his successor, Abiathar finds himself irretrievably in Adonijah's camp.

Unlike his aged father—David is 70 years old at the time of his death—Solomon is not one to let the grass grow under his feet. Upon his father's death, Solomon quickly initiates a purge of all those whom he sees as threats. First to go is his rival, his brother Adonijah.

Now King Solomon swore [an oath] *by the* LORD, *saying… "As the* LORD *lives, Who has established me upon the throne of David my father, and Who made me a House as He promised, Adonijah shall be put to death this very day!" So King Solomon sent Benaiah, the son of Jehoiadah*[54]*; and he struck him down and he died* [1 Kings 2:23–25].

---

48. *2 Samuel* 2:1–4a.

49. Unlike the realm of his predecessor, Saul, a kingdom consisting of all the tribes of Israel, the new political reality that emerged from Saul's defeat at the Battle of Mount Gilboa was that of two kingdoms: Judah to the South (comprised of the tribes of Judah and Simeon), and Israel to the North and East (consisting of the remaining 10 tribes). By becoming first King of Judah, then subsequently also King of Israel, David created a new reality: the United Kingdoms, two independent kingdoms, both ruled by one and the same person. This arrangement is called a personal union. David ruled both of his Kingdoms from Jerusalem, which belonged to neither. Rather, it belonged exclusively to David; he also held the title of King of Jerusalem. For further detail, see my *Invention of Monotheist Ethics*, Volume II, Chapters 19–22, which gives an analysis of the shifting political realities behind David's rise to power.

50. See *2 Samuel* 6:1–20.

51. Actually, the decision lies exclusively in David's hands, but for years he has procrastinated and failed to designate his heir. This has led some of his sons to take matters into their own hands, to recruit allies, and to attempt to force the issue.

52. Solomon, at this time, can have been no older than 18; possibly only 16 years of age.

53. By virtue of his office as High Priest, Abiathar holds a seat in the Cabinet.

54. Benaiah is the commander of the units of foreign mercenaries which make up the palace guard, and a key supporter of Solomon. He here emerges in a new role, that of Solomon's enforcer.

Next on the list is Joab; but he does not wait to be hunted down.

When the news reached Joab, since Joab had supported Adonijah and had not supported Solomon,[55] *he fled to the Tent of the* LORD[56] *and seized the horns of the Altar.*[57] *Now it was told to King Solomon that Joab had fled to the Tent of the* LORD*, and behold he is by the Altar. Solomon sent Benaiah, the son of Jehoiadah,*[58] *saying: "Go, strike him down!" So Benaiah came to the Tent of the* LORD *and said to him: "Thus says the King: 'Get out!'" "No," he said, "For here will I die." So Benaiah brought the word to the King, saying: "Thus said Joab, and thus did he answer me." Then the king answered him, saying: "Do to him just as he said. Strike him down and bury him...."*[59] *So Benaiah, son of Jehoiadah, struck him down and killed him; and he was buried in his own house in the wilderness* [1 Kings 2:28–31a, 34].

Solomon's hatchet man, Benaiah, seems to have some scruples about murdering a man in sanctuary. Solomon has none; after declaiming a speech for public consumption about how Joab deserves what he will be getting and how clean Solomon's hands are, he orders Benaiah back to murder him at the Altar. This time Benaiah steels himself and does it. The old warrior—brutal and bloody-handed, brilliant commander and loyal supporter of David—is, without fanfare, laid to rest at his ranch in the Southern Wilderness. He no longer merits a state funeral. In the new regime he has become a non-person.

Solomon has no intention of stopping here. Only the purge of the entire leadership of the Old Guard will do. Abiathar is next on the list.

And to Abiathar the priest the King said: "Get you to your estate in Anatoth[60]*; for you deserve to die. But today I will not kill you, for you bore the Ark of the* LORD *my God before David my father, and because you suffered all the hardships that my father suffered." So Solomon expelled Abiathar from being a priest unto the* LORD *(thus fulfilling the word of the* LORD*, spoken concerning the House of Eli at Shiloh)* [1 Kings 2:26–27].

That belonging to the wrong political party should merit a death sentence for the inoffensive High Priest would take some explaining to the public. It is never a wise policy to murder priests; it just doesn't look good, and this is probably the real reason for sparing his life. So the old man—he must be well into his sixties—is

---

55. Reading with LXX, Syr and Vulg. MT reads *Absalom*.
56. The Temple has not yet been built. The Ark has been temporarily housed in a tent, even as it had been from Sinai onward.
57. These were projections at each of the four corners of an altar, which were called "horns" since they resembled them. In the Ancient Near East anyone reaching a shrine and laying hold of the altar's horns could claim sanctuary (which is why the term "sanctuary" has become a synonym for a religious shrine).
58. LXX reads: *Solomon sent to Joab, saying: "What has come over you that you have fled to the Altar?" Joab said: "because I am afraid of you and have fled to the Lord." Then Solomon sent to Benaiah, the son of Jehoiadah, saying: "Go, strike him down!"*
59. We omit Solomon's bombastic and hypocritical justification for the murder he has just ordered.
60. Anatoth was a small town not far from Nob, located about 3 miles north of Jerusalem, and inhabited exclusively by priests. At the time of the division of the Promised Land, the town of Anatoth was one of the towns awarded to the priestly caste: *And for the sons of Aaron the priest they gave... Anatoth with the open land about it.* (Joshua 21:13, 18) Part of this adjacent territory had belonged to Ahimelech. The estate is now Abiathar's by inheritance.

thrown out of his position and exiled to his family fields, there to live out his remaining years—probably under house arrest. The priesthood being hereditary, his son Jonathan should, by rights, succeed Abiathar, but Solomon is hardly one to respect hereditary rights. What is the good of a purge, if you can't put your own supporters into the plush positions?

> *Then the King appointed Benaiah, the son of Jehoiadah, as* [Commander] *of the Army in place of Joab, and the King appointed Zadok the priest*[61] *in place of Abiathar* [1 Kings 2:35].

We return to the parenthetical remark with which the narrator closed the account of Abiathar's deposition and exile from Jerusalem:

> *...thus fulfilling the word of the* LORD, *spoken concerning the House of Eli at Shiloh* [1 Kings 2:27b].

By this remark I do not believe that the narrator meant to imply that this was part of Solomon's motivation. Solomon probably never gave it a thought. The narrator is introducing us to something that will be one of the main themes of the *Book of Kings*: that human beings, acting out of their own worldly and often sordid motives, inadvertently are fulfilling God's larger purposes. Thus the writer of *Kings* is reminding us that by this act Solomon is bringing closure to the open-ended saga of the curse on the House of Eli. Far from having run its course, the curse remains in full force, and after almost a century the final blow falls. The way the Greeks put it was: "The mills of the gods grind slow, but they grind exceeding fine."

It was into this grim heritage, some 350 years after Abiathar's exile to Anatoth, that his distant descendant, Jeremiah, was born. Under this cloud Jeremiah was destined to live out his life.

---

61. Zadok, one of Solomon's backers, was the priest in charge of the great altar at Gibeon.

CHAPTER 13

Problematic Beginnings

A prophet shall I raise up from the midst of your brethren, like you, and I will put My words in his mouth, and he shall speak to them all that I command him. And it shall come to pass, that anyone who will not listen to My words that he shall speak in My name, I, even I, will require it of him.

—(Deuteronomy 18:18–19)

As the twig is bent, so grows the tree.
—Common aphorism adapted from
Alexander Pope, *Epistles to Several Persons*

We have examined so far two instances recorded in the Bible of prophets who rebelled against God their Master: that of Jonah, son of Amittai, and that of Balaam, son of Beor. Even as the particulars of each case differ radically one from the other, so do the literary formats in which these rebellions are described. We have concluded that the example of Jonah is embodied in the format of a *fable* while the tale of Balaam is recounted as a straightforward third-person *historical narrative*. The final case of rebellion which we will consider—very different from the previous two—also differs in the literary form it takes: that of *spiritual autobiography*. And this is most unusual, for while historical narrative is ubiquitous in the Bible and fable a common conceit in the Ancient World, spiritual autobiography—letting down one's hair and revealing one's inner struggles, thoughts and feelings—was something that simply was not done.[1] So our examination of those portions of the *Book of Jeremiah*—our current concern—where the prophet bares his soul, will also be markedly different from what has gone before.

Our subject, Jeremiah, son of Hilkiah, was one of the "classical prophets" of the First Commonwealth.[2] What we know of the so-called classical prophets we learn mostly from third-party biographical sketches and editorial notes,[3] along with some

---

1. While first-person accounts telling of what one had *said* and *done* were rare but existed in the Ancient World—Xenophon's *Anabasis* and the *Book of Nehemiah* in the Bible are prominent examples—spiritual autobiography was virtually unknown. Our present case can certainly be counted as being among the very first we possess of this now common "spill it all out" literary genre.

2. The "classical prophets" of the First Commonwealth were those prophets of the eighth to sixth centuries BCE who left a written record of their sayings, and whose writings we possess in the Bible.

3. In the case of Jeremiah, the fairly extensive biographical account and the scattered notes that together provide us with a picture of his life were the work of one Baruch, son of Neriah, who served as private secretary to Jeremiah in his latter years, and who stood to him much as James Boswell stood to Samuel Johnson.

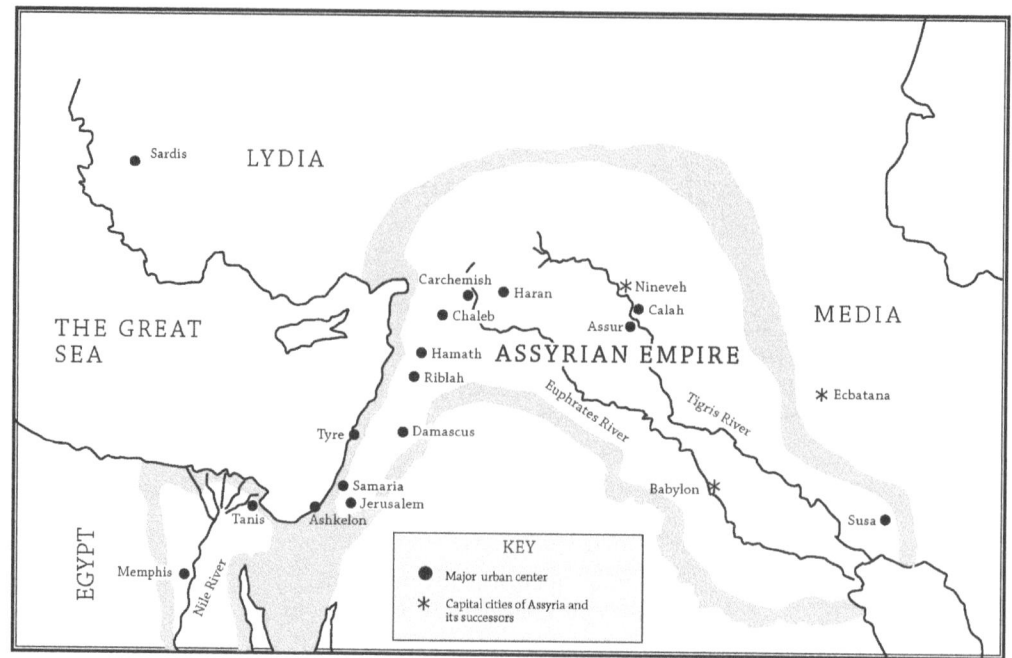

MAP 5

The Assyrian Empire at its height, c. 665 BCE.

fragmentary mentions in historical accounts of their era[4] and what we can infer from their recorded prophecies. Only with Jeremiah do we have a window into the inner life of our protagonist.

Jeremiah's Background

Beyond what we have been able to infer about Jeremiah's family heritage, and the curse that had been laid on all its members, himself included, what we know of Jeremiah's personal background can mostly be found in the first three verses of the Book that goes by his name; a brief introductory Foreword most probably penned by his secretary Baruch.[5] We are told that the name of his father was Hilkiah, that he belonged to the priestly caste, that Anatoth was the place of his birth and that he followed his calling between the years 627 and 586 BCE.[6] He was born into a turbulent era, an age in which the clash of empires on the international stage impinged on every aspect of the lives of the inhabitants of Jeremiah's homeland: the Kingdom of Judah. It is this international backdrop that, to a large extent, determined the course of Jeremiah's life.

The major phenomenon that defined the 8th century BCE—the era prior to the

---

4. Mainly the *Book of Kings* and the *Book of Chronicles*.

5. See note 3 above. This assumes that it was Baruch who edited the first draft of the collected writings of his master, an assumption which I deem to be highly probable.

6. These matters are dealt with in some detail in Appendix G: Who Was Jeremiah?

Chapter 13. Problematic Beginnings 221

one in which Jeremiah lived—was the rise of the Assyrian Empire to the status of a superpower, and its ever-increasing domination of the Ancient Near East. In the course of Assyria's relentless and ruthless expansion, Israel, Judah's sister kingdom to the North, had been wiped from the face of the earth.[7] Judah herself was invaded in 701 BCE and survived only by becoming a completely compliant vassal of Assyria. According to the practices of those times, this involved not only complete political subservience,[8] but also the acknowledgment of the supremacy of the Assyrian gods and the adoption of various religious and cultural practices of the Assyrian overlords.[9] During this dark age the voice of prophecy virtually vanished in Judah.

If we have termed the theme of the 8th century BCE the saga of Assyria's rise, then the century that followed could be described as the tale of the fall of the Empire and the struggle for the succession. With the conquest of Egypt in the third decade of the 7th century BCE, Assyria had become the first power ever to unite the entire Ancient Near East under one centralized despotism. But from this pinnacle the decline was rapid.[10] Overreach had bled the Empire white, and she now lacked the resources to hold on to her vast domain. With startling suddenness things fell apart, leading to the sack of Nineveh, her capital, by the Medes and the Babylonians in 612 BCE.[11] The colossus was gone, and a new age had dawned, the only question on the larger agenda being who would inherit what from the wreckage that remained.

Looking at this vast canvas objectively, one hardly notices the tiny dot on the map that represents the little Kingdom of Judah. Yet this kingdom is destined to play an outsized role in the drama to come. In the first place, she has been blessed with a remarkable ruler at this juncture: one Josiah, son of Ammon (640–609 BCE). In the aftermath of his father's assassination, he found himself on the throne when only eight years of age. Remarkably precocious and resolute by nature, by age 16 he and his advisors had settled on a bold program aimed at acquiring political autonomy for his Kingdom of Judah, and expunging the paganism imposed upon her by her overlords.[12] Four years later, carefully timing his moves to seize advantage from the

---

7. In 722 BCE Samaria, the capital of Israel, fell. Much of the surviving population was carried off to exile (a portion of the population escaped this fate by having fled to her sister kingdom Judah to its South), and the territory of what had been Israel was incorporated into the Empire as three Imperial Provinces.

8. For example, Judah was compelled to supply forced labor to transport building materials to Nineveh for the construction there of Esharhaddon's palace, and the Judean army had to serve as part of the Assyrian Armed Forces on Assurbanipal's 667 BCE campaign to conquer Upper Egypt. One did what one was told, no matter what the cost.

9. The King of Judah at this time was Manasseh (696–642 BCE) who, in his efforts to placate his masters, thoroughly paganized religion in Judah by importing the gods of Assyria, and ruthlessly suppressed any manifestation of resistance or protest to this policy.

10. Assurbanipal (668–632 BCE), the last of the great Assyrian Warlords, was forced to evacuate Egypt and concentrate on holding off the Medes and allied peoples to the East, and on maintaining control of Mesopotamia (see MAP 5). His death signaled the beginning of the accelerating disintegration of the Assyrian Empire.

11. Actually there was a postscript to the fall of Nineveh. A shadow state lingered on at Haran, only to be finally terminated in 608. This footnote to the fall of Assyria is important for us, as this aftermath had a traumatic impact upon the Kingdom of Judah, and hence on the life and career of our protagonist, Jeremiah. For more detail see Historical Interlude I: The Road to Megiddo, which follows this chapter.

12. *Now in the eighth year of his reign, while still a lad (naar), he began to resort to the God of David his father* (2 Chronicles 34:3), i.e., he began to pattern himself on his illustrious ancestor, David, who began his career as King of Judah by wresting first autonomy, and then ultimately independence, from his Philistine overlords. For Josiah, the eighth year of his reign was 632 BCE, the year of Assurbanipal's death; probably the triggering factor in his decision.

upheavals taking place in the larger Ancient Near East, on the death of Assurbanipal's successor, Ashur-etil-ilani (632–628 BCE), Josiah made his first overt move: smashing the images of the pagan gods and desecrating their places of worship. This was far more than simple religious iconoclasm: in the context of that era this act amounted to a declaration of independence from Assyria.[13] Then, to add injury to insult, having completed his anti-idolatry campaign in his Kingdom of Judah and its capital of Jerusalem, accompanied by his troops he moved north into the territory that once had been the Kingdom of Israel and there implemented his anti-pagan purge.[14] Josiah had invaded Imperial territory and in effect annexed it to Judah. How could he ever have hoped to get away with it?

In those four years since the death of Assurbanipal things had not gone well for the Empire. Upon the death of Ashur-etil-ilani, his successor Sin-shar-ishkun (628–612 BCE), now fighting for his very life, had had no alternative but to abandon Assyria's West Asia defense perimeter against a resurgent Egypt, in order to defend Mesopotamia proper. Into this vacuum Egypt now spread.[15] There is little question but that Josiah's moves were with Egypt's permission and closely coordinated with Egypt on the highest levels. As an ally of a resurgent Egypt, and under the umbrella of Egyptian power, Josiah was attempting to restore the United Kingdom that his ancestor and ideal, David, had once created, uniting all of the Promised Land under the rule of Jerusalem. Josiah had become a player on the big board; a minor player, but one with an agenda and big plans. And it is into this heady brew of the collapse of hated foreign domination, the resurgence of a spirit of nationalism fostered by bold leadership,[16] and the purging of paganism in the name of the ancient faith of Israel that Jeremiah grew up. Then came the event that determined the entire course of his life: God informed Jeremiah of his destiny.

The Call

What is it like to be summoned by God and be given one's marching orders? It is obviously a very personal experience, one not susceptible to external more-or-less

---

13. *And in the twelfth year* [of his reign, i.e., 628 BCE] *he began to purge Judah and Jerusalem of the high places, and the Asherim, and the idols and the molten images. Now they smashed the altars of the Baalim in his presence; and the sun-images that were above them he hewed down...* (*2 Chronicles* 34:3b-4). The "sun-images" were the symbols of the god Ashur, the chief deity of the Assyrian pantheon. Their destruction was thus a defiant throwing down of the gauntlet to Assyrian rule.

14. Josiah drove his point home by dramatically opening the graves of the priests that had officiated at the various pagan shrines in the northern territories, exhuming their bones and publicly burning them on their own pagan altars, before destroying these altars as well. Paganism was being banished and outlawed within the borders of what had once been the Holy Land. (*2 Chronicles* 34:5–7)

15. Psammetichus I (663–609 BCE) was the Pharaoh who succeeded in freeing Egypt from Assyrian rule. The shock of being conquered and occupied by a foreign power had galvanized Egypt, even as Egypt's subjugation by the Hyksos centuries before had done. Psammetichus seems to be reviving the strategy of the great fifteenth century pharaohs who created the Egyptian New Empire: since offense is the best defense, expand into Asia and create a buffer region to protect the homeland.

16. There is a current notion that what goes under the name of "nationalism" is a purely modern phenomenon. Hans Kohn has argued—to my mind conclusively—that the nationalism we know today is merely the modern manifestation of a very old phenomenon with roots in both ancient Greece and ancient Israel. The sense of belonging to and having pride in one's land and its people was alive and well in ancient Israel, the kingdom of Judah being one of its early incubators. (H. Kohn, *The Idea of Nationalism*, especially Chapter 1)

objective description. Only the person involved can possibly attempt to convey his or her perceptions of the experience. So here, in his own words, is Jeremiah's account of the epiphany that changed his life.

> Now it came to pass that the word of the LORD came to me, saying:
> "Before I formed you in the belly I knew you,
> And before you came forth from the womb I consecrated[17] you;
> A prophet to the nations have I appointed you!"
>
> Now I said:
> "Ah, Lord GOD, behold, I do not know how to speak, for I am but a boy."[18]
>
> And the LORD said to me:
> "Do not say 'I am but a boy.'
> For on all that I send you you shall go,
> And all that I command you you shall speak.
>
> Be not afraid of them,
> For I am with you to deliver you—
> [This is] an oracle of the LORD."
>
> And the LORD put forth His hand and touched me on my mouth, and said:
> "Behold, I have put My words in your mouth.
>
> See, I have set you this day
> Over the nations and over the kingdoms:
> To uproot and to break down,
> To destroy and to overthrow,
> To build and to plant."
>
> Now it came to pass that the word of the LORD came to me, saying[19]: "What do you see, Jeremiah?" And I said: "A branch of an almond tree do I see." And the LORD said to me: "You have seen well, for I watch over My word to do it!" [1:4–12][20]

This apparently simple account, as well as the one that immediately follows, seem lucid and above board, but are actually complex and multi-layered; they will require careful analysis. For the present, we will accept them as the straightforward and rather naïve accounts that they seem to be, and examine them as such. As to the first, Jeremiah tells us that one day, probably in his native town of Anatoth,[21] he was suddenly confronted by God and informed of his destiny, his true role in life. In soaring poetry he is put on notice that God has appointed him as His prophet[22] to the nations of the world, i.e., to all humanity. What is more, this is no sudden whim on God's part; Jeremiah is notified that it was before he was born—more, before he was

---

17. Consecrated: set you apart for divine service.
18. Hebrew *naar*; one under age, not a mature adult and hence unfit for the task.
19. This phrase is an exact repetition of 1:4, tying the vision of the almond branch to the account of Jeremiah's Call into one unit.
20. In this section of the book, unless otherwise indicated, all chapter and verse references are to the *Book of Jeremiah*.
21. For Anatoth see Chapter 12, note 60.
22. Hebrew *nabi*. See General Introduction, note 24.

even conceived—that he had been chosen for, and dedicated to, what was to be his role in life.

How does Jeremiah take this startling pronouncement? He tells us that his immediate reaction was to try and beg off. He pleads incapability for the demands of the task due to immaturity: he is too young.[23] God does not debate his reservations; He simply brushes them aside and doubles down on His pronouncement:

"Do not say 'I am but a boy.'
For on all that I send you you shall go,
and all that I command you you shall speak" [1:7].

This is neither a request nor an option; these are your orders and you will carry them out.

This pronouncement and exchange are followed by two symbolic visions. In the first, he experiences God touching him on the mouth, symbolically putting His word—the message that Jeremiah is to deliver—into his mouth where it will henceforth reside; much like a downloaded file.[24] God then informs Jeremiah of the purport of these words, and hence the purpose of his forthcoming prophetic ministry:

To uproot and to break down,
To destroy and to overthrow the existing order;
To build and to plant a new and better one,
Not only in Judah but ultimately worldwide.[25]

The second vision is radically different in kind from the first. It involves seeing an actual physical object and suddenly perceiving an unexpected symbolic significance in its having come to one's attention. Either immediately following his epiphany, or shortly thereafter—and indivisibly associated with it in his mind—Jeremiah's attention is arrested by the sight of a branch of an almond tree that has just burst into bloom.[26] As Jeremiah tells it, it is God Who draws his attention to the branch, insisting that there is a message for him in it. The message lies in a wordplay; two Hebrew words that are virtual homonyms, *shaked* and *shoked*.[27] God drives the message home:

---

23. How old was Jeremiah at the time of his Call? He defines himself as a "boy" (Hebrew *naar*). But this is a very indeterminate term, covering a very wide range. On the one hand it refers to someone younger than twenty. In biblical times one came of age at twenty (*Numbers* 14:29): one became liable for military service at that age, and one became eligible to have a voice in local affairs and vote in national conventions, etc. Lundbom, *Jeremiah 1-20* (hereafter *Lundbom I*), p. 233, points out that at age 16 King Josiah was still categorized as a boy (*naar*) but no longer was so at age 20 (*2 Chronicles* 34:3). On the other hand, Jeremiah has had a very good education, and that education is at the very least well along. His command of rhetoric (at that time a very central part of the formal curriculum) is very advanced, and his poetic style in his first prophecies—a style and polish that bespeaks of long and careful schooling—argues against excessive youth. All things considered, I would put him in his late teens.

24. The symbolic act recalls God's treatment of Balaam (*Numbers* 23:5 and 16), and of the prophet Isaiah's description of his Call (*Isaiah* 6:6–7). There is little doubt that Jeremiah was well acquainted with both of these accounts.

25. *"I have set you this day over the nations and over the kingdoms."* (1:10)

26. The almond tree blooms in late January and early February. As the winter draws to a close in Israel it is the first tree to put forth flowers.

27. Homonyms are words with different meanings (and often with different spellings) that are pronounced alike. (For example, in English *rain* and *reign* are homonyms.) In Hebrew *shaked* is an almond tree, while the almost identical *shoked* means "to be wakeful," "to watch over."

"What do you see, Jeremiah?" And I said: "A branch of an almond tree (shaked) do I see." And the LORD *said to me: "You have seen well, for I watch (shoked) over My word to do it!"* [1:11–12]

That is, when I, the LORD, say something—such as the words I have placed in your mouth—there is no maybe about them; *they invariably come to pass*. Never forget this.

And Jeremiah never did.

With this sight of the flowering almond branch and his sudden realization of its symbolic message—the absolute certainty of God's word that he is being charged to proclaim coming true—Jeremiah's Call comes to an end. He has been called to prophecy, but what is to be the content of the message he is to deliver? This will be related in his account of his second epiphany.

The Message

The second revelation seems to have taken place shortly after his Call.[28] It is difficult to be God's mouthpiece without having anything to say. Short of having been told that bad times are coming:

To uproot and to break down,
To destroy and to overthrow [1:10].

without specifics this is a very difficult message to deliver convincingly. The *"why?"* the *"where?"* and the *"how?"* are conspicuous by their absence. The second vision begins to provide answers to at least some of these questions.

Now it came to pass that the word of the LORD *came to me a second time, saying: "What do you see?" And I said: "A boiling pot do I see, with its face away from the North."*[29] *And the* LORD *said to me: "From the* NORTH[30] *shall the evil break forth upon all the inhabitants of the land.*[31] *For behold, I summon all the tribes*[32] *of the kingdoms of the North—[this is] an oracle of the* LORD*—and they will come, and they shall set each his throne at the entrance to the gates of Jerusalem, and against all its surrounding walls, and against all the cities of Judah. And I will utter My judgments for all their evil,*[33] *in that they have forsaken Me, and have burned incense to other gods and have worshiped the works of their hands"* [1:13–16].[34]

---

28. Many scholars lump the coming vision along with the vision of the almond branch together as one unit, but the received text (MT) refutes this categorization. In the first place, the two visions are separated by a paragraph break (indicated by a *petuhah*—a letter P—between verse 12 and verse 13). The coming account is closed by a further paragraph break after verse 19. "That v. 13 is a new beginning can be inferred also from the superscription that Yahweh's word came to Jeremiah a 'second time.'" (*Lundbom I*, p. 238)

29. I.e., a pot on a fire, slightly askew, with its open top facing south, and its steam being blown away from the North, the wind coming from that direction.

30. As distinct from the South; i.e., Egypt.

31. At this point the vision proper ends, and God's explanatory exposition begins.

32. Literally, *clans*.

33. Their *raah*, the same word used for what is about to descend upon Judah and Jerusalem: the *evil* (*raah*) from the North.

34. Some of the passages attributed to Jeremiah are written in poetry and some are in prose. There have been scholars who have contended that only the poetry is authentically Jeremiah, while the prose *[continued]*

Once again a commonplace physical object—a pot boiling furiously over a fire, a north wind both fanning the flames and blowing steam and smoke southward—is turned by God into a dramatic symbol of a terrible future: the looming evil—the impending uprooting, the destruction, the overthrow of all that Jeremiah's future listeners know and hold dear—will burst upon them from the NORTH!

This is in part a political forecast: with the impending collapse of the Assyrian World Empire already underway, and as the world comes apart, a bipolar world is coming into being. In such a world Judah, situated as it is athwart the land bridge between Africa and Asia, will be caught right in the middle of the maelstrom. What Jeremiah is being told up to this point is already obvious to astute political minds in Jerusalem and elsewhere; these are political conclusions dictated by geography. What is unique to the message Jeremiah is receiving is that, first: Judah will not be able to ride out the coming storm as she has done on numerous occasions in the past, and second: the source of the disaster will come *not* from the South—resurgent Egypt, Judah's close neighbor—but from the distant NORTH, that boiling cauldron of alien and barbarian peoples currently beginning to gain momentum beyond the increasingly shaky eastern borders of the Assyrian Empire.

From the NORTH *shall the evil break forth upon all the inhabitants of the land* [1:14].

The inheritor of the world Assyria will leave behind her will not be Egypt—a force past its prime, and indeed decadent—but one of the vigorous nations of the NORTH. So far the political prognosis.

At this point the revelation shifts from the political perspective to that of the religious. Why will Judah and Jerusalem not ride out the gathering storm? Why will the nations of the NORTH lay siege to the cities of Judah and Jerusalem?[35] The evil will come as payment for the evil done by Judah and Jerusalem; evil to repay evil. And what is the appalling evil done by the inhabitants of Judah and Jerusalem that merits the evil punishment that awaits them? It is spelled out: the people have abandoned the LORD their God, they have turned to and worship alien gods; they have worshiped the work of their hands.[36] Jeremiah has finally received the message that he has been brought forth to deliver.

---

passages—although probably based on something Jeremiah did say—were put into their present form by others at a later date, after a lapse of several generations. Addressing the perception that only the poetry is authentic Jeremiah, John Bright points out that even though he was an accomplished poet "Jeremiah in his off moments must have spoken prose (even Shakespeare did) and if he did so, it was the prose of his age," i.e., the language of his prose sermons and autobiographical passages. He also argues, to my mind convincingly, that all the evidence points to these passages being contemporaneous with the poetry, and both with Jeremiah himself. (Bright, "Prose Sermons of Jeremiah," *JBL* 70 [1951]: 27–29)

35. *And they will come, and they shall set each his throne at the entrance to the gates of Jerusalem, and against all its surrounding walls, and against all the cities of Judah.* (1:15)

36. This phrase has two levels of meaning. In the crude physical sense, it refers to the manufacturing of images of metal, wood or stone and worshiping them; i.e., adopting the pagan religious practices of the Ancient Near East. But on a deeper and non-material level it refers to the human tendency to elevate the works of man to the status of ultimate goods and to give to them the devotion only God truly merits: in those days, for example, turning the externals of religion (temples, altars, sacrifices, etc.) from religious means into ends; in our own days—a more secular era—perhaps making the state, various political and social ideologies, certain charismatic leaders, etc., into absolute objects of devotion. All these are summed up in the single word: idolatry.

Charge and Warning

This is a fearsome message to receive. It is an even more daunting proposal to go out and deliver it. The messenger who conveys it can hardly expect a happy reception. Yet this is exactly the mission that Jeremiah is now commanded to perform.

Now as for you:
You, gird up your loins[37];
And rise and speak to them everything I command you;
Don't you break down before them,
Lest I break you before them![38]

God says to Jeremiah: Now that you have your message, your part in this affair is to go out and proclaim it; *all of it*. Hold nothing back. You will face opposition. You will be under intense pressure. Don't you dare break down. Beware lest you falter, or I will make an example of you; *I* will publicly break *you*.

But you are not alone. This is a partnership. I also have a part in all this.

And as for Me:
Behold, I have made you this day into a fortified city,
And into an iron pillar,
And into a wall[39] of bronze;
Against the entire land,
Against the kings of Judah,
Against her high officials,
Against her priests
And against the people of the land.[40]

And they will fight against you,
But they will not succeed against you;
For I am with you—
[This is] an oracle of the LORD—
To deliver you [1:18–19].

After warning Jeremiah what He will do to him should he falter in his mission, God encourages him by insisting that he has made him strong enough to withstand any and all pressures. In a cascade of metaphors—He has made Jeremiah as strong as

---

37. A metaphor meaning "strip for action." As we today wear coats, in ancient Israel men wore long outer garments which, for activities more strenuous than simply walking, impeded the movement of the legs. To "gird one's loins" meant to gather up the hems of one's outer garment and tuck them into one's belt, thus freeing one's legs for whatever movements would be required of them: running, leaping, close combat etc. In the present context the implication of the phrase is "get ready, prepare yourself; your mission is going to be one long war!"

38. Lundbom (*Lundbom* I, p. 248) likens this threat—and it is a threat—to "the parental threat given to a potentially whiny child: 'Don't cry, or I'll give you something to cry about.'"

39. Reading with LXX, Syr., Targ., Vulg. and numerous Hebrew mss. MT reads *walls* in the plural.

40. In Hebrew *am haaretz*, a technical term meaning "the gentry," i.e., those who own their own land. This includes everyone from small farmers to the owners of large estates. This was the class that was politically active in the running of society. In our present context, however, the words may simply be taken literally to mean everyone who was not part of the "establishment," i.e., not royalty, court or priesthood.

a fortress city, as a pillar of iron, as a wall of bronze[41]—God tells Jeremiah that he will find within himself the firmness to stand up to his enemies, whom he now enumerates: the kings[42] of Judah, the court, the priests; indeed, the entire establishment of the kingdom. And if that is not enough, he will find no friend in the common people. They too will be his enemies. And it is not as though they simply won't listen to him. They will actively oppose him, even to the extent of resorting to violence against his person. Not one authority, not one group or class, but everyone will oppose him! He will find himself completely alone.

But they won't succeed in destroying him, promises God, because Jeremiah won't really be alone. "I will be with you." You can count on Me, says God.[43] I always will be there to save you. In this, God is simply reiterating His promise made in his original Call to Jeremiah:

Be not afraid of them,
For I am with you to deliver you—
[This is] *an oracle of the* LORD [1:8].

And decades later Jeremiah will have to admit that through all the weary turns of an embattled life God had kept His promise.[44] Even in his worst moments his persecutors had never succeeded in silencing or destroying him. Each time, somehow, they had failed and he had pulled through. And with God's help he had found the strength to persevere despite every setback. Will it or not, the conditions of the life he was to lead had been set.

The Write-Up

Having scrutinized Jeremiah's account of his Call—this series of inner experiences that launched him onto his life-long mission as a prophet of God—let us step back a bit and attempt to evaluate the background to what we have just read. The point I wish to make is that while we have Jeremiah's first-person account, it is a *written* account that we possess. So the questions arise: when was it written? And why was it written? These are two very important issues whose resolution will determine how we evaluate the significance of the account. And unlike many first-person accounts that we have in written form from the past, in our instance we are in a

---

41. Many nowadays find the phrase "a wall of bronze" a strange climax to this ascending crescendo depicting ever-increasing invulnerability, especially in an era when iron has replaced bronze. But "a wall of bronze" is no new poetic invention. It is a deeply ingrained Egyptian metaphor, left over from the Bronze Age, where it was used to convey the security and invulnerability conferred on some person by the Pharaoh (who was conceived to be a god) when he extended his protection to him.

42. Note the plural; Jeremiah will find himself opposed not by one ruler but by several kings!

43. This is the function of the phrase "An oracle of the Lord" that is periodically inserted into the divine pronouncement. The statement [This is] *an oracle of the Lord* serves as a reminder that God is here making a commitment, and as a divine promise it must be taken with complete seriousness; it is absolutely reliable.

44. *The Lord is with me as an all-inspiring warrior,*
Therefore my pursuers shall stumble and not prevail;
They are greatly ashamed because they have not succeeded;
An eternal disgrace which shall never be forgotten. (20:11)
See Chapter 15, the section entitled In the Chill of the Night.

position to propose concrete answers to these questions with a fair degree of confidence. But to be able to understand the circumstances that led Jeremiah to put into writing these intensely personal experiences, we have to first summarize more than two decades of frustration and fruitless effort on the part of Jeremiah as he attempted to fulfill his mission.

He had his message, such as it was: "Because of your *evil*—your idolatry, your abandonment of the LORD your God and your refusal to heed His commands—He will punish you by bringing *evil* upon you; *evil* as a response to *evil*. Return to the LORD your God before it is too late. If and when the *evil* does come, it will not come from Egypt in spite of its looming presence; it will come from the NORTH!"[45]

For the early years of his mission his preaching was more or less in step with the policy of the Kingdom. King Josiah had mobilized the organs of state to promote a religious reformation. Real efforts were being made to root out idolatry and the practices of paganism from the public square. The *Book of Deuteronomy*, or an early version thereof, was formally made into the law of the land. And as the Assyrian empire continued to crumble, King and court had come to the conclusion that the winner who would take all would not be Egypt.[46] But Jeremiah's views were also evolving. Royal edicts could affect public behavior. The state was no longer sponsoring paganism; indeed, it had outlawed its practice. Pagan and even partially paganized shrines could be shut down, and were. But the state was not about to police every home; and in those days there was such a thing as private religion, homes routinely containing private mini-shrines. And with the shutting down of public shrines the focus of religion became, if anything, more focused on the private sphere. And so, despite the depaganization of public religion—especially in the Temple in Jerusalem—in the homes and hearts of multitudes the worship of, and the commitment to the Baalim, the Ashtaroth,[47] and especially the cult of the Queen of Heaven continued to flourish. As the years slipped by, one can sense in Jeremiah's preaching a waning of his youthful enthusiasm for the public religious reform, and a growing disillusionment in its efficacy. More: at the core of Israelite religion lies the imperative for ethical behavior—indeed this was the central message of the classical prophets and their predecessors. While the morals of the king (and probably the upper echelons of his key officials and advisers) were a radical improvement over those of his father and grandfather (and their inner circles as well),[48] a significant change in the morals of the public at large was far from apparent. Neither public policy nor Jeremiah's preaching seem to be capable of effecting the change necessary to avert the looming evil.

---

45. Here was one of Jeremiah's sore points: he never gave an answer as to exactly who was the threat. It is not that he wouldn't, it was that he couldn't. He didn't know, because he had not been told. He was reduced to the sorry plight of denying what seemed to everyone obvious: that the real and present danger was neighboring Egypt, and warning in vague generalizations against some unspecified bogeyman in the distant North. Is it any wonder that his warnings lacked credibility in the eyes of most of his audience?

46. For the international background to all this see Historical Interlude I: The Road to Megiddo which follows this chapter.

47. *Baalim*, the plural of *Baal* (literally, "Master"), the title of the nature and fertility god who was a chief focus of surrounding pagan worship. *Ashtaroth*, the plural of *Ashtoret*, the female consort of *Baal*.

48. I think it is permissible to take Jeremiah's testimony at face value in this matter: c.f. 22:1–5 as a standard to live by, and 22:15–16 as to how Josiah measured up to the standard.

Then came the disaster of Megiddo. With Josiah dead and the Egyptian puppet, Jehoiakim, on the throne,[49] public policy reversed itself. Religious reformation halted, and while formal adherence to the worship of the Lord persisted, a new tolerance for paganism began to become evident. And of course foreign policy turned about 180° as Judah fitted herself into the Egyptian orbit. As for Jeremiah, his position became increasingly precarious. Long inured to being a figure of ridicule and one to be shunned for the grave social sins of preaching unpopular ideas, and for chastising the public for their faults, Jeremiah now found his invective deemed sedition by the authorities. Attempts to mobilize the public to oppose the policies of the new king, in favor of restoring those of his father, had forced Jeremiah into hiding. He was now a declared fugitive from justice, facing summary execution should he be apprehended.[50] Almost a quarter of a century of effort, anguish and toil have led him to this nadir.

This is how he sums up his prophetic mission to date:

From the thirteenth year of Josiah, son of Ammon, King of Judah, and up until this day—these three and twenty years—the word of the Lord *has come to me, and I have spoken to you persistently but you didn't listen* [25:3].

The year is 605 BCE. The kaleidoscope has turned once again at Carchemish. Egypt has been knocked out of the ring, and a bipolar world has collapsed into a new reality: the entire Fertile Crescent—Mesopotamia and all Western Asia—is now under the sway of Babylon. This is the twenty-fifth hour; before the Babylonian hordes arrive, Jeremiah feels he must make one last effort to warn the people, one last appeal for repentance. But how is he to accomplish this?

Prohibited from entering the temple, ascending the public pulpit and addressing the assembled worshipers—indeed, afraid even to show his face lest he be arrested—Jeremiah must find some other means of getting his warning across to an increasingly apprehensive public, one being driven to panic by the sudden upheavals on the world scene, and the realization that King Jehoiakim has linked himself to the losing side. Having no real alternative, Jeremiah determines to commit a summary of his warnings to writing and to send someone in his place to read them publicly. This will be one last effort to generate a groundswell of public opinion, to influence the king and court to revise their disastrous policies. So he summons his secretary, Baruch, and dictates to him a selection of the most powerful of the prophetic utterances he has made over the past two decades. But reading over what Baruch has written, he realizes that people will ask: what gives him the authority to make such pronouncements and utter such threats? To cope with this seemingly certain objection to taking his warnings seriously, Jeremiah decides to preface his denunciations and admonitions with an account of his Call. This is his authority: God chose him to deliver His message. The words come from God; He put them in his mouth, and God's word is a certainty. Unless the people repent and change their ways, doom will come upon them.

---

49. See Historical Interlude I. The Road to Megiddo immediately following this chapter for a description of this particular cascade of events.

50. For details see Historical Interlude II. Scandals in the Temple immediately following Chapter 14.

So twenty-three long years after the event, Jeremiah dredges up from his memory the experiences that launched him on his career as a prophet, attaches this account to the beginning of the scroll of condemnations and warnings, and on a day that the king has proclaimed a national day of fasting and prayer, a time of peril,[51] and during which the Temple courts will be jammed with worshipers, Jeremiah sends Baruch to read the scroll to them.[52]

Thus did Jeremiah's account of his Call come to be composed and begin to assume its current written form. In its factual account of the messages Jeremiah received, it probably is quite close to what Jeremiah experienced at the time. The experiences were traumatic for Jeremiah and burned into his mind. But the twenty-three intervening years cannot help but color the meaning of these youthful experiences. Jeremiah has changed. He is no longer the naïve and callow youth of those years. He had been warned of what awaited him, but at that time the warnings were mere words. Now, after twenty-three years of scorn, isolation and persecution, they have a meaning they never had then. They are now tinged with terror, the terror of a fugitive in hiding, in fear for his life.

It is in this desperate period—these last four years since the death of Josiah—and the half a dozen or so years leading up to it, that the misgivings he had experienced when first called by God, misgivings never quite stilled by His assurances, have sprouted and grown into the conviction that he was right the first time: he was not suited for the mission that had been thrust upon him. He was no good at it—in twenty-three years he had made headway with neither ruling establishment nor with the people at large. And the mission was certainly no fit for him. It is from this period in his life that his "confessions" stem: the rebellious cries and complaints that amount to an accusation against God: what have you pushed me into?

The Self-Image of a Prophet

But before we move on to Jeremiah's self-revelatory "confessions," let us take one last look at his account of his Call. So far we have examined it for its surface content, and have asked ourselves how much of its substance he truly understood at the time. I think that after the passage of twenty-three years, Jeremiah would have agreed with us that at the time that he was called to prophesy he was too immature, lacking in experience of life, to understand the full implications of either the message he was to deliver or the seriousness of the warnings he received. In those days he was young and optimistic, expecting easy remedies for the deep ills of the world. He had little appreciation of the intractability of human nature, the reluctance of human beings to admit that they are wrong and the tenacity of habit. We postulated Jeremiah to be in his late

---

51. It is a moment of crisis. The news of the Babylonian victory at Carchemish has arrived. The broken remnants of the once huge Egyptian army are pouring down the coastal road, fleeing back to Egypt. Judah, as a vassal of Egypt, is in the wrong camp, and now the cost of hitching one's wagon to a falling star will have to be paid.
52. It would appear that this original scroll dictated to Baruch and read to the crowd in the Temple consisted of what presently comprises Chapters 1–6 of the *Book of Jeremiah*. For an account of how Baruch read the scroll and what it led to, see Historical Interlude II. Scandals in the Temple, following Chapter 14.

teens when he received his Call[53]; which means that he was now about forty when he first began to commit his thoughts, experiences and even his past sermons to writing. We will now examine the style in which he framed his words for what it will tell us.

From his earliest years as a prophet Jeremiah exhibited a very elegant and urbane style of speaking and writing,[54] a style far too sophisticated to be devised out of whole cloth by a teenager. As all beginning poets (in his early years he composed almost exclusively in poetry), he patterned his works on those of his predecessors. It is from his choice of models that we can deduce not only his taste in literary composition, but something of his inner life. From this perspective, let us reexamine Jeremiah's Call, as described in Chapter 1 of his Book, in the context of Chapters 2–6, which seem to be the selections from his early sermons that Jeremiah chose to dictate to Baruch. Which exemplars did he choose as his prototypes?

His main model appears to have been the ancient poem known as "The Song of Moses" (*Deuteronomy* 32).[55] William Holladay[56] demonstrates by means of a catalog of archaic terms unique to *Deuteronomy* 32, which also appear in the writings of Jeremiah, his dependence on this great poem attributed to Moses; more heavily in his early poetry, and with decreasing frequency as his own style matures.[57] But not only had the poem served as a model to Jeremiah: It seems that it was the figure of Moses himself that loomed large in Jeremiah's eyes, and that it was this in large part that steered him to begin his poetic career by using a work attributed to Moses as his main inspiration, rather than the more recent works of his 8th-century predecessors Amos, Hosea and Isaiah.

We return to Chapter 1, the account of Jeremiah's Call as recollected and written down in 604 BCE. The wording of his description of this seminal event in his life is strongly reminiscent of God's promise to Moses concerning His future relations with the Children of Israel:

---

53. See note 23 above.

54. Inasmuch as he only began committing his words to writing at about the age of forty, how can we be certain that the style of Chapter 1 (the account of his Call) or Chapter 2 (his initial launch into denunciation of Israel for its sins), in which he exhibits an elevated form of writing of great elegance, is truly his early style? How can we be certain that he has retained the original vocabulary and diction of his youth, and has not edited and revised his early sayings into the fully developed style of a man of forty? We can largely rely on the evidence that he did not edit *the contents* of those sermons and oracles he had delivered in God's name, updating them in line with the unfolding events. For example, from the very first he warned of the coming of a kingdom from the North, but for the first nineteen chapters of his Book this kingdom is nameless. Only in 604, after the Battle of Carchemish settled the matter, does Jeremiah give a name to the menace from the North, Babylon, and give a name to God's instrument who will punish His sinning nation: Nebuchadrezzar (25:9). Only now did he know whom God had meant. But when he dictated the scroll to Baruch he did not edit his earlier sermons and put in either the name of Babylon or of Nebuchadrezzar, making specific what had once been vague. This fidelity to the contents of his early oracles—his refusal to revise and update them—give us a reason to assume that, as he did not touch the contents, so he didn't revise or edit his original style.

55. This work is popularly known among Jews as *Haazinu* ("Give ear"), from the first word of the poem.

56. Holladay, "Jeremiah and Moses," p. 19–21.

57. This does not imply that Jeremiah was necessarily familiar with the entire Book of *Deuteronomy* at this early date, i.e., 627–622 BCE. Holladay is of the opinion that "It is quite possible that it ['The Song of Moses'] circulated separately." (*Ibid.*, p.26) He notes that "It is perhaps significant that more of the parallels with the Song of Moses cited above are found in Jeremiah 2 than in any other chapter.... We may see in Jeremiah's inaugural prophecies the influence of Moses in larger measure than elsewhere." (*Ibid.*, p. 25) Jacob Milgrom, in his article "The Date of Jeremiah, Chapter 2," educes powerful evidence that Chapter 2 dates from between 627–622 and is among the earliest—if not *the* earliest—of Jeremiah's prophecies in our possession.

"A prophet shall I raise up for them, from the midst of their brethren, like yourself; and I will put My words in his mouth, and he shall speak all that I command him. And it shall come to pass, the man that does not heed My words that he speaks in My name, I, even I will require it of him"[58] [*Deuteronomy* 18:18-19].

My contention is that Jeremiah was perfectly aware of this promise in 604,[59] and that when he dictated his account of his Call he—consciously or unconsciously—articulated his description using the words and imagery of God's promise to Moses.[60]

What conclusions can we draw from all this? We can anticipate that Jeremiah came to see himself in the light of God's promise to Moses: in other words, that he was a prophet—perhaps *the* prophet—who would be like Moses, raised up by God to speak His words to a recalcitrant people. If he indeed saw himself and his mission as a sort of Moses redux, this would explain not only his using what he took to be Moses' literary style as a model for his own, but much of his subsequent behavior as well.

But Moses and his "Song" were hardly Jeremiah's only inspirations. Holladay also points to obvious echoes of Psalm 22, beginning with Jeremiah's account of his Call and continuing in several of his "confessions."[61] In due time we may find it necessary to refer to other portions of this remarkable Psalm,[62] but for our present purposes let us focus on just the following two verses:

For it is You who drew me forth from the belly,
You did keep me safe upon the breasts of my mother.
Upon You have I been thrown from the womb;
From the belly of my mother You have been my God [Psalm 22:10-11].

This passage immediately calls to mind Jeremiah's wording of God's initial call to him:

Before I formed you in the belly I knew you,
And before you came forth from the womb I consecrated you [1:4].

The use of the words "womb" (*rehem*) and "belly" (*beten*) in parallel as synonyms is no common biblical conceit. Besides its occurrence in the two examples above, it appears only five more times in the entire Hebrew Bible: three times in the *Book of Job*[63] and once in *Isaiah* 46:3—all written well after Jeremiah's lifetime[64]—and once

---

58. *Require it of him*: i.e., God will punish him.

59. This is eighteen years after the discovery of the scroll hidden in the Temple (the *Book of Deuteronomy*) and its official promulgation.

60. Holladay ("The Background of Jeremiah's Self-Understanding," pp.159-161) points to the phrase *"All that I command you you shall speak"* (*Jeremiah* 1:6) which is a clear echo of *"He shall speak all that I command him"* (*Deuteronomy* 18:18), while the phrase *"I have put My words in your mouth"* (*Jeremiah* 11:9) is almost a direct quote of *"I will put My words in his mouth"* (*Deuteronomy* 18:18). Holladay concludes, "We are left, then, with the conclusion that Jeremiah knew *Deuteronomy* 18:18 and was influenced by it in the verbalization of his call." (*Ibid.*, p. 160)

61. Holladay, "Background," p. 156-157. Here we will deal only with Jeremiah's Call. The later echoes will be put on hold until we reach the appropriate "confessions."

62. For *Psalm* 22:1-22 see Appendix H. The final 10 verses of the Psalm consist of a doxology or hymn of praise to God which are not relevant to our subject.

63. *Job* 3:11, 10:18-19, 31:15.

64. "Most scholars today would agree that the weight of evidence favors an early post-Exilic date, after Deutero-Isaiah [for *Job*]. I would assign the period between 500 and 300 BCE." (R. Gordis, *The Book of God and Man*, p. 216)

in Psalm 58:4. As for the last, while Jeremiah could have known the Psalm, considering the context, it is unlikely in the extreme that it would have inspired him to copy its language.[65] This leaves Psalm 22 as the only possible candidate for being the source for this figure of speech used by Jeremiah, always assuming that these two occurrences are not simply a coincidence: the independent coinage of this synonymous use of "belly" and "womb" by two separate poets. Such things do happen, but what argues against mere accident is that other turns of phrase and images that seem native to the Psalm reappear in the "confessions" of Jeremiah, at least one of which strikes us as being a reference back to his earlier use of the Psalm's imagery in his Call, which we have already described. We will examine these—what we deem to probably be—verbal borrowings from Psalm 22, when we arrive at the relevant passages.

What we consider to be the importance of these "borrowings"—if they indeed prove to be such—is what they reveal about the inner life of Jeremiah. What we suggest is that what attracted him to the Psalm in the first place, and led to his use of language unique to it—whether consciously or unconsciously it would be difficult at best to say—is that in the tragic picture the psalmist paints of the ongoing suffering of a righteous soul Jeremiah found a mirror which reflected what he saw as his own fate. By the fact of being born into a cursed family—exiled from his proper place in the Temple of the Lord in Jerusalem and condemned to a truncated life—and by God's decreeing for him his mission as a prophet in a dangerous time, he was doomed to a life of misery and martyrdom. If indeed this is how Jeremiah saw himself, then through Psalm 22 we can get a better understanding of the frame of mind of the author of the "confessions," to which we will shortly turn.

---

65. The Psalm is a violent condemnation of corrupt judges who are charged with being wicked from the womb.

Historical Interlude I
The Road to Megiddo: Playing on the Big Board

To understand the chain of events that led from the disaster of Megiddo to what is arguably the most significant event, at least to us, to have occurred in the last tortured decade of the 7th century BCE—Jeremiah's decision to commit to writing the deepest inner experiences, anxieties, hopes and fears of his life[1]—we need to see them in their larger historical and geo-political context. Megiddo didn't just happen; it was the outcome of a constellation of events: of a courageous intervention into the clash of empires, of a bold attempt to influence the balance of power and an unexpected turn of events that brought tragedy to the Kingdom of Judah and its inhabitants. The purpose of this short INTERLUDE is to try and organize the pieces into a comprehensible picture and trace, step-by-step, the road that led to Megiddo.[2]

We pick up our tale from where we left off our brief description of the age into which Jeremiah was born, in the opening pages of Chapter 13.[3] We left our account there with the waning Assyrian Empire drawing into itself and progressively abandoning its Western periphery; first in Africa, then in Western Asia. Into this growing power vacuum, a liberated and resurgent Egypt was expanding, and under its canopy of power the little Kingdom of Judah had asserted its independence of Assyrian domination and was attempting to establish its control over the territory of what had once been its sister kingdom Israel.[4]

As the Assyrian Empire visibly disintegrated, Egypt extended her authority over ever-increasing swathes of Syria, while the Medes to the East encroached ever more deeply into what had been Imperial territory. Then, like a kaleidoscope turning, the pieces suddenly shifted into a new pattern, and everything changed. In southern

---

1. These were to form the core of what became the biblical *Book of Jeremiah*. On the long-term influence of his writings see Chapter 16 and Historical Interlude II.

2. This section, while by no means comprehensive, will attempt to sketch a brief outline of the events that is both focused and comprehensible. It is based on multiple sources—Assyrian, Babylonian, Egyptian and biblical—and assumes their fundamental reliability. Its aim is not judgmental; it simply attempts to present the facts, as best we understand them at the present, within the framework of a theory that makes some sense of them.

3. See the section entitled Jeremiah's Background.

4. It was during this dynamic period that the discovery in 622 BCE of a scroll that had been hidden in the Temple (probably of the *Book of Deuteronomy* or an early version of it) triggered, under King Josiah's leadership, a radical intensification of the de-paganization and religious reformation already underway. It also led to the canonization of *Deuteronomy*, that is, the acceptance in National Assembly of the Book as legally binding upon all the inhabitants under the sovereignty of the Kingdoms of Judah and Jerusalem.

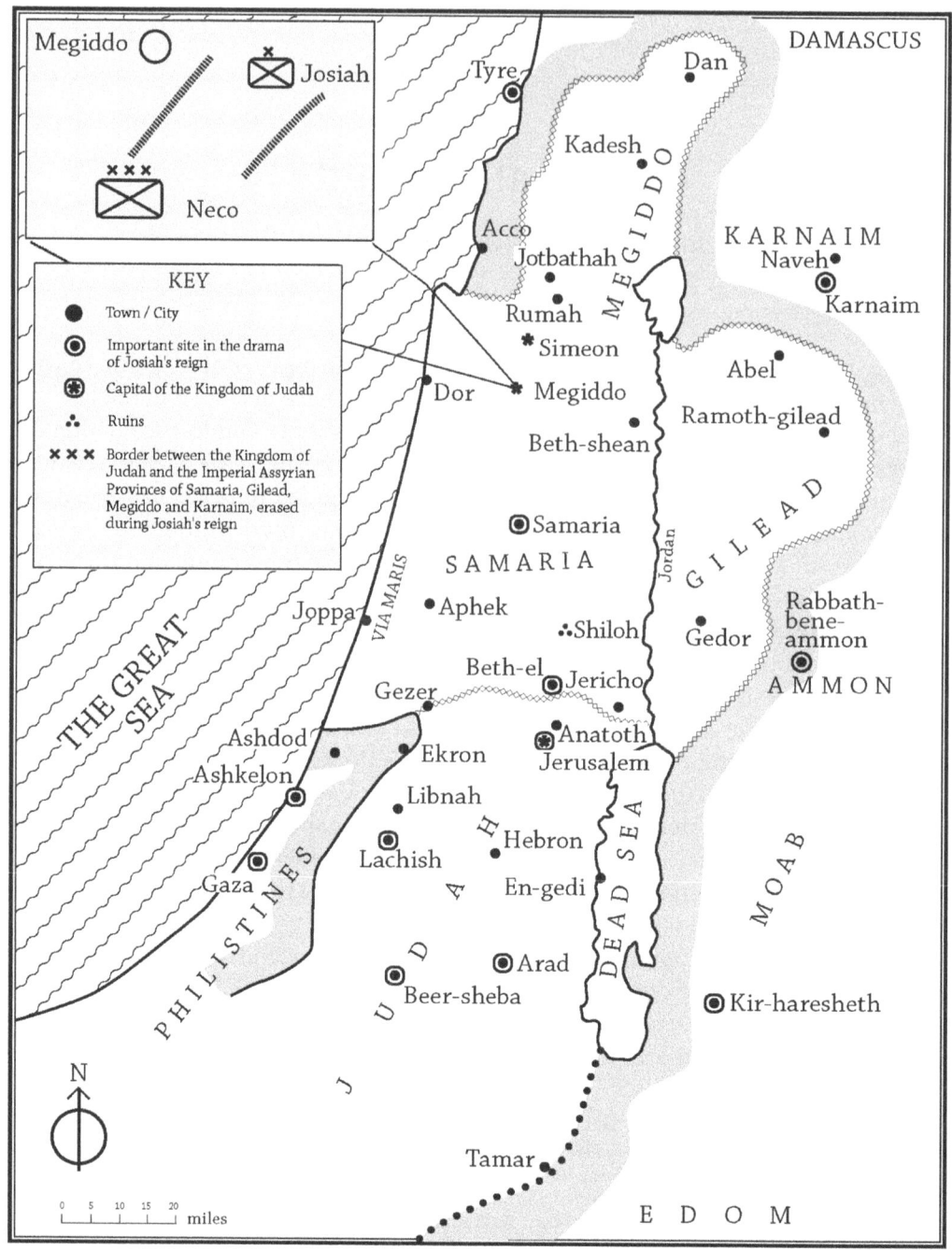

Map 6

The Holy Land during the reign of King Josiah, c. 610 BCE. Insert: The Battle of Megiddo, 608 BCE.

Mesopotamia in 616 BCE, a Babylonian general named Nebopolassar proclaimed himself "King of Akkad,"[5] raised the standard of rebellion and marched north against Assyria—only to find himself facing an Egyptian Army. New circumstances had led these ancient enemies—Egypt and Assyria—to become allies.[6] For the moment this stopped Nebopolassar, but not for long. By this time Assyria was too weakened even to be propped up. In 614 BCE, Assur, her ancient capital, fell to the Medes, and in 612 Nineveh—only yesterday capital of the entire Ancient Near East—was sacked and burned by combined Median and Babylonian armies, Sin-shar-ishkun, its current Emperor, perishing in the flames of his gutted metropolis.

What was left of the once gargantuan Assyrian Empire was a small rump state in Northern Mesopotamia, with its capital at Haran.[7] There its last emperor, Asshur-uballit II, with the remains of the once invincible Assyrian armed forces, now reinforced by an Egyptian army, was left facing the victorious Nebopolassar.[8] Circumstances had now decreed that Haran would be the key to Western Asia. Nebopolassar made finishing off Assyria his first target, while Egypt considered keeping Assyria afloat as its top priority. And with the fate of half the world at stake, at this critical juncture the Egyptian Pharaoh Psammetichus I died (609 BCE).

Psammetichus had been cautious in his commitments. His successor, Neco II (609–593 BCE), threw caution to the winds and committed the entire Egyptian home army—everything he could scrape up—to keep Assyria afloat. In 609, a massive force set forth from Egypt for Haran.

At that point in the seesaw fighting that had been taking place, Haran had fallen to the Babylonians, who had left a garrison to hold it. A joint Assyrian-Egyptian army was at the moment laying siege to it, while a Babylonian army was on the way to raise the siege. The fate of Haran and northern Mesopotamia hung in the balance. The entire issue turned on the question of who would get there first.

The Egyptian Army was following the main north-south highway, known to the Egyptians as *The Way of Horus*,[9] which connected Egypt with Mesopotamia. Pharaoh Neco, who was commanding the army personally, was driving his troops hard. They were late.[10] Arriving at the critical pass at Megiddo, the army ground to a halt. There, blocking the pass, was the entire Judean army under the command of King Josiah. What was he doing there?

---

5. The ancient title of the rulers of the third millennium Akkadian Empire, which ruled all Mesopotamia.

6. Psammetichus I, the Liberator of Egypt, had come to the conclusion that the real danger to Egypt now lay in the rising forces to the south and east of Assyria. It was now in Egypt's interest to shore up what was left of Assyria, to serve as a buffer state between herself and the rising Median and Babylonian kingdoms; hence the startling Egyptian-Assyrian alliance.

7. Haran was an important city in Northern Mesopotamia, about 230 miles west of Nineveh and slightly to its North. See MAP 5.

8. Following the fall of Nineveh, the Medes and the Babylonians divided the spoils: the Medes took everything east of the Tigris River, while Babylon received Mesopotamia and everything west of the Euphrates River as its share of the loot. This bounty, however, was largely theoretical. What was left of Assyria still held the northern third of Mesopotamia, while Egypt controlled the territories west of the Euphrates. If Nebopolassar wanted his full share of the spoils he would have to take it. See MAP 6.

9. This route is known to us by the name *The Via Maris* (*The Way of the Sea*), the translation into Latin by St. Jerome of the name given to this route by the prophet Isaiah (*Isaiah* 8:23).

10. We can only speculate on what held up the departure of the army from Egypt. Our sources are silent as to the reasons for the tardy start.

There now followed a frantic diplomatic exchange of messages[11]: What are you doing? I have no quarrel with you. My business is on the Euphrates. I have no hostile intent against you. I recognize your sovereignty. I am just transiting as my armies have in recent years. Let me through. I'm in a hurry.

But Josiah wouldn't budge. If Neco wanted to pass he would have to fight his way through. And so, having no choice, he did. In that desperate battle Josiah was killed. So far are the known facts of the matter.

One critical question is posed by these facts: whatever did Josiah think he was doing, confronting his sponsors and benefactors in this way?[12] The answer should be as obvious to us as it was to Neco: Josiah had taken a page out of Egypt's own book. Just as Egypt had switched sides, so had he, and had allied himself with Nebopolassar against the Egyptians. Just as his moves against Assyria had been coordinated with Egypt, so this present move was obviously coordinated with the Babylonians. There can be no other rational explanation. The fate of the Fertile Crescent was being decided at Haran, and Josiah was playing his part by delaying the arrival of the Egyptian Army.

Did he really think that he could stop the Egyptian juggernaut? I think that he was under no such illusion. He knew perfectly well that if it came to actual combat, the Egyptians would roll right over him.

Josiah was a bold gambler in a high-stakes poker game with heavyweights around the table, and his was a bold play indeed. All things considered, I believe that he was planning to sacrifice most of his army in order to delay the Egyptians for several days: a day at least for the battle, and one or more days to reorganize after the fight before they could get moving northward again. The time factor on the international scene must have been very tight indeed.[13] As for Josiah, he had his next step all prepared: either during or immediately after the defeat of his army he would slip away, get back to Jerusalem, shut himself into that impregnable fortress and wait—a year or even two if necessary—until the Babylonians came to the rescue of their ally. It was a bold plan that could have worked but for one unforeseen circumstance— what insurance companies used to call "an act of God"—namely, that during the course of battle, Josiah was killed. He went into battle disguised,[14] but in the hail of

---

11. We have Neco's shocked dispatch (or a summary thereof) preserved in *2 Chronicles* 35:21.

12. Many nineteenth century and even twentieth century scholars have been of the opinion that Josiah was a religious fanatic who wouldn't allow "impure" Egyptians to trespass on "holy soil." Or that Josiah believed that the Egyptian Army was somehow directed against him, and that God would intervene and defeat the Egyptians for him. This, I believe, is to completely misread Josiah's character. The more we learn about Josiah, the more we realize how levelheaded and astute a politician and statesman he was. Far from having his head in the clouds, it is the scholars who appear wooly-headed.

13. What would Josiah get from all this? Kings don't usually sacrifice their armies for others out of altruistic motives, nor do kings expect others to do so for them. Josiah was offering major assistance to Nebopolassar in a very tricky situation—assistance that would prove vital—and there was undoubtedly a serious payoff agreed between the two partners, but what the quid pro quo was to be we will never know: was it future guaranteed status as an independent ally? recognition of Judah's annexation of the three Imperial Assyrian provinces that had been the Kingdom of Israel? something else? The death of Josiah, and his replacement with an Egyptian puppet (see below), canceled all commitments.

14. This was not uncommon in those days. Kings led their troops into battle, and when they did they led from the front, not from the rear. As such they were perfect targets. To offset this liability, they often disguised themselves as junior officers or as common soldiers; their own men knew who they were, but the enemy didn't.

missile fire[15] that accompanied the hand-to-hand combat, he was hit by a random arrow and mortally wounded. He was safely extricated from the battle, transported to Jerusalem, and there he died and was laid to rest with his fathers.

Josiah did not die in vain as far as the big board was concerned. The delay was sufficient. By the time Neco and his army arrived in Mesopotamia it was all over. The Assyrian and Egyptian troops that had been besieging Haran were no more. The last vestiges of the once all-powerful Assyrian Empire in its final iteration had been erased. Egypt would have to face the Babylonians alone, with neither buffer between them nor an ally at her side. And so, a standoff ensued: with Euphrates as barrier between them, Neco consolidated his hold on Syria while Nebopolassar consolidated his position in Mesopotamia.

For Judah, Megiddo turned out to be an unmitigated disaster. Josiah proved irreplaceable. He had indeed been very much like his ancestor and ideal, David; that rare combination of commitment to the faith of his fathers, keen insight into ongoing events, unerringly acute judgment as to which path to take, the courage to take risks and an iron will that could not be swayed from a path once taken. His sons were no fit replacements, certainly not for those turbulent times. The National Assembly, disregarding birth order, chose Jehoahaz[16] to succeed his father.[17] He reigned for three months. Then, lacking the courage to keep to the policy of his father and hold out for the eventual victory of Babylon, he surrendered to Neco—now master of the entire region—and went to Riblah[18] (probably with a promise of safe conduct) to try to make his peace with the Pharaoh. Once in Neco's hands, the Pharaoh tore up the safe-conduct, had Jehoahaz clapped in chains and dragged off Egypt to eventually die, probably in an Egyptian dungeon. Neco, assuming control of Judah, placed Josiah's son Eliakim on the throne, changing his name to Jehoiakim.[19] From a former ally, Judah had been reduced to a vassal state of Egypt. Worse was to come.

The standoff on the Euphrates between the two powers lasted four years.[20] Then,

---

15. Mainly arrows and sling-stones.

16. "Jehoahaz" was his formal, or throne-name, adopted upon his assent to kingship. He is sometimes referred to by his given name of Shallum (cf. *Jeremiah* 21:11). Jehoahaz was two years younger than his half-brother Jehoiakim.

17. In Judah a king was succeeded by a son. Which son (most kings had several) was ultimately in the hands of the National Assembly (*am haaretz*). Why the Assembly decided to overrule the general practice of primogeniture has been the subject of much speculation.

18. Riblah was a city in north-central Syria, about 75 miles north of Damascus, which was serving as administrative headquarters for the Egyptian occupation of what the Babylonians called "Hatti-land," i.e., "Greater Syria." See MAP 6.

19. In the ancient world, to change someone's name was to publicly assert control over him. Beyond being Neco's vassal, Jehoiakim is now—both formally and in actuality—the Pharaoh's "property."

20. Now we are in a position to answer the question: why did Nebopolassar wait four years from the time of his victory at Haran? Why didn't he immediately move south? If the scenario we have sketched above is in any sense accurate, he probably would have had Josiah lived. It would have been in his interest to attack while an ally, Judah, was sitting athwart Egypt's lines of communication. With Jerusalem occupied by an enemy force, Neco would have found himself in an extremely awkward situation, to say the least. But by getting Jehoahaz to come out of his impregnable stronghold, and replacing him with his puppet Jehoiakim, the strategic situation had been radically altered in Neco's favor. He no longer had an enemy threatening his back. Under these circumstances, with the incentive to move quickly to take advantage of a transient situation removed, Nebopolassar understandably opted to pause, regroup and reorganize. The results of this pause were to be seen at Carchemish.

in 605, Egyptian troops crossed the Euphrates and drove the Babylonians out of a bridgehead they had established. Nebopolassar remained in Babylon and sent his son, the crown prince Nebuchadrezzar,[21] to take command of the army. In the ensuing Battle of Carchemish[22] he completely shattered the Egyptian army. Josiah had been right when he put his money on Babylon. Egypt looked impressive, but the real power lay with the Chaldeans (as the Babylonians were called). Egypt had no alternative but to abandon Syria and withdraw to within her borders. Babylon now controlled "Hatti-land."[23]

Which brings us to the crisis of the winter of 605/604 in Judah.[24]

---

21. NebuchadRezzar or NebuchadNezzar? Both spellings are to be found in the Bible, the former in the Books of *Jeremiah* and *Ezekiel*, while the latter is to be found in the Books of *Kings, Chronicles, Esther, Daniel, Ezra* and *Nehemiah*. It is the former, with the middle R that is closest to the king's name as it appears in cuneiform in all of his official inscriptions. His name was *Nabu-kudurri-usur*, which seems to mean "Nabu, defend my boundary," or possibly "Nabu, protect my son," where Nabu is the name of a major Babylonian deity. It is significant that the books of *Jeremiah* and *Ezekiel*, contemporaries of the king, get it right while the changes of R into N all appear in biblical Books written after the king's death. Some scholars believe that the change was intentional and meant to denigrate the king posthumously. While *NebuchadRezzar* means something like "Nabu, protect my son," *NebuchadNezzar* means "Nabu, protect my donkey." This phenomenon of altering the name of a historic personage to sully his memory is hardly an unknown phenomenon in the Bible. For example, *Eshbaal*, youngest son of Saul and later ruler of Israel, whose name meant "Man of Baal" (*1 Chronicles* 8:33, 9:36)—a serious embarrassment—is referred to in the book of *Samuel* as *Ish-bosheth*, "Man of shame." It is possible to postulate renaming the king as *NebuchadNezzar* as something similar, in this case an act of posthumous revenge on the man who destroyed Jerusalem and burnt Solomon's Temple. As the focus of our study is the *Book of Jeremiah*, we will use the form of the name—*NebuchadRezzar*—as it appears in all the chapters of *Jeremiah* to which we relate.

22. Carchemish was a city of vital strategic importance on the Euphrates River, about 55 miles due west of Haran. See MAP 6.

23. And at this juncture Nebopolassar died, and in September 605, Nebuchadrezzar ascended to the throne of his father.

24. For a detailed account of Jeremiah's role in this crisis, see Historical Interlude II. Scandals in the Temple which follows Chapter 14.

Chapter 14

De Profundis

Out of the depths have I called You, O Lord;
Lord, hearken unto my voice.
May Your ears be attentive
To the sound of my supplications.

—Psalm 130:1–2

Embedded in the *Book of Jeremiah* are a series of passages that comprise the subject of this short study. Through a tacit agreement of late-19th-century–early-20th-century biblical scholars, they have become known as the "Confessions of Jeremiah."[1] They appear—interspersed among divine oracles on various subjects, the proclamations, the denunciations and the snippets detailing various actions the prophet undertook—between Chapters 11 and 20 of his *Book*, but form no part of his public preaching. They are extremely intimate, opening a window into the very soul of Jeremiah. There is nothing even remotely comparable in the writings of any other prophet in the Bible. The question we need to raise at this juncture is: why do these "Confessions" even exist? We need to continually remind ourselves that the literary conventions of the ancient world ruled out the public disclosure of one's inner life. There was a clear line drawn between the public domain and one's inner world that one did not violate—a norm very different from that of our present age. What was it that induced Jeremiah to cross this line and leave a written record of some of the deepest torments and struggles of his soul?

We have dealt with the issue of why Jeremiah wrote in the first place.[2] At his Call, he had been commanded by God to speak to the people everything that his God would demand.[3] And for 23 years he had faithfully obeyed this mandate.[4] But with the onset of the reign of King Jehoiakim in 609 BCE he had effectively been silenced. Denied the public pulpit and forced into hiding, he had attempted to find an alternative way of making his voice heard: by resorting to writing God's word and having someone else read it to the public. But with the King demonstratively burning his

---

1. This designation, appropriated from the *Confessions of St. Augustine*, is widely recognized as less than fully appropriate, but in lieu of a widely-accepted alternative it remains current and, by default, we will continue its use, despite our reservations.
2. See the section entitled The Write-Up in Chapter 13, and Historical Interlude II. Scandals in the Temple, immediately following this chapter.
3. 1:17.
4. As he himself testifies (25:3).

scroll, even this course was closed.[5] As long as Jehoiakim sat on the throne, there was no way of getting God's word to the public. The issue now became one of preserving God's word, that it might enlighten future generations.

While in hiding, Jeremiah first redictated to Baruch a copy of the scroll that the King had burnt, and then to this he added numerous further divine oracles and pronouncements.[6] I would suggest that this process was a long one,[7] dredging up from memory the various communications he had received from God and preached over the 23 years of his active ministry. From the record we can see that Jeremiah had developed an intimate relationship with his God, resulting in intermittent but frequent communication. And from this same record we can see that not all the back-and-forth between Jeremiah and God consisted of oracles meant for "publication": i.e., revelations meant to be preached to the public. My thesis is that during this period of enforced silence and dictation, the conviction developed on the part of Jeremiah that *all* the words communicated to him by God were holy and deserving of preservation, and not merely those he had expressly been commanded to preach to the people.[8]

When we examine those "words of God" that Jeremiah saw worthy of preserving and dictating, we discover they fall into several distinct categories. First, there are those of his pronouncements that can stand on their own as independent compositions: the sermons that he chose for the original scroll are among those that fall into this category. Then there are those prophecies that can stand on their own, but whose value is enormously enhanced when the context in which they were delivered is supplied. Sometimes it is Jeremiah who provides the context in which the sermon was composed or delivered; sometimes he leaves this task to Baruch. An example would be the denunciatory harangue contained in 7:1–15. Here it is Baruch who supplies the context (26:1–24).[9] And lastly, there are those pronouncements that are essentially meaningless without the context that either Jeremiah or Baruch provide; Jeremiah's "Confessions" fall under this latter heading.

Put simply, in the give-and-take between the prophet and his God, Jeremiah's complaints and outpourings elicited responses from God. These divine messages were, as words of God, intrinsically holy and deserving of preservation. But without Jeremiah's original complaints and protestations God's replies are incomprehensible. So Jeremiah was compelled, in order that God's replies be intelligible, to supply the context in which they were uttered: his original outpourings, i.e., his "Confessions." In a word, my suggestion is that as far as Jeremiah was concerned, the primary

---

5. 36:26. See also Historical Interlude II, note 35.

6. This is Baruch's claim, and he should know, as it was he who was on the receiving end of the dictation: see 36:32.

7. If we are correct in our assumption that it was only safe for Jeremiah and Baruch to emerge from hiding after the death of Jehoiakim, then their underground existence stretched out for close to seven years.

8. As we have already suggested, the original scroll read in the Temple consisted of what we now know as Chapters 1–6 of the *Book of Jeremiah* (see Chapter 13, note 52), while the *many words like these* that Jeremiah had *added to them* (36:32) comprise the bulk, if not the whole, of Chapters 7–25:13 (see Chapter 13, note 54). If we exclude Jeremiah's "Oracles to the Nations" (Chapters 45–51), this covers most of the text attributed directly to Jeremiah himself.

9. See Historical Interlude II. Scandals in the Temple for details.

purpose of including his "Confessions" in the material he dictated to Baruch was to provide successive frames of reference for the specific divine utterances—"words of God"—that had to be preserved in a manner that would be understandable to future readers. That in the process the sanctity of his inner life was being violated and was being exposed to public scrutiny was collateral damage, which would have to be endured for the sake of the higher cause.

It says much about the world in which we find ourselves that we have reversed the priorities; nowadays it is the human inner torment and agony that we find of interest. We barely take note of God's responses to Jeremiah's cries of despair.

The Prophet Whom Everyone Mocks

We begin with what I take to be an early complaint of Jeremiah, which opens with a dialogue-poem featuring two speakers, Jeremiah and God;[10]

Speaker	
Jeremiah	O Lord, *the hope of Israel* *All who forsake You shall be put to shame.*
God	*Those who turn from Me*[11] *shall be written in the earth,* *For they have forsaken a fountain of living waters.*[12]
Jeremiah	*Heal me, O* Lord, *and I shall be healed;* *Save me and I shall be saved;* *For You are my praise.*
The People	*Behold, they say to me:* *"Where [now] is the word of the* Lord? *Let it but come [to be]!"*
Jeremiah	*As for me, I was in no hurry to be Your shepherd*[13]; *And as for the day of disaster,*[14] *I never desired it—You know that*[15] [17:13–16a]

Composed as a poem—most of Jeremiah's early sermons and proclamations were written in poetry and not in prose—it is framed as an exchange of views between multiple parties. Jeremiah opens with a declaration of faith: they that hold fast to their God have some hope, while those that abandon Him shall be judged accordingly.[16] But the term *mikveh*, which we rendered as *hope*, has another meaning: that

---

10. Three, if we consider the quote in 17:15 as consisting of "the people" taking part in the conversation; Our contention is that this entire composition was preserved for the sake of the half verse (17:13b), which is a direct quote of the reply of God to Jeremiah's pronouncement in 17:13a.

11. Reading with *Keri*, Q and numerous mss. MT reads *they that turn from You.*

12. MT adds here *the Lord*, which seems to be an explanatory gloss. With BHS we delete it from the poem.

13. Literally, *to shepherd after You.*

14. Hebrew *yom anush*; literally, *a day of weakness, a day of sickness* = an evil day.

15. In the division of the verses and the assignment of the speakers I largely follow Lundbom I, p. 794–797.

16. The Hebrew *yeboshu* means not only "put to shame," but also has the sense of "brought to judgment."

of a pool of freshwater from which one can drink and be refreshed.[17] Thus the opening stanza could mean "God is a pool where one can refresh oneself; all who forsake Him will go thirsty."

It is this latter meaning that God picks up on when he revises Jeremiah's metaphor.

"Those who turn from Me shall be written in the earth,
For they have forsaken a fountain of living waters" [17:13b].

God is not passive; He is active, God corrects Jeremiah. "I am not a quiet pool, I am a gushing fountain of life-giving waters. Those who turn away from Me don't just go thirsty; they die." To be "written in the earth" is the antithesis of being "written for life."[18] This editing of Jeremiah's declaration amounts to a divine rap on the knuckles—a mild rap, but a rap nonetheless. Jeremiah is attributing to God a passivity in the face of Israel's apostasy that underestimates His involvement in the affairs of the world. Turning one's back on God does not simply mean forgoing certain benefits, it means incurring devastating punishment. Jeremiah's reply to this gentle correction can be taken as an indirect apology.

Heal me, O Lord, *and I shall be healed;*
Save me, and I shall be saved,
For You are my praise [17:14].

This is Psalm language. Jeremiah is accepting the implication that he is sick, that his disparagement of God is due to his current depression; he is "down in the dumps." Please, he is appealing to God, help me out of this pit of depression; but I have good reason to be at this pass. My enemies—which seem to constitute the public as a whole—are making life a hell for me.

Behold, they say to me:
"Where [now] *is the word of the* Lord?
Let it but come [to be]*!"* [17:15]

Jeremiah is referring to the problem he has faced from day one: he has been commanded to preach the looming disaster bearing down from the North:

From the North *shall the evil break forth upon all the inhabitants of the land* [1:14].

And this he has done endlessly; the years have gone by but nothing has happened. It is Egypt that dominates the region. He has become a laughingstock: "Mr. Disaster from the North," the target of taunts.

"Behold, they say to me:
'Where [now] *is the word of the* Lord?
Let it but come [to be]*!'"* [17:15]

---

17. The term also references a pool used for ritual purification, though that meaning is probably not intended here.

18. *Isaiah* 4:3. This biblical metaphor is fully spelled out in the concept of a "Book of Life," in which one is inscribed (cf. *Psalm* 69:29) or erased (cf. *Exodus* 32:32–33).

I can't stand this ridicule and harassment much longer, Jeremiah is saying. Why do I deserve this? I never asked for this mission. And I certainly don't want the day of doom to arrive, the evil day that You force me to preach about constantly; it will destroy both everything I hold dear, and me as well.

"As for me, I was in no hurry to be Your shepherd;
And as for the day of disaster,
I never desired it—You know that" [17:16a].

Beginning with praise, this little poem of Jeremiah has morphed into a bitter complaint against the unenviable position in which he finds himself: in the office of a prophet, a position he never wanted, and forced to preach a message that revolts him. To this poem he now[19] adds a codicil:

What came out of my lips
Lies plain before You.[20]
Do not be the cause of my ruin[21];
You are my refuge in the day of evil.

May they that hound me[22] *be put to shame,*
And let it not be me who is shamed;
Let them be ruined,
And let it not be me who is ruined[23];

Bring on them an evil day,
And break them, break them twice over![24] [17:16b–18]

They Are Trying to Entrap Me!

The pressures mount. Jeremiah's complaints come as reactions to the way the public receives his preaching. As such, the changing tenor of his complaints mirrors the changes in the attitude of his listeners. In our first selection the tone was one of mockery. Jeremiah is complaining of having become a bad joke: he is being perceived as the prophet who keeps preaching that tomorrow the world is coming to an end—but it doesn't. But things do not remain static. As time passes and Jeremiah keeps delivering his message, the public perception of him begins to alter. The joke has worn thin; from a figure of ridicule he has begun to be seen as a public nuisance, and from that to a disturber of the peace. His endless denunciations are getting people's backs up. What is more, his attacks—both indirect and at times bitingly

---

19. "Now" refers to this entire unit (17:13–18) as we presently find it in the *Book of Jeremiah*, but we have no idea how much time elapsed, if any, between the composition of this poem and his writing the codicil and attaching it to his prior composition.
20. Literally, *is before your face*; i.e., is fully known to You.
21. Hebrew *mehita*, from the root *htt*, to break, to be broken.
22. Literally, *they that pursue me*.
23. The same root *htt* as in verse 17. See note 21 above.
24. Literally, *break them with a double breaking!*

explicit—upon the classes that traditionally were the molders and the arbiters of public opinion are being felt by these as increasingly intolerable. The intellectual leadership of the kingdom has reached the point where they feel that they can no longer safely afford to ignore him.

The intellectual establishment of the Israelite society of those days was threefold: the *kohanim* (the priests), the *nebiim* (the prophets) and the *hachamim* (the sages, the wise men).[25] As Jeremiah was continually propounding ideas that ran counter to the prevailing opinions and beliefs held by the intellectual elite, it was inevitable that sooner or later the intelligentsia would come to feel itself under attack and begin to respond accordingly.[26] In the next of Jeremiah's so-called "Confessions"—also, in our opinion, dating from the last years of the reign of King Josiah[27]—we find him accusing an arrogant intellectual establishment of defensively asserting their indispensable contributions to society while maliciously orchestrating a campaign of slander against him. Worse: he complains of a conspiracy to entrap him in what might eventuate in capital charges. This focused hostility of the intellectual establishment, coming on top of the increasing antipathy of the general public, seems to be disturbing him acutely. His reactions are decidedly disproportionate; indeed, they could be deemed hysterical.

> *And they said*[28]:
>
> *"Come, let us lay a plot against Jeremiah,*[29]
> *For instruction shall not perish from the priest,*
> *Nor counsel from the Sage,*
> *Nor the Word from the prophet.*[30]
> *Come, let us smite him with the tongue,*[31]
> *And pay no heed to his words."*[32]

---

25. Sometimes these are termed the "wisdom teachers." "Wisdom" (*hochmah*) involved the application of intelligence to the mundane issues of life, and the provision of counsel on how to cope with them.

26. By 608 BCE we find the priests and the prophets singled out as the leaders of the mob that attempted to lynch Jeremiah in the Temple (26:7–16). For the incident, see Historical Interlude II. Scandals in the Temple that follows this chapter.

27. In this assertion I am swimming against the current: most commentators date these passages well into the reign of Jehoiakim. I disagree, primarily because in both of these "Confessions" there is not the least hint of government persecution, something that became Jeremiah's most pressing concern with the consolidation of Jehoiakim's grip on the government, and which drove Jeremiah underground. Quite the opposite; it was the intervention of high government officials—holdovers from Josiah's regime—that, in the opening month or so of Jehoiakim's reign (26:1), rescued Jeremiah from the priest-and-prophet-led lynch mob in the Temple. See previous note. Under Josiah, the government and Jeremiah were essentially on the same page.

28. Who is the "they"? This phrase has no antecedent, and therefore must refer to the priests, sages and prophets cited in the quotation.

29. Literally, *let us plot plots against Jeremiah*, the infinitive absolute construction. See Chapter 1, note 54.

30. Probably this is a response to denunciations by Jeremiah deriding their professional shortcomings. Priests were mandated to provide instruction (Torah means "instruction," not "law") in the written record of God's past Revelation (cf., *Malachi* 2:7, but note *Jeremiah* 2:8). The sages were expected to give wise counsel (cf. 9:22, *Proverbs* 1:2–7, but see *Isaiah* 29:14). The prophets were those chosen to bring the living Word of God to His people, yet again note *Jeremiah* 2:8. All, Jeremiah charges, have betrayed their callings.

31. That is, orchestrate a campaign of innuendo and slander; possibly including false accusations and laying false charges against Jeremiah.

32. LXX omits the *no* in the final line; completely reversing the meaning: let us pay close attention to his words so that we can use them against him. Along with most modern versions we prefer to stick with MT.

Give heed, O LORD, to me,
And hear the voice of my complaint.[33]

Shall good be repaid by evil?
For they have dug a pit for my soul.
Remember how I stood before You
To speak good for them,
To turn away Your wrath from them [18:18–20].

Fair play demands that like be compensated by like; that good should be repaid by good and evil by evil. "I interceded with You for them, O LORD," Jeremiah argues. "I included them in my prayers along with all the House of Israel.[34] I stood up for these people, and this is how they repay me. Not only do they refuse to even give me a hearing and counsel others to ignore me, but they slander me. Worse: they have conspired to destroy me, to entrap me.[35] You, O LORD, are the righteous judge; give them what they deserve!"

And then Jeremiah loses all sense of proportion; he gets carried away by his emotions. He calls down a curse upon his enemies:

Therefore hand over their children to famine,
Give them over to the power of the sword[36];
May their wives be bereaved and widowed;
Their men having been killed by plague,[37]
And their young men struck down by the sword in war.

May a cry be heard from their houses,
For You will bring marauders[38] *suddenly upon them.*
For they have dug a pit to take me,
And set traps for my feet.

And You, O LORD, You know
All their counsel[39] *to kill me,*[40]
Do not cover up[41] *their iniquity,*
Their sin before You do not blot out;

---

33. Reading with LXX, Syr. and Targ. *ribi*. This is a legal term that will become central in Jeremiah's next "Confession." MT here reads *yeribai*, those who contend with me, i.e., my enemies.

34. For example, 14:7–9 and 14:20–22—prayers of intercession for the people of Israel. One of the functions of the prophet in Israel of old was to act as "counsel for the defense" when Israel faced punishment at the hands of God for its sins.

35. A pit (*shuhah*) is a deep hole dug in the ground and then covered up to camouflage it. One steps on the covering and it gives way, precipitating one down into the trap.

36. Literally, *pour them out by means of the sword*, i.e., may they be thrust through with a sword so that their blood pours out over the hand of its wielder; a vivid and dramatic word picture.

37. Literally, *the slain of death*. Targ. takes *mavet* (death) to be a euphemism for "plague," and renders it as such.

38. Hebrew *gedud*, a troop of soldiers let loose on the civilian population.

39. In the sense of their deliberate planning; the same term used in verse 18 above for the attribute so prized by the sages: wise counsel.

40. Literally, *against me for* [my] *death*.

41. Hebrew *al tichaper*.

Let them be tripped up[42] *before You,*
In the time of Your anger deal with them [18:21–23].

This frenzied appeal is to kill all the men and their children, leaving their wives to go mad with grief over the loss of their husbands and offspring, and then to turn their widows over to the tender mercies of ravaging soldiery for rape and wanton killing for the sake of killing. Why? Because they slandered me; they are trying to entrap me. This is irrational. This hysterical outburst evidences the emotional depths to which Jeremiah has been driven. Even worse is to come.

Go Sue City Hall

Jeremiah's growing panic over his situation now comes to a boil; he can no longer content himself with complaints. He feels compelled to take action, any action. He has to *do* something. So he recklessly plunges into an act that, on the face of it, is completely incongruous and downright silly to boot: he will sue God for breach of contract. At his Call he had been pushed into an agreement with the Almighty:

"Now as for you:
You, gird up your loins;
And rise and speak to them everything I command you....

And as for Me:
... I am with you—
[This is] an oracle of the LORD—
To deliver you" [1:17, 18–19].

Jeremiah feels that he has faithfully kept his side of the contract; for by any legal definition this is a simple contractual agreement. He has held nothing back; he has preached everything he has been told to preach. But God has fallen down on His part: Jeremiah has been subjected to intolerable pressures, and God has not come through with the deliverance that He promised.

Now Jeremiah is perfectly aware of the futility of such an action. Even speaking metaphorically, the party against whom he is filing suit is none other than the Judge of All the Earth before Whom the "trial" would have to take place. The Judge would obviously rule in His own favor in any such case, and against Jeremiah. Jeremiah knows full well that what he is proposing can be no more than a futile gesture, but he has reached a point where he can't help but proceed. He admits as much in his opening remark:

Righteous are You, O LORD,
Yet I will dispute with You[43]*;*
Yea, matters of justice would I raise before you.[44]

---

42. Literally, *made to stumble*. This rendition is from NRSV.
43. In the sense of lodge a complaint, enter into legal action against.
44. Literally, *speak with You*. This is legal terminology, the language of a court case: Jeremiah is calling God to account for what he considers a miscarriage of justice.

Why does the way of the wicked prosper?
[Why do] treacherous betrayers[45] live at ease?
You have planted them,
What is more, they strike root;
They grow,
What is more, they bring forth fruit.
You are near in their mouths,
And far from their minds.[46]

Now You, O Lord, *know me,*
You see me and You test my heart towards You.
Pull them out like sheep to the slaughter,
Dedicate them[47] *for the day of killing.*

How long will the land mourn,
And the grass of every field wither,
From the evil of those that dwell therein;
Beast[48] *and bird swept away.*
For they said,
"He[49] *will not see our latter end"* [12:1–4].

This is a rant against God—and it *is* a rant—composed in legal language. It is also a mark of Jeremiah's despair. The cause that he submits to the "Righteous Judge"—and Jeremiah begins by acknowledging that God *is* righteous—is not framed on a personal basis but as a universal issue: it is standard doctrine that the righteous prosper while evildoers are like *chaff that the wind blows away*. The *Book of Psalms* opens with this statement. Yet the reality is often the exact reverse. This is a basic miscarriage of justice. Furthermore, why does God tolerate evildoers in His world? Worse: God not only tolerates their existence, *He* planted them there in the first place, nourished them and permitted them to grow.[50] And to make matters even more obnoxious, they are a pack of posturing hypocrites: they pose as lovers of God, constantly mouthing pious platitudes, while deep down they are pure evil and enemies of God and man. In effect, Jeremiah is accusing God of complicity in a criminal conspiracy: in legal terms, He is an unindicted party who, from the side, aids and abets the evil that flourishes in the world![51] This is strong stuff, mitigated only by the fact that the "case" is being appealed to the very One who is being charged.

Jeremiah now switches gears: from laying charges he turns to appeal. Speaking like a defendant addressing a jury, he launches an emotional entreaty while claiming

---

45. Hebrew, *bogdai baged*. The root *bgd* means "treachery." The conjunction of two forms of the same root intensifies the charge: they are supremely treacherous individuals.

46. Literally, their kidneys: i.e., their motives. See note 59 below.

47. Or *sanctify them*, like sheep set apart for sacrifice.

48. Reading with Syr., Targ. and Vulg. MT reads in the plural *beasts*.

49. LXX and Q both specify that *He* refers to God.

50. Jeremiah seems to have *Psalm* 1 in mind: in *Psalm* 1:3 it is the righteous who are like trees *planted by streams of water, who bring forth fruit in its season*. Yet in the real world, Jeremiah claims, it is the evil-doer *whose leaf does not wither, and that in all that he does he succeeds*.

51. Lundbom I, p. 645.

to be a disinterested party. He asks that *his* motives be probed, and demands that the wicked and the treacherous that have been fattening themselves at the expense of the labor of others be treated as sheep that have been fatted for slaughter. Put them to the use for which they were intended, he demands. He concludes with an emotional description of what their kind of people do to the world in which we all must live—their depredations, born of greed, turning a flourishing and lush world into a desert—and concluding with the implication that God's forbearance is equivalent to complicity. These evil persons act as they do because they think they can get away with it, and they think they can get away with what they do because either God doesn't see where their behavior will lead, or worse, that He doesn't care:

For they said: "He will not see our latter end" [12:4].

The Plot Revealed

How does God, in His answer to Jeremiah, reply to his question of why He tolerates evil men? How does He reply to the charge of non-fulfillment of contractual obligations? How does He respond to the accusation of being complicit in the evil that is being perpetuated in the world? He doesn't. God refuses to relate to any of these issues. In His reply He simply brushes them aside.[52] He tells Jeremiah that if he thinks what he has been going through up to now is bad, he has no idea of what bad is. What he has been through is child's play compared to what awaits him. To the larger issues he has raised, Jeremiah gets no more answer then does Job.

"If with men on foot you have raced and they have wearied you,
How will you vie with the horses?
And [if] in a peaceful land you fall down,[53]
How will you fare in the jungle of the Jordan?"[54] [12:5]

The implication is that what Jeremiah has been going through is no more than a toughening-up process, preparing him for the real tests in times to come; and the times to come begin now. God tells Jeremiah: you thought that at least you could count on your family for support. Forget it; even they have turned against you. Do not trust them. You are completely alone.

"For even your brothers and the house of your father,
Even they have betrayed you,
Even they are in full cry after you!
Do not trust them when they speak fair words to you" [12:6].

---

52. Just as, in Jeremiah's Call, when instead of relating to Jeremiah's demur that he was too young and inexperienced for the job, God simply brushed it aside and gave him his orders. Another example of this type of response is Abraham raising the question of God's justice before the destruction of Sodom—*"Will You sweep away the innocent with the guilty....shall not the Judge of All the Earth not do justly?"* (Genesis 18:23, 27)—and God refuses to relate to the issue.

53. Relying on the meaning of to "fall down (flat on the belly)" for the root *bth* (Lundbom I, p. 647); accepted by RSV, NEB & NIV.

54. In antiquity the Jordan Valley, well watered by the River's periodic overflows, was a dense tropical jungle, the haunt of lions, leopards, wild boar and bears; not to mention lesser carnivora. It was an extremely dangerous region for the lone traveler.

Chapter 14. De Profundis

And now Jeremiah learns that it is not simply his family that is alienated, but the entire town of Anatoth. This is no longer merely an internal family feud; his family has joined hands with their fellow residents of Anatoth in a vicious plot directed against Jeremiah. They are determined to silence him, if needs be even to resort to the expedient of killing him. And to this his family is now willing to lend a hand.[55] This Revelation devastates Jeremiah.

> *So the* LORD *made it known to me, and* [then] *I knew;*
> *Then I saw*[56] *their deeds.*
> *And I was like a docile lamb*[57] *being led to the slaughter.*
> *I didn't know that against me they had plotted plots* [saying]:
> *"Let us put poison in his food,*[58]
> *And cut him off from the land of the living,*
> *That his name be remembered no more."*
>
> *O* LORD *of hosts, Righteous Judge,*
> *Who tests the mind and the heart,*[59]
> *Let me see Your vengeance upon them,*
> *For unto You have I laid bare my cause*[60] [11:18–20].

If we begin by assuming that Jeremiah is not just becoming paranoid but knows what he is talking about in claiming a plot against his life, it becomes incumbent upon us to wonder what could have led to a level of hatred on the part of his neighbors so severe as to bring matters to such a pass. Clarifying this issue will require a brief digression into the recent past of the Kingdom and of the part played by Jeremiah in it.

We have already mentioned in passing the religious reforms undertaken by King Josiah aimed at cleansing his kingdom of pagan idolatry,[61] a major state effort that has become known as the "Josianic Reformation." This involved much more than destroying the idols introduced into the Temple by his grandfather, King Manasseh, and purging the pagan practices associated with them.

One of the primary targets of the Reformation was the local shrines that dotted the countryside. When the Children of Israel had first entered Canaan at the end of the 13th-beginning of the 12th centuries BCE, they found the land swarming with sites of worship: shrines dedicated to the various gods of Canaan. In those areas where the Israelites were to settle the directives were clear:

---

55. John Bright (following C. H. Cornill and A. S. Peake) argues that the two sections—11:18-23 and 12:1-6—have been chronologically inverted, as 12:1-6 provides the necessary grammatical and contextual prelude to which Jeremiah reacts in 11:18-23. I find the argument persuasive, and have rearranged these sections accordingly. As can be seen, in this chronological order they "yield an excellent sense." (Bright, *Jeremiah AB*, p. 89-90)

56. Reading with LXX and OL. MT reads *You made me see*.

57. Or *a trusting lamb*.

58. Reading with LXX and Targ. MT reads *let us destroy the tree with its food* (i.e., its fruit? Its sap?)

59. Literally, *the kidneys and the heart*; in ancient times the kidneys were thought to be the seat of feelings, while the heart was considered the seat of mind and will. J. Bright renders the phrase *Thou assayer of motives and thoughts*. (*Jeremiah AB*, p.84)

60. Hebrew *ribi*. literally "case"; Jeremiah has reverted to the legal language of 12:1.

61. See Chapter 13, notes 13 and 14.

For this is what you are to do to them: you shall tear down their altars, and their sacred pillars you shall smash, and their sacred trees you shall hew down and their graven images you shall burn with fire [Deuteronomy 7:5].[62]

And so the Israelites did to some of the pagan shrines,[63] but not to all. Some they left untouched: these continued to function as places for the remnants of their former Canaanite devotees to worship the gods of old, and for Israelites attracted to this worship.[64] For the most part the Israelites simply took over the existing shrines and rededicated them to the LORD, the God of Israel. But often ancient pagan practices associated with the sites, and even the gods of Canaan themselves, lingered on, resulting in Israelites worshiping the LORD by means of pagan rituals, or even worshiping the LORD their God *along with* the gods of Canaan.[65] The outcome was that the local shrines became foci of pagan practices and breeding places of the corruption permeating Israelite religion.

In the previous century King Hezekiah had made a serious effort to close down the local shrines—the *bamot* or "high places," as they were known. The effort failed; the local opposition proved too strong. Three quarters of a century later King Josiah renewed the effort, making the eradication of the local shrines and the concentration of all public religious worship in the Jerusalem Temple the linchpin of his entire Reform program. And Josiah succeeded in this phase of his Reformation: the local shrines were not simply closed; they were physically demolished and the sites permanently desecrated and rendered unfit for religious practice of any kind.[66] With the concurrent purification of the rites performed in the Temple in Jerusalem, pagan religion was permanently banished from the public square in the Kingdom of Judah.[67]

Where was Jeremiah during these six years of intensive purging of paganism[68] which initiated the full Josianic Reformation, and what part, if any, did he play? There seems to be no question that Jeremiah was an enthusiastic supporter of the Reform program. Moreover, there is reason to believe that he was actually involved in aspects of its promulgation. Shalom Spiegel has contended[69] that during the better part of the first decade of his ministry, Jeremiah was actively engaged in Josiah's program of de-paganization of what had once been the Northern Kingdom of Israel. While

---

62. See also *Exodus* 23:24; 34:13–14; *Numbers* 33:52 etc.

63. For example, Hazor.

64. An example would be the shrine at Ophrah, where—under the patronage of one of the leading families of the town—the worship of Baal continued for almost a century after the Israelite settlement, until the sanctuary was destroyed by Gideon. (*Judges* 6:25–31) See the discussion of this paradigmatic instance in my *Judges and Saviors*, pp. 156–158.

65. This fusion of two different religions (both in belief and in practice) is what we mean when we speak of religious syncretism. See my *Judges and Saviors*, p. 54–55, for a discussion of why the Israelites felt compelled, while retaining the worship of the Lord as their central religious focus, to *also*, "on the side" as it were, pay obeisance to the gods of Canaan.

66. See Chapter 13, note 14 for an example of his draconian methods.

67. As noted in the section entitled The Write-Up in Chapter 13, while the public square had been purged, paganism lived on in the privacy of conscience and in the homes of many. The Reform, while extremely effective was, by its very nature, incapable of fully transforming the religious lives of the people.

68. These were 628–622 BCE, the years prior to the promulgation of the "Book of the Teachings of the Lord" found in the Temple. (*2 Chronicles* 34:14–33)

69. In a lecture delivered at the Jewish Theological Seminary of America in 1954.

Josiah's forces were desecrating and demolishing the paganized shrines of Israel, a parallel program of "outreach" was being pursued: an attempt to wean the former Israelites away from idolatry and to return them as members in good standing alongside their Judean brethren, to the community of the House of Israel. It was in this effort of "returning the strayed sheep to the fold" that Jeremiah—whether as an enthusiastic volunteer or as a part of a government task force recruited for this purpose would be hard to say—was heavily engaged.[70] If indeed so, being a Northerner himself,[71] Jeremiah must have made a particularly effective "missionary."

Now among the many shrines desecrated and destroyed, from Dan to Beersheba—great shrines and local altars alike—we must not forget the shrine around which the life of little Anatoth revolved. As a town of priests, the destruction of its altar would have been especially devastating to its inhabitants. For those Anatothites who were land owners,[72] the closing of the shrine did not significantly alter their economic status. But for those who were landless—probably the great majority—the results were devastating. If serving the shrine was their sole source of livelihood, they were reduced to penury. As a town of priests, its inhabitants could not look on Josiah's Reform as anything other than a curse and an unmitigated disaster. And here was one of their own—Jeremiah—who not only was in favor of the "Reform" but was actually involved in promoting it; is it any wonder that he came to be despised as a traitor to his caste and a betrayer of his neighbors? Add to this his continued preaching—his denunciations of, among others, his fellow townsmen for their multitudinous sins and his warnings that without confession and repentance they were all doomed[73]—and one can begin to understand not only how he turned himself into a pariah in his hometown, but also spawned the hatred that led to the plot whose discovery was to permanently alienate him from his place of birth. But then he could do no other. This was the path to which he had been dedicated by God. He had been warned what would be the consequences of living the life of a prophet; only now does he begin to realize what the warning really meant.

---

70. In this context, Spiegel understands the command, "*Go and proclaim these words to the North and say: 'Return Rebel Israel*—[this is] *an oracle of the Lord—I will not frown on you... etc.*'" (3:12a) as Jeremiah reporting a literal commission from God to go North and preach to the people there. He further considers 3:12b-18 as the sermon Jeremiah preached, probably many times over, to the descendants of what had once been the remnants of the population of Israel.

71. Anatoth was situated in the tribal territory of Benjamin—as the superscription (1:1) to the *Book of Jeremiah* is careful to remind us—and Benjamin was one of the Northern Tribes that together constituted the Kingdom of Israel. Its territory had been seized and annexed by the Kingdom of Judah in the course of the Syro-Ephraimite War (c. 732–731 BCE) and its aftermath. Judah, having elected to become a vassal of Assyria, was rewarded by Assyria's recognition of Benjamin as now a part of Judah, thus sparing her the nightmare of the annihilation of Israel. But in spite of her incorporation into Judah, Benjamin remained in custom and sentiment "Northern" in spirit.

72. Land, which was the primary source of wealth in those times, was entailed. This means that land came into one's ownership only through inheritance, and by law inheritance was purely by primogeniture: the oldest son inherited everything. This left younger sons (and of course their offspring) landless. One could purchase land, but in law the "purchase" was in fact no more than a long-term lease. Ultimately the land legally reverted to its true owner or his heirs. For a fuller explanation of the laws of property and inheritance in ancient Israel see my *Four Biblical Heroines*, pp. 20–24. It would appear that Jeremiah was one of the fortunate inhabitants of Anatoth: he owned land which provided him with a steady stream of income. See Appendix G: Who Was Jeremiah?

73. To get some idea of what had become their regular fare from Jeremiah, see Chapters 2–6 of his Book, which I believe comprises a selection taken from sermons delivered during this period.

Jeremiah began this episode deeply frustrated with the behavior of his God, even furious with Him; so much so that he felt compelled to commence "legal action" against Him, bringing charges of breach of contract and even of "criminal negligence." In the course of these "proceedings" Jeremiah has become aware of the depths of his ignorance about his situation. He has been shocked to discover how precarious his condition is. Abashedly he has withdrawn his previous "case" and substituted a new "case." From "defendant" the Lord has now become the "Righteous Judge" to whom Jeremiah is appealing.

O Lord of hosts, Righteous Judge,
Who tests the mind and the heart,
Let me see Your vengeance upon them,
For unto You have I laid bare my case[74] *[11:20].*

While God disdained to respond to Jeremiah's first appeal and simply acquainted him with some of the facts of life, God's response to his new petition is substantive.

Therefore thus says the Lord concerning the men of Anatoth who seek your life, saying, "Do not prophesy in the name of the Lord lest you die by our hand!" Therefore thus says the Lord of hosts: "Behold, I will punish them: Their young men[75] *shall die by the sword, their sons and daughters by famine; and none of them shall be left, for I shall bring evil upon the men of Anatoth, the year of their punishment" [11:21–23].*

Jeremiah has passed a watershed; he now knows that he has left for ever the *peaceful land* which he thought was his abode. From now on his path must be through the depths of the real world which is best defined as a *jungle* with terrors on every side.

---

74. Hebrew *ribi*, previously rendered as "cause" but literally "case." Jeremiah has reverted to the legal language of 12:1.

75. Reading with LXX and Targ. MT reads *the chosen ones, i.e.,* "the elite warriors," impossible because all inhabitants of Anatoth were priests, and priests did not fight.

Historical Interlude II

Scandals in the Temple

As we have already indicated in Chapter 13 in the main body of the book, not only was Jeremiah swept up by the tornado-like storm generated by the collapse of the Assyrian Empire—as indeed was everyone in the Ancient Near East—but as a prophet of God he felt compelled to respond to it by taking an active role and playing a part in the rush of events. At two critical moments, Jeremiah stepped onto the public stage, in desperate attempts to change the direction that the Kingdom of Judah was taking, thinking the situation to still be fluid enough for disaster to be averted. The purpose of this interlude is to examine briefly these two acts of desperation, as well as some of their consequences.

I

The first took place in 608 BCE, in the aftermath of the disaster of Megiddo.[1] King Josiah is dead. His son Jehoahaz, raised to the throne by the National Assembly,[2] has weakly given in and surrendered to Pharaoh Neco. His reward will be to be dragged off to die in Egypt. In his place Neco has put his puppet Jehoiakim, while also extracting a huge sum of money from the Kingdom as tribute. Judah is now a vassal of Egypt. As one of his first acts on the throne, Jehoiakim proclaims a fast day, calling residents of both Jerusalem and the cities of Judah to the Temple to pray for the welfare of the state and its future. And it is in this crisis that we are told[3] that God commands Jeremiah to go to the Temple, ascend the public pulpit[4] and warn the frantic assembled masses of what is awaiting them:

---

1. See Historical Interlude I. The Road to Megiddo.
2. Jehoahaz (or Shallum, to give him his birth name) will prove to be the last king to legitimately ascend the throne of Judah. His successors will all be puppets, placed on the throne by Imperial Overlords.
3. The author of this account is Baruch, son of Neriah, Jeremiah's secretary, who appears to have been an eyewitness to the events he describes. Baruch happens to be one of the handful of biblical figures of whose activities we possess extra-biblical attestation. Being a professional scribe, he possessed his personal seal with which to stamp bullae (seal impressions in clay). Bullae were used to seal documents written on papyrus or leather. After the document was rolled and secured with string, a glob of soft clay was applied to the knot, and then stamped. The documents themselves are long since gone but the bullae have survived. The Israel National Museum in Jerusalem possesses a display of bullae stamped with the seal of Baruch, son of Neriah, bearing his name.
4. Prophets had the right to address the public in the Temple, and as we shall see, full freedom to speak as the spirit moved them.

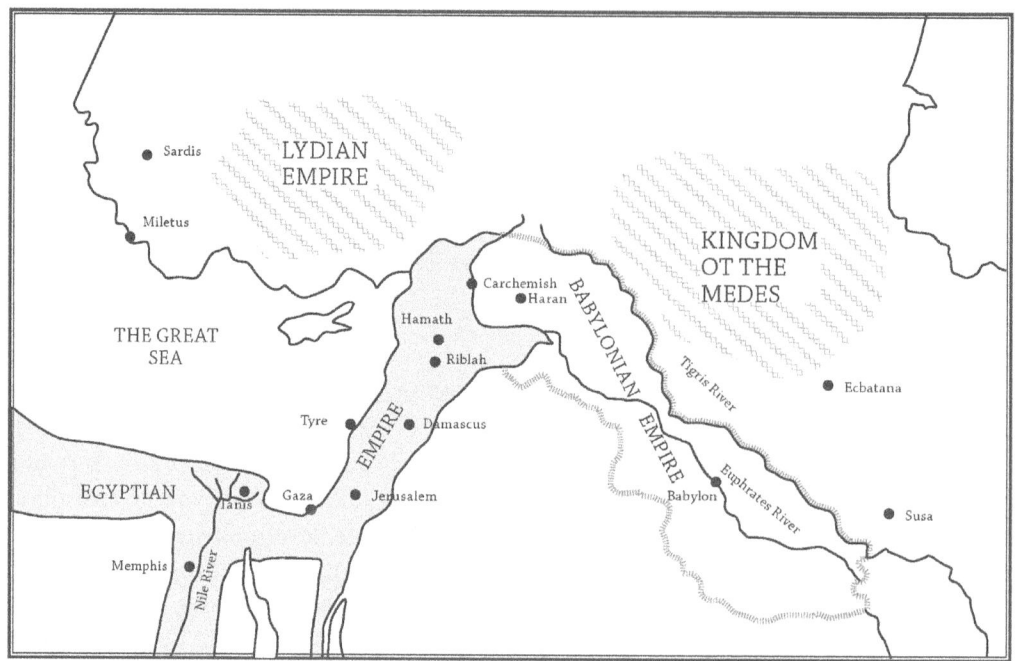

MAP 7

The Division of the Spoils I: The Ancient Near East 608–604 BCE.

And you shall say to them: "Thus says the LORD: *'If you will not listen to Me, to walk in* [accord with] *My teachings*[5] *which I have placed before you, to heed the words of My servants, the prophets, whom I sent to you, often and betimes,*[6] *but you have not heeded; then I will make this House*[7] *like Shiloh, and this city I will make a curse*[8] *to all the nations of the earth!'"* [26:4–6][9]

The packed masses—perhaps because they are in shock at his words—do not interrupt. He is allowed to finish his harangue. Only then does the crowd go wild and, led by the priests and the prophets among them, they turn into a lynch mob. As Baruch tells it:

Now it came to pass when Jeremiah had finished saying <u>everything</u> *that the* LORD

---

5. Or *in My Torah.*

6. Literally, *early and sending.* The idiom had much the same meaning as the English idiom "often and betimes."

7. The Temple.

8. Or perhaps *and* [the name] *of this city I will make* [into] *a curseword...*

9. This is a brief summary. The full speech that was delivered by Jeremiah is to be found in 7:1–15. It is explosive. In it he charges his listeners with being thieves, adulterers, murderers, false witnesses—indeed all the sins and crimes forbidden by the Ten Commandments (with the sole exception of coveting their neighbors' wives and property). He then charges the people with having turned the Temple into a den of robbers. Then Jeremiah tells them to go to Shiloh (the original national shrine that predated the Jerusalem Temple), which was destroyed by the Philistines and has remained an abandoned pile of rubble for almost 550 years. (See Chapter 12, the section entitled Confirmation: The Ax Falls.) Take a good look, Jeremiah tells them. This is what is going to happen to the Temple which you are now in, and in which you trust, and the city Jerusalem as well, if you don't change your ways! (7:1–15)

had commanded him to say to all *the people, that the priests and the prophets and* all *the people seized him, saying, "You shall surely die!*[10] *Why have you prophesied in the name of the* LORD *saying, 'This House shall be like Shiloh, and this city shall be desolate without inhabitants?' And* all *the people were gathered together against Jeremiah in the House of the* LORD*"*[11] [26:8–9].

This would have been the end of Jeremiah had it not been for the proximity of the palace.[12] Hearing the uproar, a number of government officials make haste to investigate and intervene. Imposing their authority, they defuse the situation by taking charge and convening an emergency court on the spot. Mob rule gives way to due process.

The charge laid against Jeremiah by the priests and the prophets is *false prophecy*: i.e., falsely claiming the words one has spoken to be God's words, when they really are one's own. False prophecy is a capital crime.[13] The Royal Officials serve as the judges while the mass of people in the Temple courtyard serve as the jury. Having been duly charged, Jeremiah now rises to speak in his own defense.

And Jeremiah spoke [up] *and said to* all *the officials*[14] *and to* all *the people: "The* LORD *sent me to prophesy to this House and to this city* all *the words that you have heard. And now, amend*[15] *your ways and your doings, and heed the voice of the* LORD *your God, and the* LORD *will change His mind about punishing*[16] *that He has spoken against you. And as for me; I am in your hands. Do to me as seems good and right in your eyes. Only know for certain, that if you put me to death, you will be bringing innocent blood on yourselves, and on this city, and on its inhabitants; for the truth is that the* LORD did *send me to you to speak all these words in your ears"* [26:12–15].

The courage Jeremiah displays in standing his ground, and his obvious sincerity, sway the volatile mob and the judges to take his claim seriously, but not the priests and the prophets among them; their vested interests keep them steadfast in their

---

10. The infinitive absolute construction: i.e., the maximum emphasis possible.

11. The emphasis is that of the original text, as indicated by the drumbeat of the word *kol* (all, everything), here highlighted by underlining. Jeremiah's words have provoked the entire crowd to fury.

12. The Palace Complex (which included the government center) was next door to the Temple Complex. The two were connected by a gate leading from one to the other.

13. *"Any prophet who presumes to speak a word in My name that I did not command him to utter, or who speaks in the name of other gods; that prophet shall die." (Deuteronomy 18:20)*

14. Hebrew *sarim*. Usually translated as "princes," this rendition is archaic. Nowadays the word "prince" refers exclusively to "Royals," i.e., male members of a royal family. But several hundred years ago the term "princes" meant something like "the King's men," i.e., the top men who served the King by running the kingdom: today we would term such men public servants of cabinet rank. This is the meaning of the word *sarim* as it is used here: high ministers of state.

15. Literally, *make good, improve.*

16. Literally, *the Lord will relent from doing evil.* This is almost an exact word for word quote from *Jonah* 4:2—Jonah's radical revision of classic Mosaic theology. (For the reason we follow Lindberg's rendition of this critical phrase, see Chapter 4, notes 7 and 8). The fact that the very next verse (26:14) can be read as an echo of the following verse of *Jonah* (4:3), strengthens the probability that Jeremiah knew the *Book of Jonah* and had Jonah's principled confrontation with God in mind when, with his life hanging by a thread, Jeremiah confronted the mob and stood his ground. For Jonah also, his stand had been to him a matter of life and death. (See the opening section of Chapter 4 entitled Fury Unbounded.)

demand for Jeremiah's execution. But they are overruled. The "jury" and the judges are unanimous:

> *"This man is not deserving of death,*[17] *for in the name of the* LORD *our God has he spoken to us"* [26:16b].

The priests are far from happy with his verdict, as are their allies, the "professional" prophets.[18] They may try to reignite the people to take matters into their own hands and overturn the verdict. Cooler heads now intervene to prevent just such a resurgence of mob action. A number of elders—respected members of the populace—speak up, quoting historic precedent. In the days of King Hezekiah,[19] the prophet Micah prophesied the same thing as did Jeremiah.[20] King Hezekiah did not put Micah to death; rather, he repented and prayed for forgiveness, and as a result God changed His mind about punishing His people. This precedent closes the temple incident and Jeremiah is allowed to depart.

But Baruch does not end his story here. He adds a codicil to his account: the tale of Uriah the prophet who, at roughly the same time, proclaimed essentially the same message as had Jeremiah. This time it was the king who took the matter in hand. Jehoiakim ordered Uriah's arrest. Rather than stand his ground, Uriah fled to Egypt. Jehoiakim had him extradited, returned to Jerusalem and executed.[21] This, Baruch is implying, is the fate that Jeremiah narrowly avoided. Now a marked man, his acquittal not withstanding, he was in deadly danger. Only the support of the House of Shaphan, one of the great noble families of the land, allowed Jeremiah to remain hidden from the public eye and out of danger:

> *But the hand of Ahikam, son of Shaphan, was with Jeremiah, so as not to give him into the hand of the people, to put him to death* [26:24].

II

The year is now 605 BCE. Four tumultuous years have passed since Jeremiah was nearly lynched in the Temple, years of war as two great powers—Egypt and Babylon—struggle and maneuver on the Euphrates for dominance; years of repression and inner turmoil in Judah as Jehoiakim strives to somehow implement two conflicting projects: to accommodate his overlord and master, Pharaoh Neco, and at

---

17. Literally, *There should be no sentence of the death for this man.*

18. These are two classes that are closely allied with the crown, and its current occupant, Jehoiakim, is not one who will tolerate attempts to influence him by mobilizing public opinion. Nor is he especially tolerant of free speech, as was his father, the late Josiah. This is a transition period: the high officials who intervened and imposed their authority are holdovers from the previous administration. Many of them will soon be replaced by men of a different stamp.

19. 715–686 BCE.

20. The elders quote Micah:
"Thus said the Lord of hosts:
  'Zion shall be plowed as a field,
   And Jerusalem shall become heaps of stones;
   And the Temple Mount shall [be like] the forested Heights.'" (Micah 3:12)

21. To add insult to injury, Uriah was not even accorded a proper burial. His corpse was thrown into a pauper's graveyard and left there to molder,

the same time to secure his position as ruler of Judah.[22] During this time Jeremiah has had no choice but to stay out of the public eye. The protection of the great lord, Ahikam, son of Shaphan, has kept him from harm, but at the price of silencing him. Now events are to take a turn that will once again force him onto the public stage.

In distant Babylon, Nebopolassar, Master of Mesopotamia, is ailing. He's turned over the command of the army to his son, Nebuchadrezzar,[23] and the time of inconclusive maneuvering has ended. Nebuchadrezzar goes for the jugular, and shatters the Egyptian army at Carchemish.[24] Following up his victory, he engages the Egyptians at Hamath and again defeats them. The Egyptians fall back into Syria. With the fall of Riblah, headquarters of the Egyptian army and nerve center of Egyptian-controlled Syria, the retreat turns into a rout. Hatti-land now has a new master.[25]

The shock in Judah is immense. The public is in panic; their Kingdom is allied to the losing side, and King Jehoiakim owes his throne to the Egyptian Pharaoh. At long last, after 23 years, Jeremiah's prediction has come true:

From the NORTH *shall the evil break forth upon all the inhabitants of the land* [1:14].

In this moment of crisis, Jeremiah is once again ordered to return to the fray, and in the light cast by the validation of his 23 years of scorned preaching, to repeat his warnings and give one last chance to the people to reconsider and change their direction. Unable to show his face in public, his only course will be to send someone to speak in his place; and so that the words to be proclaimed will be God's own words, they will have to be committed to writing. Summoning Baruch his trusted secretary, he dictates from memory a selection of the most powerful sermons he delivered during the days of King Josiah, prefaces them with an account of his Call (in order to authenticate the origin of his warnings),[26] and then waits for the opportune moment to act.

As expected, even as in the wake of the crisis of Megiddo Jehoiakim had proclaimed a fast, so in the wake of Carchemish he does the same. Baruch is sent to read the scroll he has written to the distraught crowds filling the Temple courtyards.[27]

---

22. The basic reality was that Jehoiakim's position as King of Judah was illegitimate. The Assembly had chosen Jehoahaz to be king. Jehoiakim had been put on the throne by a foreign tyrant and was that ruler's puppet. Placating his master, Neco, meant among other things imposing crippling taxation upon all classes of the public, which stirred up unrest and opposition. This led to the need to suppress the unrest with force, which in turn only engendered further unrest. Jehoiakim's character—the opposite of that of his charismatic and highly popular father, and probably the reason why the National Assembly had passed him over in favor of his younger half-brother in the first place—only complicated an already impossible situation.

23. See Historical Interlude I, note 21, for the name *Nubuchadrezzar*.

24. See MAP 6.

25. "Hatti-land" is the name given by the Babylonians to what we call Syria. There now ensues a pause in the rush of events. The ailing warlord of Babylon, Nebopolassar, dies. His son rushes back home to take charge and to be proclaimed King. Not long after he is back in Hatti-land to mop up.

26. See the section entitled The Write-Up in Chapter 13.

27. Baruch's account of what took place contains clear indications of collusion between Jeremiah and his protectors, the House of Shaphan. Unlike Jeremiah, not being a prophet Baruch has no right to use the public pulpit. How then is he to address the people? The answer is supplied by Gemariah, the brother of Ahikam, Jeremiah's protector: he allows Baruch the use of his office—possibly the Temple archive which is in his charge—which has a window overlooking the main Temple courtyard. It is from this window that Baruch will read out Jeremiah's words to the assembled throng gathered below. It would seem that a major political faction is providing Jeremiah with a platform, attempting to use him to help effect a change in state policy. Gemariah, of course, will not be present at the reading, and will have "no idea at all" as to how Baruch ever got access to his office.

Baruch succeeds in his mission, managing to read out the entire scroll without serious interruption. Now hovering in the background during the reading is one Micaiah,[28] and as soon as the reading is concluded he immediately leaves to report. Exiting the Temple Compound and entering the Palace, he proceeds to the office of the Scribe.[29] He finds the entire Cabinet in session,[30] and he reports to them what it was that was read out to the public. The Cabinet is shocked; this is far more than they had expected. They summon Baruch to the Cabinet room and have him read out to them what he had just read to the crowd in the Temple courtyard.[31]

> *Now it came to pass, when they heard all the words, they turned in fear one to the other, and they said to Baruch, "We have no choice but[32] to tell the king all these words." And they questioned Baruch, asking, "Please tell us, did he dictate all these words to you?"[33] And Baruch answered them: "He dictated them.[34] He proclaimed all these words to me, and I wrote them in the scroll with ink." And the Officials said to Baruch, "Go, hide yourself and Jeremiah [as well]; let man know where you are!"[35] [36:16–19]*

The members of the Cabinet are right to be terrified. The words they have just heard are incendiary. Worse, they are being reminded that the avalanche bearing down on them from the North is exactly what Jeremiah has been predicting for the last 23 years: and now it is here. Will his prediction of the destruction of Jerusalem also be vindicated? And how will the king react? This they will soon know, for they cannot delay bringing the scroll to his attention.

The entire Cabinet retires to the Palace proper. They find the king in his winter quarters—it is December—warming himself by the fire in a brazier.[36] Being informed of what has taken place, the king sends for the scroll. If the highest Officials in the land—or at least most of them—see the scroll as the word of God proclaiming the doom that is descending upon them, the king sees the scroll primarily as a threat to his autocratic rule. Upon observing their panicked reactions, he realizes that he will have to reassert his authority over these, in his eyes, spineless fools that he has governing his kingdom. He has the scroll read aloud to him. As the reader concludes

---

28. Micaiah was the son of Gemariah (see previous note). It was probably he who let Baruch into the office in the first place. It was part of his duties to observe what took place and to report back to his father and his colleagues.

29. The Scribe was the Chief Officer of the Judean Cabinet, with functions roughly similar to those of the Secretary of State in the U.S. government.

30. The text (36:12) gives a partial list of the Cabinet officials present; possibly those directly involved in the willful promotion of Jeremiah's provocation.

31. It is important to note the attitude of these High Officers of State to Baruch. They are unfailingly polite and respectful, despite the vast gap in social status between themselves and Baruch.

32. Literally, *telling we will tell*; the infinitive absolute.

33. Literally, *"How did you write all these words? Were they* [directly] *from his mouth?"*

34. Literally, *"From his mouth."*

35. Up to this point the House of Shaphan (Ahikam, Gemariah etc.) and perhaps other members of their faction have been protecting Jeremiah, but now he and Baruch have become serious liabilities. His protectors are disengaging themselves. They don't want to know them. Go to ground, they tell Baruch. Even we must not know where you are. We must be in the position of being able to take an oath that we don't know where you are. Baruch and Jeremiah have become too hot to handle.

36. A pan for holding burning coals, usually resting on a stand at elbow height.

three or four columns, the king, using a penknife, cuts off the portion that has been read and throws it into the fire! His Ministers are horrified. These are the words of God. They beg him not to burn the scroll, but he scorns their pleas. The reading, the cutting and the burning proceed until the entire scroll has been read and reduced to ashes. And with that the incident is closed, except for the matter of the author and his accomplice. Jehoiakim delegates three officials to supervise a manhunt; they are to seize Baruch the scribe and Jeremiah the prophet.

But the Lord *hid them* [36:26].

That is, it was a miracle that they managed to escape detection.

Lundbom is of the opinion that "the likelihood here is that Jeremiah and Baruch remained in hiding during the rest of Jehoiakim's reign."[37] Considering the vindictive nature of this king, I concur. And during these seven long and dreary years Jeremiah occupies himself with re-dictating the contents of the scroll that Jehoiakim had burnt,[38] and then dredging up from memory many of his other proclamations, orations and meditations, and dictating them to Baruch.

So Jeremiah took another [blank] *scroll and gave it to Baruch, son of Neriah, the scribe. And he wrote upon it from Jeremiah's dictation*[39] *all the words of the scroll that Jehoiakim, King of Judah, had burned in the fire. And besides, many words like these were added to them*[40] [36:32].

And from this secret labor was born the first draft of what was to eventually become the *Book of Jeremiah*.

---

37. Lundbom, *Jeremiah II*, p. 603.
38. Probably what we now know as *Jeremiah* 1–6.
39. See notes 33 and 34 above.
40. Probably much if not all of what is currently contained in *Jeremiah* 7:1–25:13.

Chapter 15

The Long Night

I wake and feel the fell of dark, not day.
What hours, O what black hours we have spent
This night!

—Gerard Manley Hopkins

We have remarked that the so-called "Confessions of Jeremiah"—the subject of this inquiry—are to be found scattered in the midst of other material in Chapters 11–20 in the *Book of Jeremiah*. In our examination of several of these, the reader may have noticed that we have not been following the order in which they appear in the text: we began with a selection from Chapter 17 and followed this with one from Chapter 18, only to flip backwards and continue with two short sections from Chapters 11 and 12.[1] In this chapter we will commence with Chapter 20, only to end in Chapter 15. From this treatment of the material it should be evident that our arrangement of these "Confessions" is based on the assumption that their placement in the *Book of Jeremiah*, while not necessarily random, is certainly *not* chronologically determined, but rather is based on some other criterion. For expository purposes we have rearranged the "Confessions" into what seems to us to be a developmental sequence. By the nature of things, if our sense of the stages through which Jeremiah was traversing has any validity, this rearrangement should be roughly chronological as well: the "Confessions" analyzed in our last chapter being presumed to have been uttered during the reign of Josiah—that is, before 609 BCE—while the dating of the material in this chapter, though later, is far less clear. These selections seem to be reflections of developments that followed those that provoked Jeremiah's outbursts discussed in the previous chapter, but possibly the first of them also may have taken place while Josiah was still on the throne, or more likely during the first years of the reign of Jehoiakim. What seems fairly clear is that we can date the first of the "Confessions" that are the subject of this chapter as being prior to 604 BCE. After the reading of Jeremiah's scroll in the Temple[2] he was forced out of public life and into hiding.

This having been said, we turn to the first of Jeremiah's revelations of his inner torment that will be the focus of this chapter. We begin by examining the events that provide its context.

---

1. And indeed we reversed the order of these two sections, dealing with 12:1–6 *before* 11:18–23. See Chapter 14, note 55.
2. See Historical Interlude II. Scandals in the Temple.

Meditations on Serving Time

Prologue: The Tophet

We are told that sometime in the last decade of the 7th century BCE, Jeremiah was commanded by God to assemble a group consisting of respected leading citizens and senior priests, and carrying a ceramic bottle he had purchased for the occasion, to lead them down into the Valley of the Son of Hinnom[3] to the site where the notorious Tophet[4] had once stood.[5] This had been a *bamah* or High Place devoted to the worship of the Moloch,[6] which involved the sacrifice of children.[7] As part of his eradication of the idolatrous shrines, Josiah had demolished the Tophet and at present the site stood desolate, the foundations of what had been a prominent shrine now clogged with weeds and rubbish. Into the ears of his selected audience Jeremiah pours a scathing denunciation of the horrors that had once taken place at this site at the hands of inhabitants of Jerusalem and of the Kingdom of Judah. The price of the innocent blood spilled here has yet to be paid, and paid it will be: "Take a good look," Jeremiah cries. "This is what Jerusalem will look like when a Just God exacts the retribution due for what has been done here, and what is continuing to be done in Jerusalem."

And then Jeremiah resorts to magic. He raises the bottle that he has brought with him and smashes it to smithereens in front of them, saying:

"Thus says the LORD *of hosts, 'Thus shall I break this people and this city, just as one breaks a potter's vessel so that it cannot be mended [and in the Tophet they will bury for lack of space to bury].*[8] *Thus shall I do to this place*[9]*—*[this is] *an oracle of the* LORD*—and to its inhabitants, making this city like Tophet. And the houses of*

---

3. A valley running south and west of Jerusalem.

4. The term "Tophet," always used as a proper noun, may be Aramaic, or a cognate to Aramaic, meaning "oven" or "fireplace." On the other hand, *toph* in Hebrew is a small hand-held drum, and hence Tophet might mean "the Place of Drumming."

5. The majority of scholars take the position that upon the death of Josiah the *bamot* or High Places were rebuilt by Josiah's successors, and that the Canaanite cults—including the Tophet—resumed their former activities. However no evidence can be adduced by the scholars to support this thesis. Rather they are reduced to asserting that their claim is self-evident, as for example, "although neither Kings nor Chronicles mentions a rebuilding of the high places by Jehoiakim or Zedekiah… a rebuilding of the Tophet *must have taken place* during the reign of Jehoiakim." (Lundbom I, p. 495, emphasis added) I find Y. Kaufmann's counter arguments—based on the evidence rather than on mere assertions of certainty—persuasive: that the High Places were never rebuilt and that idolatrous public worship was reduced to privately performed rites in honor of the Queen of Heaven and private roof offerings (incense and libations to the astral bodies). (*Religion of Israel*, p. 406–408, and especially note 2) We have evidence that the High Places were demolished; we have none that they were ever rebuilt. Assertions that they "must have been" are not sufficient to persuade.

6. *Moloch*, or more properly *Molek*, may possibly be a title; the proper name of the deity was Melkart.

7. This practice is described by George Foot Moore as follows:
The idol itself had the head of a calf upon a human body; its arms were extended, with the hands open like those of a man who was about to receive something from another. The image was hollow—we must suppose of metal—and was heated by a fire from within til the hands were glowing. The priests took the child from his father and laid it in the hands of Moloch, where it was burned to death; the priests meanwhile violently beating drums that the cries of the victim might not be heard… ("The Image of Moloch," *JBL* 16: 161–162).

8. This phrase is really irrelevant here, and may be a gloss copied from 7:32. LXX omits this phrase.

9. Most scholars agree that the reference here is to Jerusalem.

Jerusalem, and the houses of the Kings of Judah will be like the place of the Tophet: unclean; even all the houses upon whose roofs they made offerings to all the host of heaven,[10] *and poured out libations to other gods'"* [19:11–13].

This magic ritual—smashing a ceramic vessel inscribed with the name of a victim (accompanied by the most solemn of curses) to ensure his destruction—had been practiced in Egypt and the Ancient Near East for millennia, and was known to everyone. Jeremiah is using a universally believed superstition to drive home his message of doom. Jeremiah must have been desperate with the sense of looming disaster that, in order to get his point across, he resorts to what amounts to a gesture rooted in pagan religious practice.

His audience is struck dumb with shock. To their minds, with this act Jeremiah, as an agent of God, has irrevocably set into motion the process that will lead to the destruction of Jerusalem. This is hardly what they were expecting when they set out on their "guided tour" of "ancient idolatrous ruins." But this is not the end of the story.

Then Jeremiah came from the Tophet where the LORD *had sent him to prophesy, and he stood in the courtyard of the House of the* LORD *and said to all the people:*

"Thus says the LORD *of hosts, the God of Israel: 'Behold, I am bringing upon this city—and upon all her cities*[11]*—all the evil that I promised against her, for they have stiffened their necks, refusing to hear My words'"* [19:14–15].

Unlike the report of Jeremiah's Call, which was written by the prophet himself,[12] this third-party account of Jeremiah's visit to the Tophet, his follow-up in the Temple and its traumatic aftermath was written by his secretary and companion—Baruch, son of Neriah—who was probably an eyewitness to the events described. Taking the case of Jeremiah's harangue of 608 in the Temple as precedent,[13] I assume that the speech recorded in 19:1–9 and 11–13 was delivered in full in the Temple as well as at the Tophet, and that 19:15 is Baruch's one sentence summary of it.[14] The worshipers gathered in the Temple courts, like Jeremiah's picked audience at the Tophet, are reduced to a state of shock. Before they can recover and react, a new participant interjects himself into the drama.

Law and Order

Now Pashhur, the son of Immer the priest, who was the chief security officer in the House of the LORD,[15] *heard Jeremiah prophesy these words. And Pashhur struck*

---

10. I.e., the sun, the moon and the stars.

11. I.e., on all the cities of Judah, "Judah" being understood.

12. See Chapter 13.

13. Of this incident we have two accounts: we have the text of the speech itself that Jeremiah delivered (7:1–15) and Baruch's third-person description of the event and its consequences (*Jeremiah* 26). In his report, Baruch does not quote Jeremiah's entire speech but simply gives a thumbnail summary of it.

14. Lacking a specific report of a repetition of the bottle-shattering, I assume that this action was not repeated in the Temple; to perform this act in the Temple would really be too much.

15. Hebrew *pakid nagid*. He was one of the highest ranking officers in the Temple, with much the same responsibilities as the chief security officer of a large corporation holds today, but as the Temple precincts were autonomous, he had police and judicial powers as well within its walls.

Jeremiah the prophet! And he put him in the stocks[16] that were in the Upper Benjamin Gate of the LORD's *House[17]* [20:1–2].

This treatment is brutal, and unusual. In fact it is so unusual that the incident demands our close attention. Baruch is so shocked by the assault on Jeremiah's person that he momentarily loses his normal tight control over his language: he lets a superfluous word escape him. *And Pashhur struck Jeremiah* is all he needed to say; by adding the words *the prophet*,[18] Baruch is in effect exclaiming: but he is a *prophet*, how could he dare? Just as a prophet had complete freedom of speech, the person of a prophet was sacrosanct. Striking a prophet was equivalent to striking the Word of God! And then, to add insult to injury, Pashhur puts Jeremiah in the stocks. Given the norms of ancient Israel, this behavior is shocking beyond belief.

Normally this incident is treated by commentators as though Pashhur was no more than a nasty brute, but the matter is not that simple. Up to now we have been looking at things from Jeremiah's point of view. Jeremiah is desperately trying to arouse a groundswell of public opinion and force the government to change the direction of its policy; he is convinced that the direction the government is taking will inevitably lead to what now gets called a train wreck. But let us look at the situation in the Temple through Pashhur's eyes.

Pashhur happens to be on the spot while Jeremiah is speaking. He has heard Jeremiah's incendiary words, words that are likely to provoke a riot.[19] Pashhur intervenes because he has to; he is the chief security officer of the Temple. Here before him is an individual trying to provoke a riot. It is his duty to preserve order. Realistically, he has two options: he can treat this person as a prophet or as a lunatic.[20] If he is a prophet, then the only way to shut him up is to arrest him and charge him with false prophecy; a capital crime.[21] If a lunatic, one would punish him for disturbing the peace and then turn him loose.[22] Pashhur decides to let Jeremiah down easy: he treats him as a madman and strikes him, and as lightning does not strike Pashhur dead, he has made his point; with one bold action he has defused the situation—these are not Divine Threats, these are simply the ravings of an insane person—and so he calms the crowd. Then he follows normal procedure for such cases and puts Jeremiah in the stocks overnight.[23]

---

16. Hebrew *hamahpechet*, from the root *hpch*, to turn, to distort; i.e., a contraption that holds the body in a twisted or distorted—and hence painful—position, usually on public display where the prisoner could be reviled and pelted with dirt and garbage, the purpose being public humiliation.

17. I.e., the gate on the north side of the Temple Compound.

18. In Hebrew, one word.

19. We remember, in 608, Jeremiah's harangue which turned the crowd of worshipers in the temple into a lynch mob. See Historical Interlude II. Scandals in the Temple, Section I.

20. The behavioral line between prophets and lunatics could at times be very thin. Madmen who believed themselves to be prophets were not uncommon. Of course, Pashhur knows exactly who he is dealing with; Jeremiah is not exactly a nobody.

21. *Deuteronomy* 18:20. This was the route taken in 608 BCE, and it didn't work. Jeremiah was adjudged a true prophet and was acquitted.

22. "... *In order that there be officers in the House of the Lord to* [deal with] *any lunatic that 'prophesies,' to put him in the stocks...*" (*Jeremiah* 29:26)

23. In this too Pashhur is treating Jeremiah with a minimum of harshness. Crowds can be very cruel: the vicious harassment to which a prisoner in the stocks is usually subjected—both physical and mental—can break the subject emotionally. The Temple gates are closed at sundown, and the mob of spectators [*continued*]

But Jeremiah is not a lunatic, and Pashhur knows this. From Jeremiah's point of view, Pashhur's treatment of him is a deadly insult to both the prophetic calling and to the Word of God. And while Jeremiah probably appreciates the reasons for Pashhur's behavior—Jeremiah is not stupid—he has no choice but to respond with fury to the way Pashhur is insulting the person of a true prophet of the LORD, and dragging God's Word in the mud. Striking a prophet is an insult to the God Who sent him.

> *Now it came to pass on the morrow that Pashhur released Jeremiah from the stocks, and Jeremiah said to him: "The* LORD *has not named you Pashhur but rather 'Terror on every side!'*[24] *For thus says the* LORD: *'Behold, I will make you a terror to yourself, and to all those who love you; for your eyes shall see them fall by the sword of their enemies. And I will give all Judah into the hand of the king of Babylon, and he will carry them captive to Babylon and* strike *them down with the sword'"* [20:3-4].

You *struck* me, Pashhur. For this God will *strike* down with a sword all your loved ones—your dearest friends and companions—and as the crowd in the Temple watched me being *struck*, so will you be forced to watch your loved ones being *struck* down.

But Jeremiah does not stop here with this "appropriate punishment" for striking a prophet. In a rush he returns to his denunciation of Jerusalem, and for the first time in the Book he reveals, at long last, the identity of the "Foe from the NORTH": Babylon.[25]

> *"And I shall give all the wealth of this city, and all its assets and all its treasured possessions—even all the treasures of the Kings of Judah—I will give into the hand of their enemies and they shall plunder them, and take them and bring them to Babylon. And as for you, Pashhur, and your entire household, you will go captive; to Babylon will you come, and* there *shall you die and* there *shall you be buried—you and all your loved ones—whom you have led astray"*[26] [20:5-6].

---

is shut out. Jeremiah was only confined overnight; the next morning he was released. All things considered, Pashhur was being surprisingly easy on a fellow priest.

24. Hebrew *magor-misabib*. This is a phrase Jeremiah has used on more than one occasion (6:25; 46:5; 49:29 and most especially in 20:10). John Bright has this to say about the term: "Apparently Jeremiah had used the expression so often that it was becoming a nickname. One can imagine one man in the crowd nudging another as Jeremiah passed, and whispering; 'There goes old Magor-misabib.'" (*Jeremiah AB*, p.132–133) Jeremiah is here bestowing a new name upon Pashhur, transferring the epithet by which he has become known onto his nemesis. From now on you will be known, as I have been, as *Mr. Magor-misabib*, except that in my case it was meant to be funny, but in your case it will become tragic.

25. Did Jeremiah really intend to let the cat out of the bag at this point? Jeremiah may have come to the conclusion that in the struggle for the remnants of the Assyrian Empire it is Babylon that would emerge triumphant, but I suspect that he intended to wait until the conclusion was incontrovertible. This would have to await the outcome of the battle of Carchemish in 605 BCE. My feeling is that under the pressure of what he had undergone and the rush of his denunciation, "Babylon" just slipped out. (The formal transition between "The Foe from the North" and "Babylon" will not take place until 25:9.)

26. Literally, *to whom you have prophesied by The Lie (bashaker)*. In 3:23 the term, also with the definite article, is being used as a euphemism for Baal, and so should be taken here; hence it is rendered as "The Lie." It should also be taken in the sense of "The Big Lie," the opposite of the truth as revealed by God. As the word *to prophesy* is in the *piel* form, which is causative, this means that Jeremiah is not claiming that Pashhur is a prophet but rather that he is promoting the message of the false prophets—i.e., perhaps those whom Jeremiah denounces as *healing the hurt of My people lightly, saying, "peace, peace" when there is no peace* (6:14; 8:11)—hence our rendition of *whom you have led astray*.

In the Chill of the Night

Having rhetorically consigned Pashhur to what a practicing priest would have considered an abominable fate—to be driven from the Holy Temple into exile and from life in the Holy Land to die and be buried in "unclean soil"—Jeremiah is thrown out of the Temple and forbidden further entry to its premises.[27] With this the episode should be concluded, but it is not. We have passed over far too quickly that long chill night when for seemingly endless hours a lone figure, imprisoned in the stocks, has been left to come to terms with his condition and with his God. He has been left with no distractions and plenty of time to think, to order his thoughts and to try to sum up where his more than two decades as a prophet of the Lord has brought him. And to do this he goes back to the beginning: to his Call. The result of that dark night will be the meditation which now will follow, consisting of three separate poems, by dawn arranged—or rearranged—into a composition of stirring pathos and power.

We must picture Jeremiah, alone, locked into the stocks and chilled to the bone. The Temple court is empty, the nights in Jerusalem are cold even in the summer, and unless there is a moon it is pitch-dark. It will be a long night and he has much to ponder, as well as much steam to let off. Emotionally, Jeremiah has reached the end of his tether. As in the past, he begins to complain about his sorry lot, but never has he used language such as this to his God.

> *You have seduced me, O* Lord, *and I was seduced;*
> *You raped me and overcame me!*
> *I have become a laughingstock all the day;*
> *Everyone makes fun of me.*
> *For whenever I speak, I am mocked*[28]*;*
> *I cry, "Violence and devastation!"*
> *Because the word of the* Lord *has become for me*
> *Reproach and ridicule all the day long* [20:7–8].

Cycling back to his beginnings, he adopts the persona of a victim. He pictures himself as a young and naïve person, seduced by an older and experienced predator. Worse, when push came to shove and he tried to demur, the Lord fell back on superior strength, overcame all resistance and had His way with him. The language is overtly sexual.[29] This is not, and has never been, a consensual relationship, Jeremiah is saying. You *forced* me to become Your prophet against my will. You are the cause of my having become the butt of constant humor. I am predictably laughable. You *force me* to continually repeat Your message, and since they know in advance what I am going to say they mock me with it and hold me in contempt.

It is this that has driven Jeremiah to rebellion. Jeremiah's primary mandate was to proclaim everything that God commanded him,[30] and he has done so. But now

---

27. This may have been the reason Jeremiah could not go to the Temple in 604 BCE. See 36:5.
28. Reading with LXX. MT reads *I cry out*.
29. *Pate* in the *piel* form means "to seduce," (cf. *Exodus* 22:15), while the root *hzk* in the *kal* form means "to rape" (cf. *Deuteronomy* 22:25). As previously, Jeremiah is falling back on legal terminology. See Chapter 14, notes 44 and 60.
30. *"All that I command you you shall speak."* (1:7)

Jeremiah admits that he has crossed the line; he has made the decision to no more speak the word of the Lord—enough is enough—only to discover that in this too he has no choice. The compulsion to speak overcomes him; he is powerless to resist it.

> *And I said: "I will not mention Him,*
> *And I will not speak any longer in His name,"*
> *And then there is in my heart as it were a burning fire,*
> *Shut up in my bones,*
> *I weary myself to hold it in*
> *But cannot.*
>
> *For I have heard the whispering in the crowd*[31]*:*
> *"'Terror on every side';*[32] *denounce, we will denounce him!"*
> *All my close friends are waiting for me to stumble:*
> *"Perhaps we can entrap*[33] *him and so prevail against him,*
> *And take our revenge on him"* [20:9–10].

He can't escape his fate. His warning has become a slogan by which he is mocked. He is taunted by the phrase "Terror on every side"—a watchword he has adopted from the Psalms[34]—which has become his nickname. He has managed to alienate his closest friends and acquaintances. He can no longer trust them. Even when they encourage him he more than suspects—he is convinced—that they are trying to entrap him; to entice him into language that can be portrayed as seditious, and so present him to the authorities as a traitor to the state. Jeremiah has reached the stage where he sees enemies everywhere. This is pure paranoia, but that doesn't mean that he is delusional. It may very well be true that almost everyone has turned against him. The incontrovertible fact is that, as of this moment, Jeremiah feels completely friendless, threatened and abandoned. It is on this note that he ends part one of his tripartite meditation.

But if this is so, then how do we explain the second composition: a paean of faith in praise of the Lord his God? It is more than a violent mood swing, a reaction to the dark depression into which he has been precipitated. It is the unchallengeable knowledge that as long as he does not betray his God—he has, after all, shockingly discovered that even if he wants to, he is incapable of actually doing it—he will never be alone.

> [However] *the* Lord *is with me as an awe-inspiring warrior,*
> *Therefore my pursuers shall stumble,*
> *And they shall not prevail.*
>
> *They are greatly ashamed*
> *Because they have not succeeded;*
> *An eternal disgrace which can never be forgotten.*

---

31. So Bright and Lundbom: *rabim* has as one of its meanings "a crowd," cf. *Exodus* 23:2.
32. The phrase is a direct quote from *Psalm* 31:14.
33. Hebrew *yephute*, the same word previously rendered as "seduce." See note 29 above.
34. See note 32 above. This is not the first time we have come into contact with the influence of this remarkable *Psalm*. See the discussion of *Jonah* 2:9, in Chapter 2 above.

O LORD of hosts, Who tests the righteous,
Who sees the emotions and the minds [of men],[35]
Let me see Your vengeance upon them;
For to You have I committed my cause.[36]

Sing unto the LORD;
Praise the LORD;
For He has rescued the soul of the needy
From the hand of evildoers! [20:11–13]

 It has been suggested that this last stanza was recited by Jeremiah—or more likely sung—upon his release from the stocks in the morning. If so, Pashhur knew exactly who Jeremiah meant. Before the world Jeremiah kept up a brave front, keeping his agony and despair well hidden, only to be committed to writing years later, and to become available to public scrutiny long after that. At the time, however, the third poem in the composition records a relapse into the mood of a soul desolated by the ill-usage of the world; a lament that he ever had to have been born. If we hold to the theory that Jeremiah was subject to violent mood swings, then we can postulate that having commenced in dark depression, and that the pendulum having swung to a manic condition of joy and relief at God's perceived salvation, it should now swing back to redeposit our hero where he started: composing a bitter lament over the fate to which he has been consigned.

 But perhaps we are reading too much into what is, after all, a literary composition. We must never lose sight of the fact that Jeremiah is an accomplished poet, and the demands of his artistic spirit impose their own conditions. The composition that now lies before us—and we must never forget that it is a composition—is a composite; a compromise between the outpourings of his tormented soul and the conventions of biblical poetry to which his art is beholden. We must not assume that the order in which we currently find the three poems is the order in which they were composed. Judging by the content alone, poem number three (20:14–18) would seem to be a natural continuation of poem number one (20:7–10). We remember that after confessing to having decided to rebel and cease proclaiming the word of God, he discovered that the compulsion to speak would not be denied and that he had no choice but to continue preaching. He complains of being trapped in a world bereft of friends, a world full of enemies who both mock him and ceaselessly plot against him and attempt to entrap him. He ends on a despairing note:

All my close friends are waiting for me to stumble:

We can appreciate the irony of his referring to them as his "close friends"—

and then he quotes them:

---

35. Literally, *the kidneys and the heart*. Just as the heart was considered the seat of the mind and the will, the kidneys were thought of as the seat of the emotions. We have encountered these metaphors previously; see Chapter 14, note 59.

36. Literally, *revealed my case*; Again Jeremiah has reverted to legal language. See Chapter 14, notes 60 and 43 above.

"*Perhaps we can entrap him and so prevail against him,*
And take our revenge on him" [20:10].

Now let us see how poem number three (20:14–18) links up with these thoughts.[37]

Accursed be the day on which I was born;
The day on which my mother bore me,
Let it not be blessed.

Cursed be the man who brought glad tidings to my father, saying:
"A male child is born to you,"
Making him marvelously happy.[38]

May that man be like the cities
Which the LORD *overturned without pity*[39]*;*
May he hear a cry in the morning,
And an alarm at the time of midday.

— — — [40]

Because He[41] *did not kill me in*[42] *the womb;*
So that my mother would have been my grave,
And her womb pregnant forever.

Why is it that from the womb I came forth
To see hard labor and sorrow,
And [for] my days to end[43] *in shame?* [20:14–18]

I would suggest the possibility that it was from this nadir that Jeremiah rebounded, concluding that dreadful night with the courage to compose 20:11–13.

But then why, when he came to put into written form the poems that he had mentally composed over that long night, did he alter their natural order? To us it

---

37. In Chapter 13, in the section entitled The Self-Image of a Prophet, we discussed Jeremiah's use of terminology and imagery borrowed from *Psalm* 22:10–11 in his description of his Call, and suggested that one reason for drawing on the imagery of this particular *Psalm* might be that Jeremiah saw in the psalmist's description of his martyrdom a prototype with which he could identify. The psalmist was speaking, so Jeremiah felt, to his own situation. This possibility is strengthened by Jeremiah's return to the language of *Psalm* 22 in our present "Confession." Besides his two references to his residence in, and emergence from the *womb* (cf. 1:4), our present poem both opens and draws to its close with references to his *mother* (20:14 and 20:17), and in what we deem to be Jeremiah's final "Confession" he again refers to his *mother* (see below 15:10). Once again we are drawn to Psalm 22:10–11 for the source of this imagery. (See Chapter 13, notes 61 and 62 with related text, where these verses are quoted.) Holladay comments: "These references to birth and mother are unparalleled in the extant pre–Jeremianic prophetic literature." ("Background," p. 156) Holladay considers both these "Confessions" to "question the validity of his [Jeremiah's] call." (*Ibid.*, p. 157) When one adds to this the fact that the language of *Jeremiah* 20:7 seems also to have been lifted directly from Psalm 22:8, the case for Jeremiah's identifying his agony with that of the psalmist seems compelling. For a probable view of how Jeremiah saw himself at this time in his life, see Appendix H for the first 22 verses of Psalm 22.

38. Hebrew *sameah simhahu*; the infinitive absolute, turning the announcement into a harbinger of extreme joy.

39. I.e., Sodom and Gomorrah.

40. Both the truncated meter and defective contents argue that a line here is missing.

41. The subject of this verse is indubitably God; hence the capitalization of *He*.

42. Reading with LXX and Syr.; MT reads *from*.

43. Hebrew *vayichlu*, "they end," "they conclude"; cf. *Psalm* 31:11 and *Psalm* 102:4 for this use. Also note *Genesis* 2:1.

would seem that the poems arranged in the order of their composition would authentically mirror the stages through which his soul had moved, culminating in a revival of faith with the dawn. But to Jeremiah, the poetic conventions of his time argued differently. His priorities differed from ours. What was important about that endless night was not the despair into which he had been plunged but the triumph of the spirit that enabled him to emerge unbroken, able to look Pashhur directly in the eye, and find within himself the courage to continue functioning as a messenger of God. It was this that supremely merited emphasizing. The way one highlighted something in those days was to place it at center stage; that is, if one was composing some literary work, one would place it precisely in the center of the composition. For example, if one wants to know what the author of Psalm 23 considered the key to his spiritual gem, all one has to do is to count the words—in the original Hebrew of course—starting both forward from the beginning and backward from the end. Exactly in the middle of the Psalm, by word count, we find the phrase *For You are with me*.[44] This, the psalmist is telling us by its very construction, is what the Psalm is all about, and consequently what should be central in one's life.

Another example of this biblical literary technique is to be found in the *Book of Jonah*. In the second chapter of our book we deal in detail with Jonah's prayer, after he has been swallowed by a giant fish. Our treatment does not include a word count, but were it to do so we would discover that *Jonah*, Chapter 2, consists of 112 words, and at the midpoint of the chapter we find the couplet:

Nevertheless I will continue to look
Toward Your Holy Temple [Jonah 2:5b].

the declaration of faith born from despair, which is the pivot around which the chapter turns.[45]

My contention is that it is this convention that led Jeremiah to place the Ode celebrating the rebirth of his faith—the triumphant outcome of his nightlong struggle with despair—not at the end of his three-part meditation, where it chronologically belongs, but at its center. This is what was important: he was not broken; he could emerge from his ordeal with head held high.

Downfall and Resurrection

But this burst of courage born of a renewal of faith proves to be ephemeral. The pressures remain unremitting and the despair into which Jeremiah had fallen is too profound for him to pull himself out unaided. Without external help, he finds himself unable to turn his renewed resolution into a long-lasting commitment. As I read the record, it is not long before Jeremiah has relapsed into hopeless depression.

---

44. *Psalm* 23 (excluding the superscription *A Psalm of David*) consists, in the Hebrew, of 55 words. Counting 26 words from the opening of the *Psalm* proper and 26 words from its end, we arrive at its central three word phrase *ki atah imadi*, expressing the psalmist's core affirmation: *God is with me*. See Introduction to the Book of *Jonah*, note 26 and related text.

45. See the discussion of *Jonah* 2:4–5 in Chapter 2, the section entitled The Prayer of Jonah.

Woe is me, O my mother,[46] *that you gave birth to me,*
A man of strife and contention to the entire land!
I have neither lent nor have I borrowed,[47]
[Yet] everyone curses me....[48] *[15:10]*

Perhaps it would be helpful at this point to paraphrase Jeremiah's lament, because in it he summarizes what has become his current position. Despite his love of God and his loyalty to Him and His word—indeed the only joy in his life—his existence has become unendurable, even desperate. Because of his devotion to God and his efforts for Him, he has become isolated, cut off from friends and normal human interaction. He is constantly filled with fury at what goes on around him, especially people frivolously partying, willfully oblivious to the disaster that awaits them. No one will have anything to do with him. The words God has commanded him to proclaim are doom-laden and rob life of all joy. He is filled with rage and has no choice but to let it out, the result being a life of loneliness. He is denied even the consolations of a family life; the companionship of wife and the satisfaction of children will remain foreign to him. God has forbidden him to marry (16:1–4). He has forfeited all the normal pleasures of life, and is constantly scorned and persecuted; indeed, he is in imminent danger of losing his life. In all this he charges God with having let him down. He has looked to God for help, for support and for protection—in vain. He likens God to a wadi in the wilderness, capricious and unreliable; when needed most, He makes himself scarce.[49] God, Jeremiah charges, has failed him.

You know, O LORD*:*
Remember me and keep me in mind,[50]
And take vengeance for me on them who persecute me.[51]
Do not take me away[52] *due to Your long-suffering [nature];*
Know that for Your sake I have been scorned.[53]

---

46. For the significance of Jeremiah's return to making reference to his *mother*, see note 37 above.

47. Literally, *I have not lent, nor have any lent to me*. Owing money to others, and having others owe money to one are proverbial ways of ensuring enmity. It is a metaphorical way of saying that I don't deserve the hatred that is felt towards me, and have done nothing to provoke it. It is simply my fate to be hated.

48. The following four verses (15:11–14) do not belong here; they are a prose insertion—ostensibly God's answer to Jeremiah's complaint—that break into both the poetry and the development of Jeremiah's complaint. This was probably a marginal note that "crept into the text," i.e., originally probably a cross reference meant to clarify something in the text; in those days there were no chapter and verse notations, so the only way to reference another part of Scripture was to quote an abbreviated version of it. A later scribe probably mistook the reference for a correction, and inserted it into his copy of the text. "In common with perhaps the majority of commentators… we take verses 13f to be an intrusion from another context. The verses are a damaged variant of 17: 3f where they seem to be in place… Verse 12 is likewise a problem and is probably best taken as an intrusion like the two verses that follow it." (Bright, "A Prophet's Lament," pp. 61–62)

49. A *wadi* is a seasonal river in an arid region; with the winter rains it flows with water, at times even becomes a raging torrent, while in the summer the flow ceases and it becomes a dry riverbed. In other words, when you don't need it, the river is brimming with water, but just when you do need the water, it ceases to flow.

50. Literally, *take account of me*. This is a cry pulsating with urgency.

51. Literally, *those who pursue me*.

52. A euphemism for "allow me to die." I.e., due to your patience with my persecutors, they have time to finish me off before You get around to dealing with them.

53. Literally, *I have borne reproach*. This line is a direct reference to *Psalm* 69:8, almost an exact quote. Jeremiah often draws upon the *Psalms* for the vocabulary of his "Confessions."

Chapter 15. The Long Night

Your words were found and I ate them;
Now Your words[54] *were to me a joy and a delight,*[55]
For Your name was called upon me,[56]
O Lord, *God of hosts.*
I did not sit in festive circles and rejoice;
Because of Your hand I sat solitary,
For Your hand filled me with fury.
Why has my pain become perpetual,
And my wound incurable, refusing to be healed?
Will You be for me a wadi,
Waters on which one cannot rely? [15:15–18]

In this lament—which is more than a lament, it is an indictment—Jeremiah is in effect summing up all the complaints of his previous "Confessions" into one charge sheet. He is going back once again to his Call, and to God's promise in it:

I am with you ... to deliver you [1:19]

and charges God with having reneged on His commitment. The more he has put himself out for God, the worst things have become. Mockery and vilification have given way to physical assaults. All the immunities that are normally accorded to prophets of the Lord have been breached in his case. His life is crumbling under the weight of two decades of persecution. He has called upon his God to heal him:

Heal me, O Lord, *and I shall be healed;*
Save me and I shall be saved,
For You are my praise [17:14].

But his God has neither healed him nor saved him.

Why has my pain become perpetual,
And my wound incurable, refusing to be healed? [15:18]

Is this the way to treat one who gave his all for You? Remember:

You *put forth* Your *hand and touched me on the mouth and said:*
"Behold, I have put My words in your mouth" [1:9].

"Your words were found and I ate them[57];
Now Your words were to me a joy and a delight" [15:16].[58]

"Indeed, they were the only joy that the last two decades have afforded me. And You used these words to reduce me to misery. You are unreliable; you are capricious; when I am in desperate need You don't keep Your word. You are nowhere to be found."

---

54. Reading with *Ketib*. *Qeri* reads *word* in the singular.
55. Literally, *a gladness of heart*.
56. I.e., I became your precious possession.
57. A metaphor for "they have become a part of me."
58. There are those who take this phrase as a reference to Jeremiah's joyous reaction to the discovery of the "Book of the Torah" (*Deuteronomy*) in the Temple in 622 BCE, and his wholehearted commitment to the state religious reforms that it mandated. These two interpretations are compatible; they complement rather than conflict with one another.

These final words of Jeremiah border on blasphemy, barely mitigated by his record of devoted service and his expression of love for God's words which have inspired him. Clearly Jeremiah's battery has run down to almost nothing. He is completely played out.

Reinstatement

God's answer to Jeremiah's complaint—which comes to a tentative tender of resignation from his calling—amounts to a sharp rap on the knuckles. God neither commiserates with Jeremiah's unhappy condition, nor does He try to answer the played-out prophet's charges of abandonment. He doesn't remind him that he was never promised a bed of roses; that he was warned that thorns and briars would be his lot. All that he was promised was that God would save him from his enemies—that he wouldn't drown—and God has kept His promise. Jeremiah is still afloat. What God does is to set Jeremiah straight, and to kick-start his dead engine back into life.

Therefore, thus says the LORD:
"*If you return* [to duty], *and I* [agree] *to restore you,*[59]
[Then] *you shall stand before Me.*[60]
And if you bring forth the priceless from the worthless,
As My mouth you [again] *shall be.*
They shall turn to you,
But you, do not turn to them" [15:19].

Shape up, God is telling Jeremiah. You are not serving Me by sitting around and whining. If you want to return to My service you will have to straighten out. You need to change your attitude. Focus on your job—that is what is important—and not on how you feel. What is currently coming out of your mouth is a mixture of My word and your complaints. It is My word that is priceless. In the large picture your feelings are irrelevant.[61] If you will put your feelings to one side and give voice only to My word, then you can be My Mouth again, i.e., My prophet.

But there is a second condition: My word—all of it, pure and unadulterated—must be what you proclaim in My name. Don't you dare soften it down in an attempt to make My word more acceptable. It is your job to bring them up to your level. Sooner or later they will begin to understand and appreciate it. But don't you dare descend to their level. Unvarnished, the Truth will stand the test of time.[62] If you are willing to accept these conditions, and to recommit yourself to My service, then I will

---

59. Both "return" and "restore" in the Hebrew are different forms of the same root (*shub*); i.e., if you make the first move then I will meet you halfway, but it is up to you to make the first move.

60. "To stand before" is an idiomatic expression meeting "to serve," i.e., to be reinstated as My prophet.

61. The Hebrew root *zll* signifies something light, worthless and insignificant; the opposite of *ykr*, valuable, priceless. In reference to what has been coming out of Jeremiah's mouth, it would seem that the two main possibilities that are God's concern are Jeremiah's complaints and his demands for vengeance on his enemies. Both are unworthy of a prophet of the Lord. God is demanding as a condition of reinstatement that Jeremiah rise above such a paltry level and put such self-centered concerns to the side.

62. With the exception of a perceptive handful, Jeremiah's preaching during his lifetime gained no traction. It was only after his death that, among the exiles in Babylon, Jeremiah's message was accepted and became a beacon that sustained the exilic community and led to their return to Jerusalem.

be willing to accept you. But it is you that must make the first move by repenting your current weaknesses.

If you make that commitment, and I reinstate you as My prophet, then My promise to you will be not relief from harassment and persecution, or even peace of mind, but the inability of your enemies to silence you, and the strength to endure what you will have to endure in the long years ahead that you will labor in My service.[63]

"And I will make you to this people a fortified wall of bronze,
And they shall fight against you,
But they shall not overcome you;
For I am with you to save you and deliver you."
[This is] *an oracle of the* LORD [15:20].

We are not told explicitly what Jeremiah's response was to this cold shower, but the facts speak for themselves. Jeremiah continued to serve as his God's mouth—His prophet—through continually worsening conditions for at least another twenty years. And from this point onward the record contains not a hint of rebellion or complaint.[64] For what must have seemed an endless lifetime Jeremiah soldiered on, faithfully performing what was demanded of him by his Master.

With the exception of Moses, we know more about the life of Jeremiah than we do of any other prophet, but from the moment of his reinstatement Jeremiah had crossed a watershed. From now on—with one exception which we shall now explore—while we will have an extensive record of his words and deeds, the window to his soul will remain sealed.

---

63. In effect, a return to God's service would cancel the family curse of a short lifespan. God needs him long-term, and in fact Jeremiah continued to serve his God in continually worsening conditions at least well into his 60s. We make this connection in retrospect. Did Jeremiah at his life's end ever consider the possibility that his surprisingly long life was a consequence of his mission? We have no idea. But I am fairly confident that at this juncture of his life it is most unlikely that he conceived any connection between continuing his divinely mandated task and a mitigation of the family curse.

64. Doubts aplenty there may have been—there is only one further instance included in the record (see following chapter)—but if so, Jeremiah did not make an issue of them or share them with the public.

Historical Interlude III

Long Day's Journey into Night

1. 604–597 BCE: *The Skimming of the Cream*

We are now in the year 604 BCE. The shattered remnants of the once huge Egyptian Army have largely been withdrawn from Syria.[1] Egypt's pretense of upholding her Asian Empire has, at Carchemish, been exposed as illusion; she has been reduced to what she had been from the start: a purely African power. The pause in the advance of the Chaldean juggernaut,[2] occasioned by the death of Nebopolassar in Babylon and the crowning of his son Nebuchadrezzar as the new King of Akad,[3] has come to an end. Nebuchadrezzar is back in Hatti-land and was vigorously moving to assert his control over his newly acquired Empire. By his seizure of the Philistine city of Ashkelon[4] he cleared the last vestiges of the Egyptian presence from Western Asia.[5] It was probably at this juncture that Jehoiakim of Judah surrendered to Nebuchadrezzar and became his vassal.[6] He was hardly unique; he was merely part of the stampede of the little principalities of Hatti-land—but yesterday loyal vassals of Egypt—who had lined up to come to terms with their new overlord. And with this new reality the mad swirl of events that began with Carchemish momentarily stilled.

The hiatus lasted three years, and then in 601 BCE Nebuchadrezzar made his move: he invaded Egypt. Why he did this is far from clear. Perhaps his string of victories had gone to his head and he thought that he could emulate the Assyrians. Perhaps he just wanted to maintain momentum and preempt any Egyptian attempt at a comeback. Whatever the reason, Nebuchadrezzar received his first major setback. He was so badly beaten, that when he fell back, he didn't attempt to make a stand on the line of the old Assyrian West Asia defense perimeter, and so preserve his new-won

---

1. In Jeremiah's satiric poem mocking Egypt's defeat (*Jeremiah* 46:1–26), we have a vivid picture of the chaotic flight of the Egyptian army as it abandons Hatti-land to Nebuchadrezzar.
2. Chaldeans: an ethnic designation used as a synonym for Babylonians.
3. See Historical Interlude I, note 5, and Historical Interlude II, note 25.
4. See MAP 8.
5. From this point onward, while Egypt continued to exert sporadic influence in Western Asia, she ceased to be a power on the Asian continent. *The King of Egypt did not come out of his land anymore; for the King of Babylon had taken everything—from the Wadi of Egypt* [i.e., the border of Egypt proper] *to the Euphrates—that the King of Egypt had possessed.* (*2 Kings* 24:7)
6. *2 Kings* 23:36–24:2; *In his days Nebuchadrezzar, King of Babylon came up, and Jehoiakim became his servant* [for] *three years…* (*2 Kings* 24:1)

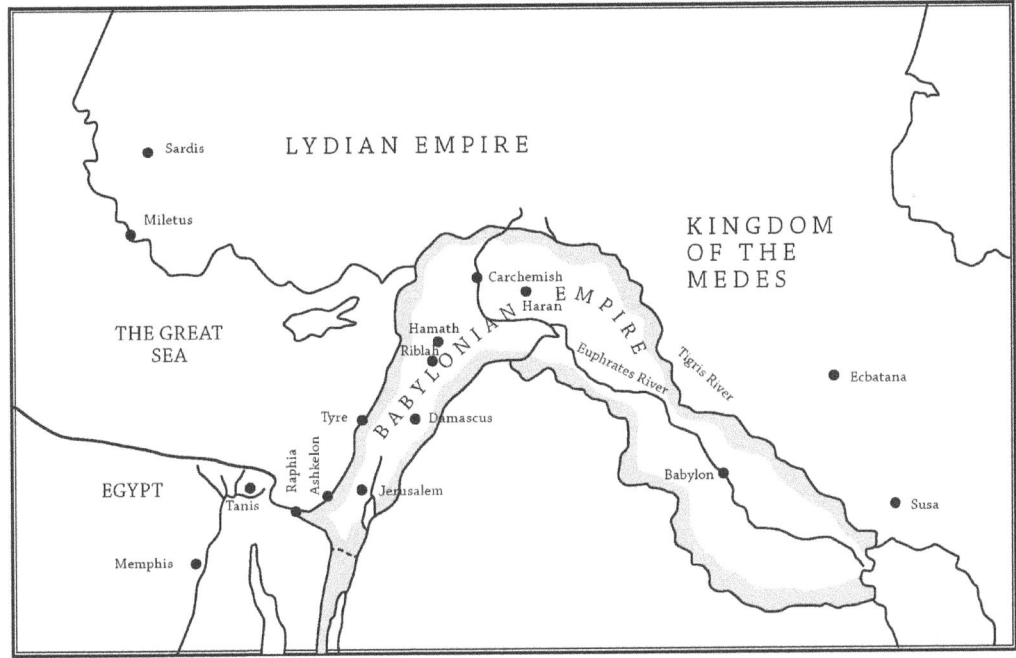

MAP 8

The Division of the Spoils II: The Ancient Near East after 604 BCE.

Empire. He pulled his army all the way back to Babylon, some 900 miles away.[7] Egypt naturally followed up by extending her influence (if not her armies) into the vacuum thus created. A new reality had been created for the Kingdom of Judah. How should she react?

This dilemma confronted all the principalities of Western Asia that had just pledged fealty to the Chaldean—or Neo-Babylonian—Empire: to remain loyal to Nebuchadrezzar or to switch back to Egypt? And Jehoiakim made the disastrous mistake of betraying his oath and, trusting to Egyptian support, declared independence from Babylon. This is something that Nebuchadrezzar would neither forgive nor forget. The oath taken by Jehoiakim was made to Nebuchadrezzar personally, and its breaking was taken personally by Nebuchadrezzar. He was at that time in no position to do much about it, but what he could do he did. Not all the states in the region had followed Jehoiakim's lead and switched back to a reliance on Egypt; some, such as Moab, Edom, and several of the Aramaean kingdoms, remained loyal to Babylon. These Nebuchadrezzar encouraged to raid and harass Judah, and he sent contingents of Chaldean troops to help keep things hot for Jehoiakim.[8]

From 600 BCE and onward, Nebuchadrezzar rebuilt his army and campaigned to reassert his control over Hatti-land. The year 598 BCE found the Babylonian army

---

7. Objectively speaking, to undertake so major an operation as the invasion of what was, after all, a major power, while so far from his own base, and with tenuous lines of supply, was ill considered to say the least. Not only would the Babylonian army need refitting and reinforcing, but the lines of supply would have to be shortened by building up bases in Hatti-land from which to operate.

8. *2 Kings* 24:2. See also *Jeremiah* 35:11.

laying siege to Jerusalem. Jehoiakim's son, Jehoiachin,[9] was now king. After a reign of but three months he surrendered to Nebuchadrezzar.[10] Perhaps his thought was that since it was not he who rebelled against the Chaldeans, Nebuchadrezzar would deal leniently with him. But Nebuchadrezzar was in no mood to forgive and forget.[11] Instead of being permitted to continue to rule Judah as a puppet, Jehoiachin, his mother, his wives and all his senior government officials were carted off to exile in Babylon. And with them are exiled 7000 land owners (i.e., almost all of the landed gentry), 1000 of the best craftsmen, and numerous other leading citizens and key military officials; about 10,000 persons in total: the "cream of the crop," as it were.[12] Along with the captives, Nebuchadrezzar carried off the contents of the Treasury and the Royal Palace, and he looted the Temple of the gold vessels Solomon had made. Stripped of its leadership and middle class, only the lower class of Judah and Jerusalem was left.[13]

To keep things under control, the Babylonian overlord placed Mattaniah, a younger son of King Josiah, on the throne as regent,[14] and changed his name to Zedekiah.[15] Officially, his nephew in Babylon was still king and he was simply his temporary stand-in.

With Jehoiakim dead, Jeremiah and Baruch were now free to come out of hiding. It was to this grim reality that they now emerged.

2. 597–586 BCE: Era's End

In the handling of his "Judean Problem" Nebuchadrezzar had made a serious miscalculation. He seems to have assumed that deprived of their leadership echelon, the lower classes of Judah would subside into quiescence. By not deposing King Jehoiachin and simply holding him captive, it appears that he felt that his replacement—the puppet, Zedekiah—lacking legitimacy, would be unable to mobilize sufficient backing to be able to cause serious trouble.[16] In this latter calculation

---

9. Otherwise known as Jeconiah, probably his birth name; also known by the shortened form Coniah.

10. The situation is confusing. From *2 Chronicles* 36:6–7 it would seem that Jehoiakim was still alive when his son surrendered the city, although very shortly thereafter he died (*2 Kings* 24:6). It is possible that due to illness or political incapacity his son had been installed as co-regent, and for the last three months of Jehoiakim's life the rule had actually been in his son's hands.

11. Actually, as Jehoiachin will learn, he *will* be treated leniently, despite being exiled to a Babylonian dungeon. When he learns what will be done to his uncle, Zedekiah, he no doubt realizes that, comparatively, he got off very lightly.

12. *2 Kings* 24:12–16. Not mentioned here but nonetheless included among the exiles was the priest, Ezekiel, later to become one of the leading prophets of the Exile.

13. This situation will be encapsulated by Jeremiah in his vision of the two baskets of figs (*Jeremiah* 24:1–10); one basket with very good fruit and the other with figs so bad as to be inedible. The good figs are those Judeans who were carried off to Babylon. What is left in Judah and Jerusalem is the "rotten fruit." The question has been raised, why was Jeremiah—a landowner, i.e., one of the gentry—not deported with the rest of his class? Probably because having been in hiding for close to seven years he had "disappeared from the radar" and had been overlooked. It is doubtful that his omission was a policy decision on the part of the authorities.

14. Jehoiachin had been exiled by Nebuchadrezzar, but not deposed. He was still King of Judah, and is so listed in the Babylonian accounts detailing the records for his food rations while in prison.

15. See Historical Interlude I, note 19.

16. Zedekiah was only 21 years of age when Nebuchadrezzar picked him to be his nephew's figurehead.

Nebuchadrezzar will be proved correct: a weak personality to begin with and effectively neutered politically, Zedekiah was incapable of steering events. Where Nebuchadrezzar went wrong was in his estimate of the tenor of the Judean populace. Deprived of their traditional leadership classes—mature, seasoned, prudent and knowledgeable—they threw up in their place a new body of leaders who were inexperienced, volatile, rash and demagogic individuals. What was needed at this juncture—both for the good of the Kingdom of Judah and for Nebuchadrezzar's good as well—was a strong figure who could take this gaggle of nouveau riche in hand. But Zedekiah was incapable of filling such a role; it is he who was to be dominated by his subordinates—parvenus all—rather than they by him. The remaining eleven years of the Kingdom of Judah were thus fated to be a tale of inexorable unfolding tragedy.

From the first, the new official class, struggling to accommodate itself to the unaccustomed responsibilities of sudden leadership, was subject to the unceasing intrigues and pressures of neighboring Egypt. It did not prove difficult for Egypt to seduce large numbers of them to a pro-Egyptian orientation, and from there to seriously considering, jointly with other kingdoms in the region, a break with Babylon—all, of course, with promises of massive Egyptian support. Zedekiah seems to have been willing to remain in the Babylonian orbit; but it was not he who determined policy, and the pressures become irresistible. In 588 BCE, Zedekiah finally gave in:

And Zedekiah rebelled against the King of Babylon[17] [*2 Kings* 24:20].

Where was Jeremiah during these nine critical years? Having emerged from hiding, Jeremiah immediately reengaged in the public arena, both by word and deed counseling submission to the rule of Babylon. His message to Judah and Jerusalem on the one hand, and to the exiles in Babylon on the other, was the same: Do not expect any change in the international situation in the short term; Babylonian rule is here to stay for the foreseeable future. Accept the reality and prepare for the long haul.[18]

Beyond incessant preaching, Jeremiah had turned himself into a living sermon, walking about the streets of Jerusalem wearing an ox yoke on his shoulders to drive home the message: Submit to the yoke of the King of Babylon, otherwise face disaster: the sword, famine and plague.[19] But unfortunately Jeremiah would be proved powerless to stem the tide of nationalist sentiment that was driving the Kingdom toward the precipice. What Jeremiah had first seen, and struggled so hard to prevent, finally occurred: the sword, famine and plague.

The two catastrophic years of the revolt—one and a half of them with Jerusalem

---

17. Probably by refusing to pay the annual tribute.

18. In a letter to the community of exiles in Babylon he counseled them: *"Build houses and settle in; plant gardens and eat their fruit. Take wives and beget sons and daughters, and take wives for your sons, and give your daughters to husbands, that they may bear sons and daughters; so multiply there and do not be diminished. Seek the peace of the city to which I exiled you, and pray for it to the Lord, for in its peace shall you have peace.... For thus says the Lord, '[Only] upon the completion of 70 years of Babylonian [Exile] will I remember you and perform for you My good word by returning you to this place.'"* (Jeremiah 29:5-7, 10)

19. Jeremiah 27-29. These events took place in the years of 594-593 BCE, a time when there was active planning of a joint uprising against Babylon by Judah, her neighboring kingdoms and Phoenicia. The uprising never came about, and it is possible that Jeremiah's public demonstrations raised sufficient opposition to rebellion to cause Judah to back out of the proposed alliance.

under siege—proved to be one long agony. The cities of Judah to the south of Jerusalem were razed, one after another, and their populations massacred. Jerusalem, which was virtually impregnable, held out in the hope of the promised Egyptian support, which of course never came.[20]

With the outbreak of the revolt, Jeremiah intensified his efforts, first preaching surrender, and when the leadership proved obdurate, declaring that individuals should save themselves and desert to the enemy. Although branded as a Babylonian collaborator, Jeremiah remarkably retained his freedom of movement and expression.[21] However, when during a break in the siege, Jeremiah attempted to leave Jerusalem he was arrested, charged with attempting to desert to the enemy, and thrown into prison.[22] While in close confinement—in which he nearly died—his public activities came to a halt, but with a relaxation of the terms of his imprisonment he was able, in a limited fashion, to resume his public preaching (as will be described in Chapter 16). He was to remain in custody until Jerusalem fell to the Babylonians.

Finally, the day came when all the supplies in the city had been consumed[23] and the city walls were breached. As the sack of the city began, King Zedekiah made a break from Jerusalem, trying to escape to the Trans-Jordan. Overtaken and captured near Jericho, he and his family were brought before Nebuchadrezzar at Riblah.[24] There Zedekiah was forced to watch as all of his sons were slaughtered, and then his eyes were gouged out. He was hauled off to Babylon in chains and there incarcerated at hard labor to the day of his death.[25]

A month after the fall of Jerusalem, Nebuzaradan, Nebuchadrezzar's deputy, arrived at the city from Riblah. Acting on orders, he put both city and Temple to the torch, and demolished the city's walls. The city of David and Solomon was reduced to a heap of smoldering rubble.[26] The survivors of the sack, the remaining craftsman, the deserters and others of the rural population were slated for deportation. Only the poorest of the landless poor were to be left behind. The Kingdom of Judah had come to an end.

---

20. This siege was temporarily lifted—from January to April, 587 BCE—when Pharaoh Apries (589–570 BCE) sent an army into Hatti-land and Nebuchadrezzar turned from Jerusalem to confront it. But instead of engaging, the Egyptian army withdrew. The siege resumed.

21. *Jeremiah* 37:4.

22. Jeremiah claimed that his purpose for leaving Jerusalem was to visit his home town of Anatoth where, due to the Jubilee (see Glossary), a redistribution of land was taking place and, as a landowner, his presence was necessary. This excuse—though probably valid—was not accepted. In the eyes of the authorities Jeremiah's pronouncements were seditious, if not outright treasonous, and here was an opportunity to shut him up. For the lifting of the siege which gave rise to Jeremiah's attempt to leave the city, see note 20 above.

23. The date given in *2 Kings* 25:3 is 9 Tamuz of the year 586 BCE.

24. Riblah was used in its day by Pharaoh Necho as the administrative headquarters of Egypt's Asian Empire. Apparently Nebuchadrezzar had taken it over as the administrative center of Hatti-land, from which he was conducting his campaigns against the various rebel states.

25. *Jeremiah* 52:7–11. For MT *house of hard labor* LXX reads *at the mill*, i.e., that he was used as a slave grinding grain.

26. The date of Nebuzaradan's arrival and his torching the city is given in *2 Kings* 25:8 as the 7th of Ab (i.e., August 14, 586 BCE), while in *Jeremiah* 52:12 the date is given as the 10th of Ab. "The Rabbis handled this discrepancy by spreading the event out. The destruction of the Temple was set as 7 Ab, and a day of national mourning for 9 Ab." (Lundbom, *Jeremiah III*, p. 519)

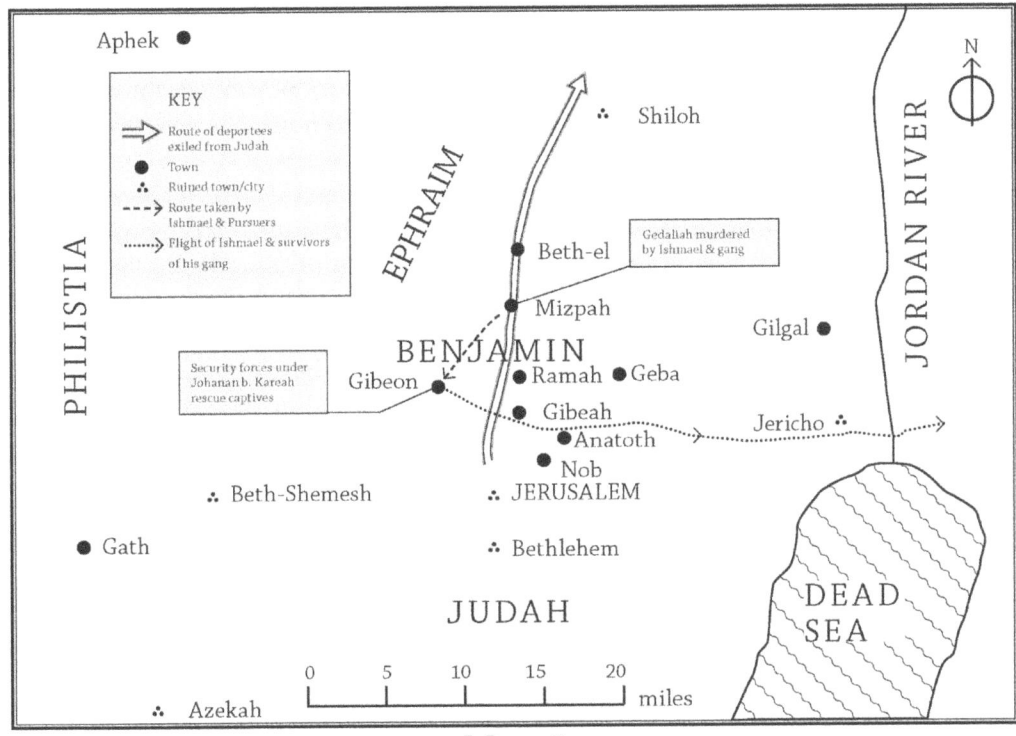

MAP 9

Northern Judah and Benjamin, October 586 BCE.

3. Aftermath: Nightfall

> *Now Nebuzaradan, the Commander of the Guard, deported to Babylon the survivors of those who had been in the city, and those who had deserted to him, and the rest of the people [of the rural population] who had survived. [Only] the very poorest of the poor—those who had nothing—did Nebuzaradan, Commander of the Guard, leave in the land of Judah; on that occasion he distributed to them vineyards and fields.*[27]
>
> —Jeremiah 39:9–10

In the midst of that miserable chained herd of survivors, the remnant of what was once the vibrant and prosperous population of Jerusalem and Judah, was to be found the bedraggled figure of Jeremiah.[28] Upon reaching Ramah[29] he was recognized, and his presence was brought to the attention of Nebuzaradan who was in command of the operation. Upon his orders Jeremiah's chains were struck off, and he was brought into the presence of the Commander. It turns out that Jeremiah was

---

27. Literally, *and he gave them on that day vineyards and fields.*

28. While not explicitly stated, Baruch must also have been there, for it was he who penned the eyewitness account which is the basis of our narrative.

29. Ramah: the first resting point of the convoy on the long trek to Babylon, about 5 miles north of Jerusalem.

well known to Babylonian Intelligence, and his decades-long pro–Babylonian activism was known to no less a person than King Nebuchadrezzar himself.[30] Nebuzaradan had his orders concerning how Jeremiah was to be treated: he was to be free to decide his own future.[31] Jeremiah's decision was to remain in what was left of Judah.

There was not much left. The cities had all been destroyed and the survivors deported. Of the rural population, the gentry and the independent farm-owners were gone, their property confiscated and distributed to the penniless indigent farm laborers and sharecroppers who had been allowed to remain. Over these barrel-scrapings the Babylonians had appointed Gedaliah, son of Ahikam,[32] as governor.[33] The regions to the south and west of Jerusalem had been devastated, but the areas to the north were less damaged. A few towns and villages were still standing. It was one of these—Mizpah[34]—that Gedaliah chose to be the seat of such government as the Babylonians would allow the Kingdom of Judah to retain. So it was to Mizpah that Jeremiah wound his way, and it was there that he made his home.

Gedaliah's main task was to restore a semblance of law and order to the state of anarchy created by the collapse of the Kingdom. Dispersed army units repaired to Mizpah to formally submit their surrender to Babylonian authority and pledge allegiance to Gedaliah. Displaced survivors began to settle into the abandoned homes of the deportees. Chaos began to give way to a sense of security. Crops began to be harvested.[35] A sense of hope began to permeate the survivors as a community began to take form, only to be nipped in the bud by diehard fanaticism.

Not only civilians had fled to neighboring lands from the terror of the Babylonian army—refugees that were now returning in droves to the region centering on Mizpah—but army units as well. Some of them had retreated to the Kingdom of Ammon, which was allied with Judah against Babylon and was as yet unconquered. One of these, a unit commanded by one Ishmael, son of Nethaniah, was not willing to accept the amnesty offered by the Babylonians to all who would accept Gedaliah's authority. As far as Ishmael and his men were concerned, the war was not yet over, Gedaliah was a traitor and the reviving territory of Judah was a Babylonian puppet state filled with turncoats. They were to be hated and despised. For their Ammonite

---

30. *Jeremiah* 39:11–12.

31. He was given the choice of coming to Babylon as a guest of the state, of remaining in Judah or going elsewhere as he wished. (*Jeremiah* 40:1–4)

32. We have met Gedaliah's father, Ahikam; he was Jeremiah's protector. And we have met Gemariah, Gedaliah's uncle, who provided Baruch with the window overlooking the Temple courtyard, which enabled him to read Jeremiah's incendiary scroll to the populace. Both these great nobleman were sons of Shaphan, who had been Secretary of State (the official title was "Scribe") to King Josiah, and one of the architects of the pro-Babylonian policy to which his House has been loyal to the very end. All of which helps explain Gedaliah's appointment.

33. We must remember that, despite being a prisoner, as far as the Babylonians were concerned Jehoiachin is still King of Judah. Zedekiah, who was his regent, was now deposed. Formally, Gedaliah was now regent in his place (*al habait* is the technical title).

34. See MAP 9.

35. Jerusalem was torched in mid–August (see note 26 above). By mid–September the Babylonian army and the mass of deportees were gone. A small garrison remained in Mizpah, but the task of restoring order and policing the region had now devolved upon Gedaliah, using the remnants of the Judean armed forces to ensure security. It was now harvest time and the economy was beginning to revive.

hosts Ishmael was an ideal instrument.[36] When he and ten of his men appeared in Mizpah, claiming to surrender and to pledge loyalty to Gedaliah, they were believed. So trusting were Gedaliah and those around him that this small contingent was able to surprise them, massacre him and his followers, and the small Babylonian garrison as well. Then rounding up all the civilians they could lay their hands on, the band and their captives started back for Ammon.[37] They got as far as Gibeon before they were overtaken by the Judean security forces. All the captives were rescued, while Ishmael and eight of his men succeeded in escaping to Ammon.

To the extent that there was a community of survivors remaining in Judah, Johanan, son of Kareah, head of the security forces was now its de facto leader. In panicked fear of indiscriminate Babylonian reprisals for the murder of their governor, Gedaliah, and the killing of their soldiers stationed at Mizpah, the decision was reached to abandon Judah and seek sanctuary in Egypt. Despite Jeremiah's desperate counsel to stay put,[38] the entire community picked itself up, and abandoning Mizpah and Judah resettled in Egypt. The last remnant of organized and recognized Israelite settlement in the Promised Land had been abandoned. Outside of a scattering of isolated individuals and families, the land was now bereft of its designated inhabitants. The three-quarters-of-a-millennium saga of the Children of Israel that we nowadays call the era of the First Commonwealth had breathed its last.

---

36. Baruch, in his account of these events, quotes Judean officers who claimed that Ishmael was an agent of the king of Ammon, sent to assassinate Gedaliah (*Jeremiah* 40:13-14). Although warned, Gedaliah refused to believe the information.

37. The purpose of taking captives was probably to sell them as slaves.

38. Jeremiah was consulted, but his advice—given in God's name—was rejected. Against his will he was carried off to spend his last years in Egyptian exile.

CHAPTER 16

The Anatomy of a Lifelong Agony

A faith which does not doubt is a dead faith.
—Miguel de Unamuno, *La agonia del cristianismo*

His doubts are better than most people's certainties.
—Philip Yorke, Earl of Hardwick; quoted by J. Boswell in his *Life of Samuel Johnson*

So what have we learned about Jeremiah in our brief perusal? Observed objectively, beyond question he was a hero. Early on he took a stand in opposition to many of the entrenched beliefs, prejudices and norms of his day and age, engendering public hatred, ostracism, physical abuse and even threats to his life. For over forty years he held his ground against waves of almost universal opprobrium and censure. That again and again events proved him right earned him neither acceptance nor respite from the pressures that assailed him. In every sense he fulfilled God's prognosis for his life: to be as strong as a fortified city, as an iron pillar and as a wall of bronze.[1] Indeed, he was a man of steel—the very picture of calm certitude—the perfect personification of a hero.

But this outward façade belied an inner reality. The window into the inner man provided by Jeremiah's "Confessions" has revealed a very different picture. In contradistinction to the posture he presented to the world, he saw himself as weak, unfit and riven with doubts. He doubted everything: himself, his abilities, the things he was commanded to say, even the validity of God's promises to him. The only thing that he never for a moment doubted was the identity of Him Whom he served and Who would not be denied.

With this lack of certainty gnawing away at the foundations of his beliefs, wherever did Jeremiah find the strength to persevere?

A Prisoner Buys a Field

We have said that with the resolution of his spiritual crisis and his recommissioning as the LORD's prophet, Jeremiah put aside rebellion and complaint; at least the public record contains no hint of either.[2] But doubts could not be banished—they

---

1. 1:18.
2. By "public record" we mean not only his own personal testimony, but also the increasingly detailed and explicit biography penned by his companion and disciple, Baruch, which we find appended to his own writings in what is today known as the *Book of Jeremiah*.

seem to have been an intrinsic part of his nature—and they remained with him to the very end of his life. This is not to say that he allowed these doubts to interfere with his public duties as God's prophet. We can venture this conclusion because Jeremiah saw fit to raise for one brief moment toward the end of his life the curtain that he had lowered to cover his turbulent soul, and so has afforded us a parting glimpse into his tortured being.[3]

We are in the summer of the year 587 BCE. The disastrously misguided policies of Jehoiakim and his successor on the throne, Zedekiah, have borne their tragic fruit. Trusting to the very end in Egypt, Judah has rebelled against Babylon, ruler of the Fertile Crescent. A Babylonian army has overrun the kingdom and is laying siege to Jerusalem.[4] Things have not worked out very well for Jeremiah either. Stridently opposing the rebellion against Babylon, he has been accused of treason and of attempting to defect to the enemy. He is currently imprisoned in the "Court of the Guard," an enclosed courtyard in the Palace Complex that has been pressed into service as a confinement area for prisoners not considered violent or particularly dangerous.[5] It is while in these circumstances that Jeremiah reports the following train of events:

> *Now Jeremiah said: "The word of the* LORD *came to me, saying: 'Behold, Hanamuel, the son of your uncle Shalum, is coming to you with a request*[6]*: Buy for yourself my field that is in Anatoth, for the right of redemption to buy is yours.'" Now Hanamuel my cousin came to [visit] me in the Court of the Guard, even as the* LORD *had said. And he said to me: "Please buy my field that is in Anatoth, in the land of Benjamin, for the right of possession is yours and the [duty] of redemption is yours; buy it for yourself." Then I knew that this was [truly] the word of the* LORD*"* [32:6–8].

Jeremiah, while serving time in prison, is subject to an unsettling series of occurrences. It begins with some sort of presentiment—perhaps a dream[7]—in which he receives a visit from his first cousin, Hanamuel, who requests that Jeremiah buy his field from him. And then a bit later, lo and behold, the cousin actually shows up[8]

---

3. We are assuming that the crisis and recommissioning of Jeremiah occurred not too long after 604 BCE, when he had been forced into hiding; and certainly well before 597 BCE when, with Jehoiakim's death, we believe Jeremiah was able to once again engage in public life.

4. Judah was not the only rebel. Several kingdoms were involved in the revolt and Nebuchadrezzar is systematically dealing with them, one after another, in his draconian way.

5. Jeremiah was not always so leniently treated. Originally condemned to close confinement, he almost died from this treatment. Upon petitioning the King, Zedekiah—unwilling to have his hands stained with the blood of a prophet—transferred him to the more open confinement of the Court of the Guard. There Jeremiah could freely mingle with other prisoners, have meetings with visitors and even conduct business affairs.

6. Literally, *to say*.

7. Jeremiah recounts this as "the word of the Lord," but at the time Jeremiah hardly considered it in the category of a direct communication from God, as we shall see. We must keep in mind that our account was only written down (or more likely dictated to Baruch) well after this chain of events had concluded. I take the phrase *the word of the Lord came to me, saying…* as a retrospective remark made in the light of subsequent events; i.e., after he had come to the conclusion that the presentiment (or dream) had to be taken seriously as a divine communication. In those days, as we have learned in the case of Balaam, it was taken for fact that God did communicate with mortals via dreams. See Chapter 7, from The Veto and onwards.

8. No easy matter; Hanamuel would have had to apply to the authorities for permission to visit a felon charged with serious crimes, even if he was confined under open conditions.

and makes the proposal that Jeremiah had envisioned! It is this startling realization of his presentiment that convinces Jeremiah not only that it was a divine communication, but that it was also an order from God to grant the request: "Buy it!"

What was Hanamuel's proposition? He owned a field. In those days, no one sold one's land—"the inheritance of one's fathers"—unless desperate circumstances forced one's hand. In this case it would seem that the war, among other things, had reduced Hanamuel to penury. Under these circumstances, the powerful sense of family solidarity mandated that a close relative make the purchase so as to keep ancestral lands within the family.[9] What Hanamuel is requesting—virtually begging—is that his cousin, Jeremiah, assume the family responsibility and serve as the Redeemer. This request is outrageous. Jeremiah has long been alienated from his family—remember that not only did they turn against him, but were involved in a plot to murder him[10]—and the land in question is for all practical purposes worthless. The land is located (as Hanamuel is careful to specify) at *Anatoth, in the land of Benjamin*, and the territory of Benjamin is currently occupied by the Babylonian army; all property there has been confiscated by the conquerors.[11] But as Jeremiah has come to the conclusion that his presentiment or dream was a divine communication, the import of which amounted to a command to buy, he will follow orders:

So I bought the field that was in Anatoth from Hanamuel my cousin, and I weighed out for him the money: seventeen shekels of silver.[12] *So I signed the deed,*[13] *and put my seal to it*[14] *and had it signed by witnesses*[15]*; and I weighed out the silver on* [official] *scales*[16] [32:9-10].

But Jeremiah does more than simply buy the legal ownership of the land at full market value. He now understands the purpose of this entire charade. The public act of the purchase of land under Babylonian occupation is, in effect, a symbolic act of faith in the future. Jeremiah now, in word and deed, spells this out:

And I took the sealed [copy] *of the deed of purchase* [containing] *the contract and*

---

9. *If your brother becomes destitute, and he sells part of his inheritance, then the Redeemer* [goel] *who is closest to him* [in relationship] *shall come and Redeem that which is brother has sold.* (Leviticus 25:25)

10. 12:6; 11:18–19.

11. Is Jeremiah Hanamuel's closest living male relative? We have no way of knowing, but probably not. Hanamuel has likely approached all his other relatives and they, quite understandably, have turned him down. Legally Hanamuel is the owner of a valuable field. In practice, however, he holds nothing. His field is in the possession of the Babylonians. His approach to Jeremiah is most likely a last desperate grasp at a straw.

12. As coins of standard value had not yet been invented, one used pieces of silver whose value was determined by weight. The shekel was a unit of weight (approximately 11.4 grams); thus 17 shekels would be 193.8 grams = 6.78 ounces, i.e., a bit less than one half pound of silver. This would seem to have been the market value of the land. For a discussion of the factors that went into determining market value of land during the First Commonwealth see my *Four Biblical Heroines*, Chapter 1, pp. 20–24 (the sections entitled The Laws of Inheritance, The Inheritance of the Fathers, and The Three Faces of the Redeemer).

13. Literally, *I wrote in the document.* The deed itself had to be written out by a professional scribe—in this case Baruch—in order to be legal. The deed then had to be signed by the principles and the witnesses in their own hands.

14. In addition to signing the document, Jeremiah had to stamp it with his personal seal for it to be legal.

15. Literally, *had it witnessed by witnesses.*

16. I.e., I had the silver used in payment weighed using official weights, i.e., weights with a royal seal attesting to their accuracy.

the conditions,[17] *and the open copy,*[18] *and I gave the deed of purchase to Baruch, son of Neriah, son of Mahseiah,*[19] *in the presence of my cousin,*[20] *Hanamuel, and in the presence of the witnesses who signed the deed of purchase, and in the presence of all the Judahites*[21] *who were sitting [around] in the Court of the Guard. And I commanded Baruch in their presence, saying: "Thus says the* LORD *of hosts, the God of Israel: 'Take these deeds—this sealed purchase deed and this open deed—and put them in a ceramic vessel, in order that they may be preserved for many days.' For thus says the* LORD *of hosts, the God of Israel: 'Houses and fields and vineyards shall yet again be bought in this land'"* [32:11–15].

In effect, Jeremiah is publicly acknowledging that he has paid out good money for a worthless piece of paper. But now comes the payoff: in the presence of everyone in the Court of the Guard—prisoners, guards and visitors[22]—Jeremiah hands over the deed to the land he has just acquired to Baruch for safekeeping,[23] and in a loud voice instructs him to take measures to ensure its safety: this deed will one day be worth good money, so take good care of it. Put it in a ceramic jar, one not subject to decay, seal the jar and bury it, so that it doesn't fall into the hands of the Babylonians when they take the city—and they will. But one day, when this is all over, our children or our children's children will return to this land and resettle it. Then this deed will be the ticket to a valuable piece of land. How do I know this? Because God has so informed me. And raising his voice still further so that all could hear, he proclaims:

For thus says the LORD *of hosts, the God of Israel: "Houses and fields and vineyards shall yet again be bought in this land"* [32:15].

And thus, in the most dramatic way possible, the prophet who has been predicting doom for most of his long life—and still insists that the war is lost and absolute

---

17. The Hebrew is *hamitzvah vehahukim*, a stereotyped phrase used in *Deuteronomy* 5:31 and 6:1 in a general sense, but here used in a legal context. Bright suggests that the force of this technical phrase might be something akin to "the contract and the 'fine print'" (*Jeremiah AB*, p. 237, note 11)

18. Legal documents were always written (and signed) in duplicate, on a single sheet of papyrus or parchment, with a blank space between the two copies. Holes were punched in this blank space, the lower copy was rolled up, tied up by strings or ribbons passed through the holes, and the binders sealed. This lower rolled part of the sheet was called the sealed copy, while the upper part, which was left open for reference, was called the open copy. Should any question arise as to whether the open copy had been tampered with or altered, the seals could be broken on the sealed copy and the two compared. Should there be any discrepancy, the sealed copy was authoritative.

19. This is the first formal reference to Baruch in the *Book of Jeremiah*, even though, chronologically, he is present and in the employ of Jeremiah in 604 BCE, when Jeremiah dictated to him the scroll that he then read in the Temple (see Historical Interlude II: Scandals in the Temple). In 36:26 and 32 he is given his full professional title: "Baruch the Scribe."

20. Reading with LXX, Syr., Targ. and many Hebrew mss. MT lacks the word *ben*, the first half of the term *ben dod* = cousin.

21. I.e., those imprisoned in the Court of the Guard who were citizens of the kingdom of Judah. Noncitizens would not be able to testify as to what was now to take place.

22. If lockups were run in those days according to the same logic by which they are today, visitors were restricted to specific days and times. This must be visitor's day.

23. As we have seen, professional Scribes—there probably was some kind of certification process—served in the capacity (among others) nowadays performed by lawyers and notaries. It was normal to deposit valuable legal documents with them for safekeeping. What is unusual about this act of Jeremiah is the specific instruction he gives Baruch for the long-term preservation of the deed, and the reason he gives for it.

disaster is right around the corner—now announces that after the darkest of nights, there will be a new dawn. For the rest of his life, in one form or another, this is the message that he will now preach.

With this startling proclamation of faith in a hopeful future Jeremiah ends the public aspect of this episode.

Second Thoughts

"Now after I had given the deed of purchase to Baruch, son of Neriah, I prayed to the LORD, *saying"*[24] [32:16]

His public duty performed, Jeremiah leaves the civic stage and retreats within himself in order to come to terms with his conscience and with his God. He has followed what he believed to be his orders, but now looking back over the past several hours he can hardly believe what he has done. It makes no sense whatsoever. Here he is, incarcerated—charged in time of war with high treason, and still alive only due to a royal indulgence that may end at any moment—in a city about to be overrun by the enemy, and he is using his last precious days throwing his money away on worthless pieces of paper and making meaningless gestures in front of an audience that couldn't care less about what he says and does. As is his wont, in time of confusion and despair he turns to his God in prayer.

Unlike former times when he prayed, he has neither the will nor the patience to compose a literary work of art. He doesn't choose his words; he just extemporaneously pours out what is sticking in his throat. He doesn't complain and he doesn't blame; he has put all that behind him. He will follow orders as they are given. But he doesn't understand; he cannot understand or believe what he has just done. He cannot even put into words the depth of his disbelief. So instead of getting to the point, he begins with a rambling historical prologue—beginning all the way back at Creation[25]—apparently to give himself time to get his thoughts in order.[26]

Jeremiah begins by extolling the omnipotence of God—*there is nothing too wonderful for You* (32:17)—You created the heavens and the earth, You took Israel out of Egypt and gave them this land, just as You had promised to Abraham, Isaac and Jacob. Jeremiah then falls back on doxology: he repeats what seems to be a liturgical version of *Exodus* 34:7 (the basic attributes of God).[27] Returning to history, Jeremiah focuses on the ingratitude of Israel: they did not listen to You, they did what

---

24. While Jeremiah's prayer followed shortly after the acts that he performed (which we have just described), this first-person account of his praying to God and the contents of his prayer—obviously not public acts—must have been reduced to writing at a later date, probably by dictating the account to Baruch. Why he saw fit to do so will become evident as we proceed.

25. In this there is nothing unusual. Rambling introductions are common in extemporaneous prayers, cf. David's prayer (*2 Samuel* 7:18–29), while harking back to Creation is also well attested, cf. Hezekiah's prayer (*2 Kings* 19:15).

26. What follows is a summary, in outline form, of the main points Jeremiah makes in his prayer, along with some running commentary. For the full text of his prayer, see Appendix H: Psalm 22 and the Prayer of Jeremiah.

27. See note 6 in Appendix H: Psalm 22 and the Prayer of Jeremiah.

You did not want them to do, so You are punishing them by bringing on the current war.[28]

And now Jeremiah has brought things up to the present: Jerusalem is under siege, the battering rams are smashing away at the city walls, famine and disease are running rampant—everything You warned against—defense is crumbling: the city will soon fall; all this is taking place before Your very eyes.

And now at last Jeremiah gets to the point:

"And yet You said to me, O Lord GOD: *'Buy for yourself the field with silver before witnesses,' while the city is given into the hands of the Chaldeans!"* [32:25]

You ordered me to buy that field and to perform that entire public charade; to proclaim that there is a future. But the war is lost; how can there be a future?

Foremost in Jeremiah's mind is the fate of the Northern Kingdom of Israel to which, as a Benjamite, he is still emotionally attached. In 722 BCE Israel's capital of Samaria finally fell to the Assyrians. Most of the surviving population was deported and Israel vanished from the world scene. Even the fall of Assyria was no reprieve: what had once been Israel simply passed into the hands of the Babylonians. Now the same thing is happening to us. Israel had no future and now we have no future.

And behold, the word of the LORD *came to Jeremiah saying: "Behold, I am the* LORD, *the God of all flesh; is there anything too wonderful for Me?"*[29] [32:26–27]

God's reply to Jeremiah comes in the form of a rhetorical question in which God throws Jeremiah's own words right back in his face. You began your prayer with the words *"there is nothing too wonderful for You!"*[30] You are the one who insisted that it was I Who created the heavens and the earth. Why don't you take your own words seriously? It is true: there *is* nothing that is too hard for Me to accomplish. Yes, the city will fall, and the Chaldeans will burn it to the ground, while most of those left from the famine and the plague the Babylonians will slaughter. Yes, the survivors (among whom you will be one, as I promised) will be driven into exile. Yes, the land will become desolate, bereft of inhabitants. Yet despite it all, My children shall return to their land and resettle it. Fields will once again be bought and sold in Benjamin, and in the cities of Judah, and in the regions around Jerusalem.

"For I will in certainty restore their fortunes;[this is] *an Oracle of the* LORD*"* [32:44b].

Be ashamed of yourself for ever having doubted me. If I *say* so, it will *be* so. No matter how improbable it may seem, the future is guaranteed.

And after having been slapped down, this became Jeremiah's message to the end of his days. Jeremiah never saw the future he now predicted; he died in exile.[31] But in place of the endless warnings of doom that had been his leitmotif up to this point,

---

28. The evil of which they had been warned (1:14–16).
29. It is because of this divine reply that Jeremiah's prayer has been preserved. This "word of God" makes no sense without the prayer to which it is an answer. See the discussion in the opening paragraphs of Chapter 14.
30. 32:12.
31. In Egypt.

with the fall of the dark night his clarion cry now became the certainty of a new dawn to follow. And it was due to his prophecy of doom having come about, and now his drum-beat of messages of hope that it finally came to be believed; that his words (in their written form) were accepted as Scripture—holy writings—and that we hold them in our hands today.

Did he still have doubts? Probably, being who and what he was. But if he did, after this point in time he never gave voice to them. Through increasing disillusionment and despair he soldiered on to the very end, leaving his vindication to his God and to the unfolding of the inscrutable destiny of His people.

Stop the World, I Want to Get Off

In the last several chapters we have been exploring what appears to be a process that led a prophet to rebel against his Master. The time is overdue to define exactly what we mean by the term "rebellion," and specifically what, in our case—that of Jeremiah—would amount to rebellion against God. In the first matter, I suggest that in the case of a prophet, an explicit refusal to carry out God's commands would constitute rebellion. This understanding has been implicit in our treatments of Jonah and Balaam. In the case of Jeremiah, from the outset his mission was defined as:

> *"For on all that I send you you shall go,*
> *And all that I command you you shall speak...."*
> And the Lord *put forth His hand and touched me on my mouth, and said:*
> *"Behold, I have put My words in your mouth"* [1:7, 9].

This primary obligation to speak the words vouchsafed to him by God is reiterated in God's second Call to him:

> *"Now as for you:*
> *You, gird up your loins;*
> *And rise and speak to them everything I command you"* [1:17].

Thus, when Jeremiah admits that he has made the decision to refuse to speak the words his Master relayed to him, or to speak anymore in His name:

> *And I said: "I will not mention Him,*
> *And I will not speak any longer in His name..."* [20:9]

he has entered into a state of rebellion against his God.

But why is he rebelling against the Lord? What is it that has propelled Jeremiah to turn his back on his Master? I would suggest a number of factors entered into this outcome, the first to make itself felt being a sense of duress. He never wanted to be a prophet. When called, his first reaction was to try to beg off.[32] Primarily, he felt inadequate and unsuited to the calling. For the entire period in which he has revealed his innermost feelings he has insisted that his relationship with his God was

---

32. 1:6, 17; 17:16a.

non-consensual; he had been forced into his role as a prophet over his protests.[33] As time went on and the pressures upon him increased, his expressions became more strident: they eventually escalated to claims that he had been an innocent who had been seduced, even raped![34] In a word, the selection of a career had never been his; he was serving under compulsion and not from choice.

Added to the resentment engendered by the role he had been forced to assume was a sense of revulsion at the life he consequently was compelled to lead. As a prophet he was obligated to preach words dictated to him, messages that deviated radically from those he wished to deliver, as well as from those his audiences wished to hear, pronouncements that provoked resentment among his listeners that over time transmuted into a fury that became life-threatening.[35] Worse, not only was he compelled to preach unpopular truths, he was forced into a lifestyle alien to his nature, a pattern of behavior that turned his person into a didactic caricature, a living sermon that misrepresented, indeed contradicted what he deemed to be his true self.

> *Now it came to pass that the word of the* LORD *came to me saying:*
> *"Do not take for yourself a wife,*
> *Neither shall you have sons and daughters in this place....*
> *Do not enter a house of mourning,*
> *Neither go to lament or to console them* [the mourning family]....
> *And do not enter a house of feasting,*
> [do not] *sit with them to eat or drink,*
> *For thus says the* LORD *of hosts, the God of Israel:*
>   *Behold, I will cause to cease from this place,*
>   *Before your eyes and in your days,*
>   *The voice of mirth and the voice of gladness,*
>   *The voice of the groom and the voice of the bride"* [16:1–2, 5, 8–9].

Jeremiah's reaction to this series of commands, which cut him off from all social intercourse and turn him into an antisocial "Dr. Doom," is explicit in his complaint to his God:

> *Your name was called upon me,*
> *O Lord* GOD *of hosts.*
> *I did not sit in festive circles and rejoice:*
> *Because of Your hand I sat solitary,*
> *For Your hand filled me with fury* [15:16b–17].

Cast in the role of one symbolically mourning the coming destruction of the people of Judah and Jerusalem, forbidden any of the normal social activities in which people interact, either in their festive moments or those of loss, Jeremiah has been transformed into a recluse. Forbidden even the joys of marriage and a family life— the satisfactions of raising one's children and through them having a stake in the

---

33. 1:5, 7.
34. 20:7.
35. 12:6; 11:18–19 and especially verse 21.

future—Jeremiah has been remade into a caricature: a lonely and irascible figure, forever shunning his fellow human beings except when denouncing them. This role was to him a lifelong misery, the very opposite of what he wanted for himself.

"Why has my pain become perpetual,
And my wound incurable, refusing to be healed?" [15:18a]

To Jeremiah, being a prophet means being mocked, laughed at and reviled[36]; it means to be hated and persecuted[37]; it means to be cut off from one's fellow human beings by an impassable barrier. Who would want a life like that? Having reached the point where he can stand it no longer, he curses the day he was born; indeed he longs never to have been born.[38] What Jeremiah wanted was a normal life, one of his own choosing. As a prophet, the pressures on him became unrelenting; he had no life. And so, unable to stand the heat he wants to get out of the kitchen.[39] His cry amounts to the words of that old Broadway musical: *Stop the World, I Want to Get Off.*

But he can't: the world refuses to stop and he can't get off. His rebellion fizzles into failure.

I said: "I will not mention Him,
And I will not speak any longer in His name,"
And then there is in my heart as it were a burning fire,
Shut up in my bones;
I weary myself to hold it in
But cannot [20:9].

He finds himself in the grip of a compulsion that will not allow him to rebel. He cannot be silent. His rebellion is stymied from the start, stillborn. God won't let him off the hook.

We spoke of Jeremiah as a hero, but he was not a hero by nature. Rather, he was forced to be one in spite of himself, a tragic hero chained to his destiny, and throughout his long life denied any choice in the matter. Finally, frustrated in his attempt to escape, Jeremiah resigns himself to his fate. He accepts that he never had any choice: he had been designated as a prophet from the start and a prophet he would be until his death; that release would be in God's hands, and not in his. With his original Call and dedication,[40] he had had no idea of what he was being pushed into; with his rededication,[41] he knew only too well, but now he also knew that he had no choice. From then on he was to do as he was told and ceased to rail against his fate. But serenity would never be his; apparently, the doubts persisted to the very end, or so the record seems to proclaim.

---

36. 20:7b-8.
37. 12:6; 11:18–20; 18:17–18.
38. 20:14–18; 15:10.
39. The aphorism—*If you can't stand the heat, get out of the kitchen*—is attributed to Harry S Truman, coined in the days when he was still a Senator.
40. 1:4–19.
41. 15:19–20.

Why Did God Choose Jeremiah in the First Place?

From this analysis two issues emerge: God's choice of unsuitable people to serve as His agents, and the failure of the prophet Jeremiah to achieve his goals. Let us give both of these matters the attention that they deserve.

As to the first, there is little doubt that Jeremiah had a point, when he argued that he was unsuitable for the life imposed upon him. The task of a prophet in his era would require a figure possessing courage, force of character and persuasive skills—all of heroic proportions—and he knew full well that he was no hero. To argue that God knew better, the proof being that Jeremiah persisted through a long life, preached God's message and was never broken, begs the question. Even a lame horse can be spurred on to finish a race, if the object is simply to stay the course, rather than to win. But then that horse should never have been in that race in the first place; if the object of a race is to win, then one should only enter contestants with the qualities of a potential winner. These qualities Jeremiah justifiably felt that he lacked.

But the case of Jeremiah is hardly unique. Time and again, the record shows God choosing deeply flawed individuals to act as His agents, persons far more unsuitable then Jeremiah. Elsewhere I have argued that Ehud, the son of Gera (*Judges* 3:14–30) was a professional assassin,[42] yet God *raised* [him] *up for them* [as] *a savior*,[43] i.e., chose him as His agent to save Israel from foreign oppression. To save Israel from the Midianite nomadic horde, God chooses Gideon,[44] a man with so low a sense of self-worth as to make Jeremiah seem by comparison a paragon of resolution and self-assurance. When we add to this lack of self-esteem that unsuspected streak of ruthlessness and savage cruelty activated by his mission, God's choice seems bizarre. Then again, by resting His spirit upon Jephthah[45]—a bandit chieftain who murders his own daughter[46]—God's choice of a man such as this to act for Him becomes inexplicable.

Let us approach this problem through an examination of God's paradoxical choice of Jeremiah's hero, Moses, to be His savior of Israel and His prophet *par excellence*.[47] Adopted as an infant by a daughter of the Pharaoh, brought up and educated as a member of the aristocracy, Moses was to all intents and purposes an Egyptian,[48] with only the knowledge of his Hebrew origins blocking a complete identification with his Egyptian identity.[49] In fact Moses was a murderer, rejected by his "brethren"

---

42. My *Judges and Saviors*, p. 71–87.

43. *Judges* 3:15.

44. *Judges* 6:11–8:28.

45. *Judges* 11:29.

46. *Judges* 11:39–40.

47. *Never again has their arisen in Israel a prophet like unto Moses, whom the Lord knew face to face* (*Deuteronomy* 34:10). See also the continuation: *Deuteronomy* 34:11–12.

48. Both his appearance and deportment led strangers to immediately identify him as an Egyptian; see *Exodus* 2:18–20.

49. The facts that Moses never circumcised his son (*Exodus* 4:24–26) and that, while under his leadership in the wilderness, the premier rite of the Abrahamic faith—circumcision of male offspring—was not performed (*Joshua* 3:5, 7) both argue that within his psyche there resided a deep-seated ambiguity and alienation from his Hebrew identity.

and informed on by them to the authorities, a fugitive from justice, married into the family of a pagan priest, and to top it off, a poor and unpersuasive speaker; we would hardly consider this man a viable candidate to be the Savior of his people, much less a prophet of God. Yet it was he whom God chose. Why? Two possibilities present themselves: either Moses possessed other qualities which outweighed his liabilities[50] or of all possible candidates he was the best (or to put it another way, the best of a bad lot). These two possibilities are not mutually exclusive; they can be complementary. Let us examine the second more closely.

When one looks at the larger picture presented by the Bible, a pattern emerges. We, who currently are the Bible's readers and who thus have a grasp of the larger biblical perspective, can see that God does not create His agents *de novo*—that is, He does not (as it were) manufacture His tools as needed—but he chooses from the material available at the time. Put in simplistic terms: if at any given moment He should be in need of a leader, or a prophet or a savior, if a Deborah[51] or a David[52] is available He will choose them. If not—which is most of the time—He will perforce make do with what is available. The result of this is that the overwhelming majority of God's agents prove to be far from the ideal persons that we would wish them to be. And because no one is perfect, even the best of God's agents have their flaws and shortcomings. This brings us back to Moses and Jeremiah—among the best of God's better choices.

In both cases, while the material chosen had most of the qualities needed for the thankless tasks they were meant to perform—most essentially, they proved both tougher and more resilient than they had ever imagined they could be—as a consequence of that very fact, they were also very refractory: they resisted being shaped into tools to be used by God. Both Moses and Jeremiah had their own ideas of what they wanted to do with their lives, and it was only by applying force that God was able to bend them to His purposes.[53] But God could win no permanent victory. The toughness and resilience that were to enable them to hold their ground and persevere over careers lasting decades also made them less-than-pliable tools in the hands of God; both continued to be refractory from time to time, and God could never be certain of willing compliance with His orders. Both prophets were a constant problem to God throughout their careers. God's forbearance in their cases, as well as in those of most of His "tools," was the necessary result of the use of flawed material in order to accomplish His purposes. And as long as God chooses to deal with human beings who are not robots but possess freedom, they will have personalities that seek their own ends. Under these circumstances resistance—even rebellion—can only be expected.

---

50. Among the elements possessed by Moses that God may have considered are the fact that, uniquely among Israelites, he grew up a free man, untainted by the character deformation that slavery imposes on its victims; that he was the product of one of the best educational systems available anywhere in that era; and that he possessed a passion for justice, a character trait on which the biblical text lays great stress (*Exodus* 2:11–17).

51. At the time, governor of Israel, prophet, charismatic leader and poet.

52. Future charismatic leader, liberator of Israel, poet and king when he was chosen.

53. When commissioned by God, both Moses and Jeremiah try to talk their way out of their missions (*Exodus* 3:11–4:17; *Jeremiah* 1:6–8).

Was Jeremiah a Success or a Failure?

The final issue to receive our scrutiny is Jeremiah's conviction that his was a wasted life, and that as a prophet he was an abject failure. There seems little doubt that from the first he sought, as the central focus of his prophetic mission, to somehow avert the catastrophe that had fallen upon the Northern Kingdom of Israel in the previous century from overtaking the current Kingdom of Judah and its people. The grim word of God—

> *"From the* NORTH *shall the evil break forth upon all the inhabitants of the land.... And I will utter My judgments for all their evil, in that they have forsaken Me, and have burned incense to other gods and have worshiped the works of their hands"* [1:14, 16].

—pronouncing doom upon Judah and delineating its cause, continued to haunt him all his life. But knowing the reason for the punishment gave him the hope that could he but convince "the inhabitants of the land" to change their ways—to return to their God and to take Him seriously, cling to Him alone, abandoning once and for all their perennial flirtations with idolatry—the doom could be forestalled. This, and the warning "Don't place your trust in Egypt; it is from the North that the disaster threatens," are the two drumbeats that from the very beginning will reverberate in his prophecy.

But as the years slipped by he made headway neither with the subjects of the Kingdom, nor with its establishment. Worse: as time passed, not only did the attitude of the populace toward Jeremiah and his message shift from ridicule to indifference, and then to active hostility, but the leadership of the state—the king, the court, the priesthood and the prophetic guilds—moved from active promotion of religious reform to what, at its most generous assessment, can be described as turning a blind eye to the private idolatry of significant segments of the people. Instead of improvement, from the death of King Josiah matters became progressively worse, and this despite Jeremiah's most ardent efforts.[54]

In the end the disaster came. As he had so often warned, the Temple was destroyed, Jerusalem gutted, the land desolate, the population slaughtered and the survivors exiled. And as a final indignity, Jeremiah himself is forced to witness the Judean refugees in Egypt among whom he finds himself turn their backs on both him and his God, and make the decision to choose idolatry as their faith.[55]

---

54. During the reign of Jehoiakim, while Jeremiah had a sizable segment of the upper aristocracy behind him—largely holdovers from the Josiah regime—it was the king who called the shots, and he was uniformly hostile to Jeremiah and the values he espoused. The regime that succeeded Jehoiakim—that of King Zedekiah—saw a reversed situation: Zedekiah was sympathetic to Jeremiah and the policy he championed, but it was not he who determined policy. A weak man—the opposite of his autocratic brother—he was dominated by his nobles and they were adamantly opposed to Jeremiah and his policies. In sum, neither by personal influence nor by persuading the masses was Jeremiah ever able to decisively influence either the policy of the Kingdom or the moral level of the populace.

55. *Then all the men who knew that their wives were burning incense to other gods, and all the wives who were present—a large assembly—even all the people* [of Judah] *who were dwelling in the land of Egypt, in Pathros, answered Jeremiah, saying: "As for the word that you have spoken to us in the name of the Lord, we will not listen to you. We most assuredly intend to do everything that has come forth from our mouths* [i.e., that we have vowed]*; to burn incense to the Queen of Heaven and to pour out libations to her, even as we did—we, and our fathers, our kings and our princes in the cities of Judah and in the plazas of Jerusalem. For then we* [continued]

Is it any surprise that at his life's end Jeremiah sees himself as an unmitigated failure?

But was Jeremiah justified when he summarized his career? From the perspective of a lifetime—even the relatively long life that Jeremiah led—and taking into account the goals he thought God had set for him at his Call and commissioning, his self-evaluation would seem reasonable.[56] But human beings are short-lived creatures, and of necessity can take in only a short-term perspective, the worm's eye view, as it were. From the bird's eye perspective—the God's eye view—things inevitably appear very different. Humans can only get a glimpse of this "bird's eye" perspective—if they are historically minded—in retrospect. Looked at from this angle, we become aware that often the tasks we are called upon to perform stretch far beyond our lifetimes. They are endeavors whose outcomes we will never see, and so what may look like failure in the short term can, in the long term, turn out to be success.

Often we are unaware of the true significance of the tasks to which we are set. We think we are dealing with one issue, while in the larger picture we are really involved in pursuing a completely different outcome. Jeremiah thought he had been mandated to save the Kingdom of Judah from disaster. But we, who currently hold the Bible in our hands and who are heirs to the larger biblical perspective, are aware that the Kingdom and its people had been doomed by God for its intractable idolatry. The entire sociopolitical framework had served its purpose, and was now unsalvageable. From the vantage point of several thousand years later we can make sense of God's need to break the mold and to make a fresh start; to give the kaleidoscope a turn, and create a fresh pattern with which to work. The destruction of the Kingdom and the Exile was the turn of the kaleidoscope that would shake things up and make a new start possible.[57]

It is a historical fact that the trauma of the Destruction and the Exile reshaped the survivors, and the Children of Israel—a small, insular and inward-looking people—were moved onto the world stage. The latent universalism inherent in their monotheistic faith shifted to the fore; idolatry ceased to be an issue—much less *the* central issue—of the faith of Israel.

> The lesson of history is that they [the people] not only endured, but that it was precisely in exile that the full stature of Israelite religion began to manifest itself. It began to prepare the forms

---

had plenty of food and were well-off and saw no evil. But from the time we stopped burning incense to the Queen of Heaven and pouring out libations to her [i.e., from the days of the Josianic Reform] *we have lacked everything, and have been consumed by the sword and by famine."* (44:15–18)

56. It would seem that Jeremiah never internalized the significance of his divinely directed purchase of his cousin's field during the last days of the siege of Jerusalem, and the message of hope that it conveyed (32:6–15; see above the section entitled A Prisoner Buys a Field). Even after God's decisive answer to Jeremiah's prayer of despair, the message, if indeed it penetrated at all, seems to have been dissipated by subsequent events. Only after Jeremiah's death does the message begin to reverberate and take hold among the Judean exiles in Babylon.

57. These are conclusions that a current reader can reasonably come to, granted that he or she accepts the premises on which the text—and, for that matter, the Bible as a whole—is based. As I promised in the Preface, this is not a proselytizing work; the reader is under no obligation to accept these premises. All that has been asked is a temporary suspension of disbelief so as to enable the reader to understand and appreciate the world from which the Bible came, and the message which it conveys.

for the second stage of its development, when it would challenge and finally overwhelm the triumphant gods.

Before Israel could declare war upon paganism, however, it had to eliminate the last vestiges of "idolatry" from its own midst.... The disappearance of idolatry in Israel took place in the first generations after the fall.... That national collapse and exile should have brought on the complete and final extirpation of Israelite idolatry is... [a] datum of tremendous historical import.... Life in exile necessarily gave birth to a radically new type of cult, a cult without sacrifice or priesthood: the worship of the synagogue.[58]

In the crucible of destruction and exile, the Israelite had been transformed into the Jew.

The Book Jeremiah, begun in deep hiding in 604, augmented by his later pronouncements and Baruch's biography of critical parts of his life, lived on after him. Brought to Babylon,[59] the Book began to develop a life of its own, its contents increasingly entering the consciousness of the exile community there. What had been ignored in Judah and rejected by the exiles in Egypt began to take root in Babylon, buoyed by the prophecy of a terminus to their current status of homelessness: that after 70 years the exile would end, and that they would be restored to their land (25:8–13; 29:4–14). And as Jeremiah's prophecies of the destruction of the Temple and Kingdom had been fulfilled, the belief took hold that Jeremiah's prophecy of redemption was also assured. The fall of Babylon in 539 BCE found what had been a rabble of broken exiles transformed into a community of believers. This rejuvenation was not only due to Jeremiah, but through the Book that circumstances had compelled him to compile, it is to Jeremiah that the credit for the initial impetus belongs. The cascade that began in 608 BCE in the Temple, and that reached its crescendo in 605, also in the Temple,[60] found its fulfillment in 538 with there being a people in existence worthy of being liberated so that a portion of them could return, rebuild the Temple and begin the reclamation and rebuilding of Jerusalem.[61]

I would suggest that in the larger picture—from the God's eye-point of view—Jeremiah's real job had been to prepare the ground for this transformation. His Message—that for their sin of idolatry, the LORD, the God of Israel, had condemned the Kingdom of Judah to destruction—had been relentlessly repeated for more than forty years. But it was only among the survivors of the catastrophe, in exile in Babylon, that the message first found acceptance and finally took root in the soul of the people. His call for repentance, and his promise that after seventy years the sentence would end and God's people—purged of their sin—would return to their land[62] was what enabled the people to endure the catastrophe.

It seems clear in retrospect that Jeremiah, and his younger contemporary Ezekiel—Jeremiah in Jerusalem, and Ezekiel in Babylon—between them provided the spiritual resources that enabled Israel not to be irretrievably broken by the calamitous

---

58. Y. Kaufmann, *The Religion of Israel*, pp. 450–451, 5.
59. It seems likely that Baruch, after his master's death, left Egypt to reunite with family who had been exiled to Babylon, bringing the manuscript with him.
60. See Historic Interlude II. Scandals in the Temple.
61. The first wave of returnees left Babylon in 538 BCE.
62. 25:8–13; 29:10–14; 30:1–25; 31:34–39 etc.

fall of the Kingdom.[63] But it is Jeremiah's teachings, through the medium of his Book, that must be credited with the initial impulse and direction that set the exiles onto the road to redemption. It is to Jeremiah, and Jeremiah alone, that the Chronicler awards the credit.

> *Now in the first year of Cyrus, king of Persia,[64] that the word of the* LORD *as proclaimed by Jeremiah[65] be fulfilled, the* LORD *stirred up the spirit of Cyrus, king of Persia, and he made a proclamation throughout all his kingdom, and also put it in writing, saying: "Thus says Cyrus, king of Persia: 'All the kingdoms of the earth has the* LORD*, the God of the heavens, given to me, and He has laid upon me the task of building Him a House in Jerusalem, which is in Judah. Whoever there is among you of all His people—the* LORD *his God be with him—let him go up'"* [2 Chronicles 36:22–23; Ezra 1:1–3a].

For all his doubts, frustrations, bursts of resentment and rebellion, all unbeknownst, Jeremiah was helping midwife the rebirth of his people, and the transformation of the Israelite into the Jew.

From God's point of view, Jeremiah's career was a resounding success.

> *And the* LORD *put forth His hand and touched me on my mouth, and said:*
> *"Behold, I have put My words in your mouth.*
> *See, I have set you this day*
>
> *Over the nations and over the kingdoms:*
> *To uproot and to break down,*
> *To destroy and to overthrow,*
> ***To build and to plant"*** [Jeremiah 1:9–10].

---

63. The exile community produced its own prophets—notably Ezekiel and the prophet known to us alternatively as Deutero-Isaiah or "the unknown prophet of the exile" (*Isaiah* 40–66)—who must share the credit for the remarkable preservation of the remnants of a people with both feet already in the grave, and in its metamorphosis from a semi-pagan "rebellious House" into a faith community.

64. I.e., in the first year after his conquest of Babylon and his assuming the rule over the entire Chaldean Empire (339–338 BCE).

65. Literally, *by the mouth of Jeremiah*.

Conclusion: A Final Accounting

Therefore, since the world has still
Much good, but much less good than ill,
And while the sun and moon endure
Luck's a chance, but trouble's sure,
I'd face it as a wise man would
And train for ill and not for good.

—A.E. Housman, *A Shropshire Lad*, LXII

Three Abortive Rebellions

The subject of our study has been two tales of rebellion placed side-by-side with a personal account of the same, stemming respectively from the dawn, high noon and sundown of the First Commonwealth; a span of more than six hundred years separating the first of our protagonists from the last. Three disparate and distinct literary formats—a historical narrative, a fable and a disjointed spiritual autobiography—confront us, embodying three unique personalities driven by radically different motives to one and the same outcome: insubordination in the face of their acknowledged Master. Two of these tales are encased in highly polished and extremely sophisticated literary compositions, of which one—the *Book of Jonah*—appears solo in the Bible as one of the Prophetic Books, while the other—the *Book of Balaam*—has achieved canonical status through its incorporation in the *Book of Numbers*.[1] The third, the so-called "Confessions of Jeremiah," comprises a collection of disparate autobiographical compositions—mostly in poetry—gathered from among the writings of the prophet in the biblical Book that bears his name.

All these we have analyzed in some depth. They have proved to be extremely complex and multi-faceted, but when we focus on the common element of rebellion, patterns begin to emerge. Let us summarize, in order of appearance.

Jonah: by the time we have reached the dénouement of the Book we have learned that Jonah's rebellion is over a matter of principle.[2] The demands made upon him vio-

---

1. As *Numbers* 22:2–24:25, with *Numbers* 21 on the one hand, and *Numbers* 25 and 31 on the other serving to frame the Book and integrate it into the larger saga of the Wilderness Wanderings.

2. The fact that the hero of the Book is a character in a tale invented by its author is irrelevant to the present argument. We are comparing three literary works in the form we currently possess them, and comparing their respective plot-lines.

late his deepest held convictions, and it is these that drive him to rebel. While he is finally compelled by force majeure to comply, yet it would seem that God fails to convince him that he is in error, and he remains faithful to his convictions to the very end.

Balaam: the issue in the *Book of Balaam* pivots not on a matter of principle but on that of ego.[3] Balaam refuses to be God's servant, insisting on having his own way. But in his case also all his attempts to free himself from divine compulsion fail. As we have it, the story of Balaam is a tale with two alternative endings. In the Book he surrenders to God, losing everything in the material sense but spiritually triumphing, becoming a prophet.[4] Conversely, in the Epilogue he intensifies his rebellion and loses everything, including his life. In a sense, the dichotomy in our current text of the *Book of Numbers* embodies a proposition that these are the two alternatives open to the human condition.

Jeremiah: as he tells it, it would appear that his motives are mixed. In the first place, there festers a deep resentment at having been forced against his will into a lifetime calling that he never wanted. Then adding injury to insult, he finds the life that he is forced to lead intolerable. Both combined lead him to open revolt, only to find that refusal is no option. Ultimately, he would seem to have made his peace with a fate, not of his choosing, that he cannot alter.

In sum, what we have are three variations on a common theme: three exceptional human beings—and they are exceptional; persons who care deeply and who are very strong-willed—who are told to do or not to do something, a mandate which they find deeply offensive and which leads to rank insubordination. Their refusals are overruled, and despite their best efforts they find that they have no choice but to do as they are told. Rebellion collapses; their attempts at charting independent paths fail.

The Tragic Struggle for Autonomy

The time has now come to discuss what has led us to group these tales together, beyond the common office their protagonists hold—all were prophets—and the joint theme of rebellion that drives these compositions. As an assemblage what do they have to tell us?

Our suggestion is that despite the real differences in the personalities, circumstances and motives of our three protagonists, there is a fundamental issue that underlies all of our cases, one which raises them from being of purely anecdotal interest to a level of universal concern. Our proposal is that what we have before us amounts to three studies stemming from three separate periods of the Biblical Age, all of which are exploring the question of human autonomy: to what degree is

---

3. In the case of Balaam we need to differentiate between the *Book of Balaam* proper (*Numbers* 22–24) and its Epilogue (*Numbers* 25 and 31), which are by two different authors. Although these authors in effect picture Balaam from very different perspectives and evaluate his actions quite differently, they both agree as to the source of his rebellion: his ego.

4. By losing everything materially, Balaam gains an unparalleled increase of freedom. He ceases being God's ventriloquist's dummy and gains freedom of expression. From a vision restricted to insight into past and present, his perspective expands to take in the future as well.

Conclusion: A Final Accounting

autonomy a practical possibility for human beings? And if it is, to what extent is it to be desired? In sum, we aver that our three heroes (or possibly in more than one case, antiheroes) are meant to do duty as prototypes of the human condition: that the authors of these compositions that we know today as the *Book of Jonah* and the *Book of Balaam* intentionally crafted their tales in the way that they did in order that their protagonists could serve as depictions of "Everyman." And in the case of Jeremiah, the way he lived his long life, continually turning himself into a living sermon, produced someone who could be seen as more symbol than man. He also can be seen as a potential prototype.

But before we can proceed to explore this matter we need to be clear in our minds as to what we mean by the term *autonomy*. The word itself comes from the Greek and means to be self-governing, without outside control; a law unto oneself.[5] In this sense autonomy is a synonym for freedom: an autonomous person is a free person, one who has charge of his or her own life.

To begin with, the very idea of autonomy is counterintuitive. We all know from experience that we can't do everything we want to do. External restraints—which include other humans—limit our options and often block us from achieving our desires. Not infrequently we are forced to act in ways contrary to what we would wish, while only rarely, if ever, can we fully get our way. Yet despite this awareness, most of us hold deep in our hearts the unrealizable dream of autonomy as an ideal desideratum. Somehow, in an ideal world, we would be free to do as we will. This basic contradiction between the ideal of autonomy and the consciousness of the restraints of reality goes to the very core of the human condition. We dream of living our lives as we would wish, and rage against both those who thwart us and the objective realities that restrain us. It is to this inherent contradiction that, at their deepest level, our three tales address themselves.

The problem is universal, but in the era in which we find ourselves it is especially acute. The temper of our times holds that personal autonomy should be more than merely a dream; in our day it is looked upon as virtually a basic right, and somehow attainable.[6] So all-prevailing is this attitude that even in disciplines—such as academic philosophy—that routinely subject cultural phenomena to critical analysis, almost universally they seem to accept autonomy or self-governance as a good, while feeling no need to give reasons for this value judgment. Such uncritical acceptance of autonomy as a positive value virtually cries out for serious consideration of so inherently problematic a subject. It is this very lack of balance that makes these three tales that are the subject of our study so timely: for in that they address our issue, and in that their protagonists—as we would contend—are cast as representatives of the human condition, i.e., "everyman," considering what they have to say may help us to achieve a more balanced and reasoned appreciation of what is involved.

Surprisingly, despite the many differences between our three texts—in subjects,

---

5. *Auto* = self + *numos* = law, hence self-law, i.e., to be a law unto oneself.

6. It was not always so. Before the 18th century it was mostly taken as a given that human autonomy was an evil that could only lead to anarchy and social collapse: man was meant to be governed. The turning point in the attitude—from bad to good—with regard to autonomy came with Rousseau (1712–1778). More on this shift in attitude further on.

settings, authorial perspectives and eras of composition—the authors are unanimous on one central thesis: that in spite of the fact that the aspiration to be self-governing seems native to human nature, autonomy is not a viable option for a human being.[7] All three of our texts, being parts of the Bible, naturally frame the issue in terms of an uneven struggle between God—Creator of man and Governor of the universe—on the one hand, and specific persons—stand-ins for humanity in general—whose sense of integrity drives them to revolt against their inability to fulfill themselves as they see fit. Because of the inherent inequality of the two contestants, the struggle is futile from the start, and hence tragic. In all three cases the battle cry of our protagonists amounts to the declaration of the poet:

> *I am the master of my fate,*
> *I am the captain of my soul.*[8]

And in each instance an unsympathetic deity dashes the illusion to pieces; man is not the master of his fate. It is God, our tales insist, Who holds the destiny of our souls in His Hand.[9]

The tragedy embodied in our tales is twofold. God has created human beings with a capacity of free choice and the resultant desire to use it. Therefore God finds humans to be refractory, disobedient and rebellious; as we would say nowadays, they are hardwired to be so. On the other hand, the humans who are designed to freely choose can be expected to want to actualize this capacity freely, and are deeply offended by being blocked from doing so. This is a conflict built into the very design of the world in which we find ourselves, a struggle seen as profoundly unsatisfactory by both parties. This is an issue that goes to the heart of the human condition, and one that first surfaces in the opening pages of the Bible, in a tale that I would contend to be foundational.

East of Eden

> *Now the* LORD *God formed the man* [from] *dust from the ground, and breathed into his nostrils the breath of life; and the man became a living being. And the* LORD *God planted a garden to the East of Eden,*[10] *and He placed there the man that he had formed* [Genesis 2:7–8].

---

7. We must never forget that two of the texts we have chosen to analyze are literary compositions, whose anonymous authors designated prophets to be their central protagonists and chose to so cast their anti-heroes as to be extreme exemplars of humankind; the implication being that if these extremely capable human beings proved unable to wrest a measure of autonomy for their lives, then who can? The real-life example of Jeremiah acts as a confirmation of this thesis.

8. William Ernest Henley, *Invictus*, final lines.

9. For those among us who do not hold a theocentric view of the universe, there is no great difficulty in reframing our issue in secular terms. For an unresponsive deity substitute an indifferent universe in which humans, driven by a compulsion to fulfill themselves, come up against a refractory environment that inevitably blocks them.

10. Hebrew *b'eden mikedem*. An alternative rendition would be: *Now the Lord God planted a garden at the beginning of time, in Eden,* taking *mikedem* in its temporal sense to mean "in primeval times." So LXX, Targ., Rashi, Ibn Ezra and Kimchi.

This mythic account from the opening chapters of the Bible—the story of the Garden of Eden—is a tale that is often misunderstood. Readers have tended to read the tale *historically*, that is, to see it as a factual account of a series of events that took place at a specific moment in time, rather than to read the tale *metaphorically*. Read thus, the story of the Garden of Eden becomes a profound meditation on the human condition: an attempt to understand why human life is so shot through with misery and tragedy. Read metaphorically, the story does not tell us what once happened so much as what *always* happens. The tale provides insight into the permanent psycho-moral condition of the human being that reasserts itself in every generation, and addresses itself to the question that persistently dodges our years: why are our lives so difficult?[11]

The tale insists that it wasn't always so. We are taken back to the beginning, the original primordial state of the emergent species from its fellow members of the animal kingdom. Like them, the prototypical human finds himself in a state of innocence. He has neither past nor future; he is only conscious of the present in which he exists, and of his primal needs: food, drink, rest, absence of pain and so forth. It is notable that sexual needs do not seem to ruffle the restful state of this innocent soul.[12] The world in which he finds himself—the Garden—supplies all his felt needs with minimum effort on his part. Even if he is aware at this point in time of his assigned occupation—*to tend the garden and to keep it* (Genesis 2:15)[13]—the task is not onerous. Life is simple and pleasant; food grows on trees and fruit is available for the picking. In sum, living is easy, self-consciousness is minimal and responsibilities few; existence is childlike and hence idyllic.

The Garden in which the man finds himself is set out as a fruit orchard, designed with man in mind for his easy living. But there is more to it then just the fruit trees. In the midst of the Garden *the* LORD *God made to grow ... the tree of life and the tree of the knowledge of good and bad.*[14] (Genesis 2:9) The ingestion of the fruit of the first grants eternal life,[15] while partaking of the second—which becomes the focus of the tale—would appear to open one's eyes to the possibility of autonomous choice between alternative courses of action.[16] The point here to be emphasized is that the Garden was not just there; it was God Who made the Garden, God Who put the

---

11. I am indebted to Leon Kass, *Beginning of Wisdom*, Chapter 2, for much of this analysis.

12. William Golding, in his first exploration of primal innocence and its tragic dénouement, cast his protagonists as a population of pre-adolescent schoolboys, thus avoiding the complication of sex in his modern re-creation of the Garden of Eden myth, *Lord of the Flies*. In the biblical tale, the one lack of the original man was companionship, and we are not told that the man originally experiences it as a lack. It is God who feels this as a dissonance: *"It is not good for man to be alone."* (Genesis 2:18)

13. Hebrew *leabdah u-leshamrah*; literally, to work it and to guard it, i.e., to keep it up, to maintain it against deterioration.

14. This phrase is often rendered as *good and evil*. The Hebrew term *ra* has both the meanings of *bad* and *evil*. *Bad* is the more general term. *Evil* is a subcategory of *Bad*: *evil* means the morally bad (sickness is bad, but not evil; rape is bad *and* evil). Just as *good* is a general category, applying equally to morally charged areas of life and morally neutral ones, so its appropriate antonym would properly be *bad*. The relevance of this difference will soon become apparent.

15. Man is made of perishable stuff: dust of the ground. It is not clear from the text whether one bite would confer immortality, or it would require a constant diet of the fruit to sustain life.

16. This simple formulation does not do justice to the complexity of the subject. See below for further elaboration.

man in the Garden, and put the two trees—the tree of life and the tree of the knowledge of good and bad—in the midst of the Garden. In other words, the possibilities of immortality and, as we shall see, autonomy were put within human reach from the start by God. All the man has to do is put out his hand and seize the opportunity.[17]

While placing the man in the Garden God addresses him directly and gives him his operating instructions, which include a warning[18]:

> *Now the* LORD *God commanded the man saying: "Of all the trees of the Garden you are free to eat,*[19] *but as to the tree of the knowledge of good and bad you shall not eat of its* [fruit]; *for on the day you eat of it, you shall certainly die!"*[20] [Genesis 2:16–17]

Of the tree of the knowledge of good and bad God not only forbids in the strongest terms the eating of its fruit, but appends to the prohibition a warning: eating of it is a capital offense: eat and you will die! But of the tree of life no mention is made. And indeed, not having had his attention drawn to the tree of life, the man seems entirely indifferent to it. In his innocent childlike state, death has no meaning for him, and he has no fear of it,[21] and thus no incentive to prevent it by acquiring immortality. God has no need to prohibit it because the man simply has no interest in it.

The tree of the knowledge of good and bad is another matter entirely. As we shall see, this tree has an intrinsic attraction. And as to the warning, death having no meaning to the man in his current childlike state, the warning passes him by, leaving no impression. All that registers is the prohibition, and by the fact of its being prohibited the man's attention is drawn to this tree. The questions, as to what the tree of the knowledge of good and bad confers and what its consequences may be, are much less clear-cut. Firstly, we must ever keep in mind that the tree is a metaphor; knowledge does not grow on trees.[22] What the tree stands for appears to be both the ability and the propensity to make independent value judgments based on personal experience and rational consideration. We are here talking not merely of moral matters but of all areas of practical life; the tree represents rational evaluation of alternative courses of action and free choice between them on the basis of which seems better and which worse. It would seem that our story starts with the assumption that humans have the built-in ability to make free—that is, autonomous—choices. After all, why would God warn against acquiring the knowledge of good and bad—i.e., the consciousness of being able to make independent choices—if the *ability* to do so was not *innate* (but as yet dormant)? The point of eating the fruit of the tree would thus seem to be a symbolic way of describing an act that brings on a conscious awareness of one's ability to choose, as well as activating the desire to use this ability. And as we shall see, the tale confirms this suspicion.

---

17. Is the tale implying that the man is being set up?

18. This is the first time in the Story of the Garden of Eden (*Genesis* 2:4–3:24) that God directly addresses the man whom He formed. God's communication is explicitly framed as a command.

19. Literally, *eating you may eat* (the infinitive absolute construction), i.e., you certainly may eat.

20. Again, the infinitive absolute construction.

21. Kass is of the opinion that "as is true of any other animal, man's immediate attachment to his own life implies an instinctive fear of death… [but] because concern with death does not penetrate the consciousness of his simple soul," he shows no interest in the tree of life. (*Beginning of Wisdom*, p. 62)

22. Kass, *Ibid.*, p. 63.

Conclusion: A Final Accounting

Now the serpent was the most cunning of all the beasts of the field that the LORD *God had made,*[23] *and he said to the woman: "Is it true that God said: 'You shall not eat of any tree in the Garden?'" And the woman said to the serpent: "We may eat of the fruit of the trees of the Garden,* [but] *of the fruit of the tree that is in the midst of the Garden God said, 'You shall not eat of it nor touch it lest you die.'" And the serpent said to the woman: "You most certainly will not die,*[24] *for God knows that on the day that you* [plural] *eat of it your eyes will be opened and you will be like gods, knowing good and bad." And the woman saw that* [the fruit of] *the tree was good for eating, and a delight to the eyes, and desirable to make one wise. And she took some of its fruit and ate; and she also gave to her man* [who was] *with her, and he ate* [Genesis 3:1–6].

Note that *eating* the fruit does not provide either knowledge or the motivation to choose. Even *before she ate*, the woman makes an autonomous choice to eat from the tree, and then does so. The eating is merely the outcome of her choice. So why did she choose to do so? We are told:

"For God knows that on the day that you [plural] *eat of it your eyes will be opened and you will be like gods, knowing good and bad"* [Genesis 3:5].

It is the lure, the promise of apotheosis—to become like gods, to become coequal with God—that tips the balance. And the promise of the serpent is no lie; it is confirmed by no less a Personage than God Himself (*Genesis* 3:22)! But the promise is not all that it seems. To become "like gods" one would have to make the *right* choices, and the ability to choose does not guarantee that the choices made will be the right ones, either for others or for oneself. Humans are emotional as well as rational creatures, and emotions often cloud one's reason. More to the point, reasoning is based on the facts at one's disposal, and these in turn are based on our experience, which is invariably limited.

And herein lies the rub: we never know enough to ensure good decisions. Human beings are short-lived creatures, and this short lifespan guarantees that most of our choices will be poor ones. Indeed, considering his lack of experience, a man could expect good choices to be merely flukes. The upshot of this line of reasoning is that gaining consciousness of the ability to make autonomous choices based on one's own experience and reasoning—partaking of the fruit of the tree of knowledge of good and bad in the language of the biblical metaphor—by itself does not confer Godlike status. Only by *also* partaking of the fruit of the tree of life—becoming immortal, and thus gaining the experience that would enable *good* choices—can man become like gods. And our text confirms this line of reasoning.

---

23. Who or what is the serpent? Remembering that we are not reading this story *historically*, as an account of past events, but *metaphorically*, we must keep in mind that just as knowledge doesn't grow on trees, likewise, snakes don't talk. As the tree is a metaphor representing the possibility of human autonomy, so the serpent is a metaphor. It is the objectification and externalization of the innate human ability to reason, up to this point dormant, that is coming awake; questioning appearances, innocent reliance on instinct and naïve acceptance of things as they are. Implied by the focused maliciousness of the serpent's intentional undermining of the woman's innocence is the dangerous propensity of reason to get things wrong and to lead astray. Also suggested is reason's tendency to erode past certainties and inner confidence in oneself and one's ways. Once unfettered reason gains sway, untroubled peace of mind becomes a distant memory. See also Chapter 7, note 47.

24. The infinitive absolute construction.

> *Now the* LORD *God said: "Behold, the man has become like one of us, knowing good and bad. And now, what if he puts forth his hand and also takes from the tree of life and eats, and lives forever?" So the* LORD *God sent him forth from the Garden of Eden to work the soil from whence he was taken. So He drove forth the man, and to the East of the Garden of Eden He stationed the cherubim and the whirling flaming sword to guard the road to the tree of life* [Genesis 3:22–24].

More; not only is the man denied the possibility of joining immortality to autonomy, thus achieving godlike status, but God also cuts the lifespan of primordial humanity—which was measured in centuries[25]—down to our current terms.

> *Now the* LORD *said: "My breath*[26] *shall not abide in man for ever,*[27] *for he also is* [merely] *flesh; so his days shall* [henceforth] *be 120 years"* [Genesis 6:3].

In other words, what this biblical tale is saying is that human beings can never become "like gods." Apotheosis is denied a priori to humans.[28] At the start, the species is seen as having had the divinely preferred option of innocence and long life (with the possibility of immortality) or the option of autonomy at the price of a short life. And, not knowing what they were doing, the prototypical humans—Adam and Eve—chose autonomy. And that is why the human condition is what it is.

There remain the questions which we left open earlier: the first being what was it that impelled the woman to make the choice that she did. We noted that she was tempted, even seduced, and that the clincher was the lure that humans could become like gods. It was the overweening ambition to be coequal with their Creator—in other words, *hubris*—that led the prototypical humans to choose autonomy over obedience. And this vaulting ambition, our tale clearly implies, was latent in the human being, present *before* tasting of the tree, and was the root cause of the choice of autonomy.

The issue remaining concerns the consequences of disobedience. To put the question differently, we know what the woman thought she would gain: she had been promised that *your eyes will be opened and you will be like gods, knowing good and bad,* and she therefore concluded that the fruit of the tree was *desirable to make one wise. And so she took some of the fruit and ate…* (Genesis 3:6)

And it was so: her eyes were opened, but the wisdom acquired was not what she had expected.

---

25. The man (Adam) is said to have lived 930 years (*Genesis* 5:3–5). Including Adam, there are ten antediluvians listed in *Genesis* 5–10. If we do not count Enoch who "walked with God and disappeared" (*Genesis* 5:24) and his grandson Lamech who drowned in the great flood at age 777 (*Genesis* 5:31) the remaining eight are reputed to have had an average life span of 926 years.

26. I.e., *the breath of life* by which God vitalized the dust from which the original human being was created. (*Genesis* 2:7)

27. Thus LXX, Vulg., Saadia and Ramban. The word *yadon* (here rendered "abide" due to the context) is a hapex (see Glossary). Rashi, Rambam and Ibn Ezra see the word as derived from the root *dyn*, "to judge." Hence they render this phrase as *My spirit will not continue to suspend judgment upon man…*

28. The Bible stands opposed to the pagan belief that not only was apotheosis possible, but was actually realized by select individuals, such as the rulers of Egypt. The Pharaoh was believed by Egyptians—and believed himself as well—to become transformed into a god upon succeeding to the throne. The Bible is proclaiming this belief to be mere delusion.

And the eyes of both of them were opened, and they realized[29] that they were naked; so they sewed together fig leaves[30] and made for themselves loincloths [Genesis 3:7].

Autonomous choice fosters wisdom; wisdom involves self-consciousness, which leads to the realization for the first time of their sexual nature, which in turn leads to their consciousness of their nakedness, and to the value judgment that nakedness is bad. Innocent self-acceptance is replaced by shame.[31] That wisdom reveals unanticipated realities was not what they had expected. Worse is to come.

Disobedience also must be paid for. Called to account, humans are sentenced to the consequences of their act[32]:

And to the man[33] He[34] said: "Because you heeded the voice of your woman, and ate of the tree from which I commanded you not to eat:
Due to you, cursed be the ground;
By painful labor shall you eat from it
All the days of your life.
Thorn and thistle shall it bring forth to you,
And you shall eat the grass of the field.
By the sweat of your brow[35]
Shall you eat bread,
Until you return to the ground;
For from it were you taken.
For dust you are,
And to dust shall you return" [Genesis 3:17–19].

In place of achieving divine freedom with autonomy, man finds himself enslaved to what we now know as the human condition. Instead of immortality, man is consigned to mortality: from now on all human beings will be stamped with an expiration date.[36] Life will now be a ceaseless struggle just to survive. And far from being masters of their fate, though human beings may harbor this illusion, they will never be in control. Instead of the dream of a life like gods, the price exacted by the choice of autonomy is a life that is nasty, brutish and short.

A Saving Grace

What we have tried to demonstrate by our very partial and selective analysis of the foundational Garden of Eden Story is an attitude toward human autonomy,

---

29. Literally, *they knew*.
30. Fig trees, as copious producers of sweet fruit, had been one of the human's favorite food trees. Now in their hour of need they find another use for it: fig leaves are large, wide and tough: ideal material for a cover-up.
31. Shame is an emotion felt upon becoming aware of the gap between one's idealized self-image and reality.
32. For the sake of maintaining focus, we skip over the sentence passed on the serpent and the woman which are species and gender specific, and concentrate on the fate dealt out to the man, which encompasses all humanity.
33. MT vocalizes the word as a proper noun, i.e., as *Adam*, as in *Genesis* 2:20.
34. I.e., the Lord God.
35. Literally, *of your face*.
36. *Genesis* 6:3. See also note 25 above.

obedience and disobedience to God, and the consequential condition of human life that permeates the entire Bible. The Bible views disobedience and rebellion against God, on the one hand, and human existence being nasty, brutish and short, on the other, as an inseparable package—two sides of the same coin. In this sense, the three tales that have been the focus of our investigation can be seen as commentaries on this biblical position. This is a stance which our three protagonists find extremely distasteful—or to be more exact, against which the authors of these tales are themselves in rebellion[37]—and we would suggest that their specific rebellions are as much a protest against the general human condition as a concern with their specific grievances.[38] The fact that three supremely intelligent and thoughtful authors—of which at least one is himself a prophet—writing in three different periods of the Biblical Age, come to one and the same conclusion, that revolt is futile, and in effect throw up their hands, would seem conclusive. This is the way things are, and there is nothing that can be done about it. Are we to accept this point of view?

Many, if not most modern readers of the Bible—myself included—would be almost instinctively repelled by this line of reasoning. As denizens of the 21st-century Western World, we have been brought up to believe that we are free to choose our paths in life, that autonomy is our most basic right, it is an absolute good; we deeply resent any overt or even implied curbs on it. This biblical position is completely alien to our sensibilities.

We have already mentioned that the father of the modern view that autonomy is a good much to be desired was the 18th-century philosopher Jean-Jacques Rousseau.[39] However, it was his younger contemporary, Immanuel Kant, who established the current conviction that personal autonomy is the highest value of all. Not only does the current sensibility hold that every human being has the innate right to make his or her own free choices, but as this is the highest value it is also incumbent upon us to respect the rights of others to make up their own minds. Just as we expect them to honor our right to choose, so must we honor theirs. This is the philosophical foundation of the liberal practice of tolerance, and hence our almost instinctive discomfort with, and dismissal of, the biblical position we have been explicating. So let us review the conclusion of our three authors in the light of the modern views of tolerance.

In the biblical view, the fundamental flaw in the ideal of human autonomy lies in the fact of the human inability to see the big picture, to be able therefore to reliably foresee the consequences—long and short-term alike—of the choices that lie before us. We lack the necessary data to make good choices, and hence one's choice cannot be good except by a stroke of luck. Because we have been created as free creatures, God often allows us to exercise our freedom and take the consequences of our choices. But God can, and at times does, override our decisions, as in the cases of our three tales; He does so ostensibly for our own good or for a higher good.

---

37. In the case of Jeremiah, the protagonist is identical with the author.

38. It is important to note that in all three tales, glimpses are provided of the larger picture—glimpses which our protagonists cannot see—which justify their having been overruled.

39. See note 6 above.

The Kantian assumption is that autonomy *is* the highest good, and that therefore it should never be aborted. But just at this point we run into a contradiction between theory and practice. What about children? They are human beings, yet we recognize that they lack the necessary knowledge to make wise decisions. Consequently parents routinely override their choices. And from the biblical point of view this is only right and proper; it is the responsibility of parents to do so to protect their young. From the biblical point of view, as all humans in the larger sense are children, their choices also often need to be overridden by God.

Returning to the primordial template of the Garden of Eden Story, because humans have never partaken of the tree of life they are mortal, and thus can never be "like gods." We lack an essential element of divinity and hence are consigned by default to the tragic human condition of being aware of the possibility of autonomy, but consigned by remorseless restraints to be unable to ever fully utilize this possibility. We are not, and can never be "like gods."

But is there no escape from the human condition? Here I would like to conclude what has turned out to be a meditation on the ambivalent and paradoxical condition that human beings find themselves in: biblically speaking, *humans are created in the image of God and know it, yet are unable to actualize that built-in capacity*. Endowed with the capacity for self-governance, humans are yet condemned by that very capability to an existence of frustration, misery and mortality. Is there no way out from this trap in which we find ourselves?

What can we learn from our three tales which are, in effect, attempts to address these very issues? In the first place we can postulate that it is often the best who will rebel, and therefore God is patient with these rebels; He doesn't just slap them down. Secondly, rebellion is futile. However distasteful it may be in our eyes, there is no escape from the human condition. And thirdly, our three tales all propose, very reluctantly, the same answer. It is the default position: to accept the inevitable and to make one's peace with it. Or to use the biblical terms in which our authors of necessity frame their answer: obedience to God.

This seems a paltry alternative to the exciting dream of autonomy, the yearning to be "like gods." But it is precisely here that I would like to close this meditation with what I consider a remarkable insight by Leon Kass. Let us recapitulate: human beings, aware of being created in the image of God,[40] are quite naturally obsessed by the desire to be like Him. In their attempt to achieve the divine capacity of free choice—so we are told in the Story of the Garden of Eden—they rebelled against His command and so plunged themselves into the condition that we know: a life that is nasty, brutish and short.

In his analysis of the Ten Commandments, Leon Kass points to an alternative.[41] God has opened to his creatures an opportunity to partially achieve their desire by means of obedience: through *Imitatio Dei*; through the imitation of God.

In creating the world, so we are told, God labors for six days and on the seventh

---

40. Twice, in *Genesis* 1:27 and 5:1–2, we are explicitly informed that both the prototypical humans—male and female alike—are created in the image of God. Their descendants can be presumed to have inherited this likeness.

41. Leon Kass, *Founding God's Nation: Reading Exodus*, pp. 348–354.

He desists from His labors, distances Himself from His work, and then, surprisingly, He blesses not His creation but the seventh day itself.

> *Now the heavens and the earth were completed and all their host. So on the seventh day God completed His work which he had made, and He desisted on the seventh day from all His work that He had made. Now God blessed the seventh day and He hallowed it,*[42] *because on it He desisted from all His work which God had created to make* [Genesis 2:1–3].

God is pleased with what he has made,[43] but His attention is now focused on time itself. It is the seventh day that is both blessed and hallowed, and is set apart from all other days. Time is being divided into units of seven days (which we will call weeks). Six of these will be regular, run-of-the-mill workdays, but one—the seventh of each unit or week—will be special, set apart and blessed. This metaphysical grouping of days into units of seven,[44] and this mysterious setting one of these temporal units apart is concretized in the Ten Commandments and given institutional form as the Sabbath.[45]

> *Remember the Sabbath day to keep it holy.*[46] *Six days shall you labor and do all your work. Now the seventh day* [is a] *Sabbath to the* LORD *your God. You shall do no manner of work: you, your son, your daughter, your man-servant or your maid-servant, your cattle and your stranger that is within your gates. For* [in] *six days the* LORD *made the heavens and the earth, the sea and all that is therein, and on the seventh day He rested. Therefore the* LORD *blessed the seventh day and He hallowed it* [Exodus 20:8–11].

In the inauguration of the institution of the Sabbath, and in commanding human beings to imitate Him,[47] His creatures are being given the opportunity to desist from the destiny of

> *"By the sweat of your brow*
> *Shall you eat bread,*
> *Until you return to the ground;*
> *For from it were you taken."*

We, among all creatures of creation, have the capacity to take a step backward and, like God, to stand down from work; to stand back and take stock of what we have achieved. To contemplate the world and be grateful for it is to distance ourselves

---

42. Hebrew *vayekadesh oto*, literally *and He made it holy*. The Hebrew word *kadosh*, usually rendered as "holy" specifically means "to set apart." Thus to hallow the seventh day means to set it apart from all the other days of the week; to declare it special and blessed.

43. In *Genesis* 1:31 we have been informed that upon completing His work He evaluates the outcome and finds it *very good*.

44. Unlike days, which are natural temporal units based on the rotation of the earth, and months which are also nature-based, i.e., on the rotation of the moon around the earth, the week—the grouping of days into units of seven—is thoroughly arbitrary in that it has no basis in natural phenomena.

45. The term *Sabbath*, in Hebrew *shabbat*, comes from the root ShBT which means *to cease, to desist*. The Sabbath day takes its name as the day on which God *desisted* from His work of creation.

46. Hebrew *lekadsho*: to keep it set apart; to keep it special.

47. Exodus 20:8–11; 31:16–17.

from the world of flux and torment. In this opportunity, for one day out of seven, we can choose to be like God.

Let Kass state his thesis in his own words.

> The existence of Sabbath rest offers a partial reprieve from the unremitting toil prophesied by the Lord at the end of the story of the Garden of Eden—a "punishment" of the human attempt to become like gods and know good and bad, undertaken in an act of disobedience.... But here, with Sabbath desisting, we are not only permitted but also obliged to pause our life of toil, sorrow and loss and accept instead the god-like possibility of quiet, rest, wholeness, and peace of mind.
>
> This rise to godlike peace, unlike the self-directed "fall" into the knowledge of good and bad, depends on obedience.... It is a harkening to a command to enter into sacred time, that we may realize our human yet godlike potential. Doing as I say, teaches the Lord, is the route to "doing as I did."[48]

In disobedience humans strove to acquire autonomy and thus be "like gods," only to achieve misery. It is through the choice of obedience that we are given this opportunity to be like God by imitating Him, and thus, at least for a time, rising above the human condition.

---

48. Kass, *Founding God's Nation*, op. cit., p. 353.

Appendix A:
When Was *Jonah* Written?

In the introduction to the *Book of Jonah* we rejected the theory that the Book is a work of narrative history[1] and instead postulated that it is a fable. This decision then became the foundational hypothesis for our study. As such, the question of when it was written becomes irrelevant. To be a fable is to exist out of time and space; it is a metaphor for human behavior and a stimulus for moral reevaluation, with neither the date nor the place of its composition having any necessary relation to its contents.

But while the historical period of its genesis has no direct connection with how we perceive either the plot line or the message of the work, it may impact our understanding of several peripheral matters that surround *Jonah*. Therefore we offer in this appendix a brief summary of some of the issues involved in attempting to date the Book, and we also come to some tentative conclusions with regard to the era of its composition.

At the outset it is necessary to repeat that, despite several centuries of intense study and debate, consensus continues to elude the scholarly world; opinions as to the date of *Jonah*'s composition cover a range of no less than seven centuries, from the 9th to the 2nd centuries BCE.[2] Once we abandon the impression that we are dealing with a work of narrative history, due to our identification of the "hero" of the tale with the historic personality of the 8th-century-BCE prophet Jonah ben Amittai—an association based on no more than a tendentious insinuation by the author—we find ourselves in the equivalent of a trackless desert, devoid of any and all unambiguous chronological markers.[3] Those scholars who favor the period of the Second Commonwealth[4] for the genesis of the Book base their conclusions almost exclusively on the discipline of philology, i.e., linguistics; the study of the language used in

---

1. See Introduction to *Jonah*, note 11 for the reasons why we reject this interpretation as well as the implications of this stand.

2. Magonet, p. 78.

3. Lacking definitive statements dating specific events, scholars are reduced to making tenuous assumptions from random phrases. Simon, for example, who dates the work to the Persian period, pounces on the phrase, "*by the authority of the king and his nobles,*" 3:7 (Hebrew *mitaam hamelech u'gedolav*), and drawing attention to the fact that "elsewhere in the Bible we find the inclusion of the King's counselors in the issuing of decrees only with regard to the kings of Persia" (p. 31), he insists that "this is an important point for determining when the book was written" (*ibid.*); a point of dubious weight considering the paucity of our knowledge of Assyrian administrative procedure. See also Chapter 3, note 35.

4. See Glossary.

the Book.[5] Pointing to about half a dozen words or expressions deemed to be "Aramaisms"—i.e., words of a late vintage (see Glossary)—they consider these decisive proof of 4th-century or later composition.

The main problem with this thesis is that the Book is not written in the style of works that can be definitely dated to the age of the Second Commonwealth; prose works of the Persian period such as *Esther*, *Nehemiah* and *Chronicles* look and read very differently than does *Jonah*. When it comes to language, form of composition and style of writing, *Jonah* finds its peers in such works as the *Book of Samuel*, *Genesis*, *Ruth*[6] and "The Elijah Saga" (*1 Kings* 17-19 and *2 Kings* 2)[7]: all compositions of the earlier part of the First Commonwealth era. This disconnect between the handful of words that philologists deem to be late and the style in which the Book is written (that virtually all commentators agree is early) compels those who insist on a late composition of the Book to claim that the author of *Jonah* intentionally wrote the Book, not in the idiom of his own day and age, but rather imitated the archaic style of a long-past era (once in a while slipping up and accidentally using current terminology). Why any writer should have taken such a course is far from clear, unless he was trying to pass off his composition as a work of hoary antiquity, a not unknown phenomenon. This would imply that the author of *Jonah* was consciously penning a fake, a conclusion that some scholars do not flinch from asserting.

At this point we must register an objection. In the first place we have a repugnance to imputing nefarious motives to a great writer, and we can hopefully agree that *Jonah* is a remarkable literary work. Unless one has irrefutable evidence of malicious intent, it is our belief that he (or she) should be accorded the benefit of the doubt. But beyond this assumption of professional and artistic integrity on the part of most great artists, when faced with a contradiction between the findings of philology and those of literary style, our preference is to choose literary style as the surer indicator. Philology, while a discipline of illustrious pedigree, has been known to make egregious errors; our knowledge of ancient languages and cultures has proved to be notoriously spotty, and over the past century more than one "certainty" of past years has been overturned by increasing knowledge.[8] On the whole, a writer's style has proven to be better evidence of when and where he or she lived and worked than almost any other indicator.

There is a common saying that is relevant to our present problem: if it looks like a duck, and waddles like a duck, and quacks like a duck then it probably is a duck. Since *Jonah* looks like an early First Commonwealth work, reads like an early First

---

5. This includes the study of the language comparatively with other Semitic languages, its grammar, etymology, morphology and semantics.

6. See note 8 below.

7. For the reasoning behind my contention that these chapters are excerpted from a probably 8th century biography of Elijah, and later incorporated in the *Book of Kings*, see my *The Elijah Enigma*, p. 14–17.

8. A case in point is the *Book of Ruth*: as recently as 50 years ago almost universally considered, despite its language and literary style being that of the 10th and 9th centuries BCE to have been written in the Persian period, due to the numerous "Aramaisms" it contained. More than half a century of scholarship has discredited this thesis. All of the so-called "Aramaisms" have been shown to have been in use in the early Biblical Age, or in earlier forms of Hebrew that preceded the emergence of the Israelites in Canaan. For an elaboration of this point see my *Four Biblical Heroines*, p. 24–25.

Appendix A: When Was Jonah Written?

Commonwealth work and sounds like an early First Commonwealth work, then in all probability it is a First Commonwealth work.

So much for linguistics and literary style.

Turning to historical analysis, what has this discipline to contribute? In the first place we can say with fair certainty that *Jonah* could not have been written prior to the first half of the 8th century BCE. If the "hero" of *Jonah* has been given the name of a real-life historic person—the prophet from Gath-hepher referred to in *2 Kings* 14:25—then the Book could hardly have been written before the "hero's" namesake actually lived.[9]

Establishing a *terminus ad quem* is more difficult, but perhaps the depiction of Nineveh in the Book may give us a clue. Here we rely on a basic principle of fiction writing, credibility; in order not to lose the reader the author must avoid affronting him or her with blatant self-contradictions or unacceptable impossibilities. To use an example I have employed before, Margaret Mitchell's best-selling novel, *Gone with the Wind*, is an avowed work of historical fiction. Its heroes—Scarlett O'Hara and Rhett Butler, and everything they do—are the creation of the author's imagination. So the author is free to make Rhett Butler a native of Charleston, a blockade runner and whatever she will. But there are limits to authorial freedom: Mitchell does not have the option of making Rhett an ace in the Confederate Air Force, if she wants to keep her readers with her, because they all know that at the time of the Civil War the airplane had not as yet been invented. It would be an affront to the intelligence of her readers; it simply would not be credible.

In light of this need of even writers of fiction to maintain credibility in the eyes of their readers, it might seem that the author of *Jonah* would have a hard time keeping the confidence of his audience while having God pardon Nineveh after 612 BCE, when everyone knew that "the Great City" had indeed been "overturned" by the Medes and the Babylonians. Further, the counterfactual depiction of Nineveh—in *Jonah* Nineveh is portrayed as an unwarlike oversized City-State beset by crime and civic violence, not as the capital of a vast predatory Empire—would also have been unpalatable after 705 BCE, when the great warlord Sennacherib turned the sprawling commercial center into the capital of the Assyrian Empire, and thus the command-center of an Assyrian war machine bent on world conquest.

Painting a sympathetic picture of the "Great City" after 721 BCE—the date of the final annihilation of the Kingdom of Israel, the sack and destruction of its capital, Samaria, and the exile of the survivors of the massacre of its population would seem to be more than a bit of a stretch. Indeed, one might argue that the years 743–738 BCE, the dates of the Western Campaigns of Tiglath-pileser III—in which Israel was stripped of two thirds of her territory,[10] and the remaining rump state reduced to vassaldom—as the time after which it would have become well-nigh impossible for

---

9. As the historic Jonah ben Amittai was a contemporary of King Jeroboam II (793–753 BCE), and most likely lived in the earlier part of his long reign, that would seem to place the earliest possible time for the composition of *Jonah* to be in the middle to latter part of Jeroboam's sway, i.e., in the second quarter of the 8th century BCE.

10. Tiglath-pileser III defeated Israel, tore off the Galilee and the Gilead, deported their populations and incorporated these territories as provinces into the Assyrian Empire.

any Israelite to look upon Nineveh, and the land of which it was a part, with anything but hatred and loathing.[11]

For what it is worth, this would seem to limit the period of time when *Jonah* could reasonably be assumed to have been composed: from the later years of Jeroboam's reign to the beginning of the campaigns of Tiglath-pileser: from about 765–740 BCE, and certainly no later than 722 BCE. But lacking hard data all this can be little more than informed speculation.

It is perhaps best to conclude with the words of Sasson:

> None of the arguments offered above, whether expressed singly or in tandem, is conclusive.... I acknowledge how little this ... contributes to a fuller understanding of this particular book.[12]

---

11. Quite a few scholars read the same clues quite differently. Holding fast to the belief that a number of "Aramaisms" in the text prove it to be a product of the 4th century BCE or later, they see the idealized picture of Nineveh in *Jonah* as a sign of the forgetfulness of the historical realities of the 8th century due to the passing of the centuries since those days and the time when *Jonah* was written. Wolff is representative of this view when he writes, "For the narrator and his readers ... Nineveh was a power belonging to the remote past—'time out of mind'" (p. 148)... "because for him [the narrator] it [Nineveh] belonged to the remote and primeval past" (p. 99). To Wolff it is only after the passage of many centuries that such an unrealistic depiction of Nineveh could emerge.

The main drawback to this point of view is the fact that Jews do not forget; they tenaciously retain the memories of the great disasters that have befallen them and of those who perpetrated them. And to ensure that they would never forget, they canonized both the *Book of Kings* and the *Book of Nahum* to preserve ever before their eyes the disaster of 721 BCE and exactly who was responsible for the atrocity that led to the disappearance of the "Ten Lost Tribes."

12. Sasson, pp. 26, 27.

Appendix B:
Who Was the Innovator and Who Were the Copycats?

*That is why I arose to flee to Tarshish, for I knew that You are a **compassionate and merciful God, slow to anger and abounding in loving-kindness, and ready to change Your mind about punishing**.*

—Jonah 4:2

Rend your hearts and not your clothing,
And return to the LORD your God;
*For He is **compassionate and merciful,***
Slow to anger and abounding in loving-kindness,
And ready to change His mind about punishing.

—Joel 2:13

– 1 –

Joel 2:13 and *Jonah* 4:2 are for all practical purposes identical in the way they rework *Exodus* 34:6, and it seems obvious that one of the two is quoting the other, but who is quoting whom? Most modern commentators are of the opinion that it is *Jonah* that is copying *Joel*, mainly on the assumption that *Joel* was written first. But this is no more than an assumption. Sasson puts the matter succinctly: "It makes little sense to solve a difficult problem (the dating of Jonah) by relying on an intractable issue (the dating of Joel). It used to be that the composition of Joel was placed in the preexilic period (as early as Jehoash's reign, late ninth century). Although there is no agreement in the matter now, Joel is generally placed in the mid-fourth century BCE."[1]

Jonathan Magonet, who has gone into our question in depth, notes that "Critical opinion gives such a wide range of dates to both books (from the 10th to the 2nd century for Joel; from the 9th to the 2nd century for 'Jonah') … that no clear-cut historical relationship can be evoked. We are thus left with an examination of internal literary criteria for our analysis."[2]

Magonet's analysis is both comprehensive and incisive; and at least to this writer

---
1. Sasson, p. 23.
2. Magonet, p. 78.

convincing. With regard to the rewriting of the *Exodus* passage into the form it assumes in *Jonah* 4:2 and *Joel* 2:13, with the phrase *ve'neeham al haraah* (*and ready to change Your mind about punishing*) being substituted for the word *ve'emet* (*and truth*)—see Chapter 4, note 7—Magonet concludes: "Whereas in Joel it [the altered passage] stands as an isolated phrase, within 'Jonah' it is part of a theme that pervades the whole book. It is therefore our contention that Joel, as in other places, extracted the two sentences from an earlier 'prophetic' book and wove them into his own material."[3] This is the basis of our crediting the author of *Jonah* with the theological revolution championed in his work, and not the author of *Joel*.

– 2 –

While *Joel* is the only place in the Bible where the specific wording of the revamped *Exodus* 34:6 pronouncement is duplicated, the application of this revised theology turns up in the prophecies of Jeremiah[4]:

> *The word that came to Jeremiah from the* LORD *saying:* "Arise, and go down to the house of the potter, and there I will cause you to hear My words." *So I went down to the potter's house, and there he was at work on the* [potter's] *wheels.*[5] *And whenever the vessel that he was working on was spoiled—as clay sometimes will be in the hands of a potter*[6]*—he would start again and make it into another vessel as it seemed right in his eyes to do.*[7]
>
> *Then the word of the* LORD *came to me, saying:* "O house of Israel, can I not do to you just as this potter does?"—[this is] *an oracle of the* LORD—"Behold, as clay in the potter's hand, so are you in My hand, O house of Israel."[8]
>
> "At one moment I may speak concerning a nation or kingdom that I will uproot, and break down and destroy it; and that nation of which I spoke turns from its evil, then I will change My mind about [the] punishing[9] that I intended to do to it.
>
> "At [another] moment I may speak concerning a nation or a kingdom that I will build up and plant it, but should it do that which is evil in My eyes, not harkening to

---

3. *Ibid.*, p. 79. Sasson, while hesitant to commit himself wholeheartedly to Magonet's conclusion, nevertheless concurs with his evaluation of *Joel*, claiming, "Joel, in fact, is a veritable anthology of venerable thoughts and sentiments." (p. 23)

4. *Jeremiah* 18:1–12 is delineated as a discrete unit, made up of five distinct paragraphs in MT, being set off from the surrounding text and divided by paragraph breaks (*petihot* and *stumot*) as follows: 18:1–4 (introduction); 18:5–6 (drawing in the parallel with 1–4); 18:7–8 (application A: God ready to change His mind and forgive); 18:9–10 (application B: the converse of A); 18:11–12 (Jeremiah commanded to proclaim this message and Israel's response). We will only cite the first four mini-paragraphs as the fifth—Jeremiah's mandate and Israel's response—is not relevant to our topic.

5. Literally, *the two stones*: twin wheels, usually made of stone, connected by a vertical axis. The clay was worked into vessels on the upper wheel, while the lower wheel was spun by the feet.

6. Reading *kahomer* (as clay) with some mss. instead of *bahomer* (with the clay) as MT.

7. Reading with LXX. MT reads *right in the potter's eyes to do*.

8. Note that the potter does not throw the spoiled vessel away; he squeezes the wet clay back into a lump and starts afresh, making from it a new vessel. This implies to John Skinner that God, the Master Potter, has "in his heart some grand design which had been thwarted once but could not be defeated finally." (*Prophecy and Religion*, p. 163)

9. Hebrew, *ve'neehamti al haraah*, c.f. *Jonah* 4:2.

My voice, then I will change my mind about the good that I said I would benefit it"
[*Jeremiah* 18:1–10]

What we have here in *Jeremiah* is the revised pronouncement of God's attributes restated as an operational principle being applied by God to the nations of the earth. The question this statement in *Jeremiah* poses to us becomes: is *Jonah's* revised understanding of God's nature being taken by *Jeremiah* and being applied to God's behavior to national entities, or conversely is *Jeremiah's* analysis of the way God treats peoples and nations being used by *Jonah* as a basis from which to deduce God's nature? In a word, is one of these works dependent on the other, and, if so, which is dependent on which?

This problem is different in one important respect from that of our previous *Jonah-Joel* question: there we had no definitive dating for either Book or prophet, while here we do. The prophet Jeremiah was active in the last quarter of the 7th century and the beginning of the 6th century BCE. This leads those scholars who postulate a Second Commonwealth date for the composition of *Jonah* to conclude that it was the prophet Jeremiah who was the radical thinker who revised the classical theology, and that it was the author of *Jonah* who took his lead from him.[10] On the other hand, if we take the position that *Jonah* was written in the 8th century BCE (see Appendix A), then it is the author of *Jonah* who is the radical reviser of *Exodus* 34:6, and Jeremiah who has absorbed and applied *Jonah's* ideas.[11]

– 3 –

The impact of this new theology does not stop with Jeremiah; it surfaces again in the prophecies of his younger contemporary, Ezekiel. And as Jeremiah insisted that—granted the right circumstances—God is willing to change His mind in His relations with the ways of nations and peoples, so Ezekiel takes matters one step further and proposes that God is willing to do the same with regard to individuals.

> *Should the wicked person turn back from all the sins that he has committed,[12] and observes all My laws, and does what is just and right, he shall surely live; he shall not die. All the transgressions he committed shall not be held against him; through his righteous acts he shall live. "Do I in the least desire the death of the wicked person"—declares the* LORD *God—"but rather that he should turn from his [evil] way[13] and live?"*
>
> *Now as for the righteous person, when he turns back from his righteousness and*

---

10. This leads the scholars to further assume that the whole scenario of *Jonah*, Chapter 3, is based on *Jeremiah* 36, and is designed as an antithesis to it. In other words, while in *Jeremiah* 36, the Israelite King of Jerusalem, Jehoiakim, refuses to either believe or repent, actually burning the words of God (*Jeremiah* 36:28), thus sealing the doom of Jerusalem (cf. *Jeremiah* 18:11–12), the pagan king of Nineveh in *Jonah* 3 believes in the word of God and leads his city to repent, thus saving it.

11. In this case, *Jonah* 3 cannot be understood in the light of *Jeremiah* 36; roughly 150 years will have to pass from the time of the composition of *Jonah* before *Jeremiah* 36 could possibly have been written.

12. Reading with the *Qeri*, the *Ketib* reads *his sin* (singular).

13. Reading with the *Qeri*, LXX, Targ. and Syr. *Ketib* reads *ways* (plural).

commits iniquity, committing all the abominations the wicked person does, shall he live? No regard shall be paid to all his righteous acts because of the treachery that he has practiced and the sin he has committed; for them he shall die! But should the house of Israel say, "That's impossible!"[14] The way of the Lord is not fair!" Now hear this,[15] O house of Israel: "Is it My way that is not fair? Is it not your ways that are not fair? When a righteous person turns back from his righteousness, commits iniquity and dies for it, for the evil acts that he did he shall die.

"And should an evil person turn back from his wicked acts and does what is just and right, he has saved his life. Because he took thought and turned back from all his transgressions that he had committed, he shall surely live; he shall not die" [Ezekiel 18:21–28].[16]

Ezekiel is here bringing to center stage a necessary implication of the revised theology we have encountered in *Jonah*, where the term *emet*—truth, reliability—is replaced by God's willingness to change His mind: that when it comes to judging the individual God does not take his past into account; He only judges him on the basis of his current status. Ezekiel is in effect insisting—in the face of popular protest—that this is an inescapable corollary of the new theology of repentance, which cancels punishment of past sins: the past has become irrelevant to God's judgment.[17] While we may bask in the idea that a moment of true repentance, if achieved, can wipe out a misspent lifetime of wickedness and sin, logic insists that this is not a one-way street. The converse must then also be true: a moment of vile wickedness can similarly wipe out a lifetime of virtue and godliness. In application, this theological revolution proves to be a two-edged sword.

– 4 –

In neither case of the passages we have quoted from the writings of Jeremiah, nor those of Ezekiel, have we taken into account the personal circumstances of these prophets. Further, we have refrained from discussing the historic and socio-political circumstances in which these pronouncements were made,[18] and even desisted from examining the textual contexts in the Bible in which they are embedded. All these matters, while vital to the understanding of the larger meaning of these texts in the history of the times in which they were first uttered and subsequently reduced to writing, are irrelevant to the aim of this study. From the start our purpose has been to trace the birth and subsequent development of a radical new theological conception

---

14. Hebrew, *lo yitachen*: a popular expression, then as now, with the sense of "that cannot be!" "That is impossible!" "That is not fair!"

15. Again popular idiom; literally, *please listen....*

16. This argument is repeated in *Ezekiel* 33:12–19, supplemented by several examples of what is involved in true repentance: such as restoring pledges to borrowers taken as collateral for loans or restoring stolen goods to their rightful owners (*Ezekiel* 33:15), i.e., making restitution for past wrongdoing against persons.

17. This is the basis of the maxim: no matter what kind of life you have led, repent one minute before your death and all will be well.

18. In both cases these pronouncements were addressed to populations undergoing severe crises, and the purpose of their messages was to help the specific people weather the storms which were besetting them.

of the power of repentance, and the progressive realization of some of the implications of this doctrine that were not evident at the time of its first promulgation. Nor do we intend within the confines of this mini-essay to move beyond the boundaries of the Bible. The history of this doctrine of repentance over the following twenty-five hundred years is a subject for another study.

Our concern has been to attempt to identify the original form in which the new doctrine was first promulgated, and then to trace some of the early stages of its absorption into the religious consciousness of biblical Israel and the early forms it took: first into liturgy (Joel), then to an understanding of the fate of nations (Jeremiah), and then to the fate of individuals (Ezekiel).

Suffice it to say that it is our contention that it was the *Book of Jonah* that brokered this new doctrine and its ever-expanding implications. The concept of repentance leading to Divine forgiveness was hardly new. But always the expiation of sin had been associated with punishment. Once the sinner had been punished, if he or she then repented, God would grant forgiveness. What was new and revolutionary was the doctrine that repentance could *substitute* for punishment; that punishment need no longer be a factor in the cleansing of the soul from sin and the bestowal of God's grace. Even though the mainstream of biblical faith never fully accepted this new doctrine, biblical religion would never be the same. All the daughter religions that grew out of the world of the Bible—Judaism, Christianity and Islam—in one way or another were deeply impacted by this understanding of the nature and the power of repentance. It is in this that the lasting importance of the *Book of Jonah* lies.

Appendix C:
North Moab: A Tale of Lost Lands

Heshbon was the City of Sihon, King of the Amorites. Now he had fought against the first king of Moab, and had taken all his land up to the Arnon out of his hand.
—Numbers 21:26

It seems fairly certain that the region that is the main setting of our tale, the southern part of the Gilead in the Trans-Jordan, once belonged to Moab. Both *Numbers* 21:6 and *Judges* 11:32 claim that the South Gilead, the territory between the Arnon and the Jabbok Rivers, was once part of the Kingdom of Moab. When we speak of the Kingdom of Moab we need to be clear in our minds as to how this kingdom was constituted. From archaeological excavations it would appear that, unlike the Bnai-ammon who consolidated into an established state—the Kingdom of Ammon—in the 15th century BCE, in the late 13th century BCE, which is the time of our tale, Moab was still mainly a tribal nomadic society that was just in the process of coalescing into a kingdom, probably due to the pressure of the movement of Amorites[1] into the region. The formation of a kingdom was insufficient to stop the Amorites. In the period not long before the appearance of the Children of Israel on the scene, our sources inform us that a segment of the Amorite people, led by one Sihon, overran the Moabite kingdom, only being halted at the Arnon. The war ended with Moab reduced to the remnant between the Arnon and the Zered Rivers, with the northern province of the Kingdom, from the Arnon to the Jabbok, becoming part of the Amorite Kingdom of Heshbon, ruled by its conqueror, Sihon.

To the notice cited above, of Sihon having conquered his kingdom from the Moabites (*Numbers* 21:26), the writer of our account now appends an Amorite victory paean celebrating this triumph.

Therefore the ballad-singers say:
  "Come to Heshbon;
May she be built and firmly established,
  City of Sihon."
For a fire has gone out of Heshbon,

---

1. The term Amorites literally means "Westerners." It was a name given by the Mesopotamians to a large ethnic group of peoples existing to their west. The movement of these groups southwestward brought them into Canaan and into the Trans-Jordan, where they became a large element of the population.

Appendix C: North Moab: A Tale of Lost Lands

A flame from the City of Sihon;
 It has devoured the Capital of Moab,[2]
  Consuming the high places of the Arnon.[3]
Woe unto you, O Moab!
 You are lost, O people of Chemosh![4]
He has turned[5] *his sons into fugitives,*
 And his daughters into captives[6]
[To Sihon, an Amorite king.][7]
The dominion of Moab has perished,[8]
 From Heshbon to Dibon[9]
Women kindled [fire][10] *against Medeba*[11] *[21:27–30].*

This historical note with its attached poem is a digression from the account of Israel's conquest of, and eventual settlement in, the South Gilead. Why did the writer decide to break off his narrative for what seems of antiquarian interest only? The reason was hardly antiquarian, but of current and pressing moment.

The Israelites had no mandate to appropriate and settle Moabite land. Indeed, they were expressly forbidden to touch Moabite territory,[12] which is why they went to such trouble to give it a wide birth when moving from Kadesh to the Gilead, and why the writer stresses that the Arnon is the northern border of Moab; everything north of the Arnon being Amorite territory.[13] But the lands north of the Arnon once belonged to Moab; the region is rife with place names that testify to its Moabite past: for example, the very area where the Israelites make their camp north of the Dead Sea prior to crossing the Jordan still bears the name *arvot moab*, the Steppes of Moab. The writer considers it essential to stress that the South Gilead—the region between the Arnon and the Jabbok Rivers—although once Moabite, had been conquered by the Amorites under Sihon and had been transformed into a new entity: the Amorite

---

2. Taking *Ar* to be here used not as a place name but as a variant of *Ir*, "city." Hence *Ar moab* = the City of Moab, a city south of the Arnon River and probably the capital of Moab before Moab was truncated, losing its northern province to Sihon; the capital then being removed away from the new border to Kir-moab. See MAP 3.

3. Reading with the LXX *baalah*; MT reads *baalei, the lords of*.

4. Chemosh was the chief deity of the Moabite pantheon.

5. I.e., it is Chemosh, the national god of Moab, who has abandoned his people to the tender mercies of their enemies, the Amorites.

6. Reading with Sam. The more usual form of the word, *bashevi*.

7. This line may be an explanatory gloss.

8. The rendering of this problematic verse (21:30) is largely conjectural: we have redivided the consonants to read *veniyr moab abad, the dominion of Moab has perished* (cf. P. D. Hanson, "The Song of Heshbon and David's Nir," p. 297–320). So Targ., Vulg. and Rashi (see Glossary). MT reads *vaniyram abad*, which might possibly mean *we shot at them* (?)

9. A city three miles north of the Arnon River.

10. Reading with LXX and Sam. *nashim naphhu*.

11. LXX and Sam. read *al, against* for MT *ad, until*. Medeba is a city in Moab about fifteen miles east and slightly south of the mouth of the Jordan River.

12. Moses is speaking: "Now the Lord said to me, 'Do not harass Moab or provoke them to war. For I will not give any of its land to you as a possession, for I have given Ar as a possession to the children of Lot.'" (Deuteronomy 2:9)

13. *For the Arnon is the border of Moab, between Moab and the Amorites.* (Numbers 21:13)

Kingdom of Heshbon. And then, as if to say, "You don't have to take my word for it; here is Amorite testimony to these facts," he then quotes an Amorite victory paean celebrating the conquest. The country Israel conquered and settled was no longer part of Moab. Thus the whole point of this digression is to legitimize the Israelite possession of the South Gilead.

This entire issue was hardly a moot point. Moab never relinquished its claim to her "lost northern province," and more than a century later[14] this issue resurfaced once again in pre-war diplomacy, with Jephthah having to go over the same ground that we have reviewed here. History never dies; it just sleeps, waiting to be resurrected. That is why it is important to put it in writing, and to have it ready for when it again becomes relevant.

---

14. This reckoning is on the basis of our currently accepted understanding of the chronology of that distant era. On the other hand, Jephthah will claim a gap of three hundred years (*Judges* 11:26), and he may have been right. After all, he was a bit closer to the events than we are. See my *Judges and Saviors*, p. 255–266 for a discussion of the issues involved in Jephthah's negotiations with the King of the Ammonites.

Appendix D:
The Geography and Ecology of the Trans-Jordan

Readers of the Bible tend, after a time, to become at least minimally familiar with the topography of the Land of Israel west of the Jordan River: its main regions and features, the location of some of its cities and more important sites. But the lands inhabited by the Israelites east of the Jordan have been *terra incognita*, a region unknown to us but by name. However, it was in this arena that the Children of Israel began the process of taking possession of what was to be their permanent home. Two tribes out of twelve decided to forego crossing the Jordan and to settle in territory to its east. A bit later almost one half of the tribe of Manasseh elected to give up their territorial allotment in and around the Highlands of Ephraim, to move east and instead take up residence in the Bashan and in the Gilead north of the Jabbok River. All in all, more than one fifth of the Israelites made their home in the Trans-Jordan. It is fitting that we pause for a few minutes to get some idea of the *mise en scène* in which our drama takes place.

Over one hundred and thirty years ago—in the last decades of the 19th century, before "modernization" had begun to dramatically alter the landscape and the land still resembled the conditions that prevailed in biblical times—the noted Bible scholar and geographer George Adam Smith explored the region and left this description of it.

> Eastern Palestine ... looks barren [but] surprises you with its fertility.... West of the Jordan no rivers run, and only a few perennial streams, but here are at least four rivers—Yarmuk, 'Arab, Jabbok and Arnon, of which the Yarmuk, with its great falls, is as large as the Jordan.[1] These rivers drain the country and the desert behind. They run in deep gorges, below the average level of the plateau, but are fed by numerous springs and streams which, with the winter snow and rains, sufficiently water the higher lands. Luxuriant vegetation is almost universal, and agriculture prosperous. In the most northerly of the three divisions of the country, from Hermon to the Yarmuk,[2] a large part of the surface, a rich volcanic soil, is tilled for wheat, the rest covered by thick herbage. This is Hauran, the granary of Syria, and the hilly district to the west of it was once thickly wooded. The middle region, Gilead, between the Yarmuk and the Jabbok, has its ridges covered by forests, under which you may march for the day in breezy and fragrant shade; the valleys hold orchards of pomegranate, apricot, and olive, there are many vineyards, on the

---

1. Before it receives the Yarmuk.
2. This is the region known in the Bible as the Bashan.

open plains are fields of wheat.... In the third division, south of the Jabbok, the forests gradually cease, and Ammon and Moab are mostly high, bare moors.... More famous than the tilth of Eastern Palestine is her pasture. We passed through at the height of the shepherd's year. From the Arabian deserts the Bedouin were swarming to the fresh summer herbage of these uplands. We should never have believed the amount of their flocks had we not seen, and tried to count them....

The Arabs had also many sheep and goats. The herds of the settled inhabitants were still more numerous. In Moab the dust of the roads bore almost no marks but those of the feet of sheep. The scenes which throng our memory of Eastern Palestine, are ... the streams of Gilead in the heat of the day with the cattle standing in them, or the evenings when we sat at the door of our tent near the village well, and would hear the shepherd's pipe far away, and the sheep and goats and cows with the heavy bells would break over the edge of the hill and come down the slope to wait their turn at the troughs. Over Jordan we were never long out of the sound of the lowing of cattle or of the shepherd's pipe.

And thus one understands why so much of the annals of this country is taken up with the multiplying of cattle, tribute in sheep and wool,[3] and the getting of spoil by tens of thousands of camels, and hundreds of thousands of sheep.[4] Bulls of Bashan and fat kine of Bashan are proverbial throughout the Old Testament.[5]

---

3. *2 Chronicles* 5:9; *2 Kings* 3:4.

4. *2 Chronicles* 5:21.

5. G. A. Smith, *The Historical Geography of the Holy Land*, p. 336–338. This quotation also appeared in a similar context in my book, *Judges and Saviors*, p. 238.

Appendix E:
The Deir 'Alla Inscription(s)

In 1967, digging in the Trans-Jordan near the junction of the Jabbok River with the Jordan, at the site of the biblical town of Succoth[1] (currently called Tell Deir 'Alla), a Dutch archaeological expedition uncovered a partially-roofed room containing fragments of ancient inscriptions. The text had been written with black and red inks upon plaster which had covered up the wall of the room.[2] This plaster had subsequently fallen from the wall—possibly due to an earthquake that had destroyed the complex of buildings of which the room was a part—and the pieces were found lying on the floor in two clusters, each one some distance from the other. This discovery aroused immense interest in the world of biblical scholarship because one line, written in red ink, clearly contained the name Balaam, son of Beor. The full line, which has been interpreted as the heading or title of the inscription, reads, "*The misfortunes*[3] *of Balaam, son of Beor; a divine seer is he.*"[4]

The building complex in which the inscription was found has been assigned by carbon-dating to near the end of the 9th century; i.e., slightly before 800 BCE.[5] At first assumed to be a temple or sanctuary of some sort, the absence of cultic appurtenances has largely demolished this theory.[6] Kitchen sums up: "There is nothing 'religious' about this room in a ninth-century dwelling; benches against the other walls may have served readers of the text as seats."[7] The language of the inscription (or inscriptions), at first glance taken to be Aramaic, is now generally recognized as a dialect of Hebrew. It is "a literary language, i.e., formulaic, poetic and traditional."[8]

But besides being, for the most part, readable and understandable, the inscription proved to be a formidable challenge. The pieces of plaster found lying on the

---

1. See MAP 3.
2. Owing to the curvature of some of the pieces, there are scholars who postulate that the plaster had been originally applied to one or more pillars.
3. The "misfortunes" seems to refer to Balaam's prophecies of impending doom, and not to any personal troubles.
4. In the original: *yizre bilam bar beor, ish hozeh elohin hu* (vowels added; ancient Semitic scripts only contain consonants). The English translation is by B. Levine, p. 242.
5. This means that the inscription was written almost half a millennium after the events related in the *Book of Balaam*.
6. "More likely, these rules and rooms served for trade, redistribution and manufacture of household crafts." (Levine, p. 263)
7. Kitchen, p. 413.
8. Ashley, p. 439.

floor amounted to nothing so much as the pieces of a large jigsaw puzzle (or perhaps two or more jigsaw puzzles mixed together), with the ink on some of the pieces faded almost to unintelligibility, many pieces missing and perhaps pieces from other puzzles mixed in. Putting the fragments together has proved a daunting task. They were originally assembled into "Combinations," then reassembled, the missing pieces leaving gaps, and lots of pieces left over (possibly from other inscriptions). The result of much scholarly work is 34 more or less legible lines with many gaps. But as Ashley notes, "Neither the translation nor the interpretation of the texts is agreed upon at the present."[9] The remaining lines are more or less fragmentary phrases, and from the middle of "Combination II" no one can make head or tail of what we have.

Taking into account the extremely problematic nature of our current understanding, what seems to emerge from the text of "Combination I" is the following:

> Balaam experiences a nocturnal visitation by the gods in which they reveal to him that a council of the gods has ordered a certain goddess, named Shagar, to cover the heavens with clouds and produce darkness on the earth. This leads to general devastation which is graphically and poetically described. After recounting this vision to the leaders of the people (of the Succoth Valley?), it would seem that Balaam intervenes and by various (magical?) means manages to avert the disaster.
>
> "Combination II," to the extent we can make any sense of it, appears to be a vision or description of the underworld, i.e., the realm of the dead. After line 17 even this fragmentary cohesion breaks down and it seems that no one can make any sense of the fragments as they are currently arranged.

It is important to note the pagan content of the inscriptions. This reinforces the picture given in the *Book of Balaam* (*Numbers* 22–24) where Balaam is depicted as a pagan pure and simple. "Neither he [Balaam of *Numbers* 22–24] nor the Balaam of the Deir 'Alla text are in any way 'Yahwist.'"[10] Further elements in the Deir 'Alla inscription(s) which corroborate the picture given in the Bible are the description of Balaam as a "seer" (*hozeh*)—the same term as used in the biblical account—his undergoing nighttime divine visitations, and a positive portrayal of Balaam in both accounts[11] (the 8th-century-BCE prophet Micah also held a favorable opinion of Balaam, *Micah* 6:5). To my mind, it is significant that both Micah and the Deir 'Alla inscription(s) place the career of Balaam in the distant past; in Micah's case, as in that of the *Book of Balaam*, in the pre-conquest period when Israel was encamped in the Jordan Valley not far from Succoth. The personality of Balaam seems to have made as great an impression on non–Israelite circles as it made on the children of Israel.

What was the reason the inscription was placed on the wall in the first place? Kitchen calls this "a question unanswered, and not answerable with certainty." He then speculates that traditions of Balaam had long endured among the inhabitants of the Gilead. Perhaps a local inhabitant had had a dream or perhaps a vision. "Seized with enthusiasm (or terrified urgency?), he quickly wrote down what he had 'seen,'

---

9. *Ibid*. For an English transcription and attempted translation with extensive notes, see Levine, pp. 244–265.

10. Kitchen, p. 413. Even Levine, who postulates an Israelite authorship for the Deir 'Alla text, admits that "we must acknowledge a pagan Spirit animating the Deir 'Alla inscriptions." (p. 271)

11. "Equally significant is that Balaam is presented in a positive light, again in agreement with the biblical story." (Milgrom, p. 476)

and had it written on the wall for others to ponder."[12] This speculation is probably far from the mark, but is as good a guess as any so far given.

What conclusions can be drawn from Deir 'Alla? Keeping in mind the highly ambiguous nature of our current understandings of what we can at present make out of the fragmentary remains discovered there, it seems more likely than not that the Balaam son of Beor referred to at Deir 'Alla and the one featured in the Bible are one and the same person. If so, then we would have extra-biblical evidence for his historicity; a figure of international reputation and a significant player on the stage of world affairs in his time. The agreements between the two accounts as to the nature of his activities and the mode of his operation would tend both to bolster the underlying credibility of the account given in the *Book of Balaam*, and at the same time caution against any romantic picture of this pagan seer being either a monotheist or a convert to the faith of Israel. As we have previously mentioned, Jewish tradition holds that the material about Balaam contained in the *Book of Balaam*—if not the *Book* entire—was not indigenous to Israel itself but rather entered it from the outside. The Deir 'Alla inscription(s) would tend to confirm this conclusion.

---

12. Kitchen, op. cit.

Appendix F:
The Plague at Baal-Peor

No less than five times the author of our text associates a "plague"[1] following or coeval with the traumatic collapse of sexual and religious discipline that took place at Mount Peor.[2] As repetition is the main means of emphasis in biblical Hebrew, a five-fold restatement of a given term virtually demands that we pause and consider the author's purpose in drawing our attention to this term. More: to exactly what is he referring by the use of this term? We have already called attention to the opinion that this term should be understood as a euphemistic reference to a bloody purge of the apostates who were seduced into betraying the Lord by the worship of Baal. The basis of this interpretation lies in understanding the aftermath of the Baal-peor debacle as patterned on the precedent of the eradication of the turncoats who participated in the worship of the Golden Calf some thirty-eight years previously (*Exodus* 32:25–28).[3]

But there is another and seemingly more straightforward way of approaching this question. One can read the text literally, taking the term "plague" in its normal meaning of a virulent and lethal communicative disease; in our case a disease that largely affected those who had been seduced into idolatry. Considering the context,[4] we would perforce seem to be speaking of a sexually transmitted disease (STD). The main problem with this approach is that there is no currently known STD that completely fits the symptomology implied by the text: a disease easily communicated by sexual intercourse with a short incubation period (one week or less), which is virulent with a high mortality rate. The only candidate known to us today that at least partially fits the bill would be gonorrhea. It is easily and almost exclusively communicated by sexual congress; it spreads rapidly and has an incubation period of only between two and six days. The problem lies in the fact that gonorrhea, as we know it today, is not a virulent disease and has a very low mortality rate. It is a noxious disease but only rarely a fatal one. This would appear to disqualify it for the role of

---

1. Hebrew, *magephah*.
2. 25:8, 9, 18, 19 and 31:16.
3. See Chapter 11, note 25.
4. See 25:1–3 and the action taken by Moses in the wake of the Midianite campaign: allowing only those Midianite women who were virgins—i.e., who had never experienced sexual intercourse and hence who would be unlikely to be infected—into the camp, and imposing a seven day quarantine on all the troops (and of course the virgins) before allowing their entrance (31:14–20).

the "plague" charged by the narrator of our episode with having caused some 24,000 fatalities. It is this lack of a suitable candidate that has deterred most modern biblical commentators from taking the term "plague" (*magephah*) literally and has induced some to read the word metaphorically.

But this may not be the final word on the subject. The crux of our problem may lie in the word "today," which we have been using liberally. Today—that is, in our present era—there may be no venereal disease that fits the description provided by our account, but this does not necessarily mean that there were none thirty-three hundred years ago. Diseases are not static; they mutate and evolve over the centuries and millennia. And the virtually universal tendency of virulent diseases is to become progressively benign with the passage of time.[5] So gonorrhea, for instance, which we know existed in the Ancient Near East three thousand and more years ago,[6] may not have been the chronic but generally non-lethal infection we know today but a virulent killer well deserving the designation of "plague."

The pathogen that causes the disease—*N. gonorrhoeae* (gonococcus)—is particularly mutable and adaptive. The intimate relationship it has had with humans for thousands of years has led to many adaptive changes, including the ability to resist many natural host defenses that normally function at sites in the human body that it infects.[7] Alarmingly, recently *N. gonorrhoeae* strains have been discovered with human genetic sequences inserted in their DNA.[8] This ability to incorporate human DNA sequences "gives us reason to expand our thought processes, as we consider the coevolution of humans and microbes and the consequences … for the physiologic and, potentially, virulence systems of the recipient.… It did not escape our attention that nL1 [the human DNA sequence] was present in strain FA6140, which was the cause of an outbreak of gonorrhea in Durham, NC, in 1983 that was refractory to penicillin therapy and has been infamously linked to the downfall of penicillin for the treatment of gonorrhea."[9] If such radical changes can occur within the short span of our lifetimes, reversing almost a century of success in reducing the mortality rate of the disease from almost 10 percent to 1 percent,[10] it behooves us to be very hesitant

---

5. The reason for this is twofold. On the one hand, the members of a host population tend to develop resistance to the disease, the weaker members being killed off while it is the survivors that live to reproduce. On the other hand, the disease itself adapts. A disease that rapidly kills off its hosts is a disease committing suicide. It is the milder strains of any given illness that sicken, but *do not kill* its host that survive. From the viewpoint of the microorganism or virus that causes the disease, it is to its benefit that its host should live. Hence over time virulent diseases tend to become progressively less lethal and turn into chronic illnesses.

6. Scientific opinion is nearly unanimous as to the condition described in *Leviticus* 15:1–12: "the only illness we know of that can be referred to here is gonorrhea." (J. Preuss, *Biblische-talmüdisch Medizin*, p. 410). It was the second century CE Greek physician Galen who gave the disease the name by which it is known to this day: *gonorrhea*.

7. Shafer & Ohneck, "Taking the Gonococcus-Human Relationship to a Whole New Level," p. 1–2.

8. Anderson & Seifert, "Opportunity and Means: Horizontal Gene Transfer from Human Host to a Bacterial Pathogen."

9. Shafer & Ohneck, op.cit., p. 2–3.

10. "The PID [pelvic inflammatory disease caused by gonorrhea] mortality rate has decreased by 90% over the past 35 years to just a few deaths per year." (Kara A. McElligott, "Mortality From Sexually Transmitted Diseases," p. 11) If a 10% mortality rate does not seem of "plague proportions," it would be well to bear in mind as a comparison the great Antonine Plague of 165–168 CE (most probably of smallpox) which had an estimated mortality of 7 to 10 percent, yet caused approximately 3.5 to 5 million deaths! (Littman and Littman, "Galen and the Antonine Plague," p. 243–255)

in assuming that the disease in biblical times, over 3,000 years ago, acted in much the manner to which we have become accustomed over the past generation or two.

Our purpose in following this line of speculation, in what is essentially an aside, is not to come to a definitive determination—I do not believe that we are currently in possession of the data that would enable us to do so—but to present the alternatives to the reader. Perhaps someday we will know more and be able to state definitively exactly what the author was referring to when again and again he refers to the "plague" that ravaged the Children of Israel at Mount Peor. For the present we leave the reader to choose between what seem to be the two main alternatives.

Appendix G:
Who Was Jeremiah?

Before one plunges into the *Book of Jeremiah* proper, with our protagonist giving his first-person account of how he became a prophet, we are confronted with an editorial Foreword (*Jeremiah* 1:1–3). A brief summary of the information it outwardly contains is to be found in the section entitled "Jeremiah's Background" in Chapter 13 of the main body of this book. But this concise reference does justice neither to the significance of the information contained in these curt three verses, nor to the artifice with which its implications are conveyed to us; nor does it begin to explain these implications. One of the purposes of this appendix is to correct some of these failings.

The passage in question, which does double duty as both Introduction to Jeremiah's Call, and to the *Book* as a whole, runs as follows:

> *The words of Jeremiah, son of Hilkiah, who was of the priests that were in Anatoth in the Land of Benjamin, to whom the word of the* LORD *came in the days of Josiah, son of Amon, King of Judah, in the thirteenth year of his reign.*[1] *It came also in the days of Jehoiakim, son of Josiah, King of Judah,*[2] *until the end of the eleventh year of Zedekiah, son of Josiah, King of Judah,*[3] *until the captivity*[4] *of Jerusalem in the fifth month.*[5]

The first thing that should strike us as we examine this editorial Foreword to a Book purporting to be a collection of the "words"—i.e., the speeches, sayings and first-person accounts—of a person by the name of Jeremiah, is its unusually convoluted phraseology. The passage appears wordy and redundant; the very antithesis of good biblical style.[6] Yet on closer examination we shall discover it is anything but.

---

1. Josiah reigned from 640–609 BCE; thus his 13th year would be 628/627.
2. Jehoiakim reigned from 609–598 BCE.
3. Zedekiah reigned from 598–586 BCE.
4. Hebrew, *galut yerushalaim*; literally, *the deportation into exile of* [the population of] *Jerusalem*.
5. Currently known in the Hebrew Calendar as the month of Av. On the seventh of Av (which corresponds to August 15, 586 BCE) the Babylonians put the city of Jerusalem, along with the Temple of Solomon, to the torch and proclaimed a decree of exile to the surviving population.
6. When one compares our Foreword to the editorial Foreword to the *Book of Ezekiel* (Ezekiel was a younger contemporary of Jeremiah) the differences in style and format are arresting. *On the fifth day* [of the month], *that is the fifth year of the exile of King Jehoiachin* [i.e., in 593 BCE] *it came to pass that the word of the Lord came to Ezekiel, son of Buzi, the priest, in the Land of the Chaldeans by the River Chebar; and the hand of the Lord was upon him.* (*Ezekiel* 1:2-3) Not only is this language straightforward, but it is far less wordy (in the Hebrew only 27 words to 47 words for *Jeremiah*.

The apparently infelicitous phrasing actually harbors allusions to a wealth of background that in straight discourse would take far too many pages to relate. We shall only attempt to unpack two or three of these allusions, ones that relate to aspects of Jeremiah's background that may serve to illuminate facets of his self-understanding that bear upon his "confessions," the subject of our inquiry.

We begin with the fact that the editor who penned the Foreword[7] introduced the author not as "Jeremiah, son of Hilkiah the priest" (the proper and conventional way of designating his station), but rather as [one] *of the priests that were in Anatoth*; drawing our attention to the particular group or family of priests of which he was a part. So what was special about "the priests that were in Anatoth" that made them different from priests elsewhere? That which made them unique was that they were all descendants of one man: Abiathar, son of Ahimelech the priest. In Chapter 12 we have gone in some detail into Abiathar's heart-rending beginnings, his rise to the High Priesthood and his ruinous fall from favor and his banishment to Anatoth, as well as a tragic heritage that he bore.

More than 300 years had passed from those days until the birth of his distant descendent, Jeremiah, but the memory of that deposition would remain green. Jeremiah's family remembered, and all Israel remembered. Everyone knew that "the priests that were in Anatoth" were, by rights, the priests that should be serving in the Temple that Solomon built; it only took the mention of the name Anatoth to trigger the association. And one can imagine the deep sense of resentment and feelings of victimhood that permeated the lives of "the priests that were in Anatoth." Just by being born into that family, Jeremiah could not but be burdened with a deep sense of historic wrong. He was a disinherited man, cast out of his rightful place which was serving God in the Temple in Jerusalem, marginalized and vegetating with all his family in rural Anatoth.

But there is yet more to the story. Abiathar was not some priestly nobody whom David rewarded with the High Priesthood in consideration of his having loyally shared in the dangers and privations of his outlaw years. Abiathar was the great-great grandson of Eli, High Priest and custodian of Shiloh, the central sanctuary of all Israel during the Age of the Judges.[8] Due to the massacre of the priests at Nob,[9] Abiathar was now the sole living descendent of Eli, and hence, by right of inheritance, the one and only legitimate candidate for the office. But this was not the only heritage that Abiathar carried. Along with the High Priesthood, he was also heir to the family curse: the curse on the House of Eli.

And the remembrance of the events that took place at Shiloh during the last days before its destruction was very much alive 450 years later during the lifetime

---

7. Most probably Baruch, son of Neriah, Jeremiah's personal secretary, who was an extremely fine stylist. See Chapter 13, notes 3 and 5.

8. From the day Joshua deposited the Ark of the Covenant (which contained the original tablets inscribed with the Ten Commandments) at Shiloh, until the site was destroyed by the Philistines around 1050 BCE, this was Israel's Central Sanctuary. Its first High Priest was Eleazar, son of Aaron the brother of Moses. Eli, Eleazar's direct descendant, held his position by right of inheritance from the very first High Priest, Aaron. By appointing Abiathar to the High Office, David was simply endorsing his legitimate right to the High Priesthood.

9. See Chapter 12, the section entitled the massacre at Nob.

of Jeremiah.¹⁰ It must have been a terrible thing to be born to a family that has been cursed, and to know that for the sin of one's ancestors to be oneself cursed to die young and by the sword.¹¹ But there would seem to be little doubt that he saw himself living under a cloud. Do as he might, in those days being part of a family that was on the one hand living with a sense of victimization, and on the other hand the bearers of an ancient curse could not help but color Jeremiah's outlook. He was a man born to live under a double cloud. And to add to all this, now he had been chosen by God to be His prophet. His emotional makeup could hardly have been simple.

If Jeremiah's inner life was, to say the least, complex and convoluted, his outer circumstances were far simpler and less problematic. Having been born into the gentry—that is, into the land-owning and propertied classes of the population—he began life with the possibility of a comfortable existence.¹² Jeremiah never seemed to run short of funds. From his early 20s when, shortly after his Call, he moved away from his home to live in Jerusalem, he seems to have lived the economic life of an absentee landlord, with a steady income flowing in from his holdings. He may not have been wealthy, but he evidently had the means to hire a private secretary (Baruch). Even during the siege of Jerusalem he proved able on short notice to come up with a sizable sum of ready cash.¹³

Being born into the priestly caste guaranteed Jeremiah an education that would prepare him for the proper performance of the professional duties of a priest; being a member of the propertied class insured that his education would be broader than merely that of a professional school, and also would be of high quality. We have already alluded to the elevated level of his schooling.¹⁴ Jeremiah was exceptionally well educated for his time.

The core of his education had been meant to prepare him for a career as a practicing priest. While the family had been ousted from what they considered their rightful position in the Temple in Jerusalem, there was a shrine in Anatoth.¹⁵ Serving the shrine would seem to have been the designated future of the young priestling.

---

10. *Jeremiah* refers to Shiloh and its fate as precedent for what eventually awaited Judah in the sermon he delivered in the Temple in 608 BCE which almost got him lynched.

11. I.e., by violence. These curses never seemed to have realized themselves in Jeremiah's life. From all indications, he lived at least into his mid-60s, a respectable age for those times. We have no evidence of his dying a violent death.

12. Being a member of the gentry class was no guarantee of either wealth or even moderate prosperity. The phenomenon of the impoverished gentry—long-established landowning families that had fallen on hard times and had been forced to sell off much or even all of their lands—was becoming increasingly common in eighth and seventh century Judah. But there is no indication that Jeremiah's family (or Jeremiah himself) had been reduced to those straits.

13. In a dramatic gesture of optimism for the future, he purchased a field in Anatoth. This was a cash transaction, and he was able to produce the not inconsiderable sum of 17 shekels worth of silver nuggets—which served as cash in those days—in order to finalize the transaction (32:6–15). See Chapter 16, the section entitled "A Prisoner Buys a Field."

14. Not only the high polish of his rhetoric and his compositional skills, but the intimate acquaintance with the classics of Israelite literature he exhibited, especially the writings of his great eighth century predecessors Hosea and Isaiah, and the compositions attributed to Moses. See Chapter 13, the section entitled "The Self-Image of a Prophet."

15. While we have no direct textual or archaeological evidence of such, it is hardly conceivable that a town designated as a priestly town for hundreds of years, and populated exclusively by priests, would be without its own "Bamah" or "high place." See Glossary.

That he would abandon this lifetime calling for that of a prophet was an outcome unanticipated by everyone, including Jeremiah himself. From that surprise turning, his relationship with his family seems to have been uneasy at best. With Jeremiah's move to Jerusalem and his concomitant adoption of an urban lifestyle, his decision not to marry[16]—a virtually unheard-of phenomenon in those days—and his escalating attacks upon the platitudes, morals and behavior of mainstream society, the breach between him and his family steadily widened until it became unbridgeable.[17] The boy who had grown up in Anatoth had turned his back on both home and upbringing to become a stranger to his past, a deeply alienated inhabitant of a tumultuous present facing an uncertain and darkening future.

---

16. 16: 1–4.

17. More on his relationship with his family when we get to his "Confessions." See Chapter 14, the section entitled "The Plot Revealed."

Appendix H:
Psalm 22 and the Prayer of Jeremiah

Psalm 22: 1–22

1. For the choirmaster: On Ayeleth Hashaḥar[1]; a Psalm of David.
2. My God, my God, why have You forsaken me?
   [Why are] the words of my cry[2] far from saving me?
3. My God, I call out by day and You do not answer,
   And by night, and there is no quiet for me.
4. Yet You are holy,
   Enthroned [in] Israel's praise.
5. In You did our fathers trust,
   They trusted and You delivered them.
6. They cried to You and escaped,
   In You they trusted and were not put to shame.
7. As for me, I am a worm and no man;
   Scorned by men and despised by the people.
8. All that see me mock me;
   They curl their lips, and shake their heads:
9. "Commit yourself to the Lord, He will deliver you.
   Let Him save him, for He delights in him."
10. For it is You who drew me forth from the belly,
    You did keep me safe upon the breasts of my mother.
11. Upon You have I been thrown from the womb;
    From the belly of my mother You have been my God.
12. Do not distance Yourself from me
    For trouble is near;
    For there is no one to help.

*　＊　＊　＊　＊　＊　＊　＊　＊　＊*

13. Many bulls encompass me,
    The mighty bulls of Bashan surround me.

---

1. Literally, *Hind of the Dawn;* most probably the name of a popular song whose tune was to be used to accompany the Psalm in its performance.

2. Literally, *my roar.* The Hebrew *sha'agati* is a term that, in normal usage, denotes the roar of a lion, hence a very loud cry.

14. *They open wide their mouths at me,*
    Like a ravening and roaring lion.
15. *I am poured out like water,*
    All my bones are out of joint;
    My heart has become like wax,
    It has melted in the midst of my guts.
16. *My strength*[3] *is dried up like a potsherd,*
    And my tongue sticks to my jaws;
    You lay me in the dust of death.
17. *For dogs encompass me,*
    A crowd of evildoers encircle me.
    <The next line is unclear>
18. *I counted all my bones;*
    And they, they gaze, they stare at me.
19. *They share out my clothes among them;*
    They cast lots for my coat.[4]
20. *Now* [as for] *You, O* Lord, *do not keep Your distance;*
    My Strength, hurry to my help.
21. *Save my soul from the sword,*
    My only one from a dog's hand.
22. *Deliver me from the lion's mouth*
    And from the horns of wild oxen—answer me.

Jeremiah's Prayer

"Ah, Lord GOD, behold! You have made the heavens and the earth by Your great strength and by Your outstretched arm; there is nothing too wonderful for You[5]; performing loving-kindness[6] to the thousandth generation,[7] and paying back the iniquity of the fathers into the lap of their children after them, the great, the mighty God, the Lord of hosts is His name; great in council and mighty in deed, Whose eyes are open to all the ways of mortals, to give to [each] man according to his ways and according to the fruit of his doings; Who did show signs and wonders in the land of Egypt—to this very day—and in Israel and among humans in general, and You have made a name for Yourself, as at this day.

Now You took Your people Israel out from the land of Egypt with signs and with

---

3. Or alternatively, *my palate has become as dry as a potsherd* reading *hki* in the place of *kohi* (a simple reversal of consonants). This emendation is endorsed by many modern scholars.

4. Literally, *my tunic, my outer garment.*

5. In the sense of "too difficult," i.e., beyond Your powers.

6. Literally, performing *ḥesed*; see Glossary. These words are a partial paraphrase of a part of God's revelatory description of the principles by which He deals with humanity (*Exodus* 34:7). During First Commonwealth times both the original version and variations of it, through liturgical use, were widely known and quoted: besides Jeremiah's appropriation of part of the formula, see Chapter 5 above for another part being taken over in an altered form by the author of the *Book of Jonah.*

7. Literally, *thousands*; the parallel text in *Deuteronomy* 7:9 reads *le'eleph dor, to the thousandth generation,* indicates that our expression *la'alaphim* is being used synonymously as a one-word abbreviation of *eleph dor.*

wonders, with a strong hand and an outstretched arm and with great terror, and You gave them this land which You swore to their fathers to give to them, a land flowing with milk and honey; and they came and took possession of it;[but] *they did not listen to Your voice nor did they walk according to Your instructions[8]; everything that You commanded them to do they did not do, so You made all this evil to happen to them.*

Behold, the siege ramps have come [up to] *the city to take it, and this city is given into the hands of the Chaldeans[9] that fight against it, due to the sword, and the famine and the pestilence; so that which You spoke has come to pass. Behold, You see it* [taking place]*!*

And yet You said to me, O Lord God: '*Buy for yourself the field with silver before witnesses,*[10] *while the city is given into the hand of the Chaldeans!*'"

And behold, the word of the Lord *came to Jeremiah saying:*

"*Behold, I am the* Lord, *the God of all flesh; is there anything too wonderful for Me?*"[11] *Jeremiah 32:17–27*

---

8. Reading with *Ketib*, the consonantal text: *betorotecha*. *Qeri* reads in the singular.
9. A synonym for Babylonians.
10. Literally, *and have witnesses witness* [the transaction].
11. I.e., too difficult for Me to accomplish?

Timeline I: Putting Things in Perspective

This chronology is based on the dating of K.A. Kitchen and E.R. Thiele, and is approximate, give or take about two or three years for the more exact dates. For a more detailed account of the concluding years of the first commonwealth (the "Age of Jeremiah,") see Timeline II.

DATE	EVENTS IN THE HISTORY OF ISRAEL	EVENTS IN WORLD HISTORY
1900–1600	The Patriarchal Age (including Joseph)	Code of Hammurabi
1690/80–1400	Israel in Egypt	Hyksos expelled from Egypt; New Empire begins
1400–1300	Israel in Egypt	Egypt rules Canaan; Amenophis IV (Akhnaten) fails in attempt to reform Egyptian religion
1300–1200	Israel Exits Egypt; Entry into Canaan[1] Prophet: Moses	The Bronze Age ends in general civilizational collapse. The Mycenaean Empire in Greece, the Hittite Empire of Asia Minor, the Mitanni, Assyrian and Kassite Empires of Mesopotamia and the Minoan Empire of the Mediterranean disintegrate and vanish. In 1177 the second invasion of Egypt by the Peoples of the Sea is repulsed by Pharaoh Ramses III, who barely manages to salvage the Nile Valley from the ruins of the New Empire.
1200–1032	Age of the Judges; Destruction of Shiloh; Age of the prophet Samuel	Age of Chaos. The Trojan War; Dorian invasions of Greece; Philistines arrive in Canaan; Arameans establish states in Syria
1032–1011	Saul king of Israel	

---

1. Sinai Covenant no earlier than 1400, no later than 1200-1180; the female tavern keeper phenomenon (cf. Rahab, *Joshua* 2) is valid down to circa 1100, after which customs changed.

Timeline I: Putting Things in Perspective

DATE	EVENTS IN THE HISTORY OF ISRAEL	EVENTS IN WORLD HISTORY
1011–971	David rules the kingdoms of Judah and Israel; makes Jerusalem his capital around 1003, conquers all the states between Egypt and Mesopotamia. Prophet: Nathan	
971–931	Age of Solomon; Temple built in Jerusalem; Davidic Empire begins to disintegrate. Prophet: Ahijah the Shilonite	Beginning of Egyptian and Assyrian resurgence
931–880	The kingdom of Israel successfully revolts against the House of David; the United Kingdoms permanently separate and the Davidic Empire collapses; Judah unsuccessfully attempts to reconquer Israel.	Egypt invades Western Asia, then collapses. Rise of Damascus as the major power in Syria; rise of Assyria.
880–741	Judah and Israel learn to live together and cooperate; continual war with Syria. Prophets: Elijah and Elisha, followed by the age of Classical Prophecy: Amos and Hosea.	Assyrian attempt to conquer Western Asia checked at Battle of Qarqar (853); effective Western resistance to further Assyrian penetration collapses; Carthage founded as a Phoenician colony in North Africa.
741–723	Decline of Israel and final destruction by Assyria (723); Judah survives as a vassal of the Assyrians. Prophets: Isaiah, Micah.	Damascus falls (732); Assyria rules all Western Asia.
723–586	Judah subject to Assyria. King Josiah implements a major religious reform (622), canonizing the Book of Deuteronomy. Judah, now subject to Babylonia, rebels. In 586 Jerusalem falls, the Temple is destroyed, and much of the surviving population is exiled to Babylon (*for details see Timeline II*). Prophets: Nahum and Jeremiah.	Assyria conquers Egypt. With the death of Assurbanipal the Assyrian Empire begins to disintegrate: Assyria is expelled from Egypt; Babylonia rebels; Nineveh falls (612). The Assyrian Empire is divided between the Babylonians and the Medes. Solon reforms Athens' laws.
586–538	Babylonian Exile; Cyrus frees Jews (538) and permits them to return and rebuild their Temple in Jerusalem. Prophets: Ezekiel and Deutero-Isaiah.	Cyrus the Great unites the Medes and the Persians, conquers Lydia (547) and captures Babylon (539) thus creating the greatest empire the world had known. Pisistratus seizes power in Athens.
538–430	42,000 Jews return to Jerusalem, rebuild the Temple (515) and re-found the commonwealth of Judea. Ezra and Nehemiah rebuild the walls of Jerusalem, canonize the Torah and institute it as the law of the land (430). Prophets: Haggai, Zechariah and Malachi. THE BIBLICAL AGE COMES TO A CLOSE	Persia conquers Egypt and the Greek states of Asia Minor, invades Greece and is defeated at Marathon and Salamis. The Greeks now start fighting among themselves. The Age of Pericles and the Athenian Empire, Aeschylus and Sophocles.
431–404		The Great Peloponnesian War. Athens looses to Sparta. Plays of Euripides and Aristophanes.

Timeline I: Putting Things in Perspective

DATE	EVENTS IN THE HISTORY OF ISRAEL	EVENTS IN WORLD HISTORY
404–338		Continual warfare in Greece and major social change. Macedonia consolidates as a major state; Philip of Macedon conquers Greece at the battle of Chaeronea. Plato.
338–323		Philip assassinated (336); Alexander the Great conquers the Persian Empire (334–323) and dies in Babylon. Aristotle.
323–200	Judea becomes part of the Ptolemaic Empire. Antiochus III (the Great) pushes the Ptolemaic Empire back to the border of Egypt; Judea becomes part of the Seleucid Empire.	The Era of the Diadochi (the successors of Alexander) who battle for the succession, and end by dividing it among the survivors of the wars, Seleucus getting Syria and Mesopotamia and Ptolemy getting Egypt. First Punic War (264–241) Rome defeats Carthage and occupies Sicily. Second Punic War (218–201) sees total defeat of Carthage. Rome now master of the Western Mediterranean.
199–165	Decree of Antiochus IV outlaws practice of Judaism; Temple profaned December 168. Revolt of Judas Maccabeus and his brothers. Temple rededicated December 165.	Rome defeats Philip V (199) and Greece becomes a protectorate of Rome. At Magnesia Rome defeats Antiochus III (190) and detaches Asia Minor from the Seleucid Empire. Rome is now the sole superpower.
164–63	Judah dies and his brothers continue the struggle against the Seleucid Empire. Judea declared an independent state by Simon (143). He and his successors (the Hasmoneans) are both kings and High Priests. Independence ends with the capture of Jerusalem by Pompey (63). Judea now a vassal of Rome.	Social and civil war in Rome: the Gracchi, Marius and Sulla; Pompey defeats the pirates, Mithradates and Tigranes (66), and annexes Syria. Rome now effectively rules the entire Hellenistic world up to the Euphrates.
63 BCE–70 CE	Herod declared king of Judea by Rome (40), rebuilds the Temple. Upon his death Rome assumes direct rule of Judea (4). The Jews revolt against Rome (66–70 CE); Jerusalem and the Temple both destroyed.	Julius Caesar defeats Pompey but is assassinated. In the resulting civil war Octavian defeats Antony, becoming the first Emperor of Rome. Persecutions of Christians begin in Rome. Nero, last of the Caesars, dies in Greece. General Vespasian declared emperor of Rome.

Timeline II:
Late 7th–Early 6th Centuries BCE

Events in the life of Jeremiah	Events in the Kingdom of Judah	Events in the International Arena
	+640 King **Amon** assassinated; **Josiah** ascends the throne of Judah at age 8	
	632 **Assurbanipal II** dies 628 **Josiah** begins to assert de facto independence. Moves North into territory that once was Israel	628 **Assur-etil-ilani** dies **Sin-shar-ishkun** evacuates Western Asia Egypt expands into Syria
627 Jeremiah called to prophecy Mission to the North?		
	622 Discovery of Scroll in Temple: **Deuteronomic Reformation launched**	
		617 **Nabopolassar** rebels; leads Babylonian army North against Assyria Assyrian-Egyptian alliance: Egyptian army blocks **Nabopolassar** 614 **Medes** take **Assur** 612 Joint **Median-Babylonian** army sacks **Nineveh** Death of **Sin-shar-ishkun**
608 Jeremiah delivers stinging denunciation in Temple; is almost lynched	+610 **609 BATTLE OF MEGIDDO**; **Josiah** killed 608 **Jehoahaz** betrayed by **Necho** and deposed; his brother **Jehoiakim** placed on throne **JUDAH NOW VASSAL OF EGYPT**	610 **Psammetichus I** dies; **Necho II** rules **Egypt** 609 Siege of **Haran**; **Necho** dispatches huge army **Siege fails: ASSYRIA WIPED OUT** **Ashur-uballit II** dies: **Nabopolassar** now master of Mesopotamia

Timeline II: Late 7th–Early 6th Centuries bce

		605 **Nebuchadrezzar** leads Babylonians to victory at **Carchemish**, then again at **Hamath**
604 **Baruch** reads **Jeremiah's** scroll to crowd in Temple; **Jehoiakim** burns the scroll **Jeremiah** & **Baruch** in hiding	604 **Jehoiakim** surrenders to **Nebuchadrezzar** **JUDAH NOW VASSAL OF BABYLON**	604 **Nabopolassar** dies; **Nebuchadrezzar** crowned King of Akad. Occupies Syria.
	600 **Jehoiakim** rebels against Babylon; Babylonian army appears before Jerusalem	601 **Nebuchadrezzar** invades Egypt and is defeated. Withdraws army to Babylon
598 **Jeremiah** resumes active public **life**	598 **Jehoiakim** dies; his son, **Jehoiachin**, surrenders to **Nebuchadrezzar** & is imprisoned. His uncle **Zedekiah** is installed as his Regent in **Jerusalem FIRST EXILE: UPPER & MIDDLE CLASSES** **JUDAH NOW VASSAL OF BABYLON**	
	588 **Zedekiah** rebels against Babylon **JERUSALEM UNDER SIEGE**	
587 **Jeremiah** arrested attempting to leave the city. Imprisoned, he nearly dies from mistreatment. His conditions improved by **Zedekiah**, he remains imprisoned till the fall of the city		
Fall 586 **Jeremiah** carried off to Egypt against his will. Eventually will die in Egypt	586 **Jerusalem** falls; is razed by **Nebuzaradan**; **Zedekiah** captured and blinded; **SECOND EXILE: EVERYONE BUT POOREST OF POOR**; **Gedalia** appointed new regent at **Mizpah**. Gedalia assassinated; remaining population flees to Egypt. **THIRD EXILE: EVERYONE THAT IS LEFT**	
		539 **Cyrus the Great** conquers Babylon: **Issues Proclamation freeing the Jews**
	538 First wave of Jews leaves Babylon for Jerusalem	

Glossary of Terms and Place Names

Words appearing in **bold** are themselves in the Glossary.
Names appearing in *italics* are in the "Who's Who" section that follows.

Abel-shittim (Abel of the Acacias): The site on the **Steppes of Moab**, at the foot of **Mount Peor**, opposite **Jericho** where the **Children of Israel** pitched their last camp prior to crossing the **Jordan River**.

Abravanel, Don Isaac ben Judah: (1437–1508 CE). Financier, philosopher and biblical commentator who lived sequentially in Spain, Portugal and Italy; his commentary on *The Twelve Prophets* was published in 1520 CE.

Acropolis: The Greek term for the fortified inner citadel of ancient cities, usually located at the site's highest point, containing the temple(s), palace and other government buildings from which the city and its territories were ruled.

Agag: 1. King of the **Amalekites** in the 11th century BCE. Defeated by *Saul* and executed for war crimes by *Samuel*.
2. Possibly name of **Amalekite** royal house, or a title designating a king of **Amalek**.

Akkadian: A Semitic language, cognate to **Hebrew**, spoken in **Mesopotamia**.

Albright, William Foxwell (1891–1971): American Middle-East scholar who pioneered the discipline of Biblical Archaeology.

Amalek (Amalekites): A semi-nomadic people based in the **Negeb** wilderness south of **Beersheba**. Their vicious harassment of the **Israelites** from the **Exodus** period onwards resulted in their becoming the archetypical enemy of **Israel**.

Amenophes II: Egyptian **Pharaoh** during the Age of the **New Empire**; conqueror of Asiatic empire.

Ammon: Hebrew-speaking non–Israelite kingdom east of the **Gilead**. See **B'nai-ammon**.

Ammonites: The inhabitants of the Kingdom of **Ammon**. See **B'nai-ammon**.

Amorites: Literally "Westerners"; the name for one of the large ethnic groups that inhabited **Canaan** before the **Israelite** conquest. The term is often used as a collective designation for all the pre–**Israelite** inhabitants of the region.

Anatoth: A town of priests about 3 miles north of **Jerusalem**; the birthplace of *Jeremiah*.

Angel: The English form of *Angelos*, the Greek word for messenger. See **Messenger**.

Arabah, The: The Hebrew term for the **Jordan Valley**. This includes the depression surrounding the **Dead Sea** ("The Salt Sea"), the lowest point on the surface of the earth. The Arabah continues south to the Gulf of Aqaba.

Arabim Mountains: A range of mountains east of the **Dead Sea**, running North-South the length of the **Moab** plateau. Viewed from the **Cis-Jordan**, these highlands jut up close to 4,000 feet from the **Dead Sea**. See **Pisgah**.

Arad: City in the **Negeb**, about 16 miles northeast of **Beersheba** and 15 miles southeast of **Hebron**, destroyed by the **Israelites** in the 13th century BCE.

Aram: A collective noun signifying the totality of the **Aramean** Peoples.

Aramaic: The language of the **Arameans**. See **Arameans**.

Arameans: A **Semitic** people that inhabited most of **Syria**, whose language, **Aramaic**, is a sister language to Hebrew.

Aramaism: A term of Aramaic province which is deemed to have entered the Hebrew language only during the **Babylonian Exile**-Persian periods, when the Israelites dwelt in an **Aramaic**-speaking environment; thus an indicator of a late (**Second Commonwealth**) dating for the text in which it is found.

Ark of the Covenant, The: The portable chest surmounted by two gold cherubim, containing the stone tablets on which were inscribed the Ten Commandments; Israel's most sacred object.

Ar-moab: The ancient capital of **Moab**, located a bit south of the Ar**non** River. After the loss of North Moab territory to *Sihon*, the capitol was transferred to **Kir-moab** further south.

Arnon River: A perennial stream flowing midway into the eastern side of the **Dead Sea** through the Wadi el-Mujib, a tremendous ravine that at one point, south of **Dibon**, is 2.5 miles wide and 1,650 feet below the tops of the adjacent cliffs. It formed the boundary between **Moab** and *Sihon's* kingdom of **Heshbon**, and later the southern border of the tribe of **Reuben**.

Ashdod: Philistine city near the Mediterranean coast.

Asher: Israelite tribe settled in the western **Galilee** north of **Carmel**.

Ashkelon: Philistine port city on the Mediterranean coast between **Gaza** and **Ashdod**.

Ashur: Name of the chief god of the **Assyrian** pantheon.

Ashurbanipal II (669–632): The last of the great **Assyrian** warlords, conqueror of Upper **Egypt** and expander of the **Assyrian Empire** to its greatest extent. His death signaled the start of the rapid disintegration of the Empire.

Assur: Early capital of **Assyria**.

Assyria: The empire created by the **Assyrians**.

Assyrians: A people centered in upper **Mesopotamia** who were among the most single-minded militarists in history. Totally ruthless, they built up one of the most fearsome military machines the world has ever known, destroying their many competitors and ultimately bringing the entire **Fertile Crescent** under their yoke.

Baal: (Often in the plural: **Baalim**). Literally "Lord," "Master"; the title of Hadad, chief god of the **Canaanites**. He was a storm and fertility deity who was thought to die each summer and be resurrected with the winter rains.

Baal-peor: The name of the god whose shrine was located at the foot of Mount Peor, bordering the **Steppes of Moab**.

Baba Batra: A **Tractate** of the **Talmud**.

Babylon: Major city in Southern **Mesopotamia** on the banks of the **Euphrates River**; the capital of the Neo-Chaldean Empire of *Nebuchadrezzar*.

Babylonian Exile: Sometimes known as the Babylonian Captivity. The historical period following the destruction of the **Kingdom of Judah** (586 BCE) during which most of its surviving population was removed from the land by the victorious Babylonians and resettled in **Mesopotamia**. This period is deemed to have ended with the proclamation of *Cyrus the Great* (538 BCE) allowing the Jews to return to their homeland.

Bamah (High Place): A local shrine, often sited on a hill top or promontory, and not uncommonly a long-standing pagan shrine that had been appropriated by the Israelites and rededicated to the worship of the LORD, the God of Israel. Often pagan traditions and practices lingered on, exerting a corrupting influence on Israelite religion. The **Bamot** (plural of **Bamah**) of **Judah** were all permanently shuttered by *King Josiah* beginning with 628 BCE.

Bashan: Area bounded by **Mount Hermon** in the north, Jebal Druze to the east, the hills east of the **Sea of Galilee** to the west and extending about six miles south of the **Yarmuk River**; conquered by *Moses* in the 13th century BCE.

Beersheba: A town approximately 45 miles southwest of **Jerusalem**, traditionally marking the southern extremity of **Judah**.

Glossary of Terms and Place Names

Benjamin: **Israelite** tribe occupying the area between **Jerusalem** and **Beth-el**.

Berith: The Hebrew term for Covenant; when preceded by the indicator for the direct object, i.e., "The Covenant," it refers to the Sinai Covenant, the foundational document embodying the ground rules of the relationship between **Israel** and its God and acting as the Constitution of the People of Israel.

Beth-el: Israelite town and shrine in the southern reaches of **Ephraim**, about 11 miles north of **Jerusalem**. The shrine was reputed to have been founded by Father *Jacob*.

Bethlehem: A town about 3 miles south of Jerusalem, birthplace of *David*.

Bicolon (pl. bicola): A line of biblical poetry consisting of two segments or cola. See **colon**.

Bikah: The Hebrew term for the **Jordan** Valley, including the area of the **Dead Sea**.

B'nai-ammon: Literally, the Children of Ammon, the name by which the **Ammonites** knew themselves.

Bronze Age: An archaeological term relating to the period of the Ancient Near East between approximately 3100 and 1200 BCE, the era when the main material used for tools and armaments was bronze. It was preceded by the Stone Age and followed by the **Iron Age**. It is usually divided into:

Early Bronze—3100 to 2100 BCE
Middle Bronze—2100 to 1550 BCE
Late Bronze—1550 to 1200 BCE

Canaan: The name given by the Egyptians to the Asian province of their Empire. This became known to the **Israelites** as **The Promised Land**.

Canaanites: 1. A collective term for the various peoples and ethnic groups inhabiting **Canaan**.
2. A designation for one of the largest ethnic groups inhabiting **The Promised Land** prior to the Israelite conquest.

Canon: The term for the official corpus of Sacred Writings; i.e., the Bible.

Canonizers: The body of individuals who decided which works were to be included in the **Canon** and which excluded.

Carchemish: A strategic city on the **Euphrates River** in Northern **Mesopotamia**; the site of the decisive battle between the **Babylonian** and **Egyptian** armies in 605 BCE that decided the fate of Western Asia for a generation.

Carmel: A mountain range stretching southeast from the Bay of Haifa.

Chemosh: Chief deity of the pantheon of **Moab**.

Children of Ammon: See **B'nai-ammon**.

Children of Israel (commonly Israelites): Literally, "the descendants of Israel," *Israel* being the alternate name of Father *Jacob*. This was the name by which the Israelites knew themselves, hence seeing themselves as a nation of blood relatives tracing their lineage from a common eponymous ancestor.

Cis-Jordan: From the Latin (cis = this side of), i.e., this side of the **Jordan**, the area between the Mediterranean Sea and the **Jordan River**; as opposed to the **Trans-Jordan**, the other side of the **Jordan**.

Cities and Daughters: The basic difference between a city and a "daughter" is that a city is defined as a *walled* urban complex whereas a "daughter" is an unwalled grouping of houses, i.e., a village. Cities, being defensible, assumed the responsibility for the defense of the population of the regional villages and thus were the seats of regional government; the "daughters" were dependent on the cities.

Colon (pl. cola): The individual segment of a line of biblical poetry, having either two or three beats.

Commonwealth, First: The six century historical period, from the settlement of the Land of Israel towards the end of the 13th century BCE until the destruction of **Judah** and the exile of the last of its surviving inhabitants by the victorious **Babylonians** and resettled in **Mesopotamia** in 586 BCE. This period is the heart of the Biblical Age.

Commonwealth, Second: The historical period comprising almost six centuries, beginning with the return from the **Babylonian Exile** in 538 BCE until the destruction of **Jerusalem** by the Romans in the year 70 CE. The first centuries of this period bring the Biblical Age to a close.

Covenant: See **Berith**.

Cubit: A standard unit of length equivalent to about 18 inches. Originally, it was the distance between the elbow and the finger-tips of the average adult male arm.

Damascus: Capital of one of the leading **Aramean** states in Syria, roughly 120 miles northeast of **Jerusalem**.

Dan: 1. Israelite tribe originally settled west of **Benjamin**; later relocated to the far north beyond the **Galilee** tribes.
 2. Name of the principal city of the tribe in its northern location.

Davidic Empire: Tenth-century Empire consolidated by *David*, stretching from the border of **Egypt** to the **Euphrates**. Upon the death of his son *Solomon* the empire disintegrated.

Dead Sea: Known to the ancients as "The Salt Sea" because of its concentrated saline nature, it is a stagnant body of water fed by the **Jordan**, **Arnon** and **Zered Rivers** but with no outflow. At 1,275 feet below sea level, it is the lowest body of water on the surface of the earth.

Dead Sea Documents (Abbr. Q): Scrolls and scroll fragments of various biblical and extra-biblical Books found in caves at **Qumran** near the **Dead Sea**. They are the oldest extant versions of biblical Books, some dating from as early as the 3rd century BCE.

Deir 'Alla: An archaeological site on the **Jabbok River** in the **Trans-Jordan**; the location of the biblical **Sukkoth**. For the inscriptions discovered there which mention the biblical seer *Balaam*, see Appendix E.

Determinative: A sign in the Egyptian system of hieroglyphics attached to a proper noun to indicate the nature of the entity named.

Deuteronomy: The fifth Book of the Bible. The raising of Deuteronomy to authoritative status in the **Josianic Reformation** of 622 BCE was the beginning of the canonization process that led to the Bible as we know it.

Dibon: The modern Dhiban in the **Trans-Jordan**, three miles north of the **Arnon River**.

Dittography: The unintentional repetition of letters or words in copying; a not uncommon cause of error in biblical texts.

Divination (Hebrew *Kesem*): The "science" of forecasting future events, universally respected and practiced in the Ancient Near East. Though deemed effective by the Bible, its practice is forbidden to Israelites (*Deuteronomy* 18:10) who are instead referred to God's prophets (*Deuteronomy* 18:15).

Eben-ezer, Battle of: Decisive **Philistine** victory over the **Israelite** tribes about 1050 BCE.

Edah: An ad hoc emergency council called together by the tribal chieftains in early **Israel** whenever a national trans-tribal issue arose. It consisted of all adult male **Israelites** who constituted themselves a National Assembly vested with legislative and judicial powers. With the rise of the monarchy the Edah fell into disuse.

Edom: A Hebrew-speaking kingdom located mainly on the **Trans-Jordanian** Plateau, south of the Kingdom of **Moab**. **Edom** took its name from the **Edomites**, the ethnic grouping that founded the Kingdom. See **Seir**.

Edrei: A town on the **Yarmuk River**, about 30 miles east of the point the **Yarmuk** joins the **Jordan**. Site of the battle where **Israel** defeated *Og* and conquered the **Bashan**.

Egypt: Ancient African kingdom and great power, separated by the Sinai from the south of Judah. Egypt ruled **Canaan** during the age of the **New Empire**.

Elder: The head of a family; as such one of the local councilmen and magistrates.

Elders in the Gate, The: The term for the governing body of a local community which also exercised judicial functions. The "gate" in the title refers to the gate in the town or city wall, which was the site where the body held its sessions.

Emek: 1. "Lowlands," "vale," "flat country"; the opposite of "Highlands."
 2. The region of the Land of Israel that runs north-south between the coast of the Mediterranean to the west and the foothills of the **Highlands** (the **Shephelah**) to the east.

Glossary of Terms and Place Names

Ephod: 1. A relatively small, portable object, manipulated by a priest, used in early **Israel** to ascertain the will of God.
   2. A linen vestment worn by priests (and sometimes laymen) when officiating at some ritual.

Ephraim: The premier among the Northern tribes, Ephraim gave its name to the **Highlands of Ephraim** which it shared with its brother tribes **Benjamin** and **Manasseh**.

Euphrates River: One of the two mighty rivers that flow through **Mesopotamia**. See **Tigris River**.

Eusebius Pamphili: Otherwise known as **Eusebius of Caesarea** (260?–340 CE). Bishop of Caesarea from shortly after 313 CE until his death, Eusebius was a Roman historian, exegete and Christian polemicist. His major work, *The Onomasticon* ("On the Place Names in the Holy Scripture"), is an alphabetical listing of all the place names listed in the Bible with, where possible, information as to their location. Written prior to 324 CE, the work reflects the situation (and the knowledge) current in the Holy Land prior to its "Christianization" during the reign of the Emperor Constantine.

Exodus, The: The name by which **Israel's** liberation from slavery and escape from **Egypt** has come to be known.

Fertile Crescent: The fertile area curving from the river valleys of **Mesopotamia** through Syria and ending in the Land of **Israel**, bounded on all sides by either arid regions or the sea. It was in the Fertile Crescent that organized agriculture and animal husbandry first came into being about ten thousand years ago.

Former Prophets: Translation of Hebrew term *nebiim rishonim*, the name given to the Books of *Joshua*, *Judges*, *Samuel* and *Kings*, which together form a continuous history of the **First Commonwealth**.

Gad: **Israelite** tribe settled in the **Gilead**, with **Reuben** to its south and **Manasseh** to its north.

Galilee: The northern region of the Land of Israel, beginning with the northern rim of the **Jezreel Valley**; home to the tribes of **Asher, Issachar, Naphtali** and **Zebulun**. Detached from Israel by **Tiglath-Pileser III** in 740 BCE.

Galilee, Sea of: See **Sea of Galilee**.

Gaza: Ancient city on the Mediterranean coast about 13 miles south of **Ashkelon**. During the Age of the **New Empire**, Gaza was the capital of the **Egyptian** Provence of **Canaan**. Upon arrival of the **Philistines** and the **Egyptian** evacuation of their Asian Empire, it became one of the five major cities of the **Philistine Pentapolis**.

Gerar: A principality in the South-West of **Canaan**, about 15 miles north-west of **Beersheba**.

Geshur, Kingdom of: An **Aramean** kingdom located to the northwest of the **Bashan**, whose western border fronted on the **Sea of Galilee**.

Gibeah: A town 3 to 4 miles north of **Jerusalem**. The hometown of *Saul* and the capital of the Kingdom of **Israel** during his reign.

Gibeon: A town about 6 miles northwest of **Jerusalem**, site of a major shrine.

Gilboa, Mount: A prominent mountain ridge on the south side of the **Jezreel Valley**.

Gilead: Technically, the region of the **Trans-Jordan** bounded by the **Yarmuk River** to the north and the **Jabbok River** to its south; but sometimes used to designate the entire **Israelite Trans-Jordan**.

Gilgal: **Israelite** shrine in the **Jordan Valley**, about 16 miles northeast of **Jerusalem** and about a mile and a half northeast of **Jericho**.

Gittin: A **tractate of the Talmud**.

Grace: See **Hesed**.

Habakkuk: A prophet who probably lived in the 6th century BCE.

Hamas: A term denoting ferocious bloody violence, mainly in urban contexts, but not in connection with warfare; a synonym for bloodshed.

Hapax: (Abr. of *hapax legomenon*; lit. used only once). A term designating a given word or phrase as unique in the Bible, appearing only once.

Haran: Situated on a major tributary of the **Euphrates River**, this ancient commercial hub was centrally located in Northern **Mesopotamia** about 230 miles north-west of **Nineveh**. From 612–608 BCE *Haran* served as the last capital of **Assyria**.

Hasmoneans: The descendants of *Simon*, brother of *Judah the Maccabee*; the dynasty that ruled the Kingdom of Judaea from 140–37 BCE.

Hatti-land: The name by which **Syria** was known to the **Babylonians**.

Hebrew: 1. A member of a widespread ethnic group in the Ancient Near East.
   2. The name of a Semitic language spoken in **Canaan.**

Hebrew Bible: The Holy Scriptures of the Jews, so known because it is written in Hebrew. It is known to Christians as the **Old Testament.**

Hebron: The premier city of the southern region of **Canaan**—what was to become the territory of the tribe of **Judah**—is located some 20 miles south of **Jerusalem**, 39 miles east of **Gaza**, and sited 927 meters above sea level. The Cave of Machpelah, the burial place of the Fathers *Abraham*, *Isaac* and *Jacob*, and of the Mothers *Sarah*, *Rebecca* and *Leah* is to be found in its vicinity.

Hermon, Mount: The tallest mountain in the land at 9100 feet, and often capped with snow, Mount Hermon lies at the northeastern-most tip of **Israel's** area of settlement; **Dan** nestling at its southwestern foot.

Hesed: *Hesed* is, first and foremost, a way God manifests Himself to humanity. His care for humans shows itself through His *hesed*: His loving kindness in giving people far more than they deserve. But human beings can manifest *hesed* through acts of unconditional kindness to others in excess of what the other deserves based on his or her own behavior. In so doing such a person is reflecting God's grace.

Heshbon: 1. An **Amorite** kingdom ruled by one King *Sihon*, situated in the **Trans-Jordan**, that was conquered by **Israel** in the last days of *Moses* and settled by the tribes of **Gad** and **Reuben**.
   2. A city, the capital of the Kingdom of Heshbon.

Hill Country or **Highlands of Ephraim** (Hebr. *Har Ephraim*): That portion of the central north-south mountain ridge located north of **Jerusalem**; the area of settlement of the tribes of **Benjamin, Ephraim** and the western part of **Manasseh.**

Hill Country or **Highlands of Judah** (Hebr. *Harai Yehudah*): That portion of the central north-south mountain ridge located south of **Jerusalem**; the area of settlement of most of the tribe of **Judah.**

Hittites: A people resident in Anatolia (present day eastern Turkey) who created a great civilization which flourished between around 1600 and 1200 BCE. Their **Hittite Empire** dominated a large part of the Ancient Near East during these centuries.

Hozeh: A visionary; a diviner, a practitioner of **divination.**

Hyksos: The name given by the Egyptians to an Asiatic people that conquered Egypt and ruled it for more than a century, from c. 1690–1580 BCE, until an Egyptian uprising terminated their domination. With the fall of their capital, Avaris (Tanis), c. 1550 BCE, Amosis, founder of the glorious Eighteenth Dynasty, finally expelled them from Egypt.

Hyrcanus, John (135–106): Hasmonean king who converted the **Edomites** (now known as Idumeans) to Judaism.

Ibn Ezra, Abraham: (1089–1164 CE); Medieval Spanish philosopher, poet, grammarian and Bible scholar.

Imperfect tense: See **Perfect tense.**

Infinitive absolute: A grammatical construction in biblical Hebrew involving a repeated verb, the effect of which is to immeasurably strengthen the action delineated. It is used to indicate powerful emphasis.

Iron Age: An archaeological term defining the era from approximately the 12th century BCE when iron (more properly steel) replaced bronze as the main metal in general use. For the Ancient Near East the Iron Age is divided into:

Iron I—12th and 11th centuries BCE
Iron II—10th through 6th centuries BCE

Israel: 1. Collective noun used to designate the **Children of Israel** as a people.

2. Abbreviated form of "**Land of Israel**."
3. The **Kingdom of Israel** (after 920 BCE).

Israelites: See **Children of Israel**.

Jabbok River: One of the main eastern tributaries of the **Jordan**. Its source is near Amman (biblical **Rabbah**). From there it flows northward, then turns 90 degrees and flows westward through ever deepening canyons until it empties into the **Jordan** 15 miles north of the **Dead Sea**. Its earlier south to north stretch served as the western boundary of the **Ammonite** kingdom, and its later east to west course formed the boundary between the two **Amorite** kingdoms of *Sihon* and *Og*. See **Heshbon, Kingdom of** and **Bashan**.

Jaffa: Major port on the Mediterranean coast.

Jahaz: A city near the SE border of the Kingdom of **Heshbon**; the staging platform for the attack on the **Children of Israel**.

Jazer: A stronghold in eastern **Heshbon**, approximately ten miles west of **Rabbath-ammon**, between the city of **Heshbon** and the **Jabbok River**.

Jenny: A female donkey.

Jericho: Ancient city, over nine thousand years old, located near the **Jordan River** about 8 miles north of the **Dead Sea**. It is listed by the Bible as the first site captured and destroyed by *Joshua* during the conquest of **Canaan**. It remained a heap of ruins all through the Age of the Judges and the Age of the United Monarchy which followed; it was only rebuilt in the 9th century BCE by *King Ahab* of **Israel**.

Jerusalem: Ancient city, the largest in the southern part of **Canaan**. Conquered by *David* in the 10th century BCE, he made it his capital.

Jezreel, Valley of: A flat fertile corridor flanked by mountainous country running roughly southeast from the Bay of Haifa to Beth-shean in the **Jordan Valley**. The term sometimes is used collectively to include its northern extension, the Valley of Acco, as well.

Jordan River: The main river of the land of Israel, running north-south from the **Sea of Galilee** down to the **Dead Sea**, a distance of about 70 miles.

Jordan Valley: The valley formed by the **Jordan River**. See **Arabah**.

Josianic Reformation: The major monotheistic reforms undertaken by King *Josiah* (641–609 BCE) which involved centralizing all worship in the Temple in **Jerusalem**, and arranging the acceptance of (most probably) the Book of **Deuteronomy** as the "Constitution" of the Kingdom of **Judah**.

Jubilee: An institution mandated in *Leviticus* 25:8–17 to be observed every 50th year by the emancipation of all Hebrew slaves, the restoration of all alienated lands to their original owners (or his heirs) and desisting from sowing and reaping all agricultural lands in that year.

Judah: The southernmost tribe of **Israel**, later a kingdom in its own right.

Kadesh-barnea: An oasis rich in springs, located over 50 miles to the southwest of **Beersheba** and about 95 miles southwest of **Jerusalem**; this was the base camp of the Israelites during the Wilderness Period prior to their entry into the **Promised Land**.

Kaufmann, Yehezkel: (1889–1963) Israeli biblical scholar, author of the monumental 8 volume *Toldot Haemunah Hayisraelit*, translated in English as *The Religion of Israel*.

Kenites: A semi-nomadic tribe allied to the **Israelites** whose main range lay south of **Arad**.

Ketib: The Hebrew consonantal text of the Bible. See **Qeri**.

Kimchi, Rabbi David: (c.1160–1235 CE) A medieval French philologist, philosopher and biblical commentator, also known by his acronym **Radak** (Rabbi David Kimchi).

King James Bible: The classic translation of the Bible into English published in 1611 CE; its official name is "The Authorized Version" (AV).

King's Highway, The: Running east of the **Jordan River** across the **Trans-Jordanian** Plateau, this was one of the two major routes connecting **Egypt** and **Mesopotamia**. See **Via Maris**.

King's Way: An East-West route branching off the **King's Highway,** connecting **Heshbon** with **Jericho.**

Kinneret, Lake: See **Sea of Galilee.**

Kir-moab: Capital of the Kingdom of **Moab.**

Kosem: A practitioner of **divination.**

Latter Prophets: The second part of the Division of the Hebrew Bible entitled "The Prophets," containing the actual writings of the prophets themselves: the books of *Isaiah, Jeremiah, Ezekiel* and *The Book of the Twelve Minor Prophets.* See **Former Prophets.**

Levi: The priestly tribe, with no designated area of settlement. Dispersed among the other territorial tribes, its religious vocation was its inheritance. Being landless, those of its members who could not find employment serving as priests at shrines formed an underclass of poverty-stricken dependents on pubic welfare.

Levite: A male member of the tribe of **Levi.**

LXX: Abbreviation for **Septuagint.**

Maaca: Aramaean kingdom directly north of **Geshur.**

Maimonides, Moses: Born Cordoba (Spain) 1138 CE, died Fostat (Egypt) 1204 CE; rabbi, physician, astronomer, philosopher, Talmudic scholar and legalist; one of the most influential thinkers in the mediaeval world and one of the greatest Jewish minds of all time.

Malach: (Hebrew for "messenger"); a representative, human or supernatural, sent on a mission. When supernatural the word is often rendered in English as **Angel.**

Manasseh: 1. **Israelite** tribe, one part settled in the Central Highlands north of **Ephraim,** the other in the **Gilead** and **Bashan** regions of the **Trans-Jordan.**
2. King of Judah (reigned 696–642 BCE), remembered for his paganization of Judah. Grandfather of King *Josiah.*

Masorites: The term for those persons who, over the generations, were concerned with the precise preservation and transmission of the holy text of the Bible. The end product of the millennia-long endeavor is the current text of the Hebrew Bible known as the **Masoretic Text (MT).**

Masoretic Text: See **Masorites.**

Matzebah (Plur. **Matzebot**)**:** A stone or wooden monument raised and dedicated to a deity. Common in early Israel, they were later banned due to their association with pagan worship. Today used to designate a "gravestone."

Mazar, Benjamin: (1906–1995) Biblical historian and recognized "dean" of biblical archaeologists.

Medeba: The modern Madaba on the ancient **King's Highway,** 15 miles southeast of the mouth of the **Jordan,** in the territory of the tribe of **Reuben.**

Medes: An Aryan people of mountain tribes related to the Persians, who dwelt in the Iranian highlands east of the **Tigris River.** Together with the **Babylonians** they destroyed the **Assyrian Empire** and divided it between them.

Megiddo: A fortress city founded in 7,000 BCE, controlling the main pass through the **Carmel** range. Site of numerous battles, including the battle in 609 BCE in which King *Josiah* perished.

Merism: A linguistic term: the expression of a totality by means of a pair of opposites; such as "from near and far," i.e., from everywhere; or "through thick and thin," i.e., through everything.

Mesopotamia: The name given to the region of the Near East watered by the **Euphrates** and the **Tigris Rivers.** The region today goes by the name of Iraq.

Messenger: The literal translation of the Hebrew word *malach*; one entrusted with a specific mission. When Jephthah sends diplomatic envoys to the King of Ammon to initiate negotiations, they are termed *malachim,* messengers (*Judges* 11:12). The Bible also depicts God making use of messengers. These are designated as either *a messenger of the* LORD or *a messenger of God.* The messenger can be either a human being or a supernatural being. When the latter, these are usually depicted as appearing human and distinguishable as supernatural beings only by their actions (cf. *Judges* 6:12–22; 13:3–21 etc.). The term "Angel," often used to translate the Hebrew *malach*, comes from the Greek *angelos*, the term used by the authors of the Septuagint (LXX) to translate the Hebrew *malach*; *angelos* is simply the Greek word for messenger.

Midianites: A conglomerate of related nomadic tribes whose range extended from the rim of the Arabian Desert to the Sinai Wilderness. *Moses* took refuge among them while a fugitive from **Egypt**, and while there took to wife a Midianite woman. Despite these early relations, over time the Midianites became inveterate enemies of the **Israelites**.

Midrash: A form of homiletical exegesis of the biblical text, usually of a fanciful nature, widely practiced by the rabbis of the **Talmudic** Age. The value of Midrash lies in the moral and ideological values it attempts to inculcate. The rabbis clearly differentiated between Midrashic interpretation and expository exegesis (*pshat*) which was meant as a serious literal elucidation of the biblical text.

Milcom: The chief deity of the **Benai-ammon**.

Minhah (Hebrew): 1. The daily afternoon offering to God of finely ground flour and oil.
2. A gift brought in token of submission, which is why the daily afternoon offering was called a "minhah," i.e., a sign of **Israel's** submission to God.
3. (Modern) The second of the three daily prayer services.

Mizpah: A town located in the Central **Highlands** in the territory of **Benjamin**, between **Jerusalem** and **Beth-el**. Because of its central location and its having been the site of a prominent shrine, it was chosen as the location for the seat of the **Babylonian** puppet government headed by *Gedaliah, son of Ahikam* following the destruction of **Jerusalem** in 586 BCE.

Moab: A Hebrew-speaking **Transjordanian** kingdom often hostile to **Israel**, bordered on the north by the tribe of **Reuben**, on the south by the Kingdom of **Edom**, and on the west by the **Dead Sea**.

Nabateans: An Arabian Bedouin people that built a sophisticated commercial civilization in the post-biblical era, displacing the **Edomites** from their homeland in the process.

Nachmanidies: See **Ramban**.

Nahal: See **Wadi**.

Negeb: "The Southlands"; the southern wilderness area of the land of Israel, roughly from **Beersheba** southward. In biblical times it was sparsely inhabited by nomadic tribes. "Negeb" originally meant "dry" or "parched," a vivid description of the region.

Neum: A term indicating that the attached material is an oracle of God; a synonym for "oracle."

New Empire, The: (c. 1567–1150 BCE comprising the 18th and 19th dynasties). The name given to the age in Egyptian history following the Second Intermediate Period when **Egypt** was conquered and ruled by Asiatics known as **Hyksos**. After expelling the foreign invaders **Egypt** expanded out of the Nile basin and carved out an empire in Western Asia which they termed **Canaan**.

New Testament: Written in Greek, it, combined with the **Old Testament**, together form the Holy Scriptures of Christianity.

Nineveh: 1. Capital of the **Assyrian** Empire, situated on the northern reaches of the **Tigris River** in **Mesopotamia**, opposite the present day Mosul.
2. Mythic megalopolis, the focus of the *Book of Jonah*.

Nob: A town of priests about one and a half miles northeast of **Jerusalem**, site of King *Saul's* massacre of the priestly House of **Eli**.

Old Testament: The Christian name for the Hebrew Bible.

Papyrus: A kind of paper made from the stems of the papyrus plant, manufactured in Egypt.

Parchment: The skin of a sheep, goat or some other animal prepared to be written on.

Paran, Mount: The Wilderness of Paran is a region in the **Sinai** Peninsula which extends into the **Negeb**. **Mount Paran** is located somewhere in this region, possibly not far from **Mount Sinai**.

Pentapolis: A union of five city-states; in particular, the union of **Gaza**, **Ashkelon**, **Ashdod**, **Ekron** and **Gath**.

Peoples of the Sea: The name given to the conglomeration of peoples that convulsed the Eastern Mediterranean during the great collapse of the **Late Bronze Age**. The **Philistines** were a part of this phenomenon.

Peor, Mount: A mountain at the southern end of the **Arabim Mountain** chain in the **Trans-Jordan**, overlooking **Able-shittim**.

Perfect tense (Grammar): Biblical **Hebrew** possesses neither a past nor a future tense, but instead **perfect** and **imperfect tenses**: indications not of *when* an action took place but whether the given action has been *completed* or whether it is *still ongoing*. In translation the **perfect tense** is usually rendered in English by the past tense, and the **imperfect** by the future; renditions that are sometimes unavoidably misleading.

Peshita: A translation of the Bible into Syriac (a late form of the Aramaic language), possibly during the 1st century CE; usual abbreviation: **Syr.**

Pethor: The homeland of *Balaam* in **Mesopotamia**.

Petuḥah: (P) (pl. **Petuḥot**) A Masoretic sign denoting a major break in the biblical text. See **Stumah**.

Pharaoh: Literally, "Great House"; the official title of the King of Egypt.

Philistines: A people of Aegean origin who seized the opportunity presented by the collapse of the **New Empire** to settle in the southwest corner of **Canaan** and establish a **Pentapolis**. They became the main competitors of the **Israelites** for the possession of **The Promised Land**.

Philo of Alexandria: (c. 20 BCE–50 CE) A Jewish Hellenistic philosopher and biblical exegete who developed an allegorical method of biblical interpretation; considered by some to be the founder of religious philosophy in Judaism, Christianity and Islam.

Phoenicia: The area known today as Western Lebanon; the one segment of **Canaanite** population and culture that escaped the **Israelite** conquest. Fronting on the Mediterranean, the **Phoenicians** were to become the greatest commercial people of the Ancient Near East. See **Sidonians**.

Phoenicians: The inhabitants of **Phoenicia**.

Pisgah: A collective term for the headlands of the **Moabite** plateau. See **Arabim Mountains**.

Plains of Moab, The: (Hebrew *Sedai Moab*) The **Moab** Plateau, an area of rich farm and grazing land.

Plural of Majesty: Since ancient times and down to the present day, it has been customary for monarchs to refer to themselves in the plural, i.e., "It is our wish that…" or "We hereby decree that…." This usage is routinely used in connection with God, "The King of Kings."

Primary History, The: The term coined by D.N. Freedman for the complex of nine biblical books—the *Pentateuch, Joshua, Judges, Samuel* and *Kings*—which purports to trace the origins of the **Children of Israel** from the dawn of history to the settlement in **Canaan**, and then to the exile of the **Israelites** from the land.

Promised Land, The: See **Canaan**.

Qeri: Literally "read thus"; the text as it is read according to the **Masorites**. See **Ketib**.

Qumran: Location abutting the northwest corner of the **Dead Sea** where the earliest known copies of some of the Books of the Bible have been found. See **Dead Sea Documents**.

Rabbath-ammon: Sometimes simply **Rabbah**. Capital of the **Ammonite Kingdom**.

Radak: See **Kimchi**.

Ralbag: Acronym for Rabbi Levi ben Gershon (1288–1344 CE). French mathematician, astronomer, philosopher and biblical commentator.

Ramah: Town in the **Highlands of Ephraim**, located about 6 miles north of **Jerusalem**.

Rambam: Acronym for Rabbi Moses ben Maimon. See **Maimonides, Moses**.

Ramban: Acronym for Rabbi Moses ben Nahman, also known as Nahmanides (1194–1270

CE); medieval Spanish biblical exegete, poet, philosopher, rabbinic scholar, cabbalist and physician.

Rashi: Acronym for Rabbi Shlomo ben Isaac (1040–1105 CE), probably the greatest of the medieval Jewish biblical commentators and exegetes.

Red Sea: (Hebrew *Yam Suf*, properly "Reed Sea"); the body of water crossed by the **Children of Israel** during the **Exodus** from **Egypt**.

Reuben: **Israelite** tribe settled in the **Trans-Jordan,** bordering on the Kingdom of **Moab** to the south, the **Dead Sea** to the west and the tribe of **Gad** to the north.

Riblah: A town in northern **Syria** used first by **Egypt**, then by **Babylon**, as the respective headquarters for their armies and administrations when each in turn occupied the region.

Saadia Gaon (Rabbi Saadia ben Joseph of Fayum): (882–942 CE) **Talmudic** scholar, biblical commentator and charismatic leader of Eastern Jewry; pioneer in systematically attempting to integrate Jewish theology with Greek philosophy.

Salt Sea: The name by which the **Dead Sea** was known in biblical times.

Sam.: Abbreviation for Samaritan Bible, the Samaritan text of the Pentateuch and *Joshua*.

Samaria: The capital of the Kingdom of **Israel**, founded by King Omri. The city of Sebastia was founded by King *Herod* on this site in the 1st century BCE.

Sargon II: (722–705 BCE) **Assyrian** warlord—successor to **Shalmaneser V**, conqueror of the **Kingdom of Israel**—who exiled **Israel's** surviving population.

Scripture: Sacred writings; often used as a synonym for the Bible.

Sea of Galilee: The large body of fresh water to the east of the **Galilee,** from which the **Jordan River** flows to the **Dead Sea.**

Seer: Visionary; diviner. See **Divination**.

Seir, Mount: Name of the high **Transjordanian** plateau south of the Kingdom of **Moab**; the heartland of the Kingdom of **Edom**.

Sennacherib: (705–681 BCE) **Assyrian** warlord, who in 701 BCE laid siege to **Jerusalem** but remarkably failed to take it.

Septuagint: The Greek translation of the Bible, usually abbreviated LXX.

Shadai: A term designating the LORD, in common use during the Age of *Abraham*.

Shalmaneser V: (727–722 BCE) The **Assyrian** warlord who took **Samaria** and destroyed the **Kingdom of Israel**.

Shekel: A unit of weight amounting to approximately 11.33 grams.

Sheol: The Underworld; the realm of the dead, where in biblical times people believed one's soul went after death.

Shephelah: The strip of foothills that fringe the western side of the **Highlands** or "Hill Country" running north-south in the middle of the land; hence, the region that lies between the Highlands and the Plain that parallels the coast of the Mediterranean.

Shilo: Town approximately 21 miles north of **Jerusalem** that served as the home of the **Tabernacle**; the central shrine of pre-monarchic **Israel**. It was destroyed by the **Philistines** approximately 1050 BCE.

Shofar: A ram's horn, blown in biblical times to sound a warning of approaching danger; also used for military signaling, as a means of rallying the public and to proclaim the crowning of a king..

Sidonians: A synonym for **Phoenicians**.

Sinai: 1. Triangular peninsula largely composed of mountainous desert that separates **Egypt** from Asia. **Mount Sinai** (Mount Horeb) is to be found in this region.

2. **Mount Sinai:** Also Mount Horeb; the spot where **Israel** entered into its **Covenant** with God and received the Ten Commandments.

Sorcerer: (Hebrew *mikashef*) One who, according to the pagan view, by drawing on forces inherent in the primordial meta-divine sphere, can manipulate both nature and the gods. (See **Sorcery**)

Sorcery: (Hebrew *keshef, keshafim*) The pagan "science" of *altering* the future by drawing on the power of the primordial realm, which underlies the realm of nature, to influence outcomes in the natural order. As the gods were considered to be part of the natural order, the sorcerer (*mikashef*) was deemed able to even coerce the gods to do his will. The practice of sorcery was not only forbidden by the Bible but is punishable by death (*Exodus* 22:17).

Steppes of Moab (Hebrew *arbot moab*): The arid region of the **Trans-Jordan** north of the **Dead Sea** abutting the **Jordan River**.

Stumah (S): **Massoretic** sign denoting a minor paragraph break in the biblical text. See **Petu**h**ah**.

Succoth: Town in the **Trans-Jordan**, located in a fertile valley on the north bank of the **Jabbok River**, about 4.5 miles east of the **Jordan River** and about 35 miles northeast of **Jerusalem**. This is the location where the **Deir 'Alla Inscriptions** were found.

Syllabary: A sign representing a syllable or part of a word.

Syria: The name given to the large fertile region northeast of the land of **Israel**, roughly bounded by the Lebanon Mountains to the west, the **River Euphrates** to the north and the **Arabian Desert** to the east.

Syro-Ephraimite War: (732–731 BCE) the attempt of a **Syrian-Israelite** coalition to impose a regime change on the **Kingdom of Judah**. The attempt failed due to the intervention of **Assyria**. The outcome of the war was the partial dismemberment of the Kingdoms of **Israel** and **Damascus**, and the annexation of the territory of **Benjamin** to the **Kingdom of Judah**, which had now become a **vassal** of **Assyria**.

Tabernacle: The portable sanctuary that was the focus of Israelite worship during the wilderness period; also known as The *Mishkan* and the Tent of Meeting.

Talmud: The 24 volume corpus of Jewish law, tradition and theology that provided the authoritative formulation of Rabbinic Judaism.

Tanach: The **Hebrew Bible**; an acronym designating the three divisions into which the **Hebrew Bible** is divided.

Targum (Plur. **Targumim**): The term designating the Aramaic translations of the Bible, usually abbreviated as Targ.

Tarshish: Probably the **Phoenician** colony of Tartessus in Spain; *Jonah's* destination when he fled the LORD.

Terebinth: Hebrew *elah* (*Pistacia teribinthus palaestina*), a large deciduous tree common on the lower slopes of hills in ancient **Israel**, usually solitary and seldom found in thickets or forests. Being a tree of considerable size and longevity it was venerated in ancient times.

Tetragrammaton: The four letter personal name of the God of **Israel**, usually rendered in English by the title LORD.

Theodotion: A Hellenistic Jewish scholar who around 150 CE translated the Hebrew Bible into Greek.

Tiglath-Pileser III: (745–727 BCE) **Assyrian** warlord who defeated the **Kingdom of Israel** and stripped it of the **Galilee** and the **Gilead**.

Tigris River: One of the two mighty rivers that flow through **Mesopotamia**. It is to the east, and roughly parallel to the **Euphrates**.

Tractate: One of the volumes of the **Talmud**.

Trans-Jordan, The: From the Latin (trans = the other side of), i.e., the other side of the Jordan, the arable region bounded on the west by the **Jordan River** and the east by the Arabian Desert; sometimes referred to in the Bible as "the far side of the Jordan."

Tuthmosis III: Egyptian Pharaoh in the Age of the **New Empire** who conquered much of **Syria**.

Ugarit: Ancient metropolis and trading hub destroyed about 1195 BCE during the great collapse of the **Bronze Age**. It was located on the **Syrian** coast about 7 miles north of the present Latakia. Important for the vast library discovered in its ruins. See **Ugaritic**.

Ugaritic: The language spoken and written by the inhabitants of **Ugarit** is a language very similar to biblical Hebrew, and the literature written in it has helped illuminate much that was obscure in the Bible. **Ugaritic** poetry in particular has proved to be one of the models upon which biblical poetry is based.

Glossary of Terms and Place Names

Urim and Thumim: A mechanical device, manipulated by a priest, used during the early period of Israelite history to determine the will of God. These **Urim and Thumim** were small objects, carried in a pouch or pocket in the "Breastplate of Decision" worn by the High Priest on his chest. We are currently far from certain as to how they were manipulated; one theory being that the priest, to achieve a yes or no answer threw these objects as lots, deriving the answer from the pattern of their fall. The use of the **Urim and Thumim** died out during the 10th century BCE.

Vassal: One who has accepted a position of political subservience to another, who is recognized as the lord and master.

Via Maris: The main highway, running along the Mediterranean coast, connecting **Egypt** and **Mesopotamia**. See **King's Highway**.

Vulgate: The translation of the Bible from its original Hebrew into Latin in the last quarter of the 4th century CE by Saint Jerome; usual abbreviation: Vulg.

Wadi: The bed of a seasonal river found in arid zones. With the winter rains it becomes a raging torrent. In the summer it is a dry riverbed.

Wasteland, The: See **Yeshimon**.

Wellhausen, Julius: (1844–1918) a highly influential German biblical scholar.

Yarmuk River: A river in the **Trans-Jordan** that flows westward into the **Jordan River** south of the **Sea of Galilee**; the traditional boundary between the **Gilead** and the **Bashan**.

Yeshimon: (Always found with the prefix denoting the direct object; thus, *hayeshimon*). The wasteland of **Judah** north of the **Dead Sea**, on both the east and west sides of the **Jordan River**.

Yom Kippur: The Day of Atonement, the holiest day in the Jewish calendar.

Zebah: A type of sacrifice: a free-will offering of which only token parts are burned on the altar and most of the animal is consumed in a communion meal by the family which made the offering, usually within the precincts of the shrine.

Zered, Wadi or River: Despite the term "**wadi**," the Zered is a perennial stream. It is the present Wadi el-Hesa, 35 miles long, whose waters flow into the eastern end of the **Dead Sea**, falling almost 4,000 feet during its course. It was the southern border of **Moab** and the northern border of **Edom**.

Who's Who

This Who's Who contains not only names that appear in the biblical Books of *Jonah*, *Balaam* and *Jeremiah*, but also some that find their place in this study. Names appearing in *italics* are themselves in the Who's Who and can be consulted. Terms appearing in **bold** can be found in the Glossary that precedes this section.

Aaron: Older brother of *Moses*, first High Priest in Israel and founder of the priesthood.

Abiathar: Son of *Ahimelech*, sole survivor of the massacre at **Nob**. Made High Priest by *David*, he was deposed and banished to **Anatoth** by *Solomon*. He was the distant ancestor of *Jeremiah*.

Abimelech: King of **Gerar**, who became involved with *Sarah*, *Abraham's* wife.

Abraham: The first of "The Fathers" of the people who will be known as the **Children of Israel**.

Adam: The original and prototypical human being. When preceded with the indicator for the direct object, thus, "*ha-adam*" simply means "the man."

Adonijah: Fourth son, by order of birth, of *David*. Supplanted by his younger half-brother *Solomon* in a palace coup, and then murdered by him.

Agag: King of the **Amalekites** in the 11th century BCE; defeated by *Saul* and executed by *Samuel*.

Ahab: (874–833 BCE) King of **Israel**, son and heir to King *Omri*. He is notorious for permitting his wife, Jezebel, to introduce the pagan god **Baal** into Israel and for sponsoring his worship.

Ahikam: Member of a great noble family in late 7th century BCE **Judah**, member of the royal cabinet of Kings *Josiah* and *Jehoiakim*; protector of *Jeremiah*.

Ahimelech: Chief priest of **Nob**; son of Ahitub and great, great grandson of *Eli*. Murdered by *Doeg* at the order of King *Saul*.

Amos: The first prophet to commit his oracles to writing, he was a poor resident of Tekoa in **Judah** who prophesied in **Israel** during the reign of *Jeroboam II*.

Asa: (910–870 BCE) King of **Judah**; a religious reformer.

Balaam, son of Beor: Thirteenth-century-BCE pagan prophet hired by King *Balak* of **Moab** to curse the **Israelites**. According to *Numbers* 21, God forced him to bless **Israel** in place of cursing them.

Balak: King of **Moab** in the days of *Moses*. Fearful of **Israel's** arrival in the **Trans-Jordan** he hired one *Balaam*, a pagan prophet, to curse the **Israelites**.

Baruch, son of Neriah: Personal secretary to *Jeremiah*; his close companion and biographer.

Bathsheba: Wife of *Uriah the Hittite*, whom *David* murdered in order to cover up their adultery, and then taking her to wife. Mother of *Solomon*.

Beniah, son of Jehoiadah: Commander of *David's* mercenary troops and his bodyguard. Killer of *Joab*, then promoted to his position as Commander in Chief of the army by *Solomon*; served as *Solomon's* hatchet man.

Cyrus II (The Great): Persian ruler (d. 530 BCE) who, by his defeat and amalgamation with the **Medes**, founded the Achaemenid Empire which conquered **Babylon**, liberating the captive **Judeans** and encouraging their return to **Jerusalem**.

David: Youngest son of *Jesse* of Bethlehem; poet, warrior, liberator of his people from **Philistine** domination, statesman, empire-builder, King of **Judah**, King of **Israel** and conqueror of **Jerusalem**: reigned 1010–970 BCE.

Deborah: Prophet and **Judge** in **Israel**, who initiated a War of National Independence against the Canaanites. Her ode of triumph, known as the "Song of Deborah," is one of the greatest works of early Israelite poetry.

Doeg: Idumean chief-herdsman of *Saul* who informed on *David* and *Ahimelech*, leading to the massacre at **Nob**.

Eleazar: Son of *Aaron*, father of *Phinehas*, and contemporary of *Joshua*. He became High Priest after the death of his father.

Eli: High Priest in **Shiloh**, and **Judge** of **Israel** during the first half of the 11th century BCE.

Eliakim: Birth name of King *Jehoiakim*.

Elijah the Tishbite: Contemporary of Ahab, this charismatic prophet made his life work the eradication of the worship of **Baal** in Israel.

Elisha, son of Shaphat: Prophet; disciple and successor of *Elijah*, who completed his work of eradicating **Baal** worship from Israel by initiating the overthrow of the *House* of *Ahab*.

Esau: Older twin brother of *Jacob*.

Ezekiel, son of Buzi: A member of the priestly House of *Zadok*, Ezekiel was exiled from **Jerusalem** to **Babylon** in 597 BCE; five years later he began his prophetic career which lasted at least twenty years. His spiritual leadership to the community of the exiles is largely responsible for their survival and the ultimate return of some of them to **Jerusalem**.

Gedaliah: Son of *Ahikam*; **Judean** noblemen appointed by the **Babylonians** as their governor of what remained of the Kingdom of **Judah** after **Jerusalem's** destruction in 586 BCE. He governed from **Mizpah** until assassinated by one *Ishmael*, a **Judean** resistance fighter.

Gemariah: **Judean** nobleman, brother of *Ahikam*, who also served on the royal cabinet; supporter of *Jeremiah*.

Gideon: Savior of **Israel** who, in a war of National Liberation, rid **Israel** of the scourge of the nomadic **Midianite**, **Amalekite**, and Children of the East invasions. Offered the crown, he refused it on principle.

Goliath: Giant **Philistine** warrior; *David* launched his career by killing him in battle.

Hanamuel: First cousin of *Jeremiah*, from whom he bought a field.

Hazael: King of the **Aramean** state of **Damascus**.

Heber: A **Kenite**; husband of *Jael*.

Herod the Great: Placed on the throne of **Judea** by Rome, and hugely unpopular, he ruled as a tyrant; he is largely remembered for his magnificent rebuilding of the Temple in **Jerusalem**.

Hezekiah: (716–687 BCE) King of **Judah**; survivor of the failed **Assyrian** invasion of **Sennacherib** in 701 BCE.

Hobab: Son-in-law of *Moses* and ancestor of the clan of **Kenites** that accompanied the **Israelites** from the **Sinai** Peninsula to the **Promised Land**.

Hophni: Corrupt son of *Eli*, killed in the **Battle of Eben-ezer**.

Hosea: Eighth-century-BCE prophet who championed a theology of care and lovingkindness.

Ichabod: Son of *Phinehas*, grandson of *Eli* and distant ancestor of *Jeremiah*.

Isaac: The second of "The Fathers"; son of *Abraham* and father of *Jacob* and *Esau*.

Isaiah, son of Amoz: Jerusalem's greatest citizen, the prophet's public career seems to have spanned the last 40 years of the 8th century BCE.

Ishmael, son of Nathaniah: Officer in the **Judean** army, member of the royal family, assassin of *Gedaliah*.

Israel: Alternative name of *Jacob*, bestowed on him upon his return to the Promised Land after an absence of almost two decades.

Jacob: The third and last of "The Fathers." Son of *Isaac* and grandson of *Abraham*; father of twelve sons and one daughter; due to his alternative name of *Israel*, his offspring and their descendants became known as "The **Children of Israel**."

Jael: Wife of *Heber* the **Kenite**; famous for having lured General *Sisera* into her tent and assassinating him.

Jeconiah: Birth name of *Jehoiachin*.

Jehoahaz: Son of *Josiah* (birth name *Shalum*), King of **Judah** (609 BCE 3 months). Deposed and deported by *Neco II*; died in **Egypt**.

Jehoiachin: Son of *Jehoiakim* (birth name *Jeconiah*), King of **Judah** (598 BCE 3 months). Deported by *Nebuchadrezzar* and imprisoned in **Babylon**.

Jehoiakim: Son of *Josiah* (birth name *Eliakim*), King of **Judah** (609–598 BCE). **Egyptian** puppet placed on the throne by *Neco II*, he switched to **Babylon**, then rebelled and died leaving his son *Jehoiachin* to pay the price.

Jephthah: **Judge** from the **Gilead** who led **Israel** to victory in a war of National Independence against the **Ammonites**; notorious for having offered his daughter as a sacrifice in fulfillment of a vow.

Jeremiah, son of Hilkiah: One of the greatest of the classical prophets. A member of the priestly House of *Eli*, the prophet's public career covered the last forty years of the Kingdom of **Judah** (626–586 BCE), and continued after the destruction of the Kingdom for several further years in **Egypt** where he died.

Jeroboam II: King of **Israel** (793–782 coregent with his father Jehoash, 782–753 reigned solo). The last great era of independent **Israelite** existence.

Jerubbaal: Alternative name of *Gideon*; quite possibly his original name.

Jesse: Father of *David*.

Jethro: **Midianite** priest; father-in-law of *Moses*.

Joab: Nephew of *David* and commander of **Israel's** army. Murdered by *Solomon* after *David's* death, and at his instigation.

Joel: A prophet of unknown date.

Jonah, son of Amittai: 1. Eighth-century **Israelite** prophet from Gath-hepher.
2. Central protagonist of the biblical Book by that name.

Johanan, son of Kareah: Officer of **Judean** army loyal to *Gedaliah*, who after his assassination led the surviving Judeans into **Egyptian** exile.

Jonathan: Oldest son of *Saul* and heir apparent to the throne of **Israel**. Close friend of *David*; died at the Battle of **Gilboa** at his father's side.

Joseph: Eleventh son of *Jacob* and his father's favorite; born to *Rachel*; ultimately viceroy of Egypt.

Joshua, son of Nun: Aide-de-camp and personal servant of *Moses*. Upon the death of *Moses* he led the tribes of **Israel** in the conquest of **Canaan**.

Josiah, King: (641–609); the last ruler of **Judah** as an independent kingdom. He is mainly remembered as the originator of the major religious reform that goes by his name. See **Josianic Reformation**.

Judah: Fourth son of *Jacob*, the progenitor of the tribe, and ultimately the Kingdom that bore this name.

Laban: Father-in-law of *Jacob*; brother of *Rebecca*, father of *Leah* and *Rachel*.

Leah: One of "The Mothers" of the **Children of Israel**. Wife of *Jacob* who bore him six sons—*Reuben, Simeon, Levi, Judah, Issachar* and *Zebulun*—and a daughter, *Dinah*.

Lot: Nephew of *Abraham*.

Micah the Morashtite: Eighth-century BCE **Judean** prophet quoted as precedent at *Jeremiah's* trial.

Micaiah: Son of *Gemariah*.

Michal: Daughter of *Saul*, wife of *David*.

Miriam: Sister of *Moses* and *Aaron*.

Moses: Prophet, lawgiver and Liberator of the **Israelites** from Egyptian bondage; the most important single personage in all **Israelite** history.

Nahor: Son of *Terah*, brother of *Abraham* and grandfather of *Rebecca*.

Nebopolassar: (616–605 BCE) **Babylonian** rebel general who successfully declared himself King of Akad.

Nebuchadrezzar: (605–561 BCE). Son of *Nebopolassar*. King of Akad, creator and ruler of the **Babylonian** Empire. The name is often spelled *Nebuchadnezzar*.

Nebuzaradan: Babylonian high official who razed **Jerusalem** and burnt the Temple in 586 BCE.

Neco II: (609–593 BCE) **Pharaoh**, son of *Psammetichus I*; ruler of **Egypt** and contender for control of Western Asia.

Obadiah: A prophet of uncertain date.

Og: King of the **Bashan**, defeated and killed by the **Israelites** in the days of *Moses*. His land was later settled by part of the tribe of **Manasseh**.

Omri: (885–874 BCE); general from the tribe of **Issachar** who founded the longest-lived dynasty of **Israel**; the father of King **Ahab**.

Peoples of the Sea: The name given to the naval marauders who ravaged the shores of the Eastern Mediterranean during the Great Collapse which brought the **Bronze Age** to a close.

Phinehas: 1. Grandson of *Aaron*; awarded the High Priesthood in perpetuity for his zealous intervention in putting a stop to the apostasy of **Baal-peor**.
2. Corrupt son of *Eli*, killed at the **Battle of Eben-ezer**; father of *Ichabod*.

Psammetichus I: (663–609 BCE) the **Pharaoh** who liberated **Egypt** from **Assyrian** domination.

Rachel: Favorite wife of *Jacob*; mother of *Joseph* and Benjamin. One of "The Mothers" of the **Children of Israel**, and the only one not buried in the Cave of Machpelah, the family sepulcher.

Ramses II: (1290–1224 BCE) the greatest Egyptian King of the Nineteenth Dynasty; probably the **Pharaoh** of the oppression.

Ramses III: Pharaoh of the Twentieth Dynasty (c. 1184–1153 BCE). Fought against the second wave of the **Peoples of the Sea** and repelled their invasion of Egypt in 1177 BCE.

Rebecca: Wife of *Isaac*; mother of *Jacob* and *Esau*.

Reuben: First-born son of *Jacob* and *Leah*.

Ruth: Daughter in law of Naomi, great-grandmother of *David* and heroine of the Book of Ruth.

Samuel: Prophet and last of the Judges, he dominated the second half of 11th-century **Israel**. He initiated the monarchy, anointing and later delegitimizing *Saul,* and anointing *David* in his place. He was the founder of the prophetic movement in Israel.

Sarah: First of "The Mothers" of the Jewish People; wife of *Abraham* and mother of *Isaac*.

Saul: First King of the People of **Israel**, he created the basic institutions of the monarchy. Initially successful, his break with *Samuel* and increasing mental instability presaged his final defeat and death at the battle of **Gilboa**.

Shaphan: Judean nobleman and Secretary of State (Scribe) to King *Josiah;* father of *Ahikam* and *Gemariah*.

Sihon: King of **Heshbon**. Refusing passage to the **Israelites** on their way to the **Promised Land** he offered battle, was defeated and killed. His kingdom was then occupied and settled by the tribes of **Reuben** and **Gad**.

Simon: Brother of *Judah the Maccabee*; founder of the **Hasmonean** dynasty in **Judea**.

Sisera: Canaanite general. His defeat at the hands of general Barak and the prophet *Deborah*, and his subsequent assassination by *Jael*, marks the end of significant **Canaanite** resistance to the **Israelite** settlement of the **Promised Land**.

Solomon: (971–931); son of *David*, renowned for his wisdom and grandiose building projects, he was the last ruler of the United Kingdoms. Delegitimized for apostasy by Ahijah the Shilonite, his one long-term accomplishment was the construction of the Temple in **Jerusalem**.

Terah: Father of *Abraham*.

Uriah: 1. Prophet, contemporary of *Jeremiah*; executed by *Jehoiakim* for sedition.
2. The Hittite: one of *David's* top commanders and husband of *Bathsheba*; murdered by *David* in order to possess his wife.

Zadok: Chief priest of the great shrine of **Gibeon**. He was appointed High Priest in place of *Abiathar* by *Solomon*, whom the king had deposed. He was a distant ancestor of the prophet *Ezekiel*.

Zechariah: Prophet of the post-exilic era.

Zedekiah: (597–586 BCE), son of *Josiah*, appointed regent for King *Jehoiachin* whom *Nebuchadrezzar* had deported and imprisoned. Revolted against **Babylon**, was deposed, blinded and imprisoned for life.

Bibliography

This bibliography is not meant in any way to comprehensively cover either the vast array of works that deal with the biblical Books that are the subject of this study, or even those works consulted in the writing of this book; either list would prove interminably long. It merely comprises a list of those works I have seen fit to quote or cite, its purpose being to enable the curious reader to easily locate them for further reference. For a more comprehensive survey of the field I refer those interested to the bibliographies of the major commentaries on *Jonah*, *Numbers* and *Jeremiah*; particularly, if one wishes to be somewhat up to date, those published in the current century.

Abravanel, Isaac. *Commentary on the Latter Prophets* (Hebrew). Pisaro, 1520, in *Commentary on the Prophets and Writings*. Warsaw, 1862.

Ackerman, James S. "Jonah" in *The Literary Guide to the Bible* (eds. R. Alter and F. Kermode). Cambridge: Harvard University Press, 1987: 234–243.

_____. "Numbers" in *The Literary Guide to the Bible* (eds. R. Alter and F. Kermode). Cambridge: Harvard University Press, 1987: 78–91.

_____. "Satire and Symbolism in the Song of Jonah" in *Traditions in Transformation: Turning Points in Biblical Faith* (eds. B. Halpern and J. D. Levinson). Winona Lake, IN: Eisenbrauns, 1981: 213–246.

Aharoni, Yohanan and Avi-Yonah, Michael et al. *The Carta Bible Atlas* (Fourth Edition). Jerusalem, Carta, 2002. Formerly published as *The Macmillan Bible Atlas* (third edition, revised). New York: Macmillan Publishing Co., 1993.

Albright, William F. *From the Stone Age to Christianity* (Second edition). Garden City, NY: Doubleday, 1957.

_____ "The Oracles of Balaam." *Journal of Biblical Literature* 63 (1944): 207–233.

_____. *The Proto-Semitic Inscriptions and Their Decipherment*. Cambridge: Harvard University Press, 1969.

Alter, Robert. *The Art of Biblical Narrative*. New York: Basic Books, 1981.

_____. *The Art of Biblical Poetry*. New York: Basic Books, 1985.

_____. *Genesis: Translation and Commentary*. New York: W.W. Norton, 1996.

Anderson, M.T., and Seifert, H.S. 2011. "Opportunity and Means: Horizontal Gene Transfer from Human Host to a Bacterial Pathogen." mBio 2(1): e00005-11.

Ashley, Timothy R. *The Book of Numbers* (NICOT). Grand Rapids, MI: Eerdmans, 1993.

Bar, James. "Man and Nature: The Ecological Controversy and the Old Testament," in *Ecology and Religion in History*, edited by Spring, David and Eileen. New York: Harper and Row, 1974, p. 48–75.

BDB *see* Brown, Driver & Briggs.

Biblia Hebraica *see* Elliger & Rudolph.

Bickerman, Elias J. "Jonah and the Whale" in *Four Strange Books in the Bible* by E. Bickerman. New York: Shoken, 1967: 3–49.

Bowman, A. T. "Jahve og Elohim I Jonaboken." *Norask Teologisk Tidskrift* 1936: 159–163.

Bright, John. "The Date of the Prose Sermons of Jeremiah." *Journal of Biblical Literature* 70 (1951): 15–29.

_____. *A History of Israel* (fourth edition). Louisville: Westminster John Knox Press, 2000.

_____. *Jeremiah* (AB). Garden City, NY: Doubleday & Co., 1965.

_____. "A Prophet's Lament and its Answer." *Interpretation* 28 (1974):59–74.

Brown, F., Driver, S. R. and Briggs, A. *A Hebrew and English Lexicon of the Old Testament*. Oxford: Clarendon Press, 1951.

Buber, Martin. *Darkah Shel Mikrah* (Hebrew). Jerusalem, 1964.

Calvin, John. *Commentaries on the Minor Prophets* (trans. John Owen). Grand Rapids, MI: Baker Book House, 1979.

Cohen, A. *The Psalms*. London: Soncino Press, 1950.

Crenshaw, James Lee. *Joel* (AB). New York: Doubleday, 1995.

Cross, Frank M. and Freedman, David N. *Studies in Yahwistic Poetry*. Grand Rapids, MI: Eerdmans, 1975, 1997.

Ehrlich, Arnold B. *Hamikra Kifshuto* (Hebrew), 3 vol. Berlin: Pepplaur, 1889–1900.

Elliger, K., and Rudolph, W. (ed.). *Biblia Hebraica*

Stuttgartensia. Stuttgart: Deutsche Bibelstiftung, 1977.

Frankfort, Henri, Frankfort, H.A., Wilson, J. A., Jacobsen, T. and Irwin, W. A. *The Intellectual Adventure of Ancient Man: An Essay on Speculative Thought in the Ancient Near East*. Chicago: University of Chicago Press, 1946.

Freedman, David N. "Archaic Forms in Early Hebrew Poetry." *ZAW* 72 (1960): 101–107.

Gane, Roy. *Leviticus, Numbers* (The NIV Application Commentary). Grand Rapids: Zondervan, 2004.

Golding, William. *Lord of the Flies*. New York: Capricorn, 1954, 1959.

Goldman, S. "Jonah" in *The Twelve Prophets* (ed. A Cohen). Bournmouth: The Soncino Press, 1948: 136–150.

Gordis, Robert. *The Book of God and Man: A Study of Job*. Chicago: University of Chicago Press, 1965.

Greenberg, Moshe. *Biblical Prose Prayer as a Window to the Popular Religion of Ancient Israel*. Berkeley: University of California Press, 1983.

_____. "Kaufman on the Bible: An Appreciation" in *Studies in the Bible and Jewish Thought* by M. Greenberg. Philadelphia: Jewish Publication Society, 1995: 175–188.

Hanson, P. D. "The Song of Heshbon and David's Nir." *Harvard Theological Review* 61, 1968: 297–320.

Heschel, Abraham Joshua. *Heavenly Torah: As Refracted through the Generations*. Edited and Translated from the Hebrew with Commentary by Gordon Tucker with Leonard Levin. New York: Continuum, 2007.

Hobbs, Thomas. *Delphi Collected Works of Thomas Hobbes*, 1 edition (June 24, 2019). Amazon.com Services LLC.

Holladay, William L. "The Background of Jeremiah's Self-understanding: Moses, Samuel and Psalm 22." *Journal of Biblical Literature* 83/2 (1964):153–164.

_____. "The Covenant with the Patriarchs Overturned: Jeremiah's Intention in 'Terror on Every Side' (Jeremiah 20:1–6)." *Journal of Biblical Literature* 91/3 (1972):305–320.

_____. "Jeremiah and Moses: Further Observations." *Journal of Biblical Literature* 85/1 (1966): 17–27.

_____. "Jeremiah's Lawsuit with God: A Study in Suffering and Meaning." *Interpretation* 17 (1963): 280–287.

Huehnergard, J. "On the Etymology and Meaning of the Hebrew *Nabi*." *Eretz-Israel* 26, p. 88–93.

Ishida, Tomoo. *History and Historical Writing in Ancient Israel*. Boston: Brill, 1999.

Kass, Leon R. *The Beginning of Wisdom: Reading Genesis*. New York: Free Press, 2003.

_____. *Founding God's Nation: Reading Exodus*. New Haven: Yale University Press, 2021.

Kaufmann, Yehezkel. *The Biblical Account of the Conquest of Canaan*. Jerusalem: Magnes Press, 1985. (Reprint of the 1953 edition with a new preface).

_____. "The Book of Jonah" in *Toldot Haemunah Hayisraelit* (Hebrew, 8 volumes). Jerusalem: Devir, 1954: Vol. IV, p. 279–287.

_____. "Paganism" in *Toldot Haemunah Hayisraelit* (Hebrew, 8 volumes). Jerusalem: Devir, 1954: Vol. II, p. 286–416.

_____. *The Religion of Israel: From Its Beginnings to the Babylonian Exile* (translated and abridged by M. Greenberg). Chicago: University of Chicago Press, 1960.

King, Philip J. and Stager, Laurence E. *Life in Biblical Israel*. Louisville: Westminster John Knox Press, 2001.

Kitchen, Kenneth Andrew. *On The Reliability of the Old Testament*. Grand Rapids: Eerdmans, 2003.

Kohn, Hans. *The Idea of Nationalism: A Study in its Origins and Background*. New Brunswick: Transaction Publishers, 2008. (Originally published by Macmillan, New York, 1944.)

Levine, Baruch A. *Numbers 21–36*, The Anchor Yale Bible. New Haven: Yale University Press, 2000.

Limberg, James. *Jonah, A Commentary* (Old Testament Library). Louisville: Westminster/John Knox Press, 1993.

Littman, R.J., and Littman, M. L. "Galen and the Antonine Plague." *American Journal of Philology* 94, no. 3 (1973): 243–255.

Lundbom, Jack R. *Jeremiah 1–20* (AB-21A). New York: Doubleday, 1999.

_____. *Jeremiah 21–36* (AB-21B). New York: Doubleday, 2004.

_____. *Jeremiah 37–52* (AB-21C). New York: Doubleday, 2004.

Luther, Martin. *Luther's Works, American Edition* (56 vol.). Philadelphia: Fortress Press, 1955.

Macintyre, Alistair. *After Virtue* (second edition). Notre Dame, IN: Notre Dame Press, 1984.

Magonet, Jonathan. *Form and Meaning: Studies in Literary Techniques in the Book of Jonah*. Sheffield: The Almond Press, 1983.

_____. "Jonah, Book of." *Anchor Bible Dictionary*, Vol. III. New York: Doubleday, 1992: 936–942.

Malamat, A. "Amm Lebadad Yiskon: A Report from Mari and an Oracle of Balaam." *Jewish Quarterly Review* 76 (July, 1985): 47–50.

Marcus, David. *From Balaam to Jonah: Antiprophetic Satire in the Hebrew Bible*. Atlanta: Scholars Press, 1995.

Mazar, Benjamin. "Canaan on the Threshold of the Age of the Patriarchs" (Hebrew). *Eretz Israel* 3 (1954): 18–32.

McElligott, Kara A. "Mortality From Sexually Transmitted Diseases in Reproductive-Aged Women: United States, 1999–2010." *American Journal of Public Health*. 2014 August; 104(8): e101–e105.

Mendenhall, G. "The Vengeance of Yaweh" in *The Tenth Generation*. Baltimore: John Hopkins University Press, 1973: 69–104.

Meyers, Carol. "Women at the Entrance to the Tent of Meeting," in *Women in Scripture: A Dictionary of Named and Unnamed Women in the Hebrew Bible, the Apocryphal/Deuterocanonical Books, and the New Testament*. Grand Rapids, MI: Eerdmans, 2000.

Milgrom, Jacob. "The Date of Jeremiah, Chapter 2." *Journal of Near Eastern Studies*, Vol. 14/2 (1955): 65–69.

_____. *Numbers* (JPSTC). Philadelphia: Jewish Publication Society, 1990.

Millgram, Hillel I. *The Elijah Enigma: The Prophet, King Ahab and the Rebirth of Monotheism in the Book of Kings*. Jefferson, NC: McFarland, 2014.

_____. *Four Biblical Heroines and the Case for Female Authorship: An Analysis of the Women of Ruth, Esther and Genesis 38*. Jefferson, NC: McFarland, 2008.

_____. *The Invention of Monotheist Ethics* (2 Vol.). Lanham, MD: University Press of America, 2010.

_____. *The Joseph Paradox: A Radical Reading of Genesis 37-50*. Jefferson, NC: McFarland, 2012.

_____. *Judges and Saviors: Reflections of a World in Chaos*. Lanham, MD: Hamilton, 2018.

Moldenke, Harold, and Moldenke, Alma. *Plants of the Bible*. New York: Dover Press, 1952.

Noth, Martin. *Numbers: A Commentary* (trans. J. D. Martin). Philadelphia: Westminster Press, 1969.

Podhoretz, Norman. *The Prophets: Who They Were, What They Are*. New York: The Free Press, 2002.

Preuss, J. *Biblische-talmüdisch Medizin*. Trans. F. Rosner. New York: Sanhedrin, 1978. (First published: Berlin: S. Karger, 1911).

Pritchard, James B. (editor). *Ancient Near Eastern Texts Relating to the Old Testament* (Second Revised Edition): Princeton, NJ: Princeton University Press, 1955.

Provan, Iain, Long, V. Philips, and Longman, Tremper. *A Biblical History of Israel*. Louisville: Westminster John Knox Press, 2003.

Rad, Gerhard Von. "Israel, Judah and Hebrews in the Old Testament" in *Theological Dictionary of the Old Testament* (ed. G. Kittel, trans. G. W. Bromiley). Grand Rapids, MI: Eerdmans, 1965: Vol. III, p. 356–359.

_____. *Old Testament Theology, The Theology of Israel's Prophetic Traditions* (trans. D. M. Stalker). New York: Harper and Row, 1965.

Reif, S.C. "What Enraged Phinehas?—A Study of Numbers 25:8." *Journal of Biblical Literature* 90 (1971): 200–206.

Rost, Leonhard. "Fragen um Bileam," in *Beitrage zur alttestamentlichen Teologie*, ed. H. Donner et al. Gottingen: Vandenhoeck und Ruprecht, 1977: 377–387.

Sacks, Robert D. *A Commentary on the Book of Genesis*. Lewiston, NY: Edwin Mellen, 1990.

Safren, Jonathan D. "Balaam and Abraham." *Vitus Testamentum* 38 (1988): 105–113.

Samuel, Maurice. "Perverted Genius," in *Certain People of the Book*. New York: Knopf, 1959: 30–69.

Sarna, Nahum. *Exodus* (JPSTC). Philadelphia: Jewish Publication Society, 1991.

_____. *Genesis* (JPSTC). Philadelphia: Jewish Publication Society, 1989.

Sasson, Jack M. *Jonah* (AB 24B). New York: Doubleday, 1990.

Shafer, W.M., and Ohneck, E.A. 2011. "Taking the Gonococcus-Human Relationship to a Whole New Level: Implications for the Coevolution of Microbes and Humans." mBio 2(3) e00067-11. doi:10.1128/mBio.00067-11.

Sherwood, Stephen K. *Leviticus, Numbers, Deuteronomy* (Berit Olam). Collegeville, MN: Liturgical Press, 2002.

Simon, Uriel. *The Book of Jonah* (trans. Lenn Schramm), JPSBC. Philadelphia: Jewish Publication Society, 1999.

Skinner, John. *Prophecy and Religion*. Cambridge: Cambridge University Press, 1951 (first published 1922).

Smith, George Adam. "The Book of Jonah" in *The Book of the Twelve Prophets* (Revised Edition), Vol. II by G. A. Smith. New York: Harper and Row, 1938: 483–528.

_____. *The Historical Geography of the Holy Land*. London: Collins, 1966. The twenty-fifth edition of the 1894 original published by Hodder & Stoughton, revised.

Sternberg, Meir. *The Poetics of Biblical Narrative: Ideological Literature and the Drama of Reading*. Bloomington: Indiana University Press, 1985.

Thiele, Edwin Richard. *The Mysterious Numbers of the Hebrew Kings*. Grand Rapids, MI: Kregel Publications, 1983.

Thomas, D.W. "A Consideration of Some Unusual Ways of Expressing the Superlative in Hebrew." *Vitus Testamentum* 1953: 209–224.

Tiemeyer, Lena-Sofia. "'Peace for Our Time': Reading Jonah in Dialogue with Abravanel in the Book of the Twelve." *JHS* 17/6 (2017): 1–23.

Trible, Phyllis. *Rhetorical Criticism: Context, Method and the Book of Jonah*. Minneapolis: Augsburg Press, 1994.

_____. *Studies in the Book of Jonah*. New York: Columbia University, 1963.

Vaux, R. De. "Le pays de Canaan." *JAOS* 88 (1962): 23–29.

Wenham, Gordon J. *Numbers: An Introduction and Commentary* (TOTC 4). Nottingham: Inter-Varsity Press, 1981.

Wolff, Hans Walter. *Obadiah and Jonah: A Commentary* (trans. by Margaret Kohl). Minneapolis: Augsburg Press, 1986.

Scriptural Index

This book contains the entire text of the *Book of Jonah* in chapters 1–4. The full text of the "Book of Balaam" and its framing narrative (*Numbers* 21:21–25:19 and 31:1–8) is to be found seriatim in Chapter 6–11. Specific verses may be found in their sequential order. All other references to biblical verses, including those additional citations for the *Book of Jonah* and The Balaam narrative that are not in sequential order, are listed below. The "confessions of Jeremiah" are indicated in **boldface** type. The order in which the Books are listed follows that of the Hebrew Bible.

Genesis
1:1—17, 20
1:26–27—20n29
1:27—309n40
1:31—310n43
2:1–3—310
2:4–3:24—304n18
2:7—306n26
2:7f—302
2:9—303
2:15—303
2:16f—304
2:18—303n12
2:20—307n33
3—127n47
3:1–6—305
3:5—305
3:6—306
3:7—307
3:13—46n48
3:17–19—307
3:19—310
3:22—306
4:10–12—94n23
5:1f—20n29; 309n40
5:3–5—306n25
5:24—306n25
5:31—306n25
6:3—306, 307n36
7:4—70n22
10:11f—35n2
12:1–3—120n18; 156n24
12:3—143n48, 179n33
14:13—44n41
14:18–20—141n42
15:7–21—124n34
18:1—138n32
18:23, 27—250n52

19:6, 16—156n29
19:12–26—69
19:21, 25, 29—69n20
19:36–38—108n24
20:1–7—21n37
20:3—119n15
22:17f—143n48
24:3—44n37
27:29—156n24, 159n52
28:14—143n48, 173n26
31:3—124n34
31:10–13—124n34
31:24—119n15
32:23–31—173n27
35:9–15—106n9
36:36—106n9
36:35—111n42
38:9—124n34
38:11—156n29
41:1–4—124n32, 134n10
41:25–32—134n10
44:8—88n46
46:1–3—141n42

Exodus
2:3, 5—58n28
2:11–17—294n50
2:16–22—163
2:18–20—193n48
3:10—37n11
3:11–4:17—38n18, 294n53
3:18—138n32
4:10—19
4:14–16—19
4:14–16—21n36
4:21–23—37n11
4:24–26—293n49
5:1–5—37n11

5:3—138n32
6:29—67
7:1–2—19n31, 21n36
15:12—51n3
14—44n39
14:16, 22, 29—44n39
14:31—48n55
15:2–18—140n38
16:1–3—149n78
17:1–7—149n78
17:8–13—162n69
17:14–16—162/3
18:21—186n15
18:23–25—98n30
20:2–3—170n15
20:8–11—310
20:18—92n8
22:15—267n29
23:2—268n31
23:22—189n29
24:18—70n22
29:9—209n22
31:16–17—310n47
31:18–32:14—92n8
32:4—91n7
32:12—73n34
32:14—75n52+53, 77
32:25–8—330
32:32f—244n18
32:7–14—21n35
32:12—75n47, 76n50
32:25–8—187n25
32:30—138n31
33:13—93
34:6—179n6; 93; 98n30
34:7—92; 93; 95; 162n30; 338n6
34:28—70n22
40:15—209n22

Leviticus
15:1–12—331n6
19:29—184n5
21:9—184n5
25—286n9

Numbers
2—153n13
3:32—187n21
10:9—189n29
10:29–32—163n74
10:35—159n49
14:29—224n23
14:39–45—105n7
16:28–34—51n3
16:32f—51n3
17:11—185n12
20:14–21—106n10
20:21+25+31—299n1; 300n3
21:1–3—106n12
21:13—323n13
21:26—323
21:27–30—323n38, 140
22–24—113
22–24—191, 195, 328
22:1—184n2
1–6—132n1
22:2–24:25—299n1n2
22:2—153, 168, 177n30
22:4, 7—189
22:6—118, 201
22:12—129n56; 171; 174n20; 196n28; 197n68; 197n72+74
22:18—129n16, 119, 197
22:20—119n15, 197n73
22:22—157n37
22:23, 25, 27, 33—117n9
22:23, 31—199n79
22:27—157n37
22:28—135n11
22:32—143
22:38—138, 197
22:41—169n10
23:1–3, 14–15—171n18
23:3—138n31
23:3, 15f—138n32
23:4—171
23:5—171
23:5, 16—224n24
23:8—172n21
23:9—147n71, 173, 180
23:9f—173
23:12—197
23:19—176
23:20—170n14; 176
23:21—175n38; 181
23:21, 23—196
23:22—175
23:23—170n14; 175
23:26—197
23:31—169n8
24:1—168; 171n19; 170n14; 177n30; 199n75; 198

24:1f—169
24:2—161n60; 169n11; 178; 199
24:3–4—169n13; 169, 178, 200
24:9—179
24:17—181
24:18f—113n9
24:20—161n62
24:20f—169n12
24:25—196
24:25—111
25:1–3—330n4
25:2—190
25:8f, 18f—330n2
25:14f—186n18
25:15—189n31
25:19—191
26–30—191n38
31—195
31:1—191
31:8—188n28; 189n31
31:14–20—330n4
31:16—185n12; 194n2; 330
33:55—189n29
33:49—184n4
34:1–15—110

Deuteronomy
Book of—229n59; 233n4; 235
1:46—105n4
2:9–—323n12
2:9, 16–19—108n24
2:26—107n18
2:33—109n30
5:6–28—92n11
5:6–7—170n15
5:31—287n17
6:1—287n17
6:5–9—92n11
7:5—252
7:9—92n13; 338n7
7:9, 11—70n22
13:9—88n44
18:10—117n11
18:15—117n11
18:18–19—219; 233; 233n60
18:20—257n13; 265n21
22:25—267n29
23:4f—115n2
25:17–19—163
27:4–7—195n66
29:22—69n20
31:27—88n46
32—232
32:21—59n36
34:10–12—293n47

Joshua
Book of 37—26; 26n9
1:1—35n1
2:9–14—115n1
3:5, 7—293n49
7:14–23—43n35
13:22—117n10; 202
21:13, 18—217n60

Judges
Book of—26; 26n9
1:16—164n77; 163n73
3:15—293n43
4:17–27—164n75
5:24—164n79
6:21–23—125n38
6:21–3—125n38
6:25–31—252n64
7:13f—124n32; 114n10
8:28—293n44
9:5—74n38
9:8–15—28
9:24—74n39
11:26—324n14
11:29—293n45
11:32—322
11:39f—293n46
13–16—49n63

1 Samuel
Book of—26n9; 26; 314
1:3—206–207
2:1—54n11
2:3—155n20
2:20—209n23
5:12–14—210n29
3:18—210
4:5—210n35
4:18—209n21
6:5—138n31
9:9—167; 129n57
14:36–45—193n52
14:38–43—43n35
15—164
15:6—164n76
15:15—88n44
15:29—66
18:11—41n26
19:11f—212; 213
21:4f—213n42
22:11–15—214
30:29—164n76

2 Samuel
2:1–4—216n49
6:1–20—216n50
7:18–29—52n5; 288n25
11:23—192n46
12:12—185n14
12:13–23—70
15:3—52n5
24:14—55n15

1 Kings
Book of—26; 26n9; 316n11
10:22—45n44
17–19—314
17:8–12—49n62
17:17–24—61n46
19:4—84
19:15—32n12
19:18—70n22

Scriptural Index

2 Kings
3:4—326n3
5:13—88n46
6:8–23—49n62
8:7–13—49n62
14:25—26n8; 26n10; 37n10; 39; 315
18:26, 8—44n41
19:15—288n25
20:1–11—70
23:36–24:2—276n6; 277n8
24:1—276n6
24:6—278n10
24:7—276n5
24:12–16—278n12
24:20—279
25:3—280n23
25:8—280n26; 480

Isaiah
Book of—25n22; 31
1:15—73n33
2:16—45n44
4:3—244n18
6:6f—224n24
8:23—237n9
13:19—69n20
14:12—159n47
18:9—54n10
19:6—58n28
19:18—44n41
23:1—45n44
29:7–18—193n53
29:14—216n30
31:4—193n53
36–39—25n3
40–66—298n63
49:10—82n27
60:9—45n44
66:19—57n14

Jeremiah
Book of—25n2; 31n22
1–6—231n52; 242n8
1:1—253n71
1:1–3—333
1:4–19—222–228; 292n40; 233
1:5, 7—291n33
1:6, 17—290n32
1:7—267n30
1:7, 9—290
1:9—274
1:9–10—292
1:10—224n25
1:14–16—259; 289n28; 298; 244
1:17–18—248; 291
1:18—284n1
1:19—273
2—232n57
2:8—246n30
2:20—185n11
3:12—253n70
3:123—266n26

6:6f—74n41
6:14—286n26
6:25—73n24
7:1–15—242; 256n9
7:1–25:13—242n8; 242n39
8:11—266n26
8:19—69n36
9:22—245n20
11:14—272n48
11:18–23
12:1–6
11:17–18—291n34
11:18–19—286n10
11:18–21—291n35
11:20—254
11:21–3—254
12:6—286n10; 291n35; 292n37
14:7–9—247n34
14:20–22—247n34
15:10—292n38
16:1–9—486
16:1–4—336n16
16–18—245
17:13–18—504–409
17:13—243n10
17:14—243; 273
17:15—243n10; 244
17:16—245; 290n32
18:1–12—318n4; 318; 319n10
18:5–8—66
18:18–23—411–413
19—19n28
19–20—292n38
19:9—55n15
19:11–15—438–441
20:1–6, 7–18—441–445
20:7—290
20:7–8—293n36
20:9—290n34; 293
20:10—266n24
20:14–18—292n38
20:11—228n44
20:16—69n20
21:11—239n16
22:1–5—229n48
22:15f—229n48
24:1–10—278n13
25:3—230; 241n4
25:8–13—297n61
25:9—232n54; 266n25
26:1–30:3—25n3
26:1–24—242
26:4–6—256
26:7–16—246n26
26:8–9—257
26:12–15—257
26:12–15—257
26:16—258
26:24—258
27–29—279n19
29:5–10—279n18
29:10–14—297n62
29:26—265n22

30:1–25—297n62
31:34–9—297n62
32:6–27—476–482
32:44—483
32:6–15—296n56; 335n13
32:12—289n30
32:15—287
32:16—288
32:17–27—338–9
35:11—277n8
36:1ff—25n3
36:12—260n30
36:16–19—260
36:26—261; 287n19
36:28—319n10
36:32—242n8; 242n8; 261; 242n6; 187n19
40:1–4—282n31
40:13f—283n36
44:15–18—295–6n55
45–51—242n8
46:1–51:64—37n13
46:1–26—276n1
46:5—266n24
46:18—69n20
46:29—266n24
50:40—69n20
52:7–11—280n25
52:12—280n26

Ezekiel
Book of—25n2; 26n7
1:1—35n1
2–3—333n6
3:27—127n46
7:4, 9—88n44
7:23—74n41
18:21–8—319–20
27:13—42n29
27:25—45n44
33:12–19—320n16
33:22—127n46

Joel
2:13—317; 318

Amos
Book of—31n22
1:3–2:3—37n13
2:3–2:16—49n16
3:7—21n14; 80
4:11—69n20

Obediah
Book of—25n1; 25
1:3–4—165

Jonah
1:1—39; 43; 55; 66n4; 86n39
1:12—47n6; 67n25; 73
1:3—68n10; 69n18
1:4—51n1
1:5—48

1:6—47; 55; 62n48; 88n45; 138n31
1:8—28n14
1:9—32; 36n7; 38; 44n41; 45n45; 91
1:10—43n36; 46n10; 79
1:11—47n52
1:14—52n5; 55
1:15—47n52
1:16—44n39; 46n49; 48n55; 48; 78n3
2:1—38n17; 83
2:2—61; 62
2:3—56n16
2:5—60; 41n95; 271
2:6—57n25
2:7—62
2:7-8—80n13
2:8—56n16
2:9—56n16
2:10—56n16
3:1—35n1
3:2—46n49; 72n25
3:4—37
3:5—38n19; 73n36
3:6—82n21
3:7—313n3
3:7f—38n17
3:9—77; 88n45
3:10—77n54; 77n2; 77; 78
4:1—82n23; 82
4:2—38n20; 79; 79n12; 81n20; 84; 86n38; 86n40; 91; 93; 95; 98; 148n72; 317; 318; 318n9
4:3—80n13; 85n16; 257
4:5—82n21; 85n35; 86n40
4:6—83n31; 85; 85
4:8—85n40; 86; 86
4:9—138n31
4:9-11—86n39; 86n40; 88
4:10—29n17; 86n40
4:11—38n17; 29n17; 75

Micah
3:12—258n20
6:5—112; 328
9-12—74n41
7:18-20—90n3

Habakkuk
1:3—145n59
1:13—145n59

Nahum
Book of—25n1; 316n11; 74n42
3:1—74

Haggai
Book of—25n1; 26n7

Zechariah
14:9—183

Malachi
1:11—49n62
2:7—246n30

Psalms
1:3—249n50
22—270n37
22:1-22—233n62; 337-8
23—32n26
24:1f—17n20
31:7—59
31:11—270n43
14—268n32
34—54n10
42:8—56n19
47—145n61
51—54n10
55:10—74n41
69:8—272n53
69:29—244n18
78:38f—78
90—54n11
95:5—44n39
98:6—145n61
102:4—270n43
103:7f—92n9
103:8—98n31
104:26—51n1
106:29—185n12
107:5—58n32
118:5—55n15
121:6—82n27
130:1f—241
116:26—44n37

Proverbs
1:2-7—246n30
23:8—64n57
25:16—64n57
26:11—64n57

Song of Songs
4:10—156n25

Ruth
Book of—25n1; 26n8; 314
1:1—35n1
1-2—111n42

Lamentations
1:3—55n15
3:8—155n19

Ecclesiastes
1:2—59n34
3:16—205

Esther
Book of—26; 44n42; 314
1:1—35n1

Job
Book of—26n21; 120; 90
3:11—233n63
10:18f—233n63
14:12—42n30
31-15—233n63
33:21—137n25
42:1-6—89n50

Daniel
Book of—44n37; 44n42

Ezra
Book of—44n37
1:1-3—208

Nehemiah
Book of—44n37; 314
3:34—161n64
8:15—82n29
13:2—195n66

1 Chronicles
Book of—44n37; 314
4:43—163n72
8:33—240n21
9:36—240n21

2 Chronicles
5:9—326n3
5:21—326n4
20:36f—45n44
34:3—221n12; 224n23
34:3f—222n13
34:5-7—222n14
34:14-33—252n68
35:21—238n11
36:6f—278n10
36:22f—298

NEW TESTAMENT

2 Peter
2:15f—195n66

Jude
11—195n66

Revelations
2:14—195n66

General Index

Aaron 107, 187, 191, 206, 208, 209, 217, 334
Abiathar 215–218, 334
Abimelech 74, 119
Abiram 51
Abraham 18, 30, 48, 98, 108, 120, 124, 141, 143, 148, 156, 159, 179, 250, 288
Abravanel, Don Isaac 43, 44, 70, 76, 80, 124, 128
accountability 94
Ackerman, J. 53, 55, 91, 178
Adam 50, 306, 307
Adonijah 216
Adulam 213
Aesop 27
Agag 156
Ahikam 258–260, 282
Ahimelech 213–215, 217, 334
Akkadian 69, 159, 237
Albright, W.F. 27, 114, 139, 141, 145, 146, 155, 156, 158, 159, 162, 166, 167, 180, 195
alphabet, invention of 8, 16, 141, 165
Altar 206–209, 217
Alter, Robert 8, 32, 127, 135, 140, 152
Amalek 161–165, 179
Amittai, son of 26, 27, 29, 35–37, 43, 66, 112, 219, 313, 315
Amman 109
Ammon, Kingdom of 105, 108, 109, 117, 121, 282, 283, 322, 326
Amorites 48, 106–110, 115, 148, 153, 160, 185, 322–324
Amos, Book of 30, 31, 37, 69, 80, 112, 232
Anatoth 6, 217, 218, 220, 223, 251, 253, 254, 280, 285, 286, 333–336
animal sacrifice 16, 185
the Apocrypha 31
Arabic 82, 187
Arad, Kingdom of 106
Aramaeans 53
Aramaic 3, 6, 69, 155, 263, 327
Ark of God 210–212
Ark of the Covenant 3, 153, 206, 210, 216, 334

Arnon River 106–108, 111, 115, 132, 160, 185, 322, 323, 325
Ashley, Timothy 144, 146, 151, 156, 158, 160, 327, 328
Assurbanipal 68, 221, 222
Assyrian Empire 43, 44, 68, 72, 74, 76, 88, 221, 226, 235, 237, 239, 255, 266, 315
Augustine, Saint 90
autonomy 2, 14, 27, 113, 127, 167, 198, 200–202, 221, 300–309, 311

Baal 136, 185, 186, 187, 189, 192, 194, 195, 198, 222, 229, 240, 252, 266, 330–332
Baal-peor 185–187, 189, 192, 194, 195, 198, 330
Babylon 159, 230, 232, 237, 239, 240, 259, 266, 274, 276–282, 285, 296–298
Babylonians 68, 221, 237–240, 259, 276, 280, 282, 286, 287, 289, 315, 333, 339
Balaam (son of Beor) 103, 299–301, 327–329; dream of 122–132, 133–135, 199; oracles of 114, 138–144, 146–149, 155–157, 161–166
Balaam, Book of 1, 3–5, 7, 11, 13, 101, 103, 118, 128, 129, 131, 135, 139, 153, 154, 167–170, 177, 180–182, 184, 189, 191, 194, 299–301, 327–329
Balak (king) 112, 115, 117–125, 130–140, 142–154, 157, 158, 161, 166, 168, 170–174, 176–178, 189, 194–198, 200
Bamoth-baal 136
Bar, James 17
Baruch (son of Neriah) 219, 220, 230–232, 242, 243, 255, 256, 258–261, 264, 265, 278, 281, 282, 283, 284, 285, 286–288, 297, 334
the Bashan 109–111, 115, 119, 148, 175, 184, 192, 325, 326, 337
Bathsheba 70, 216
Benaiah 216–218
Benjamin 110, 210, 214, 253, 281, 285, 286, 289, 333

blessed 117–120, 122, 131, 142–148, 150, 153, 154, 157, 158, 161, 164, 168–171, 174–179, 196, 197, 199–201, 221, 270, 310
Bomberg, Daniel 5
Boswell 219, 284
Bright, John 226, 251, 266, 268, 272, 287
Bronze Age 110, 166, 228
Buber, Martin 32

Caleb 149, 191, 196
Calvin, John 59, 90
Canaan 16, 30, 48, 105, 106, 108, 110, 111, 136, 149, 164, 206, 251, 252, 314, 322
Canonization 5
Carchemish 117, 230–232, 239, 240, 259, 266, 276
Carol, Lewis 112
Chaldeans 240, 276, 278, 289, 333, 339
Chebar "River" 333
Chemosh 323
Children of Israel 3, 37, 42, 48, 49, 91, 96, 97, 103–108, 110, 111, 113, 115, 117, 118, 137, 138, 144, 148, 149, 163, 164, 170, 173, 182, 184, 186–188, 190–192, 194, 197, 198, 200, 202, 208, 232, 251, 283, 296, 322, 325, 332
Christianity 3, 4, 13, 16, 27, 29, 321
Chronicles, Book of 48, 49, 163, 187, 220–222, 224, 238, 240, 252, 263, 278, 298, 314
Churchill, Winston Spencer 205
the Cis-Jordan 111, 184
Cohen, A. 56
Coleridge, Samuel Taylor 45, 166
confession of faith 32, 48, 49, 92, 148
Coole, F.C. 162
Cornill, C.H. 251
Cozbi 188–191
Craig, K. 62
Cross, Frank M. 206, 363
curse 117–122, 130–134, 136, 137, 141, 142, 144, 146, 147, 150, 153,

154, 157, 158, 161, 170–172, 174, 179, 180, 189, 195–197, 199, 201, 209, 210, 215, 216, 218, 220, 247, 253, 275, 334, 335
Cyrus 183

Damascus 37, 239, 341
Daniel, Book of 5, 48, 240
Dathan 51
David 17, 45, 47–49, 52, 53, 70, 80, 81, 161, 163, 164, 212–217, 221, 222, 239, 271, 280, 288, 323, 334, 337
Dead Sea 6, 80, 103, 105, 107, 111, 144, 151, 323
Deborah 164
declaration of faith 42, 53, 243, 271
Deir 'Alla inscriptions 112, 117, 120, 156, 327–329
de Unamuno, Miguel 284
Deuteronomy 4, 59, 69, 88, 92, 101, 105, 107–109, 115, 117, 163, 164, 170, 195, 200, 219, 229, 232, 233, 235, 252, 257, 265, 267, 273, 287, 293
Dibon 323
Dickens, Charles 30
divination 47, 117, 118, 146
diviner 117, 118, 120, 134, 151, 154, 202
Doeg the Edomite 213–215
donkey 1, 122–130, 134, 135, 147, 157, 168, 169, 173, 240
dreams 29, 119, 124–127, 129, 133, 134, 285
Dryden, John 184

Eben-ezer 212, 213
Ecclesiastes 59, 205
Edom, Kingdom of 105, 106, 159–161, 165, 179, 277
Egypt 6, 17, 37, 42, 67, 91, 103, 105, 107, 110, 111, 115, 117, 119, 123, 125, 130, 142, 145, 146, 148, 149, 154, 156, 157, 162–164, 170–172, 174, 175, 182, 184, 191, 196, 198, 208, 221, 222, 225, 226, 229–231, 235, 237–240, 244, 255, 258, 264, 276, 277, 279, 280, 283, 285, 288, 289, 295, 297, 306, 338
Ehrlich, Arnold 47
Einstein, Albert 152
Eleazar 107, 187, 193
Eli 84, 206–213, 215–218, 334
Elijah 11, 16, 26, 27, 37, 53, 61, 70, 84, 184, 314
Elisha 27, 37, 53
emending the text 7
"Emerald City" 68
the enlightenment 2, 80, 90, 142, 147, 153, 168, 169, 178–182, 196
ephod 208, 215
epidemic 185

Esharhaddon 221
Esther, Book of 6, 26, 35, 48, 240, 314
Euphrates 110, 117, 118, 237–240, 258, 276
Eve 50, 305
Exodus, Book of 4, 28, 30, 37, 42, 48, 52, 67, 70, 73, 75–77, 79, 91–95, 98, 138, 140, 148, 149, 162, 163, 170, 186, 187, 196, 209, 244, 252, 267, 268, 288, 293, 294, 309, 310, 317
Ezekiel 34, 26, 35, 46, 74, 88, 98, 127, 240, 278, 297, 298, 319, 320, 333
Ezekiel, Book of 49
Ezra, Book of 43, 48, 240, 298, 306

fable 27, 28, 30, 44, 52, 53, 69, 70, 78, 81, 95, 112, 219, 299, 313
First Commonwealth 28, 96, 137, 139, 219, 283, 286, 299, 314, 315
Frankfort, Henri 17
Freedman, David N. 206

Gad 108, 111
Galen 331
Gane, Roy 136
Gath 26, 213
Gedaliah 282, 283
Gemariah 259, 260, 282
Genesis, Book of 3, 4, 8, 17, 29, 30, 35, 48, 50, 69, 70, 74, 88, 94, 98, 106, 108, 111, 119, 120, 123, 124, 127, 138, 141, 143, 148, 156, 159, 173, 179, 250, 270, 302–304, 306, 307, 310
Gese, H. 62
Geshur 111
Gibeah 212, 214
Gideon 134, 252, 293
Gilboa, Mount 134, 216
Gilead 111, 115, 315, 322–326, 328
Gilgal 112
Golden Calf 30, 75, 77, 91, 149, 187
Golding, William 303
Goliath 213, 214
Gomorrah 69, 71, 270
gonorrhea 330, 331
Gordis, Robert 233
"Gotham City" 68
Greenberg, Moshe 13, 52

Habakkuk 145
hamas 73, 74, 94
Hamath 259
Hanamuel 285, 286, 287
Hannah 54
Hanson, P.D. 323
Haran 221, 237, 238, 240
Hatti-land 239, 240, 259, 276, 277, 280
Hebrew 32

Hebrew Bible 3, 5, 6, 8, 17, 26, 27, 31, 34, 55, 123, 130, 137, 155, 233
Hebron 216
Henley, William Ernest 302
Herder, J.G. 43
Hermon, Mount 109, 325
Heschel, Abraham Joshua 200
hesed 59, 60, 64, 79, 92–94, 338
Heshbon, Kingdom of 105–107, 110, 111, 115, 119, 140, 148, 160, 184, 192, 322–324
Hezekiah (king) 70, 163, 252, 258, 288
Hippocrates 184
Hobbes, Thomas 32, 97
Holladay, William 232, 233, 270
Hophni 206, 209, 210
Hopkins, Gerard Manley 262
Hosea, Book of 232, 335
the host of heaven 264
Housman, A.E. 299
Huehnergard, J. 27
Hyrcanus, King John 165

Ibn Ezra, Abraham 85, 90, 128
Ibsen, Henrik 203
Ichabod 211, 212
idolatries 59
imperfect tense 68
infinitive absolute construction 52, 78, 82, 93, 150, 157, 132, 208, 246, 257, 304, 305
Isaac 43, 80, 106, 124, 141, 148, 156, 288
Isaiah, Book of 6, 34, 31, 37, 48, 49, 54, 69, 73, 82, 159, 193, 224, 232, 233, 237, 244, 246, 298, 335
Ishmael, son of Nethaniah 282
Islam 4, 16, 29, 321

Jabbok River 108–110, 115, 160, 322, 323, 325–327
Jacob 3, 5, 17, 47, 106, 114, 124, 132, 141, 143, 145, 146, 148, 150, 153, 156, 159, 160, 173, 175, 180, 181, 195, 196, 232, 288
Jael 164
Jaffa 33, 35, 37, 45, 46, 49, 58
Jahaz 108
Jazer 109
Jehoahaz 239, 255, 259
Jehoash (king) 317
Jehoiakim 230, 239, 241, 242, 246, 255, 258, 259, 261–263, 276–278, 285, 295, 319, 333
Jephthah 121, 324
Jeremiah (the prophet) 1, 3–5, 7, 11, 13,19, 25, 31, 37, 55, 59, 66, 69, 74, 98, 157, 165, 185, 299–302, 308, 318–320, 333–339
Jeremiah, Book of 1, 3, 4, 5, 7, 11, 13, 28, 34, 31, 37, 55, 59, 66, 69, 74, 98, 157, 165, 185, 219, 220,

223, 225, 229, 230, 231, 232, 233, 235, 239, 240, 241, 242, 245, 260, 261, 262, 265, 266, 299, 319, 320, 333, 335
Jericho 107, 111, 115, 184, 280
Jeroboam II (king) 26, 43, 80, 315
Jerome, Saint 6, 237
Jerusalem 5, 6, 11, 32, 52, 58, 183, 206, 212, 216–218, 222, 225, 226, 229, 234, 235, 238–240, 252, 255, 256, 258, 260, 263, 264, 266, 267, 274, 278–282, 285, 289, 291, 295–298, 319, 333–336
Jesse 214
the Jezreel Valley 111
Joab 216–218, 358
Job, Book of 26, 46, 89, 90, 120, 137, 168, 233, 250
Joel, Book of 98, 317–319
Johanan, son of Kareah 283
Johnson, Samuel 219
Jonah, Book of 1, 3–7, 11, 13, 26–37, 41–56, 58–99, 112, 124, 138, 139, 148, 182, 257, 268, 271, 299, 301, 313–321, 338
Jonathan 30
the Jordan River 105, 184, 214, 323, 325, 327
Josephus 184
Joshua 188, 191, 196, 206, 213
Joshua, Book of 26, 35, 47, 115, 117, 149, 202, 217, 293
Josiah 221, 222, 230, 236, 238, 246, 259, 278, 282, 333
Jotham 27, 28, 30
Judah 75, 151, 163, 214, 216, 220–222, 224–228, 230, 231, 235, 238–240, 252, 253, 255, 258, 259, 261, 263, 264, 266, 276–283, 285, 287, 289, 291, 295–298, 333, 335
Judaism 3, 16, 165, 321
Judges, Book of 16, 26–28, 53, 74, 121, 124, 125, 134, 140, 163, 164, 166, 184, 252, 293, 322, 324
Justice and Mercy 90

Kadesh 104, 105, 107
Kant, Immanuel 308
Kass, Leon 59, 70, 127, 303, 304, 309, 311
Kaufmann, Yehezkel 13–15, 17, 111, 263, 297
Keil, C.F. 162
Kenite 161–164
keyword 32, 33, 55, 62, 168, 180, 181
Kierkegaard, S. 34
kikayon 82–85, 87, 88
Kimchi, David, 47, 80, 81, 302
King, Philip J. 206
King James Bible 7, 8, 32, 146, 351
Kings, Book of 26, 27, 37, 43, 48, 49, 53, 61, 70, 84, 88, 125, 194, 216, 217, 218, 220, 240, 263, 276, 277, 278–280, 288, 314, 315, 316
King's Highway 105
Kir-moab 323
Kiriath-huzoth 136
Kitchen, K.A. 327–329
Koheleth 59
Kohn, Hans 222
Korah 51

Laban 119
The Latter Prophets 5, 34
leitwort 32
the Leningrad Manuscript 5
Levine, Baruch 136, 137, 154, 161, 189, 327, 328
Levitical choirs 52
Limburg, James 47, 56, 62, 70, 74, 79, 81, 94
Lot 70, 108, 323
Luke, Book of 88
Lundbom, Jack R. 224, 225, 227, 243, 249, 250, 261, 263, 268, 280
Luther, Martin 90, 96, 364

Maaca 111
MacIntyre, Alasdair 90
magic 14, 15, 29, 136, 146, 147, 153, 154, 170–175, 177, 196, 197, 199, 263, 264
Magonet, Jonathan 30, 53, 62, 79, 90, 313, 317, 318
Maimonides, Moses 124
Malachi, Book of 53, 246
Manasseh 111, 221, 251, 325
Marcus, David 123
martyrdom 42, 44, 70, 71, 234, 270
Masoretic Text 5, 6, 9, 28, 80
Masorites 6, 191
Mazar, Benjamin 110
Medeba 323
Medes 68, 221, 235, 237, 315
Megiddo 221, 229, 230, 235–237, 239, 255, 259
Mendenhall, G. 191
merism 42, 73
Mesopotamia 27, 30, 72, 105, 107, 118, 140, 193, 221, 222, 230, 237, 239, 259
Micah 34, 74, 90, 112, 195, 258, 328
Micaiah 260
Michal 212
Midian 117, 118, 124, 188–194
Midianite 117, 118, 123, 124, 134, 163, 186–194, 198, 293, 330
Milgrom, Jacob 47, 113, 114, 137, 151, 159, 187, 191, 192, 232, 328
Milton, J. 31, 115
Miriam 107
Mizpah 282, 283
Moab, Kingdom of 103, 105, 106, 109, 111, 112, 115, 117–120, 123–126, 128–131, 133–135, 138–140,
143–145, 147, 151–153, 158–161, 165, 166, 169, 179, 181, 184, 185, 189, 190, 193, 194, 196–202, 277, 322–324, 326
Moldenke, H. & A. 82
monotheism 13, 42, 73
Moore, George Foot 263
Morse, Samuel 146
Moses 6, 17, 26, 28, 30, 37, 42, 54, 67, 70, 75, 77, 91–96, 99, 101, 105–107, 109–112, 138, 148, 149, 162, 163, 182, 184–195, 200, 206, 232, 233, 275, 293, 294, 323, 330, 334, 335
Myers, Carol 207
myth 14, 15

nabi see Prophet
Nahum, Book of 34, 74, 92, 316
Napoleon 164
Nebopolassar 237–240, 259, 276
Nebuchadrezzar 232, 240, 259, 276–280, 282, 285
Nebuzaradan 280, 281
Neco II 237, 238, 239, 255, 258, 259
Negeb 105, 106, 117, 162, 163, 165
Nehemiah, Book of 6, 48, 82, 161, 195, 219, 240, 314
nemesis 51, 54, 266
the New Empire 110
Nineveh 35, 37, 42–44, 47, 51, 53–55, 62, 66, 68–81, 83–85, 87–90, 94, 96, 103, 138, 221, 237, 315, 316, 319
Nob 212–215, 217, 334
Numbers, Book of 1, 4–7, 47, 55, 105–107, 110–113, 124, 132, 136, 138–140, 149, 153, 159, 162, 163, 167, 178, 184–189, 191, 194–196, 224, 252, 299, 300

Obadiah 165
Og, King 109, 115, 121
Oliver Twist 30
oracles 69, 70, 72, 113, 114, 135, 138–144, 146–149, 152–173, 177–182, 195, 196, 200, 208, 214, 223, 225, 227, 228, 232, 241, 242, 248, 253, 263, 275, 318

pagan 13–17, 27, 29, 33, 37, 42, 45, 50, 53, 54, 73, 75, 83, 93, 117, 120, 137, 138, 142, 146–149, 152, 153, 167–171, 176, 178, 179, 180, 182, 187, 194, 221, 222, 226, 229, 251, 252, 264, 294, 297, 298, 306, 319, 328, 329
Paine, Thomas 43
parable 52, 53, 61, 76
parallelism 140
Pashhur (son of Immer) 264–267, 269, 271

General Index

Peake, A.S. 251
Peor 151, 185, 187, 189–192, 194, 330–332
perfect tense 61, 63, 68
Peshita 6
Pethor 117, 118, 125, 131, 135, 193, 196, 198, 200, 202
Pharaoh 28, 37, 42, 55, 67, 123, 134, 156, 208, 222, 228, 237, 239, 255, 258, 259, 280, 293, 306
Philistines 54, 138, 210–214, 221, 256, 276, 334
Philo 191
Phinehas (grandson of Aaron) 187–189, 193, 197, 201
Phinehas (son of Eli) 206, 209–212
Pisgah 144, 172
plague 69, 107, 117, 187, 189, 191, 194, 247, 279, 289, 330–332
Pope, Alexander 219
Preuss, J. 331
primordial realm 14–17
Promised Land 104, 106, 111, 113, 191, 217
prophet 1, 26–30, 36, 37, 42, 43, 49, 53, 61, 62, 71, 72, 74, 77, 80, 84, 90, 101, 112, 125, 127, 129, 145, 154, 155, 158, 161, 165, 167, 169, 178–180, 183, 185, 195, 200–202, 205, 208, 212, 219, 223, 224, 228, 231–234, 237, 241, 242, 245–247, 253, 255, 257–259, 261, 264–267, 270, 274, 275, 284, 285, 287, 290–295, 298–300, 308, 313, 315, 319, 328, 333, 335, 336
Proverbs, Book of 64, 246
provincialism and universalism, struggle between 90
Psalm 17, 32, 48, 53–56, 58, 59, 74, 78, 80, 82, 92, 98, 185, 233, 234, 241, 244, 249, 268, 270–272, 288, 337
Psammeticus I 222, 237

Qumran 6

Rabbath-ammon 109
Ramban 128, 306
Rashi 90, 156, 302, 306, 323
rebellion 1, 37, 42, 44, 53, 58, 64, 70, 79, 81, 83, 90–92, 99, 172, 201, 202, 219, 237, 267, 275, 279, 284, 285, 290, 292, 294, 298–300, 308, 309
redemption 285, 298
Reif, S.C. 187
Reuben 108, 111
Riblah 239, 259, 280

Rosenzweig, Franz 32
Rousseau, Jean Jacques 301, 308
Rudolph, W. 5, 62
Ruth, Book of 34, 26, 35, 111, 314

sackcloth 72, 73
Sacks, Robert 70
sacrifice 16, 17, 33, 42, 51–53, 60, 64, 76, 81, 98, 136–138, 151, 164, 185, 190–191, 206–208, 226, 249, 263
Samaria 221, 289, 315
Samaritan Pentateuch 189
Samson 53, 54
Samuel 26, 45, 47, 52, 54, 55, 66, 70, 88, 129, 138, 155, 164, 167, 185, 192, 193, 207, 210, 216, 240, 284, 288, 314
Samuel, Books of 70
Samuel, Maurice 199
Sarah 30
Sarna, Nahum 70, 92
Sasson, J.M. 62, 73, 77, 79, 82, 86–88, 91, 316–318
Saul (king) 17, 45, 163, 164, 212–216, 240
Schama, Simon 12
Scripture 2, 5, 26, 29, 97–99, 127, 137, 272, 290
Sea of Galilee 105, 109, 111
seer 118, 120, 129, 133, 134, 139, 141, 147–151, 153–155, 158, 167–170, 172, 177, 179, 180, 182, 195, 200–202, 327–329
Seir 159
Sennacherib 68, 72, 88, 315
Shaddai 156
Shakespeare 29, 58, 84, 93, 94, 179, 198, 226
Shaphan 258–260, 282
Sheol 51, 55, 58
Shiloh 206, 210, 213, 217, 218, 256, 257, 334, 335
Shittim 112, 184, 193
Sihon (king) 107–110, 115, 118, 121, 322, 323
Simeon 188
Simon, Uriel 12, 46, 61, 62, 66–69, 73, 74, 78, 86, 88, 90, 313
Skinner, John 318
slavery 103, 106, 149, 294
Smith, George Adam 90, 325, 326
Sodom 69, 70, 71, 74, 98, 250, 270
Solomon 216, 333
Spiegel, Shalom 252
Stager, Lawrence E. 206
Steppes of Moab 103, 107, 111, 113, 115, 184, 190, 323
Sternberg, Meir 123

Succoth 328
sukkah 82, 84, 85
Sun Tzu 103
Syriac 6, 187
Syro-Ephraimite War 253

Tabernacle 187
Talmud 61, 68
Targum 6, 81
Tarshish 35, 37, 41, 42, 46, 49, 54, 63, 79, 81, 86, 317
Temple 5, 52, 56–58, 65, 217, 229, 231, 233–235, 240, 242, 246, 251, 252, 255–260, 262, 264–267, 271, 273, 278, 280, 282, 287, 295, 297, 333–335
The Ten Commandments 77, 91, 92, 206
Tent of Meeting 186, 187, 207
Thanksgiving 52–54, 60, 61, 63, 64, 80
Theodotion 57
Thompson, Francis 35, 55, 78
Thucydides 97
Tiglath-pileser III 315
Tigris River 68, 81
the Tophet 263, 264
Trans-Jordan 103–109, 111, 113, 116, 117, 184, 190, 280, 322, 325–327
Trible, Phyllis 85, 91

unified composition 28, 29
Uriah 258
Urim and Thumim 29, 193

Valley of the Son of Hinnom 263
Vanoni, G. 6
von Ranke, Leopold 31
The Vulgate 6

Wellhausen, Julius 155
Wolff, H.W. 62, 68, 73, 74, 79, 82, 88, 90, 316
Wordsworth, William 45

Xenophon 68, 219

Yarmuk River 109, 111, 325
Yeats, William Butler 31, 151
Yom Kippur 56, 90

Zadok 218
zebah 52, 60, 135–137, 207
Zechariah 183
Zedekiah 333
Zered River 106, 322
zevah 185
Zimri 188, 190

www.ingramcontent.com/pod-product-compliance
Ingram Content Group UK Ltd.
Pitfield, Milton Keynes, MK11 3LW, UK
UKHW051851210426
5322IPUK00025B/658